Oscar Browning

The Despatches of Earl Gower

English Ambassador at Paris From June 1790 to August 1792

Oscar Browning

The Despatches of Earl Gower
English Ambassador at Paris From June 1790 to August 1792

ISBN/EAN: 9783337014704

Printed in Europe, USA, Canada, Australia, Japan

Cover: Foto ©ninafisch / pixelio.de

More available books at **www.hansebooks.com**

THE DESPATCHES

OF

EARL GOWER,

ENGLISH AMBASSADOR AT PARIS FROM JUNE 1790
TO AUGUST 1792,

TO WHICH ARE ADDED

THE DESPATCHES OF MR LINDSAY AND MR MONRO,

AND

THE DIARY OF VISCOUNT PALMERSTON

IN FRANCE DURING JULY AND AUGUST 1791,

NOW PUBLISHED FOR THE FIRST TIME.

EDITED FOR THE SYNDICS OF THE UNIVERSITY PRESS

BY

OSCAR BROWNING, M.A., F. R. Hist. S.,
FELLOW OF KING'S COLLEGE, CAMBRIDGE, AND UNIVERSITY LECTURER.

CAMBRIDGE:
AT THE UNIVERSITY PRESS
1885

TO MY FRIEND

PROFESSOR J. R. SEELEY

THIS VOLUME IS DEDICATED.

CONTENTS.

	PAGE
PREFACE	ix—xiv
INTRODUCTION	xv—xxxviii
DRAFT OF INSTRUCTIONS FOR EARL GOWER	1
DESPATCHES OF EARL GOWER, FROM JUNE 21, 1790 TO AUGUST 12, 1792	5
MR DUNDAS TO EARL GOWER	209
EARL GOWER TO LORD GRENVILLE	210
NOTE FROM KING GEORGE III.	211
EARL GOWER TO LORD GRENVILLE	211
MR W. LINDSAY TO LORD GRENVILLE	212
GEORGE MONRO TO LORD GRENVILLE	225
MR W. LINDSAY TO LORD GRENVILLE	235
GEORGE MONRO TO LORD GRENVILLE	235
DIARY OF THE SECOND VISCOUNT PALMERSTON IN FRANCE	283
APPENDIX	311
I. LORD ELGIN TO LORD GRENVILLE	312
RÉSUMÉ D'INFORMATIONS EXACTES AU 25 JANVIER 1794	314
EXTRAIT D'UNE LETTRE ADRESSÉE À MILORD ELGIN	340
PREMIÈRE SUITE DU RÉSUMÉ	343
INFORMATIONS ADDITIONNELLES	353
II. S. FOUCHÉ À MONSIEUR D. S. CURTIS À PARIS	372
RELATION DU VOYAGE DE LA FAMILLE ROYALE À VARENNES	373
INDEX	377—400

PREFACE.

I FIRST became acquainted with the despatches of Lord Gower, which are printed in this volume, some years ago, when I was working in the Record Office on the foreign policy of the younger Pitt. They appeared to me, as soon as I read them, of great historical interest, and well fitted to be published. I therefore informed two leading London publishers of their existence and asked them whether they would undertake to print them, offering to see them through the press. The first publisher to whom I applied refused at once, saying that correspondences were a glut in the market; the second took a little time to consider, but eventually declined. Shortly after this, when I was pursuing my researches in the French Foreign Office, I was informed by two of the best authorities on the French Revolution, M. Henri Taine and M. Albert Sorel, that Lord Gower's despatches had been read by competent Frenchmen and had been declared to be of high value; and that their publication would be an important contribution to historical study. Armed with this testimony I applied to a third London publisher, sending him a specimen of the letters. After a courteous delay he also refused to have anything to do with the papers, giving as his reason that he had compared Lord Gower's account of the flight to Varennes with that given by Carlyle, and while there was nothing in Lord

Gower's description which was not in Carlyle, there was a great deal in Carlyle which was not in Lord Gower. Undaunted by these refusals, I applied to a fourth publisher of well-known liberality. He went so far as to have the correspondence copied at his expense, but after having read it he came to the conclusion that it could not be published without heavy loss. After these experiences it required great courage on the part of the Syndics of the Cambridge University Press to undertake a work so little likely to prove remunerative, and by doing it they deserve the gratitude of all serious students of history.

The publication of documents such as are contained in this volume should not be left to private enterprise, but should be carried out by the State. The State has published a number of volumes under the superintendence of the Master of the Rolls which have been of the greatest service to English History, and without them the works of Stubbs, of Freeman, and of Green could not have been written. Similarly the collection of calendars of state papers have supplied Mr Gardiner and Mr Brewer with their best materials. But the Rolls series ends with Henry VII., just at the time when English history begins to be interesting to the student of modern international politics, while the calendars of foreign papers are at present confined to the reigns of Henry VIII. and Queen Elizabeth. Surely if there is any period of history which was vital for the existence of the English nation and for its position in Europe, it is the period of the French Revolution and of Napoleon the First. During this epoch we followed an independent line of conduct based on the inherent qualities of our race and the traditions of our development. We stood aloof from Europe both in peace and war; we ratified the conclusions of our reason by enormous sacrifices, and we emerged in 1815 bruised and battered but indisputably the first power in the world, a position which we held for fifty years. We refused to join the coalition in 1791, we refused to make peace in 1800, we were the last to make peace in 1801, we were the first to break the peace of Europe in 1803, we were the soul of the coalition against Napoleon in 1815, we dominated the counsels of Vienna. Our conduct during this momentous epoch, the conduct mainly of an aristocratic government which has now passed away, deserves to be written for a national example, as much as the history of our Reformation or of our Great Rebellion. Yet the documents from which this history can be alone composed are allowed to sleep in the obscurity of the Record Office, or to moulder in the lumber rooms of country houses. It is painful to think how much material for the history of these times has been lost to us for ever. An example which we may wisely imitate is set us by foreign nations. Besides numerous publications of French and Austrian state papers may be mentioned the collections of the Prussian archives, and the volumes of the Russian Historical Society, both rich in memorials of the revolutionary period. Indeed so much attention has been paid to this subject on the Continent that we can learn the extent of our own resources better from French and German than from English writers. Sybel was the first to place the attitude of England towards the Revolution in its true light, Le Bon has narrated the curious history of the negotiations between Pitt and the *émigrés* conducted through William Wickham. Copies of English official correspondence have during recent years been sent in large quantities to Germany, and we are in danger of having our conduct in these critical circumstances described and judged by enemies rather than by friends. It is not unreasonable to ask that some part of the sum devoted by Government to publications of this character should be assigned to a period of history which must be accurately known by us if we are to form a sound judgment on the foreign complications of our own time.

The volume now offered as a contribution to this knowledge contains the despatches of Lord Gower written from Paris during twenty-six months, from June 1790 to August 1792. They are not of an exciting character, nor do they shew great insight or penetration. They are careful accounts written week by week by a competent and well-placed observer for the information of his Government, and they are perhaps more valuable because the writer did not comprehend the full significance of the events which he describes. The French Revolution has been so often lifted by sensational writers into the region of cataclysmal and almost superhuman occurrences that a narrative is specially acceptable which tends to range it among the facts which appeal to our ordinary experience. The despatches of Lord Gower are supplemented by a few letters written by Mr Lindsay, who was left as Chargé d'affaires in Paris after his chief's departure. These are followed by a number of letters written by Colonel Monro to Lord Grenville from Sept.

1792 to January 1793. George Monro was a spy in the pay of the British Government. His letters resemble the form of a newspaper correspondence, and will be found interesting and picturesque. Especially thrilling is his account of the September massacres, of which he was an eye-witness. To these documents I have been able to add, by the kindness of Mr Evelyn Ashley, a diary of the second Lord Palmerston, the father of the Prime Minister, written in France during July and August 1791. After the declaration of war between France and England in Feb. 1793 Paris was hermetically sealed. No effort on the part of our ministry or of Lord Elgin, our representative in Flanders, could penetrate the obscurity; all who were suspected of giving information were put in prison or guillotined. The veil did not lift until the summer of 1794, when an unknown but well-informed correspondent in Switzerland was able to send to Lord Elgin some remarkable accounts of the political, military, and social condition of France. These reports are printed at the end of this volume. I have added in a second appendix a document hitherto unpublished on the arrest of Louis XVI. at Varennes, which I owe to the kindness of Mr Curtis of New York.

It remains for me to state what I have attempted to do as editor of these papers. To have annotated them completely would have been to rewrite the history of the Revolution. I have therefore confined the notes to a very narrow compass, but I have included in the index a full *onomasticon* of persons and places which I hope will to some extent supply their place. My task in dealing with the orthography and punctuation of the documents has been more difficult. Lord Gower was a bad writer of English, a faulty and inconsistent speller, and a most unscientific punctuator. These original defects were increased by the blunders either of the author or the copyist. To have printed a facsimile of the correspondence as it stands in the volumes of the Record office would have driven the staunchest student to despair. At the same time it was desirable to preserve whatever was characteristic of the man or of his habits of thought. I have therefore adopted a compromise. I have altered everything which appeared to me the result of carelessness. I have preserved eccentric spelling where it seemed to be deliberate, or where it required a graphic touch, as where Robertspierre becomes first Roberspierre and then Robespierre. I have altered the punctuation so as to make the reading of the volume more easy, but it will probably be thought that I have kept too many long and rambling sentences. If after this process some bad faults remain the critic should first ask whether they are not to be attributed rather to Lord Gower than to the editor. Mr Monro's letters teem with errors of every description, and had to be corrected throughout. Lord Palmerston's diary has been left almost untouched, although it is feared that some mistakes remain uncorrected. The French documents at the end of the volume have been revised. The volume is left to the indulgence of historical students. An attempt has been made in the introduction to estimate the historical value of the documents which it contains.

KING'S COLLEGE, CAMBRIDGE.
October, 1885.

INTRODUCTION.

THE correspondence of Lord Gower opens on June 21, 1790, a year and six weeks after the meeting of the States General, a year after the Tiers État, taking refuge in the tennis court at Versailles, had sworn not to separate until they had given a new constitution to their country. Much had happened in the mean time. The three estates, disobeying the king's order to deliberate separately, had formed themselves into a National Assembly, many of the clergy and a few of the nobles clustering round the members of the commons. The king, who had expected by the duplication of the third estate to gain a firmer support to his power, had been forced to look to the army for assistance. Troops were collected round the court and the capital to repress any disturbance. The capital had begun to shew tumultuous tendencies. The garden of the Palais Royal, the residence of the Duke of Orleans, not subject to the ordinary superintendence of the police, became a centre of agitation. The court found that they could depend better upon foreign than on native troops. The attempt to collect these excited jealousy both in Paris and in the Assembly. The Assembly asked the king to withdraw his army from Paris, while Paris determined to oppose a national armament to the Royal forces. This was the origin of the National Guard. The two powers, the court and the capital, stood opposed to each other with arms in their hands. The first step of open war was the taking of the Bastille on July 14; it was a formal renunciation of obedience to the authority of the king. Louis XVI. instead of sternly reestablishing his supremacy, went the next day to the Assembly, threw himself upon its wisdom, and declared that he had given orders to withdraw his troops. The day following the king visited the capital and accepted the tricolour cockade, the union of the Bourbon white with the blue and red of the Paris municipality. Paris had conquered the king, a great revolution had been already consummated.

The submission of the monarchy involved the exile of its staunchest defenders. The Comte d'Artois left France by the advice of his brother, and became the first fruits of the emigration. It might have been thought that the crown, emancipated from the fetters of the nobles and the clergy, stood in closer union with the people. The sacrifice of feudal rights on the night of August 4 contributed to strengthen this view. But the growth of ages could not be torn up in a moment, and the wilful disregard of public law carried in it the germs of future war. The king and the Assembly left face to face with each other began to quarrel at the bidding of divergent interests. Who should command the army, the crown or the parliament? The king sought to defend himself with the troops whom he trusted. A dinner in the theatre of Versailles led to a scene which widened the chasm between the court and the people. The capital saw no remedy but to bring both king and Assembly within its walls. Hence came the disgraceful events of October 5, and the forced transference of the king to Paris. Louis XVI. exchanged the palace-temple of Versailles, where his ancestors had been worshipped as divinities, for the unfurnished barrack of the Tuilleries. The king was virtually a prisoner. The Assembly instead of being free to deliberate at leisure had to frame a constitution amidst the surging passions of a wavering mob. The royal authority was already doomed, although few had declared themselves republicans. The creation of departments in place of the ancient provinces upset the administration of the old régime. The election of the judges and of the clergy made a strong executive difficult. The throne was deprived of some of its most necessary attributes.

The emigration had attained large dimensions, the idea of revolution was exalted with growing enthusiasm. Yet at this time a war was imminent between England and Spain, and France, if she was to preserve her honour and execute engagements made only thirty years before, needed to speak in Europe with a decisive voice.

Into this tumult of interests Lord Gower found himself plunged. His predecessor, the Duke of Dorset, a fine gentleman in mind and manners, an ornament of the inner circle at Versailles, was recalled because his liveried servant had been seized by the mob and a letter from the Duke to the Comte d'Artois found in his pockets. His first despatch introduces us to the difficulties of the army, the approaching fête of the revolution, the anniversary of the fall of the Bastille. The market women who brought the king to Paris have the impertinence to invite the Comte d'Artois to return from Turin, and are received at Lyons with almost royal honours; couriers are passing to and fro between Spain and England; the family compact is still a matter of discussion. An Abbé, mistaken for the Sardinian Ambassador, is stript naked to see if he carries letters with him. Notwithstanding this, the diplomatic body think it well to assist at the fête of the federation, which goes off prosperously in the Champ de Mars. English histories of this period do not make us understand how near we were to a war with France in the autumn of 1790. In August the French are increasing their fleet and army to meet a similar increase on the part of England, the Spanish Ambassador asks explicitly whether France intends to perform the stipulations of the family compact of 1761 or not. On the 27th of that month Mirabeau, the president of the *Comité diplomatique* of the Assembly, reports that all existing treaties ought to be maintained by the French nation until they are revised or modified, that the king is requested to abide by his engagements with Spain, and that thirty ships of the line are to be commissioned. The Assembly goes beyond this request and orders the equipment of forty-five ships of the line besides smaller vessels. All parties, Lord Gower says, are agreed on this measure. Two days later Lord Gower reports that although the king and his ministers desire peace a large party in the country is in favour of war. The aristocrats hope to fish in troubled waters, others desire to violate the commercial treaty. Perhaps some members of the Assembly were influenced by Spanish gold. We do not exactly know by what means this danger was conjured. Lord Gower gives assurance of the friendly feeling of England towards France, but Pitt was able to engage in a more direct negotiation with the leading members of the Assembly. Hugh Elliot, a diplomatist of great, though erratic genius, had been a friend of Mirabeau from boyhood. Lord Gower affords glimpses of the mysterious mission with which he was intrusted. Pitt's instructions to Elliot have been lost, and we do not know what arguments he used. Perhaps English gold proved a counterpoise to Spanish gold. But the result of his persuasion was an entire change of front. Towards the end of October the "popular" party declares itself in favour of peace, and prefers an English alliance to a Spanish compact. Elliot is able to announce his triumph on October 26, and two days later in his private advice to the court Mirabeau says that England is desirous of peace, and that the armaments have reference to the Northern war then going on between Sweden and Russia, a statement for which there is very little foundation, but which may have rested on the authority of Elliot, who had himself so much to do with it. In November Lord Gower states that the prospect of peace has damped the spirit of the aristocrats, but pleased the rest of the nation.

A letter of December 3, 1790, informs us of one of the most important moments of the Revolution. The National Assembly has passed a decree obliging the clergy to take the civic oath, and all those who do not comply are to lose their rights as French citizens. The Pope was at that time expected to sanction the decree. This measure caused a breach between the

Revolution and the Church which prevented it from being accepted by the nation as a beneficial reform, and rendered futile the plans of Mirabeau for a constitutional government. The king at first expected the Pope would not object to the decree and then waited for his decision, but at the close of the year he gave his consent. The Pope eventually declared against the oath, only four bishops were found willing to take it, the greater part of the inferior clergy refused it.

As Lent and Easter approached the desire of the Royal family to perform their usual devotions with priests who had not taken the oath became stronger. This could not be done in Paris, and hence preparations were made for removal. At the beginning of Feb. 1791 the stables at Versailles are inspected to see that the king has made no preparations for flight. The king's aunts determined to spend their Easter at Rome (Feb. 18), their luggage is stopped (Feb. 20), they are themselves detained at Arnay le duc (March 4), but are suffered to proceed, by the intervention of Mirabeau. The king begins to suffer seriously from his confinement in the Tuileries, being debarred of his usual exercise (March 11), the ambassadors are not allowed to see him, and there is considerable anxiety. His recovery is celebrated by illuminations and by a Te Deum (March 18). Notwithstanding this, a month later, the King and Queen are prevented by the mob from going to St Cloud for the Holy Week (April 22). They sat for an hour and three-quarters in their carriages, subject to every insult, and were compelled to return to their prison. This might have been prevented by Mirabeau had he been alive, but he had died a fortnight before (April 8). His funeral was followed by 28,000 people and three-fourths of the population of Paris were present as spectators.

We read in the correspondence many signs of growing disorder. The language in the Assembly resembles that of the *Dames de la Halle* (Jan. 28), the bust of Desilles is carried round the hall to the tune of Ça ira (Feb. 4), when Lord Gower hears the abbé Maury exclaim *Voilà comme les Français font des lois.* Lord Gower goes to dine with Monsieur, afterwards Louis XVIII., and while they are at coffee a number of fish-women are admitted into the court of the Petit Luxembourg. The Prince assures them that he does not intend to quit Paris (Feb. 25), but they attend him even to the Tuilleries. The dropping of a hunting knife causes a disturbance in the Queen's apartments (March 4); Lord Gower finds a number of fish-women cordially embracing M. de Montmorin in his own drawing room (April 1); the same women punish several hundred nuns by a general flogging because they will not hear mass said by a priest who has taken the oath (April 15). The outrage offered to the king shewed that Bailly, the mayor of Paris, and Lafayette, the commander of national guards, had no longer any power over the mob. The king's household resign, the ambassadors see him go to mass celebrated by a single priest, Lafayette surrenders his command and takes his place in the ranks of the army (April 22). He is however persuaded to accept the command again, and thus disappoint the Jacobins who had hoped to have the nomination of his successor (April 29).

Lord Gower mentions on May 6 and on subsequent dates the discussions about Avignon and the Venaissin, which had belonged to the Pope but which had been absorbed into France by the Assembly. This was only one of the events which embroiled revolutionary France with Europe. The jealousy of other powers may have at first welcomed the Revolution as tending to weaken the power of France for mischief. But the abolition of feudal rights on August 4, 1789, struck a vital blow at the princes of the Empire. One of the first to feel it was the Elector Archbishop of Mainz, the Arch-Chancellor of the German Empire. He had metropolitan rights in Alsace which were seriously threatened. Mirabeau was one of the few members of the National Assembly who understood the relations of France to Europe. He desired to maintain existing alliances, but while the connection with Spain was not unpopular with the nation, that with Austria was an object of deep dislike. We see the storm gradually rising which was to lead to war. The Nuncio does not appear at court, the Pope is burnt in effigy, Condé is expected to invade France with his death's-head army (May 6), it is paid by Prussia, or perhaps by the king (May 13).

Two facts of considerable importance are alluded to on May 20 and 22. First the decree which prevented members of the National Assembly from sitting in the legislature, and which therefore took the conduct of the new constitution out of the hands of those who framed it and were the best fitted to wield it, and secondly the statement that Frenchmen are gone to England with a view of setting fire to the fleet or dockyards. The correspondence of this time is full of evidence that France was a nest of what would now be called dynamiters. Their operations were principally conducted against Ireland, and it is difficult to ascertain how far the defensive measures of the English Government in 1792 were occasioned or justified by the fear of their operations unless the whole evidence with regard to them were before us.

On June 17 we are informed of two precautionary measures, the administering of an oath to the officers of the army to be faithful to the constitution, and the sequestration of the property of the Prince of Condé if he refuses to disband his army. Five days later a thunderbolt bursts from a clear sky. The king has left Paris in the night of June 20 and taken the road for the low countries (June 22). The following day (June 23) Lord Gower announces that the king has been stopped at Varennes, he also states that Bailly and Lafayette had known the king's intention to leave the Tuileries some days before and had taken all possible precautions to prevent it. They stayed with the king till one in the morning and then left a double guard in the palace. Two days later (June 25) the return of the Royal family is described, the order and decorum with which the mob behaved were truly remarkable. The capture of the king at Varennes is perhaps the greatest misfortune which has befallen France during the last hundred years. Louis had no idea of leaving his country, or of joining the enemy. He wished merely to retire to a fortress, probably Montmédy, in which he would be independent of the Paris mob, and able to treat with the extreme revolutionary party on equal terms. The Queen and the *émigrés* may have desired something more than this, but there is no proof that they would have gained their object. The flight may have been a mistake, Kaunitz was opposed to it from the first. But its failure was a fatal blow to the monarchy, and to all hope of settled government. The court before weak, henceforth became contemptible. The Royal family is now strictly guarded and the ambassadors do not go to the Tuileries without special invitation (July 1).

It was just at this juncture that Viscount Palmerston arrived in Paris, and his diary gives us some picturesque details of the situation which are unfortunately wanting in Lord Gower's despatches. On Monday, July 10, he pays a visit to the Assembly and to the Jacobin club and writes a graphic account of both meetings. The members are entirely occupied with the question of the king. The procession in honour of Voltaire, which Lord Gower dismisses in one cynical paragraph, is described by Lord Palmerston at length; the same may be said of the French anniversary of the taking of the Bastille, and the disorderly scene which followed it.

The altered position of the king after the return from Varennes excited the powers of Europe to new efforts in his favour. Count Mercy, the Austrian ambassador, thought that the frontier fortresses then in the hands of royalist garrisons might be delivered up to the soldiers of his country, and France be invaded by this means. The Comte de Provence and the Comte d'Artois were afraid of a foreign intervention which might lead to a dismemberment of France. Gustavus III. of Sweden, then at Aix la Chapelle (July 22), recalled his officers in the French service and meditated a descent on the coast of Normandy and the restoration of the monarchy. The princes attempted to persuade Catherine of Russia to join 8,000 of her troops to the 16,000 Swedes. Austria would march from Flanders, Prussia and the Empire from Alsace and Lorraine, Switzerland and Savoy from the east, Spain from the south. France could make no adequate resistance, and the National Assembly would be dissolved[1]. Kaunitz disapproved of this plan, he thought that by the moral pressure of a united Europe something like a constitutional monarchy might be established in France. Catherine also refused her assistance.

In the meantime the sketch of the new constitution had been completed and was to be offered to the king for his acceptance (August 5). It was difficult to see how this was to be done. Lord Gower says "If in his present state of confinement it will be a mere mockery; if he is previously allowed his liberty it is uncertain what use he may make of it."..."It is generally believed that the king will go either to Rambouillet or to Fontainebleau, where he will accept the constitution."

On August 27 the Emperor Leopold II. and Frederick William King of Prussia met at Pillnitz. The result was an agreement between Prussia and Austria directed against the Revolution, but not of a very decided nature. These two powers did not commit themselves to any step unless the other powers of Europe would combine with them. The Emperor of Austria well knew how little he was risking. Thus the convention led eventually to war. However much the sovereigns might desire peace, the course of events was too strong for them.

Lord Gower announces on Sept. 2, 1791, that "the constitution, such as it is, is at last finished: it will probably be accepted by the king on Monday." He also expresses the wish of the Assembly that the constitution shall remain unaltered for thirty years, and that it shall not be amended or changed without elaborate formalities. He adds that "thanks to the declaration of the rights of man, a notion is spread over the

---

[1] *Feuillet de Conches*, II. 187, quoted by Ranke. *Ursprung und Beginn des Revolutionären Krieges* 72.

whole country that everybody is not only to think but to act for himself." It is difficult to teach the people what is or what is not constitutional, or who are governors and who are "to be governed." The constitution was to a certain extent a compromise. The National Assembly contained some members who desired a republic, but the majority wished for the continuation of the monarchy. The moderate democrats thought to obtain their end by making the government national and popular while at the same time they allowed kingship to continue its existence. The moderate royalists believed that the permanence of kingship was insured by the popular character of the institutions in which it was imbedded. The end of the revolution had been obtained, because the two privileged classes, the priests and the nobles, had lost their privileges, and power was firmly consolidated in the hands of the third estate. Although the king did not approve of the constitution in all respects, yet it would be untrue to say that he accepted it under compulsion. The queen probably regarded it as the least of many evils, and we cannot be surprised that Lord Gower found on Sept. 1 that "her deportment and appearance discovered a mind suffering under affliction not easily subdued." The constitution was accepted on Sept. 14, and "the king upon his passage was very much applauded by the people" (Sept. 14).

With the acceptance of the constitution the first revolution is at an end. The terrible events which followed were produced by new forces and by different combinations. The commune of Paris now steps into the place of the *bourgeoisie*. The commune had shewn itself in the destruction of the Bastille, and in the riots of October 5. It had asserted itself still more definitely on the second anniversary of the fall of the Bastille, and had on that day been crushed by the *bourgeoisie* with the help of military force. It found spokesmen in the republican faction of the Jacobin club, an organization of the most powerful character, which dominated the Assembly by its debates, and had its ramifications throughout the whole of France. The commune and the Jacobins were only too powerfully supported by the new legislative Assembly which met for the first time on October 1, 1791. Lord Gower remarks (Sept. 16) that more than half the next Assembly will be composed of country attorneys "and that not only the nobility but the commercial interest will be very much excluded," "the members of most note who are already chosen for the next legislature are not of that sort which care to argue favourably for it." The cries of *Vive le Roi* which greeted the king as he returned from closing the Constituante on Sept. 30 were the last which met his ear.

The ill-feeling of the *Législative* towards the king was shewn at once. They changed the *Roi de France* into the *Roi des Français* and suppressed the titles of *sire* and *majesté*, they gave the king an arm-chair similar to that of their president, "It shewed," as Lord Gower says, "an absurd disposition to quarrel with the king about trifles while he, on the other hand, has shewn a decided intention not to quarrel with them if he can possibly avoid it." Their differences now assumed a more serious character. The new constitution could not be a guarantee of permanent peace until it was accepted by foreign powers, nor were they likely to accept it if the *émigrés* and especially the Princes stood aloof. The King of England recognized the new constitution at once, and so did Holland, then under English influence (Oct. 14), but the King of Spain appeared to doubt whether the French king was really free either morally or physically, and the King of Sweden refused to acknowledge the new constitution (October 31). Prussia was in a difficulty —her relations to England demanded the recognition of the constitution, but her engagements with the Empire held her back. The Emperor accepted the constitution in November, and Sweden gave way at last.

The *émigrés* still remained irreconcilable; under the influence of Calonne they determined to regard the king as virtually deposed, and to raise the Comte de Provence to the post of regent of the kingdom. In answer to this the Comte was ordered to return to France within two months under penalty of losing his right to the succession. Further the Assembly decreed any emigrants remaining across the frontier after January 1, 1792, should be declared guilty of conspiracy and should suffer the penalty of death. The king urged every argument to induce his brother to return, but he could not give his sanction to a decree which treated so many of his devoted friends with unreasonable harshness. Using the right given him by the constitution he refused his consent—"the measure of refusing that decree was generally approved: the democratic party rejoice at it as it tends to prove the king's freedom." (Nov. 18). This was only true of the moderate democrats. How precarious the king's freedom was felt by Lord Gower when he tells us that the king was prevented from passing from one wing of the Tuilleries to the other to pay a visit to his sister (ib.).

Another difficulty arose with regard to the non-juring priests. Gower tells us (Oct. 28) that there are complaints of their manœuvres and machinations, and (Nov. 11) that they are creating disturbances in every part of the kingdom, more particularly at Caen, where they are in a state of civil war, and blood has been spilt on both sides. A week later (Nov. 18) we hear that the Assembly has decreed that these priests are to take the *serment civique*, and that those who refuse it are to be deprived of their pensions. The king was in a great difficulty. "The court exists in a miserable suspense between its jealousy of the emigrants and its dread of the Jacobins" (Dec. 2). At last the king determines to withhold his consent. He is encouraged to take this step by a decree of the department of Paris drawn up by Talleyrand (Dec. 5).

These two circumstances brought into strong light the antagonism between the two divisions of the Parisian populace, the *bourgeoisie* and the commune, the directory and the sections.

A civil war was ready to break out the moment the *émigrés* and their foreign allies crossed the frontier. It is difficult to follow the exact policy of the king and queen with regard to the German powers. The king, although refusing to hurl a decree of excommunication against the *émigrés*, was ready to take vigorous measures for the defence of the frontier against the German armies. The queen, though she dreaded the invasion of France by foreign troops, urged her brother Leopold to summon a European congress for the settlement of the affairs of France, and in the meantime to maintain a powerful army on the French borders which might be useful in time of need. Although the war party in Paris was ready to run the risk of war with Prussia or Austria, they were anxious to keep peace with England. The best diplomatist they had, M. Talleyrand-Perigord, was sent to the court of St James (Jan. 20, 1792). He could not appear in a public character as he had been a member of the Constituante, and a self-denying ordinance prevented any such from taking office under the new government. The Duc de Biron was first thought of as his ostensible chief, but Mr de Chauvelin was substituted at a later period. The ultimatum which eventually brought about the war was the work of Brissot and the Girondists. Lord Gower tells us that those of the Jacobins who followed Robespierre wished to avoid war by negotiation (ib.). If this is true it is contrary to the received view. Lord Gower's second despatch of Jan. 20 shews the antagonism existing between Delessart and Narbonne, a circumstance which eventually broke the ministry in pieces. On Jan. 27 we hear of the momentous sitting of Jan. 25, in which a categorical answer of peace or war was demanded before March 1. It is probable that even then the majority of the Assembly did not desire war, but they were led by the eloquence of the Girondists to take steps which could lead to no other conclusion. The difference of opinion between the parties as to peace and war was connected with a similar division as to the powers of the king. The constitution gave the sovereign the prerogative of war and peace, but the Jacobins could not believe that the king would ever declare war. They also suspected, with some truth, that the queen was in active correspondence with Austria. Suspicion began to be rife of a new evasion, and an instance of this is mentioned on Feb. 3, when Lord Gower relates that a sécrétaire made for the King of Naples was searched on being carried out of the palace, lest the king should be concealed in it. On Feb. 10 we hear of the manufacture of pikes in the Faubourg St Antoine, arms which were to be used with fatal effect on June 20 and August 10. The king felt himself so weak that he was obliged to give his consent to the decree which confiscated the property of refractory *émigrés*.

On Feb. 27 Kaunitz sent to the French government a solemn despatch technically called an "office" which was intended to be favourable to peace. It represented the views of the Emperor as in harmony with those of the majority of the French nation, but it abused the Jacobins in no measured terms as the common enemies of Europe and of France. The publication of this letter produced the worst effect. Lord Gower says (March 2) "It remains to be seen whether the Emperor's naming the Jacobins, and marking them out as the cause of his continuing to arm will tend to diminish their numbers." On March 10 the news arrived in Paris of the sudden death of the Emperor Leopold II. The same despatch notified the dismissal of Narbonne whose opinions were too extreme for him to work harmoniously with his colleagues, and also the violent attack of Brissot upon Delessart which Narbonne does not seem to have anticipated. War was now certain. It had been brought about by a number of converging events, none of them alone sufficient to cause it. The ill-judged ultimatum of Louis XVI., the imprudent "office" of Kaunitz, the sudden death of Leopold II., who had restored quiet to Europe, and lastly the unexpected break up of a moderate ministry gradually made peace impossible. In anticipation of the conflict a treaty of alliance between Austria and Prussia had been signed on Feb. 7.

A despatch of March 16 gives a list of the new ministry, as far as they are known. A week later we hear of the close relations between Lafayette and Dumouriez, and of the adhesion of Robespierre to the views of the new ministry. In view of the seriousness of the situation the red Phrygian cap is discontinued and the tricolour cockade is considered sufficient. The plan of the new ministry was believed by the court to be to separate the king and queen in order that she might be tried for corresponding with Austria, to suspend the king from his functions, and to make a simultaneous attack on Sardinia and Germany. Kaunitz was informed by Breteuil that nothing could save the monarchy but an immediate attack on the Rhine. On March 30 Lord Gower believes war to be inevitable. A new despatch of Kaunitz has been read to the Assembly which excites great indignation, as it seems to cast a doubt on the right of France to choose her own internal government. Talleyrand has sometime before returned from his first mission to England. He is now to go again with Chauvelin as his chief. Lord Gower remarks (April 6) that both Talleyrand and Chauvelin are intimate friends of Narbonne, and that it is remarkable that they have both consented to serve under a Jacobin ministry although neither of them is decidedly a Jacobin. It says much for Talleyrand's versatility and ability that he was chosen both by Delessart and Dumouriez as the most safe mediator in a difficult negotiation. The circumstances related on April 11 amply justify Lord Gower in the opinion that "it is evident that the ministry here have a most earnest desire to be upon the best possible terms with England." Two days later he reports that Paris has in the previous week enjoyed more quiet than in any week since the Revolution, but that it has the appearance of the sort of calm which portends a storm. Indeed the very next despatch (April 20) states that the king had been to the Assembly to propose the declaration of war in form against the King of Hungary and Bohemia. The king is believed to have done this with a light heart, for if the allies won he would regain his power, and if the French were victorious he would be popular as the author of the war.

The proposition of the king was adopted by the Assembly almost unanimously, indeed there were only seven votes against it. The Assembly knew that in attacking Austria they would also have to fight with Prussia, but they believed that, if England were neutral, France could cope with the rest of Europe united. Indeed Sweden could do nothing, Spain had no decided resolution, Sardinia was weak, and Russia was too selfish to risk much in such an enterprise. Austria and Prussia were hindered by conflicting rivalry. Besides the Girondists said that the war might cost a few thousand lives, but it would spread freedom all over the world. The object of the French was to conquer the Netherlands; by this they would avenge themselves upon Austria and enhance the consideration of France in Europe. Dumouriez knew that the demolition of the barrier fortresses by Joseph II. had left Flanders unprotected on the French side. He lost no time, but pushed his troops across the frontier on April 29.

The first reverses of the French are described in the despatch of May 4, the murder of Dillon at Lille and the repulse of Biron at Mons. This was attributed by the Jacobins to the treachery of aristocratic officers; many of them resign their commands (May 11) and Servan becomes minister of war (ib.). The representatives of Prussia and Russia suddenly leave the French capital (May 18). On May 25 mention is made of the "Austrian Committee" supposed to be sitting in Paris to assist the plans of the invaders. As the danger approaches the National Assembly, the governing bodies of the department of the Seine, of the municipality of Paris, and the Jacobin club determine to sit in permanence (June 1). The king's guard is disbanded, the care of the Royal family is committed to the National Guard and the Swiss (ib.). The real significance of Servan's plan for collecting a democratic force round Paris is so little perceived that it is merely treated as a means of increasing the army, the "miserable state" of which "exceeds our belief" (ib.). However, by the next week the mischief of the measure becomes apparent, and a design is hinted at of conveying the king and the Assembly to the banks of the Loire where they would be further away from the influence of foreign armies.

The decree of the Assembly to collect men from all the cantons of France was opposed by the National Guard and by Lafayette and was vetoed by the king. Roland and his wife wrote a violent letter of remonstrance to the king, but as he was supported by Dumouriez he was able to dismiss Roland Servan and Clavière (June 15). Dumouriez remained, but had for some time been wavering between a civil and a military employment (June 8). Lord Gower thinks that this change of ministry "may tend in some measure to unite the Jacobins" but "may ultimately prove their destruction." That it did at least for a time "unite the Jacobins" is shewn by Dumouriez's resignation (June 18), which is attributed (June 22) to the impossibility of carrying on the government in the face of the unpopularity produced by the king's veto.

Lord Gower's report of the attack on the Tuilleries on June 20 is interesting. The account of the king's firmness and courage is confirmed. The circumstance of his having applied the hand of a grenadier to his heart, saying "feel here if there be any signs of fear" is perfectly true. His sister Elizabeth stood by his side during the whole evening (June 29), a fact not generally noticed. The responsibility of the outrage is rightly laid to the charge of Péthion. Lafayette highly disapproved of the scenes of June 20 and wrote a remonstrance to the Assembly; Lord Gower thinks that he has "crossed the Rubicon" (June 22). This disapproval was echoed by many departments of the North. Lord Gower thinks that monarchical and antimonarchical France may be considered as divided by the river Loire.

In his despatch of July 6 Lord Gower forecasts the events which were now imminent, the departure of the king, the substitution of an aggressive republic for a constitutional monarchy. The king, he says, expects the event with courage, but the ministers have no fixed plan. The *fédérés* invited to the fête of July 14 are beginning to arrive from all quarters, from Marseilles, from Bordeaux, from Brest. "Their stay in Paris is indeed to be of short duration, but it will be long enough to answer any sinister purpose." It is evident that the ambassador fully understands the personal danger to which the king and his friends were exposed. There were at this time two chief parties struggling for power, the Girondists whom Lord Gower generally calls Feuillants, who wished to preserve the forms of the constitution but at the same time to deprive the king of all authority, and to make him merely the expression of the national will; and the Jacobins who maintained the sovereignty of the people without reference to the constitution and who wished to establish a republic. The Assembly was controlled by a committee of twelve, composed of Girondists. The Sections of Paris, the *fédérés* and the extreme Jacobins were guided by another committee in which the leading power was Robespierre. The declaration that the country was in danger (July 13), taken from Roman models, seemed to suspend for the time all regular and constitutional authorities. The *fédérés* arrive gradually (ib.), their number is not so great as was expected, but the Jacobins contrive to get hold of them as they come. The king naturally wishes to leave Paris, Lord Gower hopes (July 20) that he may be able to retire to Rouen, where he will be safe in the heart of Normandy. The ministers do not approve of this and tender their resignations, but they are not accepted (July 13). The Jacobins get rid of three regiments of regular troops in order to leave an open field for the operations of the *fédérés* (July 20). They attempt to do the same with the Swiss Guards, but they cannot effect it. By this time the number of *fédérés* in Paris has reached three thousand.

Towards the close of July matters become more serious. The king refuses to leave Paris (July 27), but it is doubtful whether he could have done so had he attempted it; a part of the garden of the Tuileries is thrown open to the public; on July 26 the *fédérés* of Brest at the moment of their arrival proceed to march with a cannon to the Tuileries, and are only dissuaded by the eloquence of Péthion and Santerre. Still worse is the character of the five hundred *fédérés* from Marseilles (August 3), the body of men in whose honour the Marseillaise was composed by Rouget de L'Isle. It is hoped that they may leave immediately for the camp at Soissons, which already contains nine thousand men.

The acuteness of the crisis between the rival parties in Paris, and the bitterness of both of them against the king, is generally attributed by historians, especially by Ranke, to the ill-advised manifesto of the Duke of Brunswick. It is therefore noticeable that Lord Gower does not mention it till August 3, and then says that it has produced very little reaction in Paris. "The *aristocrats* are dissatisfied with it, and the *democrats* affect to despise it." In the same letter we hear that the forty-eight sections of Paris have asked for the king's restitution and that the petition has been presented by the Mayor and Common Council of Paris. On the following day Lord Gower asks how he is to act. He sees that the monarchy to which he is accredited is tottering to its fall, and that the personal danger of the queen is greater than that of the king. Is he to join the other powers in taking any decisive step.

The great event of August 10 is narrated briefly in the next despatch (August 12). The king with the Royal family left the palace at ten o'clock, not at eight according to the received account, and took refuge in the National Assembly "in a room adjoining to which they have continued ever since." The Assembly declared itself permanent, it decreed the withdrawal of executive power from the king, the dismissal of the present ministers, and the summoning of a national convention to draw up a new constitution. Servan, Clavière and Roland are recalled, Danton, Lebrun and Monge become ministers.

As soon as the news of these events reached England Lord Gower was recalled. The sovereign to whom he was accredited had ceased to reign, and to have given him or any other envoy letters of credence to the Provisional Government would have been to depart from the position of strict neutrality which England had determined to observe. However in the feverish state of public feeling it was not easy for the ambassador of an aristocratic power to leave Paris. Lord Gower asks for his passports, but does not receive them immediately. Pisani the Venetian ambassador is stopped by the mob as he is leaving for England, and only escapes after a strict examination of his papers. Lord Gower is able at last to set out for England on Tuesday, August 21. He leaves Mr Lindsay behind him as chargé d'affaires, who stays long enough to see something of the September massacres.

Mr Lindsay's letters are in some respects fuller than Lord Gower's, partly because Lord Gower was a man of few words and partly because the journals of the capital no longer described occurrences with so much minuteness. He writes (August 27), that the recall of the ambassador is not considered as a hostile movement, that the town is comparatively quiet after the late events, and that although the ministers form a provisional executive government, yet the real power lay in the hands of the commune and the new municipality. He relates the house to house search for suspects, the imprisonment of aristocrats, the approaching trial of the queen, and the election of the convention. There seemed to be no fear of the Duke of Brunswick, "the ablest general in the world;" if he reached Paris the convention would retire to the south. The allied armies crossed the frontiers on August 10, Sierck was taken on August 11, and Longwy surrendered with only a shew of resistance, the heights of Verdun were reached on August 30.

In the scarcity of muskets Danton obtained leave "to search every private house in the kingdom and seize upon all arms, horses, waggons, and in general upon whatever property he judged in the present exigence useful to the public service" (August 29). The French are determined to meet invasion by invasion. Dumouriez is to march upon Bruxelles, Montesquiou into Savoy (ib.). Lindsay reckons the aristocrats in France as not more than 50,000 (ib.). On August 30 we are told that the Assembly and the municipality are at variance, and that the Jacobins have quarrelled amongst themselves; indeed the Assembly is already in a kind of imprisonment (ib.). Indeed this difference which broke into open quarrel (ib.) is the reason why Lindsay could not leave Paris, as no passport of the Assembly would be valid unless it were approved of by the commune. Lord Kerry and many other English are in the same position (Sept. 2). We feel very vividly the terror which brought about the September massacres, when Lindsay tells us on that day that as he writes the alarm guns are firing, the tocsin is ringing, and drums are beating to arms all over the town. A courier has brought the news that the Prussians are near Châlons, but Lindsay believes they must be much nearer. The next letter (Sept. 3) gives an account of the massacres themselves, but a far more graphic description is to be found in the letter of the spy Colonel Monro, who watched the slaughter with his own eyes for two hours on Monday evening.

Col. Monro's letters are extremely interesting, and they are the fuller because no public journals were likely to narrate the events which he describes. The Revolution has passed entirely from the domain of discussion and veiled legality to that of tumultuous action. It will only be necessary to emphasize a few matters which might be overlooked, or which differ materially from the view generally received. On Sept. 15 Monro expresses his belief that if a Prussian army were to appear before Paris quiet or concealed citizens who want peace, and a vast number of people who are adverse to Jacobin principles would readily declare themselves for the king (p. 231). He reckons the number killed in the massacres at seven thousand (p. 232), and believes that the murders if not set agoing by some one were at least never intended to be stopped (p. 233). The army is concentrating near Châlons (p. 233), the Parisians are making preparations to resist a siege, they are turning their iron pots into cannon balls, and leaden coffins into bullets (p. 234). The Marseillais to the number of four hundred remain in the capital. Monro believes that they are "Genoese assassins hired for the purpose" (p. 237). A poor man happening to say in the Palace Royal that soldiers were being sent to the army to be butchered was immediately killed (ib.). Not half the soldiers who stream to Châlons are either armed or clothed (p. 238). The king's body servant was imprisoned for singing Grétry's air *O Richard o mon roi.*

Monro tells us that the Assembly placard the streets with printed defences of their conduct (p. 242), and that even Roland the minister has taken this means of replying to Marat (p. 244). Marat is described as "a violent man laying himself out for what party he shall find best" (ib.). The "blackguards of Paris" begin to stop people publicly in the streets and take their watches and bracelets from them (p. 246). Monro never moves out but with pistols in his pockets (p. 247). It is probable that if the allies could have marched straight upon Paris they would have crushed opposition. The Duke of Orleans passes part of every day at Paris and goes to the country in the evening, the only *aristocrat* who is secure (p. 249). The Garde Meuble in which the regalia of France are kept is robbed and the large crown diamond is stolen. This appeared to inspire the police with new activity (p. 251). Marat again posts his handbills abusing the Assembly and the ministers (ib.). The convention meets and abolishes every shew of royalty. Tom Payne makes a speech through an interpreter (p. 253). The first news of Valmy is regarded as a defeat (p. 254). This was not far from the truth, as the position was occupied by the Prussians on the following day. The general belief is that the allies will continue their march on Paris.

The king's trial is now at hand, but it is remarkable that notwithstanding the rigour with which they were treated the Royal family are always said to be in excellent health. On Dec. 17 Monro gives an account of an English society of friends of the Revolution who meet in Paris and who received a "brotherly kiss" from the sections. Few however of the society or of the sections met to exchange it. On Dec. 26 he sees Louis XVI. appear at the bar of the convention. He was driven from the temple to the convention as fast as possible, in about ten minutes (p. 267). "He appeared to me perfectly composed and in good health: his appearance and address had a very good effect upon the people." After his retirement a stormy scene took place in which the President was threatened with clenched fists. The corner of every street is papered with notices announcing the approaching sale of the remaining property of the *émigrés*.

On Jan. 7 Monro gives it as his opinion that France is in no state to go to war with England, and that if such a war were to take place it would ruin France and the constitution (p. 273). There can be no doubt that the belief that the war with France would be a short one had much effect in overcoming Pitt's reluctance to undertake it. Also the French fleet is described as totally without officers, sailors, or discipline (p. 276). On Jan. 13 Robespierre and the sections are not strong enough to prevent a piece in favour of the King called L'Ami des Lois being performed at the Comédie Française (p. 278), yet in this very letter Monro has to announce that the king is condemned to death (p. 280). This was a great surprise. "Few," he says, "of the members who went to the National Convention on Thursday morning with a positive resolution voted as they intended" (p. 280); they were intimidated by the mob, or influenced by some desire to defy England and Spain. Monro says "I cannot express the horror that was painted even in the countenance of every individual in the National Convention, where the very worst of the worst of mankind are assembled, when Égalité gave his vote for the death of his king and relation." Yet when Monro left Paris immediately afterwards "there were some thousands of armed men parading in different parts of the city ready to commit any sort of riot, and threatening destruction should the king not be put to death." Monro reached London on Jan. 21, the very day of the king's execution. When the news of it was received by ministers Chauvelin was immediately dismissed the country, and on Feb. 1 the French government declared war against England and Holland. From that time Paris became a closed city. No authentic information of what passed within its walls reached England for a year, when Lord Elgin was able to send to Lord Grenville the most valuable papers, which are printed in Appendix I. and which deserve the close attention of every historian.

DESPATCHES, ETC.

DESPATCHES.

Draft of Instructions for Earl Gower.

Instructions for our right trusty and well-beloved councillor George Granville Leveson Gower, Esqre., commonly called Earl Gower, whom we have appointed our Ambassador Extraordinary and Plenipotentiary to our good brother the most Christian King. Given at our Court at St. James's the 7th 1790, in the Thirtieth year of our reign.

1. Upon the receipt of these our instructions and your letter of credence, you are to repair to Dover where you are to embark for Calais, from whence you are to proceed with all convenient speed to Versailles or to such other place as our good brother, the most Christian King shall keep his Court, of whom you shall ask an audience in our name, when having delivered your credentials you shall assure him of the esteem and value we have for his person, and of our sincere desire to cultivate the most perfect good correspondence between us and our said good brother, and our respective dominions.

2. You shall in like manner deliver our letter of credence to the most Christian Queen, accompanying the same with like expressions of our esteem and friendship for her.

3. You are likewise to make suitable compliments in our name to the princes of the blood, according to the stile and practice of that Court, taking care at your audiences, and all other occasions, to maintain our dignity, and that you be treated with all the honours and respects that are given to Ambassadors from Spain and other crowned heads.

4. Whereas our royal predecessor, King Charles the second, did by his order in council bearing date the 26th day of August, 1668, direct that his Ambassadors should not for the future give the hand, in their own houses, to envoys, according to what is practised by the Ambassadors of other princes; you are therefore, in pursuance of the said order in council, to observe the ceremonial therein prescribed, and to take the hand of envoys, in your own house.

5. If you should learn that any of our subjects are kept in confinement, on account of their religion, you are to press the Court of France very earnestly, in our name, that all such unfortunate persons, who suffer for a conscientious adherence to their religion, may be set at liberty.

6. You shall carefully observe the motions and intentions of that Court with respect to us and our dominions, as well as any of their neighbours; you shall observe their inclinations in relation to the present state of affairs abroad; whether they are entering into any leagues or engagements with other princes, especially such as may be prejudicial to the publick peace.

7. You shall use your utmost endeavours to discover what plans or secret designs the Court of France may have formed, or may be forming in the East Indies; what number of ships of war or land forces may have been sent from the different ports of France to the East Indies since the cessation of hostilities, what ships or land forces may be preparing to be sent thither. And also whether any, and what orders have been sent to the commanders of their forces at their several settlements in that part of the world.

8. You will make it an object of your very particular attention to discover whether any treaties are either in agitation, or, actually entered into between France and any other European state, and in case such treaties should actually exist, or be only under consideration, you will take every measure in your power to be informed of the nature and extent of such treaty, or, treaties, and to procure and transmit to me correct copies thereof.

9. And it will likewise be an object well worthy of your most serious attention to discover whether any foreign ships of war are actually in any of the ports of France, and in case such ships should be in the ports of the said kingdom, to ascertain as far as possible the number, force and destination of them respectively.

10. You shall protect and countenance our merchants trading to any of the territories belonging to France, and use your best endeavours to secure to them the full enjoyment of all those privileges and immunities which are stipulated by the several treaties now subsisting between the two Crowns—and particularly by the Treaty of Commerce concluded at Versailles the 15th of January, 1787, and to obtain relief for them on any just complaint they shall make to you.

11. You shall constantly correspond with our several ministers employed in foreign Courts during your residence at that of France, for your mutual information and assistance; but you are on no account to correspond with your private friends on publick affairs.

12. You will in general be extremely attentive in making yourself master of the interior state of the Court of France, in studying the passions and interests of the Princes of the Blood, and other great persons of both sexes, who are in anywise honoured with the friendship and confidence of their most Christian Majesties, and in making the closest enquiries possible into the dispositions and characters of the ministers of state, not only with regard to their pacifick or warlike inclinations, but to their particular connections with one another, their views, their abilities, their power, and the degree of influence each has, or may have, with their most Christian Majesties.

13. As it must ever be essentially necessary to our service at all times to be as accurately informed as possible of the interior state of France, you will not fail to pay the strictest attention to the proceedings of the National Assembly now sitting at Paris, and of any other assembly of the states or notables of the kingdom, which may hereafter be convened,

during your mission. You will use your endeavours to obtain an accurate knowledge of the characters and views of the persons who may have the lead in those assemblies, and of the factions which may prevail therein, and you will regularly transmit to our aforesaid Secretary of State all such accounts upon this subject as may appear to you to be interesting for our information.

14. On your arrival at Paris, you will receive from our minister there, the whole of his correspondence and such of our late ambassadors and ministers there, as may be in his possession, and you are to consider the instructions contained therein, as the rule of your conduct, as far as the present circumstances will admit, and you shall also at the expiration of your mission, either deliver to your successor, or transmit to the office of our aforesaid Secretary of State, the originals of the official papers in your custody and your official correspondence.

15. Of all matters you shall be informed of during your stay at the Court of France, which may be of consequence and worthy our knowledge, you shall constantly give an account to us by our principal Secretary of State for Foreign Affairs, from whom you will receive such further instructions and directions as we shall think fit to send you, which you are to observe accordingly.

Paris, *June 21st*, 1790[1].

Yesterday I had my audiences of their Most Christian Majesties and of the rest of the Royal Family now at Paris[2]. I have delivered the Duke of Dorset's Letters of Recall and my credentials, which were most graciously received.

* * * * *

Paris, *June 25th*, 1790[3].

Upon some disturbances happening at Nîmes on the 4th of this month, patroles were established, in which a party of dragoons and the Regiment de Guyenne were employed. The next day the municipality, not well affected to the Revolution, having heretofore worn white cockades but now mounting the military red tufts in their hats, insisted on forming the patrole themselves and referred the question to the commissioners appointed by the King for the formation of the Departement du Gard, who gave their opinion against them; but, notwithstanding this, the municipality took upon them to forbid the Regt. de Guyenne and the dragoons to continue the patrole. On the 13th the municipality attacked the dismounted dragoons, one of whom was killed: The citizens united themselves with the dragoons and the disorder became considerable. The King's commissioners required martial law to be proclaimed and that the Regiment de Guyenne should be put in motion. The proclamation was made, but not till two hours afterwards and the regiment was not ordered out, which occasioned the repulse of the dragoons and citizens. On the 14th the municipality recommenced the

---

[1] Lord Gower's correspondence opens on the day in which the Moniteur announced that titles of nobility had been abolished by the National Assembly on Saturday, June 19.

[2] The King and Royal Family removed from Versailles to Paris on October 6, 1789. The Comte d'Artois had left the country.

[3] The account of these disturbances is given in the Moniteur of June 17 and that of the discussion on them in the Moniteur of June 19. The disorders had begun in April and become serious at the beginning of May. The Royalists were also Catholics, whereas the town was generally Protestant.

disorder, hiding themselves in their houses, from whence they fired on the citizens and at length assembled themselves in a tower, where they fortified themselves as well as they could. On the 15th the Regiment de Guyenne came to this tower, but made no attack, they were however fired upon from thence, on which their rage was no longer to be suppressed; they forced the tower and many persons were killed. The next day the aggressors assembled in a convent, from whence they were likewise dislodged; the killed in these different skirmishes amount to about 80.

This account was given to the National Assembly by one of the deputies of Nîmes, who said that the city was desirous that the King should testify to his commissioners his satisfaction at the part they had taken in defence of its inhabitants and that he should continue their powers till tranquillity was re-established. After some altercation the Assembly decreed, that their president should immediately wait upon the King and beg him to continue powers to his commissioners and to charge them expressly to maintain the public tranquillity and to divest the municipality of Nîmes of this part of their functions.

On Saturday last a body of men, consisting of those who were the most active at the taking of the Bastille, was admitted at the bar at the National Assembly when Mr le Camus read a Projet de Décret from the Committee of Pensions, which was to this effect that, struck with admiration at the heroick intrepidity of the conquerors of the Bastille, the National Assembly decrees that every man of that body shall receive an uniform and arms[1]: upon the barrel of their muskets and upon the blades of their swords shall be inscribed—*Given by the nation to .... Conqueror of the Bastille*, and besides other marks of gratitude from their country, on the 14th of next month (the day of the confederation) there is to be a place allotted for them in the Champ de Mars where France may contemplate the first conquerors of Liberty. This decree passed

[1] See Moniteur June 21, 1790. A note says that the reward gave rise to the idea ten years afterwards of sabres of honour, which were soon afterwards replaced by the institution of the Legion of honour. During the Convention no material rewards were given, but it was only declared that a citizen had deserved well of his country.

par acclamation. The consequence however may be very serious, for, I have just learnt that, the ci-devant Gardes Françaises and the Troupes du Centre, in fact the whole of the Milice Soldee, amounting to about 8000 men conceive that they are entitled to the same honors: the conquerors of the Bastille have, in consequence very handsomely waved their new honors; but the inhabitants of the Quartier and Fauxbourg St Antoine, to which they belong, insist upon their maintaining their new dignities. Mr de la Fayette and the Mayor[1], who have been occupied with these dissentions all yesterday and this day, have sent out orders to convene the principals of the dissatisfied troops in order to compromise with them.

These dissentions, my lord, become alarming in proportion as the 14th approaches. The town having promised to give a fête to the crowd which will be assembled from all parts of France on that day, it is scarcely to be supposed that it can end without some disagreeable event, occasioned by the intoxication of many thousand people assembled together, but I am far from believing that there is any premeditated plan to create fresh disturbances. The decree of the National Assembly, which passed last Sunday, abolishing hereditary nobility and all titles whatever that do not come under the name of Grande together with the prohibition of liveries and coats of arms has not met with the expected popularity. The King however has given his sanction to it. The day on which it passed, the wives of the Spanish and Sardinian Ambassadors were insulted, with words only on account of their servants' liveries. The Corps Diplomatique have in consequence complained to Mr de Montmorin and it is in agitation to have some additional mark to distinguish us from the natives, such as, that our servants should carry canes or wear some particular feather in their hats.

Mr Fitz-herbert's courier passed through this place yesterday morning between eight and nine o'clock; the Spanish courier arrived at the same time.

Yesterday the President informed the Assembly that he had seen three deputies from Avignon that morning who desired to be received at the bar on Saturday. After a few observations

[1] Bailly.

whether as petitioners their petitions should be ordered to be presented and to lie on the table till they should have deliberated on the subject, or, whether, as foreign ministers the executive power has the sole right to receive them, it was arrêté that they should be received by the Assembly on Saturday morning.

Mr de Mirabeau[1], le jeune (as he is now called, to distinguish him from his brother since the abolition of titles) is expected here to day or tomorrow to give an account of his conduct before the National Assembly. His absurd behaviour in running off with the cravates (the streamers of the colours) of his regiment at Perpignan had nearly cost him his life.

PARIS, *July* 2, 1790.

In my last dispatch I informed your Grace that jealousies were excited between the ci-devant Gardes Françaises and the Corps des Vainqueurs de la Bastille. Those jealousies have subsided, the latter having deputed Mr Bailly the Mayor, to declare to the National Assembly that they declined all marks of honor which might distinguish them from their fellow citizens.

A deputation, of a different sort, has lately afforded much astonishment. Les Dames de la Halle have sent deputies from their body to Turin, inviting the Comte and Comtesse d'Artois to Paris, in order to be present at the Federation. At Lyons they were placed in the commandant's box at the play house,

---

[1] An account of this escapade is given in the Moniteur of June 19. The Vicomte de Mirabeau was colonel of the regiment of Touraine. Mirabeau having gone to visit it at Perpignan lodged in the house of the Marquis d'Aguylar the mayor, and the flags of the regiment were placed in the same house in a room next to that occupied by Mirabeau. Mirabeau left the town at five in the morning, and when the regiment came to fetch the colours at ten they found them without their streamers. The mayor was seized and put into prison as a hostage, and Mirabeau was himself arrested at Castelnaudary and the streamers found in his luggage. Mirabeau was set at liberty by order of the assembly. On June 27 he explained that he had gone to Perpignan to quell a mutiny in his regiment, that he found the men in great disorder, and that he carried off the streamers in order that the king might send them to some town where the loyal soldiers could rally round them. Moniteur, June 29.

from whence they harangued the spectators, between the acts. They carry with them passports signed by Mr de Montmorin, Mr de la Fayette and Mr Bailly.

The Duke of Orleans[1] has ordered a table of 300 covers for the 14th and 15th, and has written to inform his friends that he intends to be here before that time. It is supposed that he will change his mind; copies of certain papers, now at the Châtelet having been sent to him officially, which may have that effect.

Eighteen hundred people are employed in preparing the Champ de Mars which is to be disposed so as to be able to contain 300,000 people, it is with great difficulty that the workmen are kept in any degree of subordination.

It does not appear probable that the debate upon the family compact[2] will come on soon, as it does not seem to be the desire of the ministry or of the majority of the Assembly that it should, as a proof however that many of the enragés wish that the question should be canvassed, I send your Grace enclosed No. 4 of a Journal published by the Société de 1789. That club and the Club des Jacobins are the places where most subjects are debated and determined upon before they are proposed in the National Assembly. La Société de 1790 has a correspondence with people of the same way of thinking in most parts of Europe.

The last dispatch that Mr de Montmorin has received from Spain is dated the 22nd. The Spanish Ambassador told me that from it he learns that the man who stabbed Mr de Florida Blanca is a French chirurgeon; he suspects that he was once his (Mr de Fernan Nunez's) valet de chambre chirurgion: and, if so, he has lived a long time in South America.

The second battalion of the Regiment de la Guadeloupe, in garrison at Port Louis, in the Island of Tobago, has rebelled against its officers and the town has been burnt to ashes. The

[1] He was at this time in England.
[2] The question of how far the Family Compact of 1761 between France and Spain was binding upon the French monarchy under its new conditions. The risk of war between England and Spain about the question of Nootka Sound was avoided by the submission of Spain. Baron de Staël says under date June 1, "Le comte de Montmorin paraît décidé à ne présenter à l'assemblée Nationale l'affaire qui regarde le pacte de famille qu'après le 14 juillet."

National Volunteers and the soldiers mutually accuse each other of being the cause of this disaster. The battalion is embarked on board some merchant ships in order to return to France.

In consequence of this event the Assembly has decreed that their President shall desire the King to order that means of subsistance and defence shall be sent to the inhabitants of Tobago; who, it may be proper to remark, consist of nearly twenty thousand blacks to three hundred and fifty whites.

But that island does not alone suffer from intestine broils, for, in a letter from Port au Prince there is an account of an insurrection of the regiment of artillery in that town against its officers, and of a conspiracy being discovered among the blacks of Cap Francais.

It is also reported, that they are acting the same sort of scenes at Martinique. In truth it is difficult to say in what part of the French dominions there are not commotions.

Paris, *July* 5, 1790.

I write by this day's post to inform your Grace of an event that happened lately near Pont-Beauvoisin.

The Abbé Comte de Cordon, a relation of the Sardinian Ambassador at this Court, in going from hence to Savoy, was attacked by the populace at a small village near and on this side of Pont-Beauvoisin; being, on account of his name, mistaken for the Ambassador: he was stript naked to discover if he had any letters about him; none however were found.

I must here mention that he had had one, written by the Ambassador upon private business, but not knowing the contents of it, he had contrived to eat it up before he was seized. The populace were long in suspence whether they should hang him or carry him back prisoner to Lyons, before they could decide, by good luck, somebody arrived who knew his person and he was allowed to proceed. On his arrival at Turin a messenger was dispatched to Paris; the Sardinian Ambassador has presented a memorial from his Court and there the affair rests at present.

When, in my last dispatch I said there were 1800 men at work in the Champ de Mars, my calculation was short of the real number; at present there are almost as many thousands: and yesterday, being Sunday, 5000 of the bourgeoisie worked voluntarily.

Some French sailors, having seized the nets of a Neapolitan fishing vessel in the port of Martigues, the Neapolitans applied for redress, but, not being able to obtain it, they have seized the nets of a French vessel by way of reprisals. An affair of the same sort has happened at Toulon. An Algerene had taken a Neapolitan vessel, which was retaken, near the port of Toulon, by Neapolitan and French sailors and carried to the Lazaretto. The captain demanded his ship, and upon being refused, sailed for Algiers in order to lay his complaint before the Dey. In the first case, the King has ordered the Amirante de Martigues to proceed against the aggressors and in the latter he has ordered the vessel to be restored; for both these measures His Majesty has received the thanks of the National Assembly.

The Marquis de Pons, his M. C. Majesty's Ambassador in Sweden is going in the same capacity to the Court of Spain.

I send your Grace the Postillon par Calais of yesterday.

Paris, *July* 9, 1790.

In order to prevent confusion at this time when it is so much to be feared, the elections for the new municipality of Paris are postponed, by a decree of the National Assembly, to the 25th of this month.

Mr Albert de Rioms, who is appointed to command the fleet, is to be allowed to take the civic oath on the day of the Confederation for himself and for the sailors under his command with an intent to do away his unpopularity. When this was agitated in the Assembly it was opposed by Mr Robertspierre[1]

---

[1] This spelling of the name gives some countenance to the idea that Robespierre was an Englishman or an Irishman by birth, and that his real name was Robert Spier. Madame Huber in her letters to Lord Auckland (MS.) calls him Bob Spier.

and Mr Charles de Lameth; the former expressed, very strongly, his hopes that France would not side with Spain on the present occasion.

Having in my dispatch No. 2 enclosed a paper published by the Société de 1789 in favor of Spain, I think it proper to inform your Grace that I believe what is there said to be far from the general opinion of that society. They have since published the articles of the family compact with notes to prove the impossibility of maintaining that treaty with their present constitution. They say that they cannot adhere to engagements which never were just, which are incompatible with the rights of man and the principles of a free constitution and which render the nation dependant upon the will of one man and that man a stranger. They declare such treaties between Kings to be conspiracies against the people of their respective countries.

I have reason to think that the preparations at Brest proceed extremely slowly and that they are in great want both of men and ammunition: with regard to the latter, most of the municipalities, through whose territories powder and other ammunitions are to pass, have stopt them, and the Assembly has been obliged to make a decree, by way of passport for them, that of the minister not having sufficient effect.

Mr Necker on Sunday last[1] having asked for a supply of 45 millions of livres, the Caisse d'Escompte was ordered by the National Assembly to pay that sum into the treasury in notes *portant promesses d'assignats:* since which time the administrators of that bank have issued out daily notes to the amount of 3 millions and a half.

The National Assembly has decreed that justice shall be administered in the name of the King. That the venality of officers of judicature shall be abolished and that the judges shall be paid by the State. They are to be elected for the term of six years; at the expiration of which time they may be re-elected. They cannot be dismissed except in cases of *forfeiture*. They are to have suppléants to supply their place,

[1] Von Sybel says "the assignats fabricated in April had already been spent before the end of August, and no new resources could anywhere be discovered."

in case of death or dismission, till the expiration of the six years, and *assesseurs* (assistants), in case of temporary disability.

In all matters civil and criminal, pleadings, reports and judgments are to be public and every citizen is to have a right to defend his own cause by speech or writing. All criminal matters are to be tried by jury and the code of civil law is to be immediately reformed.

The town of Grenoble has written to the Assemblé Nationale that a camp of 1500 men is forming in Savoy, and that the Chasseurs de Royal-Corse now in garrison there have received orders to quit that town; they express their fears of the consequence. The President has been ordered to lay the letter before the King and to intreat his Majesty to quiet the fears of the inhabitants of Grenoble.

The zeal shewn by the Parisiens that the circus in the Champ de Mars should be finished before the 14th exceeds all belief. They go in large troops, drum beating, colours flying to assist the workmen.

Many people still doubt that the Duke of Orleans will appear on the occasion: his chancellor, Mr de la Touche read a [letter] from him to the National Assembly in which he says that if they decide qu'il n'y a pas lieu à deliberer he will certainly assist at the fête. They did not do that but called for the order of the day; how his Serene Highness will understand that proceeding remains to be known. I enclose the Exposé de la Conduite de Mr le Duc d'Orleans.

Paris, *July* 15, 1790.

The ceremony of the Confederation was performed yesterday without the least disturbance: I have not heard that a single accident has happened. I shall send the particulars to your Grace by the courier.

Paris, *July* 16, 1790.

The ceremony of the fourteenth was conducted with astonishing regularity. An event however had nearly happened which would have impeded it and might have been the cause of many peoples' death. The temporary wooden bridge over the Seine gave way in one place: the rest however remained sufficiently firm to allow the procession to pass over it. The oath taken by his Majesty was this:

I, King of the French, swear to the Nation to employ all the power delegated to me by the constitutional law of the State to maintain the constitution decreed by the National Assembly and accepted by me, and to cause the laws to be executed.

The Duke of Orleans, whose arrival last Sunday made little impression, was the only one of the Royal Family present who did not meet with applause, he finds himself not applauded by the people, and treated with insult by the nobility.

The National Assembly has ordered the following Projet de Décret from the Comité Militaire to be printed.

Art^{le}. 1st. The army shall consist of 204,619 soldiers or officers, of which 150,953 en activité, and 50,000 sedentaires dans les departemens: the proportion of foreign troops in time of peace, including the Swiss, to be as one to eight and three-fifths.

Art^{le}. 2nd. The proportion of the infantry to the rest of the army as three and one-third to four. The cavalry as one to five and a fifth.

Art^{le}. 3rd. The French army in time of war, by the addition of foreign troops shall consist of 233,730 men. The proportion of the infantry to the rest of the army will then be as five and a half to seven, the cavalry as one to five and a third. The artillery and engineers as one to sixteen seven-ninths.

Art^{le}. 4th. The proportion of officers to soldiers in the infantry in time of war as one to twenty-eight one-third, in the cavalry and dragoons as one to eighteen, in the light troops as one to twenty, in the artillery and engineers as one to ten and one-third.

It is the intention of the Committee of Pensions to reduce their amount from 58 millions per annum to 18 millions.

Letters from many of the seaport towns in Spain mention that orders have been received from government to allow the merchant ships which had been detained in the several ports to proceed to the places of their destination.

I am to acquaint your Grace that the Prince of Monaco has desired me to convey to their Majesties in the most respectful manner, his wishes for their prosperity and happiness.

PARIS, *July* 16, 1790.

On Sunday last the Spanish Ambassador informed me and the rest of the foreign ministers that he had seen Mr de Montmorin the preceding day, who told him that Mr de Bailly, the mayor of Paris, had signified to him his intention to write to the foreign ministers informing them that there would be a covered gallery prepared for them on the fourteenth. It was the general opinion that this was not a sufficiently formal invitation. I therefore agreed with the rest to return politeness for politeness; that we should leave our names in person at Mr de Bailly's door but not to assist at the ceremony. On Monday night, Mr de Ségneville, secrétaire à la conduite des Ambassadeurs, wrote to us that he was that moment ordered by Mr de Montmorin de nous prévenir, au nom de la municipalité et de l'Assemblée federative que Messieurs les Ambassadeurs et Ministres Etrangers ainsi que les Etrangers qui les accompagneront, auront à la ceremonie du pacte federatif des places reservées dans la gallerie couverte ou seront placés le Roi et l'Assemblée Nationale.

In consequence of this I waited, on Tuesday morning on the Swedish Ambassador[1], whose opinion I judged to be the same as mine, and I found that I was not mistaken; he agreeing with me that this formal notification from the municipality ought to

---

[1] Baron de Stael Holstein, husband of Madame de Stael née Necker. He gives an account of the same circumstance in his correspondence July 15. Lord Gower's account of this transaction is more full than that of Baron de Stael.

alter the determination made on Sunday, he promised to meet me at the Bureau des Affaires Etrangères, where, being Tuesday, we should meet the other ministers: from thence I went to the Nuntio, whose opinion I already knew to coincide with mine. I found him at the Bureau des Affaires Etrangères, not disposed to support his opinion with vigour. My next step was to discover Mr de Montmorin's sentiments who ingenuously enough told me that his private opinion was that we should go; but being asked what he imagined the King might wish, he declined giving any answer.

Upon the arrival of the Spanish and Neapolitan Ambassadors, they shewed an inclination to maintain their former resolution; upon their addressing themselves to me, I declared that I was ready to conform to the determination of the rest but gave my opinion for going. Upon this the Spanish Ambassador took the first opportunity of desiring Mr de Montmorin, before us all, to write to his Majesty requesting to know his pleasure. The minister's answer was that, if we insisted upon it, he would write, but, at the same time, he could tell us beforehand the answer would be that the King was indifferent and that we should do what we thought proper. Mr de Fernan-Nunez with much warmth, observed that this was the sort of treatment he had met with during the whole of this year; that if the King's answer was to that effect the whole blame of our proceeding should fall upon Mr de Montmorin. Upon this the minister retired to his cabinet, wrote to the King and, without waiting for the answer, ordered a letter to be written to the mayor desiring a guard for every foreign minister's carriage, all carriages not so attended being forbid on the day of the ceremony. His Majesty's answer was that he should be happy to see the foreign ministers at all public ceremonies at which he himself should assist. We accordingly went the next morning in a body, all being present except the Dutch Ambassador whose state of health was a sufficient excuse. It seems to be a general opinion that our absence might have occasioned serious consequences, and I flatter myself that my conduct upon this occasion will not incur the censure of his Majesty and his confidential ministers.

PARIS, *July* 23, 1790.

The day of Confederation has been followed by a week of conviviality. Panem and Circenses have been bestowed with a most liberal hand, and the deputies are about to return to their respective departments well pleased and in good harmony with their fellow citizens of the capital. They have been desired to exhort their countrymen to pay their shares of the patriotic contribution, twenty-eight thousand municipallities not having as yet subscribed, and, lest exhortations should fail, the National Assembly has ordered the Committee of Finance to prepare a Projet de Décret which may empower the municipallities to fulfill that part of their duty and by coercive means to procure exact payments of the patriotic contribution, and also to enable the districts and departments to oblige the municipallities so to do with all the diligence that the public good requires.

As soon as one cloud has passed without falling another appears on the horizon; the elections for the new municipallity begin next Monday and, it is supposed, they will continue some weeks, during which time there will be great need for the exertions of Mr de Bailly and Mr de la Fayette, exertions which of late have deserved the greatest commendations, for to them probably is owing the wonderful tranquillity that has subsisted.

It is reported that the King of Sardinia has ordered all French subjects to quit Nice and every part of his dominions bordering on France. I omitted to inform your Grace, in my last, that Mr de Bonne-Savardin, who is accused of a conspiracy with Mr de Maillebois against the present government, has made his escape from prison. I enclose a letter of Mr Guignard, ci-devant Comte de St Priest, to the President of the National Assembly, which he sent to me for that purpose: your Grace will find by it that he has been impeached by the Comités de Récherches both of the town and of the National Assembly of having entered into the same conspiracy. It is supposed that they were to be supplied with men and money by the King of Sardinia to enter Dauphiné, while ten thousand men, raised by the Prince of Hesse and other German Princes who have possessions in Alsace, were to invade the last mentioned province.

The National Assembly has, after many debates on the subject, decreed that East India goods are to be allowed to be imported only at Port de l'Orient and Toulon. They have also decreed that in every session upon the proposition of the executive power the number of individuals of every rank both in the army and navy shall be determined by a decree of the legislative body sanctioned by the King.

A letter has been read by one of the secretaries from Mr de la Luzerne demanding money for the equipment of the fleet which the Assembly has authorized, but no notice has as yet been taken of it. I take the liberty of informing your Grace that, on the same day, a letter of compliment was read from Lord Stanhope, as president of a society in London who call themselves Friends to the French Revolution, merely to shew what effect the reading of it had on the Assembly. Mr C. Lameth moved that it should be printed and also that the president should be ordered to write an answer to the society, and declared that, in his opinion, it might tend to the tranquillity of Europe. Another member opposed it, and whenever he spoke of the two nations as rivals he was called to order with much clamor. Mr Lameth's motion was carried.

To the few accidents that happened on the 14th I have to add the oversetting of a boat by which some persons were drowned, among the rest two deputies, sons of the mayor of Aurillac. This has been thought a sufficient occasion for the attendance of deputies from the town of Paris to attend the obsequies and a decree to that purpose from the National Assembly.

Paris, *July* 30, 1790.

Alarms of a very serious nature, and ill founded suspicions have of late occupied the attention of the National Assembly. An express arrived on Tuesday from the department of the Ardennes informing them that the commandant of Mézières had received orders from Mr de Bouillé at Metz to allow Austrian troops to pass through Mézières, in their way to the Low Countries; in consequence of a requisition to that effect from the Comte de Mercy, that Rocroy, Charleville and Avesnes were without troops, that the whole country was in the greatest consternation, that, instead of attending to the harvest the peasants were arming themselves and that the navigation of the Meuse was interrupted. A decree was passed in consequence appointing six commissioners to examine, at the war office, the King's orders to the several commanders of the frontier-towns, and also to require from the Minister of Foreign Affairs a communication of the intelligence that he has received relative to the political situations of the neighbouring Powers. I must observe that, during the debate, one of the members, Mr Martineau, expressed no small suspicions of the conduct of the British Cabinet; he imagines that there subsists a good understanding between the Courts of London and Madrid and dreads the consequence.

By the report of the commissioners it appears that Mr de Bouillé's letter was written by his Majesty's orders in consequence of a convention made between the two Powers in 1769, although a decree passed the Assembly on the 28th of February forbidding the introduction of any foreign troops without a decree of the legislative body, that, with regard to the troops in the frontier-towns it appears that there are but 150 men at Rocroy and one battalion of the Regiment of Esterhazy at Charleville, the Regiment of Berchigny being lately sent from thence to the frontiers of Champagne. Alsace and the three bishopricks have as many troops as in time of war, and the frontier of the Alps was never better guarded and will be still more so by the regiments which are sent to Lyons, for, I have to inform your Grace that, in consequence of the late disturbances and the impossibility of levying the taxes, five regiments have been sent there.

With regard to the political state of foreign Powers, the commissioners learnt from Mr Montmorin that England was arming with the greatest activity, that our ships were too large to pass the Sound and that it appeared improbable that so large a fleet was intended against Spain alone. In the Journal des débats et des décrets it is thus worded, il est impossible aussi qui ces armemens regardent l'Espagne seule. Il est bien probable qu-elles ménacent également les possessions Françoises. As that paper carries with it a certain degree of authenticity, I thought proper to write to Mr Montmorin to know if he had used such expressions, I have received an answer, copy of which I enclose to your Grace.

They learn also that Spain is arming with great activity, but that nothing is to be feared from that quarter. That the minister believes the King of Hungary is inclined to peace; that if he concludes the treaty with Prussia,[1] &c., he will turn his force to the reduction of the Belgic provinces and, upon being asked whether the Cardinal de Rohan was intrigueing with the Princes of Germany who have possessions in Alsace, he said that he had received information from Ratisbone to that purpose. He told them that the alliance of Prussia with England was certain and that its influence over Holland was very great. That, with regard to the King of Sardinia's dominions, he knew but of two battalions at Nice, but, that it was true that the French were ordered into the interior parts of the kingdom; he said he believed there were not above two thousand men at Chambéry. This report produced a decree to the following effect. That in consequence of a decree of the 28th of February last the orders of the Secretary of the War Department to the commanders in the frontier-towns were to be regarded *comme non avenus*, the National Assembly reserving to itself to decree with regard to the passing of the Austrian troops when it shall know the number of men, the different kinds of arms and implements of war, the order of their march and the object of their destination. Another decree has passed desiring his Majesty to give orders that the most strict police may be observed and to prevent any infringement of the law of nations and that every step shall be taken with the belligerent powers to maintain freedom of commerce and particularly on the Meuse. The King has been also desired to issue orders for the speedy manufacture of all sorts of instruments of war and his ministers are to inform the Comité Militaire of all demands

---

[1] A treaty eventually concluded at Reichenbach.

of arms and ammunition that shall be made to them by the municipalities on the frontiers and to give in an account of the arms distributed by them.

In the course of the debate it was asserted, by one of the commissioners, that Mr Montmorin had said that the Prince of Condé was the most dangerous enemy to the Revolution; that he had money but he knew not by what means, and as a farther corroboration of this a *denonciation* against him, from the municipality of Cette in Languedoc, for having published a manifesto was offered to be produced. A motion was moved by the Duc d'Aiguillon to censure the ministers and another by Mr Mirabeau the elder to declare the Prince of Condé a traitor to his country and to confiscate his estate in case he did not disavow the manifesto in the space of three weeks; but neither was carried. A committee has been appointed to examine the treaties between France and other countries and the respective engagements which may result from them.

Accounts are arrived that Mr de Bonne-Savardin has been retaken by two of Mr de la Fayette's aid de camps at Châlon sur Marne, in company with the Abbé Barmont, a member of the National Assembly, passing with a deputy to the Confederation from Strasburgh as his servants: the latter had a large packet of letters from the Cardinal de Rohan: a detachment from hence is sent for them. This event adds to the fermentation, which I fear it will be very difficult to quell, and which renders the situation of affairs in many respects alarming.

In consequence of Mr de la Luzerne's application the Assembly has granted but one million for the navy.

The General Assembly of St. Domingo has declared that they will acknowledge no other authority than that of the King. It may be worth while to observe that MM. Curt and Guibert were received by the Assembly as representatives of the Island of Guadeloupe in September last upon condition that they should be acknowledged as such by their constituents; they however have chosen others and the Assembly has agreed to admit them all.

PARIS, *August* 2, 1790.

I am sorry to inform your Grace that his Majesty has been confined, for some days past, with a tooth-ache and swelled face accompanied with a slight fever; the account from St. Cloud yesterday says that the fever is rather abated.

I enclose an extract of a bulletin officiel, which the Swedish Ambassador has received from Stockholm, giving an account of a victory obtained over the Russians on the ninth of last month by their flotte-legère; some compensation for the defeat of their grand fleet, of which only fourteen sail of the line are returned to port.

I also send your Grace copies of a second letter from Mr de Montmorin and of a letter from Mr Friteau to the former, by which it appears that Mr Friteau's private opinion was falsely attributed to Mr Montmorin.

PARIS, *August* 6, 1790.

I have the pleasure of informing your Grace that his most Christian Majesty is almost entirely recovered from his late indisposition. I have also that of being able to say that, not only Paris, but all parts of the kingdom are at present without disturbance. The elections for this municipality proceed with a tranquillity that was not expected. Mr Bailly is re-elected mayor to the satisfaction of all parties and there is no doubt that Mr la Fayette will be continued commandant general. A letter was read, on Monday last, to the National Assembly, from Mr Montmorin, containing his most Christian Majesty's orders to acquaint them that England was encreasing her armament; that it would be therefore necessary (although a good understanding continued to exist between the two nations) that France should also encrease hers; and inclosing a letter from Mr Fernan Nunez dated the 16 of June last, which Mr Montmorin observes, contains the state of the negotiations at that time between England and Spain. He says that, in hopes of their coming to an understanding his Majesty had postponed urging the Assembly to a decision but that he could no longer delay that measure. The Spanish Ambassador's letter asserts that the speedy and exact performance of the Treaty of 1761, called the Family Compact is become an indispensible preliminary to treat with success; that, under that necessity, Spain is obliged to have recourse to the aid of France and that the King his master has ordered him to ask explicitly what France can do, in the present conjuncture, in order to assist Spain. An immediate determination is required and the measures which the Court of France shall adopt must be active open and positive so as to avoid the least occasion of distrust. If otherwise, his most Christian Majesty must not be surprized if Spain should look for other friends and other allies among all the powers of Europe, without excepting any, upon whose assistance she can depend in case of necessity.

Under these circumstances it being the general opinion that the Assembly would decide in favor of the family compact, I thought it was my duty to send to Mr Montmorin copies of the declaration and counter-declaration which I had just received from Mr Fitz-Herbert[1]. They have been communicated to the Assembly; in consequence of which a further delay of their decision has been obtained.

The National Assembly, having blended the plan of the committee with that of the Minister for the War Department, have at length decreed that the standing army shall consist of from 150 to 154 thousand men. The infantry being from 110 to 112 thousand, the cavalry from 30 to 31 thousand 500, the artillery and fortification from 10 thousand to 10 thousand 500. The Swiss regiments are to be continued. Your Grace will observe with what reason the Ministers of the War Department and of the Navy complain of want of subordination, (in the enclosed postillon par Calais) both in the army and navy.

---

[1] Mr Fitz-Herbert was English minister in Spain. The declaration and counter-declaration had reference to the dispute of Nootka Sound.

Paris, *August* 13, 1790.

A general want of subordination, proofs of which occur every day forebodes a short continuance of the present tranquillity. In the navy, it has forced Messrs Guy and Pondevès to return to France from their cruises in the Mediterranean and off the Leeward Islands. In the army, it bears a still more formidable aspect, seven regiments have formed a military congress and, at Metz, the soldiers have threatened to destroy Mr de Bouillé and the rest of the officers under his command. In the strong language of Mr de la Tour du Pin, France, which cannot exist without soldiers, may soon be unable to exist with them. While the friends to the present constitution are daily discovering fresh causes of alarm from abroad, an universal relaxation of discipline and a want of energy in the executive power are forming real dangers at home.

An event has lately happened which proves the fears of plots against this country from foreign parts that possess the minds of the people and the little attention that is shewn by them to the executive part of government.

A courier from Vienna, with letters directed to the Post Master General at Paris, has been stopt at a very small town, (but a municipality) near Bar le Duc. The packet was opened; it contained a letter for Mr Montmorin and two others, one for the Spanish Ambassador, the other for the Comte de Florida Blanca: the direction of the two last being written in Spanish to men dignified with the title of Count which in that language happens to be written Condé, the letters were supposed to have been sent from the prince of that name and accordingly opened. The only satisfaction the Spanish Ambassador has obtained is a decree of the National Assembly disapproving the conduct of the municipality and expressing their regrets on the occasion. The judges of the Châtelet have impeached two of the members of the National Assembly for being concerned in the affair of the 6th of last October. They had the delicacy not to disclose their names, but it is generally known that the Duke of Orleans and the elder Mirabeau are the persons accused. This business is before the Comité des Rapports.

In consequence of harsh expressions which had been used in the Assembly on the preceding evening between Mr Barnave and Mr Cazalès, they met in the Bois de Boulogne on Wednesday morning. The latter received a shot in the head[1] but the wound is pronounced to be not dangerous. If Mr Barnave had fallen the resentment of the people might have been fatal to others as well as to Mr Cazalès.

Paris, *August* 20, 1790.

The executive and legislative powers have at length united their endeavours to restore discipline and subordination in the army and navy.

A most alarming insurrection of the garrison of Nancy has obliged the National Assembly to give to the King the full power of the sword in case persuasion may not have the desired effect. The three regiments, Du Roy, Mestre de Camp cavalry and de Chateauvieux a Swiss regiment, in short the whole garrison of Nancy, have risen against their officers, broke open the military chest and divided the money contained in it. The Assembly have unanimously decreed that the instigators of this rebellion as well as the soldiers are guilty of the crime of lèze-nation: that those who have taken any part whatever in it and who shall not have declared, by writing, if it is thought necessary, within the space of twenty-four hours after the publication of the present decree, that they acknowledge and repent of their error, shall be punished accordingly and, in order to enforce it, they have requested his Majesty to appoint some general officer with power to collect together the troops and national guards of the Département de la Meurthe and all the neighbouring departments. The King has, in consequence, named Mr Malseigne, a Maréchal de Camp and Brigadier des Carabiniers, to that post.

The Regiment du Roy is remarkably well furnished with cartridges but the cannons have fortunately no carriages.

---

[1] Bertrand de Molleville says that he was protected by the thickness of his hat. Fashionable society crowded to pay its respects to M. de Cazalès.

The Assembly has made great progress in the code of penal laws for the navy, in which they have instituted a military jury.

The formation of the army proceeds upon the bases laid down jointly by the minister and Comité Militaire, of which I gave your Grace an account in my dispatch No. 7.

A courier, it is said, arrived on Sunday last from Bordeaux with letters to the ministry complaining of want of specie; that without it it was impossible to provide themselves with the necessaries of life that being in great distress for want of corn, they had sent to the Upper Languedoc to purchase it, but the people of the country would not accept of assignats, in consequence of which they desire leave to stop and apply to their own use the supply of piastres expected from Spain.

There is another report, to which I fear there is too much reason to give credit, that the Comité Diplomatique are of opinion in favour of maintaining the family compact.

The appanages are taken from the Princes of the Blood, by a decree of the National Assembly, in place of which they are to be allowed a million of livres per annum.

The accusation against Mr de Mirabeau and the Duke of Orleans, who is fortunate in having the assistance of the former's abilities, it is supposed, will not affect in any considerable manner either of the accused persons.

The only agreeable news that I have to send to your Grace from this country is that the harvest, at least in this neighbourhood had been got in extremely well.

PARIS, *August* 27, 1790.

The day before yesterday Mr Mirabeau the elder reported to the National Assembly the opinion of the Comité Diplomatique with regard to the family compact. It consisted in advising the Assembly to empower them to examine that treaty in order to form out of it a national compact by leaving out all the articles offensive and, at the same time to request the King to order his minister at the Court of Madrid to enter into a negotiation with the Spanish ministry upon those grounds. They proposed two decrees.

1st. That all existing treaties shall be maintained by the French nation untill it shall have revised and modified them. 2nd. That, before the thorough examination of treaties which the nation may think proper to continue or alter, the King shall be requested to make known to all the Powers with which France is connected the justice and love of peace are the bases of the French constitution; that the nation cannot admit in her treaties any stipulations which are not purely defensive and commercial. That accordingly they request the King to inform his Catholic Majesty that the French nation, in taking all proper measures to maintain peace, will abide by the engagements which her government has contracted with Spain. That they also desire the King to order his ministers to negotiate accordingly with the Court of Spain and to commission thirty ships of the line, eight of which at least to be fitted out in the ports of the Mediterranean.

This report was taken into consideration yesterday morning and, after a short debate, the Assembly decreed that they would abide by the defensive and commercial engagements which the government has contracted with Spain; that the King should be desired to order his Ambassador to negotiate with the ministers of the Catholic King in order to strengthen, by a national treaty, tyes useful to both people and to fix with precision and clearness all stipulations which may not be entirely conformable to the views of general peace and to the principles of justice, which shall always be the politics of the French and also, taking into consideration the armaments of the different nations of Europe, their progressive encrease, the security of the French colonies and commerce, they decree that the King shall be desired to order into commission forty-five ships of the line with a proportionable number of frigates and small vessels.

Thus your Grace perceives that my notions with regard to the decision of this question have proved too true. How, in the present state of their finances, they can think it possible to equip so large a fleet surpasses my conception. They must either expect money from abroad or by voting what they can never execute endeavour to compensate with a useless shew of zeal for not entirely abiding by the family compact. Certain it is that at this time when both parties are most exasperated against each other, upon this one point they are most thoroughly agreed.

Upon my expressing my surprize, yesterday evening to Mr Montmorin, at the number of vessels voted, he declared himself as much so as I could be ; he assured me that the King and his ministers wished most ardently for peace, that in consequence of the decree of the National Assembly they should send orders to commission more ships but that it would be done (this he said in the utmost confidence) avec la plus grande lenteur.

The last accounts from Metz and Nancy are favorable; at the latter the soldiers, by the intervention of the National Militia, have declared their repentance.

As I wish your Grace to receive an early account of the decision of the National Assembly, I send the messenger with this dispatch at five o'clock A.M.

PARIS, *August* 29, 1790.

I had a conference this afternoon with Mr Necker, at his desire, in which he added his assurances, to those I had received before from Mr Montmorin, of the sincere wish for peace entertained by his Majesty and his ministers.

If the decree had been worded according to their intention, thirty instead of forty-five would have been the number of ships voted : he desired me to observe that it authorized them to put into commission, forty-five ships but did not oblige them to fit out so large a number.

I lead him to confess that the fear of disobliging Spain was the real cause of so extravagant a decree and, having hinted that what was intended to sooth Spain might irritate England, he acknowledged his fears of it and promised to endeavour, when it is ratified by his Majesty, to have some expressions made use of, which, though not contrary to the decree, might tend to weaken the unfavorable impression it may have made in England.

Although peace may be, and I believe it is, the sincere wish of his Majesty and the ministry there is certainly a very large body of men, in this country inclined to war. The aristocratical party has little to hope from peace and shews evident signs of wishing to profit by the confusion which a war would certainly occasion. Some look for an opportunity of breaking the commercial treaty[1]: others, and that not a small number from mere jealousy. I will not take upon me to say that Spanish money has had influence on any members of the National Assembly, although there are appearances which might in some degree give rise to such an opinion.

Mr Gouvion, major general of the Garde Nationale and a confidential friend of Mr la Fayette is gone to Brussels, it is supposed, to negotiate with Mr Van-der-Noot[2].

Mr de la Tour-du-Pin has this day informed the Assembly that, in spite of the efforts of Mr Malseigne and of the municipality, the insurrection still continues at Nancy. On the 24th the Regiment du Roy and that of Mestre-de-camp signed their submission to the decrees of the National Assembly, but on the 26th they became again refractory and the Swiss Regiment of Chateauvieux has continued throughout to be disobedient. Mr de Bouillé is determined to compel them to obedience and has accordingly called together the National Guards and the troops in the neighbourhood in order to fight against the garrison in case it should be absolutely necessary.

Paris, *September* 3, 1790.

By the activity and good conduct of Mr de Bouillé the insurrection of the troops in garrison at Nancy is supprest, but not without considerable slaughter. On the first day of this month he appeared before the town with all the troops and Gardes Nationales he could collect in the neighbourhood: the latter requested to be placed in the first ranks, which was

[1] The Treaty with England concluded in 1786.
[2] The leader of the revolutionary party in Belgium.

granted, in hopes that their appearance might prevent the seditious soldiers from firing; but unfortunately this had not the desired effect: some of the regiment having fired it soon became general. The Regiment du Roy, the first which capitulated, is sent to Verdun, of the Regiment de Chateauvieux those who are not killed are taken prisoners and the Regiment de Mestre de Camp is ordered to Toul. The following event had obliged Mr de Bouillé to send to the Assembly requesting them to appoint commissioners to assist him in enforcing their decree.

Mr Denoue, who commands the Regiment du Roy in the absence of their colonel Mr de Châtelet, was forced into a dungeon and Mr Malseigne, to avoid the same fate, had escaped by force out of the town and was pursued but not overtaken before he had joined the Carabiniers at Lunéville who after a slight engagement were obliged to bring him back; but what principally operated with Mr de Bouillé was a report industriously spread about, not only at Nancy but throughout the country, that he was sent by the ministry and the aristocratical party in order to effect a counter-revolution. He is now reproached by the club of the Jacobins and some few members of the Assembly for having approached the town before the arrival of the commissioners, but his conduct is applauded by all impartial men.

The populace collected together last night with an intention of insulting Mr de la Tour du Pin, whose son, Mr de Gouvernet has been active at Nancy but, by the vigilance of the guards they were dispersed.

The National Assembly received on Wednesday last the notification of his Majesty's sanction of their decree of the 26th in which they were informed that, in order to fulfil gradually their intentions, the King had determined to begin by arming 16 ships of the line, which added to the former put into commission would make the number of commissioned ships 30: at the same time he would take proper steps to have the whole number 45 completed with all the haste that the turn of affairs might require and that this arrangement made no alteration with regard to the calculation of the expence laid before them by Mr de la Luzerne, viz. 21 millions: but that his Majesty would take care that the money which should be voted by the Assembly should be called for in proportion to the armament. The Assembly has postponed their decision with regard to the further issuing of assignats till the 10th of this month. Mr de Mirabeau's plan of issuing to the amount of two thousand millions seems not to be generally approved of. Three frigates with troops on board have lately sailed from Rochefort to Tobago.

I am this instant informed that the Assembly has decreed a vote of thanks to the National Guard of Metz to the troops and to Mr de Bouillé.

Paris, *September* 10, 1790.

I received your Grace's dispatch No. 4 on Saturday last and on that evening I delivered a memorial to Mr de Montmorin, copy of which I inclose; I at the same time observed to him the obvious impossibility of harmony remaining uninterrupted between the two countries if France should think itself bound to take part in support of any claims, however unfounded, which the Court of Spain may chuse to advance.

I have this instant received a letter from Mr de Montmorin with a copy of his dispatch to Mr de la Luzerne, both of which I inclose.

Quiet is restored at Nancy, but the means taken to effect it have not been approved of so generally as might have been supposed considering that if that insurrection had not been timely suppressed it would probably have been the beginning of a civil war. Mr de la Fayette having signified his approbation of it his enemies les enragés, or as they may be now called the Duke of Orleans's friends have tried to hurt him by rendering that opinion unpopular, but that is not the only means they have taken, money in no small quantity has lately been distributed among the lower class of people, and they have so far succeeded that it was believed yesterday that he meant to follow the example of Mr Necker, whose resignation has pleased all parties.

Fanaticism and insubordination have united in the Vivarois at the Château de Jalès[1] and have formed a confederation which calls for all the energy of government to suppress it. Tormented with internal foes and constantly alarmed at dangers abroad, particularly from the eastern frontiers I believe the ministry wish sincerely to see peace established between England and Spain; I also believe that the moderate people and the Club of 1789 have the same wish; the aristocrates and enragés look for confusion let it arise from what quarter it may and in the present state of the finance of this country a foreign war is almost a sure way of effecting it. Among other causes however of the vote which passed on the debate upon the family compact, I should have added the fear of losing the West India Islands, all of which have shewn great disaffection to the present government; the same fear and a desire of profiting by a neutrality may operate, in case a war between England and Spain should be unavoidable in making them discover that Spain has been the aggressor.

It is generally supposed that fourteen ships of the line are in tolerable readiness at Brest; the want of men is what distresses them most. The arsenal is furnished with stores sufficient to fit out sixteen more in every article except hemp.

The Assembly has postponed the decision upon the subject of the assignats to the 17th of this month.

Paris, *September* 17, 1790.

I have reason to believe that the utmost exertions are making at Brest and that twenty-one ships of the line are now almost ready for sailing, the original fourteen and seven additional since the decree of the Assembly: for of the sixteen lately put into commission there are seven at Brest and nine at Toulon, so I am informed by Mr de Montmorin.

The spirit of sedition, which clogs the wheels of government in every part of the French dominions, has shewn itself very

[1] At this place the national guard of the department of Ardèche, Hérault and Lozère had encamped and renewed as an embodied army the oath taken at the Federation.

strongly at Brest: the National Assembly has not listened to the wishes of the mutineers and it remains to be seen whether prompt payment and soft words will satisfy them.

The money in specie which Government is obliged to procure to pay both sailors and workmen costs at least 12 per cent.

The last accounts from Saint Domingo are very alarming. The French part of that island is in a state of actual rebellion.

At Angers there has been a riot upon the old pretence of the dearness of corn: it is certain that there are people who are using their utmost endeavours to make an artificial scarcity of it; men go about the country and buy large quantities from the farmers at a considerable price a quarter of which they pay and oblige them to lay up the corn in magazines till a fixed time when they are to receive payment for the other three quarters.

Mr de la Fayette's popularity, which was considerably sunk by the money and calumny of his enemies, is again rising and he is daily visited by large bodies of National Militia from the different Sections of Paris and from the neighbouring municipalities who come to assure him of their attachment.

In consequence of your Grace's instructions I omit no opportunity of letting it be understood that nothing but necessity can occasion any views to be entertained in England hostile to France or to the settlement of their present constitution. I at the same time signify that any assistance afforded to Spain will oblige the British Cabinet to adopt such measures as may be most likely to render that assistance ineffectual and I flatter myself this language has made some impression on the popular party.

I send your Grace Mr Necker's[1] last report to the National Assembly which has been presented this morning.

---

[1] Mr Necker had left Paris on Sept. 3 and presented a letter to the National Assembly on the condition of the finances before his departure.

Paris, *September* 24, 1790.

The arrival of le Léopard at Brest from Saint Domingo, with above eighty members of the Colonial Assembly on board, has increased the disturbances in that port: the crew of the Patriote have risen against their captain and it is feared the rest of the fleet will follow their example. The King, at the desire of the National Assembly, has sent commissioners, who are to use every possible means in order to restore discipline in the fleet and order in the town of Brest. An arduous undertaking if one may judge from Mr Albert's letter to Mr la Luzerne.

Government has been trying to get money at Lyons for the arsenal at Toulon but without success.

The subject of the Assignats occupies the attention of every body; the wellwishers to Mr Mirabeau's original plan for the emission of twenty hundred millions, by which they would probably have made large fortunes at the expense of the nation, have been making exertions in every part of the kingdom to obtain addresses in favor of it, at Paris they have so far succeeded that all the Sections have declared in favor of it, but, as there is no chance of its being carried in the Assemby Mr Mirabeau has given up the attempt of issuing at once so great a quantity, eight hundred millions it is supposed will be the largest amount.

The affair of the 6th of October[1] last is to be debated in the Assembly on Monday next, in case the business of the Assignats is finished by that time: the Judges of the Châtelet have published, by order of the Assembly, their Procédure Criminelle upon the subject, which I send to your Grace as it is a matter of no small curiosity.

There are accounts received from different ports in the Mediterranean that the Spaniards are bombarding Tangiers.

The Spanish Ambassador is in hourly expectation of a courier from his Court; he supposes their fleet is returned to port.

---

[1] This was the official enquiry which had been held at the Châtelet into the circumstances of the attack on Versailles and the removal of the King to Paris.

PARIS, *October 1st,* 1790.

Yesterday I communicated your Grace's dispatch, No. 7, to Mr de Montmorin, in consequence of your instructions to that effect; I had not an earlier opportunity, as that minister has been in the country, from whence he returned on Wednesday night, when he informed me that he could not see me till after the Council on Thursday. I must therefore wait some days for the result of that communication.

Many English residing at Paris having applied to me for an exemption from the Capitation Tax which they are now levying in this town, I wrote to Mr de Montmorin a letter, copy of which I inclose together with copies of his answer and of a letter to him upon the subject from Mr Lambert; I have, since the receipt of these letters, represented to him, in conversation, that, as long as the Treaty of Commerce of 1786 subsists, the Arrêt du Conseil can in no ways affect the subjects of His Britannick Majesty and consequently their exemption from the Tax cannot be considered in the light in which Mr Lambert sees it, but proceeds expressly from the 12th Article of the above-mentioned Treaty of Commerce. The Minister has, in consequence of my representation, promised to reconsider the subject. I wish in the mean time to be informed whether my conduct on this occasion meets with the approbation of His Majesty and his confidential ministers.

The important business of the Assignats is at last decided: eight hundred millions of livres in Assignats without interest have been decreed in addition to the former four hundred millions. They have not yet however determined their quotas.

The affair of the 5th and 6th of October last is now before the Assembly; if one may judge from the present complexion of things the Duke of Orleans and Mr de Mirabeau will not be found guilty.

The last accounts from Brest state that order is re-established there, the most seditious being sent away; but I believe the officers have little reason to trust to the present disposition of the crews.

I should not omit to mention to your Grace that Mr de

Montmorin seemed eager to inform me yesterday that the Spanish Ambassador's dispatches, lately arrived, gave him great hopes that our negotiations with the Court of Spain would be soon terminated to the satisfaction of both parties.

Paris, *October 5th*, 1790.

I send inclosed an official letter which I received yesterday evening from Mr Montmorin, in consequence of the communication I made to him according to your Grace's instructions.

The spirit of disobedience continues at Brest: *La Forme* however, a vessel of 74 guns has at last quitted that port, in order to replace the Léopard on the West India Station. It was with the greatest difficulty that the captain Mr de Rivière could prevail upon the crew to sail: in a letter to Mr Hector, Commandant la Marine in that port, he says that he has seized the first moment to put to sea when he found the crew at all disposed to obey his orders.

I must repeat to your Grace that I firmly believe that nothing but want of discipline could prevent this country from sending to sea a fleet of twenty or one and twenty sail of the line immediately if it were thought necessary, not to mention the ships fitting out at Toulon.

Mr de Moustier, minister plenipotentiary from this Court to the United States, is appointed to succeed Mr d'Esterno in that capacity at the Court of Berlin.

Paris, *October 8th*, 1790.

The National Assembly begins to feel the bad consequences of having abolished the late Courts of Justice before they had established new ones in their place.

The rioters in Languedoc having done much damage to the canal and interrupted the free circulation of grain they have been obliged to empower provisionally the former Judges to try them and all other disturbers of the public peace.

Most of the Chambers of Vacation of the Parliaments have protested against the decree which suppresses the former Judicature: that of Toulouse, having in an Arrêté censured in the strongest terms the proceedings of the Assembly, has refused to register the Letters-Patent of its suppression.

The party of the Jacobins and the friends of the Duke of Orleans prevail so much in this place at present that the new municipality have required Mr la Fayette and Mr Bailly to take an oath that they have not received money from the Government or any person whatsoever: the former has taken it but the latter spurns at the idea.

Mr Albert de Rioms has sent his resignation, finding it impossible to preserve order in the fleet. It is supposed he will be succeeded by Mr d'Estaing.

The highest of the new Assignats is to be of 2000 livres, the lowest of 50 livres.

PARIS, *October 15th*, 1790.

By the last accounts from Brest it appears that the officers have lost all hopes, in the present circumstances, of restoring discipline in the navy. At Toulon, though in a less degree, the same spirit prevails. The Assembly will very soon take some decisive measure upon that subject.

The deranged state of the finances has obliged them to make a present use of part of the 800 millions, which were intended to pay off so much of the Dette constituée. It having been proved to them that the probable expense for the three last months of this year will amount to above two hundred and thirty millions, and that the receipt will be less than ninety-four millions, they have decreed that of the 800 millions in Assignats, thirty-one millions odd hundred thousands should be employed for the use of the Public Treasury for the month of October, with an intention of voting above fifty-two millions for November and above forty-eight for December.

There is every reason to suppose that the Administration in this country will soon be changed; but whether the new

Ministry will consist of the friends of Mr la Fayette or of Mr Mirabeau remains to be known; if of the latter, the decree of the Assembly which prevents its members from holding offices under Government will be repealed.

PARIS, *October 22nd*, 1790.

Although the popular party has been unsuccessful in an attempt to obtain an address to the King, from the National Assembly, requesting him to remove his Ministers, their popularity and influence are by no means diminished: the majority of the Assembly were undoubtedly for the dismission of the present ministry, but objected to the mode proposed to effect it. The two clubs, the Jacobins and the Club of 1789, and the different Sections of Paris have declared themselves highly dissatisfied at the continuance of the ministers, and I understand, that in consequence of this very marked unpopularity, they have all signified their intention of resigning, except Mr Montmorin, whose conduct in office has met with the approbation of the popular party. I think it my duty to inform your Grace that that party has signified to me, through Mr Elliot[1], their earnest desire to use their influence

[1] The mention of this name throws light on a very obscure passage of diplomatic history. In the Life of Hugh Elliott by Lady Minto, p. 335, this passage occurs. "In 1790 Mr Elliott came home on leave and was sent by Mr Pitt on a secret mission to Paris in 1790 and 1791. Beyond the bare fact that he was so sent the correspondence tells nothing of this mission. In one letter only there is an allusion which throws a light upon its nature and success. A brother diplomatist writing to him some years afterwards concerning a delicate negotiation then pending says, "If you could have been sent to conduct it as successfully as you did your mission to Mirabeau,"" &c. Also in the Preface, p. ix, Lady Minto says "the only paper which my grandfather had been anxious to recover was a private memorandum in Mr Pitt's handwriting containing instructions for his guidance, and this, on regaining it, he sent to the Foreign Office." It is probable that these instructions of Pitt's referred to the same mission. I have inquired of Sir Edward Hertslet and am told that no paper of this kind exists in the Foreign Office. I am also informed by Mr Kingston that no direct trace of Mr Elliott's mission exists in the Public Record Office although search has often been made for it. We can easily infer from the mention of Mr Elliott's name in connection with the foregoing and following dispatches what the object of his mission was. A serious dispute which might at any time lead to war was raging between Spain and England on the question of

with the Court of Madrid in order to bring it to accede to the just demands of His Majesty and, if supported by us, I am induced to believe, they will readily prefer an English Alliance to a Spanish Compact.

The debate and decree of yesterday will probably tend to incline the minds of the sailors at Brest towards those who will soon hold the reins of government, and will consequently promote some degree of subordination in the navy.

It is reported here that the Ministry at Madrid is changed, and that the Spanish Ambassador here, who has been passing some days at Fontainebleau, will have some considerable office in the new administration.

Nootka Sound. By the *pacte de famille* France was bound to give Spain assistance in an offensive or defensive war. Pitt was using the strongest and most haughty language to compel Spain to submit to us, but if France joined her these remonstrances would be ineffectual and a European war would break out. Mirabeau was not a minister and therefore Lord Gower could have no communication with him, but he was chairman of the *comité diplomatique* of the National Assembly in whose hands, rather than in those of the minister, lay the issues of peace or war. It was important to secure that Mirabeau should not only maintain the principle that France was not bound to assist Spain under the present circumstances, but should do all he could to urge Spain to submit to the demands of England. If Elliott was authorized to use any other arguments to Mirabeau of a more delicate or secret nature it would be a reason for the correspondence having completely disappeared. Elliott had been an intimate friend of Mirabeau from boyhood. Baron de Stael says under date of October 10, "Si la guerre est déclarée entre l'Angleterre et l'Espagne reste à savoir si la France s'en mêlera ou non. Le parti populaire voudrait conserver la paix, mais les sentiments de la cour sont très différents, à ce que je crois." Some additional light is thrown on their negotiations by the correspondence of Mirabeau and La Marck on Oct. 24, 1790, La Marck wrote to Mirabeau "Pourquoi donc n'êtes-vous pas venu hier ?..........La marquise de Vauban *Elliott*, Louis de Seques Biron et moi nous vous avons espéré et attendu fort longtemps." In his "Note pour la cour" of October 28 Mirabeau advises peace and says with regard to England, "La paix n'est point, quoi qu'on en dise, difficile à maintenir. L'Angleterre et surtout le cabinet de saint-James ne veulent pas la guerre: ils ont voulu se préparer à tout événement dans le cas où la loterie qui se tire dans le Nord [the war between Sweden and Russia] amènerait un quine à l'entreprenante Russie et se mettre en mesure, si contre leur vœu, la guerre arrivait, d'en tirer partout et envers tous le plus grand parti possible. Cette pensée vague a été réchauffée par quelques circonstances particulières qu'il serait long de déduire ici: mais, au fond, ils ne sont point décidés à la guerre, et même ils penchent fortement à la paix." He goes on to say that Spain cannot fight without France.

PARIS, *October 26th*, 1790.

Mr Elliot being very anxious that your Grace should be informed, without loss of time, of the disposition of the leading men of the prevailing party with whom he has had communication I shall send Morley to London to-night who will be the bearer of this dispatch.

I must observe to your Grace that the opportunities which Mr Elliot has had of conversing with the members of the Comité Diplomatique, and which from my situation it was not in my power to have, have enabled him to convince them of the pacific intentions[1] of His Majesty; and, I can add with pleasure, that they seem anxiously inclined to co-operate with His Majesty's Ministers in order to induce Spain to comply with his just demands.

I shall tomorrow communicate to Mr Montmorin your Grace's dispatch, No. 10.

A letter was this day read to the Assembly from the King's Commissioners at Brest; by which it appears that there are great hopes of restoring quiet and discipline in the navy, the alteration of some articles in the Code Pénal being the only thing now required by the sailors.

The consideration of those articles will come before the Assembly tomorrow.

PARIS, *October 29th*, 1790.

Mr Fleurien, a Capitaine de Vaisseau and esteemed as an active and intelligent man, is appointed Minister of the Marine: the Colonies are to be in a separate department.

The command of the fleet at Brest is given to Mr Bougainville; this appointment, it is supposed, will be popular with the sailors, but may excite the jealousy of the officers, as he has not passed through the regular *Grades*.

---

[1] The susceptibilities of the French had been excited by the preparation of the English Fleet to act against Spain, fearing it might be directed against France.

In the last conference I had with Mr Montmorin that Minister informed me that, owing to the present unquiet state of the Colonies, it was found necessary to send immediately two ships of the line and two frigates to the West Indies and that he would write to Mr La Luzerne to notify this to your Grace.

At a time when there is great reason to hope that discipline will be restored in the navy, there are fresh appearances of the want of it in the army: the scene which passed last year at Versailles[1] upon the treat given to the Regiment de Flandres has been renewed at Béfort in Alsace upon a similar occasion: the Regiment of Royal Liégeois gave a repas de corps to two hundred soldiers of the Regiment de Lauzun Hussars lately arrived in that garrison: at the conclusion of which, having trampled upon the National and reassumed the white Cockade, they were proceeding to acts of violence, but were prevented by the timely interference of the Civil Magistrates and the National Guard.

Mr Bouillé, who arrived there the next morning has ordered the regiments to quit the town. They are both foreign regiments.

The Spanish Ambassador informs me that three hundred soldiers have been destroyed by an earthquake at Oran, but that the fortifications have not suffered very considerably. A seventy-four gun ship has been burnt at Carthagena by the overturning of a cauldron of boiling tar, which he attributes to the same cause.

The National Assembly has resolved that the English, Scotch and Irish religious houses established in France shall not be considered as national property.

---

[1] This was the famous dinner in the Salle d'Opéra when the Royal family entered and the band played O Richard o mon roi, l'univers t'abandonne. It is described in all histories of the revolution.

PARIS, *November 5th*, 1790.

I received last night a letter from Sir Robert Ainslie[1], an extract of which together with a copy of an article of intelligence from the Black Sea I send inclosed to your Grace.

The prospect of a continuation of good harmony between Great Britain and Spain, upon which I most sincerely congratulate your Grace, has thrown a visible damp upon the hopes of the aristocratical party, but is very pleasing to the rest of the nation.

In consequence of the King's not having as yet accepted the resignation of any of his Ministers, except Mr La Luzerne, a convocation of the forty-eight Sections of Paris is advertised by the Mayor to be held this afternoon.

The Queen has been indisposed for some days past with a sore throat, but Her Majesty was sufficiently recovered to have a Drawing Room yesterday evening.

PARIS, *November 12th*, 1790.

L'Illustre, a ship of the line, is arrived at Brest from Martinico and brings an account that the island is entirely in the hands of the soldiers, seven hundred of which have possessed themselves of Fort Bourbon which commands Fort Royal; Mr de Damas, the governor, has escaped, but is said to be dangerously wounded.

As the pay of the Guards, at present about his Majesty's person, and which is at the expense of the municipality of Paris, will cease at the end of the year; the King has consulted Mr la Fayette upon the subject; and it is understood that it is intended His Majesty should receive into pay the Gardes soldées of the Paris Militia, chiefly composed of the late Gardes-Français as his body-guards. This has excited the jealousy of the democratic party, and, in consequence of it, a very warm debate took place yesterday in the National Assembly, and a motion was carried that, the Military and Constitutional

---

[1] British Minister of Constautinople.

Committee should make a report on the subject. This arrangement of a *maison militaire* for the King and the late publication of Mr Calonne, which is regarded as a manifesto of the Comte d'Artois and the Prince of Condé, have given the greatest alarms to the democratic party, and, as they perceive their popularity on the decline they seem determined to take some strong measures in order to bring the unsettled state of affairs to a speedy crisis, a crisis perhaps of the greatest misery to this unfortunate country, occasioned by the alliance of metaphysics with politics, the fanaticism of liberty and democratic rage.

The resignations of the ministers for the Home and War Department and of the Keeper of the Seals[1] have been accepted, but I cannot with certainty inform your Grace who are to succeed them.

PARIS, *November* 19*th*, 1790.

Mr Duportail, an officer who served during the last war in America, is appointed Minister for the War Department. His political opinions are supposed to be entirely, what is here called, au sens de la Revolution; and his letter to the National Assembly to notify his appointment is a strong proof of it; for, in it, after some compliments to, what he calls, that august Assembly he expresses his desire to take an active part in a revolution which will be the most memorable epoch in the history, not only of France but, of the whole world. The Keeper of the Seals has not yet resigned.

Two hundred families have applied for passports to the Mayor since the pillage[2] of Mr de Castries's house; he obtained one under a feigned name and is now out of the French dominions.

---

[1] St Priest was Minister of the Interior, Latour du Pin Minister of War, and the Archbishop of Bordeaux Keeper of the Seals. Latour du Pin was succeeded by Duportail, the Archbishop by Dupont du Tertre, a bourgeois, and St Priest's office was taken by the Foreign Secretary Montmorin, who was the only one of the old ministers left.

[2] The Duc de Castries' house was pillaged in consequence of his having wounded Charles de Lameth in a duel.

While the National Guard continues to be unanimous there is little cause to fear the mob of Paris, but, as endeavours are not wanting to foment dissentions in that body, the peace of the capital may, with reason, be supposed to be in danger. It is the intention of the democratic party to force Mr la Fayette from the command and to substitute in his place Mr de Biron and Mr Charles de Lameth; the former to command the milice soldée the latter the non soldée; and it is also in contemplation that there should be, in France, as many soldiers of the milice soldée as of regulars.

Much mischief has been done by the overflowing of the Loire and the last courier, who passed through this place on Wednesday morning, in his way to Madrid may very probably be retarded by that accident, as the Spanish Ambassador's courier is not yet arrived from Madrid.

Mr Montmorin omits no opportunity of expressing to me his anxiety at not hearing that the disarmament is begun in England.

P.S. Above 200,000 weight that is above 100 ton of gunpowder is expected to pass through here in its way to Brest from the magazines at Metz, Strasbourgh &c.

PARIS, *November 26th*, 1790.

Mr Montmorin sent a letter yesterday to the National Assembly, copy of which taken from an accurate journal I send to your Grace; but he did not inform them, as I understood from him on Tuesday last it was his intention to do, that six sail of the line, four in addition to the two I formerly mentioned to your Grace, with frigates and five or six thousand soldiers were to be immediately sent to the West Indies. When he communicated this to me he told me that he should instruct Mr la Luzerne to notify it to your Grace, and, at the same time expressed his readiness to notify it in any other manner or to give any further explanation that his Majesty's confidential ministers might desire.

Mr Duport Dutertre, an advocate of probity, but of no eminence before the Revolution, to which he professes himself a sincere friend, is appointed Ministre de la Justice et Garde du Sceau de l'Etat. The opinion of Mr La Fayette has evidently had great weight in the appointment of the present ministry.

Your Grace's last messenger past through this place about five o'clock this evening in his way to Madrid.

Paris, *December 3rd*, 1790.

Mr de Lessart has succeeded Mr Lambert in the office of Controleur General.

The National Assembly has passed a decree, which has been sanctioned by the King, obliging the clergy to take the civic oath and declaring that every ecclesiastic who shall act contrary to that oath either by refusing to obey the decrees sanctioned by the King, or by exciting opposition to them shall lose the rights of a French citizen and be incapable of exercising any office. A letter is expected from the Pope enjoining them to comply. In consequence of the troubles in Martinico and the request of Mr Peynier governor of Saint Domingo the Assembly has at last desired the King to send six thousand men to the West Indies with four ships of the line in addition to the two already ordered with a proportionable number of transports.

A merchant ship lately arrived from the East Indies met on its passage a vessel from which they learnt that there was an insurrection in the Isle de France.

A great number of forged Assignats have already got into circulation: the maker of them, after much pains and difficulty, is discovered, he is a prisoner in the Châtelet, and, during his confinement in that prison he has contrived to engrave, without detection, no less than ten copper-plates for taking them off.

PARIS, *December 10th*, 1790.

It has been proposed in the Assembly to tax the public Funds, but, upon a motion of Mr Barnave, they have declared that the invariable principles of public faith must ever prevent them from being the object of a particular tax. They have risen surprizingly within these few weeks: the loan of 125 millions, which two months ago was at 11 per cent. loss, were yesterday at 10½ above par.

The lands and houses formerly belonging to the clergy continue to be sold much higher than their valuation, but they were, for political reasons, evidently rated too low.

The two French regiments which conducted themselves so shamefully at Nancy are ordered to be cashiered, the common soldiers however are to be allowed three months' pay.

It is reported that Mr Conway is on his return to this country from the Isle de France and that the troops are to go back from thence to Pondicherry.

PARIS, *December 14th*, 1790.

I take the opportunity of Mr Fraser's return to England to inform your Grace that Mr Montmorin assured me positively this morning that there is no foundation for the report that the troops are returned from the Isle de France to Pondicherry. He also told me that the Ministry might possibly send fewer vessels and troops than they had intended to the West Indies: it appears indeed that, at this very critical time, they may have sufficient employment for all their troops at home.

I was mistaken when I informed your Grace that the King had sanctioned the decree which obliges the clergy to take the civic oath. His Majesty I understand waits for an answer from Rome.

PARIS, *December 17th,* 1790.

The inclosed paper will prove to your Grace the great alarm which the discovery of a company of forgers of Assignats in London has occasioned in this country. Mr Montmorin, when he yesterday mentioned the subject to me, stated it as a matter of the utmost importance; and assured me that the assistance of His Majesty's Ministers on this occasion would be regarded as a strong proof of good-intelligence between the two countries, and would insure reciprocal assistance whenever it should be required.

At Mr Montmorin's request, I shall take the liberty to write a letter recommending the business and the bearer to your Grace's protection: which letter that Minister will deliver to the person who is to manage this affair in London for the French Ministry.

The aristocratic party express openly in public their hopes of a speedy counter-revolution. It is certain that the capital is regarded with a jealous eye by the provinces; which jealousy is industriously fomented by all those, a considerable number indeed, who are dissatisfied with the present Government. Three people have been lately taken up and sent to the prison of Pierre Encise near Lyons on account of the discovery of a treasonable plot; and between hope and fear many people attached to the former system are daily quitting Paris.

PARIS, *December 31st,* 1790.

The King has notified, by a letter counter-signed by the Garde du Sceau, his acceptation of the decree relative to the civil constitution of the clergy; in consequence of which the Bishop of Autun[1] and most of the inferior clergy, members of the Assembly, have taken the oath prescribed by that decree. The late constant rain is supposed to have delayed the return of the courier from Rome.

A serious but premature plan for a counter-revolution has certainly been discovered at Lyons. The story of a number of

[1] Talleyrand.

men having arrived there from Auvergne with led horses which they left in order to return precipitately home I find to be absolutely true.

It is certain that there have been considerable dissentions among the French of the aristocratical party at Turin. The Prince of Condé, having spoken disrespectfully of the conduct of the King of Sardinia, has been obliged to leave that country, and is now at Nyon in Switzerland: the Comte d'Artois remains at Turin; but his return to Paris is expected by many. In case of that event the Temple will probably be his place of residence.

The Assembly has voted one hundred thousand livres for the works at Cherbourg the Minister of the Marine Department having promised to lay before them the plan of those works, which, he calculates, will cost, for the year 1791, only nine hundred thousand instead of four or five millions of livres, the usual annual amount of the sum expended on them.

PARIS, *January 7th*, 1791.

It is difficult to believe that Government has not as yet been informed of the sentiments of the Court of Rome with regard to the decree of the 27th of November, although the long-expected courier is not arrived.

All the Bishops[1] except those of Autun and Lydda and the Abbé Expilly, elected bishop according to the new constitution by the Department of Finisterre, have refused to take the oath. I understand that it is intended that they should be allowed 10,000 livres per annum. In order to induce the Comte d'Artois to return it will very probably be proposed in the Assembly that the nation, in addition to the traitement already allowed him, shall pay him a sum of money for certain mines and forges which belonged to him before the last decree upon the Apanages. The Prince of Condé is, it is said, returned to Turin.

---

[1] Of 131 bishops only 4 took the oath.

The commandant of the Garde Nationale at Marseilles has been taken up on his way to Nice being strongly suspected of being concerned in the plan of counter-revolution lately discovered at Lyons.

I think it my duty to inform your Grace that Mr Simolin has of late had frequent conferences with Mr de Montmorin.

PARIS, *January* 14*th*, 1791.

In consequence of your Grace's instructions No. 14 I have communicated to Mr de Montmorin the circumstances of Mr Dawson's complaint: that Minister having desired me to state it in writing I have sent to him a memorial; copy of which I inclose. In case it should appear that Mr Landolph has been authorized by the French Government to act in the manner mentioned in Mr Dawson's memorial, I shall desire to be informed what is the ground or nature of the claim of France to the exercise of such rights in the place in question, and I shall lose no time in transmitting to your Grace the answer of the French Ministry.

The King of Sardinia having absolutely refused to give any assistance to the French emigrants the Prince de Condé will pass the remainder of the winter in Switzerland and the Count d'Artois is waiting at Venice for such offers from the Assembly as may induce him to return to France.

The greater number of the curates of Paris took the oath last Sunday: some however, having another week allowed them to consider the subject, declined taking it at that time; in the mean while no official answer is arrived from Rome; but there is good reason to beleive that Government is apprized of the unfavorable sentiments of that Court.

Above sixteen millions have been voted for the current service of the present month.

Paris, *January* 21st, 1791.

On the arrival of Mr Groves with your Grace's instructions, I wrote immediately to Mr de Montmorin desiring his authority and assistance in order to enable him to receive and convey to England Claude Fini alias Chameron.

That Minister informed me yesterday, in the course of conversation that in the present state of things, it was impossible for him to authorize the conveying of Claude Fini to England: he expressed his wish that it were possible; although, he remarked, he knew that the British Government could not, in case it were requested afford reciprocal assistance. Mr de Montmorin having promised an answer in writing, I shall send it to your Grace by the next messenger.

No answer from Rome has been as yet made public. The curates in the capital who have refused to take the oath have been permitted to retire without bloodshed, but not without insult from the populace. In the provinces particularly in the south some cruelties have been committed, and in one place the mob cut off the curate's head and, having placed it on the altar, sprinkled it in derision with holy water.

The regiments of Soissonois and of Penthievre are, by a decree of the National Assembly recalled from Avignon. Some soldiers of those regiments have together with the National Guard of that town been guilty of the most horrid barbarities. Their first intention was to beseige Carpentras in order to destroy the Assembly now sitting in that town, but, finding it too strong, they turned their rage against Cavaillon, which they pillaged, after having murdered many of the inhabitants and having committed all sorts of indecencies. Your Grace may judge of the alarming state of the southern provinces from a letter of Mr du Portail to the National Assembly, in which he says that the number of regular troops is much inferior to the wants and desires of every department, particularly in the south of France. He insists much on the difficulty of sending them to the places where they are wanted. Sometimes the regiments themselves shew a spirit of resistance which it would be dangerous to put to a trial; sometimes municipalities and administrators of departments declare that they will not permit the regiments in their departments to go away, or, that they will not receive some others destined to be sent to them, and at other times they stop the troops that have orders to pass through their territories.

The Prince of Condé has left Switzerland and is now at Stutgard.

I inclose a copy of a French translation of a letter said to be written (in Latin) from the Emperor to the King of France a notion that His Imperial Majesty, is preparing to act in conformity to that letter has occasioned a considerable fall in the funds here.

The frigate la Nymphe arrived at l'Orient on the 12th and is said to bring an account of a victory gained by Tippoo Saib in the East Indies. I send your Grace a translation of that account from one of the public papers. Mr de Montmorin, when I mentioned the subject to him yesterday, assured me that he had received no official intelligence which could at all corroborate the report, and told me that he remained with the Minister of the Marine and Colonies upon business till ten o'clock the night before who at that time had received no account of it. I have this morning seen a gentleman who has received a letter from a friend at Pondicherry dated the 26 of July in which there is no mention of this victory.

Paris, *January 23rd,* 1791.

I forgot to inform your Grace that Mr de Mirabeau, instead of quitting Paris as he had once intended, mounted guard last week at the Thuilleries as commander of a battalion of the National Guard; he has since been obliged to quit that station, being chosen one of the administrators of the department of Paris, an office which is not tenable with any other: the Bishop of Autun, for the same reason, has resigned his bishoprick. A very large importation from England of buttons for the national uniform has made it necessary for every possible precaution to be taken in order to prevent tumults in this town: the journey-men manufacturers having threatened to destroy the shops of all those who sell English goods.

Those who are best acquainted with East India affairs give little credit to the report of Tippoo's victory. The accounts however from Chandernagor are unfortunately too true; the inhabitants of that place having deposed the officers appointed by the King, dispersed the magistrates, and pillaged the archives.

The spirit of opposition in Alsace to the decrees of the National Assembly joined to the Emperor's letter to the King has occasioned a proposal from one of the sections of this capital which has been approved of by the rest, to form a body of twelve thousand men in order to march to the frontier on the first alarm of hostilities from that quarter.

PARIS, *January 28th*, 1791.

In order that your Grace may know the sort of language that the Princes of Germany, who have possessions in France, hold to this Court, I inclose a printed copy of the Bishop of Spire's answer to a ministerial note of the Baron de Groschlag, the King's Minister Plenipotentiary to the circle of the upper Rhine, which I received from that Princes minister at this Court. I inclose also a copy of the Emperor's letter in the original Latin. The Prince of Condé's and Mr de Calonne's journey to Stutgard increase the suspicions of designs from that quarter hostile to the present Constitution of France. In addition to which the state of the minds of the inhabitants of Alsace add much to the general alarm. The prevalence of the Protestant religion in that country cause the Catholics to be extremely strict with regard to their religious tenets, and of course much dissatisfied with the decree concerning the civil constitution of the clergy: some former decrees of the Assembly in favor of the Protestants having before given them impressions not favourable to that body. Many of the Protestants, on the other hand, being farmers of the lands of the clergy, use every possible means to prevent the sale of those lands.

It is intended, in consequence of these alarms, to increase the number of regular troops, which consist now of one hundred and twenty thousand men, to one hundred and fifty thousand, and to raise in addition one hundred thousand auxiliary troops, that are not to do garrison duty but to be ready in case of necessity, and to be enlisted for three years.

The Assembly of Carpentras, in proof of whose loyalty and attachment to their Sovereign I inclose a declaration sent to me by their president, have been obliged to place on the gates of their town the arms of France, not however without having first sent to the neighbouring departments to know if they might expect any assistance from the National Guard.

The accounts from Martinico state that island to be in the most deplorable situation, the governor, Mr de Damas, having thought fit to put arms into the hands of the slaves. Two ships of the line sailed some time ago for that colony, and the other four with six thousand troops, if they have not been prevented by contrary winds, have by this time left Brest.

I rejoice to find that the disagreable reports brought by la Nymphe from the East-Indies are entirely without foundation.

The violence of party is at present so great in the National Assembly that no terms of abuse are omitted by the speakers on either side, and the style of language which used to be confined to the markets, and therefore called *le langage des halles*, is now very frequently adopted in that place.

The club of the Jacobins and another lately established called des Amis de la Constitution Monarchique are at open war. The house of Mr de Clermont Tonnerre, the president of the latter club, has been threatened to be pulled down by the populace, which being notified yesterday by a member to the Assembly, the president wrote to the mayor, who immediately went to the spot, which prevented the threat from being put into execution.

During the course of this week, there has been frequent occasion to call for the aid of the National Guard. Some days ago a party of Chasseurs, a body of men established principally with a view to prevent smuggling, insisted, without any order from the civil magistrate, upon entering the house of a person who was known to have smuggled goods, in the village of la Villette adjoining the barrière leading to St Denis, and, entrance being refused, they proceeded to acts of violence and were fired upon by the people within, who were possessed of fire arms, as they belonged to the National Guard. They fired in their turn, and this sort of engagement continued till the arrival of Mr la Fayette with a large (*sic*) of guards and canon. The Chasseurs have, by this proceeding rendered themselves extremely unpopular, and they are on that account unable to do their duty, the consequence of which is that every night some barrière is forced and prodigious quantities of smuggled goods, particularly wine and brandy, are brought into the town, which must occasion a considerable decrease of the public revenue.

An assistant of the police was yesterday extremely ill-treated by a mob in the faubourg St Antoine but he was at last rescued by the interference of the guard. I hope to be able to give your Grace an account of the present state of the finances of this country in my next dispatch.

PARIS, *January* 30, 1791.

I omitted to inform your Grace that the King last week appointed Mr de Lessart Minister of the Home Department. The thousand auxiliaries are to act instead of the militia and are to receive three sous a day during the three years of their engagement, unless called upon active service. In that case they will be incorporated with the other regiments. The regular troops, when compleated will amount to 150 thousand men; the National Guard to 300 thousand.

The administrators of the department of la Drome, which bounds the Pope's territories on the north, having resolved to send succours to the inhabitants of Carpentras, causes some uneasiness, but it is hoped that orders to the contrary from the Minister of the War Department will arrive in time to prevent any bad consequences.

I inclose the Moniteur of this day as it contains two very interesting speeches[1] one of Mr Alexander Lameth, the other of Mr Mirabeau. The latter gentleman is at last chosen president of the Assembly.

PARIS, *February 4th,* 1791.

There is good reason to believe that the quiet which we at present enjoy will not be of long duration. The party of Mr Barnave and the Lameths omit no opportunity of giving the spur to a popularity which they perceive to be declining: on the other hand, the new club[2] shews a degree of firmness, which has as yet been wanting among those who profess their principles. It is certain that they intended to acquire a popularity by causing bread to be sold to the poor, considerably below the market price: which, being done in too open a manner, has had, in some degree, a contrary effect, and has given to the club of the Jacobins an opportunity of denouncing them as a society formed by a faction, and dangerous to the Constitution. The club of 1789, through fear of being implicated in this accusation, has declared that they reject from their society all those who continue to be members of the Club Monarchique, for so they call by abbreviation the Societé des Amis de la Constitution Monarchique, who took that appellation in contradistinction to the Societé des Amis de la Constitution, the regular appellation of the Jacobins. The last society having imprudently published a letter in which they accused the Chasseurs of having designedly caused the late disturbances at the barrière of la Chapelle, leading to St Denis, and that they had received pay to act in that manner, the mayor found it necessary to

[1] Lameth's speech was delivered as president of the military committee, Mirabeau's as reporter of the diplomatic committee. It dealt principally with international relations and urged that there was nothing to be apprehended on the side of England. The English nation was substantially in harmony with the French Revolution and the Minister would not dare to run counter to its views. He professed a complete ignorance of the private views of the English ministry, and naturally spoke so as to avoid all suspicion of Eliott's mission.

[2] The club of the Amis de la Constitution Monarchique was founded towards the close of 1790.

issue a declaration, entirely exculpating them, and the Jacobins were obliged to retract their opinion in a second letter.

I inclose Mr Malouet's well written answer to Mr Barnave's *Denonciation du Club de la Constitution Monarchique*, at the end of which there is printed the first letter of the Jacobins contrasted with that of the Club Monarchique upon that subject. In order to compensate this error and to turn men's minds from a subject not favourable to them towards one which might hurt the other club, a report was industriously spread by the Jacobins that there was a plan to carry off the Royal family and that horses were in readiness in the stables at Versailles for that purpose. They accordingly sent commissioners to inspect and report: in one stable, it is true, they found 120 horses, in another 140, but one number belonged to a regiment of horse, the other to the Chasseurs; nor was the number of horses found to be encreased in those stables since the revolution. Another cause of alarm is the intended journey of the King's aunts to Rome. The reason assigned for this resolution is a point of conscience not to attend mass performed by a priest who has taken the new oath; if this is the only reason it may be easily surmounted; certain however it is that they have asked for passports and that preparations are making for the journey. In the mean time the friends to the Constitution at Sève[1], near which town Mesdames reside, are corresponding with the club of the same name at Paris, the Jacobins, and beseeching them to use their influence and authority in order to prevent their departure.

The Bishop of Orleans and the Cardinal Bishop of Sens have taken the oath: the Cardinal de Bornis, having taken it with a restriction, *sans manquer à ce que je dois à Dieu et à la religion*, will probably be deprived not only of his bishoprick but of all the offices that he holds under Government. The lands of the clergy continue to be sold for at least a third more than their valuation; the difficulty of employing assignats in any other manner, and the prospect of the great improvements which may be made on those lands, heretofore much neglected, are the most probable causes of this advantageous sale.

[1] *Sève* is the usual manner of spelling Sèvres at that time.

An East India merchantship, the Amphitrite, on its return to France, has been wrecked off the coast and almost within sight of l'Orient: out of 108 men five only were saved.

The last accounts from Martinico are dated the twenty-fifth of December: at that time the rebels were still in possession of the forts. The colonies of Cayenne and Guyanne shew the same spirit of opposition to their governors; so that there is scarcely a single colony belonging to France that is not in a state of insurrection.

There are reports of disturbances in Britanny but there are no accounts that can be depended upon.

I inclose an abstract of the expences of the three first months of this year: the whole expences of the year will soon be laid before the Assembly of which I shall give your Grace the earliest account.

I am informed, by the Minister from the Republic of Geneva, that the heads of the French party there have been gained by giving them *droits de bourgeoisie* and by other means.

I cannot conclude without mentioning a circumstance on account of it's singularity. I happened to be at the Assembly, on Saturday last[1], when a funeral pageant was performed there to the memory of Mr Desilles, whose bust was carried in a sort of triumph round the room accompanied by a procession of soldiers with martial musick: a speech was made on the occasion by one of the members and another by the president; as soon as the last was concluded, the ears of the legislators of France were amused with the favourite air of Ça ira, performed by this martial band: the Abbé Maury, who happened to be near us, exclaimed *voila comme les français font des lois.*

[1] This happened at the evening sitting. A detachment of the grenadiers of the battalion of St Joseph was introduced, drums and a band headed a deputation, in the midst was carried the bust of Desilles, who died at Nancy of his wounds in trying to spare the blood of his fellow-citizens. M. Gouy and the President made speeches, the bust was placed on the Secretaries' table recovered with oak-leaves. A large painting of the action of Desilles was ordered to be made. Immediately after this Mirabeau was declared President of the Assembly. Nothing is said in the Moniteur about Ça ira.

PARIS, *February*, 11*th*, 1791.

During Mr de Mirabeau's presidency more essential business will have been dispatched by the Assembly than has been done by that body in the space of months before. Among other things are to be reckoned 1st. the conclusion of the organization of juries; and 2nd. the formation of a High National Court to try those who are accused by the legislative body. It is to consist of four judges taken from the Tribunal de Cassation, the formation of which now occupies the attention of the Assembly; the jury of this court is to be composed of citizens having the qualifications requisite to be a deputy to the National Assembly: two to be chosen at every election for a new legislature by every department, and to continue during the duration of that legislature. The place where it is to sit must be distant at least 15 leagues from that of the National Assembly.

3rd. The reduction of the number of municipalities, a consummation most devoutly to be wished for by all who are enemies to anarchy and confusion, would have been agitated before this time in the Assembly had it not been for the interruption which a remonstrance from the city of Paris, and the business brought forward in consequence of that remonstrance has occasioned.

The municipality has stated to the Assembly that Paris is no longer able to bear the weight of those taxes which the former abuses of Government enabled it to pay: that in proportion to their decrease of wealth they suffer an increase of expence. That they are obliged to maintain twenty-seven thousand adventurers and needy persons, (the fact is that, under the name of workmen and labourers those people receive fifteen sous a day although they scarcely work at all). That they have still to pay four millions for the expence of the revolution, and one million two hundred thousand livres for the works in the Champ de Mars for the Federation. That it is unjust that they who were the most active in bringing about the revolution should be the greatest sufferers by that event. In this state of distress they request the Assembly to decree that six millions should be paid to them by the public treasury; they being able to prove that fifteen millions are owing them by the public.

The payment of the six millions has accordingly been decreed, and Mr Dupont, by order of the Comité d'Impositions, has laid before the Assembly a plan for levying taxes to be paid at the entrance of towns in proportion to their population; according to which plan it is calculated that every inhabitant of Paris will pay annually eighteen livres per head instead of forty livres ten sous. The towns of France formerly paid in droits d'entrée seventy millions per annum, of which forty-six went to the service of Government, the other twenty-four were employed by the towns themselves. Paris alone contributed thirty-six millions, twenty-eight of which were paid to the public. It is now proposed to reduce the forty-six millions, which were formerly paid to Government, to twenty-four and that of Paris from twenty-eight to ten.

The expences of the new Government, for the present year, are estimated at 658 millions: as they are now printing tables of these expences I shall delay enlarging upon that subject till next week.

The King's aunts seem determined to leave this country: they have employed people to buy gold coin for them in Paris to so large an amount that it has considerably increased the price of it.

The sentiments of the inhabitants of Alsace have occasioned great uneasiness to the King's Commissioners: they found the minds of people so adverse to them at Strasburg that they hastened to Colmar where they were saved from the fury of the people by the interference of the National Guard. *Vive Mr d'Artois: les Commissaires à la lanterne* were the expressions with which they were saluted on their arrival at the last place.

The troubles in Britanny have not been very considerable; some lives have been lost and many people taken prisoners by the National Guard in order to prevent the further burning of castles in that country.

In Quercy quiet is at last restored, but there also the rioters have done much mischief. At Chantilly they have destroyed the Prince of Condé's park and gardens. In Paris necessity has obliged the municipal officers to interfere in order to suppress the gaming-houses in the neighbourhood of the Palais-

Royal which were swarming with thieves and pick-pockets. The Bishop of Autun has published a curious letter in which he acknowledges that he has lately been guilty of the vice of gaming, but that he has not won so much as his enemies are pleased to say.

The four remaining ships destined for the West India colonies did not leave Brest till the fifth of this month. That armament will cost Government near nine millions.

The curates whose conscience will not permit them to take the oath are to be allowed 500 livres a year: it is not yet determined whether the bishops who are in the same predicament are to have so much as £10,000 a year: the sum given to those whose bishopricks were suppressed upon the late reduction of them.

The Prince of Condé has left Stutgard and is gone, it is said, to Brunswick.

PARIS, *February*, 18*th*, 1791.

According to the instructions which I received from your Grace, by the last courier, I have delivered to Mr de Montmorin a memorial in favor of the Tobago creditors. I inclose an answer to one which I delivered to that Minister some time ago upon the subject of Claude Fini alias Chameron.

Five 74 gun ships, two frigates of 18, and nine of 12 guns, with five store ships having on board twelve battalions of infantry is the exact number of vessels that sailed for the West-Indies. I reckoned only four of the line, supposing that two had sailed before, according to the information which I had received from Mr de Montmorin of the intention of the Ministry at that time: the single ship which sailed then had been destined already for that station, and was therefore fitted out at the expence of the ordinary establishment. Mr de Bougainville is returned from Brest, I have good reason to believe, well pleased at having been able, though not without much difficulty, to prevail upon the sailors and soldiers to embark upon that expedition; two million one hundred thousand livres have been spent to buy piastres in order to pay them three months advance in specie.

The King's commissioners in Alsace leave no means unemployed in order to effect their business in that country: one is not surprized that they converted eight professors at a theological disputation when one knows that they carried with them from hence arguments to the amount of one million of livres; they have however been obliged to call for the additional aid of a military force. The same arguments probably and certainly the same military aid have been employed by the commissioners in Britanny; where twenty six parishes had united to defend the curates who had refused to take the oath. The Bishops of Treguier, St Pol and Vannes, who are accused of instigating these troubles, are ordered *de se rendre à la suite de l'Assemblée Nationale*. But one of the most effectual measures which have been taken in order to conciliate the minds of the inhabitants of Alsace is the late decree of the Assembly permitting them to cultivate tobacco; a measure however which will be attended with a considerable decreace of the revenue. The 1st article of this decree, the permission to cultivate tobacco, subject to certain duties on the manufacture, and sale of it, passed by a majority of ten only, the 2d prohibits foreign snuff, the 3d lays a duty on foreign tobacco in leaves of 25 livres pr quintal, excepting what is brought directly from America in French vessels, upon which three fourths only of that duty is laid; it is referred to the committee of contributions whether the duty should be lessened in the same manner upon tobacco from the Levant. The 4th allows tobacco in leaves to be stored, for a year, in the ware-houses of the *Régie* and to be re-exported duty free. The 5th which taxes the manufacture is adjourned, the 6th establishes a *Régie Nationale* subject to the same duties as private manufactories.

Another decrease of the revenue, the diminishing the duties on the entrance of towns, is not yet decided upon: many members of the Assembly object to the plan of the committee and are of opinion to take them entirely off. The duties on spirituous liquors, a considerable branch of the revenue, is no longer to exist.

The tradesmen's companies are abolished which will cost the public a very large sum in indemnifications. I inclose a state of the public expences for 1791 published in the name of the committee of finances.

In order, in some degree, to supply these various diminutions of the public revenue, it is decreed that all merchants tradesmen manufacturers &c. shall be obliged to take out a licence, the price of which is to be in proportion to the rent of their house or shop and according to their trade; those of luxury are rated the highest and those that are absolutely necessary the lowest, bakers for instance are to pay but half the common price.

A decree of the Assembly has taken from Mr and Mme de Polignac their estate of Fénétranges, bought by those of the Crown with money, which it appears was given them by his Majesty for that purpose, and has sentenced them to refund 800000 livres given them also by the King during the administration of Mr de Calonne, whom they have declared answerable for the whole payment. This decree among many others prove the violence of party. Mesdames continue to declare their intention of leaving this country, altho' after the remonstrance that has been made to the Assembly by 32 sections of Paris against their journey, and the general impression that it has made in the country it is difficult to say how they can venture to put their intention into execution.

I find that I was misinformed with regard to the Prince of Condé who I understand is, or at least was very lately, in the neighbourhood of Stutgard. Mr de Calonne has past a few days at Vienna and is now at Venice.

The King and Queen of Naples, and it is said the Emperor purpose to go to Italy in the beginning of the next month. Madame du Barry, who has been robbed of jewels to the amount of near fifty thousand pounds sterling has heard that some of them have been offered to be sold in London; she left this place yesterday in order to endeavour to regain them. It appears that they were stolen by a gang of eleven people whose next attempt was to have been upon the jewels of the Queen of France.

From the complexion of things I shall not be surprized if I shall have to inform your Grace that the Cardinal Bishop of Sens is elected to the See of Paris.

PARIS, *February 20th*, 1791.

The King's aunts left their country house at Bellevue last night at ten o'clock on their way to Italy and have since been heard of at Fontainebleau: it is supposed they will reach Auxerre this day. A party of people chiefly Poissardes arrived at Bellevue about an hour after their departure and have stopped their baggage.

Accounts have been received from Geneva of disturbances in that place the country people having approached the town in a manner that alarmed the inhabitants, the gates were shut upon them and they have been obliged to retreat.

The Assembly has decreed that after the first of May next all *droits d'entrée des villes* shall cease.

PARIS, *February 25th*, 1791.

The departure of the King's aunts has been the cause of two considerable mobs, but which, owing to the vigilance of Mr la Fayette, have been attended with no bad consequences. The first gave me an opportunity of being witness to great firmness and presence of mind in the King's brother, I happened to dine, on Tuesday[1], at the Luxembourg with a company which

---

[1] Bertrand de Molleville gives the following account of this event III. 35. "It was rumoured that Monsieur the King's brother also intended to leave Paris accompanied by Madame. It was to this Prince Barnave alluded in his motion. An immense mob, chiefly composed of women, set out for the Luxembourg, and a large detachment of them after some slight resistance made their way into the Palace and were introduced into Monsieur's apartments, where they expressed the uneasiness of the people and solicited him not to go away. Monsieur declared to them that it never had been his intention to separate himself from the King and that he would never quit his majesty. So solemn an assurance excited the liveliest acclamation of joy and Monsieur, immediately setting out with Madame to go to the Tuileries, was accompanied thither by the whole mob."

was honored by his presence: while we were at coffee, one of his attendants, with signs of the greatest alarm, rushed into the room and informed us that the mob threatened to force their way into the Petit Luxembourg[1] where Monsieur resides, declaring that they were certain that he intended to quit Paris that night: he immediately without the least signs of emotion gave orders for a *députation* to be admitted into the court, where he went and informed them that they were perfectly mistaken, and at the same time gave them his word of honor that he would not leave the kingdom at present. This deputation consisted entirely of women. Having done this, he proceeded to the Thuileries, where he goes regularly every Tuesday, in order to attend the *Jeu de la Reine*, accompanied on this occasion by a troop of *Poissardes* and populace. When Monsieur entered the gates the guard endeavoured, but in vain, to prevent their following him into the court; upon this Mr la Fayette ordered the cavalry to force them out of it, Mr Bailly and some municipal officers arrived at that instant and insisted upon their sheathing their swords, but informed the mob that, if they did not retire, it would be impossible for them any longer to prevent the guards from firing upon them: this had the desired effect! they retired, and Monsieur was suffered to return quietly to the Luxembourg. I understand that Mr de la Fayette complains much of Mr Bailly's want of resolution, last night when the latter was giving a circumstantial account of the different disturbances to his Majesty the King was heard to say: It is impossible to continue to act any longer in this manner, something must be done! or words to that effect. The disturbance of yesterday, which ended in the same manner as the former, was owing to a request from Mesdames to the National Assembly for a passport; they are stopt at Arnay lé duc, a sorry town in Burgundy, by the *Commune* of that place. Upon a motion of Mr Mirabeau the Assembly has decreed that, considering that no law of the kingdom forbids Mesdames from travelling *il n'y a lieu à délibérer* and refers that affair to the

---

[1] Monsieur resided in a small pavilion of the petit Luxembourg now occupied by the Sécrétaire du Sénat.

executive power. The manner[1] in which the first opposition to their passage at Moret was overcome is much blamed and the person who is responsible for the orders given to the Chasseurs will suffer under the lash of the popular party. Mr de Montmorin who commands at Fontainebleau is a near relation of the minister.

The National Guard of L'Orient with the assistance of 150 soldiers of the regiment of Walsh have quieted the peasants in Britanny. Above eighty of them have been taken prisoners, the number of killed is uncertain but it amounts at least to between twenty and thirty.

In Alsace also every thing is quiet four hundred regular troops have entered Colmar, and the military preparations in that province prove that Government has no great confidence in the continuance of tranquillity in that quarter.

The palace of the Elector of Mayence is prepared as a residence it is said for the Prince of Condé who declares his resolution of entering France with an armed force whenever an opportunity shall offer.

The Comte d'Artois it is expected will return to Turin.

Your Grace will recollect the Confederation encamped at Jalès in the Cevennes, which was dispersed by a decree of the Assembly in the month of August; the camp however has always subsisted, and is now composed of about eight thousand men. To that camp, after the late affair at Uzes, where the dragoons at last restored tranquillity but not without some bloodshed, the Catholics and discontented have retired, for those skirmishes in the south which pass merely for disputes between the Catholics and Protestants are in fact engagements between the enemies and friends to the present constitution. The activity of Mr Du Portail, seconded by a decree of the Assembly, will probably find force sufficient to make head against that otherwise very formidable body of men. The accounts from Toulouse are very unfavorable to the present system.

The Republic of Geneva suffers much from the neighbourhood of France, and the contagion of the principles at present in fashion in this country. The late attack upon the town by

---

[1] The gates were forced open by their escort.

the peasants, chiefly from the Pays de Gex and probably excited by a correspondence with the Jacobins and certainly encouraged by those called *natifs* who are mostly descended from strangers and consequently have not the *droits de bourgeoisie*, had nearly overturned the constitution of that town. Mr de Roverai who governs the popular opinion within the town, having shewn himself in opposition to the peasants, saved the republic. Fresh concessions and *droits de bourgeoisie* granted even to the natives of a certain standing they flatter themselves will preserve the present Government.

Three of the principal people employed in the Bank of Vienna having been detected in forging notes on that bank and informed against by the Austrian Minister have fled to Huningue in Alsace: the municipal officers secured their persons and papers. Mr de Lessart gave orders for the delivery of the prisoners into the hands of those who were appointed to receive them by the Austrian Minister; but, upon their appealing to the tribunal of Alkirch, that body decided that they should remain in prison till the demand should be laid before the National Assembly, and, having learnt that the Comité Diplomatique were deliberating upon that business they forbad the municipality to obey the orders of the minister.

The Assembly has referred this affair to a fresh examination of the united Comités de Constitution et Diplomatique in order to form a decree upon the necessary formalities for the restitution of fugitives reclaimed by foreign powers.

PARIS, *March 4th*, 1791.

A Mr de Court, a gentleman from the West Indies, having by accident let fall from under his coat a short couteau de chasse in the Queens appartment at the Thuilleries last Monday morning[1] was the cause of the extraordinary scene which passed there on that evening. On the Tuesday and Thursday preceding when, on account of the mobs that surrounded the palace, it was supposed that the persons of the Royal Family

[1] Feb. 28.

might be in danger, many gentlemen, from motives of duty or principle, went to the royal apartments, and being in haste were of course in undress, but, as it is usual at present, had pistols in their pockets, and many had short couteaux de chasse or daggers, in so doing they shewed greater marks of zeal than prudence, it being contrary to law to enter the palace thus armed. On account of what had happened in the morning, the National Guard thought themselves entitled to search the persons of those who had arrived that evening: the search was very productive; many baskets being soon filled with pistols and daggers: this however was not done without violent opposition from the wearers of them, some of whom declared they would sooner die than give up their arms: the King, seeing the danger of this resolution, laid his commands upon them to deliver them up, saying that he would be defended only by the National Guard. Some of those who were most obstinate have been sent to prison, many have suffered much from the ill-treatment of the soldiers. The measure was right, the means were undoubtedly wrong.

In the midst of this scene of danger to all present, for had any one pistol gone off by accident a massacre must have ensued, Mr de la Fayette arrived from Vincennes[1]. He thanked the Guard for their conduct and congratulated them that for the future there would not be a body of men between their Sovereign and them. The next day he signified in writing, the language of which is curious on account of the novelty of some of the expressions, that he had given his Majesty's orders to the *chefs de la domesticité*, a new term for the chief officers of the household, to prevent the introduction of arms into the palace; it being the will of the King of the Constitution to be guarded only by the soldiers of liberty.

The King's person is now completely in the hands of Mr de la Fayette: the Government of the kingdom seems to be going fast into those of Mr de Mirabeau, whose conduct since

---

[1] Some repairs having been undertaken at the Château of Vincennes the people were afraid lest it should be converted into a new Bastille. They therefore marched from Paris and began to demolish it. Lafayette had great difficulty in quelling the tumult.

his presidency and his election as one of the administrators of the department of Paris has been much and deservedly applauded. His avowed opposition to Barnave, the Lameths, and the thirty who follow them implicitly per fas et nefas, has conciliated to him the minds of the friends of Government and the lovers of peace, who flatter themselves that his great talents may at last prove of service to his country.

In the mean time anarchy and insubordination, encouraged equally by the aristocratical and democratical factions continue to prevail. The late affair at Vincennes serves to prove how easily and upon what weak pretences a very formidable mob may be raised.

The accounts from the neighbourhood of Jalès state that the department is collecting very considerable forces of regular troops and National Guard, which they doubt not will soon disperse that dangerous assemblage of fanatics and discontented people. In Alsace, a fresh conspiracy is thought to have been discovered: a deserter having addrest himself to a Mr Defresney, a secretary of the Cardinal de Rohan, in order to obtain his pardon and leave to return to France, was intrusted by him with a letter for the Abbé d'Ezmar; the contents of which and the soldiers confession have caused the Assembly to order Mr Defresney and his son to be brought prisoners to Paris. I shall not be surprised if it should turn out to be a forgery. I inclose to your Grace a copy of the letter.

The municipality of Arnay le duc, not trusting to Mr de L'Essarts letter, would not allow Mesdames to leave their town till they had received an answer from some deputies, whom they had sent to Paris to enquire into the truth of things; as that answer must now be arrived they have probably proceeded on their journey.

The Assembly has decreed that no tobacco is to be imported by sea except directly from the United States, the Spanish Colonies, Russia and the Levant; that from America either in American or French vessels, the Spanish in Spanish or French, that from the Ukraine in Russian or French, and that from the Levant in French vessels only. Foreign tobacco in leaf is allowed to be brought into the kingdom at Strasbourg, Valenciennes and Lille paying a duty of 25 livres per quintal. The same duty is laid upon all that is imported in American, Spanish or Russian vessels; 18 livres 15 sols upon what is brought in French vessels. They have not yet fixt the duty upon tobacco the produce of their own colonies.

They have laid a duty of 70 livres per quintal upon foreign linen cloth; upon that imported by land from Austrian Flanders and Germany 36 livres; and upon fine linen 45.

Upon oils and soap the duty is to be 6 livres.

Mr le Chev. de Ternant, who has been negotiating in Germany, is appointed minister to the United States. Mr de Ste Croix goes to Poland.

PARIS, *March 11th*, 1791.

The King of France, naturally of a full habit of body, has never been sufficiently abstemious in his diet; but, while he resided at Versailles, a constant course of hard exercise prevented the bad effects which an excess of food would otherwise have produced: at Paris he has been debarred the advantage of exercise; to this cause and perhaps, in some degree, to agitation of mind in consequence of what happened lately at the Thuilleries, is to be attributed a fever under which he has suffered for some days past. On Sunday[1] we were informed that, on account of a slight indigestion, his Majesty could not see us, but on Tuesday the disorder had risen to an alarming height, and on Wednesday his throat was so swelled that he articulated with the greatest difficulty. The fever is since considerably abated and there is every reason to suppose that he is now out of danger. Those, eight in number, who were sent to prison for being refractory on the 28th at the Thuilleries, are to be sent to Orleans with the rest of the prisoners at the Abbaye accused of crimes of Lèze-Nation, and to be tried there

[1] March 6. On March 9 Montmorin writes to Mirabeau "ceci est une maladie qui à la vérité ne se présente pas sous un aspect très grave mais cependant elle peut le devenir d'un moment à l'autre." There was considerable fever and spitting of blood.

by the Tribunal Provisoire, which is to be composed of Judges elected by the fifteen districts nearest to Orleans, and to continue till the formation of a Haute Cour Nationale. There are at present not less than eighteen hundred prisoners at Paris, but it appears to be the opinion of the Assembly that the prison at Vincennes can be dispensed with, relying I suppose upon the dispatch of the New Courts of Justice, and that it is becoming a free nation, that the towers of that castle should suffer the fate of the Bastille; in the mean time the reparation of it is ordered to be stopt.

The camp at Jalès is dispersed almost without bloodshed and some of the leaders are seized. The hopes of the aristocrates are now turned towards Alsace, where the neighbourhood of the Prince of Condé keeps the minds of people in agitation. A manifesto is soon expected from that Prince.

The Bishop of Spires' answer to Mr de Groschlag's second letter, both of which I inclose, is a curious specimen of good humour and perseverance. The Duke of Wirtemberg is expected here in the course of next week, to the no small concern of his minister at this Court.

A great number of bishops have been elected to supply the place of those who have refused to take the oath: the election for Paris comes on next Sunday. The curate of St Eustache, who is the King's confessor, will most probably be chosen. The Cardinal de Brienne is otherwise provided for and in a manner which equally proves the instability of popular opinion; being re-elected bishop[1] of Toulouse.

The Assembly has decreed that the King is to have the power of appointing and dismissing the Ministers, who are to be six in number: the minister of Justice, of the Interior, of the Colonies, of War, of the Marine, and of Foreign Affairs. The finances are to be administered by a board consisting of six members who are to preside in turn for the space of a month. Such is the precarious state of the colonies that the Assembly was afraid of admitting at the bar a deputation *des gens de couleur*.

The law against emigrants, against those at least who do

[1] Loménie de Brienne was Archbishop of Toulouse.

not come under the denomination of *fonctionaires publics*, has met with so much opposition, both in the committee and the Assembly that, unless some fresh popular motive shall occur, it will probably be dropt.

PARIS, *March* 18*th*, 1791.

The King is so far recovered from his late indisposition that no bulletin's have been given out since Wednesday. There was a general illumination last night, by desire of the municipality; on Sunday there will be another and Te Deum will be sung in the cathedral, at which the new bishop will officiate: although the King's recovery is the ostensible reason the election of the bishop has a great share in these proceedings.

It is difficult to discover what virtues or talents have raised the Bishop of Lydda[1] in partibus infidelium to the See of Paris. His appearance at the Jacobins immediately after his election and before which he was not a member of that club is highly censured by all those who are not blinded by party.

The desire of quiet was the cause of the Cardinal's election to that of Toulouse which his refusal will probably disturb.

In my dispatch, No 6, I mentioned the demand of six millions which the municipality of Paris had made to the National Assembly and which I erroneously supposed to have been granted: on the contrary, they have taken all this time to consider the subject, and have allowed only three millions, one to be paid upon the publication of the decree, another on the 10th of April and the third on the 10th of May.

By taking away the Clermontois from the Prince of Condé they have reduced his income to 300,000 lrs. a year.

They have decided the great business of the contributions. By the contribution mobiliaire they are to raise, for this year, 66 millions; 60 of which for the Treasury, 3 at the disposal of the Legislature and 3 at that of the Administrations of Department. The contribution foncière is to amount to 240 millions, all of which is to be paid into the treasury: nobody however

---

[1] The Abbé Gobet.

is to be rated at more than a sixth of his clear income: besides this a certain number of sols in the livre, not exceeding four, are to be raised, forming a *fonds de non valeur* of 12 millions, 8 of which for the Legislature and 4 for the Administrations of Department.

I send your Grace inclosed a printed copy of an *avis requisitorial* of the Diet of Ratisbonne and the Prince de la Tour-Taxis's answer which made their appearance here on Wednesday and have occasioned no small degree of uneasiness. The Comité Diplomatique having desired Mr de Montmorin to inform them what he knew about it received for answer that he had no official knowledge of any such papers and that the context of them was not in the usual form; he added that, after having considered the matter, he had every reason to suppose that they were forged and, that without doubt, Mr Bérenger, the French minister at the Diet would not have failed to communicate to him those papers had they been authentick. In a letter, he wrote to the Assembly some days before, he informed them that four of the Princes, the Duke of Deuxponts and his brother, the Duke of Wirtemberg, who is arrived here, and the Prince of Linange had agreed to enter into a negotiation, that the rest were endeavouring to obtain the protection of the Emperor and Empire and that their reclamations had occasioned much fermentation at Ratisbonne; he, at the same time said that, as the suppression of the diocesan and metropolitan jurisdictions were not susceptible of any negotiation, it was to be hoped that time and reason would make them drop those reclamations, to which the new constitution would not allow them to have any regard.

The fleet, which has been in the roads during the whole winter has entered into the harbour of Brest having suffered considerably by the frequent storms. The department having announced to the Assembly that the persons in prison on account of the disturbance at the Thuilleries had no accusers, the Assembly passed to the order of the day and the prisoners are released.

PARIS, *March* 25*th*, 1791.

The King is entirely recovered from his late indisposition.

It is now certain that the *avis requisitorial* is not authentic. The authenticity of the inclosed letter from the Pope to the Cardinal de Brienne is doubted by some people, I believe however that it is genuine: but it is generally believed that his letter to the King is arrived; in which he declares that if the present civil constitution of the clergy continues he shall consider France as separated from the Catholic Church. He seems to have omitted no argument that can favor his cause, for his letter is said to consist of 102 pages.

The new Bishop of Paris, having been refused institution both by the Cardinal Bishop of Sens, to whom he applied in person, and by the Bishop of Orleans, from whom he little expected a refusal, has appealed to the directoire du departement, which body, if one may judge from the general sentiments of its members would easily be induced to dispense with that ceremony. The late Bishop of Autun can, if it thought necessary, make that matter easy. A decree to regulate future regencies has been the chief business in the Assembly during this week. In case of a minority the regency is to devolve to the nearest relation on the male side, provided he is a Frenchman, that he inhabits the kingdom, that he has taken the civic oath, and is not a presumptive heir of another crown.

(Women are excluded: the mother however is to be the guardian.)

In case of failure of any relation answering this description a regent is to be elected by a body of electors chosen by the people for that purpose. The Marechal de Broglio having written from Trèves expressing his surprize at his son's motion in the Assembly with regard to him and contradicting in strong terms what he said upon that occasion places the Prince de Broglio's conduct in a ridiculous light.

On a motion of Mr de Mirabeau, a deputation, of which he was one, was sent to Mr Du Portail to know if it were true that there were but 7000 men in the department of the Lower

Rhine and 2000 in that of the Upper. They brought for answer that in the two departments there were between 9 and 10 thousand, but, that about the 15th of April they would amount to about 12 thousand infantry and 4 thousand cavalry. The minister has since said that he was misunderstood, that he meant to say there were but 8 or 9 thousand in the department of the Lower Rhine. That, in the beginning of March, there were 12 thousand 8 hundred men and that in two months there will be twenty thousand. Mr de Mirabeau seems to wish to prove that he alone can be an efficient minister.

It appears that the sale of the church lands amounts, at the present time, to above two hundred millions.

The municipal officers of Douay, who were sentenced by the Assembly to be carried prisoners to Orleans for having refused to proclaim martial law, during the late riots in their town, had, as it is natural to suppose it would happen and as it has always happened in the like cases, left the country before the arrival of the decree.

The troubles continue in Martinico.

PARIS, *April 1st*, 1791.

By a late decree of the Assembly, all *fonctionaires publics* are obliged to residence unless it is dispensed with by the body of which they are members, by their superiors or by the corps administratifs.

The King, *premier fonctionaire public*, cannot absent himself above 20 leagues from the place where the legislative body is sitting, but, when it is not sitting, he may go into any part of the kingdom. If he should leave the kingdom and not return after a proclamation to that purpose by the legislative body it is to be understood that he has abdicated the crown.

The presumptive heir of the crown may, with the King's permission, travel in any part of the kingdom, but he cannot go out of it without the authority of a decree of the Assembly.

Mr Cernon having stated that the deficit for the three first months of this year amounted to above seventy-four millions moved that one hundred and twenty-nine millions should be *versé dans le trésor public* but he could obtain only fifty.

I send, by this messenger, Mr Dufresné's *apperçu des recettes et dépenses* for this year, and also a *tarif general des droits d'entrées et de sorties.*

An impudent publication made its appearance yesterday, which I inclose in order to have your Grace's real instructions.

There is something in the Pope's letter, which certainly arrived on the 20th, which prevents the Ministry from making it public; it is said that the conduct of the late Bishop of Autun is extremely censured in it and that they have sent to Rome to desire a letter more fit for publication in the present circumstances.

The Bishop of Sens's return of his Cardinal's hat has restored to him that degree of popularity which his refusal to give institution to the bishops would otherwise have taken from him. I inclose his letter to the Pope in answer to that which I sent to your Grace last week and for the publication of which we are indebted to the Abbé Maury.

I yesterday had a singular proof of the degree of licence which the inhabitants of this country at present enjoy. Having gone after dinner to make a visit to Mr de Montmorin I was surprised, at my entrance into the drawing room, to see it uncommonly full of company, and my surprize was considerably increased when I perceived that the female part of it consisted of those ladies who in this town go under the denomination of *dames de la halle or poissardes:* they were at that moment taking leave of the minister with the most cordial embraces, having already performed that ceremony to most of the corps diplomatique who had the misfortune of dining there and of the newly appointed foreign ministers, which appointment is very much condemned by the Jacobins, although their secretary Mr de Bonne Carrère is included in it. Mr de Ségur goes Ambassador to Rome and is succeeded at Petersburg by Mr d'Osmond who was appointed last year to go to the Hague, where Mr de Gouvernet, son to Mr de la Tour du Pin is to go. Mr de Vibraye goes Ambassador to Sweden and is succeeded at Dresden by Mr de Montesquieu, son to the late President of the

National Assembly. Mr de Darfort changes his mission at Florence, where there is no longer to be a minister, for the embassy at Venice in the room of Mr de Bombelle who refused to take the oath. All these except Mr de Ségur who is of no party, are, if not aristocrats, impartiaux and of the persuasion of the club of 1789. But to sum up the whole, Mr de Bonne Carrère, a gentleman of whom I believe your Grace has some knowledge, as he has been more than once in England, a man of an intriguing spirit and not without abilities, is to go to Liège.

The Count Oraczewski is arrived here in the capacity of Envoy Extraordinary and Minister Plenipotentiary from the King and the Republic of Poland.

A man possessing the greatest talents, which, if accompanied with good principles, might have rendered him not only an ornament of the age but the saver of his country was this morning[1] cut off in the midst of his career of ambition by a putrid fever. The Jacobins will no longer be curbed by Mirabeau and the friends of Government will feel the loss of his abilities, for, as Mr de Montmorin well observed to me yesterday, men of great talents without principle may be of service to their country, but little talents with little intrigues are sure to be the bane of it.

A disturbance at Toulouse has caused the death of three or four men and is quelled for the present. At Strasburg the minds of people are in great fermentation, and the arrival of imperial troops in the country of Porentrui, although only between four and five hundred, is looked upon with a jealous eye.

The inhabitants of Avignon have voted themselves the 84th department of France.

The death of Mr Macnamara proves the unsettled state of the Isle de France.

[1] Mirabeau died on the morning of April 2.

Paris, *April 8th*, 1791.

Accordingly to your Grace's instructions I have taken the first opportunity of stating to Mr de Montmorin the motives for the additional armament which His Majesty has thought proper to order: at the same time I mentioned the anxiety of the Tobago proprietors and desired an answer. He said that that business was now before Mr de Fleurien and that he would inform him that I had renewed my representation, he took occasion to lament the number of wheels that are employed in the complicated machine of the present Government of this country.

The death of Mr de Mirabeau, which I announced to your Grace last Friday, did not take place till the next morning. It was as remarkable as his life, and, though perhaps opportune for his glory, much and sincerely lamented by his country. His body was attended to the grave by twenty-eight thousand people, and it may fairly be reckoned that three-fourths of the inhabitants of Paris were spectators at his funeral. A remarkable instance how easily vice may be overshadowed by a sense of public utility.

The inspection of his body by thirty physicians has entirely done away a report that was gaining ground that he was poisoned, which was in some degree corroborated by the wonderful manner in which he retained his mental faculties to the last moment of his life.

The want of his advice is conspicuous in the last degree of the Assembly, which declares that no member of the present or any future Legislature shall, till four years after the expiration of his function, have any place in the ministry or receive or even ask for any place pension &c. and, in order I suppose to render these places less desirable, in a *code pénal* upon the crimes and punishments of ministers, the galleys and the carcan, a sort of pillory, are esteemed a proper correction in certain cases.

Owing to the great difficulties attending it, the question about wills is adjourned sine die; without one, children are to inherit in equal proportions.

Mr d'André and some others are of opinion that the great business of forming a constitution for this country will be finished in the course of the month of July and they have accordingly proposed that the King should take the necessary steps for the convocation of a new Legislature.

The party of the Lameths and Barnave are visibly on the decline. Charles Lameth has given a severe blow to his popularity by refusing to attend a deputation to enquire after Mirabeau's health, who, when he heard it, said, *Je le savois maladroit mais je ne le croiois pas si bête.*

The six commissaires du trésor public are named; they are Messrs Lavoisier, Condorcet, Tremblay, de Vayne, Rouillé de l'Etang, and Huber[1]. The appointment of Mr de Condorcet was disapproved by all the ministers, but the King said, *Je le veux, je l'ai promis à Mirabeau.* Mr Huber is a gentleman of Geneva, connected with Mr Necker, and who has lived a considerable time in England, where he married an English lady of the name of Sturt. The decree which condemns the Cardinal de Rohan and his accomplices to be tried at Orleans, will serve rather to increase than diminish the fermentation at Strasburg.

PARIS, *April 15th*, 1791.

I inclose a letter from Mr de Montmorin to me conveying a copy of a letter from Mr de Fleurien to him, by which your Grace will perceive that the business with regard to Tobago rests entirely in the Committees of Commerce and the Colonies.

In the article Paris in the inclosed Gazette de France your Grace will see the means which Mr de Montmorin has taken to disavow that impudent publication, Memoires d'Instructions, &c.

He informed me, in the course of conversation, that the naval armament in England occasioned disquietude in the minds of many people; that he had been applied to by the members of the Diplomatic Committee to inform them what

---

[1] He and his wife were constant correspondents of Lord Auckland.

he knew concerning it: he answered that I had notified it to him and that I had told him that it was for the purpose of adding weight to His Majesty's representations and to negotiations the object of which is to procure a general peace in Europe. The size of the vessels which they deem unfit for the Baltic gives occasion to various surmizes; and Mr de Montmorin said that they might think fit to encrease their armament at Brest.

The only remarkable event that has happened here during the course of this week is the flagellation of the Sœurs Grises and other nuns, to the amount of some hundreds, by the Poissardes, because they chose to hear mass celebrated by priests who have not taken the oath. Such is the feeble state of the police as well as of the Government that the offenders have been suffered to escape without punishment. But an Arrêté du Directoire, drawn up by the Abbé Siéyes, it is hoped will prevent such proceedings for the future and the Roman Catholic religion will be tolerated in this country.

The soldiers of the regiment of Languedoc have seized the military chest; but people are grown so accustomed to acts of insubordination that this event is scarcely talked of.

It is reported that the Prince of Condé has obtained six thousand men from the Prince of Hesse-Cassel with which, and about as many more volunteers he is determined to enter Alsace.

The Duchess of Orleans left Paris suddenly last Sunday: she is gone to her father the Duc de Ponthieu in Normandy, and it is said that articles of separation between her and the Duke of Orleans are about to be drawn up.

In the present anarchy, in and out of the Assembly, it is impossible for me to give your Grace any certain account of the state of parties: thus much however is evident, that there is a sett of men whose object is the total annihilation of monarchy however limited. The heads of this party are: Robertspierre, Péthion, Buzot, and Prieur; in the other extreme are Maury and Cazalés; as for Barnave and the Lameths their consequence, as a party, is so much destroyed that they are wavering whether they should give themselves to the Republicans or the friends to a limited monarchy. The present constitution has no friends and cannot last. It remains for the new Legislature to new model it into a genuine Republic, if the Republican party should prevail, or if the other happen to be strongest many decrees of this Assembly must be annulled and new ones substituted in order to give some energy to the King[1] and the executive power.

I know that Mr de la Marck has communicated to Mr de Montmorin some papers left by Mirabeau which may enable him, if properly supported, to stem the torrent of republicanism.

PARIS, *April 22nd*, 1791.

The extraordinary events of this week have given manifest proofs of the absolute anarchy under which this country labours. An endeavour to compel the King to attend mass celebrated by priests who have taken the oath has caused the constitutional laws and liberty of the country to be violated by those who were especially armed for the defence of them: for it was the National Guard, not the mob, which prevented the King from going to St Cloud.

On Sunday, it was with the greatest difficulty that Mr la Fayette could persuade them to do duty at the King's Chapel: during which time, those who attempted to enter the Church of the Theatins, where the late curate of St Sulpice was to officiate, were threatened with the fashionable punishment of flagellation. The next day when His Majesty, the Queen and the Royal Family entered their carriages in order to go to St Cloud, where they had, some days before determined to pass the Holy Week; they were surrounded by a multitude of people, who insisted that they should not depart. Having remained an hour and three quarters in his carriage, having seen the few nobility that remained about his person ill treated, and having heard, during all that time, the Queen abused with the most harsh and indecent language the King was obliged to return to his palace or rather to his prison. The presence of Mr Bailly had, as usual, no effect upon the people, and Mr de la

---

[1] Unfortunately the Legislature took a different line.

Fayette discovered that Commandant General was become an empty title. The National Guard confessed that they were acting against the law but insisted that the *premier fonctionaire public* should obey the supreme will of the people.

The next morning the Directory of the Department issued a proclamation for assembling the sections in order that they should decide whether the King should be desired to fulfill his intentions of going to St Cloud, or whether he should be thanked by them for having preferred to remain at Paris least he should disturb the public tranquillity.

The majority of the sections wisely agreed that *il n'y avoit lieu à deliberer*.

The Directory at the same time presented an address to the King requesting him, in strong language to dismiss the *refractaires* who surrounded his person, and advising him to announce to foreign nations the glorious revolution which has taken place in France and that he is King of a free people.

The King went to the Assembly and read a speech, a copy of which together with the President's answer I inclose.

The only measure which the Assembly took upon the subject was to order them to be printed by way of a proclamation for the reestablishment of public tranquillity.

The next day the chief officers of the household the King's and Queen's almoners and most of the inferior officers of the court sent their resignations, and yesterday the King received us accompanied by a few remaining attendants on his way to a mass celebrated by a solitary priest.

Mr de la Fayette having resigned his command, his house is constantly full of deputations from the several battallions and from the municipality entreating him not to desert them at this critical time if he can assure him of their obedience he will be prevailed upon to conform to their wishes; if not the prospect will be alarming. In the mean time Mr la Fayette and his Aids de Camps have entered themselves as private grenadiers. The Abbé Sieyes and many of the members of the club of 89 have joined the Jacobins; whether they hope by their influence in that meeting to moderate their proceedings or whether they intend to go with the current remains to be seen.

I inclose an after thought letter from Mr de Montmorin, suggested to him, I imagine by the diplomatic committee: he seems determined if possible to continue in office, but, with the rest of the Ministers he is severely treated by the Jacobins and it is very doubtful that they can resist much longer.

Paris, *April 29th*, 1791.

In consequence of your Lordship's instructions, I shall have the honour of addressing my official letters to you[1], untill I receive further intimation of His Majesty's pleasure in that respect.

Mr de la Fayette's re-acceptation of the command of the National Guard has given great satisfaction to the wellwishers of the present constitution and to all those who are interested in the tranquillity of Paris. The Jacobins, whose plan was to have one of their party chosen commander, shew evident marks of disappointment. They say that he has exacted a degree of submission which it is improper for free citizens to agree to; and they make an absurd distinction between the passive obedience of a regular soldier and the *raisonée* obedience which alone ought to be required of the National Guard.

Mr la Fayette's first act of discipline has been to break that company of Grenadiers, whose indecent behaviour to the King and disobedience of orders was so conspicuous on the 18th of this month[2]. The late Bishop of Autun[3] and the Abbé Sieyès return to the Jacobins has as yet had no apparent good effect, and I have reason to think it occasions no small jealousy in the

---

[1] This letter is addressed to Lord Grenville who had become Foreign Secretary on the retirement of the Duke of Leeds.

[2] It was on this day that the King was prevented from going to St Cloud to spend the Holy week. On the following day Lafayette resigned his position as Commander of the National Guard. The soldiers disbanded formed the Grenadier company of the bataillon de l'Oratoire, belonging to the *Gardes soldés* formerly called the French Guards.

[3] Talleyrand.

minds of those with whom they are principally connected, I mean Mr de la Rochefoucault, Dandré Chapellier and others.

A curious circumstance has come to my knowledge with respect to the address of the Department[1] presented to the King on the 18th.

Mr de Montmorin continued with the directors till four o'clock the next morning entreating them not to print it. The Abbé Sieyès, seeing that the late Bishop of Autun and the rest of the directors present were going to comply with the request of the Minister, went immediately to the printing office, bought some hundred copies and had them instantly circulated. This is the man who has undertaken, by the assistance of papers in the possession of Mr La Mark which I mentioned in No. 15, to follow up the intentions of Mirabeau, and by so doing to defeat the faction of Barnave and the Lameths. The instruction to the Ministers at the foreign Courts comes from that shop: and, the address being published Mr de Montmorin was obliged to sign it or resign. Upon my complimenting him upon the applause with which it was received by the Assembly, he gave me to understand that it was not merited on his part. The Ministers of the other departments are equally obliged to sign whatever is offered to them for that purpose by the leading members of the committees.

The consideration of the important business of Avignon, which has been twice adjourned because the report was not prepared, will certainly come before the Assembly tomorrow. The Comtat in the mean time is suffering all the horrors of a civil war and it will be in a state of desolation before the Assembly can agree to receive it as the 84th department. The minds of people are so much occupied by the state of things at home that the massacre of Mr Mauduit and the insubordination of the troops sent to St Domingo are scarcely noticed.

At a time when the price of provisions must necessarily decrease, for the *Droits d'Entrée* will cease next Sunday, for which the treasury will be fully compensated by the *Droit sur le*

---

[1] An address presented by the department of Paris, drawn up in part by Talleyrand, begging the King to dismiss his present ministers, and to choose such as are favourable to the Revolution.

timbre which is wonderfully productive, the journey-men of all sorts shew an alarming disposition to insist upon the increase of their wages.

The Diplomatic Committee has informed the Assembly that the King of Spain has ordered the formation of a line of troops in the provinces of Catalonia and Arragon, in order to prevent *brigands* and vagabonds entering that country from France. I inclose the Spanish Ambassadors letter to Mr de Montmorin with a translation of his dispatch upon that subject that quiet is established at Porentru[1] and that in general there are no preparations on the frontiers which can give just cause for alarm. An emission of assignats as low as five livres has been proposed and will probably be adopted by the Assembly.

The disturbance at Versailles upon the departure of the Regiment de Flandres has been much exaggerated a few men were pelted with stones, some straggling shot was fired and one man only was killed.

PARIS, *May 6th*, 1791.

Since the National Assembly has declared that it hopes to finish the constitution of this country in less than three months it has made scarcely any progress in that important business. The last week has been employed about the constitution of Avignon and the Comtat Venaissin[2], which, if not protected by the greater Powers, will certainly be included in the French Government. The Assembly has come to a declaration, supported by a majority of 180 members, that they do not form an integral part of the French kingdom; but it by no means declares that they *ought* not, and, if it can be fairly proved that the majority of the inhabitants desire that that country should be incorporated with France, the Assembly will readily accept of the department of Vaucluse. In the mean

[1] Porrentrui on the frontiers of the Empire.
[2] This belonged to the Pope. The report of Menou on this question in the *Moniteur* (May 1, 1791) is full of interesting information.

time Carpentras sustains the siege of the Avignon army and 80 deserters from the Regiment de Soissonnois with great firmness they happen to be tolerably well supplied with Artillery, and, having fired with mitraille they have killed some hundreds of the besiegers, having suffered very little loss on their side. Some emissaries from Avignon going to raise recruits in the Cevennes have been seized and imprisoned at Tarascon.

The Pope's conduct in the present crisis is not to be accounted for by the rules of cool policy. Why he should refuse to receive an Ambassador because he has taken the Civic Oath, distinct from, but which he seems to have confounded with, that which the clergy are obliged to take, it is difficult to account for; the more so as he suffers the present Chargé d'Affaires to transact business at Rome although equally stigmatized in that respect. His Holiness, they say, begins to doat; his *bref*, a copy of which, in print, and of a second, which is lately arrived, I send to your Lordship, rather favors that opinion. The Nuncio did not appear at Court yesterday; he pleaded illness, which is in part founded, for the irksomeness of his situation has had a visible effect on his health his decent behaviour in these ticklish times has gained him a general esteem. The effigy of his master drest in robes ridiculously costly was publickly burnt the other day in the Palais-royal, not by the mob but by a set of wild enthusiasts of what is called the better sort.

Although I give little credit to the assistance that the Prince of Condé is said to expect from German troops yet I have reason to believe that he will attempt to enter France with his death's head army, for it is literally true that the uniform of his soldiers is so ornamented, about the end of this month. Want of money as well as want of prudence will prevent a longer delay. That your Lordship may have some notion of the reception he is likely to meet with in case he make the rash attempt I inclose a copy of a letter from Mr Kellerman, who commands in that country, to his friends the Jacobins.

Mr de Fleurin having resigned the Department of the Marine, because it is to be united with that of the Colonies, has been very much prest by all parties to continue in office; but without success; a Mr de Hoc or Mr de Moustier, if he can be spared from Berlin, will probably be his successor.

The Convoy for Martinico is arrived there and Mr de Behague has taken the command of Fort Bourbon, which is now guarded by two companies of Grenadiers of the Regiments of Forez and Touraine.

If Mr de Montmorin should be obliged to resign, of which there is a great probability, Mr de Choiseul Gouffier it is supposed will succeed him.

I mention the forced resignation of Mr Huber, one of the *Commissaires* de la *Tresorerie*, as it gives me an opportunity of correcting an error I made in a former dispatch in which I called that gentleman a Genevois; it appears that he was born at Lyons, where his family, of Swiss origin, has been established for more than a century. On account however of a connection with the house of Graff in London, which proved bankrupt, his enemies have obliged him to quit his employment.

The Russians have obtained a victory over the Turks at Brailow but Mr de Simolin has not received the particulars of it.

From what has passed to day in the Assembly it appears that we shall be deluged with assignats of 5 livres to the amount of one hundred millions; a very perishable commodity.

P.S. I inclose a copy of the Decret de Commission Imperiale of the 26 of April.

PARIS, *May 13th*, 1791.

The state of affairs has suffered no alteration during the course of the last week.

The Nuncio remains quietly in his hotel till he shall receive further instructions from his Court. The inhabitants of Carpentras sustain the seige with great firmness, and indeed they have little to fear from the enemy's army as it is totally in want of ammunition.

The Prince of Condé's little army, ridiculed, in its present state, by men of sense, is still a bugbear to many; some of whom are members of the committees: and it is difficult to persuade them that it is not paid by Prussia; some even go so far as to surmise that money from His Majesty's Civil List has found its way into that quarter. It is said that the Comte d'Artois is going to reside somewhere between Francfort and Mayence.

Mr Thevenard, a *Chef d'Escadre* who commands at l'Orient, it is now said will have the Marine Department: Mr Moustier however is still expected from Berlin. I shall not be surprized if I have soon to inform your Lordship that Mr de Montmorin is appointed *Chef de la Domesticité*: as I understand that in the projected arrangement and reform of the household, there is to be one chief officer with that title.

The army also is about to be reformed, all confidence between the present officers and the soldiers being destroyed. The last letters from St Domingo bring an account of the death of Mr de Villages, *Commandant de la Station*. The alarming situation of the West India Colonies has for the last three days occupied the attention of the Assembly, and has occasioned very interesting debates: for the particulars of which I must refer to the Moniteur which I regularly send for your Lordship's perusal. Mr Barnave, who has, for some time past, taken upon himself to act as Minister for the Colonies, has, by so doing, contrived to destroy, or at least very much to diminish, his ill deserved popularity. His friend, Charles Lameth, in order to avoid the same fate, was obliged to vote contrary to him yesterday, although he has an estate in that country. The language of the *Colons* is that if they do not carry the question with a large majority they must *se jetter dans les bras de l'Angleterre*.

The Funds sink daily and the price of money increases: silver is at nine, gold at twelve and a half per cent.

I inclose a copy of a letter from the Prince Galitzin to Mr Simolin together with one from the Prince Repnin to the former.

Paris, *May 20th*, 1791.

The decree of last Sunday by which the mulattos born of free parents are admitted into all colonial and parochial assemblies if they have the other requisite qualifications, has separated the West India Colonies from France. The planters of St Domingo wish to be independent; but they would not insist upon a total independence, if, by so doing, they could insure protection against their mother country. A gentleman will probably soon wait upon your Lordship, who will be able to give ample information upon this subject. The deputies of all the West India islands have resigned their seats which is regarded as a rash measure: the assembly has however thought fit to overlook it. I enclose exact copies of their letters addrest to the Assembly.

There is a visible confusion of parties since the decree which prevents the present members from being reelected for the next legislature. That of yesterday, worded in a confused manner, declares that *Les membres d'une legislature pourront être réélus à une Legislature suivante et ne pourront être elus de nouveau qu-après l'intervalle de deux ans.* This does not affect the former decree with regard to the present Assembly. The renewal of the legislative body is to take place without a letter of convocation from the King, and every new legislative body is to meet on the first Monday in May wherever the preceeding one shall have sat. That body however may determine where it will sit and continue to sit or adjourn as it shall think proper. They have not yet decided whether ministers or members of the directories of departments shall be eligible.

The Committee of Finances has at length been obliged to disclose an unpleasant truth to the Assembly, the 12 hundred millions are nearly exhausted: a fresh emission of assignats is therefore necessary: one hundred millions in addition have already been decreed in assignats of five livres, and an emission of six hundred millions more is expected. A new copper coinage, the greatest quantity possible is also decreed. They flatter themselves that the national property will be proved to amount to three thousand millions, according to the rate of the present sale of those lands, a third of which is already sold;

so that the resource of assignats is still in full vigour. No taxes are however as yet collected, except that productive one of the stamps for the impôt sur les patentes has not been sufficiently inforced to produce much, and the land tax cannot be raised before the autumn. The high price of money, which increases daily, owing to the persecution of the vendors of it, is not only a grievance to individuals, but a great distress to government: the treasury was obliged to buy ten millions for the last month for which they paid seven hundred thousand livres. The article of secret service money; which has not yet appeared is, I believe a great drain to them. The public funds, which of late have fallen considerably, begin to rise, owing to the fresh emission of assignats. The exchange with England is almost at twenty-eight per cent. In spite of the general distress, it is certain that the manufactories of Lyons and Rouen are in a flourishing state.

The inhabitants of Carpentras, having encouraged the enemy to approach the town fired upon them *à mitraille*, which seems to have cooled their courage for the present. The neighbouring departments are taking part, some with the besieged others with the besiegers. And the town of Avignon is afraid of admitting its own army within its walls.

PARIS, *May 22nd*, 1791.

I have this instant received the inclosed *signalement* of the people who are supposed to be gone to England with an intention of setting fire to the fleet or dock yards. Mr Fergusson will have the honor of delivering this letter to your Lordship.

PARIS, *May 27th*, 1791.

The Assembly has finished the organization of the legislative body, which it has declared the King cannot dissolve. The persons as well as property of it's members are to have, in civil cases, no privileges distinct from those of other citizens.

Mr Buzot's project of dividing, by lot, the Assembly into two sections to deliberate separately, in order to prevent rash and hasty decrees has not been adopted, but the Committees of Constitution and Revision have unanimously agreed that it is desireable to find some means to hinder the impetuosity and haste of future legislatures. I am not surprized that they speak with feeling upon the subject, for a levity in decision, especially of late, has done little honour to the present Assembly.

They had desired their committees to draw up an instruction to be sent with the decree to the colonies: upon their neglecting so to do, Mr Du Port proposed one of his own composition, which your Lordship may see in the Moniteur of the 22d. of this month. But it was agreed that the *travail* of the committees upon the organization of the colonies would best answer that purpose. The trading-towns have taken the alarm and the language of the colonists at Bordeaux has induced the administrators of that department to lay an embargo upon all the vessels bound for the colonies. In their address to the Assembly, which was received with great applause, they state that the district, the municipality, the chamber of commerce and all the patriotic clubs united with them in an ardent desire to enforce the decree, and that many of the National Guard had entered their names as volunteers to be sent to restore peace in the West Indies.

The two battalions which are arrived from Saint Domingo were not suffered to land there by Mr Blancheland, judging, as it is natural to suppose, from the behaviour of the troops in the island, that their arrival would be detrimental to the mother country.

On Tuesday a *projet de décret* of the committee concerning Avignon, was rejected by a majority of twenty voices, which, it was thought, had decided that question; but, the next day a second decree declared that the former did not at all prejudice the rights of France to Avignon and the Comtat, and desired the King to take provisional measures to restore peace in that country.

The price of specie continues nearly the same, for, although many sections have allotted particular spots for the free sale of money, few vendors are to be found. The new copper coin and assignats of 5 livres will soon be in circulation. They certainly think of a naval armament but they have not yet come to a resolution upon that subject.

Paris, *June 3rd*, 1791.

The *Code Pénal* has occupied the attention of the Assembly for the greatest part of this week. On Tuesday however their attention was drawn off to another subject; their own conduct or rather misconduct, by the reading of a letter addrest to them by the Abbé Raynal[1], full of unpleasant truths and wholesome advice. The Abbé not knowing in what manner it might be taken, has thought proper to quit Paris. I inclose a printed copy of this remarkable letter. With regard to the *Code Pénal* they have as yet made little change in the mode of punishment, excepting that they have decreed that death shall be inflicted without torture, and that criminals shall be beheaded instead of being hanged, and that as a re-integration in civil rights may take place after a certain time, no durable marks of infamy are to be inflicted.

They have agreed that the instruction drawn up by Mr Dupont (not Du port as I inadvertently wrote the name in my last dispatch) shall be immediately sent to the colonies. Some vessels have been already allowed to sail there from Bordeaux. A letter having been read from Mr Montmorin, complaining of some false and improper insinuations with regard to the King's intentions of leaving the kingdom, printed in the Article Allemagne in the Moniteur no. 151, they thought fit to pass *à l'ordre de jour*.

Necessity will enforce them to disband the army in order to form it in a new manner. A measure which Mirabeau had in contemplation. Mr Duportail, in giving an account to the Assembly of the subalterns and soldiers of the regiment de Dauphiné having obliged their officers to quit their command,

---

[1] He was now nearly eighty years of age. The letter is a very remarkable production and well deserves reading.

says, that this event does not bear the character of one of those which hazard and unforeseen circumstances occasion ; that ordinary measures are insufficient to prevent the evil and that it will require all the wisdom of the Assembly. The soldiers will not obey their officers because they consist of the *ci-devant noblesse* and the same spirit operates in the fleet. The directors of the department of the Lower Rhine have requested of the Assembly the assistance of five thousand of the National Guard in order to constrain the zealous fanaticism of the inhabitants of that country and to resist the manoeuvres of the Prince of Condé and the Cardinal of Rohan. The Assembly has taken no step with regard to military assistance but they have disapproved the conduct of the majority of the members of the directory of the department of the Upper Rhine and have ordered them to be replaced and declared their Arreté void: for the particulars of this business I must refer to the report of the committee which your Lordship will see in this day's Moniteur.

The assessment for the *Contribution* fonciere et mobiliaire is completed and Mr Tarbé is appointed *Ministre des Contributions publiques*. This appointment is universally approved. A society has deposited a security at the Hotel de Ville of twelve millions and issue notes of five livres value, which, en attendant the assignats are of considerable use ; but the price of money continues nearly the same.

The demand for the manufactures of this country increases prodigiously.

It is certain that the Count d'Artois has been expected in Germany but it is also certain that he had not left Italy on the 20th of last month.

The Nuncio quitted this place last Monday. A letter from the mayor and many of the municipal officers of Carpentras, declaring their wishes to be united to France has raised the hopes of those who wish for an 84th department.

An attempt was made yesterday to have mass celebrated by a priest *non assermenté* at the Church of the Theatins, but without success, although backed by a decree of the Assembly, an arreté of the department and the wish of the municipality. Some people, for they were too few to be called a mob, meeting with no resistance, overturned the altar and dispersed the congregation.

A decree passed the Assembly yesterday to desire the King to order a new Treaty of Commerce with the United States of America, and Mr Ternant set off this morning with instructions from Mr Montmorin for that purpose.

I communicated last week to that Minister a memorial of the Mortgage Creditors of Tobago (copy of which I inclose) which he promised to send immediately to the committee. I believe it is in consequence of this measure that Mr Chapelier told Mr Balfour yesterday that he should be ready to make the report in a very few days. If he should fail to do so, I shall, according to your Lordship's instructions, desire Mr Montmorin to write to the President of the Assembly upon the subject.

PARIS, *June* 10*th*, 1791.

Mr Balfour informed me yesterday that Mr Chapelier had not only not made the report of the committees upon the Tobago business, although he had promised to do so in the course of a week, but that he had said he could not make it for some days nor till he had finished some important business with which he is occupied at present. I communicated this circumstance in conversation to Mr de Montmorin and desired him either to lay the affair before the Assembly or to find some other means to facilitate the success of the just pretensions of the parties concerned. He said that Mr Chapelier had told him that the report was in readiness, but that, after what I had mentioned, he would speak to him again upon the subject and do all that lay in his power to expedite the business. At his request, I have sent him a letter, a copy of which I enclose. I have very good reason to believe that the expectation of a bribe has been the cause of this delay.

This week has made little or no difference in the dismal appearance of public affairs. The Comtat continues to suffer all the calamities of civil war. Money in specie has sunk but little in it's price; the taxes are not levied; few assignats remain in the Treasury, and they are afraid of moving a decree for a fresh emission of them, till they can obtain a more regular account from the several departments of the value of the lands already sold: only two hundred and seven districts have as yet sent in their accounts.

The discontented nobility are tending daily towards Worms, where the Prince of Condé may soon boast of an army composed almost entirely of officers.

The attendance at Constitutional Clubs has occasioned a general disposition among the soldiers to cashier their officers; and, among the many new experiments now making in this country that of an army in which the soldiers are to have the command seems not to be the most promising.

Six committees have given their opinion against disbanding the army and seemed to flatter themselves that a proper severity with regard to the regiment de Dauphiné would be sufficient to preserve discipline; but some late accounts from Alsace will perhaps prove to them that it will not be sufficient. A member was yesterday beginning to give an account of a motion, made by the subalterns in one of the popular meetings at Strasburg, to dismiss their officers, but the National Assembly would not permit him to proceed and referred that affair to the six committees appointed to draw up a report upon the means of reestablishing order in the army.

Want of energy in the Civil Government encourages seditious language among the journeymen tradesmen and workmen who demand an increase of wages, and the same cause has hitherto prevented the opening of the Theatins for nonjuring papists. The Comte d'Artois, it is said, is at Ulm: he seems inclined to deliberate twice before he passes the Rubicon.

PARIS, *June 17th*, 1791.

The only measures as yet taken with regard to the army are. A decree of the Assembly obliging all officers to sign a promise upon honor to be faithful to the nation the law and the King, and to oppose with all their power any plot or conspiracy against the present constitution. Camps of instruction ordered to be formed. The regiments on the frontiers to be on the war establishment; and an enrolment for volunteers of the National Guard (who are to act only in a case of necessity) to be opened in every department. By another decree the Prince of Condé is summoned to return into the kingdom within the space of a fortnight, or to retire from the frontiers, having formally declared that he will undertake nothing against the constitution or the tranquillity of the kingdom. In case of disobedience his estate and goods are to be confiscated, or, to use their own words, sequestered.

In Alsace, the distress for want of specie is still greater than in the interior part of France, the market of Strasburg being, in a great measure, supplied from the other side of the Rhine, where assignats are far from being current.

The late Bishop of Autun is to communicate to the Assembly a plan to prevent the great loss which this country suffers by the exchange with foreign nations. I understand he proposes to liquidate the public debt by paying the creditors with *Obligations Nationales or Quittance de Finance.*

The committees have at length drawn up a long instruction for the colonies, containing a plan for a constitution consisting of about three hundred articles, which, however, is not to affect any former decrees of the Assembly and is to be sent there merely as a memorial and instruction. The *Procès Verbal* of the Colonial Assembly of Martinico of the 17th of March last an extract of which I inclose, gives a faint hope that the decree of the 15th of May will not be ill received in that island. The Assembly of Guadeloupe has written to that of Martinico desiring them to appoint Commissioners to treat in common upon the constitution of those islands and particularly upon that important article the political and civil state of the free mulattos and slaves.

Paris, *June* 22nd, 1791.

I take the first opportunity of informing your Lordship of the surprizing event which happened yesterday, no person whatever having till this moment been permitted to leave Paris.

Between seven and eight in the morning it was discovered that the King and all the Royal Family had left the Thuilleries unknown to the Guard. It is supposed that they quitted the Palace between one and two o'clock, and it is imagined that they have taken the rout through the forests of Compiègne and the Ardennes to the Low Countries but nothing certain is as yet known. Monsieur and Madame have also left the Luxembourg.

Owing to the activity of the National Guard the exertions of the municipality and the prudent deliberations of the National Assembly, for the heat of party, has, for the present entirely subsided, the tranquillity of this town has been perfectly preserved.

As soon as the Assembly was met, the President informed them that he had received from the mayor intelligence of the departure of the King and of the Royal Family: couriers were immediately ordered to be sent to every department with orders to prevent any body from quitting the kingdom and the Ministers were summoned to attend the Assembly.

The *Ministre de la Justice* was authorized to continue to make use of the Seal of the State, which measure was thought necessary, as a letter had been delivered to him that morning signed by the King forbidding him to do so till further orders. That Minister delivered a memorial which Mr la Porte (*Intendant de la Liste Civile*) had put into his hands, having had the Kings orders to communicate them to all the Ministers.

The National Assembly sits night and day, and the Ministers transact business in an adjoining appartment.

I send inclosed the Logographe which gives the most accurate account of every thing that passes in the Assembly, and some other printed papers by way of supplement. In the Postillon of this morning there is mention made of the fears of some of the Ambassadors for their personal safety: if any of them have exprest such fears they have had very little reason for so doing: for myself I never had any.

I wait with impatience for instructions from your Lordship at this critical period.

P.S. The inclosed notes from Mr Montmorin will prove to your Lordship the difficulty I had to obtain a passport for my messenger.

Paris, *June* 23, 1791.

I received the inclosed paper from Mr de Montmorin last night.

The most recent account of the King's situation was brought this afternoon by a Mr Mangin, son to a member of the Assembly, who resides at Varennes, a small town between Stenay and Clermont in Argonne. He says that early on Wednesday morning the King and Royal Family passed through Sainte Menehould in a Berline with six horses but with only two attendants on horseback: the postmaster of that place suspected that they were not common travellers and questioned them particularly about their rout; they said that they were going to Verdun the first town on the great road, he followed them but seeing them take the bye road which leads to Varennes, he rode in haste to that town and gave the alarm: when the King arrived at the inn the inhabitants insisted that he should not proceed on his journey untill they knew for certain who he was and the motives of it. His Majesty was therefore obliged to enter the inn where he was seen by Mr Mangin who, being acquainted with his person, informed the astonished multitude that they possess their King.

A courier arrived at the Assembly last night about nine o'clock with an account of his Majesty's being stopt at this place, he at the same time delivered a letter from the municipal officers of Sainte Menehould informing the Assembly that Mr Bouillé, who commands at Metz, had sent detachments of troops to that town and other places in the neighbourhood, having given out that a large quantity of money for the pay of the garrisons on the frontiers was expected to pass that way and that they were to convoy it. It appears that when the King was first stopt some hussars were seen riding through the town who finding the alarm too general passed quietly on. The Assembly has given orders to secure Mr Bouillé and it has also appointed three of its members Mr Barnave Mr Pethion and Mr la Tour-Maubourg commissioners with power to give orders to the troops the National Guard and the administrative bodies: their principal business however is to protect the persons of the Royal Family on their return to Paris. According to Mr Mangin's account, the King slept last night at Chalons and intends to sleep this night at Epernay; it is therefore possible that he may arrive in the capital tomorrow, but more probably on Saturday. Monsieur and Madame are safely arrived at Mons.

The way in which the Royal Family contrived to leave the Thuilleries is not yet known; the thing is wonderful and the more so because the Mayor and Mr la Fayette had been apprized of their intention for some days before and had accordingly taken all possible precautions to prevent it: they both staid with his Majesty till one o'clock, when they retired perfectly secure that no attempt of the sort could be made that night; having left a double guard and an extraordinary number of officers upon duty against whom there is no suspicion of corruption.

The Assembly continues to sit night and day adjourning sometimes for an hour or two and in the intervals of urgent they proceed with the ordinary business.

The late Bishop of Autun, finding that his scheme would not succeed, entertained the Assembly with a discourse upon finance and the balance of trade and so that matter ended. Six hundred millions more have been decreed, one hundred and sixty only of which are to be emitted at present, the quantity that has been already burnt, in order to adhere to their former decree that twelve hundred only should be in circulation at one time. Twenty eight millions have been ordered to the public treasury. The tranquillity in and out of the Assembly has been astonishing but I this moment learn that the quiet of the Assembly is likely to be disturbed by the riotous rejoicing of the Poissardes and the inhabitants of the

Fauxbourg Saint Antoine, an unpleasant prognostic of what may happen on the King's arrival.

His Majesty's Memorial, which your Lordship will see in the Moniteur 173 has contributed much to unite the sentiments of all parties on the present occasion; the least that can be said for that measure is that it was precipitate. Almost all the members of the Assembly have taken the new oath and Mr la Fayette and his friends have joined the Jacobins.

PARIS, *June* 25, 1791.

The King and Royal Family arrived this evening at seven o'clock. The order and regularity with which the whole of their entry was conducted was astonishing. They were carried round the outside of the walls of the town till they came to the Grille of Chaillot from thence they proceeded in a direct line through the Champs Elysés and the Place de Louis Quinze to the garden of the Thuilleries; unfortunately some of the crowd forced their way into the gardens when the carriages entered which occasioned the Royal Family's hearing some unpleasant language when they arrived at the palace: in all other respects the greatest decorum has been preserved.

A separate guard, under the command of Mr la Fayette, has been ordered by the Assembly for the King, the Queen and the Dauphin; for the latter a Governor is to be appointed by the Assembly. It is said that the convent of the Val de Grace will be destined for the residence of the Queen. A declaration is to be demanded from the King and Queen in order that the Assembly may be better able to judge how to act with regard to them.

The decrees of the Assembly are to be valid without the King's sanction and the ministers and the other branches of the executive power are to continue to do the business of that part of the Government till it shall be otherwise determined. Addresses come daily from the frontiers full of friendly sentiments to the present constitution but expressing their fears of an invasion and their want of means to resist the enemy. The number of National Guard which the Assembly has decreed to be *en activité* and which will receive better pay than the regular troops, fifteen sous instead of ten, will amount to about three hundred thousand.

The great events which have occurred during this week have made me forget one of less importance, the insurrection at Bastia. General Paoli will easily be able to quell it when he receives the assistance of two frigates and some additional troops which are ordered to be sent to him. The Duc de Choiseul and the Comte Charles de Damas are taken and are in prison at Verdun: it is not known whether Mr de Bouillé has escaped; his son was at Varennes but finding the game lost he thought proper to retreat. The father had trusted too much in the obedience of his soldiers and it was imagined the inhabitants of the country would be less eager to prevent the King's departure. Mr de Fersen the principal contriver of this scheme is safely arrived in Flanders.

Had the King forced his way through Varennes he would have found the bridge beyond the town barracaded in such a manner that it would have been impossible for him to have proceeded on his journey.

Paris, *June* 27, 1791.

As almost every circumstance which can afford matter of intelligence for your Lordship must now come before the Assembly, I send, and shall continue to send, the Logographe, which journal not only gives the most accurate and litteral accounts of the debates but gives also exact copies of the most interesting papers that are laid before the Assembly.

The affair of the passport, which had nearly caused the destruction of Mr Montmorin's house, is simply this. That minister had given the duplicate of a passport to a Baronne de Corff, a Livonian lady, having been informed by Mr Simolin, who was persuaded of the fact, that *par distraction* she had burnt the original. Mr Montmorin has been publickly declared irreprochable in this affair.

Some of the King's and Queen's principal friends were yesterday permitted to approach them. It is supposed that the Duc de la Rochefoucauld will be appointed Governor to the Dauphin.

Three commissioners are appointed to receive the declarations of the King and Queen: they were with their Majesties last night for the space of three hours but the result of that interview is not yet known.

Mr de Bouillé is out of France.

PARIS, *July* 1, 1791.

The party of Barnave the Lameths and Duport, having almost entirely lost their ill-deserved popularity, shewed, before the late event, an inclination to change their system of politics, in order to preserve their importance: the present state of things has afforded them an opportunity of adopting a new line of conduct, and a sort of coalition has taken place between them and the aristocratic party which will probably not last long.

When Mr Duport proposed last Wednesday in the name of the Committee of Constitution, which was attended on that occasion by Mr Cazalès, a confederation on the fourth of August, the time calculated for the completion of the Constitution and the consequent dissolution of the Assembly he had in view a solemn federative reintegration of the King upon his acceptance of the Constitution. The loss of this motion in the Assembly, where the Republican party is much less considerable than in the country at large does not augur well in favor of the supporters of that system. I inclose printed copies of the King's and Queen's Declaration; by the former it appears that it was his Majesty's intention to proceed no farther than Montmédi, where he expected to be protected by the troops under the command of Mr de Bouillé. In a most imprudent letter from that commander to the Assembly it is asserted that it was by his instigation that the King was persuaded to this measure: he trusted, without sufficient reason in the obedience of the troops, and I fear the King trusted too much in the attachment of his subjects out of Paris.

The Royal Family, though strictly guarded, have their usual intercourse with one another and give a list to Mr la Fayette of those persons whom they wish to see. It has been signified to the King through Mr de Montmorin that, in the present circumstances, the Ambassadors think it their duty not to appear at the Thuilleries without his Majesty's orders to that purpose.

The Assembly have not yet elected a Governor for the Dauphin: they have declared that no member of their body shall be eligible, which prevents the nomination of Mr de la Rochefoucauld. The *partie droite* has taken no part in the debates upon this subject nor indeed scarcely upon any other since the King's return.

The primary Assemblies are almost all finished and no inconsiderate corruption has been used to influence the choice of electors. The electoral Assemblies are suspended till the fermentation all over the kingdom shall be subsided. The Judges lately chosen for the Criminal Tribunal of Paris and many of the electors for the next Legislature are the *Élite* of republicanism: the same spirit I believe does not pervade the kingdom.

The members of the General Assembly of Saint Domingo are permitted to return to their island, but an advance of money which they requested has been refused. The troubles in Corsica are nearly quelled your Lordship undoubtedly knows that the Count d'Artois has met his brother at Brussels.

Paris, *July* 4, 1791.

I take the first opportunity of sending to your Lordship a letter I received on Saturday evening from Mr Montmorin inclosing copies of one from Mr Thevenard to him and another from Mr le Chapelier to Mr Thevenard.

I have received your Lordship's instructions by Mr Moore to which I need not add that I shall pay the greatest attention. As the Assembly is now become the great channel for information I shall for the future take the liberty of sending the Logographe regularly by this day's post. In No. 67 there is an interesting letter from the commissioners appointed for the Departments of the Meuse, Moselle, and Ardennes: as a supplement to which I inclose extracts of two letters which have been communicated to me.

The Duke of Orleans has declared publickly that he would refuse the Regency if it were offered to him: it is reported, as another proof of his humility, that he has signified to the Duchess that since there are no longer Princes in France she must expect a pied à terre instead of a palace at Paris, and that the state of his affairs obliges him to reduce her pin money to a thousand livres per month.

In the present situation of things in this country one is not surprized that slight occurrences should afford matter for serious alarm: but one cannot help smiling when some few vessels are mistaken[1] for the British fleet and that by so egregious a mistake a whole country should be in arms.

The fears that the inhabitants express of a Spanish invasion are equally well grounded.

PARIS, *July* 8, 1791.

Having received a letter from Nantes stating that on the 29th of June a body of national troops had come on board the Endeavour of London, and the Commerce of Newcastle, and demanded their sails which they took away, although they had no article on board which had not been regularly entered at the Custom house; I wrote immediately to Mr Montmorin desiring him to procure orders for the restoration of the sails and leave for the departure of the vessels: the next day I

---

[1] This refers to letters from Nantes expressing fear of an English descent in conjunction with the flight of the King and a belief that it had already taken place.

received a note from him inclosing a decree of the National Assembly, both of which I send to your Lordship. I have this instant received a letter from the master of one of those vessels informing me that their sails are brought back to them and that they have permission to leave the port. The cause of their detention was the appearance of some French West India men off the coast between Belleisle and Noirmoutier which were supposed to be part of the British fleet: the appearance of these vessels and an attempt made by about a hundred aristocrates in Britanny to embark for Jersey, (which embarcation was somehow mistaken for a debarcation of six thousand English,) were sufficient to alarm the whole coast from Brest to Rochefort: from thence to the Mediterranean the country was alarmed by a report of an irruption of the Spaniards occasioned by a skirmish with the smugglers on the frontiers, a strong proof how much this country is at present on the *qui vive*. The real cause of the report of the English invasion was known almost as soon as the report itself; but with regard to the other, the Spanish Ambassador thought himself obliged to write to Mr Montmorin in order to satisfy the minds of people of the falsity of that report: your Lordship may see his letter in the Logographe No. 70.

Nothing of any moment has passed either in or out of the Assembly except the declarations signed by two hundred and ninety members of the Assembly which I inclose a decree concerning the emigrants will probably be passed tomorrow.

The delicacy and prudence necessary to be observed in any ulterior measure with regard to the King and the Royal Family have occasioned a suspension of any deliberation upon that subject.

It appears, by the accounts of the commissioners sent by the Assembly to the several departments, that in all the regiments many of the officers, and in some a few of the soldiers have quitted the kingdom. The former having signified to the soldiers of their regiments that if they would leave the kingdom and join them they had full power from the King to give them advanced rank his Majesty has written to the Assembly denying that he has given any such powers and he takes the opportunity of repeating that his intention was to go no farther than Montmédi.

The Republican party certainly looses ground and conscious of their weakness some of the heads of that party declare that they will be contented with *une monarchie sans monarque ou une régence sans regént.*

It is said that the Empress of Russia has proposed a treaty with this country and the very long conferences which I observe between Mr Simolin and Mr Montmorin favor that supposition.

Paris, *July* 15, 1791.

I send inclosed to your Lordship a printed copy of a petition presented to the National Assembly by Mr Roume de Saint Laurent in which he styles himself charged by the Minister of the Marine to answer the complaints of the English creditors.

The decree of last Saturday which subjects to a treble taxation those emigrants who do not return within a month is generally considered as the best measure that could be adopted in the present circumstances of the country.

The army, according to Mr Duportail's papers laid before the Assembly, will only amount to about two hundred and forty thousand men including infantry cavalry artillery and the National Guard.

The commissioners who were sent to inspect the frontiers have given a very unfavorable report of the state of the fortifications particularly at Metz and the garrison towns in the department of the Ardennes; at the former there is one place entirely open and defenceless: they complain also of a great want of military stores and ammunition excepting cannon, with which they are abundantly supplied.

The procession in honor of Voltaire which took place on Monday seemed more calculated to give entertainment to children than to have any good or even bad effect excepting that it afforded an excuse for one whole days idleness; a thing which he himself used often to lament.

The celebration of the fourteenth consisted of a procession and a Te Deum sung before the altar *de la Patrie* in the *Champ de Mars*, which appeared to be almost as crowded as it was at this time last year. It has been occupied this morning by a large concourse of people who assembled there in order to sign a petition to the National Assembly requesting them to bring the King to a trial. A great majority of the Assembly, consisting of the moderate party, the aristocratic party and that of the Lameths and Barnave during the two days that have already been employed in debates upon this subject have shewn themselves determined to support the plan of the seven united committees: which is to respect the inviolability of the King but to suspend his functions till the completion of the Constitution: when they propose to offer the Charter of the Constitution for his acceptance or refusal.

I this moment learn that the Assembly has decided that the King shall not be *mis en cause*.

Mr Duveyrier who carried the decree of the Assembly to the Prince of Condé has not been heard of since he followed that Prince to Coblentz.

PARIS, *July* 18, 1791.

The proceedings of the National Assembly on Friday last with regard to the King having occasioned much fermentation and the next morning a crowd of people assembled round the *Autel de la Patrie* being harrangued by deputations from the club of the Jacobins, who not only spoke of the King and the Royal Family in the most opprobrious terms but reviled the Assembly, they gave directions to the Ministers, the Department and the Municipality to use every possible exertion in order to maintain peace and enforce the laws.

Yesterday morning two unfortunate men were discovered concealed under the *Autel de la Patrie* it is supposed out of a mere frolic, for which they payed dear. It was spread about that they were concealed there with a design to blow up the altar, and summary justice was executed upon them: their heads being severed from their bodies were carried on spikes and the mangled bodies dragged in a horrid manner along the streets; a troop of cavalry to the amount of some hundreds and infantry arrived time enough to prevent this horrid spectacle from being exhibited in the midst of Paris; but as soon as they were departed the crowd reassembled in the Champ de Mars, and it was judged expedient that Mr la Fayette and the Mayor of Paris should go there with a considerable force and proclaim Martial Law. Being, not only insulted but pelted with stones the Guards were at length obliged to fire: ten or twelve men are said to be killed about as many wounded and some are carried to prison. Paris is at present perfectly quiet. I intend to send Flint with more particulars in the course of this day, or tomorrow at furthest.

PARIS, *July* 18, 1791.

It has been stated in the Assembly that, so far from being hasty to give orders to fire upon the people in the late affair at the Champ de Mars, the National Guard had received repeated volleys of stones and a musket had been discharged at Mr la Fayette before he gave orders to fire: the man who attempted this desperate act was seized but released at Mr la Fayette's desire, but, by a decree of the Assembly his person is ordered to be secured: the activity of the National Guard has maintained the peace and tranquillity of Paris, of the continuance of which there is a most flattering prospect: one cannot however help being anxious to hear that the same order has taken place in the provinces.

A considerable number of suspicious foreigners have been taken up today but none, as your Lordship may easily imagine, are English: the most conspicuous is one Ephraim a Jew, supposed to be employed by the King of Prussia; cyphers were found in his possession but, as he declares he is employed about a commercial treaty, he may have made use of them without an improper design. Although I am convinced that none of the many English who are here are in the least personally concerned in the politics of this country, I endeavour to persuade them to use all possible caution in words as well as action, the more so as an opinion is gone abroad that both Government and Opposition in England have tampered with the democratic party here. The members of the Jacobins who are deputies, except Mr Roberspierre Mr Buzot and Mr Pethion, have quitted that club and have composed another at the feuillants. They have also written addresses to all the provincial societies connected with the club of the Jacobins in order to prevent the bad effects which the addresses sent by that club may otherwise have in the provinces.

PARIS, *July* 18, 1791.

The chief advantage that Government has obtained by the coalition with the formerly popular party is more visible in the metropolis than it can be expected to be in the provinces, the strong [Forts de la Halle] men of the market and the suburb of St Anthony and the most wealthy bankers here appear to be still at their command, and, feeling secure of the National Guard, they have exerted the public force in a manner in which they otherwise could not have ventured to act.

Though the rage of republicanism may be overcome, it will be difficult to conquer the disgust the King's conduct has inspired.

PARIS, *July* 22, 1791.

As long as the red flag continues to be displayed at the Hotel de Ville we may expect to feel the effects of that energy which military law has given to Government. A wonderful change has taken place since the disturbances of the 17th compelled the majority of the Assembly to be sensible of its power. It is calculated that two hundred people have been imprisoned since that event, upon suspicion of fomenting sedition by writing or by other means. Danton is fled and Mr Robespierre the great *Denonciateur* and by office *Accusateur publique* is about to be *denoncé* himself. Ephraim the Jew is set at liberty; but a woman of the name of Etta Palm, who used to assume the title of Baronne d'Aelders, is confined upon the same suspicion.

Some addresses are arrived in favor of the decree of the 15th[1]: the strongest of which is that from Rouen; there can be no doubt that the country at large approves of that decree but it will be wise in the Assembly to hasten the business that remains for them to finish and to make way for their successors for in a short time *tempus abire tibi* will be told them from all quarters; and their resemblance to the Long Parliament begins to be a common topic.

The alarm of an invasion from Germany is in no degree diminisht; and the stay of the King of Sweden at Aix la Chapelle, who has recalled all the Swedish officers in the French service, is regarded in an unfavorable light. Although implicit faith is not to be given to Mr de Montesquieu's account of the bad state of the fortifications, for there are many reasons to suppose it exaggerated, yet, on the other hand, Mr du Portail, in his contradiction of that report, is possibly in the other extreme. The most alarming circumstance in the situation of that country is the total insubordination of the soldiers which Mr Emmery was obliged to state yesterday to the Assembly in order that speedy means may be taken to render them subordinate to their officers; for the few who have not either given their dismission, been dismist by their men or gone over to Germany complain that it is impossible, in the present state of things, to expect obedience from the soldiers. Many regiments have been treated much in the same manner as that of Nassau, of which your Lordship will see an account in this day's Logographe. It is certain that an engagement had nearly taken place at Metz between that regiment and the regiment de Condé.

The Swiss troops have received orders from their Cantons not to take the new oath; which will place them in a predicament very different from that of the rest of the army.

[1] This decree, passed on July 15, declared that the King was to be considered to have abdicated, and summoned Bouillé and his accomplices for trial.

Upon the whole the National Assembly was never more puzzled how to act than in the present crisis and the confusion of parties impedes the action of the seven committees in whom resides the executive power.

Considerable quantities of copper, originally intended for copper-sheathing men of war, have been sent to the Mint from all the dock yards.

Mr Duveyrier is at last arrived; according to his account, he was detained 22 days at Luxembourg without having permission to write to France: but, for further particulars, I must refer your Lordship, (for want of time) to this evening's Postillon, in which there is a speech of Mr Alexandre Lameth worth your Lordship's notice.

PARIS, *July* 29, 1791.

At the end of eight days after the first proclamation of Martial Law it ceased, of course, to be in force: but the Assembly has passed a decree resembling our Riot Act which will tend to prevent future disturbances. Of those who have been lately arrested all the foreigners and most of those who are of a democratic persuasion have been released. It is said that prudential motives more than want of sufficient grounds of accusation have caused them to set at liberty Ephraim and Madame Aelders who plume themselves much upon this proof of their innocence.

Since it has been publicly known that Mr de Bouillé has entered into the service of the King of Sweden and that considerable preparations are making on the other side of the Rhine, the approaching war is mentioned without mystery and, in spite of Mr Lameth's statement the notoriously defenceless state of the frontiers gives cause for serious alarms. Three thousand five hundred National Guards, half of which number are now encamped in the Plaine de Grenelle close to this town, will set out from hence in a few days for the defence of that part of France; they are composed of young raw undisciplined but otherwise able bodied men: their pay 15 sols per diem is so much superior to that of the regular troops that it may occasion a jealousy productive of bad consequences during the present want of discipline in the army: another cause of discontent among the regulars is an order given to pay the Swiss soldiers in specie in consequence of their having received orders from their Cantons not to receive assignats in payment of their solde, a distinction very liable to create a jealousy. Landau is thought to be the place most easy to be taken, and the more so since three engineers, who were employed in putting it into a state of defence, have escaped to Luxembourg.

Mr du Veyrier's mission having failed in all respects, the leading members of the Assembly wish to try what effect a sort of remonstrance by way of ultimatum may have upon the Princes, which it is proposed to have presented to them by the Chevalier de Coignie their intimate friend and one who professes the principles of the aristocratic party; the only certain effect of this measure is the procuring to the Chevalier an opportunity of quitting the kingdom.

The Committee of Revision have finished the *Charte Constitutionelle* which will be soon offered to the King for his acceptance. I understand he has seen it and has made some few observations upon it but which, according to the French phrase *ne tireront pas à consequence.*

A great number of false assignats have lately appeared which at present embarrass only individuals but in the end they may affect public credit. The demand for the principal manufactures of this country is so great that the manufacturers complain only of the want of a sufficient number of journey-men who are willing to work.

I have this moment received a letter from Mr Montmorin inclosing one from the Departement de la Loire inferieure, both of which I inclose to your Lordship.

PARIS, *August* 5, 1791.

I send inclosed a letter from Mr de Montmorin inclosing one from Mr Thevenard by which your Lordship will perceive that Mr Landolph has no authority whatever from the French

Government to demand a duty from vessels which frequent the river Formosa; and that in general the French claim no pretentions to restrain the freedom of commerce of other nations on that part of the coast of Africa.

Mr Thevenard adds that he will make further inquiries concerning that business in order, if it found proper, to oblige Mr Landolph to make restitution.

Some officers of artillery just arrived from Martinico having imprudently landed at l'Orient, where the colonial regiments which have been sent from the West-Indies are quartered, had nearly occasioned a very alarming disturbance: the soldiers accused them of having treated them with the most shocking barbarity and demanded their immediate punishment: it was with the greatest difficulty that the municipality, by the assistance of some troops of artillery and the National Guard, conveyed them to a place of safety. Tranquillity was not restored when the last accounts left that place.

At Douay the dissentions among the regular troops had arisen to such a height that they were proceeding to take the cannon from the barracks in order to come to an engagement. But the Department and municipality have, by their influence, prevented them from proceeding to this extremity. In order to avoid as much as possible any cause of jealousy between the troops of the line and the National Guard, it was yesterday decreed that the *Troupe Soldée* of the National Guard of Paris, consisting of nine thousand men, shall be considered as regular soldiers and enjoy their present pay, but that, if they shall act on the frontiers they shall receive only the pay of the rest of the army and that every three months they shall receive a surplus to the amount of their present pay by way of gratuity.

The history of the formation of our small camp is rather curious: it has remained for ten days at the walls of the metropolis, a sufficient time to destroy the health and morals of the soldiers, but it is now removed nearer to the frontiers: it appears that it was formed by the orders of the Department without the authority of either the Commandant General or the Minister of the War Department. Mr de Rochambeau having declined to accept the command of the whole eastern frontier, General

Luckner will have the command in Alsace and Franche Comté.

Two hundred men of the Regiment de Berwick have accompanied their Colonel and Lieutenant Colonel into Germany.

I inclose a printed copy of the *Projet de la Constitution Française* which the Committees of Constitution and Revision have presented to the Assembly. It is supposed that it will be debated for some days in the Assembly before it is offered to the King for his acceptance. The great difficulty seems to be how this is to be done; if in his present state of confinement it will be a mere mockery; if he is previously allowed his liberty it is uncertain what use he may make of it; so far however from that being the case at present the guard at the Thuilleries has been increased within these two days. It is generally believed that the King will go either to Rambouillet or Fontainebleau, where he will accept the Constitution, but after that it is not expected that he will continue long in that situation.

The public funds, the exchange with foreign nations, and the value of assignats have fallen considerably since Mr Friteau informed the Assembly that the hostile preparations in Germany have a very alarming appearance. The suppression of all orders of knighthood, in which proof of nobility are required, has at last been decreed; being in the spirit of the present Constitution it would have taken place sooner had it not been for some difficulty with regard to the Knights of Malta who are to be debarred the rights of French citizens.

Whenever the Prince of Condé's business has been mentioned in the Assembly a debate upon the subject has been postponed upon some frivolous reason, because they do not yet despair of having some answer from that quarter through the means of the Chevalier de Coigny. Vain hopes.

The Assembly has shewn a determination to treat the refractory priests and monks with little tenderness: it is proposed to send them thirty leagues from the frontiers, and in other instances ten leagues from the place of their former residence, or even to oblige them to reside at Paris.

P.S. The elections for the new Legislature are to begin on

the twenty fifth of this month so that by the fifth of September a new legislative body will be chosen.

Paris, *August* 12, 1791.

I was in an error when I informed your Lordship that martial law had ceased to be in force at the end of a week after it was proclaimed: it was not till last Sunday that the red flag was taken down; the immediate consequence of which was that groups began to assemble as usual in the Palais Royal; but, finding the activity of the National Guard in no manner relaxed, the orators among them have not ventured to preach sedition as formerly. The dilatoriness with which they proceed to bring to trial those people who have been imprisoned on account of the late riots proceeds from a hope that an amnesty, in consequence of the King's acceptance of the Constitution, will save them all further trouble in that business. If one may be allowed to conjecture, the person who most of all must desire to have the prisons emptied without the trial of the prisoners is the Duke of Orleans.

Mr Barnave seems to have undertaken to carry through the Assembly the *Acte Constitutionnel* as proposed by the committees: it will be owing to his abilities if no democratical amendments are introduced into it. He resisted with success the attempt of the Republicans who wished to prevent the King from being acknowledged a representative of the nation, and yesterday he defended with superior abilities the plan of the committee, to require no other qualification for a member of the Legislature than that of being *citoyen actif*, but to augment the amount of the contribution which it is necessary to pay in order to have the qualification of an elector.

The alarms which Mr Freteau's speech occasioned have considerably subsided and the public funds have risen accordingly. The divisions which are known to subsist among the emigrants render the preparations on the other side of the Rhine less formidable than they would otherwise be: it is known that they are divided into two parties; that of the Prince of Condé and

Mr de Calonne, and that of the Baron de Breteuil and Mr Bouillé: the Queen is as adverse to the former as she is partial to the latter: this occasions another division in the party of the Princes and accounts for the coolness which subsists between the Comte d' Artois and the Prince of Condé. Notwithstanding Mr de Bouillé's assertions in his letter, Mr de' Breteuil was the soul of that undertaking; the chief part which the General performed was the contriving to keep the towns under his command in the worst state of defence possible.

To judge by the little progress that has been already made in it, the Assembly will employ three or four days more in debating upon the Acte Constitutionnel. They have not yet decided how it shall be offered to the King for his acceptance: there seems to be little doubt that he will accept it. While Mr de Coigny is negotiating with the Princes, the Abbé Louis, a friend of the late Bishop of Autun, is sent with a mission of the same sort to Brussels.

The Spanish Ambassador purposes to leave this place soon, in order to visit his relations the Duke and Duchess of Rohan who are ill at Nice.

The language that Mr le Chapelier holds to those who have conversed with him concerning Tobago gives them but faint hopes that he will make the report upon that subject, notwithstanding the letters I had the honor of sending to your Lordship. Mr Roume de Saint-Laurent, the British creditors' principal adversary, is appointed Commissioner to Saint Domingo; whether that is meant as a reward it is difficult to say; considering the state of that island, his office is not to be envied.

The Swedish Ambassador does not positively deny the authenticity of the King of Sweden's letter in the Logographe of yesterday.

PARIS, *August* 19, 1791.

I have communicated to Mr de Montmorin the reply of the mortgage creditors of the island of Tobago to the answer on their claims, and I have obtained a fresh assurance from that minister that Mr le Chapelier shall make the report upon that business, or name some other person to make it, before the expiration of the present National Assembly.

The Abbé Louis is returned from Brussels, where he found the Comte de Mercy not disposed to treat with him: the Abbé scruples not to say that if the King does not accept the present Constitution he may be sure of support from that quarter. The fears of an invasion from Spain have compelled the ministers to confess unpleasant truths: their confidence that the King of Spain will not break his alliance with France, and the small number of Spanish troops as yet on the frontier, amounting not to above six thousand men, are the only reasons that they offer against any alarms upon that subject. They own that the Spanish Minister will not treat with their Minister at the Court of Madrid, they acknowledge the defenceless state of that frontier and the impossibility of sending any number of regular troops into that part of France, owing to the greater necessity for them in other parts of the kingdom, they acknowledge also the danger of trusting some of the regular regiments on the frontiers; they have been obliged, for instance, to order into the interior part of the kingdom the regiments of Berwick and Nassau, or rather what remains of those regiments, lest the fancy should take them to join their fellow soldiers on the other side of the Rhine. A total want of subordination will render useless the regiment of Auvergne which is now at Phalsbourg.

The detachment of Parisian National Guard, in their progress to the frontiers, have proceeded no farther than Gonnesse, within nine miles of this place, where they are now encamped, and where they suffer from the vicinity of the capital almost as much as in the Plaine de Grenelle.

The Assembly has finished the revision of the Constitution, excepting those Articles that were adjourned during the course of the revision, the debates upon which Articles may still employ some days; it is calculated that the *Acte* may be offered to the King for his acceptance on the twenty fifth, the day of Saint Louis a solemn festival in this country.

Accounts have been received from Saint Domingo, which

left that place since the news of the decree of the fifteenth of May had reached it; the effect of which was to unite the white men of different parties, who were determined to burn that decree as soon as it shall arrive officially. At Cap François they have disarmed the blacks and mulattos and it was hoped that they would be able to do the same thing in the other parts of the island, although their proportion is greater there than at the Cape. In order to preserve tranquillity where it is much threatened, the Assembly had decreed that two Commissioners shall be sent to the islands of France and Bourbon, and from thence they are to proceed to Pondicherry and Chandernagore.

The rise of the public funds, which I mentioned to your Lordship in my last dispatch, was of short duration; they are at present as low as ever: the demands for the principal manufactures of this country continue to be great; but how long their forced flourishing state will last, for which they are indebted to the low value of assignats in foreign countries, it is difficult to calculate.

The wisdom of the Assembly has decreed two hundred thousand livres as a reward to those who stopt the King at Varenne, and it's policy and delicacy has timed that decree a few days only before it is to present to him it's *Acte Constitutionelle* for his *free* acceptance.

PARIS, *August* 26, 1791.

The additional Articles of the *Acte Constitutionnel* having given rise to long discussions, it will not be ready for the King's acceptation before the end of the next week and possibly not so soon.

The King's guard is to consist of twelve hundred foot and sixteen hundred horse, composed of men who have served in the army or National Guard and to be paid at the expense of the Civil List. According to the original plan of the Committee the members of the Royal Family were not to exercise any of the rights of a *citoyen actif*: this gave the Duke of

Orleans an opportunity of attempting to gain popularity by declaring that if he should be obliged to chuse whether he would enjoy the rights of a French citizen or those which were given to the Royal Family he would renounce the latter in order to be able to enjoy the former: but this fond hope was of short duration; the next day, yesterday, the plan was changed; they are to have the rights of a French citizen, except that of being chosen to any office by popular election; and, in the presence of the Duke of Orleans, it was observed that the nation might still hope to see him command it's fleets or be employed in some important negotiation in England or elsewhere. That star is sank never to rise again.

The thorough want of subordination, which has infected the whole army, is pathetically described by Mr Du Portail in a letter which he addrest yesterday to the National Assembly and for which I refer your Lordship to this day's Logographe; but it is hoped that these undisciplined troops will not have to contend with a well disciplined army, and the journey of the Comte d'Artois to Vienna and the known want of harmony among the emigrants beyond the Rhine gives little reason to expect a formidable invasion from that quarter at present.

The electors of this department are now assembled in order to chuse deputies for the next legislature: although many of the most democratical of them are in prison or fled, yet a sufficient number remains to allow one to believe that the members chosen by this department will be for the most part, of the democratical party.

By letters which arrived here yesterday from Saint Domingo it appears that that colony is entirely lost if the Assembly does not revoke the decree of the 15th of May. The white inhabitants of all parties are united and the two regiments of Artois and Normandie lately arrived there from France have taken an oath of fidelity to that island, in consequence of an increase of pay. All vessels are examined before they are allowed to enter their ports and orders are given that those which arrive from Bordeaux shall be suffered to take fresh water, but nothing else, in order to return without unloading to their own country. This is mixing water with their wine with a vengeance! Your Lordship will recollect the Address from that town to the National Assembly and the offer of raising six thousand men to enforce their decree.

The commissioners who are to carry this ill advised decree have, I believe, not yet quitted the kingdom, so that there is still room left for repentance. Whether there is for pardon your Lordship will be the best judge; as I understand that commissioners are to be sent from Saint Domingo to England. The proprietors of that island who are resident here and who have been dreading a civil war in that country rejoice at the present situation of things and exult in not being French citizens.

PARIS, *September* 2, 1791.

The Constitution, such as it is, is at last finisht: it will probably be accepted by the King on Monday: the Acte Constitutionnel is to be presented to him by a deputation from the National Assembly, and if he accept it, he will be desired to regulate the forms of the ceremonial and to appoint a day on which he will declare his acceptance before the National Assembly.

According to the plan of the committees no other qualification except that of being *citoyen actif* is necessary in order to be chosen a member of the legislature, but an elector in towns containing above 6000 souls must prove that he possesses a revenue equal to the value of 200 days labor or that he lets a possession equal to 150: in towns which do not contain that number of inhabitants he must prove a possession equal to 150 or a *location* equal to 100. And in the country an elector must have property equal in value to 150 or farm an estate equal to 400 days labor.

The Assembly has asserted that the nation has an incontestable right to examine its Constitution, but at the same time it has declared that it is for the interest of the nation that this right should be suspended for thirty years, and, in order in some measure to effect this, it has decreed that no legislature shall enter into the examination of the Constitution, unless it has been voted expedient by three prior legislatures, and in order to gain a longer delay, in the last article concerning National Conventions, it is decreed that no motion to examine the Constitution shall be made before the third legislature.

The committees shewed a desire to give more energy to the executive power, but all attempts of that kind have been strenuously resisted by the Assembly.

Whether the decree concerning the colonies is to be suspended revoked or enforced has not yet been determined: in the meantime addresses arrive from the seaport towns stating the dreadful consequences that must follow if the Assembly shall persevere, and your Lordship will see letters from Saint Domingo in this day's Logographe which strongly corroborate their opinion. The merchants of Bordeaux have assembled and acknowledged their error, but the administrators of that department remain firm and declare the merchant's meeting at the exchange unconstitutional; but since, thanks to the Declaration of the Rights of Man, a notion is spread over the whole country that every body is not only to think but to act for himself. It is difficult to teach the people what is or what is not constitutional, or who are governors and who are to be governed.

Mr Duportail has been obliged to obtain a decree authorizing him to oppose the National Guard to the regular troops in case no other means can be found to bring them to an observance of their duty: it is possible that the town of Phalsbourg, in the possession of the regiment d'Auvergne, will stand a siege before it submits.

Letters giving accounts of disturbances are frequently received by the Assembly without any notice being taken of them; a massacre, for instance, which took place last week at Toulon, owing to a dispute about some cannon, has not yet been mentioned.

I shall be able, at the expiration of this Assembly, to send your Lordship a regular statement of the finances to the first of this month: at present I can only give you a slight notion by the expenditure and income of the month of July: in that month the expense was above fifty four millions, the receipt something more than five millions and a half; no inconsiderable deficit.

The elections proceed slowly. Garran de Coulon, a man of democratical principles, is the first chosen for this department; the most remarkable in the provinces is the late Archbishop of Sens.

Paris, *September 5, 1791.*

At nine o'clock on Saturday the Constitution was presented to the King at the Thuilleries by a deputation from the National Assembly consisting of sixty of it's members. His Majesty received them very graciously and informed them that he would examine the Constitution which the National Assembly had ordered them to present to him, and that he would make known his resolution in as short a time as the examination of so important an object would admit. He said that he had determined to remain at Paris, and that he would give such orders to the Commandant General of the Parisian National Guard as should appear to him to be necessary for the service of his guard.

Paris, *September 9, 1791.*

The day before the deputation from the Assembly presented the Constitution to the King, the extraordinary guard which had been placed about his person by Mr la Fayette was removed and the Thuilleries were guarded in the same manner as it had been before the 21st of June, and as it will continue to be till his Majesty shall have ordered otherwise. On Tuesday last the foreign Ministers were received by the King and the Royal Family. His Majesty's health does not seem to have been impaired by his confinement: the Queen received us with her usual dignity but her deportment and appearance discovered a mind suffering under affliction but not easily subdued.

The King, it is believed, will declare his acceptance of the Constitution in the presence of the Assembly on Monday next. He has already written to the Emperor and the Princes informing them of his intention and exhorting the latter to return peaceably and enjoy what yet remains to them to be enjoyed in this country.

From what we can learn from that quarter instead of a compliance with the King's wishes we have to expect a manifesto and an armed force to which they will be the more encouraged by the increasing price of corn, owing to a bad harvest in the southern parts of the kingdom, and the difficulty of transporting that article from one part of the country to another, added to the low value of paper money. A prospect of famine, though more distant than in the year 1789, is nevertheless extremely alarming, and the activity of the National Guard has been exerted more than once during the course of this week in order to prevent riots in the markets.

The troubles of Avignon and the state of that country will be laid before the Assembly tomorrow; and in the latter end of the next week a business of much greater consequence to this country, the repeal or inforcing the decree of the fifteenth of May respecting the colonies, will be decided. It was the wish of many to lay the burthen of that business upon the shoulders of the next legislature, but Mr Barnave has compelled the present legislators to bear the whole of it themselves.

Paris, *September* 14, 1791.

Yesterday the *Ministre de la Justice* delivered a letter written by the King to the National Assembly of which I inclose a printed copy.

The King having expressed a desire that a general amnesty should be granted to all persons prosecuted on account of the revolution, this wish was confirmed by a decree past this morning previous to his Majesty's arrival in the Assembly. He came in a state coach attended by the ministers, and having said, that in order to add to the solemnity of his acceptation he thought it should take place in the Assembly, he repeated the words of the oath prescribed by the Constitution and returned to the Palace of the Thuilleries through the garden on foot attended by the members of the Assembly. The King upon his passage was very much applauded by the people. The Queen was present at the ceremony.

This morning the Assembly declared Avignon and the Comtat Venaissin a part of the French empire.

Paris is in a state of perfect tranquillity and a general illumination and rejoicings have taken place on this occasion.

PARIS, *September* 16, 1791.

Although it was very generally believed that the King would accept the Constitution, yet it was not generally imagined that he would have expatiated so much upon the improvements which it had received since his intended journey to Montmédi. The sincerity of the acceptation is nevertheless doubted by many, and a fall instead of a rise in the public funds affords good reason to suppose that those who are concerned in them do not think that what has taken place this week tends to give much additional security to the Constitution.

A circumstance happened at the Assembly which gave the King a momentary embarrassment. It had been agreed, before his arrival, that they should receive him on their legs, but that they should be seated while he was taking the oath: they continued standing when he began to take it, but, upon a sign being given by one of the members, they all suddenly sat down; this interrupted the King, who, looking about and perceiving what had passed, seated himself in a chair which was prepared for him on the left hand of the President and continued his speech; his presence of mind on this occasion was much applauded.

The Spanish Ambassador intends to leave this place tomorrow, he talks of going to Nice but his postillions will first carry him to Brussels. Having taken leave of the Court previous to the King's acceptation he has not seen his Majesty since that event.

A late decree of the Assembly having divided the National Guard of Paris into legions and having declared that every *chef de légion* should have the command by turns for the space of a month, Mr de la Fayette can no longer continue to act as Commandant General: it is said that he will have the command at Metz; he has ordered a farm house which he possesses in Auvergne to be fitted up for his reception; it is certain that his private fortune is very much impaired by the expense which his situation at Paris (and for which he receives no emolument) has unavoidably occasioned.

The general amnesty which has taken place will probably secure the election of the Abbé Fanchet for the department of Calvados of which he is Bishop: he promises to be the most turbulent member of the next legislature unless he be exceeded by Brissot the author of the most republican journal that is published here, who, though opposed by all the force that Ministry and the coalition could collect, has at last succeeded in being chosen for this department. It appears that more than half of the next Assembly will be composed of country attorneys; not only the nobility but the commercial interest will be very much excluded.

The Comte de Ségur has solicited to be appointed to succeed Mr de la Luzerne in case his health will not allow him to continue in England.

Paris, *September* 23, 1791.

The King has of late omitted no opportunity of gaining popularity and of convincing the people that his acceptation of the Constitution was free and voluntary. On Sunday the Thuilleries were magnificently illuminated and the King and Queen went in their carriages to the Champs Elysées to see the fireworks and illuminations which the municipality had ordered in that place: on Tuesday they were at the Opera, for the first time since the revolution, and they intend to honor the other theatres with their presence.

I inclose a printed copy, which I believe to be genuine, of letters from the Princes beyond the Rhine to his Majesty with the declaration signed by the Emperor and the King of Prussia at Pilnitz. As it is almost certain that the Princes knew at that time the King's intention of accepting the Constitution there are little hopes that they will embrace the opportunity which the amnesty affords them of returning peaceably into the kingdom.

The National Assembly will expire on the thirtieth of this month: the members of most note who are already chosen for the next legislature are not of that sort which inclines one to augur favorably of it. The late Archbishop of Sens is not elected, as it was reported: I have good reason to believe that Mr Necker tried the inclinations of the electors of Paris, but found that he could not succeed.

The *Comité des Finances* have shewn great unwillingness to publish their *Compte Rendu;* they are resolved to keep back their *Piéces Justificatives* which are to remain in the Archives of the Assembly: the article of secret service money is the chief cause of this mystery. The Minister of the Marine has resigned and there is no small difficulty to obtain a successor: Mr de Bougainville has refused, but I understand he has recommended a Mr le Brasseur who, it is supposed, will accept the place. Mr Duportail, it is said, will also resign and Mr Dumas is talked of for the War Department in his room. I should mention another resignation, that of Mr Bailly, which is not to be accepted till the beginning of November, when the new municipality will be chosen. It was moved to day in the Assembly to adjourn the affair of the colonies to the next legislature but it was carried against the adjournment by 307 against 191.

Paris, *September* 30, 1791.

The decree of the 15th of May respecting the colonies is virtually repealed by another which was past last Saturday asserting the right of the National Assembly to make laws exclusively for the *régime extérieur* of the colonies, and, after having known the wish which the colonial Assemblies have been authorized to express concerning their Constitution, for the *régime intérieur*: but the laws concerning the state of persons not free, (for the delicacy of French freedom will not permit the word slave to be mentioned,) and the political state of the mulattoes and free negroes, and also the regulations for enforcing those laws are to be made by the colonial Assemblies and are to be put into execution provisionally, with the consent of the Governors of the colonies, for the space of a year for the American, and of two years for the Asiatic colonies; and they are to be offered immediately for the King's sanction notwithstanding any anterior decree which might have opposed an obstacle to the full exercise of the right, conferred by the present decree on the colonial Assemblies.

With regard to the Tobago business, a report has been drawn up in the name of the united Committees of Commerce and of the Colonies, a copy of which, printed in the national press, I inclose. A more favorable report the British mortgagee creditors could not have drawn up if they had dictated it, but I find the committees have contented themselves with the mere printing and distributing copies of it to the members: the report has not been made to the Assembly and consequently no decree has been past upon that subject.

The honor which the Assembly has conferred upon Avignon and the Comtat Venaissin in declaring them part of the French empire has not had the effect of quieting the troubles in that country, and at Arles they are in a state of civil war unless tranquillity has been restored by the decree condemning the proceedings of the electors of the department *des bouches-du-Rhône*, who had voted themselves permanent, and forbidding the march of the National Guards ordered by the directors of the department at the instigation of the electors. These frequent disturbances, owing to the deliberations of clubs and other political societies, have at length convinced the Assembly of the necessity of putting a stop to what was of temporary service to them during the revolution but what must be of infinite prejudice to any Government: they have accordingly decreed that the members of any club or society who shall, as a body, offer to oppose any act of legal authority, shall lose the rights of a French citizen for two years, and if not *citoyen actif* they are to be subject to a small fine.

As a return for the applauses which his Majesty has lately received from the people of Paris he gave orders that the Thuilleries and the Champs Elisées should be illuminated a second time on Sunday last at his own expence: this illumination exceeded the former in point of magnificence; the next day the sum of 50000 livres was sent to the Mayor in the name of the King and Queen to be distributed among the poor.

The inclosed Proclamation has been published by the King's heralds in the most public places of the metropolis. While I am writing this, the King is at the Assembly where he is to make a speech which will close the *Assemblée Constituante*. Tomorrow the members of the new Assembly are to take their places.

It is now said that Mr Bertrand de Molleville, formerly Intendant of Britanny, when Mr de Montmorin was governor of that province, will have the Marine Department. The offer of that of Foreign Affairs has been sent to Mr de Moustier at Berlin.

The Spanish Ambassador has altered his plan, and instead of making some stay in Flanders, in a letter which was received from him yesterday dated at Antwerp, he says that he intends to proceed to Holland. It is believed that the Princes have received pecuniary assistance from the King of Spain.

October 7, 1791.

I am extremely happy that any attention on my part in conveying the earliest intelligence of the most important events can have merited his Majesty's approbation, and I beg leave to assure your Lordship that it shall be my constant study to continue to deserve it.

His most Christian Majesty went on Friday last to the National Assembly and closed the business of that Assembly by a speech, a printed copy of which I inclose. In returning from thence he had the satisfaction of receiving the applause of the spectators, and of hearing a frequent repetition of *Vive le*

Roy, but the very people who were heard to cry *Vive le Roy* the most hastened from thence to offer civic crowns to Mr Péthion and Mr Robertspierre, the chief fautors of republicanism in the last Assembly, and whom they chose to style *les Héros de la Constitution.*

The new Assembly has not yet given any proofs of it's wisdom; of it's rashness and ignorance it gave a convincing one last Wednesday: it shewed an absurd disposition to quarrel with the King[1] about trifles, while he, on the other hand, has shewn a decided intention not to quarrel with them if he can possibly avoid it. Their rashness disgusted even the crowds in the Palais Royal, and an alarm occasioned by a fall of the public funds brought them to resipiscence; the next day they annulled their decree, and the majesty of the King of the French remains not less degraded than it was at the expiration of the Corps Constituant. For the particulars of the debate of Wednesday I must refer to the Logographe: it seems to augur that the fanaticism of liberty will be prevalent, but it may have proceeded from an impatient desire, in those members who took the lead in it, of taking the first opportunity of shewing their importance and of proving what they might be capable of doing if not prevented.

Mr Bertrand de Molleville is appointed Minister of the Marine Department. I have not heard that Mr de Moustier's answer is yet arrived.

The decree of the Assembly has had the effect of quieting the troubles at Arles.

The King has been this day at the Assembly and has made a speech, a printed copy of which I shall send to your Lordship by Monday's post.

Paris, *October* 14, 1791.

According to your Lordship's instructions, I have delivered to Mr Montmorin his Majesty's answer to the most

[1] The King had signified his intention to attend the Assembly, and the Assembly passed a decree to withhold the titles of *sire* and *majesté*. They began their sittings by taking an oath *vivre libre ou mourir*.

Christian's King's letter notifying his acceptance of the new Constitution, and I accompanied it with assurances of his Majesty's sincere desire to maintain and improve the good-understanding which subsists between the two Courts. Mr Montmorin informed me that it was the second answer that he had received: that from Holland having arrived last Saturday. I understand that his M. C. Majesty's acceptation is mentioned in it in a style of approbation that was not expected from that Court the answer from Spain is couched in a different language and his most catholic Majesty seems still to doubt of the French King's liberty either moral or physical. That from Berlin appears to correspond with the answer I had the honor of delivering from his Majesty.

I received, a few days ago, the inclosed dispatch which Mr Trevor sent open to me desiring me to convey it to your Lordship by the first messenger.

Mr de Moustier has refused the *Département des Affaires étrangères*, he was however expected to leave Berlin on the 4th of this month on leave of absence. Mr Duportail, if one may judge from his report to the Assembly which your Lordship will see in yesterday's Logographe, seems at present inclined to continue in his office.

The *déficit* for the month of September was only seven millions odd thousand livres, to which however must be added ten millions odd thousand for the extraordinaries. So that eighteen millions of capital will serve to cover the expences of that month.

Mr de la Fayette is gone to Auvergne; the command of the National Guard for this month devolves on Mr Chaton formerly a silk merchant at Lyons.

It has been a matter of doubt whether this Assembly would continue the practice of the former in appointing permanent committees: they have agreed to day to abolish some but they have preserved the most efficient. Among others the *Comité diplomatique*, which Mr Montmorin flattered himself would not be continued, is to remain.

PARIS, *October 28th*, 1791.

I send inclosed the Duke of Orleans's answer to his Majesty's letter notifying the marriage of his Royal Highness the Duke of York.

I also inclose a letter which I received some days ago from a number of English gentlemen detained at Boulogne, and a copy of one which I immediately sent to Mr Montmorin upon that subject: that Minister's successor, it is now supposed, will be Mr de Ségur, and report sends Mr de Moustier to England.

Complaints of the manoeuvres and anti constitutional machinations of the clergy *non assermenté* and debates upon that subject have occupied a considerable part of the time of the Assembly during this week, the rest has been chiefly employed in debating, with more coolness and judgement than one had reason to expect, the means of preventing future emigration and of inducing those, who have already emigrated, to return: to day they are to come to a final determination upon that subject.

The continuation of the high price of bread is very alarming, but the numerous orders which have been sent to purchase corn abroad, it is hoped, will at least have the effect of preventing any further increase of price.

Many of the municipal officers of this town are going to retire; they complain of a want of confidence in the sections and of the consequent irksomeness of their situation: and in truth to be a *fonctionaire public* of any sort in the present state of this country requires more than ordinary patience.

Mr de Brissac is appointed *Commandant en chef de la maison militaire du Roy*. Mr d'Hervilly is to command the infantry and Mr Pont-l'Abbé the cavalry.

The account in the public papers of the massacre at Avignon is too true. Those, who at that place call themselves patriots, with Jourdan at their head, whose delight is the spilling of human blood, thought proper to revenge the murder of Mr l'Ecuyer, one of their party, who had fallen a sacrifice to the bigotry of the other party, by the slaughter of at least sixty people. Whatever faults may be laid, deservedly perhaps, to the charge of the Abbé Mulot in this business, it is certain that if Mr Ferrières had marched into the town with twelve or fifteen hundred men who are under his command, this massacre, which for the horrid circumstances which attended it may be compared to that of Saint Barthélemy or the Sicilian Vespers, would not have happened. Taught by this example it is to be hoped that other countries will have the prudence to avoid being *Avignonized*.

No official letters have as yet been received from Saint Domingo. The accounts brought by the Triton are probably much exaggerated, but, by a ship which left les Cayes the first of September and arrived at Bordeaux the 21st of this month, we learn that the day it left that harbour, the municipality of les Cayes received a letter from the General Assembly at Cape François informing them that near fifteen thousand negroes had assembled in the neighbourhood of Limbé and Acul and had destroyed the habitations and massacred the white men, but that the soldiers who were sent against them had dispersed them and killed about a hundred of them. Upon this authority, without waiting for official information the Ministry have determined to send as soon as possible two ships with two battalions to Saint Domingo, and to dispatch a frigate immediately in order to give notice of their speedy arrival.

Paris, *October 31st*, 1791.

No official intelligence has yet been received from Saint Domingo: but as accounts from England confirm the former alarming reports his most Christian Majesty has given orders that the number of troops destined to be sent to that colony shall be encreased to 2300.

The King of Sweden's answer to his M. C. Majesty's notification of his acceptance of the new Constitution is arrived: he refuses to acknowledge it.

Mr Montmorin's resignation of the Department for Foreign Affairs will be accepted tomorrow, and Mr de Ségur will be appointed to succeed him.

PARIS, *November 4th*, 1791.

Your Lordship will undoubtedly be surprised to hear that this Government has not yet received any official intelligence from St. Domingo, nor indeed has news arrived in France of the insurrection in that colony that could at all be depended upon.

Owing to contrary winds, I did not receive your Lordship's instructions No. 8 till this morning: I immediately wrote to Mr de Lessart who has the *Portefeuille des Affaires étrangères* until a successor be found for Mr de Montmorin, whose resignation was accepted by his most Christian Majesty last Monday, and I inclosed to him a translation of a part of Lord Effingham's letter to Mr Dundas and, at the same time, I informed him of that Governor's conduct with regard to the assistance which he had given to the French Government at Saint Domingo having met with his Majesty's approbation. I am extremely happy at this opportunity of giving a proof of British generosity, as there are not wanting men who industriously propagate a notion that the English have, by underhand means, fomented the dissensions in the French colonies. The speech that was delivered to her most Christian Majesty last Wednesday by a deputation from the colonists of St. Domingo now at Paris is as attic as it is laconic: "Les colons de St. Domingue, au moment d'une grande infortune, ont besoin de voir votre Majesté pour trouver aupres d'elle la consolation et l'example d'un grand courage!"

With regard to the emigrants, the only measure which the Assembly has thought proper to take has been to summon Monsieur to enter the kingdom within the space of two months; failing which, he is to be esteemed as having abdicated his right to the regency in conformity to the second Article of the *Acte Constitutionel*.

Mr de Ségur had certainly agreed to accept the Department of Foreign Affairs, but owing to the behaviour of the Assembly towards Mr du Portail or to some other cause, he went into the country on Monday morning. Mr de Narbonne, it is now said, will be appointed to that office. I inclose a letter from Mr de Montmorin inclosing another from Mr Bertrand which I received last Tuesday, concerning the mortgagee creditors of the island of Tobago.

The Dey of Algiers having shewn an inimical disposition towards this country, orders are sent to Toulon to fit out a squadron sufficient to protect the French commerce in the Mediterranean.

PARIS, *November 6th*, 1791.

Dressins having left this place last Friday at noon on his way to Madrid: I re-dispatch Wiffen with your Lordship's packet No. 1, having forwarded the packet No. 2, by the ordinary post.

The frigate La Meduse which left the Isle de France about the middle of August brings an account that the spirit of insubordination rages there to an alarming degree. The Governor of that island writes that he had received a letter from Mr Du Fresne who commands at Pondicherri dated the middle of June which contains the following account. That on the 15th of May Lord Cornwallis with his army being arrived within eight leagues of Seringapatam had been attacked by Tippoo; that after having lost between 4 and 5 hundred Europeans and a much greater number of seapoys he had been obliged to retire towards Bangalore, leaving behind him a part of his heavy artillery. The firm resistance of a large body of Mahrattas prevented Tippoo from annoying the army during their retreat. Several private letters from Pondicherry give the same account.

As no mention is made in what manner the intelligence reached Pondicherry from which place Lord Cornwallis's camp is distant 300 leagues, and the passage over land rendered difficult by Tippoo's troops it is presumed it came first to Mahé and from thence by sea to Pondicherri.

An order has been sent to Brest to embark a battalion of the Regiment de Provence and another of the Regiment de la Perche upon the frigates *la Fine* and *la Réunion* and the brigs la Normande and la Moselle, which four vessels happened to be in readiness, in order to proceed immediately to St Domingo. The last accounts from Brest mention that the troops have refused to embark.

PARIS, *November* 11*th*, 1791.

The only accounts at all to be depended upon, from St Domingo, are those which have arrived through England and indeed, owing to the embargo which Mr de Blanchelande has laid upon all the vessels in the ports of the French part of that island no direct intelligence is expected from thence.

The blow which that insurrection has given to the commerce of this country may possibly determine some of the principal commercial towns to act for themselves, seeing how little they have to expect from the wisdom of their National Assembly or the power of their King. Nantes may command the commerce of the Loire, Rouen and Havre de Grace that of the Seine, and Dunkirk may wish to enter into a sort of Hanseatic confederacy with them.

Since the arrival of Mr de Blanchelande's letter, a printed copy of which I inclose, Government has determined to send a larger force to St. Domingo than it at first proposed. Two ships of the line are to be immediately sent from Brest with part of the troops about six thousand, in all, and with provision of all sorts which the arsenal and magazines of that place can afford; the rest are to be sent as soon as possible in three frigates four *flûtes* and merchant ships from the ports of l'Orient, Havre, Nantes or Rochefort; Bordeaux has since offered all the ships that are ready at that port, which I understand amount to forty nine.

The Assembly has thundered a decree against the emigrants, who if they remain assembled *au delà des frontières* on the first of January next, are to be declared guilty of a conspiracy and are to suffer the punishment of death. I have not yet heard that the King has sanctioned this decree.

The refractory priests have to expect a decree equally strong against them; it is true that they are creating disturbances in every part of the kingdom, that at Caen is the most serious, where they are in a state of civil war and blood has been spilt on both sides. I forgot to mention that the constitutional Bishop of Rouen had conscienciously resigned his bishoprick, which affords much matter for exultation to the clergy *non-assermenté*.

The appointment of a Minister for Foreign Affairs will not be decided till after the council on Sunday, two new names are mentioned for that office, Mr O'Dun, who was formerly his most Christian Majesty's Minister at the Court of Portugal and Mr de Vibrage, who was appointed last spring Ambassador to Sweden.

PARIS, *November* 18*th*, 1791.

From the character and sentiments of Mr de Rochambeau the younger, who is of the society of the Jacobins, it appears not improbable that some design[1] of the sort to which your Lordship alludes may be entertained by him: if such a scheme does really exist, it must be believed that this Government has not as yet given any countenance to it; but, when one considers that the object of it, that part at least which regards Holland, is of great national importance, and is a point in which the honor of the nation has been offended. *Hæret lateri lethalis arundo.* One should be less surprized than hurt to find, if it should be suffered to ripen, that it should be adopted by this Government, especially when one reflects that a diversion of this sort abroad would tend to compose matters at home. It is certain that this Court has some hidden object in view, for

---

[1] Probably an attack on Holland, which was now entirely in the hands of England.

otherwise it would not so tamely and with such apparent contentment, submit to what it at present suffers, without the comfort of some distant hopes. I shall use my endeavours to acquire all possible information at this place upon the subject, but I believe your Lordship will be able to learn more from any traveller in Flanders than I can procure for you from hence. The Swedish Ambassador and Mr de Simolin have received a *congé* from their Courts *pour voyager*. We still continue without a minister for foreign affairs, but I believe that Mr de Lessart will retain the *Portefeuille* and resign the Home Department. When the minister informed the Assembly that his most Christian Majesty would examine the decree against the emigrants, which is the formal manner of giving the *veto*, they refused to hear what measures the King had adopted in lieu of it: the public however were instructed the next morning by a proclamation, a printed copy of which I sent to your Lordship by last Monday's post.

The measure of refusing that decree is generally approved; the democratic party rejoice at it as it tends to prove the King's freedom. A singular circumstance however has occurred in the Palace of the Thuilleries which is not so favorable to that appearance of freedom. Madame Elizabeth has lately changed her apartment, which is now in a part of the palace very distant from that of the King: his Majesty, wishing to see his sister, was proceeding towards her apartment, but was stopt by a centinel who had received a *consigne* not to allow him to pass after nine o'clock at night till that hour in the morning; upon enquiry, it appeared that this order was given by a corporal who is taken and imprisoned.

Mr Péthion is chosen mayor. A great triumph for the Jacobines! All the principal municipal offices in Paris are now held by members of that society. Mr de la Fayette was so confident of being elected that, it is said, he came to Paris, as certain of that event; but I believe he is returned to Auvergne.

A vessel is arrived at Bordeaux which left Cap François the ninth of October. The southern and western parts of the island were at that time quiet owing to an agreement that the whites of that part of the island had made with the mulattos to abide by the decree of the fifteenth of May. At the Cape they had made frequent sallies, killed many negroes and destroyed their camp at Galifet, it appears that they were in expectation of receiving speedy assistance from the United States both of men and provisions; from the Spaniards they have obtained neither although they are bound by treaty so to do. Mr Blanchelande complains much of the insubordination of the battalions of Artois and Normandie. The frigate la Fine is sailed from Brest with four hundred men and they are making every possible exertion to send off the rest of the troops that are destined for the defence of that colony. The French troops have entered Avignon and as Jourdan and the chiefs of the brigand are in prison it is hoped that unfortunate country will be restored to peace.

The Assembly has decreed that the priests shall take the *serment civique* instead of their former oath. Those who refuse to take it are to be deprived of their pensions and they are to be expelled from their Department if suspected of any designs against order or peace.

PARIS, *November 25th*, 1791.

As soon as I received your Lordships instructions No. 12, I sent a letter to Mr de Lessart, copy of which I inclose; that Minister has accepted the Department for Foreign Affairs, but nobody has yet ventured to undertake the Home Department, which in truth requires the shoulders of an Atlas and the strength and courage of a Hercules, but as this is not an age for such heroes it is plainly to be perceived that the general fermentation throughout the kingdom is at a height and of a kind, which it is impossible for the Government, constituted as it is at present to repress. In the northern provinces, more especially much mischief is to be expected from the dangerous alliance of religious zeal with party spirit. At Marseilles and Montpelier it already rages, and the fanatics of the Cevennes are disarming with insult their bigoted antagonists. The conduct of the National Assembly gives little room to hope that it will be able to stem the torrent: they begin to entertain serious fears of the emigrants since they have learnt that they are supplied with the means not only of subsistance but of obtaining ammunition and cavalry, by the liberality, as it is supposed, of the Empress of Russia; and to those fears, and not on account of the *dénonciation* against the Sieur Varnier is to be attributed the hasty formation of an *Haute Cour Nationale*.

Your Lordship will observe that not only the municipality but the *ouvriers* of Nantes have chosen to address, not the Assembly but the King, who, in his answer, said, that he would do all in his power to restore tranquillity in the colonies and that he *hoped* he should be seconded by the National Assembly. The arrival of the frigate l'Embuscade at Rochefort is a strong proof of the insubordination of the French sailors as well as soldiers. That ship was sent from Martinico in order to convey the Commissioners at Guadeloupe to Saint Lucia, where, owing to the disturbances in that island, their presence was thought necessary, but the crew thinking their own presence more necessary in France in order to refute the denunciations made in the patriotic clubs against the soldiers, confined their captain and set sail for this country where they expect to receive the applause of all true patriots. Mr la Fayette is elected to the command of one of the six legions of the National Guard at Paris; the report of his having been here at the time of the election of the mayor is without foundation.

The Swedish Ambassador and the Russian Minister were both at Court yesterday.

Paris, *December 2nd*, 1791.

In order to find occupation for the *Haute Cour Nationale* the Assembly has formed a *Comité de Surveillance* which, to judge by the conduct and sentiments of the members who compose it, will be as active and inquisitorial as the late *Comité des Récherches;* for their party seems to acquire acrimony in proportion to it's loss of followers.

A man has at last been found bold enough to undertake the

Département de l'intérieur: Mr Cahier de Gerville, who since the revolution has executed the office of *Procureur Syndic de la Commune* with general approbation, is appointed Minister of that Department.

An universal expectation of an approaching crisis prevails. Every body acknowledges that France cannot long continue in it's present state; but what the *dénouement* of this tragi-comedy will be remains to be known.

The moderate party is daily gaining ground, and waits for some event which may enable it to shew it's strength. In the mean time the Court exists in a miserable suspense between it's jealousy of the emigrants and it's dread of the Jacobins. The private answer which his most Christian Majesty has received from his brothers proves that their party has received too much encouragement to return peacably at his summons, and the public language of the democratic party, (for a specimen of which I refer to last Tuesday's debate well worth your Lordship's perusal) shews that they are ready to pursue strong measures in support of their sentiments. Mr Isnard's speech in that debate seems to have placed him at the head of that party in the Assembly. I hope to be able to send your Lordship a state of the southern whale fishery carried on from this country by the next messenger; but as I have been obliged to send to Dunkirk for information upon that subject, I may be unable to send it so soon.

P.S. The decree concerning the priests is not yet sanctioned.

Paris, *December 5th*, 1791.

I forgot to mention to your Lordship that the Dey of Algiers has declared his intention of continuing in friendship with France; all fears therefore have ceased of the French trade in the Mediterranean being molested from that quarter.

Two thousand eight hundred men are already embarked for Saint Domingo; but a circumstance has happened at Brest which gives the Minister considerable embarrassment. Mr de la Jaille who was appointed to the command of the Dugue-

Trouin, one of the vessels destined to carry assistance to Saint Domingo, had not arrived three hours at Brest before the lantern-rope was prepared for him, the multitude conceiving that his intentions were to assist the aristocratic party in the colonies, but he was lucky enough by the assistance of the civil magistrates and the military to escape with life to the castle of that town.

About the middle of September last Mr de Rochambeau the younger addrest some of the *Patriots Brabançons* who were present at a meeting of the friends of the Constitution at Maubeuge in the following manner. Patriots, you knew how to value liberty, you desired it; but unfortunate events have prevented your obtaining it. The friends of the French Constitution comprehend the whole world in their system of philanthropy, and on that account they hope that when you return into your own country you will sow the seeds of our benevolent intentions that they may produce an abundant harvest. The Austrian Government having complained to this Court of these proceedings, the Minister of the *Intérieur* wrote to the department in which Maubeuge is situated to investigate the matter: a *Procès verbal* of this affair was accordingly required from the municipality: this has produced a most curious letter from those friends of the Constitution to the municipal officers of Maubeuge, copy of which I inclose. Mr Duportail has resigned the War Department: his successor is not yet named.

An extraordinary council is to be held this evening when it will be decided whether the King shall give his sanction to the decree against the non-juring clergy. This department has addrest him not to give it. The address, I understand, was drawn up by the late Bishop of Autun.

The report of the King's having left Paris was industriously spread on the frontiers in order to create confusion: the plan of spreading at the same time a report of an armed entrance of the emigrants into France was timely prevented by the Minister's having informed the Mayor that he had reason to suppose such a scheme was in agitation.

Nobody seems to doubt that the inclosed letter of the Empress of Russia is genuine.

Paris, *December 9th*, 1791.

I send inclosed a copy of a letter which I have received from Mr Delessart concerning the Tobago creditors. I have communicated to that Minister Mr Trist's case; and I have desired him to give such orders for the recovery of his property as he may be entitled to. With regard to resuming the negotiation which was begun in the year 1787 for settling a six-days post, which is undoubtedly a very desirable object, I see no impediment if the French Ministers are willing to resume it: as soon as I can learn their sentiment upon that subject your Lordship shall be informed of it.

Mr Louis de Narbonne is appointed Minister of the War Department: he is a young man of spirit and abilities as well calculated for that office as any person who would accept it at present.

The petition of the administrators of the department of Paris, a printed copy of which I inclose, will probably be productive of others of the same sort: the present Assembly has the faculty of forming decrees in a manner which gives the French King a fair opportunity of exercising his veto. The last concerning the colonies which was drawn up by Mr Brissot comes under that description.

The critical situation of this country becomes every day more apparent; the general alarm drives the little money in specie that remains out of the kingdom; the price of it, of course, daily increases, and the value of assignats diminishes: a national bankruptcy is more than ever to be expected.

It is believed that the King will go to the Assembly to-morrow.

Paris, *December 16th*, 1791.

The National Assembly has, as usual, employed the last week in the most frivolous manner; hearing and applauding petitions from the several sections of Paris against that which the administrators of the department have presented to his most Christian Majesty. They had decreed that these petitions should be sent to the 83 departments, but, the next day, they were persuaded by some members who belong to the club of the Feuillans to repeal it. A decree of the same sort was suffered to pass the Assembly a few days before with regard to an address which was presented to them in the name of that meeting in London which goes by the name of the Constitutional Society: it was ordered to be printed in English and French and sent to the 83 departments and also to be presented to the French King. The weighty business of last Tuesday began by listening to a discourse of one Cloots, a Prussian who styles himself Anacharsis from a resemblance that he imagines he possesses to the Scythian philosopher of that name; in addition to which he has assumed the title of *Orateur du Genre humain*, and *as such* he was admitted to the bar of the Assembly: the members of which, as if they wished still more to degrade their dignity, consumed the rest of the night, for they did not break up till seven o'clock the next morning, in examining drunken witnesses about a drunken drummer whom the *Comité de Surveillance* suspected of being guilty of enlisting men for the army of the Princes.

His most Christian Majesty, whose presence had been expected for some days, went the next day to the Assembly, and made a speech[1], a printed copy of which I inclose; the president answered dryly that the Assembly would take into consideration the propositions which he had made and would communicate its determination by a message. It is rather singular that Mr Le Montez should have so cautiously avoided using the words *Sire* and Majesté, as he is reckoned a moderate and sensible man; these words however occur in the message which has been since delivered.

Mr de Narbonne afterwards informed the Assembly that he had taken measures to have one hundred and fifty thousand men on the frontiers in less than a month, that they would be formed into three armies to be commanded by Mr Lukner Mr

[1] He said that he had informed the princes who protected the *emigrés* that they must cease all enrolment of troops from now till Jan. 15, and that if they did not they would be regarded as enemies.

Rochambeau and Mr la Fayette; that to the two former the King wished to give the title of Maréchal de France, but that a decree of the Assembly would be required for that purpose. He likewise said that he should go himself in a few days to visit the frontiers.

Since it has appeared that a foreign war is the plan and policy of the Ministers, the Jacobins begin to use every plausible argument against it: the Swedish Ambassador and Mr de Simolin were both yesterday at Court; but it is believed that the King of Sweden has again refused to attend to the letter of the French King. The genuineness of the Empress of Russia's letter to the Maréchal de Broglio is doubted.

A fresh fabrication of assignats, one hundred millions in assignats of 25 livres and one hundred millions of 10 livres have been decreed; and it is proposed to issue one hundred millions in assignats below five livres as low perhaps as 10 sous.

A club is instituted at Maubeuge under the protection probably of Mr Rochambeau the younger, the title of which is La Societé des Amis de la Liberté Brabançonne.

―――――

Paris, *December* 23rd, 1791.

I flattered myself I should have been able to have sent your Lordship this week an account of the southern whale fishery as it is at present carried on by this country: but as I have not yet received all the information I expect upon that subject, I am forced to postpone it.

As the last decree for the emission of three hundred millions in assignats makes the whole already decreed amount to two thousand one hundred millions and when the most accurate and impartial calculators suppose that the whole of the national property does not exceed three thousand millions, it is not surprizing that their credit should be shaken and if it should be expedient for this country to undertake a war, instead of the former flattering prospect of paying off the unfunded part of the national debt, a new loan must be opened.

Mr de Ségur, who retains his character of Ambassador at Rome, sets off to-day for Berlin : it is very uncertain whether Mr de Choiseul Gouffier will accept the embassy to England, if he should refuse it, it will probably be given either to Mr de Ségur or Mr de Moustier the latter, if he accepts, will go to Constantinople. Mr de Sainte Croix is appointed Minister Plenipotentiary to the Elector of Trèves and Mr de Marbois succeeds Mr Berenger at Ratisbonne.

A report of the Emperor's determination to adhere to the *Conclusum* of the Diet has given fresh spirits to the aristocratic party which had been considerably deprest by an official note of the Elector of Trèves, which your Lordship will see in the inclosed *Gazette Universelle,* which also contains an extract of a letter from Mr Walkiers well worth your Lordship's perusal as it accounts for the arrival of a large body of Brabançons in French Flanders. The Assembly has prudently issued a decree against their forming meetings. Mr de Narbonne did not leave Paris till Tuesday night.

PARIS, *December* 30*th*, 1791.

The *déficit* for the last month is eighteen millions which together with thirteen millions for the extraordinaries of that month the Assembly has decreed to be paid into the treasury from the *Caisse de l'extraordinaire:* they have also voted the twenty millions extraordinary for the army.

The continuance of the decrease of assignats has occasioned a very considerable rise in the price of all foreign merchandize: the cotton and woollen manufactures will suffer the most from this circumstance in the article of Spanish wool the rise is not less than forty sols per pound. Mr de Lessart notified yesterday to the Assembly that the King of Sweden's Minister had at last received his most Christian Majesty's notification of his acceptation of the French Constitution: there are people, who connecting this with Mr de Lessart's submitting to the Assembly the utility of secret service money, flatter themselves that a war may still be prevented; while others regard this measure as a system of procrastination founded on good policy.

The declaration drawn up by Mr Condorcet, which your Lordship will see at the end of this day's Logographe, was intended to have been sent to all the powers of Europe, but an apprehension that it might be understood as a declaration of war prevented the Assembly from adopting that measure, and made them confine the publication of it to the interior of the kingdom.

It is said that a man has been taken up at Worms, it having been discovered that he had an intention to assassinate the Prince of Condé, and they say that many people were concerned in the plot: that Prince, it is believed, is gone to Coblence.

The club of the Jacobins has gained a temporary victory over that of the Feuillans, for, by occasioning disturbances at their meetings, they have obliged the Assembly to order them to quit the Church of the Feuillans which belongs to and is contiguous to the Assembly.

A new fabrication of counterfeited assignats has just appeared: they are of 500 livres and so well done that the only discernible difference is a circumflex instead of an accent over the word *conformément*: no trace has as yet been discovered of their origin.

PARIS, *January 6th*, 1792.

The only effect of the contents of the two inclosed papers has been to impress people's minds with a notion that it will be very difficult to avoid the impending war; the French King's astonishment appears however to be greater upon this occasion than that of his subjects.

The debate which terminated in a decree that has placed His Most Christian Majesty's brothers, the Prince of Condé, Mr de Calonne, Mr de la Queille, and Mr de Mirabeau, *en état d'accusation*, not having been inserted in the Logographe of last Monday, I took the first opportunity of sending the next number of that paper, which I hope your Lordship has received.

I have again prest Mr de Lessart to have the Tobago business brought to a discussion: he has promised me that he will desire the Minister of the Marine Department to write a second time to the President, if that affair should not come before the Assembly in a few days.

With regard to a six days' post between London and Paris, he says, he is informed there are difficulties which may render that measure impracticable at present, and he, at the same time, informed me and lamented that it is impossible for the French Ministry to deliver up Oxon because the present laws and constitution of this country will not permit it. From the private letters which have been received from Mr de Narbonne and Mr de la Fayette it appears that the whole of the army, regulars as well as National Guard, is in a state of insubordination not very promising at the eve of a war; and to these accounts is to be attributed the speech of Mr Isnard in yesterday's debate, in which he strongly recommends union at home, a cultivation of ancient and an endeavour to form new alliances. The release of the soldiers of the Swiss Regiment of Chateauvieux, who were confined at Brest, by which they have certainly infringed their last treaty with the Swiss cantons, will hasten Mr Barthélémy's[1] departure from hence.

The last official accounts from Saint Domingo are far from being satisfactory: the blacks have again begun to destroy the plantations in the northern part of that island, and the inhabitants of Port au Prince, who have sent troops against them, express their fears that they may want them at home.

From the Isle de France there is a report that Mr de la Peyroux has been heard of, but little credit is given to it.

PARIS, *January* 13, 1792.

The report which Mr de Narbonne made to the Assembly last Wednesday, and which is accurately copied in yesterday's Logographe, gives a true account of the state of the fortifications and army on the frontiers; making allowance for a certain heightening of the favorable and a softening of the unfavorable parts; the jealousy between the regulars and National Guard, which must continue as long as the latter receives a pay

[1] He was French Minister to the government of Switzerland and negotiated the treaty of Bâle in 1795.

superior to that of the former, and the great want of discipline in both are not so much insisted on as truth might require. Of the want of discipline a very dreadful proof had nearly occurred at Verdun, where, owing to some dispute, the grenadiers of Poitou and the dragoons of Condé had fired upon each other and were proceeding to a regular engagement, when Mr de la Fayette arrived and persuaded them to desist.

Such being the state of the French army, the *Comité Diplomatique* and Mr de Lessart are intent to avert a war or at least to gain strength by negotiation. Mr de Périgord, the late Bishop of Autun, is upon the point of going to England. Having been a member of the late Assembly he can assume no public character. It was at first intended that he should be accompanied by Mr Bonne-Carrère, the person whom the Bishop of Liège refused to receive last year from this Court: he was at that time conspicuous as a secretary of the club of the Jacobins and having been formerly in England and well acquainted with our manners and language he was employed, during the last war, in the East Indies *pour surveiller les Anglois*. The measure however of sending this gentleman to England at present is dropt, and they are now employed in finding a more proper subject.

Mr de Jarry, who was Professor in the Military School at Berlin, and who at that time, had courted the favor of the present King of Prussia, is gone or is going there: the object of his mission is to accomplish something in which it is supposed Mr de Ségur may fail, it having been discovered that he had taken with him Bills of Exchange to a very considerable amount, and means having been taken that the King of Prussia should be informed of it perhaps even before his arrival at Berlin.

Mr de Bourgoing is, I believe, sent for from Hamburg to go to Spain in a private character, that Court having refused, last year to receive in any other.

The Swedish Ambassador's servant, Anselm is returned from Stockholm. He brings with him a congé for his master, who purposes to leave this Court in less than a fortnight, but no answer to this Court from the King of Sweden. Mr de Simolin is in daily expectation of a similar congé.

The discredit into which assignats are fallen, and which the frequent discoveries of fresh forgeries of them, if there was no other cause, will probably increase, is such that in Britanny they no longer pass in currentcy.

A vessel is arrived at Bordeaux which gives an account of the total destruction of le Port au Prince: according to an account of an officer on board, for it brings no letters, they began to burn the town on the twenty first of November: on the first of December that vessel (le Sincère) escaped from the road notwithstanding the embargo: at that time there were but six or seven houses remaining at Port au Prince, the plain had not then suffered: the inhabitants had united under arms at la Croix des Bouquets. The rebels, in addition to the blacks consisted of *petits blancs*, mulattoes, and free negroes and many soldiers of the battalions of Artois and Normandie who had joined them. He attributes the destruction of the town to the decree of the twenty-fourth of September.

The Stocks and Exchange have fallen to-day three per cent.

Paris, *January 20th*, 1792.

I informed your Lordship, in my last dispatch, of the late Bishop of Autun's intended mission to England: that measure however was not communicated to me by the Minister of Foreign Affairs till yesterday at dinner at my house. He told me that it was not absolutely resolved upon till last Sunday, that he had called upon me on the following day with the intention of conversing with me upon the subject, but not finding me at home, and not having been able to receive the foreign ministers at his own house on account of the debates in the Assembly, the subject of which rendered his constant attendance there necessary, he took that opportunity of mentioning it to me, and he said, he believed, as the Bishop was to make a *détour* that my dispatch of this day would reach your Lordship before his arrival in London. I have reason to think his calculation is not accurate. Mr de Périgord however carries with him letters of recommendation from the Minister, for they cannot be called of credence since it would be unconstitutional for him to appear in any public character. The Duc de Biron, I believe will accompany him to London, but of this I was not informed by Mr de Lessart.

From the speeches of Mr Brissot and Mr Vergniaud, in the debates of this week, it must appear that the Jacobins are desirous of war; but there is a considerable body of them, the followers of Mr Robertspierre, who wish to avoid it by negotiation.

Mr de Ste Croix's last dispatches from Coblence give reason to suppose that the French troops will not be able to find an excuse for passing the Rhine at present: the emigrants are dispersing or at least retiring. Monsieur, whose *décheance* has been declared by the Assembly, it is supposed, will go to Turin.

The *déficit* for the last month amounts in all to above thirty-five millions. It is to be hoped however, for the interest of other countries, more than it is to be expected, that a national bankruptcy may still be avoided.

In addition to the inconvenience which arises from the great number of false assignats a quantity of false louis have got into circulation, but the forgerers of them have been discovered and taken at Romainville, a village near Paris. The Assembly has not yet decided whether it is proper to declare war against the Emperor or to try whether an accommodation may not be brought about by negotiation.

PARIS, *January 20th*, 1792.

I have stated in my dispatch of to-day what Mr de Lessart said to me yesterday at dinner at my house, concerning the Bishop of Autun's journey to England; I think however it is proper you should know what Mr de Narbonne said to me at the same time upon that subject. He exprest his astonishment at Mr de Lessart's having delayed so long to notify to me Mr de Périgord's mission, and he assured me that he had desired him to mention the subject to me when it was first in agitation, he added that he believed the Bishop would be arrived in England some days before my dispatch; in fact the détour that he is to make is no farther out of the direct road than Valenciennes, where he is to meet the Duc de Biron, who will probably proceed with him to England; an alliance between France and England has, to my knowledge, been long a favorite object of Mr de Biron, and, having in former journeys to London, made an extensive acquaintance there, he will be able to introduce the Bishop of Autun to people of all descriptions and parties: it was once reported that Mr de Ste Foy was to have accompanied him for that purpose; the choice of Mr de Biron is certainly preferable in all respects. But to return to Mr de Lessart, his natural indolence contrasts so strongly with the activity of mind and enterprize of Mr de Narbonne that it will require all Madame de Stael's abilities to preserve a good harmony between them.

Paris, *January 27th*, 1792.

I inclose a letter which I have received from Mr de Lessart inclosing a copy of one to him from Mr de Richebourg *Président du Directoire des Postes*, by which your Lordship will perceive that this Government objects to a six-days post between London and Paris, but that it is ready to agree to the establishment of a four-days post between the two metropolis's.

The peace of this town has been threatened to be disturbed, during the course of this week, by mobs which have assembled before grocers shops and insisted upon a reduction of the price of sugar; but the proper behaviour of the National Guard and the conciliatory advice of the Municipal officers have prevented any very considerable mischief. Mr la Borde, the banker, who is possest of a large stock of sugar, the product of his own estate in St Domingo, has judged it necessary for his personal safety to quit the kingdom.

A notion, which is industriously kept up, that the royal family have an intention of attempting, a second time to leave the kingdom, occasions suspicions and jealousies which, at present, only tend to increase the number of spies and informers about the palace and even in private houses.

ARRANGEMENTS FOR RECRUITING THE ARMY.

The National Assembly, upon the report of the Minister of the War Department, that fifty one thousand men were wanting to compleat the army for the war establishment, had decreed that they should not be raised out of the volunteers now on the frontiers, but, upon the minister's declaring that he should resign if speedy measures were not adopted for raising them, as without them he would not be responsible for the success of a war, they decreed that, as soon as possible, a register should be opened in every district of the kingdom to receive the names of those who wisht to enter into the army on the following conditions. That every foot soldier should receive a premium of 80 livres and be engaged for three years: for the cavalry and artillery that the premium should be 120 livres, and the term 4 years: if the army should be reduced to the peace establishment before the expiration of the terms, they are to be at liberty to retire. The Assembly likewise decreed that the soldiers who have served their time should, if they chose to inlist again, receive immediately a premium of 25 livres for every year of their new engagement, and 30 for the cavalry and artillery, and after the reduction of the army these engagements are only to be binding for one half of the time then unexpired.

The King has since ordered the minister to propose to the Assembly an addition of 8 legions destined to form the vanguard of the army, when upon march in the enemy's country, each of which to consist of 1722 foot and 832 horse, one third of the infantry to be National Guards; and to form for every one of the three great divisions of the army a brigade of 843 artillery men with a train of artillery to serve on all occasions with the cavalry. It is the opinion of the minister, as well as of the three generals, that it will be necessary to pay the army in specie. Mr de Rochambeau insisted much upon this measure in a speech which he made on Wednesday in the Assembly.

A deputation from the National Assembly has desired the King to declare to the Emperor that he cannot treat with any power except in the name of the French nation, and to ask him, whether, as head of the house of Austria, he intends to live in good intelligence with the French nation and to renounce all treaties and conventions contrary to the sovereignty independance and safety of the nation, and at the same time to declare to the Emperor that unless he gives to the nation full and entire satisfaction upon these points before the first of March, his silence or any dilatory or evasive answer shall be construed as a declaration of war: the King has answered that he will take this message *en très grande consideration*. In consequence of this, Mr de Marbois, the French Minister to the Diet of Ratisbonne, is to go to Vienna, where they hope he will succeed better than Mr de Ségur has done at Berlin. His last letter from thence dated the 17th being far from satisfactory, his speedy return to Paris is expected.

The probability of a war appears so great that this Government is buying in specie in Holland and other places at an enormous price.

Paris, *February 3rd*, 1792.

A decree has past the Assembly obliging all persons who travel in France to provide themselves with passports from the municipality from whence they begin their journey: this decree, which contains articles that will prove extremely vexatious and inconvenient to all possible descriptions of travellers, and consequently detrimental to the commerce and trade of the country, has not yet received the King's sanction.

Upon a report of the Committee of Marines the Assembly divided upon the question that the minister of that department had lost the confidence of the nation, which question was lost by only 208 to 196: it is therefore probable that that minister will not remain long in office: he possesses a steadiness of character ill-calculated to conciliate the good-graces of the National Assembly.

To the continuation of the report of the King's intention of leaving the kingdom is to be attributed the non-attendance of his own guard at the Thuilleries, for the men are in complete readiness for doing duty and it was intended that they should begin to mount guard on the first of this month. In the mean time the National Guard cannot be accused of want of diligence, a ridiculous proof of which occurred the other day. The King was desirous of seeing a curious *secrétaire* which has been made here for the King of Naples and which is calculated to hold a great quantity of papers, when it arrived there was no difficulty in allowing it to be brought into the royal apartment, but, when it was to be carried back, the guard insisted upon searching it accurately least his Majesty should be concealed in it.

The day before yesterday Mr de Moustier received a letter dated the 21st of January from his secretary whom he has left at Berlin, and who resides in the house now occupied by Mr de Ségur, informing him that Mr de Ségur was found in his cabinet weltering in his blood, having stabbed himself in three different places with a knife which he had obtained for that purpose. He adds that the wounds do not appear to be dangerous and that there is little doubt of Mr de Ségur's speedy recovery. The cause of this desperate act he attributes to the unfavorable reception which that Ambassador has met with from the King and Court of Prussia. Yesterday however Mr de Lessart received a dispatch and Madame de Ségur a letter from her husband written by himself, both dated the 24th in which there is no mention of this affair; in consequence of which his family and the friends of this administration contradict the former report most strenuously.

A singular circumstance happened about a fortnight ago to a Prussian courier who was bringing instructions here to Mr de Goltz. Conscious of the importance of his packet and probably overheated by the journey, he thought that every person he met was going to assassinate him, his fears at last arrived to such a pitch that he thought fit to destroy his dispatch, and he arrived here in a state of mind which rendered it necessary for him to keep his bed for some days. Mr de Goltz was able to obtain from him what was sufficient to authorize him to inform this Court that his master was determined to protect the empire and the Emperor's dominions in the Low Countries in the event of a hostile aggression on the part of the French. Mr de Goltz denies in public the destruction of his instructions by the courier, but he has confessed it to me in confidence and with leave to communicate it to your Lordship.

The Swedish Ambassador leaves this place to-morrow, and I believe Mr de Simolin will go the day after. As for Mr de Bourgoign, he remains here, waiting for further instructions before his departure for Spain.

PARIS, *February* 10*th*, 1792.

I have received His Majesty's additional instructions on the subject of foreign secret-service money, to which I shall punctually conform myself upon all occasions which may arise during my employment abroad.

I have communicated to Mr de Lessart, according to your Lordship's instructions, His Majesty's determination strictly to inforce that part of the Navigation Act which will prevent the considerable inconveniences that have arisen from the importation of tobacco in foreign vessels into the ports of His Majesty's dominions, and I have also again urged that minister to take proper and active measures to bring to a conclusion the business concerning the Tobago creditors which is now before the National Assembly.

The Jacobins are acquiring popularity in a degree and manner that are truly alarming. The inhabitants of the Faubourg St Antoine have already made for themselves about thirty thousand pikes; the manufacture of which continues, and seems to be encouraged by the Municipality, although they are more calculated for pillage than for the protection of the property of citizens. The royal family become every day more unpopular. In order to render it practicable for the King's guard to do duty at the Thuilleries, that part of it which is ready for service is to take the constitutional oath at the Hotel de Ville before the municipal officers.

The unpleasant dispute about etiquette between the King and the Assembly, which has terminated in the former submitting to the latter, at least for the present, had nearly occasioned the destruction of the present ministry: in the council which was held upon that subject Mr Cahier de Gerville, whose political sentiments are apt to coincide with those of the Jacobins, differed from his brother Ministers and threatened to resign if the point of the folding doors was not given up; the others, on their side, threatened the same, but the mezzo termine *for the present* I believe, has preserved the ministry entire, but, to judge from every appearance, it's final dissolution is not far distant.

The Assembly has determined that the estates of all the French absentees who can assign no satisfactory reason for their absence shall be placed in the hands of the nation in order to indemnify it for the expence which they have occasioned, but it is much doubted that the King will give his sanction to this decree.

Upon the whole, the rapid increase of anarchy, not only in the metropolis but in every Municipality of this disjointed kingdom, renders a war of some sort necessary, and if a bankruptcy should insue it is to be hoped that France will not remain entire.

PARIS, *February* 17*th*, 1792.

The Municipality, instigated by a letter from the King to that purpose, has at length felt itself called upon to endeavour to prevent the ill consequences that might arise from the use, or rather the abuse, of that enormous quantity of pikes that they were making in the Faubourg St Antoine and its environs: they have accordingly issued an *arreté*, to that effect. Some of these instruments however made their appearance last Wednesday evening in the Faubourg St Marceau, in a riot which was occasioned by the emptying a magazine of sugar in order to convey it to the retail dealers, to whom it had been sold; this riot had so alarming an appearance that the Assembly held an extraordinary sitting; but it was quelled by the arrival of the mayor and twelve hundred National Guard with artillery.

The inhabitants of Noyon and the neighbouring villages are in arms, in order to prevent some boats laden with corn from descending the Oise. Mr Gouy d'Arcy, finding that the troops which he commanded were not sufficient to enforce the law, returned to Paris in order to procure additional force from the Minister of the War Department. This he has obtained, but the National Assembly has also thought proper to send four of its members as commissioners to persuade them to submit peaceably to the law.

The decree which places the estates of the emigrants in the hands of the nation has received the royal sanction. His Most Christian Majesty has written a letter to the Municipality of which I send your Lordship a copy inclosed. His guard has not yet taken the oath before the Municipality as prescribed to them by a decree of the Assembly, owing to an unwillingness in the officers, if not in the private men, to bind themselves in that manner.

The *Comité de Surveillance* has received such strong proofs of the aristocratical sentiments, for so they term it, of the *Regiment Dauphin* cavalry at Gray and the Regiment de Navarre at Besançon, that it has submitted a project of a decree to confine their service to the interior of the kingdom. The officers of these regiments may esteem themselves happy to have escaped the fate of the brother-officers at Perpignan who have been carried in handcuffs from that garrison to Orleans to the Haut-Cour Nationale.

The Minister of the War Department has the mortification to find all his plans counteracted by the want of regard which the Assembly shews to his proposals and requests, and the Minister for Foreign Affairs finds his schemes prevented by the unconstitutional interference of Municipalities who receive the applause of the Assembly. One of his spies a Mr Belport, who was carrying letters from Mr de Lessart into Germany has not only been stopt but many of his papers have been read by the Municipality of Stenay who have been applauded for this act of patriotism.

The *déficit* for the last month with the *dépenses particulières* amount to about forty two millions.

PARIS, *February* 24*th*, 1792.

It has long been the wish and object of the ministers of this country to introduce the mode of debating in general committees, in order to prevent the bad consequences which result from the sort of influence which crouded galleries have often exercised over the members of the Assembly. In order to obtain this end, as it were by stealth, for their friends could not venture to propose it openly, Mr de Moysset, formerly a member of the Jacobines, informed the Assembly that three hundred of it's members, who do not attend the committees, had formed a plan to unite in order to confer upon public affairs, and moved that on those days on which there were no evening sittings the hall of the Assembly should be open for all those deputies who might chuse to assemble in it: this motion was lost by a majority of 371 to 263.

The military committee having stated to the Assembly the propriety and advantages of the several proposals submitted to them some time ago by the Minister of the War Department, the following regulations are agreed to. 1st. In order to prepare the army for the campaign, it is enacted, that as soon as orders shall be given for that purpose, the following sums shall be advanced to the volunteer National Guard, and infantry. To lieutenants and *sous lieutenants* £300 tournois, to captains £400, to lieutenant-colonel £500 and to colonels £800. (Cavalry and artillery.) To lieutenants and *sous lieutenants* £400, to captains £500, lieutenant-colonels £700 and colonels £900. To generals £6000 and to lieutenant-generals and *maréchaux de camp* £3000. 2ly. During the campaign the lieutenants and *sous-lieutenants* are to receive an addition of $\frac{1}{2}$ to their present pay, captains and lieutenant-colonels $\frac{1}{3}$ and all officers above that rank $\frac{1}{4}$. Only every inferior officer and soldier is to be allowed, as soon as the campaign opens, 28 ounces of bread p^r diem, for which 32 *deniers* are to be retained upon his pay and $\frac{1}{4}$lb. of meat for 18 *deniers* more.

The Assembly has likewise heard the report of the committee upon the proposal for raising six legions and the forming a train of artillery to act with cavalry alone; but the decree proposed is not yet adopted. The Maréchal de Luckner and Mr de la Fayette are expected to day at Paris in order to confer with the Maréchal de Rochambeau, (who has been here for some time on account of his health,) and the ministers upon the plan for the approaching campaign.

The four commissioners who were sent by the Assembly to Noyon, finding that their presence could have no good effect are returned, and two battalions of the National Guard *soldée* have been sent there from hence: it is said that some of the private soldiers of these battalions are returned to their families. Mr de Wittenhoff, who commands them has declared his intention of attacking the rioters in two days in case they should persist till that time.

The last accounts from St Domingo give a most deplorable description of the state of that colony, and it is feared that it will not receive sufficient relief from this country, as many of the vessels which were sent out with provisions and some of those which had troops on board have, by stress of weather, been obliged to return to different ports of France.

Mr Barthélemy's cool reception at Soleure does not give him reason to hope that his negotiations with the Swiss cantons will have a speedy and successful termination.

Paris, *March 2nd*, 1792.

I inclose a copy of Mr de Lessart's answer to my letter of the ninth of last month: your Lordship is the best judge of the meaning of the latter part of it. I took occasion yesterday in the course of conversation, to assure that minister that I was convinced it was the determination of His Majesty's Ministers to maintain inviolate the treaty of commerce between the two nations: I again mentioned the Tobago business, but, being told by him that the Bishop of Autun was to arrange that affair, I dropt the subject.

I shall endeavour to send, by this day's messenger, the copies, which are ordered to be printed, of the dispatches which Mr de Lessart laid yesterday before the Assembly and which were read by one of the secretaries: but as it is probable that they will not be printed in time I beg leave to refer your Lordship to this day's *Logographe* in which they are copied with tolerable accuracy. The publication of these papers has not had the effect of lessening the general opinion of the difficulty of avoiding a war, for it remains to be seen whether the Emperor's naming the Jacobins and marking them out as the cause of his continuing to arm will tend to diminish their numbers.

The interior state of the kingdom becomes daily more distracted: the inhabitants of the neighbourhood of Noyon have been forced to a temporary submission by the quantity of troops sent for that purpose, and the troubles at Dunkirk and other places are appeased for the present, but it is in the south of France that the danger of a combustion is the greatest.

PARIS, *March 9th,* 1792.

The general anarchy, which has been for some time increasing in this country, seems at present to be nearly arrived at its greatest height. From the northern departments accounts are daily received of riots and disturbances, the pretence for which is the monopoly of corn, the price of it however is, in that part of the kingdom, far from dear; the real cause is a total dissolution of government. In the markets, even in the neighbourhood of the metropolis, the farmers are obliged to sell their corn at a price fixed by armed peasants in large bodies. In the Department of the Eure there is a body of them consisting of not less than six thousand. At Estampes the mayor has been massacred. In order to quell the disturbances in that town six hundred National Guard with cannon have been sent from hence, and another party of two hundred have been also sent with cannon into the neighbourhood of Versailles. But the proceedings in the south are still more violent and alarming: it is a singular event that a mixt body of two thousand people should arrive from Marseilles at the gates of Aix so unexpectedly that the inhabitants should not be able to make any defence against them. The fact is that the National Guard of that town was unwilling to oppose them, and the commanding officer having, through pusillanimity, ordered the soldiers of the Swiss Regiment d'Ernest to surrender their arms to the *brigands*, that regiment has given a painful proof of it's good discipline. The effect that this will have upon Mr Barthélemy's negotiation is easy to be imagined. Mr de Ste Croix is returned from Coblence: from what I could learn from himself, many of the emigrants remain there but they have laid aside every martial appearance. The indignities that he suffered and the menaces that he received from them during the whole time of his residence there, were such that he never could venture to admit any person into his presence, unless he had loaded pistols lying on his table and in other parts of the room: to the very circumspect manner alone in which he left that town he attributes his safe return to Paris. In the evening on which he privately quitted Coblence he left a dispatch with orders to have it sent in the usual manner the next morning, and his servants were told not to leave the town till twenty four hours after his departure. Near the frontier, he says, they were stopt by a party of horse-men who enquired for Mr de Ste Croix, but, being assured by them, that they were only his servants and that he himself was by that time arrived in France, they suffered them to continue their journey.

Mr de Maillé, who is appointed to succeed Mr de Blancheland, will set out for his Government as soon as the ships which were driven back by stress of weather are refitted. I shall soon have to inform your Lordship of the appointment of a new Minister for the Department of the Marine and Colonies, for, in addition to the ill-will which many of the leading members of the Assembly have exprest to his continuance in office, it appears that his political sentiments are obnoxious to Mr de Narbonne. For some genuine letters upon that subject I refer your Lordship to this day's Gazette Universelle, which paper I send your Lordship regularly as it is in fact the Ministerial Gazette.

The *déficit* for the last month is twenty millions, the *dépenes particulières* eighteen millions, and nineteen millions for the expences to be paid by the departments. I send inclosed to your Lordship a copy of Mr de Lessart's letter to me, inclosing another from Mr de Flaming to the Minister of the

Marine concerning Mr Trist's business by which your Lordship will see the result of that affair.

PARIS, *March* 10*th*, 1792.

I think it my duty to dispatch Staley with the interesting intelligence which reached Paris to-day of the sudden death of the Emperor, who was taken ill on the 25th of last month with a violent vomiting of blood and expired in thirty-six hours.

I also take the opportunity of sending your Lordship inclosed a letter from Lord St Helens which was brought here by Mr de Bourgoing's first dispatches to Mr de Lessart.

That Minister has been impeached to-day in the Assembly: thirteen articles of accusation have been brought against him and the executive power has had orders to secure his person and his private papers.

Although I thought it very probable that Mr de Narbonne would not continue long in office, I own I did not expect that, when I was informing your Lordship that Mr de Bertrand would not remain long in the ministry on account of political disagreements between him and Mr de Narbonne, the latter had received His Most Christian Majesty's orders to resign his *portefeuille*. This however was the case, and for a proof of the king's desire that Mr Bertrand, who has resigned, should remain in office, I am obliged to refer your Lordship to His Majesty's letter to the Assembly upon that subject as it is copied in a printed paper for want of a more authentic copy at present.

The harsh treatment which Mr de Lessart has received this morning seems to have affected Mr de Narbonne and the more so as it is generally known that, although they came into the ministry under the same auspices, they have since shewn considerable shades of difference in their politics. It was Mr de Narbonne's intention to join his regiment immediately at Metz, but a decree of the Assembly, which confines ministers to Paris till they have settled their accounts, renders that measure impracticable. The Jacobins are paying their court to him *en attendant*. Mr Cahier's resignation is expected to follow and probably that of the Minister of Justice. Mr de Talleyrand arrived here this morning and expressed himself extremely satisfied with his reception in England.

The appearance of the National Guards has dispersed the rioters in the neighbourhood of Paris.

PARIS, *March* 16*th*, 1792.

In consequence of your Lordship's instructions No. 6. I shall take the first opportunity of representing the case of the Tobago creditors to the new Minister for foreign affairs, Mr du Mouriez, a *Maréchal de Camp* formerly *Commandant* at Cherbourg and employed in the diplomatic line in the administration of the Duke of Choiseul. Mr Dietrich mayor of Strasbourg, it is said, will have the Home Department. These two gentlemen have both been members of the Society of the Jacobins. It is also said that Mr Clavière, who is still a member of that Society and the intimate friend of Mr de Condorcet and Mr Brissot, is to be appointed *Ministre des Contributions*, he is a countryman of Mr Necker, his rival in abilities and knowledge of finance. Mr de Grave, the minister of the War Department is a gentleman esteemed in private life, he has some reputation in the literary world and was employed in the education of the children of the Duke of Orleans. The Minister of the Marine, Mr la Coste was formerly *Chef du Bureau*, of the department of which he is at present minister. The fate of the Minister of Justice is not yet determined. Mr de Lessart is arrived in safety at Orleans, but it will be a considerable time before his trial can commence. His public papers are submitted to the inspection of the Comité diplomatique. The banditti who have infested the markets in Normandy and in the environs of the metropolis are dispersed and it is hoped that the vigorous measures which have been adopted will prevent any effusion of blood in the South of France; the situation however of Arles, Avignon and the Départment de la Lozère affords sufficient reason not to be over sanguine. Some forgers of assignats have been discovered at Passy near Paris; forged assignats, to the amount of five millions of livres were already completed and so like the true assignats that it is impossible to distinguish them: the expence of this fabrication is calculated at not less than four hundred thousand livres. They imagine that the presses and plates were made in England. The *Maison Militaire du Roy* mounted guard at the Thuilleries for the first time, this morning, having previously taken the oath prescribed to them, at the Hôtel de Ville.

The generals are returned to the frontiers: the Maréchal de Luckner speaks everywhere in terms the most unfavourable of the Maréchal de Rochambeau.

Paris, *March 23rd*, 1792.

I was in an error last week when I informed your Lordship that the generals were gone to the frontiers: at that time Mr de Luckner alone had left Paris: it was Mr de la Fayette's intention to go at the same time, but his departure has been delayed from day to day. I accidentally happen to know that he past the whole of last Tuesday with Mr du Mouriez at the *bureau des affaires etrangéres*, at least from nine in the morning till three in the afternoon; for, as that was the day appointed for the foreign ministers to transact business with the minister, there was no hour in that space of time in which some one of our body was not at the office, and upon comparing accounts we discovered that Mr de la Fayette was present at every interview. The preceding evening Mr du Mouriez attended the meeting of the Jacobins and delivered a patriotic speech which was much applauded by the whole club and worked so strongly upon Mr Roberspierre's feelings that he could not resist embracing the minister. The Jacobins that evening, but not till after Mr du Mouriez had worn one, put a stop to the newly-adopted folly of wearing red caps, which had already been attended with some disagreeable circumstances to individuals; a letter from Mr Péthion corresponding with the sentiments of Mr Roberspierre upon that subject, the Society agreed that the national cockade was a sufficient token of the love of liberty.

Mr de Narbonne keeps aloof from this Society, which may now undoubtedly be called the Ministerial Club, for Mr Clavière is appointed *Ministre des Contributions* Mr Rolland de la Platrière, a Jacobin of Bordeaux, Minister for the Home Department, and Mr Garnier Minister of Justice.

The minds of those who feel for the blood of their fellow creatures are shocked at the horrid policy of the Assembly in passing an Act of Amnesty, in order to preserve the valuable lives of Jourdan and the other malefactors of Avignon. Mr Thuriot's speech upon that occasion deserves your Lordship's attention: one of his arguments in favour of the amnesty is that it will tend to encourage the revolt of the Brabançons. The soldiers of Châteauvieux, who are coming from Brest are to be received here with patriotic honours and a fête, in order I suppose to encourage insubordination. The exchange has risen in favour of this country and the price of specie decreased very rapidly of late, but indeed every thing here proceeds by fits and starts.

Paris, *March* 30*th*, 1792.

I inclose copies of two official papers which were yesterday communicated to the National Assembly by Mr Dumouriez and which have given a sufficient proof that the politics of the Court of Vienna with regard to the affairs of France are not in the least altered by the Emperor's death, but that on the contrary the same measures will be adopted, perhaps with more energy, considering the youth and enterprizing spirit of the King of Hungary and considering at the same time the change that has taken place in the French administration. For if this ministry should continue, and there is every reason to suppose it will, as it is supported by the majority, comprehending the most active and ardent of the people, war will be inevitable, however ill-prepared this country may be for it It is true that they are not in want of men, for the number of recruits that have offered themselves are so far superior in number to the fifty-one thousand that were wanted, that they are distrest to know what to do with them, but real soldiers will undoubtedly be scarce, for, from the absurdity of their conduct, it is possible that none of the Swiss regiments, by far the best they have, will remain in their service. That of Ernest has been recalled by the republic of Berne.

I inclose to your Lordship French copies translated from the German of two official papers upon that subject which I have procured from the Minister of Geneva to this court. The administrators of the department of Paris are endeavouring to prevent the intended *fête* for the forty soldiers of Châteauvieux, in honour of their having disobeyed orders, but the Municipality is desirous that it should take place and it will probably prevail. They are expected to-morrow at Versailles. They seem to be playing the game for the Spanish negotiator who is arrived in Switzerland. But to return to the probability of war. Mr Dumouriez, before the dispatches were read, thought proper to animadvert upon that part of the Prince of Kaunitz's answer in which he appeals to *la partie saine et principale de la Nation*, by which, he said, that minister understood the aristocracy, a remark not of the most conciliatory nature: he concluded by desiring the assembly to restrain its indignation till he should receive the definitive and categorical answer which he had demanded from the court of Vienna and which he expected would arrive in a few days, (it will be at least a week before they will probably arrive). Now it is well known that his dispatches to that court as well as to those of Berlin and Madrid are written in a style more calculated to inflame than to persuade.

As for the court of Spain your Lordship may perceive by the report of the diplomatic committee, which is printed in last Wednesday's Logographe, and in which the politics of England with respect to that country are invidiously glanced at, that conciliatory measures are not even thought of. With regard to the interior state of the kingdom, disturbances, for which corn is always the pretence, break out in some one part of the northern departments of the kingdom as fast as they are quelled in other parts; in the south they are in a state the nearest possible to that of civil war: luckily for the town of Arles, a battalion of the regiment of Languedoc and three hundred dragoons of that of Lorraine, which were sent there in order to preserve tranquillity and to inforce the decree of the Assembly, arrived there before the National Guards, which were also sent there for the same purpose: for the inhabitants would certainly have opposed by force the entrance of the latter into their town, but they have received into their walls the regular troops even with demonstrations of joy. At Mendes it will be well if the *Décret d'accusation* of the Assembly against the Bishop, the mayor, and six officers of the National Guard of that town be inforced with equal tranquillity. In the department of Cantal many *Châteaux* have been burnt and the *Lieutenant Criminel* of Aurillac massacred.

The decree which the Assembly has lately passed against the emigrants and which authorizes the municipalities to manage their estates and even subjects those who have returned since the ninth of February to pay the triple contribution and not to be entrusted with any public employment for the space of two years, and also subjects those who do not return in the course of a month not to enjoy the rights of a *Citoyen actif*, or the power of holding a place under government for ten years, has occasioned the return of some of those who have a large property at stake.

The new Minister of Justice is not yet named, but it is supposed it will be a Mr Duranteau of Bordeaux. Mr Rolland is not of that town but of Lyons. These two gentlemen are both lawyers. Some mode must be soon adopted for replenishing the *Caisse de l'extraordinaire* as it is calculated that it will otherwise be empty by the beginning of April. In order to keep up the exchange, the Assembly has prohibited any further emission of *Billets de Confiance* in exchange for assignats and has authorized the Municipalities of the several places where banks for that purpose have been established to examine their accounts and to oblige them to keep by them a sum equal to their emission either in assignats or in specie. The Assembly has also annulled the decree of the 24th of September respecting the West India Colonies and it has decreed that all *Gens de Couleur* and free negroes shall enjoy the political rights of free citizens and they have accordingly authorized the executive power to send commissioners to those colonies with orders to dissolve the present Colonial Assemblies and to convoke new primary Assemblies.

I understand it is in contemplation to send immediately to England with the character of Minister Plenipotentiary Mr de Chauvelin, one of the *Maitres de la Garde Robe du Roy*, a young man of anti-aristocratical principles and a friend of Mr de Narbonne and Mr de Périgord. The latter is to accompany him, in order that his abilities for negotiating may be employed without infringing the self denying decree of the late Assembly.

I inclose a copy of Mr Dumouriez's answer to my note about the Tobago creditors.

PARIS, *April 2nd*, 1792.

Mr de Chauvelin informed me last night that His Most Christian Majesty has appointed him his Minister Plenipotentiary to the Court of London. Some articles of accusation having been exhibited against Mr de Narbonne with regard to the state of the Spanish frontiers he is to be heard this day at the bar of the Assembly.

The report of the articles of accusation against the late Minister of Justice is to be made on Wednesday.

One of the first Banking-Houses that of Monneron has broke for a considerable sum, this event so much affected one of the Messieurs that he has destroyed himself. The other brother has resigned his seat in the Assembly. Mr Clavière being his *suppléant* has had his choice of being a Minister or a Legislator and has chosen to continue in his present situation.

The Assembly has decreed that a copy of the treaty between the French King's brothers and the Prince of Hohenlohe shall be sent to the High National Court and it has ordered the Grand Procurators to give an account of their procedure against the Princes whom they have impeached.

It is believed that the Volunteers of Marseilles are in possession of Avignon.

PARIS, *April 6th*, 1792.

The National Assembly has pronounced that Mr de Narbonne is perfectly innocent of the crimes and misdemeanours laid to his charge by the Prince Charles of Hesse and his Aide de Camp, Mr du Bois de Crancé. The public was not in the least surprised at this, as the accusations were undoubtedly frivolous and ill-founded, but it was rather remarkable that the Abbé Fauchet, who till that time had always acted the part of a *dénonciateur*, should appear so conspicuously eager in his defence: this however is to be accounted for when one considers the court which the Jacobin party has invariably paid to him since his disgrace and the sort of connection which he holds with them. Mr de Talleyrand and Mr de Chauvelin are his intimate friends and, though neither of them is decidedly a Jacobin, yet they have submitted to act with those ministers who have individually declared at their public meeting their deference and respect for that Society, which in fact is the Council of this Administration of which it is very probable Mr de Narbonne himself may be one day a member. Mr du Port is in all respects in a different predicament and his friends are not without fear that he will be sent to Orleans.

Mr de Lessart has answered the interrogatory of his judges and is, of course, no longer *au secret*, but he has signified to his friends that motives of prudence oblige him to deny himself the satisfaction of being visited by them.

Your Lordship will see the interrogatory and the answers in yesterday's Logographe. In this day's Logographe there is a report of the diplomatic and Colonial Committees concerning Captain Colmin who, contrary to the orders he had received, carried and left on shore near a British port in the Bay of Honduras two hundred and seventeen black slaves from the Island of St Domingo: in consequence of which report the Assembly has decreed that the French King shall be desired to order that Captain Colmin shall be tried for this offence and to indemnify the British Government and at the same time to give it assurances that the French Nation disapproves of the conduct of Captain Colmin. This decree was passed unanimously.

The Assembly heard yesterday with satisfaction a pacific answer from the King of Sardinia, but it seemed also to hear with equal satisfaction that there were disturbances at Turin.

The answer from Vienna is now anxiously expected: it is

difficult to suppose that it can be of a nature to prevent a war, upon which the Jacobins, with the exception of Mr Roberspierre and a few others, seem to have set their hearts.

The *Fête Civique* intended to be given to the soldiers of Châteauvieux will be a good criterion of the strength of that party in the metropolis. If that should take place without disturbance their preponderance will be undoubted. The *Caisse de l'extraordinaire* has received a temporary aid of fifty millions: that sum in assignats having been decreed in addition to the sixteen hundred millions in circulation. The miserable state of the finances has occupied the thoughts of several Members of the Assembly who have stated their sentiments upon that subject. I shall not fail to send your Lordship the plans for retrieving the finances by Mr Cambon and Mr Cailhaisson as soon as they are printed. The three millions which the Assembly was forced to lend to the Municipality for the assistance of the *Caisse de Secours*, by keeping those notes in circulation have prevented the disturbances with which we were threatened. And except the house of Monneron no bankruptcy of consequence has taken place, owing to a subscription among the bankers to assist one another, but credit has received a severe blow.

Mr du Roveray, who intends, if his health will permit him, to return to England with Mr Talleyrand and Mr de Chauvelin, was offered a place in the present administration, that I believe of *Ministre de la Justice*, which he refused.

Paris, *April 11th*, 1792.

Slater arrived here last Friday night with your Lordship's Dispatches No. 9. No. 10. and No. 11. On Sunday Mr Aubert du Bazet, an officer of cavalry who served in America during the last war and who is of the *Côté droit*, having said that he was certain that the report of the Resolue being taken by the Phœnix was well founded, for he knew from very good authority that I had received an extraordinary courier to inform me of that event, moved that the Minister for foreign affairs should give an account to the National Assembly of what measure had been taken by the Government to obtain redress. The Minister assured the Assembly that he had no knowledge of that affair except what he had obtained from a newspaper, but he promised to give a detail of that business as soon as he should receive an official account of it. I am at a loss to know how Mr du Bazet received his information, as I had told that circumstance to nobody.

On Monday the Minister wrote to me, desiring me to communicate to him freely what I knew upon the subject; I wrote for answer that I expected a messenger every hour and that I should give him, as soon as possible, every information in my power. I wrote to him again yesterday morning to inform him that, my messenger being arrived, I was ready to communicate the official intelligence I had received either that evening or the next morning as it suited him best. He fixed upon that evening, in the beginning of which he arrived at my house, and as I had not had time to translate the papers which your Lordship had sent to me, we agreed to defer conversing fully upon the subject till the next morning. I accordingly went to him this morning and delivered according to your Lordship's instruction an *office*, of which I inclose a copy, and the two papers with translations of them. Having read them, he exprest very freely his sentiments of the improper behaviour of the French officer, and said that the conduct of the English was completely authorized by the 26th and 27th Articles of the Treaty of Commerce. He told me that he would immediately communicate the papers to the Assembly, but that it could not be expected that they would come to a final decision upon the subject till they had received their own official accounts. He did not mention to me the prior dispute in the road of Mahé, but I am sorry to have to inclose to your Lordship a letter which I have this moment received from him inclosing one from Mr la Coste to him with a letter from some merchants of Dunkirk and a copy of a declaration of a Captain Mollegaert and his crew complaining of ill treatment which they have received from the Captain of the Nemesis.

It is evident that the Ministry here have a most earnest desire to be upon the best possible terms with England, which is a sufficient reason for inclining the *Côté droit* to be otherwise.

When Mr du Mouriez communicated the *office* and papers to the Assembly Mr du Bazet and some others of that Party attempted to begin a debate, but finding a great majority against it they agreed that it should be sent to the Diplomatic Committee. In the course of conversation with Mr du Mouriez he told me that if no answer should arrive from Vienna before the 15th of this month they should regard themselves as *en état de guerre* with the King of Hungary: I found with him when I arrived Mr de Bethune-Charost, upon his leaving the room Mr du Mouriez remarked with a smile that a Minister was obliged to admit even *un fou* into his house. I asked him what he thought of Mr de Luckner's letter which your Lordship will see in this day's Logographe, he said, 'twas not the Maréchal's writing, but that it was *un tour de l'ennemi* who had persuaded him to put his name to it. He added that it was absolutely necessary to have a considerable force in the south; that Mr de Muy being unfit to command there that they had sent Mr de Witgenstein but finding that he was too fond of German tactics for soldiers in their present state of discipline the King had appointed Mr de Montesquiou to that command, who is known to your Lordship as a writer on the finances of this country. It appears that Arles and Avignon are both in the hands of the Patriots, for so they call them, whose numbers increase most rapidly. I inclose a copy of a letter from Mr du Mouriez concerning the Tobago creditors, and another informing me that His Most Christian Majesty has given orders to the Departments of the Seine inferieure the Loire inferieure and Morbihan to allow the goods which were shipt before the publication of the decree of the 24th of February to leave the kingdom. Mr Lomas's cotton wool &c. can therefore now proceed to their place of destination.

The soldiers of Châteauvieux had the *Honneurs de la Séance* in the Assembly last Monday. Their fête is to take place on Sunday next. Mr de Narbonne is dangerously ill in consequence of a fall from his horse. Mr Emanuel de Maulde succeeds Mr de Gonvernet at the Hague. Mr le Hoc goes to Hamburgh in the room of Mr de Bourgoing who will remain at Madrid. Mr de Vibrage goes to Copenhagen and Mr Villars to Mayence.

PARIS, *April* 13*th*, 1792.

During the last week this metropolis has enjoyed more quiet than perhaps in any other week since the Revolution, but it has the appearance of that sort of calm which portends a storm. The majority of the National Guard, especially those who are attached to Mr de la Fayette, murmur at the indecency and impropriety of leading as it were in triumph those soldiers of Châteauvieux whose sole merit consists in having disobeyed orders, but who are now used as tools to render Mr de la Fayette and the Feuillants unpopular.

Mr de Narbonne's fall from his horse will probably be attended with no other bad consequences for him than the loss of a finger: it has been observed upon this occasion *qu'il est à un doigt de sa porte.*

Mr D'Abbadie, an Englishman settled at Rochefort as broker and interpreter for the English captains coming to that port, informed me, by a letter of the 26th of July 1791, that, contrary to the 18th Article of the Treaty of Commerce, the *Directeur des Douanes* had refused to receive his report of an English vessel, assigning for reason that he was not a sworn broker and interpreter. I applied to Mr de Montmorin, who, the 16th of October following, informed me that the above mentioned Article of the Treaty of Commerce was so evidently in Mr D'Abbadie's favour that the minister *des Contributions* had given orders to the Custom House to receive his reports equally with those of the sworn Brokers. On the first of December following, Mr D'Abbadie having a report to make, it was received by the Custom House but absolutely rejected by one Mr Maureau *Juge de l'Amirauté* : I applied a second time to this government and on the eleventh instant I received the inclosed answer from Mr Dumouriez. I must observe that I have never received a communication of the observations of Mr Bertrand.

P.S. I inclose a copy of a letter to me from Mr du Mouriez inclosing sundry papers relative to the late affair in the Bay of Honduras.

Paris, *April 20th*, 1792.

Owing to the moderation and proper behaviour of the National Guard, the absurd *Fête*[1] of last Sunday concluded without any disturbance: upon the whole it has tended more to affect the popularity of the promoters of it than of those against whom it was aimed. The same party, of which are almost all the Municipality, had determined upon removing the busts of Mr de la Fayette and Mr Bailly, but the threats of the National Guard have prevented them from executing that project.

At a time when the National Guards in the South are not only permitting, but assisting in the destruction and pillage of the *Châteaux* of those unhappy proprietors whose political sentiments are not *à la hauteur de la Constitution,* the Minister of the War Department asks and obtains the permission of the Assembly to withdraw the regular troops which he had lately sent to that part of the kingdom. The inhabitants of Lyons tremble for their property nor does the consideration that the Minister of the Interior is their country-man at all diminish their fears. Orders are sent to conduct back to prison Jourdan, who is at Arles in triumph and exultation: it will be well if they can obtain *force à la loi.*

Mr Duranton of Bordeaux is at last appointed Minister of Justice: in his speech upon the occasion to the Assembly he boasted much of having past twenty years in retirement occupied in the study of Rousseau and other great political writers, and promised to act upon the true principles of the present happy Constitution of France: he has however already incurred the censure of some patriots for having countersigned His Most Christian Majesty's letter notifying to the Assembly that he had appointed Mr Fleurien Governor to the Prince

---

[1] The *fête de la liberté* held on April 15, 1792.

Royal. Eleven millions extraordinary for the army have been voted this week, since which it has been decreed that the soldiers shall be paid entirely in specie, an increase of expence to the Treasury of at least eight millions per month. [The amount of money in specie in the Treasury is twenty-four millions of livres.] Six-hundred thousand have been also voted for Cherbourg; it will soon be decided by the Assembly whether the prosecution of that work according to the original great plan is advisable at present. Other reasons besides the miserable state of the finances must be brought against it, for we are taught by the *charlatans* in finance who are friends to the present Government, that the sale of the forest lands will render the state of the finances absolutely flourishing; in the meantime the various drafts upon the national treasury are enormous. The commissioners at St Domingo have taken the liberty to draw upon the treasury for three millions and, by their dispatches to Government, it appears that they require a much more considerable sum to be sent immediately for the assistance of that colony.

The Duguay Trouin having been forced back by contrary winds, the soldiers on board have demanded an additional pay of two months which has of course been complied with. Six thousand men, four of which, National Guards, are to be sent immediately to St Domingo and two thousand to the other West India Islands.

Two letters from Mr de Noailles, which are printed in this day's Logographe, were yesterday communicated to the National Assembly by Mr du Mouriez, in consequence of which, the Assembly being convinced that the instructions of the Minister have been properly attended to by that Ambassador, they have revoked the Projet de Décret of impeachment which was proposed against him last Saturday. But this communication was the prelude of an event of the greatest consequence.

By a letter from the King the Assembly was informed that His Majesty would be there the next day. I shall send to-morrow by an extraordinary messenger the detail of this day's debate, for after the *Rapport des Ministres au Roy* had been read and the King had informed the Assembly that, in consequence of it, he was come to propose to declare war in form against the King of Hungary and Bohemia, it was found necessary to adjourn till five o'clock in order to clear the Hall of strangers who had placed themselves in every part of it. I can only add to what your Lordship will see in the inclosed *Journal du Soir* that there can be no doubt that the Assembly will coincide in opinion with His Most Christian Majesty's ministers and that war will be immediately declared against the King of Hungary.

PARIS, *April 22nd*, 1792.

I have received your Lordship's Dispatches No. 14, 15, and I shall not fail to observe punctually the instructions contained in the last of them.

In order to send your Lordship an accurate account of the debate on Friday evening in the National Assembly, I have delayed dispatching Staley till this day.

Your Lordship will see by the account of the debate in the inclosed Logographe that the Assembly was almost unanimous for war. Although any mention of the King of Prussia was cautiously avoided in the Minister's memorial, the Assembly is sufficiently aware that by declaring war against the King of Hungary they have involved themselves also in one against the King of Prussia; but I find it to be a very general notion, at least in the Assembly, that if France can preserve a neutrality with England she will be able to cope with all the rest of Europe united. This notion is encouraged by a persuasion that the influence of the Jacobins and an inoculation of their principles will occasion an insurrection, which according to their language is *le plus saint des devoirs*, in every country whose Government shall dare to oppose them in arms.

Their first military plan seems to be an attack upon Ostend and Liège; and, in order to embody their friends in that part of the world it is in contemplation to raise three Legions: one to be called *La Legion Brabançonne* another *Liégeoise* and the

[1] This was the successor of Leopold II, Francis II. who was not yet formally elected Emperor or crowned.

third *des Patriotes Hollandois*. Mr de Béthune-Charost is still here but I have reason to think that he will leave Paris in the course of this day. Your Lordship will recollect the proposal that he made to Government two years ago with regard to Ostend.

Mr de Narbonne, who is perfectly recovered from his fall without even the loss of a finger, having obtained leave from the National Assembly, will go to-night to Metz: he expresses hopes of great success in the beginning of the campaign but I believe he confines his hopes to that period.

The Maréchal de Luckner, to judge from his letter which was read in the Assembly on Thursday night, and which your Lordship will see in yesterday's Logographe does not seem to think that his army is perfectly in a condition to begin the campaign.

Mr du Mouriez, in a letter to the Assembly has shewn some anxiety for the personal safety of the Chargé des Affaires of the court of Vienna, but it is rather singular that although it is as long ago as last Monday that Monsieur de Blumendorf desired from him a passport for a courier whom he wished to dispatch to Vienna, that minister has not yet complied with his request. Mr de Chauvelin will probably be in London before Staley, as he left this place last night. Mr de Talleyrand is to follow him in a few days.

Paris, *April 27th*, 1792.

With this dispatch I send one to your Lordship from Mr Trevor: as a supplement to which I have to add that Mr du Mouriez communicated yesterday to the National Assembly the circumstance of Mr de Sémonville having been stopped at Alexandria and that the court of Sardinia had refused to permit him to proceed into the interior part of Piedmont. Mr du Mouriez's dispatch to Mr de la Lande, in consequence of this event was then read and much applauded by the Assembly. In this dispatch the Minister complains, in a very unreserved manner, of the insults offered to the French nation in the person of Mr de Sémonville and instructs Mr de la Lande to demand that the orders given by the Sardinian

Government to prevent Mr de Sémonville from proceeding on his journey should be recalled and that the Court of Turin should give an explanation of its conduct in twenty-four hours. He is also instructed to go to Alexandria in order to receive Mr de Sémonville and to present him to His Sardinian Majesty, but, in case the Court of Turin should refuse to comply with these demands, he is to accompany Mr de Sémonville back to Genoa.

Mr de Barthélemy has been negotiating, without success, for a revocation of the recall of the *Régiment d'Ernest:* the Government of Berne, with great temper and firmness, insists that the French King shall order the recall of that regiment to be put into immediate execution. The state of the French army on the frontiers is such that in no other time or country it would be possible to suppose that it could venture to oppose a regular well-disciplined army although far inferior in number; and it is believed that the impetuosity of the Ministry will be counteracted by the prudence of the Generals; both seem to place their greatest confidence in the desertion of the enemy's forces. Corruption of every sort and in every manner is employed without reserve, and this mode of making war seems to be the boast of the Assembly as well as of the Ministry; it has decreed six millions of secret service money.

It is believed that Mr de Biron, who has the command at Valenciennes, will make the first attack in the enemy's country, his popular manners joined to some military experience in America render him perhaps the most proper person they could have chosen for the business in which he may be engaged. Mr Walkiers, whose ambition was disappointed in the late revolution in Brabant, will probably act under him. We expect every hour to hear that the army of Mr de Luckner has marched to occupy the pass of Porentrui.

While there is every reason to believe that dissensions subsist between the Generals and the Ministry there is a certainty of very ill blood among the members of the Jacobin Society who employ themselves in reciprocal denunciations. Tantaene animis caelestibus irae!

G. C.

Paris, *May* 3rd, 1792.

In hourly expectation of official accounts of the engagements which have taken place between the French and Austrians near Tournay and Mons, in both of which the former have been entirely defeated, I have been prevented from sending to your Lordship an extraordinary messenger.

The official intelligence from Mr de Biron which was this day communicated to the National Assembly, is so very similar to the first reports which must have reached London before this time, that I am induced to send this dispatch by the ordinary messenger tomorrow, especially as it is most probable that the very interesting event of Mr de la Fayette's enterprize against Namur will be known before that time.

By the Maréchal de Rochambeau's journal it appears that he had orders to form three camps; one of eighteen thousand men at Valenciennes, another of four or five thousand at Maubeuge, and a third of three or four thousand at Dunkirk. On the 24th he received dispatches from Mr de Grave and Mr Dumouriez with instructions to place under the command of Mr de Biron a body of men consisting of ten battalions of infantry and the same number of squadrons of horse who were to present themselves before Mons before the 30th. The same number of horse under the command of a *Maréchal de Camp* were to arrive at the same time before Tournay and a detachment of twelve hundred men were to go from Dunkirk to Furnes. The Maréchal had also orders to assemble all the forces that could be spared from the garrisons in order to be ready to march with them as soon as possible to support Mr de Biron, of whose success against Mons there could be little doubt, considering the correspondence that the Ministry had with that country. Your Lordship will observe that these instructions gave virtually a command to Mr de Biron, superior to that of Mr de Rochambeau, and that the former received *direct instructions* from the Minister of Foreign Affairs as well as from the Minister of the War Department which were not communicated to the Maréchal. Mr Dumouriez has in fact assumed the office of

Prime Minister and he would have taken the title had it not been contrary to the constitution of this country.

The Assembly not trusting entirely to the *dons patriotiques* for the support of the war, has voted an additional *création* of three hundred millions in assignats, fifty millions of which are to be paid immediately into the National Treasury by the *Caisse de l'Extraordinaire*.

It was the intention of the Ministry that this new *création* should be employed only in the support of the war, but they were not able to obtain that point.

I enclose two dispatches to your Lordship from Mr Trevor.

Mr Tronchin, the Minister to this Court from Geneva, informs me that his republic have exprest to him their alarm at the present critical situation of things in that neighbourhood, and especially since they have heard that a camp is to be formed between Lyons and Geneva, for they have certain knowledge that the Jacobins have intrigued with those who are disaffected to their present government, and particularly with one Grenus, against whom Mr Tronchin has been instructed to present a reclamation to the French Government, a copy of which I inclose. He presses me strongly to mention to Mr Dumouriez the good intelligence which subsists between the Court of St James and the Republic, which I do not think myself authorized to do unless I receive instructions from your Lordship to that purpose.

Mr Truguet is appointed to the command of a squadron consisting I believe of seven sail of the line fitting out at Toulon, and the American and eleven smaller sail consisting of frigates and sloops are fitting out at Brest under the command of Mr Kerkalin.

Mr de Blumendorf is still here, having been instructed by the Comte de Mercy to remain till he should receive further instructions; he did not obtain a passport for his courier till last Friday night. The troubles continue in St Domingo and the greater part of the plantations in the Plaine des Cazes have been destroyed.

May 4th, 1792.

By the most authentic accounts of Mr Dillon's catastrophe it appears that the destruction of his little army was occasioned by his own imprudence. Totally unprepared for an engagement which he was instructed not to risk, he had ventured so near the enemy that he was attacked while his horses were grazing. The suspicion of treachery which was the cause of his cruel death as well as that of some officers under his command is entirely done away, and the horrors committed by his worse than cannibal soldiers are attributed even by the Jacobins to the discourses and writings by which the minds of the soldiers have been perverted within the last three years.

This is at least one step gained, and it is to be hoped for the sake of this country that they will at last discover that even in civil society, subordination, good-order and morals are necessary for its well-being.

With regard to Mr de Biron's affair before Mons, we must wait for the particulars of it in his next dispatch: it appears by what we know of it at present that he shewed more abilities and more of the experienced officer than Mr Dillon; he however seems with the instructions of Mr Dumouriez to have imbibed too much of his impetuosity. Till he had left Quievrain all appeared prosperous. A small body of Houlans abandoned that town upon his approach, which gave him an opportunity of erecting the tree of liberty in the enemies' territory, and his troops that of getting drunk and dancing to the tune of *ça ira*. The next day however when he arrived near Mons he discovered that General Beaulieu had occupied the high ground near the town which he fondly imagined would have been left for him to possess, and on that account the town could not be taken by the force which he had with him. He determined therefore to rest his army for a few hours and then to retreat, having at that time learnt the fate of Mr Dillon. At five o'clock P. M. he had a slight skirmish with the enemy. At ten the regiment *de la Reine Dragons* retreated crying out they were betrayed; Mr de Biron followed them and brought back the greater number; upon his return finding the whole army in confusion, he immediately began the retreat, which he effected without much loss, till he arrived at Quievrain from whence the Houlans had driven the French garrison: he retook the place after an obstinate resistance but was obliged to abandon it immediately. His whole army was completely routed, and fled in the greatest confusion to Valenciennes, where he narrowly escaped the fate of Mr Dillon, leaving their baggage, tents, artillery and military stores.

The news of these two total defeats which arrived within the space of a few hours, stunned the Jacobins; Mr de Grave proposed the establishment of courts martial to try military offences without the intervention of a jury; this however was not sufficiently relished to be immediately adopted, and the only proof that the Assembly has given as yet of its disposition to suppress licence is the *Décret d'Accusation*, which was past yesterday against the authors of the periodical papers called *l'ami du roy* and *l'ami du peuple*. It is probable that the present Ministry will not be able to withstand the shock. Mr Dumouriez informed the Assembly this morning that Mr de Rochambeau, in consequence of the Minister's direct orders to Mr de Biron his inferior officer, has refused to correspond with them, but that he has written to the King and sent him his resignation. The Minister also said that the plan of attack was that the Maréchal de Luckner's army should take possession of the passes of Porentrui. This I find has been effected by Mr de Custine, who at first refused to obey the Maréchal's orders, owing to a want of confidence in his soldiers; he has however since that occupied the passes which had been relinquished by the Austrian troops. Mr de la Fayette was to attack Namur: no account is as yet arrived of that expedition. The business of the army of the Maréchal de Rochambeau and its success or rather want of it is well known. By advancing thus on all sides into the enemy's country, the intention, said the Minister, was to kindle a general insurrection; at this expression even the Assembly murmured. Mr de Luckner is to succeed Mr de Rochambeau in the command of the northern army. Between six and seven millions have been voted for the naval armament.

Mr de Walkiers has not left Paris. It was my intention to have sent your Lordship an account of the number of troops on the frontiers. I hope to be able to send it by the next messenger.

Paris, *May 11th*, 1792.

I inclose to your Lordship a letter from Mr Trevor.

The repulses before Tournay and Mons have been attended with circumstances which oblige the French army to adopt defensive measures. In the northern army many of the officers, especially those of the Artillery, have resigned their commands, and to this circumstance is in a great measure to be attributed Mr de Graves' resignation. His successor, Mr de Servan, brother of the last Attorney General of the Parliament of Grenoble, unites to much activity principles which render him very well qualified to associate in council with the rest of His Most Christian Majesty's present Ministers. At Valenciennes the soldiers are obliged to remain in cantonments until tents can be provided to supply those which were lost at Quievrain. There has been a slight skirmish between the outposts near Maubeuge.

At Lille the military begin to be ashamed of their late atrocious conduct and the town is become quiet. The only force which remains beyond the frontiers is a body of three thousand men, which Mr de la Fayette sent to Bouvignes under the command of Mr de Gouvion, and which remains there in order to obtain forage, of which among many other essential articles that army is in great need; it is not improbable that this small body may be surrounded and taken by the Austrians: the rest of that army is in a state bordering on insurrection, encamped near Givet in a position secure from any immediate attack.

Mr de Luckner is at Paris.

Mr de Rochambeau throws the blame of the disgrace which the French arms have incurred, upon Mr Dumouriez; that Minister however holds firm and shews at least that he possesses the virtue of courage. For Mr de Rochambeau's opinions I must refer your Lordship to his letter to the National Assembly in this day's Logographe: he and Mr de la Fayette agree that they were egregiously deceived with regard to the good dispositions of the inhabitants of the Low Countries towards the French.

The proceedings in the south of France are not of a nature to conciliate the minds of those who wish to trust their property and personal security to the protection of the Executive Power. In an official letter to Mr de Grave, Mr de Montesquiou says: *J'espère que nous n'entendrons pas parler d'Avignon, il s'exercera vraisemblablement quelques vexations dans ce malheureux pays, par le Parti quelque temps opprimé et aujourd'hui triomphant, je crois que c'est là que se borne l'ambition marseilloise dont on a voulu nous effrayer.*

This is the sentiment of a man entrusted with the command of an army to enforce justice and maintain peace.

Ubi solitudinem fecerunt pacem appellant. The Assembly has however ordered to their bar the Commissioners of the *Bouches du Rhone* who attended and partook of the triumphal entry of Jourdan and his banditti into Avignon, and the Ministers, contrary to their disposition, are compelled to give force to the law against that band of murderers.

For the whole of the extraordinary expences for the last month the *Caisse de l'extraordinaire* is to pay into the National Treasury between forty-five and forty-six millions.

Paris, *May* 18*th*, 1792.

I have endeavoured to procure for your Lordship's information, but without success, an exact account of the present state of the French army: the result however of my inquiries is that the number of private soldiers is nearly the same as it was when Mr de Narbonne gave his statement to the Assembly, that is to say that there are still fifty thousand deficient, for although a considerable number of recruits have been obtained, that number has been counterbalanced by desertion. The proportion of officers that have quitted their regiments is still greater. All the four armies are extremely ill provided. The regiment of Royal Allemand, cavalry, except seven men, has joined the Austrians. The regiment of Saxe, Hussars, had set them the example, but 92 of the latter have returned with 88 horses. Many of the men and the officers of the regiment of Berchini have also quitted France. Nobody can be surprized at Mr de Riccé's resignation, who has read his account of the insurrection in the camp of Tiercelet printed in the Supplement No. 3 of the *Gazette Universelle*, which I sent to your Lordship by last Monday's post.

Mr de Luckner went on Monday to Valenciennes, he has not, I believe, been able with the splendid and singular offer of serving as his Aide de Camp, to persuade Mr de Rochambeau to remain in command, but it is supposed that he will immediately conduct a second attack against Mons.

The Comte de Goltz has received orders to quit this court without taking leave, and he intends to accompany Mr de Blumendorf out of France in the beginning of the next week. The Russian Chargé d'Affaires has also received orders to leave this court.

Mr Bertrand, the late Minister of the Marine has entered a prosecution against Carra the journalist for having asserted at a meeting of the Jacobins that he is a member of the Austrian Committee which meets at the Thuilleries. In order to encourage the belief of this pretended Committee, an invitation was sent to Mr Renaud de St Jean d'Angely to meet Mr Malouet and Mr Bertrand at the Princesse de Lamballe's apartment in the Thuilleries, at a time however when the princess happened to be in the country. Two men who were haranguing the group in the Palais Royal against the Royal Family, being carried before a Justice of the Peace, produced their tickets for admission to the club of the Jacobins, in order to prove their integrity, but, this not satisfying the justice, he ordered them to be uncloathed, and their shoulders betrayed marks that they had been whipt and branded.

In order to render less rapid the consumption of the 300,000,000 lately decreed, and which is already reduced to 187,000,000, the Assembly has decreed that the *Créances exigibles* not amounting to more than 10,000 livres shall be paid in assignats, the rest in *Quittances de finance,* bearing an interest of 4 per cent.

Paris, *May 25th*, 1792.

I have presented His Majesty's letter to the Most Christian King in the usual form.

It appears that the reason why Mr de Luckner has not yet made his projected attack upon Mons, is the total impossibility of Mr de la Fayette's co-operation (without which such an attack would be hazarding another defeat to little purpose) owing to the miserable state of his army in every respect.

Mr de Rochambeau and his son arrived here last Tuesday; the Maréchal, in public conversation attributes his own resignation to his infirm state of health, and in general condemns the conduct of those officers who have resigned since the affairs of Mons and Tournay, and he expresses a wish that his son would return to his post.

Among the many officers who have resigned I should mention to your Lordship the son of the Duke of Crillon.

The army in the south under the command of Mr de Montesquiou is to form three camps, one near Lyons, another at Barraux, near the fort of Ecluse, and the third on the Var. That army is in the same state as the others on the frontiers, in want of everything. The Minister has been obliged to acknowledge a *déficit* of 2000 men in the Artillery. The Minister of Justice has informed the Assembly that the *brigands* of Avignon have fled from that city and *que tout est rentré sous l'empire de la loi;* a weak empire where the most flagrant crimes are suffered to pass unpunished, and where magistrates are sent to prison for daring to do their duty. The Justice of Peace la Rivière having proceeded in a regular course of justice against the libellous authors of the report of a pretended Austrian Committee has been sent to the prison of Orleans, and is to be tried by the High National Court for having summoned three members of the National Assembly to appear before him. Messieurs Gensonné and Brissot undertook upon that occasion to prove to the Assembly the existence of an Austrian Committee, and that Mr de Montmorin and Mr Bertrand deserved to be tried for high treason; for the force of their arguments and the clearness of their proof, I must refer your Lordship to the Wednesday's debate in the Logographe of this day. It is probable that Mr Brissot will not succeed in this attempt of sending more Ministers to Orleans, especially since Mr Duranton has, inadvertently I believe, rendered himself liable to accompany the Ex-ministers, by having countersigned His Most Christian Majesty's letter to the Assembly upon that occasion. Mr le Cointre, a member of the *Comité de Surveillance,* having of his own accord written to the Municipality of Béfort, in the name of that Committee, to stop and search some Swiss soldiers, who were returning with passports to their own country, has been ordered by the Assembly to pass three days in the prison of the Abbey of St Germain, as a punishment for this infraction of the Constitution, a mere shew of justice.

The deportation of Catholic Priests who shall refuse the civic oath, has been decreed by the Assembly as a measure of police.

The premium of fifty livres per tun, which was granted by a Decree of the Constitutional Assembly to foreign whale-fishers in order to encourage the Nantucket people, is now extended to French southern and northern whale-fishers.

Paris, *June 1st,* 1792.

In order to impress into the minds of the people an apprehension of imminent danger to the State, occasioned by the machinations of the pretended Austrian Committee, and, by that means, of effecting the destruction of the King's Guard, the National Assembly voted itself permanent last Monday, and has continued in that state. The Assemblies of the department and Municipality, and the still more efficient Assembly of the Jacobins have followed its example.

The accusation against Mr de Montmorin and Mr de Bertrand, having at least for the moment failed of its success, the battery has been turned against another quarter; the next object was the disbanding of the King's Guard. From the first formation of that body a natural jealousy has subsisted between it and the National Guard, which has been industriously fomented, and the indiscreet conversation of some of the young men, who have been admitted into it, has tended to excite the minds of the populace against it. These circumstances and the prevailing influence of the Jacobins, has induced the National Assembly to decree that the King's Guard should be disbanded, and Mr de Brissac impeached and sent to Orleans. This Decree immediately received the Royal sanction, and has of course been put into execution. Upon the whole this measure has been approved of, but not by a large majority, by the National Guard, who have again the honor, together with the Swiss, of guarding the Royal Family in the interior of the Palace, but the service of the Swiss will probably be but temporary, every occasion is taken to affect the public mind against them. A drunken conversation at an alehouse has been quoted and made the most of for that purpose; the white predominated over the blue and red in their cockades, but it is not true that they were entirely white. Another event, for the purpose of giving credit to the belief of an Austrian Committee, was brought before the Assembly, the burning of thirty large bales of papers at the manufactory at Sèves, which proved to be no more than an awkward mode of destroying printed copies of an infamous publication.

To the Princess de Vandémont's journey to England I attribute the absurd report of Mr de Montmorin being gone there in company with the Princess de Lamballe.

It appears to be the mutual wish of the King of Hungary and this Government, that no letters of marque and reprisal should be granted.

The miserable state of the army of this country exceeds all belief. In order to increase the number of soldiers, it has been proposed by the Minister that every department should raise one thousand men to receive a pay of three sous per diem and to be ready when required. They embrace the offers of any foreign officer who is willing to serve, and in fact they are absolutely reduced to this measure from the great scarcity of French officers who remain.

I received a visit the other day from the Vicomte de Noailles who informed me that His Most Christian Majesty having accepted his resignation, he had determined to go to England, but with no other motive than that of living in a country whose Constitution and Government he admired, when it was impossible, from his peculiar political situation that he could continue in his own country, and he assured me in the most positive terms that he has, and would continue to have, no political connection with any of his countrymen who may be supposed to have views adverse to the present Government in England. According to his own account, the Maréchal de Luckner will find it difficult, if not impossible to introduce discipline among his soldiers; their indecent behaviour to an English woman of the name of Nash has given a second proof of the degree of insubordination to which they are reduced. I am informed by him that an account of that affair will be sent to your Lordship.

By the resignation of the Vicomte de Noailles, it is agreed by those who do not think favourably of his political conduct, that the army has lost an able officer, and that his place will not be sufficiently supplied by the Duke of Orleans, who is gone to join the army having beforehand written to the Minister of the Marine to offer his services to his country in his naval capacity: of this I was informed by Mr Dumouriez who at the same time said, that he had prevailed upon him to delay his journey to Valenciennes for some days, having suggested that it might be proper to know Mr de Luckner's opinion upon that subject; but I believe the journey was undertaken before the arrival of the Maréchal's opinion.

A plan of a strong police is in agitation and of a sort of dictatorial power to be given to Mr Péthion and the Comité de Surveillance.

The Polish Minister at this court is gone to Geneva, and from thence he is to proceed to Genoa, in order to negotiate a loan at those places, the security for which are to be the Starosties.

The permanence of the National Assembly has ceased, and the capital is again tranquil.

———

Paris, *June 8th*, 1792.

I inclose a copy of a letter from Mr Dumouriez to me concerning the 217 French negroes which were landed by Captain Colmin at English Key, and inclosing a copy of an *Arrêté* of the Colonial Assembly of St Domingo upon that subject.

Mr Dumouriez was upon the point of resigning at the end of the last week, but, finding that all parties were desirous that he should continue for the present in office, and the responsibility for the six millions being no longer imposed upon him he has consented to remain in the Ministry. His projects however of offensive war continue to be frustrated by the contrary opinion of Mr de la Fayette, and the impossibility of either that General's army or that of Mr de Luckner being, for some time in a condition to act offensively. It is calculated that the army of the Maréchal will consist of between fifty and sixty thousand men, and may be fit for action by the twenty-fifth of this month. Although that army is well disposed towards the Duke of Orleans he is expected at Paris. The disposition of the other army is probably not so favourable to him if one may judge from the well known sentiments of Mr de la Fayette and Mr Gouvion. Mr de Custine will command the army in Alsace.

The frivolousness and absurdity of the last denunciations in the National Assembly have thrown a ridicule upon that mode of attacking the Feuillants: a more serious and formidable measure is now in agitation. Preparations are making to convey in case of necessity His Most Christian Majesty and the Assembly to the banks of the Loire, if not timely prevented by the alarms of the proprietors in the capital. Having disbanded the King's Guards which they may hereafter have occasion to discover is not tantamount to dispersing them, their next plan is to controul the National Guards by a superior force, and for that purpose the Assembly has decreed an augmentation to the army of twenty thousand men to be raised in all the Cantons of the kingdom, and to be assembled at Paris on the fourteenth of July. The National Guard has taken the alarm, and the Assembly will possibly be obliged to repeal this decree. The army in general, I understand, is dissatisfied at His Most Christian Majesty having given his sanction to the decree which disbanded his Guard.

The Dutch patriots are to raise a body of between four and five thousand men; their uniform, except that of the Chasseurs and Sapeurs, is to be black turned up with light blue, owing to the scarcity of white and coloured cloth. Mr Abbema who is the richest man among them, although nearly equalled in that respect by Mr de Witt undertakes to provide the money for this purpose.

Mr Yriarté conversed the other day for some time with considerable earnestness with Monsieur Dumouriez, but I have seen no other symptoms of a Spanish mediation. Mr Dumouriez however takes every opportunity to boast of the frankness which exists in his correspondence with Mr D'Aranda. A son of Doctor Priestley, who is come here to be naturalized has been received to-day with great applause, by the National Assembly.

PARIS, *June 15th*, 1792.

A change has taken place in the Ministry of this country, which though it may tend in some measure to unite the Jacobins may ultimately prove their destruction.

Messrs Rolland, Servan and Clavière have been dismissed from His Most Christian Majesty's council. Mr Dumouriez succeeds Mr Servan in the War Department, and he is to be succeeded in that of Foreign Affairs by Mr de Naillac, a gentleman who has lately travelled in Spain, and who was formerly employed in the diplomatic line at Vienna, he is at present the French Minister to the Duke of Deux-Ponts. Mr Mourgues formerly *Directeur des Travaux* at Cherbourg is appointed to the Home Department: that of the Finances remains vacant.

I informed your Lordship in my last dispatch that Mr Dumouriez after having hesitated for some time, had determined to continue in office. When he talked of resigning his plan appears to have been to have joined the army, if he could have obtained the permission of the Assembly, and from thence to have sent an account of the wretched condition of the army and the defenceless state of the frontiers, which would have had more effect than the *Mémoire sur le Département de la Guerre*, which he read to the Assembly upon his acceptance of that department. I am therefore induced to believe that a notion, that without his presence, energy would be wanting and resolution fail, and consequently the dismission of the three Ministers, which has since been effected, might not have taken place, confirmed him to the metropolis.

The blow is now struck, but it is to be doubted that he will be able to maintain his ground. He relies however upon the impression which the public will receive from the infamous conduct of his three greatest enemies, the lately dismist Ministers and their adherents, and, considering his own account of the army, he certainly expects more from negotiation, than from the sword, and I can easily believe that his dispatches from Madrid have in a great measure prompted him to undertake a task, similar and equally difficult to that of clearing the Augean Stable. His activity and his courage are equally extraordinary.

On Tuesday last, an hour after the change in the Ministry was resolved upon, but of which I was at that time ignorant, in the course of a private conversation, he desired me to inform your Lordship, that if Mr de Talleyrand's mission was in any manner disagreeable to His Majesty or his Ministers, he should be recalled; this I promised to do, but I avoided all comments upon the subject.

Against Mr Rolland and Mr Servan he means to prove the plan of carrying off His Most Christian Majesty to the southern provinces, and in addition to that, against Mr Clavière he has a most infamous tale to unfold with regard to a plan of employing the six millions of secret service money for his private use. Mr Clavière having a million in the French funds, which he had borrowed at Genoa was a great promoter of the scheme of the assignats in order to occasion a temporary rise in the funds: in this he succeeded, but the exchange with foreign countries fell so low that his profit in the rise of stocks was not equal to the loss by the exchange, it was therefore necessary to raise the latter before he could pay his debt at Genoa. The means of his friend Mr Bidermann being nearly exhausted by this sort of *agiotage*, he employed as much as he could venture of public money, he next insisted that he should have the use of the six millions of secret service money till called for by Mr Dumouriez; but the latter minister, being apprized that Mr Bidermann had very lately placed that sum in the East India Funds, discovered the plan and resisted, in consequence of which the house of Bidermann is on the brink of bankruptcy. A failure of still greater consequence is likely to take place, the house of Tourton and Ravel.

The déficit for this month, for one is naturally led from private to public bankruptcy, is above thirteen millions; the whole to be paid by the *Caisse de l'extraordinaire* is fifty-three millions. It is calculated that of twenty-four hundred millions, already *en création* only one hundred will remain for the expences of the next month.

The suppression of casual feudal rights without indemnification unless proved to be a concession in virtue of a *titre primitif* has been decreed by the Assembly; a violation of property to the amount of six hundred millions.

The Duke of Orleans is returned to his country seat. The loss of Mr Gouvion in the late skirmish is deservedly lamented, by the movements of both armies a general engagement may be expected sooner than the time I mentioned to your Lordship last week.

Paris, *June 18th*, 1792.

I omitted, in my last dispatch, to inform your Lordship that Mr Morris has delivered his credentials to His Most Christian Majesty as Minister Plenipotentiary from the United States.

A new change has taken place in the Ministry: Mr Dumouriez having resigned, is succeeded in the War Department by Mr la Jarre formerly Aide de Camp to Mr la Fayette and Adjutant-General in the National Guards of Paris; the Department for Foreign Affairs is given to Mr Chambonas formerly mayor of Sens and commandant of this department: Mr d'Ormesson, formerly Contrôleur General has the *Département des Contributions.*

Paris, *June* 22nd, 1792.

The resignation of Mr Dumouriez is to be attributed to His Most Christian Majesty's refusal to sanction the decree relative to the transportation of the clergy who refuse to take the oaths, and that which had been proposed by Mr Servan for raising twenty thousand men: that minister having judged that the sanction of those decrees was absolutely necessary in order to preserve sufficient popularity to carry on the government. His successor in office is, like him, a member of the Jacobin club, but, like him also, he is intent on its destruction.

The Minister of the War Department is devoted to Mr de la Fayette. I misinformed your Lordship with regard to that of the finances; that department is given to Mr Beaulieu, one of the *Commissaires de Comptabilité,* motives of prudence having prevented the appointment of Mr d'Ormesson to that office, and, in that light, his having been a member of administration during the former Government was a sufficient reason. Mr Terrier de Monciel, President of the Department of Jura, and connected with the Lameths, is Minister of the Interior. Mr Duranthon and Mr la Coste remain for the present. Upon the whole it is to be expected that the measures of the new administration will be according to the principles of the Feuillants.

The late attempt[1] of the Jacobins to intimidate His Most Christian Majesty has failed entirely and has served only to impress more strongly on the minds of those who wish for order and good government an abhorrence of their principles and practices. The majesty of the throne was sullied, but it gave the King a

---

[1] The attack on the Tuileries of June 20, 1792.

happy opportunity of displaying an extraordinary degree of calmness and courage, which may be of infinite service. The circumstance of his having applied the hand of a grenadier to his heart, saying "feel here if there are any signs of fear" is perfectly true.

As your Lordship will see in the Logographe the several accounts which the deputies gave the National Assembly of the transactions in the palace, I shall not enter into a detail of them, I shall, however, inform your Lordship of all the particulars not mentioned by them, which have come to my knowledge. The King, finding the mob determined to force the door of the antechamber of his apartment, ordered his attendants to withdraw, and placed himself in the recess of one of the windows, where, attended by a few grenadiers, he suffered the mob to approach him, accepted from them a red cap with tricolor ribands, which he wore during the whole time that they remained in the palace, and, upon their expressing a wish that he should drink to the health of the nation, His Majesty condescended to comply with their request, and drunk the remains of some wine in a cup, out of which a grenadier had previously drunk. During this time the Queen and the Dauphin with their attendants were in the council chamber guarded by a table from the too near approach of the mob. It is singular considering that the populace was in every part of the royal apartment except the King's private bedchamber, that no other mischief should have been done except taking away the locks, and breaking the panels of the doors.

The admission of the mob is entirely to be attributed to the infamous conduct of the municipal officers: the commander of the National Guard had in his pocket an order from the administrators of the department to oppose force by force, but the orders of the Municipality were wanting. A dreadful responsibility would have awaited Mr Péthion had any unfortunate event taken place. Courtray being taken, it is imagined that the Maréchal de Luckner's next object will be Ghent.

The command of the army in Alsace was intended to have been given to Mr de Biron, not to Mr de Custine, although that was generally believed, but it may be doubted whether the present ministry will place that command in the hands of an intimate friend of the Duke of Orleans.

Mr de la Fayette after the letters which he has written to the King and to the National Assembly, an exact printed copy of which I enclose, may be said to have past the Rubicon. The letters which your Lordship will see in the Logographe from Mr la Morliere and Mr de Broglio, shew that the same sentiments actuated the officers of the army in Alsace: it remains to be seen what line of conduct Mr de Luckner will take, but it is scarcely possible to suppose that he will support the Jacobin faction.

I have discovered the reason why I could not decipher your Lordship's dispatch No. 22; the sixth octavo edition was consulted instead of the ninth which is the one I received from your Lordship. With regard to any apprehensions that may be entertained in Holland respecting the legion of Dutch patriots, so called because the officers are of that country, and which is not yet formed, I conceive them to be perfectly ill-founded. The measure seems to have been adopted by the French Government, simply as a means of raising four-thousand two-hundred and fifty men. So far from the legion being raised entirely at the expence of the Dutch, as was reported, I find that Mr Dumouriez advanced seven hundred thousand livres for that purpose out of the six millions of secret service money. It is remarkable that, of those six millions, only nineteen hundred thousand have been expended, twelve hundred thousand soon after the decree and seven hundred thousand more, just before Mr Dumouriez's resignation.

With regard to the Dutch legion, I understand that recruits are too scarce, for it to be in any considerable forwardness. It is to be commanded by the man who attempted to defend Amsterdam against the army of the Duke of Brunswick, which circumstance alone will account for the apprehensions entertained in Holland.

Paris, *June 29th*, 1792.

In consequence of your Lordship's instructions I delivered a letter last Tuesday to Mr Chambonas, a copy of which I enclose. I had again mentioned the subject to Mr Dumouriez a few days before he left the ministry and I had received a promise from him that he would press Mr Vergniaud to make the report without any further delay. I have reason to believe that if a reward had been promised to the members of the committee, it would have been made before this time.

Considering the sentiments exprest by Mr de la Fayette in his letters to His Most Christian Majesty and to the National Assembly, your Lordship will not be much surprized to hear that he appeared yesterday before the Assembly to acknowledge himself the author of the letters and to declare his opinion and that of his army with regard to the transactions of the 20th at the Thuilleries. His speech which was totally destitute of that eloquence which excites a popular assembly, had that effect which his friends had expected, that of intimidating the Jacobin party.

Among the many addresses which have arrived from the administrations of departments in the neighbourhood but principally to the north of Paris declaring their abhorrence of the proceedings of the 20th and their readiness to support the government and constitution against factions, the most conspicuous is that of the Somme which offers the support of two hundred battalions of National Guards. By observing the dispositions of the several parts of the kingdom, one is induced to allot a republican form of government to that half of it which lies south of the Loire and a monarchical one to the other half.

His Most Christian Majesty has proposed to the Assembly to raise forty two battalions of national volunteers in order to form a camp between Paris and the frontiers, in the neighbourhood of Soissons, but the committee to which that proposal was referred, has not yet made its report upon the subject.

By a report of the extraordinary committee of twelve, it appears that the *déficit* in the regular troops is only near twenty seven thousand, but one may be allowed to doubt the accuracy of that calculation.

From information which I have since obtained I must retract my opinion that apprehensions entertained in Holland with regard to the Dutch legion are *perfectly* ill-founded. It was originally to have consisted of four thousand two hundred and fifty men but it is now to be augmented to six thousand. Your Lordship may rely upon the authenticity of the inclosed paper No. 1 as it has been drawn up by Mr Abema himself, the other I have also obtained from good authority.

Mr de Valence, who was sent here by Mr de Luckner to desire an additional force of ten thousand men, is returned to the army but with what answer it is not known.

The Minister of the War Department and Mr de la Fayette had a long audience of His Most Christian Majesty before the Levée this morning, since which that Minister has informed the Assembly, that he has received a letter from Mr Luckner dated the 26th which from motives of prudence he wishes to communicate to a committee rather than to the Assembly. He at the same time read a letter from that general to His Most Christian Majesty expressive of the indignation which he and his army felt at the proceedings of the twentieth, and their admiration of His Majesty's courage.

Give me leave, my Lord to take this opportunity of mentioning what I am ashamed to have omitted in my last dispatch, but which was owing to my not being absolutely certain of the fact, the magnanimity of Madame Elizabeth who did not quit her brother's side for an instant during the whole of that infamous evening, and whose presence and dignified behaviour contributed essentially to keep the populace in awe. The dialogue which your Lordship has seen between His Most Christian Majesty and the Mayor of Paris past nearly as it is expressed in the Gazette Universelle.

Since Mr de la Fayette has left his army an engagement has taken place, in which according to the account read to the Assembly the French have taken eighty three prisoners, among which are five officers, but the French accounts are apt to be so erroneous that I feel always ashamed of writing them to your Lordship.

Although we enjoy perfect tranquillity in this capital at present, we have reason to doubt the continuance of it, for it is certain that the members of the mother club have sent pressing invitations to the affiliated members, to assist at the fête on the fourteenth of July.

The Assembly takes every possible measure to oblige the Ministers to send to the frontiers, before that period, the three regiments of regulars which are here at present.

PARIS, *July 6th*, 1792.

We are at the eve of a great crisis. The two contending parties must soon make the experiment which has the greatest force: in the mean time both sides shew signs of fear. His Most Christian Majesty expects the event with that courage which religion is known to inspire, but his Ministers seem to act without any well concerted or fixed plan. Mr de la Fayette's conduct during his stay in Paris was not sufficiently bold and energetic to affect the Jacobins with that degree of fear which it was intended to have produced, and it has only served to make them more active in sending for the assistance of their friends from all parts of the kingdom. Those friends are accordingly arriving from all quarters, from Marseilles, from Bordeaux, from Brest, and their arrival is legalized by a decree of the National Assembly which has received the royal sanction. Their stay in Paris according to that decree, for which I refer your Lordship to the Logographe No. 276 is indeed to be of short duration, but it will be long enough to answer any sinister purpose. On the other hand it may be doubted that Mr de la Fayette will be able, if he should think it necessary, to bring his army to the assistance of the metropolis. In this awful state of suspense, the inhabitants of Paris are waiting for the celebration of the fourteenth, at which the King and the National Assembly will assist. For my own part having the honour to represent a King universally revered and beloved, I consider myself in as little danger as it is possible to be in the anarchical state of this country: there are however members of the diplomatic body, who, not having the same cause for security, exprest to me yesterday a desire that we should continue assembled together in one house during the time of danger. My answer, which I hope your Lordship will approve, was that I should remain at my post which I considered to be my own house, or the Palace of the Thuilleries, at the time when His Most Christian Majesty receives the foreign ministers, and in fact to do otherwise would be insulting unnecessarily the French nation as well as acting contrary to the dignity of that nation whose sovereign I have the honor to represent at this court.

Your Lordship will observe that the Assembly has past a decree, which subjects the *état major* of all the corps of National Guards belonging to towns containing 50,000 souls or upwards to be re-elected, by which means the prevailing party in the Assembly hope to get rid of the present officers of the National Guard, at least of the greater number who are of the Feuillant party. Another decree which has been made this week respecting the mode of declaring that the country is in danger is also aimed against the Feuillants.

Mr de Joly, formerly *Secrétaire de la Commune* and lately appointed Secretary of the Council has succeeded Mr Duranthon as Minister of Justice.

The Minister of Foreign Affairs has notified this day to the Assembly the march of the Prussian troops.

I enclose a copy of a letter which I have received from Mr Chambonas relative to Tobago together with a copy of another from that minister to Mr Koch President of the Diplomatic Committee.

PARIS, *July* 13*th*, 1792.

I congratulate your Lordship most sincerely upon the very satisfactory intelligence which has been received from the East Indies.

Nobody was the dupe of the feigned coalition which served only to amuse the spectators who were present last Saturday during that farcical proceeding in the National Assembly. Perhaps I should except His Most Christian Majesty, the goodness of whose heart leads him to expect good from quarters and by means totally inadequate.

'The solemn declaration of the Assembly that the country is

in danger has had very little effect at least in the metropolis where the minds of the inhabitants are entirely occupied with providing lodgings for the *Fédérés* as they improperly call those who are arriving for the approaching ceremony, and with the *arrêté* of the administration of the department which has suspended the Mayor and *Procureur de la Commune* on account of their improper conduct with regard to the proceedings on the twentieth of last month. This sentence after some days' consideration has been confirmed by the King, and to-day the National Assembly has taken off the suspension of Mr Péthion, and has postponed their decision on Mr Manuda until they shall have heard his defence.

The number of people from the provinces as yet arrived, is not so great as was expected; great care is taken to provide accommodation for them by the Jacobins, lest they should be influenced by the Feuillants. Mr de Narbonne and indeed almost all the principal general officers in the armies of the Maréchal de Luckner and Mr de la Fayette are here.

The ceremony in the *Champ de Mars* will be similar to that at the federation in the year 1790. The Assembly will walk in procession, but the King will go in his carriage.

I refer to the Logographe of this day for the minister's report on the state of the nation: that part of it respecting the armies is not to be relied upon. They are increasing that of the Rhine which will be again commanded by the Maréchal de Luckner and diminishing the others. Twenty battalions are to be sent to it from the southern army, which will weaken it so as to render it almost useless. It will still however be sufficiently strong to take the Castle of Bannes in the Department of the Ardêche which is occupied by a Mr Saillant with a body of near two thousand aristocrates the remains of the camp of Jalès.

The plan of raising a Dutch legion has been communicated to the Assembly, but the committees to which it was referred, have not yet made their report upon it. The *déficit* for the last month, including everything, is in the usual proportion above fifty millions.

All the ministers resigned last Tuesday. They however

continue in office till His Most Christian Majesty can fix upon a new ministry.

Mr de Sémonville, it is said, will be appointed Ambassador to the Porte.

Paris, *July* 20*th*, 1792.

I have communicated to Mr Chambonas the papers which your Lordship has sent to me in justification of the conduct of the captain of the Nemesis and I make no doubt that the French Minister will see that affair in its true light.

Your Lordship's note to Mr Chauvelin in answer to his of the 18th of June has been communicated to the National Assembly, it has had the effect of rendering prevalent a notion that His Majesty is willing to act as mediator: an event generally wished for, since all parties are sensible of the impossibility of resisting the combined forces of the Emperor and the King of Prussia.

From a want of resolution on one part and from a regularly conducted system on the other, the situation of His Most Christian Majesty becomes daily more and more perilous. I have reason to believe, that the resignation of the present ministers, is to be attributed, when it came to the point, to a refusal to retreat from Paris. Notwithstanding which, from the present posture of affairs, I shall not be surprized if I have to inform your Lordship of His Most Christian Majesty's arrival at Rouen where he will find a great majority of the inhabitants ready to support his cause.

The Jacobins finding that the three regiments of regular troops in this town, were not sufficiently indisciplined to be relied upon by them, have contrived that they should be sent to the frontiers. There remains one regiment of Swiss which it will be difficult to dispose of in the same manner, owing to the treaty with the cantons, and to the sentiments of the private soldiers, as well as of the officers of that regiment.

The ministers who have resigned except Mr Terrier de Monciel, continue to act, as nobody has yet been found to supply their places; that minister having absolutely refused to act any longer, the Minister of Justice transacts also the business of his department *pr. interim.*

Owing to French levity and impatience, Mr de Saillant has met with an untimely end having neither fallen in the field nor suffered to sustain a regular trial. Your Lordship will see the details of this affair in the Logographe. By a decree of the Assembly, a number of National Guards is to be raised sufficient to make the army amount to four hundred and forty or fifty thousand men: the execution of this decree will meet with innumerable difficulties. Of three thousand *fédérés* who are arrived here, only two thousand have entered their names for the camp at Soissons.

Paul Jones died here on Wednesday night of a dropsy in his breast.

Many, if not all, of the administrators of this deqartment have resigned.

The Maréchal de Luckner is gone or is immediately going to join his army at Metz. Mr de la Fayette is to command the northern army and Mr de Biron that of Alsace.

I cannot conclude without expressing to your Lordship my happiness that His Majesty should have approved of my conduct with regard to the proposition that was made to me by some of the diplomatic body.

Paris, *July 27th*, 1792.

I inclose for your Lordship's information a copy of a letter to me from Mr de Bonchage, the new Minister of the Marine, and also for Foreign Affairs per interim.

Mr Champion is appointed to the Interior and Mr d'Abancourt to the War Department.

The measure employed by the generals who command in Alsace for increasing their army by repuiring from the several departments in their neighbourhood a considerable reinforcement of National Guards has been approved of by the Assembly and adopted as a means of reinforcing the other armies. In consequence of which and considering that the ministers had been prevailed upon to detatch only ten instead of twenty battalions from his army, Mr de Montesquiou, for whose report I refer your Lordship to the Logographe No. 299, returns to-day to the south. The committee of twenty-one before whom that general was examined, had agreed to report a project of a decree to declare that the Crown was forfeited, but, upon his assuring them, that not only every officer but every soldier would oppose them, they desisted: this sufficiently accounts for the speech made by Mr Brissot yesterday in the Assembly. It does not however follow that from the abortion of this scheme, His Most Christian Majesty is to be considered in a less dangerous situation than formerly; I rather fear the contrary. I understand that notwithstanding the opinion of his friends, at least of many of them, His Majesty is determined to remain at Paris. A fresh insult was offered to him on Saturday night, by the Assembly decreeing that a part of the garden of the Thuilleries adjoining to the Hall of the Assembly, and which is called *la Terrace des Feuillants*, from the neighbouring church, belongs to the nation, and is subject to the police of the Assembly. By this means the garden is open to all those whom the Assembly may choose to admit, unless a wall or an iron-rail be erected to separate the royal from the national part of the garden.

Between two and three thousand *Fédérés* are gone to the camp at Soissons, but many still remain in the capital and an additional number is expected, especially from Marseilles: those from Brest arrived yesterday, and after having partaken of what they choose to call a fraternal *fête-civique* on the ruins of the Bastille, they seized upon some canon in a neighbouring church and were proceeding to the palace, but Mr Péthion and Mr Santerre, the leading man in the Faubourg St Antoine harangued the mob and dissuaded them from their wicked purpose.

Mr la Croix having yesterday read a private letter from England by which he was informed that a very considerable naval armament was begun there, the Assembly decreed that the Minister for Foreign Affairs should inform them of such of the particulars of this armament as were come to his knowledge;

and the necessity of immediately arming thirty ships of the line was mentioned. In the evening the minister communicated to the Assembly a dispatch from Mr Chauvelin which was referred to the committee, and at the same time informed them that there was no serious cause for alarm, since the English fleet of observation had provisions on board only for a fortnight. To-day Mr Rouger said that although he was too much convinced of the generosity of the English, to suppose that they intended a perfidious attack yet being informed that there were two fire ships in the English fleet, he should move for further information upon that subject from the Minister for Foreign Affairs.

The taking of Bavay by the Austrians, has considerably deranged the plans of the French generals as it will cut off the communication between Valenciennes and Maubeuge. At the moment when I was going to dispatch the messenger I was informed that there was a considerable disturbance in the garden of the Thuilleries, I accordingly delayed his departure till I could learn the particulars of it. It appears that Mr D'Epresménil was seen by the Fédérés walking on the *Terrace des Feuillants*. He was immediately surrounded by them and dragged from thence to the Palais Royal at which place and in his way thither he received many wounds from the mob who were armed with sabres and other weapons. With great difficulty the National Guard conveyed him to the Hôtel *du Tresor Royal* where he is at present well guarded, and it is hoped that his wounds are not mortal. The National Guard are all under arms and there is a strong guard at the Thuilleries. The Assemblies of the Sections are permanent, their permanence was yesterday declared legal by the National Assembly.

PARIS, *August 3rd*, 1792.

Since the cruel ill-treatment which Mr D'Epresménil experienced on the *Terrace des Feuillants* the populace who frequent that part of the garden of the Thuilleries have contented themselves with uttering imprecations against the royal family and those who are styled *aristocrates*: that they should have refrained from approaching the palace or even putting their feet on any other part of the garden which is separated from the terrace only by ribands which they themselves have placed there, is a singular circumstance, and carries the appearance of a sentiment worthy of a free people, but it may be accounted for on other principles: it being the interest of their leaders that they should not at this moment offer violence to the royal family. They may have had the good policy to form this silken separation, which strengthened by opinion is stronger than one of stone or iron, for whoever should venture to pass those limits would be regarded by the rest as an Austrian or an *aristocrate* and treated accordingly.

The ferocious disposition of the five hundred *Fédérés* from Marseilles was but too conspicuous on the very day of their arrival: Mr Du Lamel a young man of a good character, by trade an exchange broker, fell a victim to their barbarity. It will be well for this town if they can be prevailed upon to join the projected camp at Soissons, where there are about nine thousand men already arrived. It is to be commanded by Mr de Custine, under whom Mr Servan, the late minister, is to have a command.

The republican spirit of the south has shewn itself in a conspicuous manner in the *arrêtés* of the *Départment des Bouches du Rhone,* and of the municipalities of Marseilles and Aix which have ordered the public money of that department to be employed in raising six thousand men for the southern army instead of being sent to the national treasury: but the Assembly has interfered and informed them that they have more zeal far than knowledge of the constitution.

The National Assembly has decreed that five hundred and eighty thousand livres shall be allowed for carrying on the works at Cherbourg, which it appears to be their design to complete, so as not to be demolisht by the sea.

A fresh *création* of three hundred millions has been decreed without any debate, for which they have mortgaged some religious houses not formerly included, the bishops' palaces, and scattered parts of the forest lands.

The Duke of Brunswick's declaration, which has not been officially notified, has produced very little sensation here. The *aristocrates* are dissatisfied with it, and the *démocrates* affect to despise it.

We have reports from the northern army that many Austrians have deserted and come over to them, and they assert that the evacuation of Bavay was rendered necessary by a plan of a desertion of three thousand men being discovered by the Austrian general. These reports serve to keep up the spirits of the Jacobins.

Mr Bigot de Sainte Croix, the late minister at Coblence and formerly at Stockholm, has, after mature deliberation, accepted the Department for Foreign Affairs. He is esteemed a man of abilities, of information, and what is essential at present of courage.

At the end of this day's Logographe, your Lordship will see a curious letter from the Duke of Orleans to the Assembly, in which he complains that this country will probably cease to be benefited by his services.

In the inclosed journal of this evening your Lordship will see that the National Assembly has refused to order the printing of a letter from His Most Christian Majesty, and that it has sent to the examination of a committee a petition presented by the Mayor and Common Council of Paris in the name of the forty eight sections for the King's destitution.

Quo tanta dementia cives!

Paris, *August 4th*, 1792.

In the present extremely precarious state of the royal family, I have been desired to express to the Minister of Foreign Affairs the sentiments of His Majesty with regard to the proceedings of the National Assembly and the Municipality and sections of Paris derogatory to and attacking the safety of Their Most Christian Majesties. I have declined to act in this business till I can receive instructions from your Lordship. The person of Her Most Christian Majesty is certainly in imminent danger. On Thursday the extraordinary committee is to make its report upon the King's destitution. I wish therefore to receive your Lordship's instructions as soon as possible.

Paris, *August 12th*, 1792.

Staley arrived this morning with your Lordship's dispatch No. 27.

The inclosed letters will prove my anxiety to dispatch a messenger with an account of the late proceedings and they will at the same time shew your Lordship the cause of the delay.

The Assembly having on Wednesday last acquitted Mr de la Fayette of the several charges which had determined their *Commission extraordinaire* to propose a decree of impeachment against him, gave rise to a considerable discontent among the people. This disposition which first appeared by threats and acts of violence against the members who had voted in favor of the general continued during the following day, when in the evening they learnt that the great question of His Most Christian Majesty's deposition fixed for Thursday, had scarcely been mentioned. The numbers assembled in the Faubourg St Antoine increased considerably during the night which past in the midst of the alarm occasioned by the beating of the drums and the sound of the *tocsin*, but without any accident.

The greatest part of the regiment of the Swiss Guards, and a considerable body of National Guards were placed at the Palace of the Thuilleries.

Early on Friday morning, the people having first taken possession of the arsenal moved towards the Thuilleries with a train of artillery: on their road they put to death several persons who had formed a false patrole. At ten o'clock the danger being imminent, the King with the royal family left the palace, and crossing the garden by the advice of the members of the department, took refuge in the National Assembly, in a room adjoining to which they have continued ever since. A short time after the action began between the people and the Swiss, who were left to guard the palace; the

National Guards having either retired or gone over to the other side, a very sharp fire was kept up for near twenty minutes, when the Swiss were overpower'd and almost all killed at their posts or in their flight: the number of killed on both sides is not yet known, but cannot be less than fifteen hundred: several persons of distinction, among whom was Mr de Clermont Tonnerre were put to death in different parts of the town : the furniture of the palace was destroyed by the people, and the out-buildings adjoining to it are all burnt to the ground. The Assembly having first declared itself permanent, decreed, in the course of the day, that the executive power was withdrawn from the King, that his ministers had lost the confidence of the nation and that, for the present, the government should be trusted to a ministry named by themselves: that the primary assemblies should be convened for the twenty-sixth of this month, to which all *citoyens* should be admitted without distinction of rank or property in order to appoint a national convention to meet at Paris on the twentieth of September to decide ultimately upon the forfeiture of the Crown and the mode of establishing an executive power : that His Most Christian Majesty should be lodged in some place of safety and that the civil list should no longer be continued.

The Assembly has named for Ministers, Mr Danton *pour la Justice*, Mr le Brun *pour les Affaires Étrangères*, Mr Monge *pour la Marine*, Mr Servan *pour la Guerre*, Mr Clavière *pour les Contributions*, and Mr Roland *pour l'Interieur*. Commissioners have also been named by the Assembly and sent to the several armies with very extensive powers. The people of Paris on their side have named a new Common Council which has already broke the municipality except Messrs Péthion and Manuel.

Mr Mandat the late commander of the National Guard is I believe put to death, and they have given his place to Mr Santerre.

The people having begun to destroy the statues of Louis XIV and Louis XV, the Assembly by a decree ordered all the statues of Kings to be taken down.

The Assembly has ordered a Court Martial to be formed to

inquire into the conduct of the few remaining Swiss officers and soldiers and has issued a decree of impeachment against Mr D'Abancourt, the late Minister of the War Department, for not having removed the Swiss soldiers from the capital.

Mr Dundas to Lord Gower.

Whitehall, August 17th, 1792.

In the absence of Lord Grenville, I have received and laid before the King your Excellency's dispatch No. 40 *by Morley.*

His Majesty learns with the deepest concern the heighth to which the distractions in Paris have been carried and the deplorable consequences to which they have led, which are doubly affecting to His Majesty from the regard which His Majesty invariably feels for the persons of Their Most Christian Majesties, and his interest in their welfare, as well as from the wishes which he forms for the tranquillity and prosperity of a kingdom with which he is in amity.

Under the present circumstances as it appears that the exercise of the executive power has been withdrawn from His Most Christian Majesty, the credential under which your Excellency has hitherto acted can be no longer available: and His Majesty judges it proper, on this account, as well as most conformable to the principles of neutrality which His Majesty has hitherto observed, that you should no longer remain in Paris. It is therefore His Majesty's pleasure that you should quit it, and repair to England, as soon as you conveniently can, after procuring the necessary passports.

In any conversation you may have occasion to hold previous to your departure you will take care to make your language conformable to the sentiments which are now conveyed to you: and you will particularly take every opportunity of expressing that, while His Majesty intends strictly to adhere to the principles of neutrality in respect to the settlement of the internal government of France, he at the same time considers it as no deviation from those principles to manifest by all the means in his power, his solicitude for the personal situation of Their Most Christian Majesties, and their royal family; and he earnestly and anxiously hopes, that they will at least be secure from any acts of violence which could not fail to produce one universal sentiment of indignation through every country of Europe.

LORD GOWER TO LORD GRENVILLE.

PARIS, *August* 18*th*, 1792.

Your Lordship's instructions in your dispatch No. 27 were precisely such as I expected and desired to receive, but I thought it my duty to have the authority of such instructions before I could give a decided answer.

The inclosed newspapers will inform your Lordship, as fully as it is possible in the present circumstances, of the proceedings in this metropolis; I have only to add that Their Most Christian Majesties and the royal family are placed in the tower of the Temple, the only building in which the Municipality would answer for their security, and in order to render that still more secure, they are now forming a *fossé* round it.

It appears that the National Assembly waits to see what impression the papers discovered at the Tuileries and which the new commissioners will communicate to Mr de la Fayette may have upon his final plan of conduct.

I inclose the *procès verbal* of the proceedings at the English and Irish seminary and a letter to me upon that subject from the commissioners of the *Conseil Général de la Commune*.

Note from King George III.

WEYMOUTH, *August* 18*th*, 1792.
4.11 P.M.

The drafts to Lord Gower and Mr Lindsay transmitted to me by Mr Secretary Dundas, which were drawn up in consequence of a Cabinet meeting, have my fullest approbation, and I perfectly subscribe to his opinion, that the note delivered by Mr Chauvelin renders the measure the more necessary. I see no objection to the sending copies of them to him, with a note acknowledging the receipt of his note.

G. R.

Lord Gower to Lord Grenville.

PARIS, *August* 23*rd*, 1792.

Staley the messenger arrived here early on Monday morning with Mr Secretary Dundas's letter of the 17th inst. signifying his Majesty's pleasure that I should quit Paris and return to England as soon as the necessary passports could be procured. I lost no time in communicating the contents of the above dispatch to Mr Le Brun, the person appointed Minister for Foreign Affairs by the National Assembly, and he assured me that passes should be ready by the next day, Tuesday; I have however not yet received them.

On Tuesday last His Excellency the Chevalier Pisani, Ambassador from the Republic of Venice to the Most Christian King, set out from hence with his family on his journey to England: in a few minutes after his departure his carriages were surrounded by the people and he was forced back to the Hôtel-de-Ville where he underwent a long examination as to the cause of his quitting Paris in the present critical situation of affairs. After being detained several hours he was permitted to return to his hotel, four commissaries of the Municipality being ordered to accompany him and to examine his papers, which they accordingly did. The above event needs no comment and will give your Lordship a just idea of the present state of this unfortunate capital as well as of the strength of the present government.

Advices were yesterday received from the department of

Ardennes that Mr La Fayette accompanied by most of the field officers of his army quitted the troops under his command and retired on the 19th inst. beyond the frontier.

Yesterday Mr D'Afry the commander of the late Swiss guards was brought to his trial before the Haute Cour Nationale for his conduct on the 10th inst. and was acquitted.

Mr Montmorin formerly Minister for Foreign Affairs and who since the disturbances of the 10th had thought proper to hide himself, was discovered the day before yesterday in disguise, was brought to the bar of the National Assembly and examined, but nothing of a criminal nature appearing against him he was discharged.

Your Lordship will see in the inclosed journals the proceedings of the National Assembly since I had last the honour of addressing myself to you.

As I am every hour in expectation of receiving my passports, it is of course unnecessary for me to trouble your Lordship at present with a long letter.

PARIS, *August 27th*, 1792.

After having gone through a number of forms, perhaps necessary in the present circumstances, I am in hourly expectation of receiving my final passport from the Municipality, and I hope in a few days to be able to pay my respects to your Lordship in London.

MR W. LINDSAY TO LORD GRENVILLE.

PARIS, *Aug.* 23, 1792.

My Lord,

I received on Sunday last a letter of the 17th from Mr Dundas signifying that His Majesty judged it improper for me to stay any longer at Paris in the present circumstances and desiring me to concert with Lord Gower the time and manner of my departure from this place, and I have the honour to inform your Lordship that I am quite ready to return to England and only wait for the necessary passports to set out.

PARIS, *Aug.* 27, 1792.

My Lord,

Although Lord Gower has not yet been able to procure a passport he is in expectation of receiving one every hour, and as his Excellency has directed me to remain two or three days at Paris after his departure, I think it my duty to address myself to your Lordship, as well to keep up the regularity of the correspondence, as to send as much information as has come to my knowledge since the post of Thursday last. I have the pleasure to assure your Lordship that the wise and dignified sentiments set forth in the dispatch of which Lord Gower gave in a copy to the Minister of Foreign Affairs a few days ago on the subject of the system of strict neutrality adopted by His Majesty and his confidential servants with respect to this country have had every good effect that could be expected from them, and the recall of the English mission from Paris in the present circumstances is considered rather as the necessary consequence of the above mentioned system of neutrality than as the forerunner of hostility.

The situation of Paris is more quiet than could be expected after the late violent convulsion; and as the people are all armed and the Government extremely feeble, the present tranquillity of the town is a strong proof of how much pains must have been taken to instigate the multitude to the unwarrantable proceedings of the 20th of June and 10th of August. The Jacobins seem to have gone farther than they at first intended, and not to have foreseen that the mob, the instrument with which they overturned the old government, was likely soon to become formidable to themselves; the Assembly itself being now a good deal under the influence of the rabble; for though the six ministers form what is called a *conseil executif provisoire,* the real power is transferred to the Municipality and different sections of Paris. The Municipality has been entirely occupied since the 10th in collecting as much evidence and as many proofs as possible to inculpate the conduct of Their Most Christian Majesties. For this purpose every suspected house has been searched and seals put on all papers belonging to the emigrants or their relations; many hundred people connected with the court and the aristocracy have been thrown into prison, and two or three of the most obnoxious have been executed. It is generally thought that Her Most Christian Majesty will be brought to her trial in the course of a few days, and your Lordship must not be surprised at hearing the most disagreeable account on her subject; for she is regarded as the cause of all the late misfortunes and is held in such general detestation that hardly anybody will be bold enough not to find her guilty.

It being contrary to the Constitution to try the Most Christian King, the fate of that unfortunate monarch will probably be left undecided by the present Assembly; but the people will take effectual care that nothing shall divert the attention of the new Legislature from concluding the great business of the King immediately after it meets. It is supposed that His Majesty will at least be confined for life, his family excluded from the throne, and the new Government assume the form of a republic. The Primary Assemblies (where every individual except servants has a vote) met yesterday to choose the electors. These are to elect the deputies next Sunday and the Convention is to meet at Paris on the Tuesday sennight following for the dispatch of business. Almost all the members of the late and present Assemblies who have distinguished themselves by espousing the cause of the people in opposition to the court and the aristocracy are likely to obtain seats in the Convention National.

Your Lordship will be surprised that these measures should be carrying on at a time when a great and formidable army commanded by the ablest general in the world is penetrating the country; it is however equally true and unaccountable that the approach of the Duke of Brunswick does not excite that alarm which might be expected. The public declarations of His Serene Highness have only served to irritate, and nothing can exceed the unanimity and confidence which prevails through the country. As to any party which might second the views and facilitate the operations of the combined armies, I have reason to believe that if any does exist it is too insignificant both in numbers and power (except perhaps just on the frontier) to merit attention. It is thought that if the Duke of Brunswick winters in France, his army will be enervated and lose its discipline, and if he returns to the frontier he will be obliged to begin everything again on the opening of a second campaign. They say it is very possible he may penetrate to and conquer Paris, but in that case the Convention will remove to the south, where the enemy will find much difficulty in following them. I have reason to believe, my Lord, that these are the sentiments of the ablest people and of those who have at present the most influence in this country. I regret much not being able to write to your Lordship in cypher, as the present circumstances afford much curious and interesting matter which prudence forbids me to commit to the common post.

Your Lordship will perhaps be surprised at Lord Gower's being detained so long after he has received his orders to quit Paris, but it would be ridiculous to talk of dignity or even of propriety to the present Government in the present circumstances unless in obedience to particular orders from your Lordship. A report prevailed the day before yesterday that Longwy had surrendered to his Parisian Majesty's arms, no official account however of that event is yet received at Paris.

It is also rumoured that Mr Bartélemi is imprisoned by the Swiss Government on account of the affair of the 10th inst.

Paris, *August 29th*, 1792.

My Lord,

His Excellency Earl Gower set out on Tuesday morning with part of his family on his return to England. I have not yet been able to obtain my passport but am in expectation of receiving it every hour.

An authentic account of the surrender of Longwy having appeared in the Bruxelles Gazette, which arrived here on Monday last, the event could of course be no longer kept secret, and your Lordship may judge of the impression it has made on the public mind, by the conduct of the National Assembly, who, immediately after receiving the intelligence, came to a Decree "que les dangers de la Patrie s'accroissent", and that 30,000 men be forthwith raised in Paris and its environs, to reinforce the army.

Some orders which were lately given by this Government for arms from England and Holland not having been executed, the scarcity, particularly of musquets, is so great, that yesterday evening the Minister of Justice, Mr Danton, applied, in the name of the Executive Power, to the National Assembly for leave immediately to authorise the different Municipalities to search every private house through the kingdom and seize upon all arms, horses, waggons, and in general upon whatever property be judged in the present exigence useful to the public service. He prefaced his speech by stating the alarming situation of the country which called for the most vigorous exertions, and seemed to intimate that in his opinion the public danger was much greater than generally imagined. After a short discussion the proposition of the minister was agreed to and decreed.

Preparations are carrying on to fortify the hill of Montmartre which commands most of the town of Paris, and a camp is marked out extending from the Bois de Boulogne all round the north part of the town. The accounts of the combined armies are so vague and contradictory that it would be impertinent in me to mention them but as mere reports to your Lordship who must be so much better informed from other quarters. It was rumoured yesterday that some of the Prussian Cavalry had been seen in the neighbourhood of St Ménéhoud (nearly half way between the frontier and Paris). I rather think however, notwithstanding the rapidity of the Prussian motions, that they cannot yet have penetrated so far; having a large river to pass, and no accounts of the capture either of Thionville, Metz, or Verdun, being yet arrived; though from the tenour of the Minister's speech last night in the National Assembly (which I heard delivered) and from the strong colours in which he painted the public danger, I am inclined to think he knew of worse news than he dared mention. It is in contemplation to form a camp between Meaux and Châlons which is to be commanded by Marshal Luckner, while General Kellerman is left on the frontier. Mr Du Mouriez is said to have orders to penetrate into the Netherlands towards Bruxelles, on the principle, that Rome acted wisely in carrying the war to the gates of Carthage whilst Hannibal was at her own door. I am also assured that Mr de Montesquiou has been directed to enter Savoy, which province is supposed to be very disaffected to its present sovereign, and likely to become an easy convert to the cause of liberty and equality. Mr de Montesquiou has about 42,000 troops of the line under his command, but as they are dispersed in the different garrisons along the South and South-east frontier, he cannot easily or quickly collect above 12 or 15,000 men.

In addition to what I had the honour to state in my last on the insignificancy of any party in the interiour of France likely to co-operate with or facilitate the progress of the Duke of Brunswick I must observe that since the revolution in 1789 the political sentiments of almost every individual are pretty generally known, and the best informed people agree that almost all the aristocrats or friends to the old despotic form of government are either out of the kingdom or are with the Princes, and do not amount altogether to above 50,000. But, my Lord, notwithstanding this appearance of unanimity such is the levity of disposition of the people of this country that it is impossible to judge what effect a rapid progress of the combined armies might have on the public opinion and conduct. With respect to the National Convention about to assemble, the election of the deputies is carried on precisely in the same manner as that of the late Assembly, except that the right of voting which was confined to the *citoyens actifs* is now extended to every individual indiscriminately, servants excepted. This mode is thought to be more perfect as being more comprehensive, and persons *en état de domesticité* are excluded only because their suffrages might be supposed to be influenced by the people whose wages they receive. The only material alterations which will probably be made in the Constitution by the National Convention are 1° the abolition of the twenty-five millions now allotted to the Civil List, and 2°, the transferring the executive power from the King to the Conseil du pouvoir executif consisting of the six Ministers who are to be responsible to the nation for their conduct. Paris is at present fixed upon for the meeting of the National Convention, but if the enemy should approach too near they will remove to Tours or Bourdeaux.

In the course of the present week the National Assembly has decreed the suppression of all feudal rights. I don't know if Lord Gower mentioned to your Lordship that a person of the name of Noel, a clerk in the office of Foreign Affairs, is about to be sent to England with a commission similar to that lately entrusted to Mr de Talleyrand.

The Dutch ambassador Mr de Berkenrod has received orders from T. T : H. H : M. M : similar to those lately sent to Lord Gower, and His Excellency intends, I believe, to apply to-morrow for the necessary passport to enable him to quit Paris. Mr Morris, Minister from the United States of America to the Most Christian King, had a meeting this morning with the French ministers on the subject of some money owing by America to France, but as he has no credentials to the new executive power he of course refused to enter into any negociation with them until he should be more fully acquainted with the sentiments of his superiours on the new order of things established here since the 10th. I have the pleasure to assure your Lordship that Their Most Christian Majesties and the rest of the Royal Family are in as good a state of health and spirits as can be expected in their present unfortunate situation. In reading this letter I must intreat your Lordship to make allowances as well for the shortness of my residence at this Capital as for the difficulty, in the present state of confusion, of sifting out any thing like truth from amidst the variety of contradictory and exaggerated accounts continually in circulation.

PARIS, *August 30th*, 1792.

My Lord,

The confusion in this unfortunate city increases daily; an insurrection of the inhabitants of the Fauxbourgs was expected yesterday evening, but the whole body of the National

Guard being under arms all night in order to execute the Decree for searching private houses for arms &c. no material disturbance took place. The Assembly and the Municipality, jealous of each others' powers, are at variance, and the Jacobins have quarrelled among themselves. A decree having passed the day before yesterday that the barriers of Paris should be thrown open and a free communication be reestablished through the interiour of the kingdom, which has been interrupted since the 10th by the difficulty of obtaining passports and the impossibility of travelling without them, two or three of the leading demagogues who are afraid of not being elected to the Convention if the Assembly should change its present quarters, and who wish to exclude some of the moderate people such as Messrs Condorcet, Kersaint &c. from being reelected, have made the people believe that the measure of opening the barriers is only a pretext to enable the Assembly and deputies to fly from Paris to the south and make a bargain with the enemy in case circumstances should render such a conduct necessary to their own safety. In this persuasion many of the Fédérés are averse to leave Paris or join the army notwithstanding the urgency of the moment. The Assembly may be regarded as in a sort of imprisonment and the Convention will soon be in a similar situation if it should meet in this capital. In order that your Lordship may be enabled to judge of the language, sentiments and conduct of the *men of the people* in this country I have the honour to inclose an account of a speech delivered a few days ago in the Jacobin Club. All the 83 departments have now sworn to adhere to the new order of things and support what is called Liberty and Equality.

 I am in hopes of obtaining my passport this evening and of proceeding on my journey to England in the course of to-morrow.

PARIS, *August* 31*st*, 1792.

My Lord,

 I had the honour to mention in my last that the Assembly and the Municipality of Paris were at variance in consequence of the latter having arrogated to themselves more power than is allowed them by the constitution, and having acted in open defiance to the orders of the Legislative and Executive Power in many instances, but particularly in having stopped for several hours the business of the War office under pretence of searching for some suspected people supposed to have been concealed in the house of the War Minister. Yesterday evening the quarrel between them was brought to a sort of crisis by a vigorous determination and decree of the Assembly to break the commissaries of the Municipality and to order them to appear at the bar and answer for their conduct. This decree was no sooner announced to the public, than addresses were sent from most of the sections of Paris to the Municipality, expressing their approbation of the conduct of those who had incurred the displeasure of the legislature, swearing adherence to the municipal officers, and obedience to their commands. The Municipality thought proper however to obey the orders of the Assembly, and, attended by a great concourse of people, appeared this morning, with Mr Péthion at their head at the bar, where after reading a long justification of their conduct, they informed the Assembly, that as the Municipality enjoyed the confidence of the people, who had sanctioned all its proceedings by the more general approbation, they desired the Legislature to reflect whether it would not be more prudent in them to *reconsider* the decree passed yesterday. The President of the Assembly in his answer to them made use of the most conciliatory language, represented to them the fatal effects which must ensue from the continuation of any misunderstanding in the present moment, between the Legislature and the Municipality, and told them that the very existence of the country depended upon the unanimity of the different members of the Government. He promised, however, that their case should be taken into immediate consideration and exhorted them to obey whatever the Assembly in its wisdom might judge right. The affair has, I understand, been made up within these two hours, the Municipality has been persuaded to give way, in consequence of Mr Péthion having exerted all his influence to bring his fellow citizens to reason, and the sections are now proceeding to elect new commissaries according to the decree of the National Assembly.

Mr de Montmorin late governor of Fontainebleau was yesterday acquitted of some charges brought against him for his conduct on the 10th. He is however still detained in prison. Mr de Montmorin the Ex-Minister for Foreign Affairs was yesterday *décrété d'accusation* on account of his behaviour during his Ministry, and is now in the prison of the Abbaye. A report prevailed last night that Longwy had been retaken; I only mention it to your Lordship lest you should hear it from other quarters, as there is every reason to believe the report is unfounded and is circulated by the Government merely to keep up the spirits of the people. An account is arrived that d'Etain, a small fortified place near Verdun, surrendered to forty Prussian Hussars. It is not thought Verdun can make much resistance, being a place of little natural strength, and its fortifications in very bad order; from thence to Paris the country is quite open.

A new marriage law was decreed yesterday by which divorces are allowed of, nearly in the same manner as in Switzerland and Poland, on the mutual consent of the husband and wife.

A courier arrived this morning from Mr de Biron, who commands near Strasburg, with intelligence that everything was quiet in that neighbourhood. Madame de Tarente, Dame d'honneur to Her Most Christian Majesty, was arrested yesterday, and taken to the prison of the Abbaye. She has been several times strictly examined, and as she was known to be much in the confidence of Her M. C. M. the High Court are in hopes that something which may drop from her may tend to criminate her Royal Mistress.

PARIS, *September 2nd*, 1792.

My Lord,

I have reason to believe that my being detained so long in expectation of receiving a passport does not proceed from any wish or intention of the people in power here to insult the

English Mission, but is merely in consequence of the late quarrel between the Assembly and the Municipality which of course suspended for a time all intercourse between them, and it is necessary according to a late decree of the Assembly that all passports given by the Executive power should be revised at the Municipality before they can be of any use. As, however, it is now near a fortnight, since, in consequence of your Lordship's directions, I made my first application to Mr Le Brun for a passport, and as I have taken care to remind that Minister every two or three days that my orders to leave Paris were as precise as possible, and as I have as yet obtained no satisfactory answer on the subject, I thought proper to write to Mr Le Brun a letter of which the inclosed is a copy.

I likewise inclose a letter I have just received from Lord Kerry, and have only to observe on it that there are many English here at present in a situation similar to that of his Lordship.

In case I should receive no answer from the Minister for Foreign Affairs I humbly intreat your Lordship would be pleased to send me orders how to conduct myself; whether it would be right to remain quiet at a time when the Government is so disorganized that it would be ridiculous to talk of justice, propriety or the Droits des Gens, or whether it would be expedient for me to take any step either with respect to myself or the rest of the English who cannot obtain passports. While I am writing, my Lord, the alarm guns are firing, the Tocsin is ringing, and drums beating to arms all over the town. I understand that a courier is just arrived who brings an account that the Prussians are near Châlons. I fancy however that the whole truth is not made public but that the enemy is much nearer.

This event will probably occasion so much confusion that I shall not obtain my passport for some time longer.

Paris, *September 3rd*, 1792.

My Lord,

I had the honour to mention in my last letter that a courier arrived here yesterday afternoon with an account that the Prussians were some leagues on this side Verdun. Immediately on receiving this intelligence the National Assembly decreed that as universal an alarm as possible should be spread through the whole country in order that no time might be lost in preparing for the general defence; in consequence however of the fermentation excited in Paris by the sounding the Tocsin, firing the alarm guns and beating to arms, the people assembled in different parts of the town in a very tumultuous manner, and at about seven o'clock in the evening surrounded the church called l'Église des Carmes, where about 160 Priests *non sermentés*, and taken into custody since the 10th, were confined. These unfortunate people fell victims to the fury of the enraged populace and were massacred with circumstances of barbarity too shocking to describe. The mob went afterwards to the prison of the Abbaye, and having demanded of the jailors a list of the prisoners they put aside such as were confined only for debt, and pulled to pieces most of the others. The same cruelties were committed during the night and continue this morning in all the other prisons of the town. When they have satiated their vengeance, which is principally directed against the refractory Priests, and those who were concerned in the affair of the 10th, it is to be hoped the tumult will subside, but as the multitude are perfectly masters, everything is to be dreaded. The Assembly deputed some of its most popular and most eloquent members to endeavour to bring the people to reason and a sense of their duty. These gentlemen escaped being insulted but were not listened to. The Royal Family were all safe and well late last night. It is impossible to describe to your Lordship the confusion and consternation which at present prevails here. The Prussians are advancing rapidly, they have already cut off the communication between the armies of Messrs

Luckner and Dumouriez; and intelligence is just arrived that a detachment of 2000 men lately sent from hence to reinforce Verdun is fallen into the enemy's hands.

P.S. It is confidently reported that Mesdames de Lamballe, de Tourzelle and de Tarente were among those who fell victims to the popular fury, and the number of people already massacred are said to amount to four thousand. I have received no answer from Mr Le Brun.

George Monro to Lord Grenville.

September 4th, 1792.

About one o'clock on Sunday fore-noon three signal guns were fired, the Tocsin was rung, and one of the Municipality on horseback proclaimed in different parts of the city, that the enemy was at the gates, Verdun was besieged, and could only hold out a few days. The inhabitants were therefore ordered to assemble in their respective sections, and from thence to march to the Champ de Mars, where they were to select an army of sixty thousand men.

The first part of this proclamation was put in execution, but the second was totally neglected; for I went to the Champ de Mars myself where I only saw M. Péthion, who on finding no one there returned home. During the time the officer of the Municipality was making the proclamation, two others attended at the bar of the National Assembly to acquaint them with the steps that had been taken by the direction of the Conseil de la Commune. The Assembly applauded their conduct, and immediately passed a decree, directing that those who refused their arms to those that wished to serve, or objected serving themselves, should be deemed traitors and worthy of death, that all horses of luxury should be seized for the use of the army, and that those who refused to obey the orders of the present executive power should be punished with death. It concluded by decreeing that twelve members of the National Assembly should be added to the other six that at present compose the executive power. As soon as these decrees were passed, the carriages and horses of gentlemen were seized in the streets (agreeable to the spirit of the decree). Their owners were obliged to walk home, and the horses in general were sent to the École Militaire, and the carriages were put under the care of different guards. The proceedings with the beating of drums, firing of cannon, and the marching up and down of armed men of course created no little agitation in the minds of the people. That however was nothing to the scene of horror that ensued soon after. A party at the instigation of some one or other declared they would not quit Paris, as long as the prisons were filled with Traitors (for they called those so, that were confined in the different Prisons and Churches), who might in the absence of such a number of Citizens rise and not only effect the release of His Majesty, but make an entire counter-revolution. To prevent this, a large body of sans-culottes attended by a number of Marseillais and Brestois, the hired assassins of a Party, proceeded to the Church de Carmes, rue de Vaugirard, where amidst the acclamations of a savage mob they massacred a number of refractory Priests, all the Vicaires de Saint Sulpice, the directors of the Seminaries, and the Doctors of the Sorbonne, with the *ci-devant* Archbishop of Arles, and a number of others, exceeding in all one hundred and seventy, including those that had been confined there since the tenth. After this they proceeded to the Abbaye, where they massacred a vast number of prisoners, amongst whom were also many respectable characters. These executioners increasing in number, different detachments were sent to the Châtelet, the prison de la Force, de Ste Pélagie, and the prisons of the Conciergerie. At all these places a most horrid massacre took place, none were exempted but debtors, and many of these fell victims to the fury of the people. During this sad scene, the more humane, which were but few in number, hurried to the National Assembly to obtain their interference for stopping such melancholy outrages. They immediately decreed that six of their members should go and see if it was possible to prevent such cruelties. With difficulty these members arrived at the Abbaye ; when there, one of them got upon a chair to harangue the people, but neither he nor the others could make themselves heard, and with some risk, they made their escape. Many of the Municipality attended at the different prisons, and endeavoured to quell the fury of the people, but all in vain ; they therefore proposed to the mob a plan of establishing a kind of Court of justice in the prisons, for the immediate trial of the remaining offenders. They caught at this, and two of the Municipality with a detachment of the mob, about two on Monday morning, began this strange Court of justice. The gaoler's list was called for, those that were confined for forging assignats, or theft, with the unhappy people that were any way suspected to be concerned in the affair of the 10th, were in general massacred; this form took place in nearly all the prisons in Paris. But early on Monday morning a detachment with seven pieces of cannon went to attack the Bicêtre. It is reported that these wretches charged their cannon with small stones and such other things, and fired promiscuously among the prisoners. I cannot however vouch for this, they have however not finished their cruelties there yet, and it is now past six o'clock Tuesday evening. To be convinced of what I could not believe, I made a visit to the prison of the Abbaye about seven o'clock on Monday evening, for the slaughter had not ceased. This prison, which takes its name from an adjoining Abbaye, stands in a narrow street, which was at this time from a variety of lights, as light as day : a single file of men armed with swords, or piques, formed a lane of some length, commencing from the prison door. This body might consist of about fifty ; these people were either Marseillais, Brestois, or the National Guards of Paris, and when I saw them seemed much fatigued with their horrid work. For beside the irregular massacre that continued till two o'clock on Monday morning, many of them delighted with their strange office continued their services when I left them, which was about nine on Monday evening.

Two of the Municipality were then in the prison with some of the mob distributing their justice. Those they found guilty were seemingly released, but only to be precipitated by the door on a number of piques, and then among the savage cries of *vive la nation,* to be hacked to pieces by those that had swords and were ready to receive them. After this their dead bodies were dragged by the arms or legs to the Abbaye, which is distant from the prison about two hundred yards; here they were laid up in heaps till carts could carry them away. The kennel was swimming with blood, and a bloody track was traced from the prison to the Abbaye door where they had dragged these unfortunate people.

I was fortunate enough to be present when five men were acquitted. Such a circumstance, a by-stander told me, had not happened in the operations of this horrid tribunal; and these inconsistent murderers seemed nearly as much pleased at the acquittal of a prisoner as they were at his condemnation. The Governor of the Invalides[1] happened to be one of those I saw acquitted, the street rung with acclamations of joy, but the old man was so feeble with fear, and suspense, and so overcome with the caresses of his daughter, who was attending to know his fate, that they both sunk lifeless into the arms of some of the spectators, who carried them to the Hospital des Invalides. The same congratulations attended the others that were acquitted and the same those that were condemned. Nothing can exceed the inconsistency of these people. After the general massacre of Sunday night many of the dead bodies were laid on the Pont-neuf to be claimed, a person in the action of stealing a handkerchief from one of the corpses was hacked to pieces on the spot, by the same people who had been guilty of so much cruelty and injustice.

One of the Municipality was fortunate enough for that night to save some of the women, but many of these underwent the same mock trial next day; and the Princess Lamballe, after having been butchered in the most shocking manner, had her head severed from her body, which these monsters carried about, while others dragged her body through many of the streets. It is even said they attempted to carry it to the Queen, but the Guards would not permit that. Mademoiselle de Tourzelles was also reported to have been murdered, but I understand that she and Madame de Ste Brice were saved from the fury of the people, and carried *à la section des droits de l'homme*. Many other women of family were killed and others escaped. Major Bauchman of the Swiss Guards was beheaded on the Place de Carouzel early on Monday morning. Mr Montmorin, Governor of Fontainebleau and nephew of Mr Montmorin late Minister, who was killed at the Abbaye, had been regularly tried and acquitted on Friday, but not being released was also massacred at the Conciergerie. Monsieur d'Affry was acquitted by the people and escaped. In all it is supposed they have

[1] This was M. de Sombreuil about whom the apocryphal story is told that he was released upon his daughter drinking a glass of blood. The account here given by an eye-witness disproves this legend.

murdered four thousand, some say seven, but I think that exaggerated.

By what I can understand it was late on Sunday evening before Mr Péthion took any steps to prevent the progress of this unexampled outrage, and the National Guards of course made no opposition to such irregularities. The Mayor however at last sent to the Temple the Commandant General of the National Guards, and I am happy to inform you that in the midst of all this confusion, though there was a crowd in the street, yet the court of the Temple was quiet. The Section du Marais has sworn not to permit any violence to be exercised against the prisoners in that place, and the National Assembly have also appointed six of their members as a safe-guard to the sacred persons of Their Majesties, and a number of the Municipality also attend. A motion was made last week to confine Their Majesties in separate apartments; that right was however found to rest with the Municipality, and I have the pleasure of saying that Their Most Christian Majesties still enjoy the comfort of being together, and were, not an hour ago, in perfect good health.

I ask pardon for giving such a detailed account of such uncommon barbarity, which I am sure must be as disagreeable for you to read as it is for me to commit such acts to paper, but they ought to be particularized to the eternal disgrace of a people who pretend to be the most civilized among the nations of Europe.

Wednesday, half past 2 o'clock.

The proceedings of the dispute that existed between the National Assembly, backed by a section or two, and the Conseil de la Commune has no doubt been explained by Mr Lindsay. That affair after having been carried to a considerable length, from conciliatory measures being adopted by both sides was almost dropped: and on Sunday from the critical state of the Nation the Assembly on a motion of Mr Thuriot's decreed that the Council General de la Commune should be augmented to two hundred and eighty-eight, including the Municipal Officers, the Mayor, the Procureur de la Commune, and his substitutes; that the Commissaires which had been appointed on the 10th of August should however be members of the Conseil General, without the sections wished to displace them.

A decree on the same day authorized the Ministre de la Guerre, to take the cavalry's carabines, and arm the troops that wanted them at the camp of Soissons, which is the case with most of them that are there.

On Tuesday a report was circulated that the National Assembly meant to replace His Most Christian Majesty on the throne, or invite his Royal Highness the Duke of York to occupy his place. The Ministre de la Guerre complained much of the evil occasioned by such reports, which only tended to agitate the minds of the people: the Assembly on this decreed that some of their members should be sent to the different sections to contradict such reports, and soon after Messrs Dubayet et Lavivière made a motion which they all swore to, that no stranger should ever give laws to France, and that no King should ever sully their liberty.

While such proceedings were carrying on in the National Assembly, a Mons. Moras in the Club of the Jacobins was inciting them in the strongest language to address the National Assembly for the immediate trial of His Most Christian Majesty, and avowedly persuading them to establish a republican Government. As this motion, though received with approbation was not seconded, I had the satisfaction of seeing it dropped.

On Monday the address of a Monsieur Mossy, a citizen of Marseilles, to the electors on the approaching National Convention was read in the same club: this man follows the same steps as Mr Moras, but with greater insolence recommends it strongly to the electors to make choice of no one to represent them that will not insist upon the prompt punishment of Their Majesties, and in strong language he likewise directs them to stipulate with their representatives that they will adopt no Government but a Republic.

Nothing else material has happened in either of these two houses, if you except an account of plots and risings in different parts of the country, many of which I am afraid are imaginary;

and different detachments of armed citizens, who were going to the army, that had the honour of marching through the hall of the Assembly: as also their decreeing that all the gold and silver belonging to the Royal Palaces, or the Hôtels of the Emigrants, should without loss of time be sent to the Mint for the purpose of being made into money. I must likewise add they have passed a decree, that the Municipality, the Conseil General, les Corps administratifs, and the commandant of the National Guard &c. with all the citizens of France are invited to take an oath to defend the lives and property of the people, *et la liberté, l'égalité*. Extraordinary couriers have also been sent into the different departments to *cherish the spirits et échauffer les cœurs* of all the inhabitants. Such things, with an account that the Russians are marching twenty-two thousand men to their frontiers, and that with a fleet they have in the Black Sea they mean to attack their coasts, formed the chief of their proceedings till Wednesday morning. In the mean time the different sections of Paris have been forming and are still forming their respective quotas for the army. This has created a good deal of inconvenience to the inhabitants, and of course some discontent. I however cannot but observe on the whole, that the party is strong in opposing the combined powers; but they are all conscious, that undisciplined troops can make no stand against such as they have to oppose; and I have no doubt, were a Prussian army once to appear before Paris, that many of the King's friends, who are either quiet or concealed citizens that want peace, and a vast number of people that are averse to the Jacobin principles, would readily declare themselves for the Royal party. Twelve of the National Assembly are directed to attend daily some works they have begun to throw up on the heights round Paris; of these and the citizens that are gone and are still going I shall be able to give you a better account in my next. I cannot help adding that, notwithstanding a tolerable unanimity, there exists a general complaint of some kind or other. The Ministers of every department are complaining of being unable to carry on the routine of their different offices for the interference of people who are ignorant of the nature of them; in short they all wish to be directors, but except the poor people that have been compelled to go to the army none wish to be actors, and, from what I can see and hear, they want a confidence in their army, which is not a little increased by the loss of Verdun.

As I expected Mr Lindsay to go every day, to show you I was not idle I meant to have begged him to have taken this, but that gentleman did not acquaint me with his departure till he was gone.

Paris, *September 6th*, 1792.

I find the massacre at the Maison de la Force only ended this morning at seven o'clock, and that of the Bicêtre yesterday; one may therefore have some idea of the number by the time they took to murder them: at the Maison de la Force they began on Sunday evening and at the Bicêtre on Monday morning, and continued killing at both places with little interruption, till nothing more was left for their yet unsatiated vengeance. On the whole I find at least seven thousand have actually been destroyed. I am however happy to learn that many of the women have escaped, and that amongst these are Madame de Tourzel and her Daughter, and Madame de Ste Brice, both of Her Most Christian Majesty's household. The fate of poor Madame Lamballe is but too true, as well as that of their carrying her mangled body to the windows of the Temple. Mr Péthion and the Ministre de l'Interieur, in their addresses to the public, seem much hurt at this shocking event, though it is certain the former took but little pains to prevent it, and the latter's influence without the assistance of the Mayor was really I believe of little consequence. But as Mr Péthion by a decree of the National Assembly had the whole military force of Paris at his direction, it was therefore certainly in his power, from that, and his popularity with the mob, to have prevented, at least in some degree, the sad scenes that have happened; particularly as he has been since boasting that the citizens of Paris have such respect for the laws, that a ribbon tied across what is most sacred is a sufficient barrier; and in fact while there was a mob collecting in the Rue de Temple on Wednesday night, that system was put in practice, and by these singular people was perfectly respected. That amounts I think to a clear proof that these massacres, if not set agoing by some one, were at least never intended to be stopped.

The prisoners that were confined at Orleans were brought here (notwithstanding an order given by the National Assembly to the contrary) on Friday, but were immediately sent back to Versailles; the people at Rheims have also massacred some prisoners that were confined there.

On Wednesday evening dispatches were received from General Luckner, acquainting the Ministre de la Guerre, that after having made an unsuccessful attempt to relieve Verdun with the advanced guard of the national troops, he had fallen back upon Châlons. The object of the French seems at present to be that of uniting as much of their force as possible to make what stand they can at that place; for that purpose most of the armed citizens, and other troops that have as yet left this place, and which this morning amounted to forty thousand, twelve thousand of which are armed with piques, are ordered to join what force is already there. A great part of the army at Soissons are also moving to that point, and Rheims; the whole if attacked will I daresay fall gradually back till they come near the Capital, where if they make a stand at all, their vanity will of course prompt them to do it, for I would fain flatter myself that all the opposition they can make at Châlons will be too late at least for any operations of consequence, for there seem authentic accounts that the Duke of Brunswick was at Clermont on the 5th, which is only eleven leagues from Châlons. One must therefore naturally conclude, if he means immediately to push forward, which one would wish him to do, that none of these people, the great body of which began to march on the third, can possibly be at that place before His Highness; and if they are unaccustomed to march, or carry arms, they can therefore only add confusion to anything General Luckner may have with him that is regular. Be that as it will, three of the National Assembly left this last night for Châlons to arrange with General Luckner what is necessary for their defence, as well as to give confidence to the troops, and to organize that swarm of people, that are gone and are yet going from all quarters; for they were taken from their respective sections and departments without being formed into regiments. It is also hinted, and indeed I have it from pretty good authority, that Dumouriez is to take the command of that army and Luckner is to command the camp at Paris. For the present however the following officers are named for the chief command of that camp, Mr Beureyer Lieut. General and Commandant General, Archile Duchâtelet Lieut. General second in command, Messrs Charton et Jarjaye Maréchals de Camp, Messrs Rolland et Capes Commissaries of arms and ammunition. Most of these, I am informed, the people have little or no confidence in. I went this day to see the kind of works they are carrying on about Paris, and I found they were constructing lines, which began at the village Clichy Garenne on the banks of the Seine, and crossing the Picardy road went over Mount Belleville to the Marne at Vincennes. This of course occupies an immense tract of country. When I rode over the whole there were about six working parties, each party consisting of about five hundred, and when you looked at their works, at least that part you could see from Mount Mater[1], though they had been working four days, they seemed scarce to have done anything; nor indeed do I think it possible that such lines can ever be completed. The National Assembly have decreed that three of their own Members, three of the executive power, and three of the Municipality shall have the direction of these works; some of the civil power are constantly attached to all their military operations, for I am more convinced than ever that they put but little confidence in their Generals although they strongly profess the contrary.

Had a supply of gunpowder not been obtained from Rouen they would have been badly off for that, and shot, although they have now also got some of that, with cannon, howitzers, and some firelocks from Rochefort. The inhabitants are giving in their iron pots to supply the place of shot, and are depriving the dead of their coffins to make musquet balls; and it has

---

[1] Montmartre.

even already been proposed to kill all the dogs in the capital as so many useless mouths, but notwithstanding the cruelties they have committed, yet they revolted at this act of barbarity.

General Kellerman was at Metz the fourth instant, and after leaving six thousand men before Thionville he proposed moving immediately towards Châlons with the rest of his army, but I should suppose he will scarce be permitted to do this. But it is really so difficult to get at the real operations of the army, which they try to conceal as much as possible from the people, that I can scarce venture to affirm anything respecting it.

Friday night, *September 7th.*

W. LINDSAY TO LORD GRENVILLE.

WHITEHALL, *Sept.* 8, 1792.
Saturday, 1 o'clock p.m.

My Lord,

I have the honour to inform your Lordship that having received my passport on Tuesday last from Mr Le Brun I set out the next morning and am just arrived in London. I am sorry to say that when I left Paris, the town was still in great confusion though the tumult was in some measure subsided.

The Royal Family were all safe in the Temple on Wednesday[1] morning.

Madame de Lamballe was massacred on Monday in a manner too shocking to describe to your Lordship; the other ladies confined in the Prisons escaped.

The Duke of Brunswick was, according to the latest accounts made public, between Châlons and Bar le Duc: it was confidently reported also that the garrison of Verdun having made some resistance had been put to the sword to the amount of four thousand men.

G. MONRO TO LORD GRENVILLE.

Saturday, *Sep. 8th.*

I think it necessary to acquaint you that there is a considerable scarcity of grain in many parts of this country, particularly in the south, Normandy, and Haute Guyenne, and

[1] September 5.

the National Assembly have agreed to give a premium to encourage its importation.

The barriers have been open for some days, and passports are even now dispensed with, excepting you mean to go within ten leagues of the frontiers. Last evening Mr de la Rochefoucault, President du Directoire du Département de Paris, who was making his escape, was stopped near Gisors, by a detachment of the National troops, and making some resistance was killed. A quantity of money was also stopped the same day; and it has been discovered that people have been coining their money in imitation of the Spanish coin, in order to carry it out of the country. They have therefore passed a decree of the National Assembly prohibiting any kind of coin to be carried out of the country.

There is an account arrived from Charleville that the people of that place have risen, and killed the Officer and detachment, that were conducting two waggons loaded with arms for Châlons under pretext that they were for the Austrians, and that the people, when the express came away, were threatening to burn all the magazines that contained arms. Should this take place it will be a serious loss to the French.

Dispatches were received to-day by the Ministre de la Guerre from General Kellerman, saying that he was upon his march for Pont-à-Mousson, but the General declines communicating his present plan, but the Ministre de la Guerre says he has the greatest confidence in it, as well as in General Dumouriez, from whom he also received a dispatch this day, which beside the private business it contained, stated that the Prussians were still encamped at Oudeville under Verdun. General Luckner has also wrote, but their dispatches are all secret. The Ministre de la Guerre even declined communicating them to the Assembly, but the Duke of Brunswick I daresay will soon clear it all up, as some stroke must be struck then, if he means to come directly on.

As you may hear such reports from other hands, I think it necessary to inform you of the ridiculous reports that are in circulation here. Last night it was said there had been an action near Stenay, in which the combined forces had been beaten and lost more than three thousand men, among whom was the Prince Royal of Prussia. There has likewise been a report to-day which has gained much ground among the people, and which has been twice mentioned to the National Assembly; it comes from a strange side of the country, the department of the Meuse, and states that the English are off Brest with twelve sail of the line, and have made a disembarkation of twenty thousand troops. The National Assembly passed the order of the day each time the report was made, but the people's minds are much agitated about it. There has likewise been a report this afternoon which gained still more ground; this states that the King of Prussia riding out with a detachment of dragoons was nearly shot by a peasant, and that his horse was killed under him, but that he fortunately escaped.

Mr Payne is chosen one of the Deputies for the Dèpartement de l'Oise, and Mr Robespierre one of those for Paris, Mr Péthion for the Dèpartement d'Eure et Loire, and Messrs Grégoire et Chabot for the Dèpartement de Loire et Cher. The elections go on very fast, and I am sorry to find that the principles of the Jacobins have extended much into the interior part of the country. Two hundred of the Swiss Guards who escaped the affair of the 10th and the late massacre, have consented to be incorporated in the National Guards, in order to save their lives. The Marseillais still remain in Paris. They consist of about four hundred, and there is not the smallest doubt but they are Genoese assassins, hired for the purpose. We are also in daily expectation of five thousand of the National Guards of Bourdeaux, who are little better. I can assure you as a fact that many of the citizens are in daily fear of a general pillage, and sooner or later it will certainly take place. The National Assembly have directed the Mayor to make a report of the state of the city every day, but his report is not to be attended to, for the police of the city is entirely annihilated. The other evening in the Palais Royal, which was always bad but is now intolerable, a poor man happened to say that sending all these citizens to the army was sending them to be butchered. He had scarcely pronounced the word, when he was killed by the blows of a hundred swords and clubs.

PARIS, *Sep.* 9th, 1792.

The number of men, for I cannot call them troops, that have left this for the army is prodigious. Exclusive of the adjacent villages, Paris alone has sent seventy thousand, and they are still enrolling; many of whom, as the Hôtel I live in joins that of L'Hôtel de la Guerre, I had an opportunity of seeing, and I am convinced as a military man that they must tend more to create confusion in a regular army than to be of any advantage to it. As the Duke of Brunswick of course has good intelligence, he knows this. I have heard to-day that the multitude of people that are besides this either at or going to Châlons is beyond belief. As not half of these can however be armed or clothed, and none of them scarcely disciplined, they must therefore be so many useless mouths. Indeed General Luckner and the Ministre de la Guerre are aware of this and have made several applications to the Assembly to prevent people going that have not arms.

The cause among the lower order of people is more popular than I imagined, I cannot therefore help thinking the Duke of Brunswick ought to get before Paris as quick as he can. There has been a report flying about to-day, that Thionville is taken, and that Metz is besieged, but I cannot vouch it as a fact, as it comes from no authority. Horses and waggons have been impressed in vast numbers to-day to carry provisions, camp equipage, and other things to the army. I don't know how they mean that Paris should stand a siege, for they seem to be carrying most things out of it. A quantity of assignats were again burnt on Friday, but neither gold nor silver nor yet even copper is scarcely to be seen. The National Assembly from the multiplicity of complaints that were made have put a stop to their taking any more of the coffins of the dead, and have given directions that the prison de Châtelet should be taken down, which will add much to the beauty and health of that part of the town.

Doctor Priestly, it is announced to the Assembly this day, has been elected one of the Députés for the Département of the Somme.

The deplorable state of Landau has this day been represented to the National Assembly; which is without provision or ammunition. I however have the honour of inclosing you the paper which is this moment come from the press, and which contains most of what is new that has happened to-day which I have not mentioned. I am however sorry to inform you that it is said the King has been for some days confined in a separate apartment from Her Majesty. I have however the pleasure of adding that the whole Royal family are in perfect health. The King's valet de chambre was confined for singing *O Richard, O mon Roi.*

Sunday evening, 7 o'clock.

Monday, *Sept. 10th* to Wednesday, *Sept. 12th.*

The same evening I had the honour of closing my last, the unfortunate prisoners that had been removed from Orleans were massacred at Versailles, by a party of the guard that had conducted them, and of a detachment of the Paris sans-culottes. Amongst those murdered were the Duke of Brissac, who resisted these villains for a considerable time. The late Bishop of Perpignan and the Governour of the same place shared a like fate, as also Monsieur Bertrand, late Ministre de la Marine, and Monsieur Delessart, late Ministre de l'Interieur. This last they seemed to have a particular dislike to, as they dragged his mangled body about the streets; besides these three there were many other people of consequence, and a number of the late Gardes de Roi, with a Juge de paix. In all they amounted to fifty-three, exclusive of thieves and other prisoners they put to death, that were confined in other prisons of Versailles.

Notwithstanding this Mr Péthion reported to the Assembly this evening, that Paris was perfectly quiet, and that the law reigned in its full plenitude. This transaction has not been mentioned in the National Assembly, nor are half of the irregularities mentioned publicly that are going on. I only mention this to show you the little attention that is to be paid to the Mayor of Paris's reports.

The dispatches received from General Kellerman this day, acquaint the Ministre de la Guerre that he is now arrived at his destination between the Duke of Brunswick's army and Paris, that is he is at Vry, Boulay and St Arold, which are almost upon the frontiers, near Sar-louis, and that General Dumouriez is ready to join him; he adds that these two, with Generals Luckner and Labourdonnaye, who commands at Soissons, are on the very best terms, though this is known not to be at all the case; but the whole of this account is inconsistent, and seems a bait for the people. The Ministre de la Guerre likewise informs the Assembly that he has letters from General Moreton dated the 9th, which acquaint him that the detachment taken from him by General Dumouriez's order, had so weakened him, that in a council of war it was thought expedient to quit Maulde, that this was done with the greatest courage, and good order; that both in that, and the evacuation of St Amand, though much harassed, they had lost but few men, though people talk here of their having lost two thousand. He also adds that the Commandant of Lisle writes that he has his fears about that place, which the Austrians begin to threaten. As all this has happened nearer you than me, you of course have much better information on that head, but it has created a universal alarm, and discontent here. The Ministre de la Guerre finished the detail of his dispatch by contradicting an assertion, contained in a letter signed or pretended to be signed by the officers of the garrison of Landau, stating the place was without provisions. He assured the Assembly that the direct contrary was the case, that there was near fifteen thousand sacks of flour in the garrison, and that other stores were in proportion; it is however said this is far from being the case, in point of *munitions de bouche* they are pretty well off, but in other respects not at all sufficiently provided.

A Commissaire from the army of the Rhine informed the Assembly that the Commandant of Huningen was stopped as he was quitting that place to join the Emigrants, and that Monsieur d'Aiguillon was suspended, as they had strong suspicions he meant to do the same; le Ministre l'Interieur likewise informed the Assembly that Messrs. Victor, Broglie, and Briche were arrested. The money coined out of the silver, brass, and bills of the late suppressed Monasteries amounts in all to thirty-eight millions and three hundred thousand livres; and they have passed a decree this day, directing that within twenty-four hours after the publication of the decree, the Municipality of the different Departments all over France, shall choose among themselves a certain number, who shall visit and give in an exact state of all the furniture or utensils either in gold or silver, that belongs to any Cathedral, Parish Church, or other places of worship, and that whatever was found should immediately be sent, by the shortest and safest way to the nearest Mint to be made into money.

They seem apprehensive that the scarcity of grain will breed much confusion, and its effects I believe have already begun to be felt, towards the South; the Ministre de l'interieur has stated to the Assembly that Lyons, and Nevers, with many other parts are far from being supplied as they used to be, and that riots and murders on that account are continually happening. This however he does not impute to the badness of the crops, but to the schemes of their enemies, added to the vast demand of grain for the army and the capital, as also the last year's scarcity in the South; though it is well known they have had bad crops this year in many places, and the troops and cavalry who were without subordination destroyed a vast deal of grain while green, and in addition to that a good quantity has been carried out of the country.

As I saw, when I had the honour of writing you last, that though apparently otherwise yet there existed a want of confidence in their generals; this has now begun to shew itself, and a public complaint has been made by one of the Commissaires at Châlons to the Municipality of Paris (for they have also three of their body there), and they by a deputation communicated it to the National Assembly. This complaint states that they found Châlons in the greatest confusion and agitation, and that the same spirit that surrendered Longwy and Verdun reigned there, that there was only one good patriot in the whole place, and that on asking General Luckner some questions respecting these things they got nothing but insignificant answers: that the General had then taken no steps to form the camp, and that there was plenty of saltpetre but scarce any gunpowder and only tents for eight thousand men; they also added that on their way there, they met a detachment of Walsh's regiment (who had been taken at Verdun) on their march to Meaux, by General Luckner's order; they sent this regiment back escorted by the gendarmerie: that this corps had spread a report wherever they went, how well they had been treated by the King of Prussia, and that white cockades were found to the amount of three hundred in their baggage. The National Assembly sent this complaint to their commission extraordinaire, and except the discontent it has raised I have heard no more about it; it is however supposed they have sent to arrest Luckner, should they find the complaint well founded, on the spot. Soissons and Rheims are also I understand in the greatest disorder. In every place where prisoners are confined the mob seem to take the law into their own hands: at Châlons it was with much difficulty the Deputies of the executive power could save the prisoners there, and in Paris the mob seized two soldiers whom they suspected to have robbed the regimental chest, and it took even all the influence of the Mayor to prevent their being put to instant death. This conduct of course displeases even the most violent, who sincerely wish success to the Revolution, but who dread to be governed by the mob; and I am certain if these scenes continue, the most inveterate enemies of the old Government will gladly embrace any other than the present. I see this in a great degree already here, and it will of course extend to every one that has the smallest property. The dread of a general pillage is so great that they are forming associations to defend their property.

The complaints this day (Tuesday) are much increased, Luckner is now openly abused, and they complain they have too many of the late nobility in their army; should they meet with any considerable check I dread the fate of these officers, for they will certainly be massacred. The National Assembly are quite the reverse from being unanimous. The walls are covered with their different hand-bills, for that is the way they take of referring their opinions to the public; I would fain hope the King will find his party stronger than may be expected, although I am afraid there is but little chance of that. I think it a pity the Duke of Brunswick had not if possible approached nearer the city; it perhaps would have awed the King's enemies, and have encouraged his friends. We are kept perfectly in the dark here about his intentions, but every moment that is lost is of consequence, as the French are not only daily getting more strength, more arms, and better discipline, but will also soon make the works about Paris respectable; and if they can get the better of the present licentiousness of the mob, which they will of course by degrees try to do, things will then wear a different appearance, and what would be an easy conquest at this period, may in the course of a month be a very difficult one.

The Ministre de la Guerre informs the Assembly that he has received letters from General Kellerman, who is arrived at Ligny. That General must have made a rapid march from Boulay, Vry and St Arold, almost on the frontiers, now to be at Ligny; if he is there it is a tolerable position.

Monsieur Marbeuf late Archbishop of Lyons was arrested this afternoon about seven leagues from Paris; Monsieur Chabot one of the Deputies has arrested what he calls a counter-revolutionist with a large sum of money in gold; the name of this person is concealed as he has accomplices whom they expect to seize.

Monsieur Amelot reminded the National Assembly that many of the members had neglected to pay their subscriptions for carrying on the war, most of them out of their eighteen livres a day I am afraid will find that a hardship.

The authority of the Pope in the French colonies which they had forgotten when they made their last attack on that Pontiff are, by a decree totally annihilated. It is firmly believed that their army in the South means to attack the King of Sardinia's dominions at Poncharra and Chapariellan, and that our Royal Master as Elector of Hanover means to supply the Emperor with six thousand Hanoverians.

Sept. 12*th* to Friday Morning *Sept.* 14*th.*

There is but little going on to-day; the town, excepting the complaint of the inhabitants respecting the little progress their arms make, is as quiet as a place can be where the mob are masters. The people of Paris since the Duke of Brunswick has made a halt think no longer of the defensive; they even blame their favourite, General Dumouriez, for not attacking the combined army; but things cannot remain much longer in this situation, a stroke must be struck.

The interior dissentions amongst people in power seem daily increasing. Monsieur Rolland, the Ministre de l'interieur, has been obliged to stick his defence up against the walls: it fills a large sheet of paper, most of which is in praise of himself. What made him take this step was a paper stuck up in the same manner signed Marat, "a friend of the people and a good citizen." This affiché attacks the Ministers, many of the members of the Assembly, and the generals of the army; he insinuates that most of these are in correspondence with the enemies of France, and that a letter of Monsieur Rolland's to the National Assembly was a complete piece of craft and perfidy.

This Marat was one of the Municipality, a violent man laying himself out for what party he shall find best; he was prosecuted by Lafayette, and a number of citizens have since petitioned the Assembly that the prosecution might be dropped, which I believe is done, and he is elected one of the Deputies at the approaching National Convention.

A complaint has been made to the National Assembly that vast quantities of cattle are daily exported from the coast of Normandy to the islands of Jersey and Guernsey, where many emigrants and refractory priests have taken refuge; the Assembly upon this have prohibited the exportation of cattle from any part of France. They have also decreed that the fathers and mothers of emigrants shall be obliged to furnish two soldiers completely armed and clothed, and that they shall also be obliged to subsist these two men, at the rate of twenty-five sols during the war; three weeks are allowed them to prove where their children are, and if absent on account of commerce, education or any other good reason, they, as well as poor widows who can prove this, are to be excused.

General Dumouriez acquaints the Ministre de la Guerre, that a part of the combined troops have made a precipitate retreat from one of their camps (he does not say which), and that he seized this opportunity to take possession of a very advantageous piece of ground; he adds that General Kellerman is now at St Dizier. It is almost difficult to follow this general upon paper; he marches from Vitry, St Arold and Boulay, to Ligny, and from thence to St Dizier as if it was nothing. It is almost impossible to get at the real situation of the French troops, for this is seldom mentioned, and, when mentioned, is again contradicted: I however now find that General Luckner is at Châlons, that General Kellerman is on his right at St Diziers, and General Labourdonnay is on his left at Soissons. General Dumouriez is encamped at Grand Pré, with an advanced guard under the command of General Dillon at St Ménéhould, and that the detachment that was taken from the army at Maulde, had arrived and halted at Rhétel; these different armies amount to about eighty thousand of what can be called soldiers, and they are getting much encumbered with volunteers unarmed, who are daily coming in.

Although the law respecting divorces has scarcely been passed a week, and that respecting the situation of the children in such cases is not yet made, yet the juges de paix have already separated many unhappy couples, for the law proceedings are so simple that it comes within their jurisdiction. They have given General Bruyer who is to command the camp at Paris the Hôtel d'Egmont which belonged to Monsieur Pignatelli, who has at present a command in the Emigrant army. It is reported that General Clairfait is killed, and that the combined army are in great want of provisions. I only mention this as a report.

The departments of the North have proposed raising and arming twenty-thousand men, and I find that a vast number of the volunteers that went from here are gone to the South.

The Ministre de l'interieur is again making heavy complaints to the National Assembly of the Municipality of Paris; he says they send a deputation of their members about the different departments, who exercise an authority that creates so much discontent that he will soon be able no longer to answer for the consequences. He says they enter people's houses which they call suspected, and take their plate, and other valuables. The Municipality of other places are now copying that of Paris, and even rival the executive power in authority; he particularly mentions two who went to the Assemblée electorale at Meaux (he makes an apology for using their language which I do also) and after making use of a great deal of improper language, concluded their harangue, by directing that a cannon should be cast of the calibre of His Most Christian Majesty's head, that in case of an invasion they might fire the head of that traitor at the enemy.

The Cardinal de Rohan has written a letter to the National Assembly, which is accompanied with the Duke of Brunswick's manifesto; he abuses the revolution, and declares he will make the Deputies answerable for his property which they have confiscated; he concludes his letter by hoping he will soon see an exemplary vengeance inflicted on them.

The want of small assignats is very much felt, and the people begin to be very clamorous about them. The poor men that the mob were going to have put to death for robbing their military chest, have this day been tried, and found perfectly innocent.

FRIDAY 14th to MONDAY *Sept. 17th*, 1792.

The want of police has got nearly to the height I expected it would; the blackguards of Paris have begun this day to stop people publicly in the streets, and take their watches and buckles from them; they have even taken the ladies' rings from their fingers, and from their ears: my traiteur was obliged to bring me metal spoons for fear of the others being taken; a general pillage as I said before will at last take place. The Mayor has exerted himself a little in this business, and the people have assisted in protecting themselves. One woman killed one of these villains with her scissors. I myself never move out but with pistols in my pocket, as I find them more necessary here than in Turkey.

Information is arrived this day, that a general massacre of the prisoners at Lyons has taken place, and that although the Municipality did everything in their power to save them, yet it was found impossible and a vast number have suffered. In other parts their treatment of the refractory priests is as shameful and cruel as the rest of their conduct. In many places they shave, and duck them, and those who wish to get out of the country are refused passports, although it was decreed by the Assembly that they should leave France in a given time, and that those who were found in the country afterwards should be transported to Cayenne; those that cannot escape will I daresay be soon massacred.

It is reported here that the combined army has been repulsed before Thionville, and that they have lost five hundred and fifty killed, among whom is the Prince of Waldeck, and other two, whose names they do not know. This is the report made by Mr Merlin one of the Deputies whose father resides in Thionville; he however makes no mention of what loss the garrison sustained, or at least makes it so trifling, as to make me suspect very much his partiality.

The Ministre de la Guerre says he received letters from General Kellerman dated the 12th inst., that he had at that time advanced to Bar-le-Duc and that the advanced guard of the Prussians had on his approach fallen back upon their main body. A letter from General Luckner inclosing a note from General Dumouriez says that the combined army attacked him on the 13th inst. by attempting to penetrate at the Abatis de Croix aux Bois, at the same time that they attacked his right and left wings at Marel and Mortand; he adds that this attack was only made by the light troops and that he had dispatched General Chazot with seven batallions, five squadrons, and some artillery, and hopes by this time he has dispersed them; for the affair was not finished when General Dumouriez dispatched the note to Luckner. General Kellerman on hearing this fell back to St Dizier to cover Châlons and Paris whatever might be the event. I hope I shall be able to give you a satisfactory account of this action before I dispatch my letters; a decisive one would give this business nearly a final blow at least on this side of Paris.

I need not inform you of the proceedings of the Diet of Ratisbone; the Ministre des affaires étrangères has informed the Assembly that the Emperor has pressed the Diet to declare war against France, and that the Hanoverian ambassador is the Ministre that has made a progress through the different circles to solicit their adhesion to the Emperor's wish and that of most of the Germanic Body. He added with much emphasis, for I was present when the letter was read, that the intentions of a certain Power began now after having been long suspected to discover itself. He added that the French Minister at Ratisbone was warned to quit it, and that the Emperor was trying to get any other French Minister in Germany sent back. Upon this, Mr Merlin made a motion to recall all their ambassadors, which was referred to the Comité Diplomatique.

I need not also tell you, that the French have commenced hostilities by this time against the King of Sardinia. Orders were dispatched from Paris to General Montesquiou, the 10th inst. for that purpose, and he had been prepared some time before, and only waited for the arrival of the order to put the plan in execution. It has also been reported to the National Assembly by the department of the Hautes-Pyrénées, that the King of Spain had declared war against France on the 2nd inst. and that he had appointed Generals Rabi, Alvares, and Delasny to command the army of invasion. The Ministre des affaires étrangères has this day (Sunday) given the particulars of the proceedings of the Diet of Ratisbone, and confirmed the certainty of the members almost unanimously agreeing to declare war against France. He however observes that the formation of their respective contingents, cannot take place for some time yet, they have therefore nothing to fear from this campaign. Complaints have been made in the National Assembly against the Commissaires of the executive power, who when sent to the Departments exceed the instructions they are sent with, and dismiss at their pleasure people in public employments, and appoint others as they think proper. The Assembly have therefore decreed that in future they shall be obliged to shew their instructions, before any one shall be bound to obey them, they also decreed at the same time that no municipal officer can exercise any authority out of his Municipality, and that if they attempt it after this decree they are to be prosecuted for rebellion.

The Swiss Cantons have demanded an official account from Mr d'Affy of the affair of the 10th of August and have desired him to collect the remainder of the Swiss Guards, and return with them; he will find a difficulty in collecting them, for those that remained were glad, poor people, to save their lives by entering into French regiments.

A decree respecting the houses in the Palais Royal has been passed at the instance of the Duke of Orleans, who passes a considerable part of the day at Paris, and goes to the country in the evening. It is very long and as it was private business I scarce looked at it.

Letters are at last arrived from General Dumouriez, in which he talks of an advantage gained, but which nowhere appears; on the contrary by his falling back to cover Rheims and Châlons, I think it appears quite the reverse from an advantage; as the Ministre de la Guerre's letter will best prove this, I shall take the liberty of translating the whole account, and you can then judge for yourself.

"Monsieur Filassier, the Secretary, read a letter from the "Minister of war, in which he tells the Assembly that Mr "Dumouriez after confirming the news of the advantage that "we gained sends him the following note of General Chazot's.

"My Dear General,

"After having the greatest success yesterday I have just "been attacked by a force much superior in number to mine, "and it is not possible to suppose that my small army of five "thousand men could be able to withstand one of ten or twelve "thousand.

"We have had a few men killed and about twenty wounded,

"the enemy has lost a great many more than we; you see that
"what I feared has happened, I hope we shall be more success-
"ful another time.

Signed Chazot.

"Mr Dumouriez," continues the Minister of War, "afterwards
"gives me an account of the measures he has taken to prevent
"the enemy from advancing. He has marched with his army
"to cover Rheims and Châlons, and he now occupies a position
"in which two French generals prevented, during a whole
"campaign, the enemy from proceeding in their intention to get
"to Paris.

"Prince Charles de Ligne was killed in the last action and
"we have taken a secretary of the King of Prussia's carrying
"dispatches to the Duke of Brunswick; Mr Dumouriez is
"getting these dispatches translated, and will send them imme-
"diately to the National Assembly. The Assembly sent the
"Minister's letter to the Committee of Extraordinaries."

There appears to me no advantage got here and I have never seen any other account of this affair; there was a report in the streets that General Dumouriez had killed four thousand Prussians, and that the King himself was besieged in Verdun; but this was all nonsense; I therefore understand that the whole advantage was, that General Chazot stood his ground the first attack, which was perhaps more than was expected. After a seeming hesitation they have at last directed that the Playhouse of the Tuileries shall be fitted up for the National Assembly, and as soon as two hundred of the members of the Convention assemble, the powers of the National Assembly shall then cease. Tom Payne I find by Mr Mason, who only arrived here last night, is on his road to take his seat; I have heard nothing of Dr Priestly, he has perhaps more sense than to come among such fools. What must a nation come to that can have so little discernment in the election of their representatives, as to elect such a fellow? For he has been chosen for three or four places.

Last night the Garde Meuble, where everything that was valuable in the palaces was kept, and amongst those the Regalia of France, was broke open and robbed of a variety of things of the greatest value, amongst which was the remarkable large diamond. The people that committed this robbery broke in at the back part of the house, and the guard in the front heard nothing of it. The particulars are not yet known, but it has happened on an unlucky day, as I am afraid they will search Mason, as they search everyone that goes out at the barrier; as it will however be the same tomorrow and for many days to come, I shall however dispatch him.

half past 4 o'clock, P.M.

Sept. 20*th*, to the 22*nd*.

Nothing happened on Monday although the whole day was a day of alarm; the sections were all extremely attentive, and seemed unanimous in keeping the peace. The streets were constantly patrolled with strong patrols, and when they chose, the police seemed again to exist. I flatter myself from the order that was kept, that Their Majesties were even ignorant of the horrid plans that were talked of without some of their attendants were ill-natured enough to inform them, which is not at all unlikely. During the day frequent proclamations were made, and the people were advised to be on their guard against the enemies that were dispersed among them, and were entreated to protect the lives and property of every individual. The great gates of the garden of the Tuileries were also shut, so that no one could have access during the day to the National Assembly but by the small passages, and when it grew dark every avenue but that of the Feuillants were shut, and the guard there was reinforced, and the sentries doubled. Lafayette's deputies were sadly alarmed and I really believe not without reason; I was acquainted with two, who expressed their fears to me, and their anxiety to get away never to return. Marat the associate of Robertspier, in order either to complete what was dreaded, or to add still more to the universal alarm, had stuck up hand bills in every place they could be stuck, abusing as before most of the National Assembly, the Ministers and generals, and exciting the people in the plainest terms to punish the traitors (as he termed it) when there existed so much treason; the Ministre de l'interieur he was particularly severe upon; and poor Madame Roland, who they say has great influence with her husband, and whom he addressed as the real Minister, had everything said against her that could excite the people instantly to destroy her.

The National Convention met agreeably to order on the 20th, but did little else that evening than mention the authority they were assembled by, name Mr Péthion for their president, Messrs Camers, Vergniaod, Brissot, Rabant, and Lasource for their secretaries, and call over the names of three hundred and seventy-one members which was all that were then present, and which after some little conversation was agreed to be a majority.

Next day after some little ceremony between them and the National Assembly, as the hall of the Tuileries was not quite finished they adjourned to that of the Assembly; their coming there was announced some time before by a deputation from the Convention, of which number was Philip Joseph Egalité *ci-devant* Duke of Orleans, so that everything was ready for their proceeding immediately to business which was done by Mr Manuel moving that the president of the Convention should be lodged in the palace of the Tuileries and every time he opened the sitting, the members should rise, that they might never forget their rights, nor the respect due to the Sovereignty of the people. The previous question was passed upon this motion without any opposition; and after a variety of other debates, some wishing to declare all the powers of the old government null and to reappoint them, others opposed this, and the debate turned chiefly upon the Sovereignty of the people, and the attention that ought to be paid to their wishes in forming a new constitution, and that they should almost individually sanction such an act. Upon this Mr Danton after resigning his place of Ministre de la justice, said it was impossible to have any constitution, but that which was accepted by a majority of the people in the Assemblées primaires; and that all persons and property of whatever kind should be put under the safeguard of the people. This was passed, and they also decreed that all laws that were not repealed, and the powers that were not suspended, were still provisionally to exist, and that all taxes and public contributions should be collected as before. The Convention was then going to adjourn for an hour or two when Mr d'Herbois, one of the members for Paris, said there was a declaration they could not dispense making that night, which was the abolition of Royalty; this after a very short conversation was unanimously agreed to, and on Saturday the suppression of every attribute of Royalty wherever it might be, and the destruction of everything that recalled the idea of such a government was decreed; the seal was to be changed and to bear a Roman fasces surmounted with a cap of Liberty, and the exergue La République Française, and all public deeds were in future to be dated from the first year of the Republic. The rest of the day was passed in regulating the tribunals, and in renewing them, and all the corps administratifs, among which was to be included the Municipality and justices of the peace; after a good deal of conversation on this business in which Mr Danton again took the lead, and in which Mr Thomas Payne took part by the means of Mr Gonpillian who was his *truchement*[1], for he speaks little or no French, it was decreed that the people should choose their own judges and from among whatever class of people they thought proper, not caring whether they were acquainted with the forms or nature of the law or not; indeed it seemed particularly wished that lawyers should not be chosen. It would however be doing injustice to a whole nation to say such an absurdity was decreed without opposition. I forgot to tell you in my last that a number of departments insist upon dismissing and re-electing their members as they think proper, and some of them have actually dismissed those that they had chosen for the Convention. This right must of course now be discussed.

---

[1] I.e. trucheman, dragoman, interpreter.

Sept. 22nd to 23rd, 1792.

On Thursday evening the Ministre de la Guerre informed the Assembly that the armies of Dumouriez, and Kellerman had formed a junction some time on the 19th; but by dispatches received from General Kellerman, I find his army which was encamped upon the heights of Valmy was attacked on the 20th and that after an action of twelve hours, he was obliged to fall back to Dampier a village to the left of Châlons, and the Duke of Brunswick continued his march followed by a column of Hessians and Emigrants as was supposed for Rheims.

General Kellerman by his own account in this action (which is the first they have yet acknowledged any loss), says he has only lost about two hundred and fifty killed and wounded, among which are some officers of rank; but I understand their loss is really very considerable, as well as the loss of cannon, which they make no mention of, or have ever yet done in any of their actions. General Dumouriez who also writes the same day says,—" I shall not remain long in the position "I now am, but follow the march of the enemy." He has sent back the fourteen volunteers that behaved ill in his last action, they are the sons of respectable bourgeois; what will be their fate is yet unknown. Two batallions are also daily expected for the same crime, this I daresay will cool the military ardour of the Parisiens a little. The different sections have however been making what they call a review of their batallions to-day, I saw a number of them, and not one quarter of them have fire locks, and at least one half of them are old men.

General Luckner is returned to Paris. Whether he has been recalled or is come to resign is not yet known, as he only came here last night. General Montesquiou of whose army we have yet heard nothing since the declaration of hostilities on that side, has been some nights ago denoncé or impeached in the club of the Jacobins, as well as his whole état major. I have therefore no doubt but he will likewise soon be recalled, as I understand the matter has been taken up in another quarter very seriously. Mr Fauchet bishop of Calvados, a member of the late Assembly and of the present Convention, has been expelled that society, and I daresay will soon be expelled the Convention, if he gets off only with that. His alleged crime is that of assisting Mr Narbonne to make his escape: during this enquiry Madame Staël's name has been brought much upon the carpet, luckily she got off about the time of the massacres and is now with her father who I think is Mr Necker.

I imagine the French are getting arms from England, they will also get corn if they can, indeed I know some has already been procured; if it is therefore wished to prevent the exportation of these articles, they cannot be too strict on the coast of England, Scotland and Ireland, as I know the French will almost give any price for them.

Just before the authority of the National Assembly ceased, Mr Theodore Lameth wished to intercede for his brother Charles, who has been confined at Rouen as an accomplice of Lafayette's for this month past, but the order of the day was passed on the motion; and it was also decreed, as some Bishops who were Deputies received pay for both appointments, those that had, should be obliged to reimburse the allowance of one of those places.

A scarcity of everything still prevails at Lyons, the magistrates have been obliged to lower the price of bread and other articles, and the farmers of course now bring nothing to market. Troyes and Rouen also complain much, but are as yet quiet, but only till they can get an opportunity to break out. Orleans is in an absolute state of civil war; the sections had suspended the Municipality, and they refused to comply with this suspension, and defended themselves in a house with cannon. A deputation of the National Convention have been sent to arrange this, and are not yet returned. The inhabitants of Versailles have refused to allow the different furniture of the palace &c to be taken away agreeable to an order of the National Assembly, and the Convention have been obliged to decree that it shall remain there in place of being put into the Museum here, which was decreed by the Assembly. I forgot to say the women at Lyons were the people that broke into the different magazines, and took everything they could lay their hands upon. There are a good many English here who have entered the service of this country, but who seem to do little else than walk about the streets in their uniforms. By their appearance I take them to be rather low people.

To-day I find General Montesquiou's command has been taken from him during the night's sitting of the National Convention; they are now to have two armies in the South, one to make head against the King of Sardinia, and the other to watch the motions of the Spaniards. Perpignan and Bayonne are I understand at present perfectly defenceless. They also mean to attack Sardinia from Corsica; I think they begin to have their hands pretty full.

I should have sent you an account of what has passed lately before this, but M. is not yet returned. I should be uneasy about him, did I not know his steadiness. I hope you received my two last by the post dated from the 17th to 20th. Their Christian Majesties are perfectly well, the Convention begin to talk of deciding their fate, which I think they have pretty well done already. Marat has begun to attack Mr Péthion in affichés; Robespierre has as yet not opened his mouth, no Mayor has yet been chosen, but some shock I am sure is at hand. One of the thieves who was going to be beheaded yesterday, on condition that they would pardon him, said he would discover where many of the diamonds were concealed that were stolen from the Garde Meuble, which was accordingly done, and they have found to the amount of some millions laid at the bottom of a tree in the Champs Elysées.

Monday half past 12 o'clock, A.M.

PARIS, *Dec.* 17th, 1792.

After some trifling difficulties, which I shall have the honour of explaining when I have the pleasure of seeing you, I saw my friend Mr Martin at Chambley. He shewed me every kind of attention, and I daily expect to have the happiness of seeing him in Paris, as he told me he should follow me next day, or next again; he readily accepted the remittance, for which I have his receipt, and said it was about what was due to him. I must also add that he was much affected and cried like a child, and repeatedly told me to take care of myself. I told him I ran no sort of risk as I was upon no public business, that I had always made it a practice to correspond with my friends, and to write them what was going on in any part of the world I had yet been, and that I should still continue to do so, and be happy to get any information I might think it worth while to convey to them. The newspaper I had the honour of sending you from Chambley will convince you of the dignity and propriety of most of the King's answers to the different charges that were brought against him by the National Convention on the 11th inst. I assure you this conduct has made a considerable revolution in the minds of the people here, and those that were perhaps indifferent to what had passed before begin now to regret the approaching and most probable loss of a sovereign, whose life they considered as sacred: papers are publicly hawked about saying in his praise what would have cost a man his head, had he dared to utter so much some weeks ago; I have the honour of inclosing an abstract from one of these papers.

The trial of His Most Christian Majesty was to have come on last Friday, but after much confusion and violent debates it is now delayed till the 26th inst. Messrs. Tronchet and Malesherbes are to be his counsel; many have offered and only one named Target has refused; on his refusal the King fixed on the above two: the gratitude of the one and the propriety of the other's letter make me take the liberty of enclosing them. Ladies ambitious of defending their Sovereign's cause have even offered their services and were anxious to obtain that honour.

The National Convention have decreed that His Majesty should again be permitted to communicate with the Royal family, but with that barbarity that has marked the whole of this Revolution, add that he shall not see them all together; if he sees the Royal children first, they are not to be seen afterwards by Her Majesty or Madame Elizabeth, but in the presence of some of the Municipality. The absurd reason they assign for this cruelty is that no messages may pass between the Royal family by means of the children; they are all in perfect health, and I am happy to find people more interested about them than they were.

General Kellerman by this time has taken the command of the Southern army; I spoke to one of his aides-de-camp this day, who told me he left Nancy for that purpose on Wednesday last. I understand General Anselme's situation begins to be very embarrassing, and his having taken, evacuated, and again retaken Sospello, shows the necessity of his having this post, the trouble it occasions him to keep it, and the impossibility of his doing so. His army as well as all the others are extremely ill off for all kind of clothing, and the volunteers are quitting them daily in large bodies. The National Convention have taken up this very seriously and passed several decrees to prevent it, but as yet all their efforts have been in vain. Parties run extremely high here at present. The conduct of the Municipality of Paris, who addressed the Convention to empower them to make the most strict search of the persons of the council of the King every time they went back and forward to His Majesty, created much confusion, and was almost universally scouted by the Convention.

Robespierre's party is still strong; Rolland's is strengthening with Brissot's, and Péthion within these few days has considerably altered his tone. Ministers I understand have been privately threatened by Robespierre's party, and Marat is suspected to be on the eve of deserting it: Chambon, the present Mayor, is reputed to be a moderate man and averse to the proceedings of the Municipality. Rolland and Brissot's party are certainly struggling to save the king in order to humble Robespierre's party, and I myself from everything I can learn have not the smallest doubt but they will succeed.

You have of course heard of the retaking of Frankfort by the combined armies long before this. General Custine in his official dispatches says he lost only 300 killed and 1158 taken prisoners, but it is confidently reported that he lost no less than ten thousand men. There was a report to-day that the French had retaken it, but upon enquiry I find the report entirely without foundation.

General Miranda has taken Ruremonde and the whole of Austrian Guelders; he adds in his official account that the navigation of the Scheldt is now open.

A decree was passed on Saturday regulating the treatment of the conquered countries, the principal parts of which are as follow; that in those countries of the enemy occupied by the French armies, all imposts, tithes, personal servitude, corvée, and all feudal privileges and particular rights should be abolished: they declare to the people of these countries that they bring them peace, brotherly love, succours, liberty and equality; they immediately, by way of convincing them of this, decree the suppression of all nobility, and other privileged orders, as also the then existing authority, and direct the people of these countries to assemble in *assemblées primaires* to form a provisional constitution; the generals are then directed to put all the property of Princes, and other absent people under the safeguard of the nation, and they conclude this strange piece by declaring that they will treat those as enemies who will not accept what they are pleased to call liberty and equality, as also those that enter into any treaty with their former sovereigns, and declare they will not lay down their arms till they have established liberty in all the countries they have entered. This is certainly to all intents and purposes forcing their present constitution upon these provinces they have entered, without consulting their wish or asking their consent.

I have this moment had a visit from my friend Mr Martin and enclose a note he has given me, which he desires may be given to the person that wrote him. He seems positive the life of His Majesty will be saved, and tells me that a decree will soon be passed entirely to expel all the Princes of the blood royal from France; this blow is intended at the Duke of Orleans, who is the soul of Robespierre's party. I find this has actually taken place, and it was decreed last night that every branch of the Bourbon family except those in the Temple should quit Paris in twenty-four hours, and the Republic in three days. Rolland and Pache, the Ministre de la Guerre, are likewise to be dismissed; these decrees were passed in the greatest tumult and confusion that has ever taken place in the Convention. They are busy in all their dockyards fitting out ships but are particularly so at Brest. I thought it better to be here than at my old Hôtel, should you therefore have occasion to write me you will address me at White's Hôtel, No. 7 Passage des petites Prêtres, Place des Victoires.

Paris, *December 17th*, 1792.

The party of conspirators here have now formed themselves into a society, the principles of which I have the honour of inclosing; they have however as yet met with but few subscribers; many of them that signed the late address heartily repent it.

Mr Merry, who married Miss Brunton the actress, and who is the author of some pretty poetical pieces, is the present president of this society, he however seems ashamed of his associates, and but when on business is never with them. Sir Robert Smith, Messrs Raymond, Sayer, Joyce, and two Mr Sheares with a Mr York are the leading men, the two Sheares are Irish gentlemen and brothers, and Mr York brought an address from Derby to the National Convention: those three are violent men and great Republicans, but men neither of weight or abilities to do much mischief. Doctor Maxwell has at last obtained a company in the French service, and I understand is soon to leave this to join the army; a Doctor Edwards of his party is just arrived here to pay him a visit.

Mr Frost has left this house and seldom makes his appearance; he is however one of the society: he appears however a good deal alarmed at his situation, as he told me a reward was offered for apprehending him. Tom Payne is in the country unwell or pretending to be so. Mr Stone has left this and is now in England.

The society met yesterday to receive a brotherly kiss from the Municipality of the different sections, but few either of the society or the sections attended. I cannot as yet discover that they at present are encouraged by any people in power in this place, indeed they have too much on their own hands to attend to the wishes of this society or any other at present.

Mr Joel Barlow is gone with the Commissioners to Savoy in order to assist in the organizing of that new department.

Government have many friends in this house who exert every nerve in the defence of our happy constitution: those consist chiefly of half-pay officers of the army and navy.

PARIS, *December 20th*, 1792.

Since I had the honour of writing you last I have nothing very material to communicate but what you will find in my friend Mr Martin's note which I have the pleasure of enclosing: I think I may however add that things are getting to that crisis that the massacre of a part of the National Convention or a civil war are consequences unavoidable.

There is a scheme at present in agitation to expel all the *ci-devant* nobility; should such a thing take place the confusion it will create can easily be imagined: you will however see by the journal I have the honour of inclosing that the National Assembly are afraid to proceed farther in the expulsion of the Bourbon family at present, and have therefore postponed the discussion of that business till after the trial of His Most Christian Majesty. The forty-eight sections of Paris attended to present an address in favour of that family, but although the Mayor was at the head of this deputation they would not admit it.

You of course know that armed ships have gone up to the Scheldt, and of the demands that the French have made.

Letters are also received from General Beurnonville, but they contain little else than the praise of his army in general, and of some officers in particular; at the time he wrote, he occupied Mertzieg, Fredenburg and Saarbruck, and General Pully had been attacked on his left wing at Kavel by the troops of Grevenmaker, which he obliged to retreat.

General Miranda writes that he has pursued the Austrians

as far as Herkelens and Bergen, where he found they were upon their march for Cologne. What remains of Custine's army is in the greatest want of everything; the whole of their armies are badly off, but this is the worst. Most of the generals complain of a want of assignats; Dumouriez does not correspond with the Ministre de la Guerre; General Vallence has taken Aix-la-Chapelle, and General Kellerman has arrived some days past at Chambéry, where he is making every preparation to proceed farther against the king of Sardinia.

Considerable preparations are making at Brest and Toulon, to fit out what ships they can; different quotas of seamen are moving towards these places, and they talk of being able to fit out thirty sail of the line, exclusive of the squadron they have in the Mediterranean, but this I do not altogether believe.

At the request of Mr Martin I have presumed to give him 400 livres (about ten pounds), which he means to lay out for our mutual advantage in trade, I therefore hope you will have no objections to what I have done. He talks of leaving this on Monday, and I hope you will have an opportunity of talking to him on this business some time next week.

White's Hotel.
No. 7. Passage des Petits Pères, Place des Victoires.

Since I had the honour of writing you yesterday I have nothing new to communicate but what is contained in the inclosed papers, which I take the opportunity of sending by young Mr Woodfall, who leaves Paris this afternoon.

You will see by the Journal du Soir, that the confusion in the National Convention is, if it is possible to increase, daily increasing: such anarchy I think can only end one way.

I have been informed this day that five or six sections have presented similar discourses to the one I had the honour of inclosing yesterday to Mr Hammond; but I have not been able to procure copies of them; I am however well informed they all contain the same sort of violent language, and that they are cheerfully received by the *friends* of our constitution here.

I have been told, and indeed I know it to be true, that these proceedings have occasioned Sir Rt. Smith to quit their party, as well as many others. And they have been heard to say that if England declares war now, it will in a great measure defeat their purposes, as they are not yet thoroughly prepared for such a circumstance. I however once more add that although England ought to be on their guard against all such parties, this appears to me to be wishing to make themselves of much greater consequence than they really are. Their dispositions are such that I am however sure they would, with the assistance of France, put anything in execution that could injure their country, let the measure be never so desperate.

Paris, *Dec.* 21*st*, 1792.
9 o'clock p.m.

A person from Manchester has arrived this day from that place, and brings letters from Mr Coopper; I don't yet know his name but shall find it out before Monday's post.

Paris, *Dec.* 24*th*, 1792.

You will of course receive my letter of the 21st inst. which I had the honour of transmitting you by Mr Woodfall before you can possibly receive this; in the course of the two days that have succeeded nothing particular has happened.

General Beurnonville after a variety of actions has had some little success, and it is reported has taken Graven-maker; his own account of this business is perhaps the most replete with *gasconnade* you ever heard. Having in three columns on the 15th inst. attacked his enemy who was posted on the heights of Wavren, which at that time were covered with snow three feet deep, they had on that day a very considerable advantage, and slept all night on their arms; the action was renewed next day, and the Austrians, though reinforced during the night, were chased from all their posts, and the whole country between the Sarre and the Moselle, as far as the bridge of Consaarbruck, has fallen into his hands. He concludes these two dispatches by saying he has only lost one grenadier in the first day's action, when on the same day the loss of the Austrians was very considerable; on the second day he lost five men, but took fifty-eight of the enemy prisoners, fourteen deserted and five hundred were killed; he also adds that the French were twelve hundred strong, and the Austrians three thousand. Such are the official accounts of this officer, while private information that I can almost depend upon assures me his loss must be very considerable. This general in a third dispatch continues to add, that after a cannonade of seven hours he broke down the bridges of Consaarbruck, and put to flight three thousand Austrians. This last letter is dated the 20th inst., prior to which he mentions two other actions, which he says were only disputes of position. The Austrians were however beaten in all these actions and lost a number of men, while the French lost only the little finger of a chasseur. He however adds that he could not take that useless place Traves (for these are his own words), and that some of his gendarmes were surprised, and cut off; he makes the number only five, but I understand they were nearer fifty. In the actions of the 15th and 16th he complains much of a party of his army, under the command of General Humbert, who commanded the third column, behaving ill. He has particularly mentioned the battalion of Loth, and has sent it to Sarre Louis till he can make an example of it. He concludes the whole of this official account by saying that in seven actions fought since the 6th inst. he has always been victorious, and has killed or taken 1200 of the enemy and three pieces of cannon with scarcely any loss.' General Anselme having lost the confidence of his army is superseded by General Brion; and it is reported here that Custine has met with another serious check, and that it is now in agitation to recall him. There is a report that General Dumouriez has resigned, this wants confirmation; while Marat is accusing him of having the most ambitious views on the Low Countries.

The department of the Lower Rhine is in the greatest confusion; this has originated at Strasbourg and is still at the greatest pitch there: the Convention have sent three of their members to quiet and enquire into this; how far they will succeed is a question here.

Troops in small detachments are daily arriving in the capital, amongst which are a battalion of Marseillois; this is without the order of the Ministre de la Guerre. Great disturbances are expected on Wednesday; although it is generally supposed the King's trial will not come on yet, the sans-culottes it is said are determined either to have him acquitted or condemned at the sitting of that day. The French propose making a treaty offensive and defensive with America, and for this purpose have appointed Monsieur Genest their Minister. He is to set out for that part of the world without loss of time. Some of the States of Flanders are much discontented with the French; they allege that in place of leaving them the liberty of making a constitution of their own, they have dictated the outlines of one to them in the most arbitrary manner; the French have however their party there.

They are at present extremely industrious here in circulating a report, that all letters coming from England are opened at the General Post-office in London, or if they are sent by private hands at the Custom-house at Dover, or whatever other port they may come from. So much pains has been taken to circulate this idea that I am sure they mean to use it as a pretext for retaliation, and I now expect that every letter will be opened. A son of Sir John Blackwood's, an officer in the British navy, who has lately left Bruxelles, brought some letters here. This gentleman has been taken up and examined before the Comité de Sûreté. This Comité not approving of the style of the letters, have confined him for the present a prisoner in his own hôtel.

I have not seen Mr Martin since Thursday last; on that day he agreed to set out for London, as yesterday everything was settled, and it was agreed he should have the cabriolet I brought from Calais. I hope nothing has happened to him; if I do not see him to-morrow I shall write to him. I take the liberty of sending you some journals.

11 o'clock A.M.

PARIS, *December* 27*th*, 1792.

It is in agitation, and has been indeed proposed in the National Convention, to withdraw the greatest part of the French armies from the countries they have taken, and put them in winter quarters in their own frontier towns; a certain number of these troops are however to remain in the countries they are now in, to protect the liberty of the inhabitants, as they are pleased to call it. This scheme is not to be put in execution till the different generals have finished the expeditions they have undertaken. When that is done, and the troops cantoned, the different commanders in chief are then to repair to Paris to consult on a plan for the ensuing campaign. This scheme is held out to the people for no other purpose than to deceive them, for I can scarce suppose the National Convention capable of adopting such a prudent plan. The fact is, Dumouriez's army in want of everything must from necessity soon fall back. General Custine's army, it is confidently reported here, has been entirely defeated, 16,000 have been killed, and 6,000 taken prisoners. The army on the Var is so harassed by the inhabitants and peasants of the country, that their daily loss is considerable, added to that they are ill supplied with everything. Kellerman's army is making no progress, it is scarce possible to do anything among the mountains of that country at this season. His volunteers are daily quitting him, and his army is badly off for everything; added to all these things, the difficulty and expense of supplying these armies at such a distance, in the winter, when the roads are cut up, is scarce possible, and even I believe beyond the resources of France. What they are therefore obliged to do from necessity they wish the people to believe originates from prudence.

The capture of Mayence is said to have followed the defeat of Custine's army. The Convention however make no mention of all this, nor have they mentioned for some time past a word respecting that army. As the report is however current and generally believed, I think it my duty to mention it, and sincerely hope it may prove true.

They are as busy in their dock-yards as they can be; at

Toulon they have lately launched the Sans-culottes of a hundred and ten guns, and are now busy upon another of the same rate. I understand they import quantities of hemp from England, and as I had the honor of mentioning before are very busy at Brest.

The Municipality here directed the Churches to be shut from the evening of the 24th to the morning of the 26th inst. As this is a feast of great consequence amongst the Catholics this arbitrary measure enraged the people to such a degree, that they broke open the Church doors, tore the scarves of the Municipality, and otherwise handled them very roughly; they however did no other harm, and attended their midnight mass with much decency. His Most Christian Majesty made his appearance yesterday at the bar of the National Convention. He left the Temple about nine o'clock, and as he went as fast as the coachman could drive, he arrived at the Convention in about ten minutes. He appeared to me perfectly composed and in good health; his appearance and address had again a very great effect upon the people. He left the Convention about twelve o'clock, and returned to the Temple in the same style he left it, no disturbance of any kind happened, and everything at this moment is perfectly quiet. After His Majesty and his Council retired, the debates that ensued in the Convention were attended with the most extreme violence and confusion. A motion was made by Monsieur Manuel to suspend any farther proceedings on the business before them till the opinion of the eighty-four Departments was taken upon it. This was opposed by Robespierre's party, and increased the confusion. The president attempted to take the voice of the members on the motion, but eighteen or twenty of Robespierre's party flew from their seats, and with their fists clenched threatened the president in the most violent manner. Similar scenes continued till near five o'clock, when they adjourned and are to continue the same business to-morrow. The King makes no farther defence, so that the Convention have only to decide whether he is guilty or not, and what shall be his punishment. This I am confident embarrasses them much, and I have every reason to hope if he is not massacred his life will be saved, which I most fervently pray to the Almighty may be the case,

The greatest confusion imaginable happened in all the coffee houses. Whenever the King's friends and his enemies met they came to blows, but no other accident happened. I saw my friend Mr Martin two days ago, he positively leaves Paris on Sunday. Should I want a little money I shall take the liberty of drawing upon Mr Lamb for it. Our countrymen that were in such strength here begin to change their sentiments; from being levellers and enemies to our constitution, many are now become friends of Royalty. Mr F—t and Tom Payne are not on such good terms as they were; the Député treats his friends with much *hauteur*. We have however still many enemies here, who would stand at nothing to ruin their country, but the National Convention and all the Ministers are too much occupied with their own affairs to attend to anything else.

There was a report that General Dumouriez was in Paris, but from every enquiry I have made I cannot ascertain the truth of this report; I therefore suspect the veracity of it, as no one I know has seen him. I have the honour of inclosing some journals; that of the National Convention is the most authentic, as it is published by their direction.

I cannot help remarking that while the Counsel of the King was addressing the Convention, one of Robespierre's party called out, " Monsieur le Président nous demandons que vous faire taire ce gueux la."

PARIS, *December 31st*, 1792.

Our countrymen here, who have been endeavouring to ruin their country, are now really much beneath the notice of anyone; struggling for consequence among themselves, jealous of one another, differing in opinions, and even insignificant in a body, they are, excepting a few, heartily tired of politics and addresses. Tom Payne's fate and the unanimity of the English has staggered the boldest of them, and they are now dwindling into nothing.

Another address was however proposed for the National Convention; this motion I understand was made by Tom Payne, and seconded by Mr Mery; it was opposed by Mr Frost, seconded by Mr Mc Donald. High debates took place on the occasion, and the further discussion of it was postponed till yesterday; the debates then nearly ended in blows, and I cannot as yet say how it has been carried; as they are ashamed of their proceedings they keep everything as secret as possible.

Mr Raymond scarcely attends any of their meetings, I have an idea he has got employed here in the finance department; many others have left them, and those that remain are constantly quarrelling among themselves.

Some American gentlemen belonged to this society; from their abilities they engrossed too much consequence, a motion has therefore been made to expel them as subjects of another state; in short their debates and conduct are not worth mentioning. Frost's remittances I suppose are not large from his employers, for he has left this hôtel, and gone to one where he lives extremely cheap. Mr Yorke is a very violent man, as I had the honor of saying before he brought an address from Derby; if possible he merits to be punished, he is constantly with Frost.

I have heard nothing of the Manchester address, I therefore suppose it has not been presented, indeed I have every reason to believe the Convention are tired of such nonsense, seeing the insignificancy of the people that present them.

Should I however see anything worth mentioning in the proceedings of such a wretched society I shall lose no time in giving you my opinion of them.

PARIS, *December* 31*st*, 1792.

The debates respecting the fate of His Most Christian Majesty have been carried on with still more indecency and violence since I had the honour of writing you on the 27th inst. Their debate on this business had scarcely begun on Thursday, when after a variety of opinions Monsieur St Just proposed putting His Majesty to death without waiting for the opinion of the different Departments (for the referring his fate to them had been proposed by many). This unjust, and inhuman proposal gained universal applause from the Tribunes, which was even encouraged by some of the Deputies; the majority however resented this savage conduct, and the remainder of the day from 12 o'clock till six in the evening, in the midst of this melancholy transaction which occupies even the mind of the most thoughtless, was spent in debating whether applauding on this occasion should be permitted or not. After blows, and the most scandalous behaviour that can possibly be conceived, it was decreed that applauding should be permitted, but that one of the members should be reprimanded for having encouraged it.

The debates since that have been carried on with a little more decency, though the bloodthirsty party of Robespierre exert every nerve to excite the Convention and the people to terminate the days of their unfortunate monarch: whether this will take place or not is however yet undecided. A majority of the Convention is clearly for sparing his life, and should it be referred to the Departments most of them are decidedly in his favor; much however is to be dreaded from the populace of Paris, whom Robespierre's party is exciting to the most execrable and most horrid act.

Women who pretend to have lost their husbands or children in the affair of the 10th of August have been induced by that party to present addresses to the Jacobin club, insisting upon the execution of the King, and threatening the Convention should such an act not soon take place. A part of some sections, from similar instigations, have followed similar steps, and even gone greater lengths; no tumult of any consequence has however yet taken place, and I sincerely hope a majority of the people of this capital are averse to any such step, and that the National Convention will not be intimidated by any threats.

A new president was named on the evening of the 27th. Monsieur Treilhard, not of Robespierre's party, is nominated by a great majority for that. Péthion, who I understand the other day narrowly escaped being assassinated, has not yet spoke, though he has attempted it once or twice; he and Monsieur Manuel have been expelled from the Jacobins, and the latter has also been denounced by the section of the sans-culottes. In short

Robespierre, the nephew of Damier, who attempted to assassinate Louis the Fifteenth, with his bosom friends Marat and Egalité, will stop at nothing to assassinate those who wish to save the life of Louis the Sixteenth. Complaints are daily increasing respecting the state of their armies; the Ministre de la Guerre has been denounced for this by one or two members of the Convention. I hear nothing more of General Dumouriez; if he is however not in Paris, he is daily expected here. General Custine is not mentioned by the Convention either one way or another; as the report I had the honor of mentioning to you last is not contradicted, I therefore hope it is true. The inhabitants of Liège and other countries complain much of being pillaged and ill-treated by the French troops; and report assures us that the combined armies have received very considerable reinforcements indeed. A Dutchman has proposed raising a Dutch corps; this however was opposed on account of offending that republic, with whom they were not at war. The man that made this proposal, as far as I can trace him, seems to be a man of no consequence, and perfectly unknown to some Dutch gentlemen who are here.

By the Journal I have the honor of inclosing, you will see the note of the Spanish Chargé d'Affaires presented to the National Convention by the Ministre des affaires Etrangères. This piece was treated with very little ceremony; some members proposed its being sent to the Comité diplomatique, others that no official papers should be read in the Convention till the fate of the King was decided; and others again proposed that they should hold no communication with "qu'on appelle *têtes couronnées*" till they formally acknowledge the French Republic.

I observe some people in England have advanced that the lands and goods of the emigrants have not been sold; I am sure this assertion may be easily confuted on your side of the water, by many an unfortunate Frenchman, who lost everything he once possessed; and I can assure you from this side that many of their estates and goods have been sold, others are selling every day, and the corner of every street is papered with *affichés*, announcing the approaching sale of the remaining property of these unfortunate but loyal people.

Tom Payne has proposed banishing the royal family of France, and I have heard is writing his opinion on the subject; his consequence seems daily lessening in this country, and I should never be surprised if he some day receives the fate he merits.

There are vague reports flying about this capital stating that a great part of the province of Normandy are protesting against putting the King to death, and that many of the towns are in an absolute state of counter-revolution; although I cannot in the smallest degree vouch for this, yet as the disposition of the greatest part of Normandy is well known to be attached to their Sovereign, I think it not at all improbable, and I should not be surprised to see other provinces follow their example, for by a letter I received yesterday from the secretary to the Russian Embassy at Madrid (who is on his way to Spain) I find the whole of the provinces he has passed through are in general much discontented with the violent proceedings against the King and the emigrants. Mr Martin I presume will be with you before this letter: he told me at parting that a gentleman would call upon me from time to time, but I have as yet seen nothing of him.

I have taken the liberty of drawing upon your friend Mr Lamb for fifty pounds sterling, which I hope will be honored; the bill is at sight and payable to Mr White.

The moment his most Christian Majesty's fate is decided, I shall not lose a moment in communicating it to you, whatever it may be, and I pray to God that it may be as I wish it.

half-past 11 o'clock, A.M.

PARIS, *Jan. 7th,* 1793.

The National Convention is now so torn to pieces by party, and their time so much taken up with abusing each other, that the King's business is attended but by starts. This is no doubt done by one party with an intention of gaining time, that the different Departments may express their sentiments in favor of his Majesty, and I am happy to find this plan begins to succeed, and that some of them have already presented addresses to the Convention requesting the dismission of Robespierre, Marat, Chabot, Merlin and some others; whether their good example will be followed by others or not, is uncertain, but there remains no doubt but the King has a great majority in his favour; when his trial will be finished is however uncertain, for there are a great number of deputies for and against him yet to speak. That with the different interruptions gives us every hope that things may take a favourable turn, and his life to a certainty be saved.

The people of Paris are at present quiet, and I flatter myself there is a party strong enough to protect the lives of Their Majesties in case Robespierre's party should arm his Banditti against them: but from every appearance at present, assassinations are more likely to take place in the Convention than anywhere else. To effect, or avoid that, I understand the deputies of both parties in general carry concealed arms about them.

I have the honour of inclosing you Péthion's speech, and by the Journal of yesterday, which I also inclose, you will see to what a shameful height their debates are carried, and I assure you from any reading it is impossible to form any idea of that without being present, and then any one would be convinced that it far surpasses any country cock-match, or other place where the most irregular and riotous meetings are held.

The prospect of a war with England of course creates a good deal of conversation here, the people speak for and against it according to the party they are of. The King's friends of course wish it, in hopes of creating a counter-revolution; and the Republicans sensible how materially it may affect their strange Constitution wish by every means to avoid it, though at the same time they talk exceeding big, and even seem to threaten England. Notwithstanding all this you may rest assured they are in no state to go to war with England, and, should such a war take place, it is the opinion of most people here that it will effectually ruin France and their new Constitution.

The latest accounts we have from Savoy are dated from Chambéry the 30th ult. They state that the music of the 79th regiment had been denounced for playing a variety of airs out of Richard Cœur de Lion[1], and that General Kellerman had put the Colonel of the regiment in arrest and confined the band of music; this official account states nothing else, but it is currently reported that on this account a misunderstanding arose between the troops of the line and the National Guards, in which many lives were lost on both sides. A letter of the same date states that a revolution has taken place in Geneva and that the citizens of that Republic have abolished the great and lesser Council; the letter stating this is extremely short and adds nothing else.

Letters are at last received from General Custine and that part of them which they think proper has been given to the public. They give an account of his retreat from Francfort to Mayence, which if one may believe him was conducted in the most masterly manner, and in which as usual he lost but few men, but the Prussians a vast number. He bestows much praise on his army, but adds he cannot help saying they are in want of everything and are justly making the most serious complaints. Most people believe here that Mayence by this time is either taken or near it.

General Lamorlière writes from Ruremonde that he has finished the plan of the campaign that was allotted to him, and gives an account of the contributions he has levied on the following places, viz.: Prussian Gueldres 200,000 florins, the principality of Meurs 100,000, the city of Crevelt 225,000, and Closter-camp 80,000, making in all 605,000 florins, part of which he has received, and taken hostages for the rest. In his letter he affects great delicacy for the Dutch territories and such affectation begins to be pretty common here, since we have declared the part we should take, in case they made any encroachment upon the United States[2].

Even the Commissaries sent to the army of the Var give the most dreadful account of the want of all kind of discipline in that army, which has committed the most horrid brutalities and

---

[1] An opera of Grétry's. The favourite royalist air was "O Richard o mon roi, l'univers t'abandonne."
[2] The United Provinces of the Dutch Republic.

excesses of every kind. They have therefore suspended General Anselm and General Brune commands till Biron's arrival.

General Dumouriez is at last arrived in Paris; he has not however been at the National Convention, nor does he mean to go till they send for him: it is however supposed that the present Ministre de la Guerre will be dismissed as it is said Dumouriez wishes to succeed him. Some one or other is constantly denouncing the present Minister, so that the way is perfectly paved for Dumouriez' plan. He wishes to save the life of the King and is connected with the proper party so that such a change will do no harm.

Considerable damage has been done in the camp of Meaux by fire which begun in one of the hospitals, but no lives have been lost.

Monday half past 11 o'clock A.M.

Paris, *January* 10*th*, 1793.

On the same day I had the honour of writing you last, the National Convention from an immense number of members having put their names down to speak on the subject of His Majesty's trial, came suddenly to the determination of finishing the debate, and voted that judgment should be finally passed on him on Monday the 14th inst. This was passed without much difficulty, and there is little doubt but on that day, whatever their sentence may be, it will be referred to the Departments: this, as I have always said, I hope will gain time, and in order to secure success large bodies of armed men are daily arriving here from the different provinces; and it is generally reported that exclusive of the troops that are now in Paris, no less than one hundred thousand men will be in this capital from the Departments prior to Monday; and it is generally supposed that these men are intended to protect the decision of the National Convention whatever it may be, and that there is a majority really wishing to save His Majesty's life is not to be doubted.

The official report made by the Commissaries that were

sent to the Belgique army are as deplorable as can well be conceived. It is in want of forage, provisions and clothing of every kind; in short they acknowledge that they are in such a situation, that the Generals have pronounced it impossible to go forward; when such a thing is publicly advanced by authority one can scarcely doubt that, if they have not already fallen back, they will soon do it: and when they put that in execution, they are in such a situation, that they will be obliged to make their retreat extremely rapid: for the Liègeois are extremely discontented, and the Brabantees, notwithstanding the addresses of some individuals, are still more so.

I have the honour of inclosing you General Dumouriez' official letter to the National Convention; there seems not the smallest doubt but that officer will be Ministre de la Guerre, and it is then supposed that a certain party will denounce him; but I flatter myself that his party is so well taken, and his principles so much as I wish them, that whatever they are he will carry them through.

Various reports have been this day circulated here, most of which I suspect to have originated in stockbroking finesse; but, whatever they are, I think it necessary to mention them. One says a cessation of arms has taken place for three months between the Emperor, the King of Prussia, and the French; and another says that England, Holland and France have arranged matters so that there will be no war.

The Royal family are in perfect good health, and His Majesty as well as the Queen and his sister are perfectly reconciled to their fate whatever it may be; I understand His Majesty has been in better spirits since his trial began than he has ever been since he entered the Temple.

Notwithstanding every effort they are using to put their fleet in some sort of order, they are totally at a loss for officers; and for that reason are giving the command of what ships they can fit out to the captains of merchantmen. Their inferior officers are ignorant sailors, and every ship they have, I understand, is totally without discipline.

I think it necessary to acquaint you, that one, Thomson, a bookseller, who was Delegate to Division No. 5 of a society, that I became a member of in order to see what was going on there, and at similar societies arrived here last week. As you may perhaps be unacquainted with this circumstance, Mr Nepean will explain it to you. This man recollected my face and reported that I was a spy in London and that I was here for the same purpose. I of course checked him personally for this, and others that have assisted him in spreading this report, but in all the coffee-houses it still gains ground. You may however assure them whom I have the honor of being employed by, that however much my character may suffer or my person be in danger, nothing will ever force me to commit them; they may therefore rest perfectly easy on that head, and I flatter myself I have taken such steps, that, whatever may be done in a legal way, (if the mob does not interfere) will perfectly acquit me of whatever may be alleged against me. But I do'nt think there is the smallest prospect of its going to that length; but in case it should I have taken every precaution that prudence could dictate.

Before this I presume you have seen Mr Martin; I have seen nothing of the gentleman that was to call upon me since he left me, if he will give me his address, or that of any of his other friends I will call upon them, as they might be useful to me in many respects.

The society of our friends here presented an address to the Jacobin Club last night, and mean to present a similar one to the National Convention to-day; the nature of these addresses I have not been able as yet to learn, but hope by next post to give you some account of them. I think I told you that Mr Frost and a number of our other friends have withdrawn from this society, but they have been reinforced by Captain Perry, who means to publish his Argus here.

Half past 11 o'clock A.M.

PARIS, *January* 13*th*, 1793.

I embrace this opportunity of writing you a few lines by a friend of Mr Somers's who leaves Paris for England this evening.

JANUARY, 1793.

Mr Brissot in his official report from the Comité Diplomatique states that France as a powerful Republic has been grossly insulted, and treaties infringed and broken by some late proceedings of the Court of St James's, that the Republic ought therefore to insist upon the immediate repeal of the Alien Bill, the bill respecting the paper currency of France, and a revocation of the embargo laid upon a variety of ships in different ports of England and Ireland, laden with corn and provisions for France; and that the executive council ought also to direct their Minister in London to insist upon a speedy reparation for the insult offered to France by the first mentioned bill. The impression of this report was ordered, and the executive council are charged to direct the Minister of the Republic at the Court of St James's to insist upon a prompt and categorical answer to the above specific demands. You may therefore expect this to be made directly, if it has not taken place before you receive this.

The preamble to this report states how vulnerable the British Empire is in a variety of places; our possessions in the East and West Indies are immediately to fall, Ireland is to revolt, Canada and Nova Scotia are to be attacked, the resources of England are almost exhausted, its inhabitants are in general discontented with its present constitution, and the people so oppressed with taxes that they will not contribute to the expense of a war. The whole of this nonsensical report ends with the thread-bare story of the war: "should it take place, it ought to be considered as the war of the Minister, and not of the British nation, and that the Republic of France will refer it to their justice"; I forgot to say that they also insist upon England disarming immediately.

Robespierre made a trial of his strength last night at the Comédie Francaise. The Municipality of Paris had decreed that a new piece called L'ami des lois which was very popular should not be again performed. This is a very aristocratical piece, and a severe satire upon the present anarchy, and the unjust proceedings against the King. The piece notwithstanding the decree was performed. Robespierre's party opposed it, but were much too weak; the Mayor was sent for, and General Santerre arrived with twelve hundred horse; both the Mayor and he were obliged to sit in a box till the opinion of the National Convention was taken upon the business. They passed the order of the day upon it, and the play again commenced and continued till the end without any further interruption. The Mayor and General Santerre were obliged I understand to stay till its conclusion. Similar riots were attempted in other quarters of the town but with as little success; no lives have been lost and everything is at present quiet: disturbances are however expected tomorrow, but I flatter myself such precautions are taken that nothing will happen.

As soon as the King's business is finished I shall lose no time in communicating the result of it to you by Mr L—g. I am this moment informed from very good authority, that a counter-revolution has commenced at Rouen, they have burnt the tree of Liberty, mounted the white cockade, and have sent the Republic to the Devil, while they are shouting Vive le Roi. At this exact period such a circumstance is unlucky.

General Custine has met with another defeat in which he has lost seven thousand men and is now besieged in Mayence. Excuse this hasty scrawl which I have scarce time to finish, as the gentleman is just going and I have only known an hour of his intended departure.

January 21st, 1793.

I am sorry it has fallen to my lot to be the messenger of the most disagreeable intelligence, that I, or any one else was perhaps ever obliged to communicate. The National Convention after sitting near thirty-four hours on Thursday[1] night, voted that the punishment of death should be inflicted upon His Most Christian Majesty. This unjust, and iniquitous judgment was carried by a majority of rather more than a hundred; fifty of this number, though they voted for death, differed in opinion from the rest in respect to the time it should be inflicted; some thinking it should not be put in execution till the war was finished, and others proposing it should be postponed, till the

[1] Jan. 17.

voice of the people was taken: Péthion and many of the leading members voted for death with these restrictions.

The sudden turn the opinions of the majority of the National Convention took, after what I at different times have had the honour of communicating to you can be more easily imagined than described; the King's friends were confounded, and amazement was strongly painted in the face of most men I had an opportunity of speaking to: few of the members who went to the National Convention on Thursday morning with a positive resolution voted as they intended; this sudden change in their sentiments can therefore only be imputed to fear or some such other base principle: that there was however some reason for this must be allowed, for, notwithstanding a report made to the Convention to the contrary, the mob had become very alarming, and had even threatened some of the members, particularly Mr Villette, whom they threatened to massacre if he did not vote for the death of His Majesty.

If this was not the cause of such a sudden change in opinion it can then only be imputed to political views, which had for their object England and Spain making some proposals to save the life of His Majesty. For this reason they came suddenly to the resolution of passing sentence of death upon him, in hopes if possible to intimidate these two nations, whom they naturally suppose much interested for the life of the King. For this reason also, it is supposed death will not yet be inflicted upon him, in order to give these nations an opportunity of making proposals if they wish it: but should either of them declare war it is said His Majesty will immediately be put to death. This opinion Mr Somers had from some of the members of the Comité de défense général; I however think it my duty to remark that this worthy and well informed gentleman is so much attached to His Royal Master, that on this occasion he may perhaps have thrown out such a hint in hope it might at least be tried by one of these powers in order if possible to save the life of the King. I am however myself really much afraid if His Majesty is not already dead he can scarcely be saved. The day I left Paris there were some thousands of armed men parading in different parts of the city ready to commit any sort of riot, and threatening destruction should the King not be put to death.

I cannot express the horror that was painted even in the countenance of every individual in the National Convention where the very worst of the very worst of mankind are assembled, when Égalité gave his vote for the death of His King and relation; Manuel in a very proper and spirited manner attacked him upon it. This execrable branch of the House of Bourbon has had a remittance of more than twenty thousand livres sent him lately from England; this in some manner contributes to the payment of the assassins he and Robespierre have now in pay.

The King is perfectly reconciled to his fate, the situation of Her Majesty, Madame Elizabeth, and the Princess Royal is melancholy indeed. The last mentioned of this Royal Family has for some time past been unwell, and the indelicate conversation that took place in the Convention upon the Queen applying for her physician is not to be described. The Dauphin is perfectly well and universally beloved by all ranks of people. Should they attempt to put the King to death horrid scenes will then happen in Paris, indeed every one's mind is already prepared for it, and in order to intimidate the Royal party nothing but proscriptions and massacres are held out by Robespierre's party. One list is said to contain the names of more than forty thousand people. Many of the members of the National Convention I have spoke with never expect to escape, and fear possesses the mind of the strongest.

The counter-revolution that was begun in Normandy was so miserably conducted that it scarcely merits being mentioned: the ringleaders were soon seized, and are now in prison, but that province as well as a majority of the others are for saving the life of His Majesty, and discontent and the dread of war with England reigns through them all.

As I could commit nothing regularly to paper in Paris, I shall have the honour of communicating the remainder of my intelligence to you some time to-day, as I can extract it from the almost unintelligible notes I have.

Monday morning 7 o'clock.

LONDON, *January 21st*, 1793.

Mr McDonald who I think writes for the Morning Post, and two other men who call themselves Sheares and are brothers, set off from Paris on Wednesday with an intention of going either to England or Ireland by way of Ostend. These three people particularly the two last are men of the most violent disposition, and are capable of executing the most desperate designs. If they cannot succeed in breeding disturbances in Ireland, which I think they mean to attempt, I am sure they will not hesitate in attempting to set fire to the dockyards or in doing this country any other kind of injury in their power.

The Sheares are tall men, about six foot high, and the eldest has a large purple scar upon the right side of his face. Mr McDonald is perfectly known in London.

As I passed through the provinces, more than three-fourths of every Department I spoke to were very averse to putting His Majesty to death, and I am confident that France has never been so torn to pieces by party since the Revolution began as it is now, and I am well convinced that, if they were left to themselves for a short time, the unavoidable consequence would be a civil war. If it was possible to prevent the exportation of horses it might put the French to a considerable inconvenience, as they procure vast quantities of horses from England; on the road I met with several strings. Many of their regiments are at present dismounted for want of horses and before the winter is at an end there will be still more.

DIARY

OF THE SECOND

VISCOUNT PALMERSTON

IN FRANCE.

July 6—August 31, 1791.

DIARY.

1791, *July 6th.* Set out for Dover at half past one, arrived there at ten. Found the Packet just going to sail, embarked and got out of the harbour a little after twelve. Fair wind but very little, great swell. Got to Calais about four. Went to bed at Dessains.

July 7th. Set out about two o'clock for Paris by the Flanders road, received a pass from the municipality of Calais, which is granted of course without any further trouble than sending a "Laquais de Place" for it, but which is examined often on the road. To Ardres 2 Posts, La Recousse 1, to St Omer 2, to Aire 2.

The road is very good and the country in general after you pass Ardres fine and prettily diversified. The crops upon the ground are very fine.

We were advised at Calais to put national Cockades in our hats, which we did, but I believe it was not necessary. Aire is a dull melancholy town and the inn bad. Day fine. Miles 35.

July 8th. To Lillers 1½ Posts, Béthune 1½, Touchet 2, Arras 1½, Hervillers 2, Bapaume 1, Sailly 1, Péronne 1½.

As far as Péronne the road lies through a fine rich country, generally open but beautifully diversified with woods villages and inequality of ground. We passed several fine abbeys situated on commanding eminences whose appearance is magnificent. All these I was told are broke up and together with their estates are upon sale. This idea gave me concern and impressed me with those melancholy reflexions that attend the destructions of ancient splendid institutions. The present Government of France may subsist for a while on those spoils, but it appears to me that the country must suffer, as these possessions cannot fall into the hands of such good landlords as the last, and the numerous poor who were assisted by them must either starve or become a charge upon the publick. The fortifications which we saw seem going to decay, and we have not seen the face of a custom house officer who used to stop passengers at the entrance of most of them. Beyond Péronne, which is properly the ancient limit of France, we found the country much worse, less beautiful and less well cultivated. In all the former part of our journey we were much struck with the goodness of the crops of all kinds of grain. We likewise saw much flax and great quantities of poppies of which they make oil. To Marche le Pot 1½ Posts. To Fonches 1. To Roye 1.

Some rain in the morning: fine afterwards. Miles 80.

July 9th. To Conchy 1½ Posts. Cuvilly 1 P. Flat, ugly country greatly inferior in every respect to what I saw yesterday. Gournay 1 P. Bois de Lihen 1½ P. Pont St Maxence 1½ P. Country much improved, Pont St Maxence a town on the Oise with a handsome new bridge and the Seine round it pretty.

Senlis 1½ P. Chappelle en Serval 1 P. Lanvres 1½ P. Bourget 1½. Paris 1½. The journey from Senlis is uninteresting till you come near Paris, when the prospect opens and presents several interesting objects, such as the Abbay of St Denis, Château d' Ecouen belonging to the Prince of Condé, the Hill of Montmartre and several others, together with the town itself which however does not show itself on that side in a very conspicuous manner.

I found the roads good and the Posts well served, and as my carriage was light I was driven at the rate of nearly a Post and a half which is equal to 7½ miles in the hour. Weather fine. Miles 55. Went to the Italians where I heard a very pretty comick opera as far as relates to the musick and the acting. The musick is very Italian but the stile of singing quite French and a severe strain upon ears that are not in the habit of hearing it. No good company there. Went to take a turn in the Palais Royal which is the great rendezvous of all sorts of people at night and indeed throughout the day. Excessively bad company and in a much worse stile than anything I remember here formerly.

Sunday, *July* 10*th.* Went with the Vicompte de Noailles to the National Assembly, not a day of much business but was glad to see their forms and appearance by that means at my ease. The room is very long, fitted up with rows of benches something like our House of Commons or perhaps something more like Westminster Hall during a trial, though infinitely inferior. The president sits in the middle of one side and the tribune or desk from which reports and regular speeches are made is opposite him. At each end are great galleries raised which hold large numbers and are filled with very low people. On the sides are smaller galleries which are rather more select in their company and more difficult to get admittance to. The confusion and want of order is very extraordinary at first and the president's bell has a very odd effect. There are several officers of the Assembly who walk about in the middle and endeavour to keep silence. All the end of the house on the president's right hand is given up to the malcontents and his left to the supporters of the new order of things. The great question that agitates the minds of people at present is the decision upon the measures to be taken respecting the King, who since he has been brought back remains in confinement with his family, not separated though obliged to have an officer constantly in the next room with the door open, and all his functions in a state of suspension by a decree of the Assembly, till some further determination is come to. The question of what is to be done is referred to a committee who are to make their report in a day or two. Their opinion and that of a most decisive majority of the members of the Assembly is known to be in favour of the King, and for passing over what has happened, and restoring him to the same situation in which he was before, except that I suppose he will be better watched. The committee to whom this was referred consists of all the members of the other principal committees united, and amounts to 80 or 90 persons, being the principal men of business in the Assembly; of these only three were against the King. Out of the Assembly the opinions (of those at least who declare them) seem as violent and as prevalent the other way, and the addresses sent up daily to the Assembly breathe nothing but resentment against the King and an eagerness that the most violent measures should be taken against him.

In the evening I went to a meeting of the Jacobins Club which is extremely numerous and consists indifferently of those who are and those who are not members of the Assembly. It was extremely full, not much less than 1000 persons. The question to be debated was an adjourned one, it consisted of several points, viz, can the King be tried? ought he to be tried? who should try him? and how should he be tried? Two speeches took up the whole time. The first was by a Monsr. Goupel, an old man who spoke for the King; very diffuse and without method, and very indiscreet as he rested chiefly on the absolute inviolability of the King in all possible cases, an argument and a position not at all suited to the present temper of the times. He was heard or rather not heard with a kind of indignation and tumult that can scarce be described. After him Monsr. Brissot, (both of them members of the National Assembly) read a speech very violent and inflammatory to prove that the King's person was inviolable only for those Acts of Government which are transacted through his Ministers, that there was a case in which he was personally answerable, that he ought to be tried for his conduct and that there was no danger to be apprehended from foreign powers on that account. His speech was lively and full of declamation, well suited to the temper of his audience who received it with such continued bursts of applause as almost deafened me for the rest of the evening. He was very deficient in point of argument and totally passed over what are considered as the most material grounds by those who hold the other opinion. These are first how the King can be said to have committed any crime by withdrawing himself, it being clear that there is no decree or existing law to make it so, the only one that could have had that effect not having passed or been presented for the King's sanction. The argument therefore is this; The King has made himself perfectly contemptible and shewn he cannot be trusted, but he is not guilty of any breach of the law, therefore he cannot legally be punished or deposed, and if he could, it would be highly inexpedient to do so, because in addition to the general resentment of all foreign powers such an attempt would divide the country and produce a civil war at home. Monsr. Brissot's speech however was perfectly satisfactory to his audience, and the shouts of applause given by so many hundred people on such a subject shewed a kind of ferociousness of disposition which was infinitely disgusting to a moderate mind. It was ordered to be printed and distributed over the country which I doubt not will be much inflamed by it. This transaction of last night and the similar spirit which seems to prevail among the people at large puts the National Assembly in a very awkward and difficult situation, and is very likely to create a division between them and the people at large and the " Gardes Nationales." If that happens to a serious degree, and sooner or later it must happen, their power and authority is gone and they will be turned out, as the English Parliament was who voted for treating with King Charles. If that should happen I do not see what is to succeed them but confusion, anarchy, weakness, ruin, and as the natural consequence of all this, despotism. Much rain in the night.

Monday, *July* 11. The procession of Voltaire which was to have taken place early this morning was deferred on account of the bad weather. Breakfasted at Lord Sheffield's. Made some visits. Dined with Monsieur de Noailles, Pelham and Tarlton, at Robert's a Restaurateur or tavern-keeper in the buildings of the Palais Royal famous for his good cookery. The dinner was very well dressed but dirty and ill-served. The conversation as usual political. The plan of many in the Assembly is to restore the King to the same nominal situation he possessed before, but to give him a council who are in truth to act for him, and as far as I understand are to be responsible for that part of his conduct as King, which is separate from the functions of his ministers. The queen is now scarce mentioned and her excuse for her flight, viz., that she attended the King her husband, is fully admitted, so that those who wish to try the King have no view against her. In reality the true object of most of them who are professed republicans is by a formal sentence of deposition to put a final end to the monarchy, and the idea of declaring the Dauphin King with a regency is only held out to draw on those who are less decided. Monsieur de Noailles was one of the two deputies of the Assembly sent out on the alarm of the mob who had surrounded the coach when the Queen was to get out at the Tuilleries. The pretence was to prevent the Gardes de Corps from being torn to pieces but the real object was to secure the Queen. When they came they found all order at an end and the National Guards absolutely inactive in keeping off the people, who were between the coach and the steps in such temper and numbers as would have made it very dangerous if practicable to have conveyed the Queen through them. La Fayette, who, though personally brave, has no presence of mind or decision, was haranguing them to little purpose and holding up his sword with both his hands, and declaring he would break it (i.e. give up his command) if he was not better obeyed. The deputies however by proclaiming in the name of the Assembly and the law that every good citizen must draw back, at length with difficulty made such an opening as enabled them to convey the Queen, one having hold of her arm on each side, in safety to the steps.

This afternoon the procession of Voltaire took place though the weather was very unfavourable as it was found inconvenient to defer it. It was very long, but a great part of it consisted of very shabby, ill-dressed people whose appearance was made worse by the mud and dirt they had collected. Great quantities of National Guards attended; but in disorder and without arms, except such as were on duty. Deputations of different orders of people and among others the Academy. A figure of Voltaire, very like him, in a gown was carried first sitting in an elbow chair, and afterwards came the coffin on a very fine triumphal car drawn by twelve beautiful gray horses four abreast. The coffin was covered and over it a waxen figure was laid on a bed. After having made a great circuit round the town they came to the house of the Marquis de Villette, who is married to Voltaire's niece and where he died. There the figures stopped, a kind of hymn was sung, Madame Villette and her child came down, mounted the car and embraced the figure and then with several other ladies followed it on foot, during the remainder of the procession, to the new Church of St Geneviève where it is to be deposited.

There is a Committee appointed to revise all the Decrees of the Assembly and to select and arrange such as are permanent and out of them to form a plan of a Constitution; and the idea of many persons is to present this to the King, supposing him restored to his situation, and to give him his choice whether he will accept it or not and if he declines it to give him full liberty to retire.

Wednesday, *July* 13*th.* On this day the report of the Committees, to whom united the consideration of the King's flight and the measures to be taken thereon was referred, made their report. The tendency of this was to consider the whole business as a plot of Monsieur de Bovillé who had deceived the king and, by filling his mind with false apprehensions, induced him to leave his capital in order afterwards to overturn the Constitution and introduce foreign armies into France. It proposed therefore that the Assembly should decree that Monsieur Bovillé and all the other persons concerned in the king's flight should be proceeded against, and such of them as were in custody should be tried by the High Court established for that purpose at Orleans. At the same time the Rapporteur said that the Committees did not consider the king's flight as a constitutional crime in him, and that if it was so the Inviolability belonging to his person did not allow his being tried for it. This report, on which the Committees were almost unanimous, was well received by the Assembly. Motions were made to put off the consideration of it till it was printed which was rejected, and it was determined to be proceeded on immediately and that no other business should intervene. Accordingly Monsieur Pétion, a popular leader, made a violent speech against the report and for bringing the king to a trial. When he had finished the Assembly adjourned.

Thursday, *July* 14*th.* The Assembly continued their debate and adjourned it again. A violent party is rising in Paris among the lower class of people against the plan of not trying the king.

This was the anniversary of the Federation and was again celebrated in the Champ de Mars. Mr Pelham and I got an order to go into the École militaire, which commands the whole scene. There were by all accounts considerably fewer troops than last year and the bridge over the Seine and the triumphal arch were not there, but the weather was fine and the concourse of people on that account was greater than before. The procession as it entered passed before the École militaire, but the fine object was the general coup d'oeil of the whole multitude when collected. So many troops and such a number of people were I dare say never assembled before in a place so formed to shew them to advantage without a possibility of any considerable inconvenience from the crowd. The area is 900 yards long and about half that extent in breadth. The great altar, which is a building raised high from the ground to which four ample flights of steps in a circular form lead up, and on which altogether I doubt not but 2000 persons might stand, is in the middle. The École militaire, a very handsome building, is at one end; the other extends nearly to the Seine. The whole area except in front of the École militaire is surrounded by a bank of a breadth and size proportionable to the place, sloping inwards down to the area, on which last year there were benches placed. This year the people stood. The numbers it would contain cannot be estimated. The people of Paris were pouring out to it the whole morning and yet it was not half full, though at a little distance it appeared to the eye of a spectator tolerably well covered. The troops which consisted of large detachments of the Gardes Nationales of Paris and all the neighbourhood I should suppose might amount to 20,000. They made no great figure in the area but they kept the people out. The procession consisted besides of great bodies of troops which marched with them, of detachments from all the great bodies of people concerned in all the departments of the government, the Courts of Justice, the Academies and various Societies of the Capital. The National Assembly who last year attended in a body sent this year a deputation of 24 members. The whole procession marched to the altar where were already placed about 60 priests, all in their white robes of ceremony; and as candles could not be used four fires were kept burning at the corners in vases raised on vast tripods in antique forms. The whole altar was now a cluster of people; and the banners which every Corps carried before them formed a circle completely round it. The Mass attended with musick took up some considerable time and afterwards the banners were carried in procession round the altar for a great while and every one in its turn was presented and had a long ribbon with the national colours tied to it. This closed the business, and those who had formed the procession marched back as it happened without much order. A little before the end the people contrived to get into the area which they appeared to fill and by that means presented a new scene which was curious in a different way.

The Assembly this day continued their debate and several members delivered regular speeches from the Tribune. The debate was again adjourned. Great fermentation prevails in the town where great pains are taken by persons who do not give themselves so much trouble gratis to exasperate the people against the King and to induce them to take measures to compel the Assembly (whose intention is now well known to be more favourable to him) to bring him to a trial, and in consequence of that to proceed to his deposition at least. Republican principles are now avowed in every street; and the Palais Royal, which is the centre of discontented politicians, is filled with groups who are listening eagerly to a number of little orators who are zealous and indefatigable in propagating sedition. Plans were proposed for assembling in great bodies and signing on the altar at the Champ de Mars petitions, or rather requisitions, to the Assembly not to proceed to decide the question before them till they had received the sense of the people. It was observable that, though the numbers were great in the Palais Royal and the groups large, yet the speakers and applauders were few. The rest were silent and gave no marks of their opinions.

Friday, *July* 15*th.* The Assembly began by reading an insolent petition of the kind before mentioned, signed by about 120 names quite obscure and some of them ridiculous. No notice was taken of it and the debate was resumed. Two speeches were made in favour of the report of the Committee, one by Monsieur Salle, the other by Monsieur Barnave which were very good and produced (particularly the first) a very great effect on the Assembly. Monsieur Salle, who maintained the inviolability of the king's person for the advantage of the State, proposed however that the Assembly should decree that in future a King who should make war upon the country or who should retract the oath he had taken should not be tried, but considered as abdicating his throne and that he should become liable to be tried for any acts committed after such abdication. These propositions which were to have no retrospect met with general approbation and were directly voted. After Mr Barnave's speech the Assembly determined to finish the discussion; the question was put and the proposal of the Committee was adopted by a very great majority. Those who were of a different opinion scarcely shewed themselves as it is not the custom to proceed to any division or to number the votes except in very nice cases.

The members of the opposition, or côtè droite, of course approved of this measure in preference to any more violent, but, in conformity to their resolution to take no further part in anything but what affects the King personally and only as far as is necessary for his service, none of them spoke in these debates. In the evening great violence was shewn by particular people about the town, and great anxiety seemed to prevail among the inhabitants at large as to the consequences. The Jacobins met and came to very violent resolutions against the decrees of the Assembly and voted addresses to the other clubs of the kingdom to join them. Detachments of mob went to the different theatres after the representations were begun in order to stop them. In some they succeeded, in others they were prevented by the Guards. At night there were great assemblages of people in the Palais Royal. To disperse these the method used was, to march detachments of Grenadiers up and down the gardens and always through the thickest of the crowd, by which means the orators were perpetually interrupted.

Saturday, *July* 16*th*. This day the town was much in the same state as yesterday. Matters seem to be ripening for tomorrow, when petitions and associations are to be signed at the Champ de Mars. The Assembly have directed the municipality to preserve the publick peace by all the means the law puts into their power.

Sunday, *July* 17*th*. This morning early there were gatherings of people in the Champ de Mars, and very unfortunately two men were discovered to have got into the great cavity under the Autel de la Patrie where they had carried their dinner and seemed to have proposed passing the whole day. They were discovered by boring holes through the steps and sides of the place; and the only conjecture that seems to have any probability with regard to their intentions, is that they thought they should see what might happen without being crowded, and that they should have a good prospect of the women's legs who might come up the steps. One of them is said to have been an invalid with a wooden leg, but a young man. This frolick however cost them very dear for the mob immediately decided that they were placed there to blow up with powder the altar with all the most zealous friends of the *Patrie*, and seized and carried them before some little inferior magistrates of the Quarter. But finding these doubtful and undecided what they should do, they took them away again and executed them themselves with many circumstances of inhumanity. The Municipality of Paris, having had information the day before that a large body of people were to meet early at the ruins of the Bastile and from thence proceed to the Champ de Mars, had met early at the Hôtel de Ville and their chief attention had been directed to the quarter of the Bastile. There however nothing passed nor was any mob assembled. When they received the first information of the murder at the Champ de Mars, they immediately sent some of their body with a battalion of Guards to act as the occasion should require. The accounts they received from these Commissioners were unsatisfactory and at length they returned to inform their brethren of the very disorderly state of affairs. That they had met the mob carrying the heads of the two men (which is a favourite amusement) on poles, that one of the bearers had been seized but afterwards rescued, that a man had attempted to shoot Monsieur de la Fayette, but had been prevented, that the man had been seized but released at the desire of Monsieur de la Fayette, that on proceeding to the altar they had found a number of persons signing petitions against the Decree of the 15th, that the National Guard had been repeatedly insulted and driven away, that on the Commissioners presenting themselves to remonstrate they had been very ill received, but that the mob had insisted on sending 12 persons on their part as deputies to the Hôtel de Ville who were waiting without. The Municipality who had determined immediately before the arrival of their Commissioners to hang out the drapeau rouge which, accompanied with a proclamation is an establishment of martial law, and to proceed in a body accompanied with a very strong force to the Champ de Mars, agreed, however, to stop in order to hear what the mob ambassadors had to offer. These, however, on the sight of the drapeau rouge and of the troops and cannon prepared had stepped off and were probably gone back to apprize their friends. The expedition now proceeded. It was seven in the evening when they reached the Champ de Mars—in all the environs of which they found great crowds of persons who appeared as spectators. The bank, or glacis, as it is called, on each side the opening through which they were to enter was covered with people who began to insult them by calling out, à bas les bayonettes, à bas le drapeau rouge. The Mayor made a stop just in the entrance, and was proceeding to have the usual proclamations made when they were interrupted by a volley of stones from the bank and a pistol fired at the Mayor, which narrowly missed him and wounded a soldier just behind him. On this the troops without waiting for orders, as it seems, began to fire but probably in the air as it does not appear that any-one was killed by the first discharge though it was a pretty considerable one. The firing was stopped and the march continued into the Champ de Mars. The altar in the middle was now deserted so that the allied corps of civil and military continued their course between it and the bank which was now covered with people who had resumed their courage on finding no one killed, and renewed their attacks with stones and pistols. A more serious fire then took place from the troops and the cavalry began to charge with their swords, by which some execution was done. It is difficult to know the exact numbers that suffered, but the most probable accounts say about 16 killed and as many wounded who remained behind. Several of the troops were wounded with stones etc. and three were killed who are said to have been single when attacked. A complete dispersion now took place, the mob all flying into the town where they threaten the most violent revenge with fire and sword, that the National Assembly shall be driven out and Monsieur de la Fayette not suffered to live another day. Their fire however spent itself very much during their running, and the people of Paris were so little disposed to be inflamed by them that (proper guards being posted in various parts of the town) the remainder of the evening and night passed off with the utmost tranquillity.

Monday, *July* 18*th*. This day the town seems perfectly quiet. The Mayor and his brethren came to the Assembly to give an account of the transactions of yesterday. Their conduct was approved: they were directed to proceed with the utmost vigilance and firmness to preserve the publick peace and punish the disturbers of it, for which purpose the drapeau rouge is to continue displayed at the Hôtel de Ville. The Assembly ordered strict search to be made after the man who presented his piece at Mr la Fayette; and afterwards they proceeded to pass some strong Decrees against any persons who should either by voice, publication or affiche incite the people to any acts of violence, and likewise a long imprisonment to any who should insult the National Guards or endeavour to induce them, either by threats or persuasions, from doing their duty when under arms. This was opposed by Monsieur Pétion as much too arbitrary a decree and an infringement of public freedom and the liberty of the press. Pétion together with Robespierre had been for some time distinguished for their Republicanism and had been the great leaders of the violent party at the Jacobins and were now become very unpopular in the Assembly, so that Pétion could scarce obtain an hearing and met with no support. The Jacobins had proceeded with so much violence both before and after the decree of the Assembly respecting the King and particularly afterwards when they came to resolutions which amounted to little less than a protest against the Assembly and an invitation to all the other debating societies of the kingdom, which are become innumerable, and to the country at large to join them, that all the members of the Assembly who belonged to them except two or three and a great number of moderate men who were not of the Assembly quitted them, and those who were members of the National Assembly instituted a new society who met at the Feuillants. The first intention seems to have been not to admit any but members and to make a kind of committee of the Assembly to prepare and debate business that must come before the Assembly, much mischief having been experienced from the indiscriminate admission to the Jacobins, where by that means the most violent people had got the ascendancy and taken the business out of the hands of the members of the Assembly. However it is now proposed, but not yet determined, to admit other persons by ballot. It is worth notice that the Jacobins' Club was instituted or at least supported in opposition to the Quatre vingt neuf which was a much more respectable and moderate society who used to meet to debate publick business, but who have for some time ceased to have any regular debates, though they still continue a club.

Tuesday, *July* 18*th*. Perfect tranquillity continues. Many persons are taken up on account of the late disturbances, and among others a Jew who is an agent of the King of Prussia.

Wednesday, *July* 20*th*. The party of the Assembly seems to have entirely prevailed. The country, as far as can be known, appears well satisfied with their Decree. The street orators are all vanished and the Palais Royal, though thronged, is silent as to politicks. Guards are continually there, who whenever they perceive any particular groups march directly through them by way of dispersing them, and repeat this measure continually. The plan of the Assembly seems now to be to get the report of their Committee of revision ready as soon as possible. Their business is to select out of the confused mass of Decrees something that may bear the appearance of a regular constitution. This, when it is approved by the Assembly, is to be presented to the King and he is then to be at full liberty to accept it or refuse it; and if he chooses the latter he is to be free to retire from the kingdom or even to remain in it, if he will, as a private man subject to the law.

Thursday, *July* 21*st*. Many of the members of the Quatre vingt neuf Club have joined the Feuillans. The remaining

Jacobins are endeavouring at a reunion and have offered to select 30 of each side who shall strike out all obnoxious names.

Friday, *July* 22nd. The theatres here are become innumerable, as since the Revolution all privilege is abolished and all who will may open theatres. There are at least 20 established theatres and more preparing. They have all good actors and seem to have tolerable audiences. Went to-day to a theatre of an individual Mademoiselle de Montansier, where I saw an entertaining piece called Le Sourd very well acted. It is something upon the idea of our deaf lover.

Saturday, *July* 23rd. Went to see some of their painters, Daniel Vincent and La Grenice, all in the historical line. They seem to draw well and finish with care but their colouring is cold and there is a tameness and insipidity in the whole composition. Many persons are taken up upon suspicion of being concerned as instigators of the late disturbances; but most of them are found innocent or at least no proof is found against them. The men however who put to death the two unhappy victims in the Champ de Mars are taken up and, I understand, upon clear evidence.

Sunday, *July* 24th. The Assembly, while they are waiting for the report of the Constitution, are much taken up with the state of the frontier and the attack with which they are threatened from without. Had the King escaped I find it is scarcely denied that all the regular troops in that part would have joined him; but that being over and the officers gone who were his friends, the case is very different and nobody can say how the troops will act. They profess adherence to the Assembly. They are numerous enough; but they have few officers and no discipline. The accounts of whether anything and what is preparing to attack them are so uncertain that no dependence can be placed on them. Monsieur Duveyrier, who was sent with a summons to the Prince de Condé and who has been lost for a great while, is returned. The Prince de Condé contrived to give him no answer and frightened him away with apprehensions of what would happen to him from the officers in his suite. Afterwards he was put into prison at Luxemburgh upon some frivolous pretence and kept there 3 weeks, after which they sent him with a guard to the frontier of France and turned him loose; from whence he returned to Paris as wise as he went. Detachments of National Guards in addition to those of the districts are going towards the frontier and about 1,800 were yesterday mustered at Paris. The Assembly have ordered the proper officers to proceed to the sequestration of the Prince of Condé's property.

Monday, *July* 25*th*. The most authentick reports seem to give some credit to the projected attempt upon the frontiers. In the meantime the Assembly are hastening as much as possible their plan of a Constitution, which they wish to have accepted before any new event happens, and they are trying to form some plan which may bring back their troops of the line to something like military discipline. Saw this evening a very pretty French Opera at the Italians called "Raoul barbe bleu." It is very interesting and Mademoiselle Crétu, who acts the wife, does it admirably. The present stile of musick at Paris is very good as the composers have adopted the Italian stile, tho the performers adhere too much to the old French method of singing.

Tuesday, *July* 26*th*. Went to the National Assembly. They were passing a report of 40 articles concerning the manner in which the military force should be called in to assist the civil power. Went to Grand Prè, a picture dealer, who has some of the finest Dutch pictures I ever saw, but most enormously dear, 4, 5 or 600£ apiece. I have before been with my old acquaintance Donjeu, who is in a very bad state of health. He has some very good pictures and his prices much more reasonable. Lebrun has parted with his collection. Hammond in the Palais Royal has some good ones. Went to see Racine's "Athalie" at the French theatre. It is a finely written piece but heavy in the performance, and rendered more so by the Choruses being set to dull noisy French musick. The performers of the Italian and French theatres have joined to perform this play, and exhibit it alternately at the two theatres. The musick makes it so long that there is no time for any after piece. The theatre was extremely full. It is much the finest theatre at present in Paris in all respects, as the approaches and rooms attached to it are really magnificent. The busts of the principal dramatick writers are in the great room which is very proper. The front has a large portico and on the stones of the columns which are numerous are stuck the titles of favourite plays which is perfectly ridiculous.

Wednesday, *July 27th.* Went again to Grandprè with Lord Gower and Lady Sutherland. Saw a vast number of fine pictures I did not see before. I had no idea of any dealer having such a capital lying dead in pictures. The prices he asks are enormous. Went to the French Theatre to see the "Coquette corrigée," a good comedy written about 30 years ago. Molé, Mademoiselle Raucoux and Mademoiselle Contat acted in it. Molé, whom I remember an excellent actor in the lively parts of comedy and a very pretty figure 25 years ago, is now grown old and clumsy, and is so much changed that I should not have suspected him to be the same man. He goes on to perform lovers' parts and by use does not appear to the people here so unfit for them in appearance as he does to me. He is however a very good actor. Mademoiselle Raucoux is a fine actress both in tragedy and comedy, but her figure would not suit very young parts. The character of the Coquette was played by Mademoiselle Contat, who is a charming actress full of spirit and elegance. She appears to have a very fine face and is young enough for most characters on the stage; but she is very large and I understand is much increased lately in size.

Thursday, *July 28th.* Saw a piece at the Italians called Mirvah and Adelaide. It is interesting and well acted. The latter part resembles the deserter and the distress is carried farther to a degree highly disgusting, as the hero of the piece is actually placed on his knees with his eyes covered and his hands tied, and the party who are to shoot him are just levelling their musquets when the reprieve arrives.

Friday, *July 29th.* Dined at Auteuil, about two miles out of Paris, with Madame Helvetius, widow of the celebrated author of L'Esprit. They were both very amiable and were among my earliest acquaintance at Paris. She lives very comfortably in a little retirement where she seems to have a pleasant society about her and never comes to stay at Paris. Went in the evening to some of the little theatres on the Boulevard, which seem to be very low both as to performance and audience. There is one at the corner of the Rue de Bondy called Theatre Comique and Lyrique, which seems to be a very pretty one. They have got a favourite performance there called " Nicodème dans la lune " which has little or no merit but being written for the time has great success.

Sunday, *July* 13*th*. Rode in the morning to Montmartre, where the view of Paris and all the adjacent country is extremely fine. It is so near that the town almost reaches to it. Dined with Monsieur Suard at a small house at Fontenay aux Roses about 4 miles from Paris. The country about it is very beautiful and his garden commands a pleasing view over a valley prettily diversified with villas, gardens and woods. Monsieur Suard is a literary man of a moderate and amiable character; and as I knew some sensible well-informed men were to be of the party I was in hopes to have got more amusement and information than has hitherto fallen to my share. But in this I was as much disappointed as usual. Eternal politicks and political disputes ingrossed the whole attention of the party. The French Revolution seems to me to level people's understanding as much as their ranks and situations: blind and violent zeal seems to have taken place of reason, and he who harangues in the Palais Royal garden talks with just as much wisdom and clearness on these subjects as the people of the first understandings of the country. Two Monsieurs Garats were there, brothers, and both of the Assembly and of very opposite principles. I was told their politicks had no effect upon their friendship which I believe is true; but they disputed so violently that people in England in the same case would probably have come to an open quarrel. The younger one, who is a Democrate, was quite furious; the other kept his temper much better and now and then introduced some little stroke of humour, which served to take off something of the edge of the dispute. I was diverted with a repartee which was told of the elder Garat, who being at some ceremony when a new bishop, who had just taken the oaths and was acquainted with Garat, said to him with a triumphant kind of sneer, Bonjour Aristocrate; to which the other instantly replied in the Masquerade stile, Bonjour beau Masque. The Democrates seem much out of spirits as they have lately received alarming accounts of a very serious League that is forming against them by the neighbouring powers, and feel every day more and more the weakness of their means of defence and the insufficiency of their Government. The weather is so hot as to be quite inconvenient. At seven in the evening it was impossible to walk with any sort of comfort and the thermometer, which has been for these two days above 87, was today very near 89.

Monday, *August 1st.* Went to the National Assembly. Complaints having been made by some of the members the day before that the decrees of the Assembly met with great difficulties and delays in the execution, it was ordered that some of the Ministers should attend the Assembly, at least every other day, to give an account if called for or to state any difficulties they met with in the execution of the decrees of the Assembly in their departments.

Tuesday, *August 2nd.* Rode thro' the Champs Elisees, which consists of a wood of young trees planted in rows with an excessive broad strait road thro' the middle of it. The dust is excessive and the soil being like pulverised mortar the trees themselves are quite white in dry weather. The whiteness of everything about Paris (except the complexions and linen of the inhabitants) is a great inconvenience, as all the buildings are stone and all the soil like mortar; and the very little grass that is to be seen is generally parched with the sun and whitened with the dust. At Neuilly there is a fine new bridge over the Seine of five arches wide and very flat. By means of the flatness of the arches and the height of the banks above the river, the upper line of the bridge is perfectly strait without any elevation whatever. Procceded along the road which leads towards St Germains, and turned off to the left to ascend a remarkable hill which is the highest and most conspicuous spot on the horizon of Paris. It is called Mont Valerien and Mont Calvaire. There is a religious house upon it and some chapels and hermitages, which used to draw a good subsistence from the religious zeal of the adjacent country whose inhabitants made frequent visits to the holy brotherhood. At present the visitors are so few that the Hermits are gone for want of company. The prospect from this place is very fine. The Seine winding through a large extent of country just below it, the bridge of Neuilly, the Château de Madrid, the Bois de Boulogne, the palace and woods of St Cloud, the full view of Paris and Montmartre form the principal objects of this delightful view. Went on to St Cloud. This palace built by the Duke of Orleans, brother to Louis XIV., has been a few years ago sold, improved and new fitted up. The ground Salon, the Gallerie d'Apollon and the Cabinet de Diane, which form a fine apartment highly ornamented and painted, remain as they were. There are no good pictures, but some portraits by Mignard of the characters of the time of Louis XIV., that are interesting. The prospect from the house is fine but glaring. The gardens are well-wooded but still formal, tho less so than many. They run along a rising ground over the Seine which is the best circumstance belonging to them, not excepting even their artificial cascades. They look very handsome from without. Rode home thro' the Bois de Boulogne, which is the great resort of the riders and drivers of Paris. It is extensive and has a wild forest-like appearance but not much beauty. This and the following evening saw two operas both called Lodoiska, both formed upon the same story and both brought out nearly at the same time at the Italian Theatre and the Theatre de Monsieur. The musick of the Italians is much the most pleasing, and I think the piece the best written. The scenery of the other is superior. The characters are Poles and Tartars, and both pieces end with the burning and blowing up a castle, which is performed upon the stage with an effect of fire far beyond anything I ever saw attempted.

Saturday, *August 6th*. Saw a French opera, called Raoul de Créqui, extremely interesting and admirably acted. The management of their scenery has a great effect; particularly in a method they have adopted and often make use of dividing their stage lengthwise into two parts. Thus in Raoul de Créqui there is the dungeon where he is confined and the jailor's apartment, where much of scene passes, both open at once to the audience.

Monday, *August 8th*. The Assembly entered upon the discussion of their new Constitution as formed by their Committee out of the various decrees which the Assembly have passed.

This Constitution, which is to be the French Magna Charta it is supposed, is never to be altered by any future Legislature; but if ever necessity should call for any alteration it is to be made by something which they call a National Convention. The business therefore of the Committee is to select such things as are purely Constitutional points, to simplify as much as possible, to avoid details and to omit everything that is not absolutely essential or which is likely to require alteration or modification. The Committee consists of some of the most prudent men they have, and are supposed to have fulfilled their task as well as the violent materials they have to work with will allow them. Some small progress was made today with great appearance of heat and animosity.

Wednesday, *August* 10*th*. Rode to Bellevue, a house built by Madame de Pompadour, purchased of her by Louis XV, and now belongs to the Mesdames who are gone to Italy. The house is a very good one and has been newly fitted up by them. The ornaments are elegant without being shewy. The chief merit of the place is its prospect, which is extremely fine. It is placed on a continuation of the same rising ground over the Seine on which St Cloud stands: many of the objects are the same. On the whole I think the prospect of Bellevue preferable. Immediately below Bellevue is the village of Sève remarkable for its Porcelain manufacture, which is beautiful and carried on with more experience and in a greater stile than any of the other manufactories which have arisen since. The King being the proprietor, and of course greatly out of pocket every year without reckoning what he takes or gives, which is or at least used to be considerable. There are some of the most beautiful vases of blue porcelain with gilt bronze ornaments about 7 feet in height, the price of which is about £800 each.

Thursday, *August* 11*th*. I saw a new piece at the French Theatre, called Les victimes cloîtrées. It is one of those pieces called dramas which are generally extremely affecting as this is thro' great part of its progress, tho it ends happily. It is the severest attack that can possibly be made upon the Clergy, and one can hardly believe oneself in a Catholick Country while one sees it. The applause with which it is received is excessive and if there was anything more to be taken from the Church or anything more severe that could be inflicted on the religious Orders, such a representation would be sufficient to excite the violence of the people against them.

Friday, *August 12th.* Saw the Hôtel de Salm, built at an enormous expense by the Prince of Salm, a petty German sovereign. The entrance is very fine, some of the apartments are elegant and magnificent, but it is not half finished and is to be sold. In the evening saw a pretty comedy excellently acted, called L'Intrigue Epistolaire, at the Variétés, a very elegant new theatre in the Palais Royal opening to the Rue de Richelieu.

Saturday, *August 13th.* Went with the Pelhams and Madame d'Astorgue and Monsieur Alexandre de la Rochefoucault to see Mademoiselle Devreux's house, which is the most celebrated thing of the kind in Paris for the expense and elegance with which it is fitted up. She is a lady who with very little beauty has had the good fortune to have a succession of rich lovers and the wisdom to realise a large fortune out of their prodigality, notwithstanding she has always lived well and behaved generously on many occasions and is much liked by those who are of her society. Her house is small but convenient and well disposed, and the fitting up and the furniture in the highest stile of elegance. It is said she is almost ruined by play and must sell her house.

Wednesday, *August 17th.* Went to see the Hospital des Enfans trouvés. They receive all children that are presented, which are given as soon as possible to nurses out of the country, who must come to receive them and must bring a certificate of their characters. The nurses at first are given 12 f. per month, which is diminished if the child stays with them beyond a certain age. The nurses often keep the children till they are six or seven years old, and sometimes adopt them entirely when all payment ceases. Those who are returned to the hospital are kept principally in a large place on the Faubourg St Antoine, where they are instructed till they can be placed out. About 6000 children on an average are received every year. The house where they are taken in is near Notre Dame. When I was there there were about 140 who had been received within a few days, and were none of them a week old. They are fed by hand till the nurses come for them. The greatest part of them appeared healthy, and nothing can exceed the neatness and care with which they seem to be managed. They are under the care of women of a religious order called Sœurs de la Charité, who deserve much credit for the zeal and humanity with which they execute their office. Near this place is the great hospital of the Hôtel Dieu, where all sick persons are admitted, and of the bad air and unwholesomeness of which, from the patients being overcrowded, so much has been said and written. Some reformation particularly in the lower wards has been effected since Madame Necker's time, who gave much attention to it. And in those wards more than two are never placed in the same bed, and in some parts only one, but upstairs it remains in the same state that it was, excepting that more care is taken by the attendants to preserve cleanliness as far as depends on them. I went through most of the wards. The beds are extremely good and the space very large with windows on each side, so as to make a thorough air. It being warm weather all the windows were open and as all who were able to be out of bed were so I was not sensible of the inconveniences to which the patients are exposed when the beds are full and the windows obliged to be shut. The Foundling Hospital and I believe the Hôtel Dieu have both suffered a diminution of their revenue by the revolution, as they were in part supported by the duties imposed on goods and provisions brought into Paris.

Went to the Jardin du Roi, which is at the same time a botanical garden and a publick walk, the choicest plants being within enclosures. It is on the skirts of the town, and from its size, airiness and situation on the bank of the river, is the finest publick garden in Paris, but being in a remote quarter is little frequented. Went to the General Hospital or Salpêtrière, which is an immense building or rather collection of buildings. It is entirely for females, and there are great establishments for the care and education of children and for the maintenance and support of such as are passed their labour. There is a large place for mad women who are but ill taken care of. Women of disorderly lives used to be sent here by the police to be confined for a time, but that is over. There is still a part appropriated for the confinement of female criminals who are sentenced to be confined for a certain time in consequence of particular crimes. The young and the old seem to be well taken care of.

Saturday, *August* 20*th*. Went to see the Hôtel de Marbœuf, which is newly fitted up in a very expensive manner by the owner who is a rich widow; it is not on the whole in good taste though there are fine parts of it.

Went to the Duke of Praslin's, which is a large hotel; some of the rooms and one in particular are magnificently fitted up and furnished. The floors are the most elegantly and expensively inlaid I ever saw. But what chiefly deserves attention in the house is a very valuable collection of pictures, particularly Flemish.

Sunday, *August* 21*st*. Dined at Raincy, a seat of the Duke of Orleans about 9 miles from Paris. It is on the whole a fine place, the house is very good with handsome stables and various offices. It is situated at some distance from the road with an avenue of large poplars. There is a forest adjoining to it and an extensive pleasure ground about it, of which a large part is laid out in the English taste. This is the worst part, as all the trees are young and do not thrive, the water trifling, and the grass, of which there is too much, in such bad order by the heat of the summer, the badness of the soil, and the want of rolling and mowing, that it looks like a very rough poor field.

Thursday, *August* 25*th*. Received from Monsieur Suard an *académicien's* ticket to attend the annual meeting on St Louis's day for the distribution of prizes etc. Marmontel took the chair and opened with a speech, in which he declared that the spirit of politics had so far overpowered the spirit of literature that the Academy had not found any performance worthy of a prize among those sent in for the present year. The prizes were therefore reserved, except that for the most distinguished act of virtue, which was decreed to a little association of the servants of a man in very extensive business. The master met with heavy losses, broke, and died insolvent. The servants who had lived with him long were all losers of considerable sums due for wages which they had left in his hands. Notwithstanding which they united their industry and their little possessions and maintained among them with the utmost care and attention a child of their late master who was left totally destitute and incapable from severe infirmity of supporting himself. There being no prize productions to be read, Monsieur de la Harpe read a dissertation on the state of literature from the age of Augustus to that of Louis 14th. Then Monsieur Florian repeated some fables, and the Abbé Delisle some parts of a poem on imagination, which it is to be hoped he soon means to publish. These performances had all much merit in their different ways.

Saturday, *August 27th.* Went to see St Denis. The Abbey is fine and the quantity of tombs of the different kings and other remarkable persons well worth seeing. The treasure is curious enough and does not take up much time, as the priest who shows it has as little inclination as the spectators can have to give more than is necessary.

Sunday, *August 28th.* Went to see the Duke of Orleans' house and garden on the skirts of Paris, called Monceaux, which is well worth the trouble. The house is not good but has many rooms, is fitted up with expense and in a very whimsical manner, and is well adapted to parties and entertainments. The gardens are extremely pretty, in the English taste, with much variety and a great number of buildings, some of which are in very good taste.

Tuesday, *August 30th.* Went to a breakfast at Mr Morris's. He is an American, a gentlemanlike sensible man of property and estimation in America. He was concerned in the line of finance during the war. He has only one leg, having been obliged to undergo an amputation in consequence of jumping from a window in an affair of gallantry. Made an acquaintance with Madame de Flahaut, a very sensible agreeable woman. Her husband and she have apartments in the Louvre, where they live much at home and have a small society most evenings. The chief purpose of the meeting was to hear the Abbé Delisle read some passages of his poem on the imagination, which he did. They were very beautiful, and from what I have heard the poem must be a delightful work. It is hoped it will be published this winter.

Wednesday, *August* 31*st*. Went to see the Bicêtre, about two miles out of Paris. It is a very large respectable looking place. It is a prison and at the same time an hospital for various kinds of objects, and particularly madmen and idiots, and it is likewise a kind of workhouse for poor infirm people who live there and have an allowance. The prisons consist of a great number of small cells, where the people are confined separately. Each has a window with iron bars, through which the prisoner can converse with any person in the courts and yard. Strangers are admitted very freely, and the entrance of a new visitor seldom fails to bring the inhabitants of all the cells to their grates, where they have all something to ask or something to offer for sale. Those who are so situated as not to have a good view have little looking glasses which they hold out at windows and catch a sight of the objects of their curiosity by that means. We found that notwithstanding the new laws in favour of liberty this prison was full of people who had been there many months and some of them years without being brought to any trial or having any hearing. The truth is that hitherto the machine does not move. The destruction of old institutions has been complete enough, but the substitution of new ones is very imperfect and in many cases quite ineffectual. Rode afterwards to Vincennes crossing the Seine by a ferry at Charenton. Vincennes has a great appearance of ancient grandeur.

APPENDIX.

I.

Lord Elgin to Lord Grenville.

This letter shews the extreme difficulty of obtaining information as to the state of affairs in Paris after the outbreak of the war in Feb. 1793.

[Most secret.]

BRUXELLES, *Feb.* 14, 1794.

My Lord,

In consequence of the verbal instructions which I received in London, and from the prospect of ultimate success, which a variety of private considerations led me to hope for, I have used every means in my power, since my return from England, to establish in various ways channels of information from Paris and different parts of France. Hitherto the innumerable obstacles I have had to contend with have made me silent on the subject: but I forward to your Lordship by this day's post, what I trust will be the best proof that I have not been ill-advised in my perseverance.

My endeavours, as long as they were confined to this frontier, were fruitless: I had frequently sent to Paris, without success; I had placed persons in different points for the purpose of communication; but they have all hitherto, in a very short time, been thrown into prison. The person whom I especially employed to establish correspondencies in France has tried various directions: he is now as far as Switzerland, and he sends me the enclosed memorial as the result of his first researches. Your Lordship may rely upon it, as containing nothing, but on authorities worthy of credit, and compared with much care. Fugitives from the army, who have quitted their country one, two or three months; fugitives, from the smaller administrations, from the Convention, from the principal towns in France, and from Paris itself, have been all repeatedly consulted: and they have been found to correspond in the result of their observations, notwithstanding their being connected with discording parties.

All agree in representing the evil as of the greatest magnitude, but all equally agree in the possibility of discovering effectual remedies.

The second memorial that is promised me shall be forwarded to your Lordship the moment I receive it.

I have the honor to be, with the utmost respect,

My Lord,
your Lordship's
Most obedient
humble Servant,
ELGIN.

Endorsed,
BRUSSELS, *Feb.* 14*th*, 1794.
Lord Elgin
R. 18*th* (Most Secret)
By Mason.

RÉSUMÉ D'INFORMATIONS EXACTES
AU 25 JANVIER 1794.

Le Gouvernement de la Révolution a changé de caractère : ce n'est plus une constitution idéale, abandonnée, comme en 1791 et 1792, à la désobéissance publique ; ni une anarchie interne, entre deux factions, divisées sur le régime à donner à la République, comme en 1793 ; ni la confusion résultante du triomphe d'un parti toujours menacé et mal affermi, comme durant l'été dernier.

Pendant ces trois périodes, la Convention nationale étoit encore indépendante ; chaque voix comptoit plus ou moins ; l'autorité exécutive exercée par les Ministres, rognée à chaque instant par les comités, et divisée, pour ainsi dire, entre chaque membre de l'Assemblée, chaque corps populaire, chaque administration, chaque agent révolutionnaire, chaque clubbiste, manquoit de force, d'harmonie, de secret, de centre d'unité.

Un autre régime est survenu, par l'institution, et par la toute puissance, du Comité de Salut public ; le péril de la République, et la défiance du pouvoir exécutif lui donnèrent naissance : son influence s'agrandit avec les dangers ; elle s'est perpetuée et affermie par les succès.

Ce Comité exerce la Dictature dans toute son étendue ; il rédige les plans, et les exécute ; les Ministres ne sont que ses commis ; la Convention qu'une machine à décrets, pour sanctionner les décisions de ce conseil. Il dispose souverainement des armées, du généralat, des fonds publics, des tribunaux révolutionnaires, des autorités secondaires, des agens innombrables de la force publique, des capitaux, des revenus, des biens meubles et immeubles, de la vie de chaque citoyen, des inquisitions, des Comités de surveillance, même des clubs.

Il a légalisé sa tyrannie, et l'a rendue méthodique, par l'adoption du Gouvernement révolutionnaire, devant lequel se taisent les droits de l'homme, la souveraineté du peuple, les constitutions précédentes et toute liberté. Ce régime a rencontré des oppositions parmi les anarchistes; mais le crédit du Comité a fait trembler les murmurateurs; et ce pouvoir épouvantable a été monté à tour de bras, sans qu'un seul Jacobin ait osé lui disputer l'existence.

De ce moment la puissance populaire s'est anéantie; ou du moins se trouve entièrement suspendue; les assemblées électorales, les administrations de district, les Municipalités ont disparu; le pouvoir des Directoires de Département est assujettie dans chaque détail de son exercice.

Des Délégués conventionels nommés par le Comité font les fonctions de proconsuls absolus dans ces Départemens. Des agens nationaux encore nommés par le Comité, les secondent dans les districts; et y font exécuter leurs ordres; ces Commissaires cassent à volonté les directoires, et les corps Municipaux; destituent les officiers du peuple, sans le consulter; remettent l'administration, à qui il leur plaît, et ont ainsi prévenu les conflits d'autorité, ceux d'opinion, de parti et l'anarchie qui en résultoit.

En leur absence, les Commissaires sont représentés par ces *agens nationaux* de la création du Comité qui ont succédé aux Procureurs Syndics, nommés jadis par le peuple, dans les districts, et les communes. Derrière ces Administrations et celles des Départemens, se placent les clubs; le moindre bourg, les gros villages ont chacun le leur. De leur sein est tiré un comité de surveillance, qui exerce l'inquisition publique non seulement sur les simples individus quelconques, mais encore sur les corps administratifs, lesquels, toute exécrable qu'est leur composition actuelle, sont en masse et en détail journellement contrôlés par les surveillans. Pour surcroît de précaution, le Comité de Salut public, et les propres clubs, dont ils sont extraits, les entourent d'espions et de dénonciateurs, chargés de rendre compte et d'observer la conduite des comités inquisitoriaux.

Cette chaîne de satellites correspondans, et mutuellement délateurs les uns les autres, répondent de leur fidélité aux Comités de Salut public, et de sûreté générale: ce dernier est le bureau d'informations, la sentinelle du comité de salut public auquel il est subordonné. Nous en parlerons ailleurs. Par la défiance nécessaire, qui les domine tous, ils ont pour instruction générale de dénoncer et de faire arrêter comme suspect quiconque est soupçonné de professer en secret, ou *d'avoir professé* le royalisme, l'amour de la religion, le feuillantisme, le fédéralisme, et le modérantisme.

Dans cette dernière classe sont compris tous ceux qu'on nomme *gens paisibles:* les arrêtés des Commissaires conventionnels, dans les divers Départemens, qualifient ces citoyens d'*égoïstes*, de *vampires*, d'*agitateurs secrets:* presque tous sont propriétaires; la grande majorité d'entre eux sont détenus ou guillotinés, sequestrés ou condamnés à des contributions énormes et arbitraires pour les frais de la guerre.

On ne peut se former au loin une idée juste de la soumission et de la terreur qu'a produit ce nouvel arrangement de tyrannie: personne n'ose réclamer une loi, un droit, un principe, une possession. Les supplices sont aussi fréquens dans les provinces qu'à Paris; et dans les campagnes que dans les villes. Pas une parole, pas une démarche, pas une fortune n'échappent à cette armée de délateurs, tous animés de l'émulation de renchérir en atrocité les uns sur les autres. Le mois dernier, en voyant passer quelques jeunes gens de la première réquisition, qui se rendoit à l'armée d'Alsace, un paysan octogénaire et aisé de la Franche Comté, s'écria: *Ces pauvres enfants, ce sont des veaux qu'on mène à la boucherie.* Dès le soir il fut arrêté, et huit jours après guillotiné; on citeroit mille exemples pareils.

Insensiblement et graduellement depuis quatre mois, il s'est donc formé une organisation d'abord invisible; aujourd'hui régulièrement montée, indépendante de toute espèce de pouvoir populaire, en tenant lieu, et recevant son existence, comme sa conservation, des chefs du Comité de Salut public. Tous les Jacobins modérés, les républicains incertains, les caractères froids, ceux en qui pouvoit s'élever encore un repentir, un sentiment de pitié, une idée de crainte ou de retour vers un autre ordre de choses, ont été expulsés des emplois; à force de placer, et de déplacer on est parvenu à avoir des hommes capables et bien prononcés, soit dans les armées, soit dans les administrations.

A Paris, ainsi que dans les départemens, ces divers agens sont exclusivement *des sans-culottes* dans la force du terme: plus rien de l'ancienne bigarrure: ces nouveaux parvenus foulent sous leurs sabots et font trembler les propriétaires de toute classe: ils ont réduit le reste des habitans à la nullité la plus absolue; un intérêt commun, un fanatisme atroce, ou une scélératesse sans bornes, sont les garants de leur zèle à remplir leurs fonctions et à concourir énergiquement au maintien du despotisme actuel.

Le pouvoir révolutionnaire, dont l'exercice leur est confié, agit maintenant par des règles fixes et avec une violence habituellement systématique. On ne craint plus de choquer l'opinion ni les principes de la première révolution.

Les Commissaires de parti ont pris l'appareil, la représentation, le langage des bachas; trainés dans des carosses à six chevaux, entourés de gardes, assis à des tables de 30 couverts, mangeant au bruit de la musique, avec un cortège de courtisannes, d'histrions, de prétoriens; toujours menaçans, et ne perdant jamais le ton du commandement ni celui de l'enthousiasme, ils ont frappé le peuple subitement de terreur; le même esprit, les mêmes formes extérieures distinguent proportionellement les sous ordres; en un mot, ci devant, les ministres de la puissance nationale affectoient auprès du peuple le ton de l'égalité, de l'humilité, du respect, et semblant obéir en ordonnant avec faiblesse; aujourd'hui on parle en maître, et la moindre désobéissance est un crime irrémissible.

Les trahisons, les complots, les réactions, les soulèvemens que facilitait jadis la multiplicité des autorités et l'incohérence de leur exercice sont maintenant physiquement et moralement impossibles.

Trois, quatre personnes, à moins d'être les complices même du Comité, ne sauraient se rassembler ni s'entretenir sans danger; soit à la promenade, soit dans leurs maisons. Le fermier est espionné par son valet de charrue, le maître par son domestique, le mari par sa femme, le fabriquant par ses ouvriers, le marchand par ses commis.

Les retraites les plus impénétrables sont à tout moment décelées. Rabaut de St-Etienne[1] et son frère, cachés depuis cinq mois à l'extrémité d'un fauxbourg, dans une loge recouverte d'une boiserie à trape, et où leur hôte seul leur apportoit à manger, ont été enfin trahis, arrêtés, et exécutés. La crainte fait autant de délateurs que l'intérêt ou la fureur du parti.

On ne peut plus ni parler, ni écrire. Le Palais Royal, cet ancien rendezvous des révolutionnaires, est absolument désert : on a vidé le jardin, et les maisons, même les caffés; pas un groupe n'ose se former; à la nuit, chacun se retire chez soi : on appelle cette retraite *aller coucher sa Liberté.*

Toutes les boutiques sont fermées avant huit heures du soir; les lieux de ralliement, les entretiens les plus indifférens, la solitude, les affaires privées, les correspondances, sont également dangereuses. Chaque section dans les villes a son comité de surveillance : lorsqu'on lui échapperait, on seroit investi des sbirres de la Commune ou du comité de sûreté générale qui sortent de dessous les pavés.

[1] He was guillotined December 5, 1793.

Tout ce qui pouvoit conserver quelque influence par sa fortune, par un ancien crédit, par des services rendus même à la Révolution ; quiconque dont le nom offriroit une addresse, une espérance aux mécontens, est arrêté, fugitif, ou assassiné. Les prisons de Paris et les maisons d'arrêt en renferment 18 mille : chaque ville de province à proportion : un exil volontaire a dérobé, et en dérobe encore, un grand nombre à la Guillotine : il en sort toutes les semaines au travers de mille périls ; plusieurs auxquels j'ai parlé ont fait à la lettre le tour de la France sous divers déguisemens, sans avoir pu trouver une issue ; ce n'est qu'à la suite des aventures les plus romanesques qu'ils sont enfin parvenus, à vol d'oiseau, à gagner la Suisse : seule frontière encore un peu accessible à cette foule d'infortunés.

Ce sont la plupart des habitans des villes ou contrées reassujetties par la convention, des fédéralistes, des anciens constitutionels, et des royalistes de toute dénomination.

Lorsque les élémens d'une insurrection, lorsque la faculté de la préparer, celle d'en rassembler les instruments, et *la volonté de la faire* ne seroient pas radicalement détruits, il n'y auroit aucune possibilité de l'exécuter ; car en ce moment, *le peuple entier est désarmé*. Il ne reste pas un fusil, ni dans les villes, ni dans les campagnes. Si quelque chose atteste la puissance surnaturelle dont jouissent les meneurs de la Convention c'est de voir dans un instant, par un seul acte de leur volonté, et sans que personne ose leur résister ni s'en plaindre, la nation ramenée, de Perpignan jusqu'à Lille, à la privation de toute défense contre l'oppression, avec une facilité plus inouïe encore que celle dont se fit en 1789 l'armement universel du royaume.

Voici un trait remarquable de cette facilité. On se rapelle les fières annonces de la ville de Bordeaux après la journée du 31 Mai dernier, qui abbatit le parti-Girondin ; on voulait marcher sur Paris ; on menaçait, on insultait la Convention, on rompit avec elle, on la provoqua au combat. Tous les *muscadins* de Bourdeaux, et des villes voisines s'étaient équipés, montés, exercés : ils étaient si enivrés de leur bravoure que le général Wimphen, après sa déroute en Normandie, étant allé leur porter des propositions d'alliance avec la Vendée, ils les rejettèrent comme incompatibles avec leurs idées sur la Monarchie.

Au commencement d'Octobre quatre Commissaires de la Convention se mirent en marche de La Réole, avec 1800 paysans et brigands : un hérault alla ordonner de leur part aux braves de

Bourdeaux, de sortir de la ville en bataillons, et de venir les recevoir à la porte. Personne n'ignorait qu'ils étaient suivis de bourreaux, de geôliers, et de coupeurs de bourse. Néanmoins, 12,000 Bordelais, gens de commerce, ou d'industrie, ayant fait depuis l'origine de la Révolution le service de Gardes Nationales avec un grand étalage, obéirent à cette requisition ; ils se rendirent à la porte, armés, en uniforme, et leur chefs à leur tête. Pour mieux célébrer l'arrivée de leurs assassins, ils avaient préparé des couronnes de chêne au Commissaires. Aussitôt Tallien, le principal de ces délégués, après une harangue foudroyante et outrageuse, ordonna à un détachement de ses bandits d'aller arracher à la troupe dorée ses branches de chêne, ses épaulettes, ses cocardes : l'exécution s'étant faite, sans aucune résistance, Tallien cassa les bataillons Bordelais, et entré en ville avec sa troupe de gueux il proclama l'ordre à tous les habitants sans distinction, d'avoir a déposer en 36 heures, et *sous peine de mort*, leurs armes sur le glacis du Château Trompette : avant le terme, trente mille fusils, les épées, les pistolets, jusqu'aux canifs furent livrés : une poignée de scélérats conduits par quatre magiciens désarma une cité en rebellion ; 100,000 citoyens reçûrent la loi, sans oser proférer un murmure ; les arrestations, et les supplices commencèrent le lendemain ; ils n'ont pas discontinué ; Bordeaux est aujourd'hui aux fers et pour toujours ; il sera démoli comme Lyons et Marseilles.

Il est superflu d'ajouter qu'on a détruit tout principe de soulèvement, toute confiance dans les puissances étrangères, toute opinion, tout désir de révolte par l'abandon à jamais déplorable de Lyons, de Toulon, de la Vendée. Quiconque serait tenté de croire aux promesses du dehors, à des espérances fallacieuses, à des invitations mensongères, à la possibilité du moindre succès tournerait ses regards sur les ruines de Lyons baigné du sang de ses citoyens égorgés ; il se convaincrait bien vite que le sort d'une rébellion appuyée sur le concours de la guerre étrangère, est cent fois plus horrible que la soumission au rasoir national et au despotisme de la Convention.

Ainsi, il sera prudent de renoncer à toutes chimères à ce sujet, de fermer l'oreille aux menteurs, aux flatteurs, aux colporteurs de fausses informations qui viendront imprimer, ou dire aux Cabinets, que les opprimés les invoquent, et qu'on peut compter sur leur assistance. Je démens à l'avance ces allégations emphatiques, et j'affirme que les puissances ont égorgé l'année dernière toute faculté d'insurrections intérieures en France, à moins qu'elles ne s'ouvrent l'intérieur du royaume à force ouverte.

Les Jacobins ont profité, avec leur habilité ordinaire, de leurs victoires sur les révoltés : elles ont ranimé le zèle de leurs partisans, rendu la confiance aux plus timides, tourné contre les puissances la haine des opprimés sacrifiés, généralisé le mépris et l'horreur de la Royauté, rallié à la Convention les incertains, subjugué la masse du peuple, et extirpé par l'énormité des vengeances exercées toute semence de soulèvement. On n'a plus d'amis, plus de parens, plus de communications verbales ou épistolaires : la moitié de la nation est effacée et ne compte plus que pour servir aux besoins du fisc et des armées.

Les plans et les décrets prenant tous leur source dans le Comité de Salut public, il exerce l'initiative de la législation : il jouit en même temps du droit de décision par l'asservissement où il a plongé l'Assemblée Nationale ; elle ne renferme pas 200 ou 250 membres ; le reste a été guillotiné, arrêté ou mis en fuite. La parole est à peu près exclusivement réservée à trente ou quarante montagnards au plus ; *Robespierre, Danton, Couthon, Billaud-Varennes* tiennent les armes, les langues, les poignards dans leurs mains : on ne permet plus ni débats, ni discussions ; chaque représentant étranger à cette phalange dominatrice tremble pour sa liberté ou pour sa vie, et rachète l'une et l'autre par une soumission silencieuse aux volontés des chefs.

Au nombre des absens, il faut mettre encore les commissaires envoyés aux armées et dans les départemens. Le Comité pouvant les révoquer à toute heure arbitrairement, et cette révocation devenant le prélude d'un arrêt de mort, ces députés ambulans n'ont qu'un intérêt, qu'un vœu, qu'une pensée ; ils s'accordent tous à se montrer dans leur commission aussi inexorables, aussi forcenés que leurs commettans et à leur prouver un dévouement illimité.

Le Ministre prend les ordres immédiats du Comité, lui réfère les moindre détails, exécute ponctuellement ses ordonnances, et loin de contrarier sa puissance, en est l'instrument passif, servile, et avili : on n'y place que des valets ; leurs bureaux sont leurs surveillans ; chaque commis un peu important est à la dévotion des Dictateurs. Bouchotte[1], Ministre actuel, est un imbécile, il n'a que sa signature et sa responsabilité. Pache quoique Maire de Paris est encore le véritable chef du Département. Les autres Ministres ne méritent pas d'être nommés.

[1] Minister of War till April 1, 1794.

Finances. L'emploi illimité des fonds publics est abandonné aux décisions du comité du salut public. C'est un abîme impénétrable : la profusion des dépenses est calculée sur la fécondité, sur la promptitude, sur la nature des ressources. Les finances se divisent en revenus et en capitaux, les revenus se tirent des impositions exigées à usure des propriétaires ; eux seuls acquittent les taxes ; le peuple proprement dit ne paye rien et on ne songe pas encore à l'y obliger : la régie et l'usufruit des biens nationaux invendus forment une autre branche de revenu : l'une et l'autre sont des gouttes d'eau dans l'océan ; mais à l'aide des contributions arbitraires et locales, qu'on impose sans mesure sur tous ceux qui ont quelque fortune visible, elles suffisent aux dépenses courantes ordinaires dont le montant a diminué et diminue chaque jour.

Cette diminution résulte, 1°, de l'extinction graduelle et maintenant énorme des rentes sur l'état. On ne paye plus celles qui sont dues aux créanciers de sujets des puissances belligérantes : on a gagné le capital et les intérêts appartenant aux émigrés : la guillotine et les confiscations en éteignent successivement : on a suspendu le paiement des rentes dues aux communautés ; les pensions allouées au clergé sont supprimées, ainsi que les traitemens assignés au clergé constitutionnel ; enfin l'établissement du *grand livre* où les parties prenantes sont obligées de faire enregistrer les titres de leurs créances diverses sous un même n° a fourni le moyen de profiter des négligences, de mettre en discussion toutes les créances, de connaître celles qui appartiennent aux gens suspects et de couler à fond tout ce qu'on voudra anéantir de la dette publique.

2°. Les dépenses du culte sont nulles. 3°. Celles d'administration locale sont rejetées sur les départemens. Une multitude d'autres branches telles que les secours de charité, les établissemens publics, l'entretien des routes sont également supprimées ou très réduites.

Les dépenses extraordinaires, rendues inévaluables, sont acquittées par les ressources extraordinaires qui ont quadruplé depuis un an.

Ces ressources consistent en créations d'assignats, en confiscations de capitaux, en spoliations de tout genre, et dans l'emprunt forcé d'un milliard.

Quant au premier objet, il est impossible d'en savoir la valeur, puisqu'il se fait au besoin des créations clandestines, et qu'en divers lieux les commissaires délégués ont usé et usent encore d'une planche d'assignats. Le total de ce papier en circulation a diminué depuis qu'on a démonétisé les assignats royaux.

Il ne paraît pas, au surplus, que la quantité plus ou moins considérable des billets ait influé sensiblement depuis six mois sur le cours des changes ni sur le prix de l'or et de l'argent.

Il faut attribuer les variations à d'autres causes; l'état des affaires à l'extérieur, les chances de la guerre intestine, les manœuvres des gens de banque, les soldes plus ou moins considérables d'achats et de services payés au dehors par le gouvernement, y ont eu une part plus spéciale. Ainsi du mois de mai au mois d'octobre, les assignats étaient tombés de 60 à 75 pour 100 de perte; ils sont remontés maintenant à 33 à 35 dans Paris, à 45 ou 50 dans les pays qui soutiennent encore des rapports commerciaux avec la France. Ce dernier prix se soutient depuis deux mois; mais depuis la reprise de Toulon, les avantages en Alsace et la défaite de la Vendée, les assignats ont encore haussé un moment de valeur dans le royaume. Il est des départemens où ils ne perdent que 25 ou 30, et ils seroient encore plus bas à Paris sans les fréquens achats de numéraire qu'a faits la trésorerie nationale dans le mois de décembre et le commencement de celui-ci. Mais les deux causes actives du crédit des assignats sont: 1°, La défense d'exporter les marchandises de France à l'étranger, défense qui a rendu les assignats inutiles à celui-ci. 2°, L'émigration immense des capitalistes et des négocians qui ne pouvant exporter l'or et l'argent, font sortir l'assignat dont le nombre surcharge l'étranger. Par ces deux causes le papier monnaie ne tardera pas à retomber. Au surplus, depuis la loi du *maximum* qui par son extension à la plupart des denrées et des marchandises embrasse toutes les consommations essentielles, la dépréciation des assignats n'est plus onéreuse au gouvernement que dans l'acquisition des fournitures étrangères. Cette loi s'exécute avec rigueur: personne n'ose plus s'en plaindre: elle a délivré la république de toute la dépense équivalente à l'excédant du prix qu'elle payait ci-devant pour ses consommations: c'est une économie énorme; la convention ne pouvoit prescrire à l'opinion de prendre les assignats au pair; mais elle a rempli le même but en soumettant à un tarif invariable la valeur des denrées et des marchandises.

Lorsqu'on est parvenu à forcer le citoyen non seulement de vendre, mais encore de vendre à un prix indépendant de la valeur que le papier monnaie peut perdre au cours de la place, et que la nature même du papier monnaie doit laisser toujours au-dessous du numéraire, il est fort indifférent que ce papier ait plus ou moins de crédit. La convention a donc fait à la fois une opération très économique et une opération très populaire ; car les sans-culottes consommant et ne possédant pas, il leur est fort doux d'acheter un papier à un prix qui lèse exclusivement celui qui vend.

L'essentiel à considérer, c'est qu'aujourd'hui, malgré l'énormité des dépenses, les nouvelles créations d'assignats sont moins nécessaires parce qu'il en faut une moindre quantité pour solder les besoins du gouvernement et parce que, ainsi que je le dirai dans l'instant, il paye en argent ce qu'il tire de l'étranger. D'ailleurs le comité de salut public ne regarde plus ces émissions nouvelles que comme une ressource subsidiaire : il la ménage et la ménagera : ses efforts tendent au contraire à soutenir et à élever le papier, à en diminuer l'emploi, à restreindre la masse en circulation, et à faire remonter les changes par des paiemens en espèces.

C'est dans cette vue que le comité de salut public s'est emparé dernièrement de l'actif et du passif de la banque de Paris, et du royaume ; en prenant tout le papier sur l'étranger qui se trouvait chez les banquiers, et en se chargeant de payer leurs créanciers au dehors. Vraisemblablement le but de cette opération qui se consomme en ce moment avec peu de succès, est, ou de spolier le commerce de ses créances dans l'étranger, ou de faire hausser les changes en faveur de celles-ci, en offrant, ainsi que le fait le comité, d'acquitter les remises en argent ou en assignats.

En général, on doit conclure 1°, que le discrédit des assignats est et sera, toutes choses égales d'ailleurs, moindre qu'il ne fut l'année dernière ; 2°, que la convention en fera des émissions moins fréquentes, 3°, que la masse circulante, jointe à celle de numéraire qu'elle possède, suffit à ses monstrueuses opérations.

Ce sont autant de vérités de fait qui deviendront sensibles en apprenant les ressources indéfinies que la convention s'est ouvertes depuis trois mois.

Elle a mis à sa disposition toutes les propriétés du royaume, capitaux et revenus. Les substances, les matériaux de fabrication nécessaires au service public, toiles, draps, métaux, fruits de la terre, denrées coloniales, tout est reconnu, vérifié, pris ou mis en réquisition. Elle vole une partie de ces consommations, elle paye l'autre au prix du *maximum*. Quiconque possède six chemises est obligé d'en donner une, pour les besoins de l'armée, des fournitures de souliers, de guêtres, de bas, de chapeaux, sont exigées des propriétaires de toute classe. Les détachemens de l'armée révolutionnaire escortant des commissaires en tournée dans les départemens font des visites domiciliaires jusque dans les hameaux ; ils se font délivrer, outre les articles déjà indiqués, toute la fonte, le cuivre et le fer (excepté celui des instrumens aratoires) : on a enlevé jusqu'aux marmites des pâtres ; ils ont raflé de même tous les bijoux, la vaisselle et le numéraire des particuliers, en donnant cependant des assignats en échange ; mais seulement à ceux qu'il leur plaît de ne pas déclarer *suspects*.

Vous voyez donc que non contente de posséder les métaux et le papier monnaie qui sont les signes des choses, la convention s'est emparée des choses mêmes qui constituent la richesse réelle. Ses immenses spoliations *privées*, ajoutées aux spoliations *publiques*, au numéraire acquis par l'échange des assignats, et la faculté de graduer à volonté cette richesse de papier monnaie depuis qu'on a déterminé le prix des choses que cette monnaie représente, ouvrent à la convention autant de sources intarissables de thésaurisation et de dépenses. Je le répète ; généralement tout ce qui est dans la sphère de ses besoins et de ses crimes est en *état de réquisition permanente*, c'est à dire en sa pleine puissance ; car personne ne disposerait de ce qui lui appartient dans ce séquestre provisoire, sans encourir une confiscation totale ou l'assassinat.

Maintenant si vous desirez connaître les vols effectifs, les appropriations au fisc, déjà exécutés par la convention, indépendamment des fortunes, des revenus, des immeubles, des produits de la terre ou de l'industrie qui restent encore précairement dans les mains de leurs possesseurs, et assujettis à la condition qui les rend exclusivement disponibles pour la *nation* vous devez récapituler :

1°. Toute l'argenterie, les ornemens, les monumens métalliques des églises de ville et de campagne.

2°. La vente ou la saisie du mobilier des émigrés de toute époque depuis 1789 à 1794, tout ce qu'on trouve dans leurs maisons, dans les dépôts notariaux, chez les banquiers, dans les fouilles répétées des caves, des souterrains, des murailles : nombre de maisons ont été démolies uniquement sur le soupçon qu'elles recélaient des effets cachés dans les murs ; on continue ces découvertes sans interruption.

3°. Les enlèvemens faits à force ouverte par les commissaires et les détachemens révolutionnaires dans les départemens de toutes les matières d'or et d'argent fabriqués ou monnayés appartenant aux particuliers.

4°. Les dépouilles des villes soulevées telles que Lyon, Bordeaux, Strasbourg, Marseille ; cet article est d'une valeur immense : à Lyon la presque totalité des négocians des marchands et des fabricans aisés a été enfermée, mise en fuite, guillotinée et spoliée. Par une ruse digne d'eux, les vainqueurs en entrant dans la ville, affectèrent les paroles de modération et rassurèrent les habitans. Le commerce reprit de la sécurité, on rouvrit les magasins, on sortit de leur cachette les grands livres de recette, les portefeuilles, les marchandises précieuses.

Peu de jours après, le glaive se leva, les prisons et le trésor du fisc se remplirent; l'imprudence des négocians combla la rapacité des commissaires, et le butin fut plus considérable qu'il ne l'aurait été si les massacres eussent commencé à la reddition de la ville. Les meilleurs négocians de Marseille et de Bordeaux, ici les respectables Gradis, là des Tarterons, ont été assassinés et leurs biens confisqués. Tous ceux qui ont fui ont laissé une grande partie de leurs propriétés aux confiscateurs. J'ai vu la 32ième liste des émigrés de Marseille seulement, dont les biens ont été confisqués et mis en ente; il s'en trouve 12 mille, et les listes ne sont pas achevées.

5°. La fortune des particuliers quelconques guillotinés, est également acquise au fisc: or comme il est peu de propriétaires riches qui échappent au supplice, ou à la détention, qui en est le prélude, l'opulence de la convention n'a d'autres bornes que celles de son avarice et de sa cruauté. Notaires, fermiers généraux, banquiers, Caisse d'Escompte, Compagnie des Indes &c., toutes les corporations sont confisqués en gros et en détail. Suivant les états que je me suis procurés, il paraît que, sans compter les grands massacres, les foudroiemens à coups de canon, tels que ceux qui ont eu lieu à Lyon, et les submersions artificielles des bâtimens chargés de détenus, qu'on a coulés bas dans plusieurs rivières, il parait, dis-je, que la guillotine fait périr en France 350 à 400 personnes par semaine. Nous voyons tomber sous ce rasoir, outre les aristocrates, les contre-révolutionnaires, les fédéralistes, beaucoup de francs républicains et de sans-culottes enrichis. Aussitôt qu'un révolutionnaire, qu'un des employés publics, qu'un des membres même de la convention a fait, et a laissé paraître une fortune nouvelle, il est arrêté, jugé et tué. Fabre d'Eglantine, quoique l'un des douze du comité de salut public, expie[1] en ce moment, son carrosse, ses festins, ses maîtresses, sa maison de campagne. Les administrateurs des vivres, des chariots de l'armée, les fournisseurs quelconques, les généraux, les états-majors, les agens de finance une fois enrichis, subissent cette loi. La convention spécule savamment sur ces fortunes de parvenus; elle ne met aucun obstacle à

[1] He was accused Jan. 13, and executed April 5, 1794.

leur formation ; elle s'en empare aussitôt qu'elles sont formées ; son système consiste à piller les citoyens riches, et à piller ensuite successivement tous ceux qui le deviennent: on a vu des biens nationaux retomber quatre fois dans une année aux mains de la nation, par des confiscations successives ; une grande partie des domaines ecclésiastiques déjà vendus depuis 1791, se retrouve encore aujourd'hui à vendre, par cette navette de brigandages qu'entretient la convention à la plus grande satisfaction des sans-culottes ; en guillotinant ainsi les agens divers qui ont accepté des entreprises pour les divers besoins publics, et qui ont fait des bénéfices, elle fait rentrer ses assignats peu de temps après les avoir dépensés.

L'emprunt forcé d'un milliard se perçoit, et est recouvré en grande partie, par une taxation impérative sur les revenus, taxation dont on a vu le tarif exorbitant dans un décret de l'été dernier ; on crut cette perception impraticable, ou du moins tellement lésive que les contribuables y échapperaient par ruse ou par force. Vaine conjecture ! la terreur et les délations ont fait payer, même avec un empressement que les propriétaires ont considéré, à tort, comme moyen de sûreté.

Je ne parlerai que pour mémoire des contributions extraordinaires, exigées révolutionnairement ; elles s'appellent *taxes sèches*. A Strasbourg elles ont été de 9 millions 33,000 livres, repartis sur chacun de ceux qui possédaient quelque fortune; à Marseille de douze millions.

Il ne m'a pas été encore possible d'obtenir une récapitulation approximative du produit de ces divers articles ; des gens instruits m'ont seulement certifié et démontré par des pièces justificatives la probabilité que, du 1*er novembre* 1793 *au premier janvier* 1794, il était entré, ou qu'il existait, de *trois* à *quatre cent* millions de matières d'or ou d'argent en fabrication ou monnayées aux hôtels des monnaies et d'espèces au trésor public. Chaque mois, la dépense extraordinaire emporte environ 300 millions : cet état dure depuis le milieu de l'été dernier ; on n'y comprend pas l'usage des assignats illégitimes c. à d. frappés sans décret, et dont la quantité est un mystère. La convention ni le peuple n'osent plus demander, ni on ne leur présente de comptes détaillés. L'immensité des brigandages et leur fécondité faisant croire à des ressources inépuisables, personne ne s'occupe de la dépense.

Celle-ci augmentera, loin de diminuer. Le comité souverain a pris pour base de conduite des "efforts sans bornes": on doit s'attendre qu'il tiendra parole, et ne pas s'étourdir sur la certitude de sa résolution à ce sujet. Encore bien des mois il soutiendra le fardeau sans épuisement. Sa méthode (et c'est la bonne) est de ne jamais regarder à une dépense, lorsqu'elle est nécessaire. Il considère cette nécessité d'abord, et la somme ensuite : Qu'un objet coûte cent écus ou cent mille écus, si le service public l'exige, la différence est annullée et l'on va en avant. J'ai une infinité de preuves de fait à cet égard. Par exemple, le comité achète en Suisse à 20, 25, 30 louis d'or payés *en espèces*, des chevaux qui n'en valent pas 10 à 12. Il fait couper en ce moment les forêts de la Savoie pour les chantiers de Toulon, quoique ces bois vendus en province doivent coûter trois fois ce que coûtaient les bois d'Albanie ou du Nord. Depuis quelques mois le comité s'est appliqué avec son infatigable zèle à acheter de l'étranger, non seulement ce qui lui manque, mais encore ce qu'il veut conserver dans le royaume pour des besoins urgens. Genève et Bâle sont les deux grandes artères par où elle fait circuler son or, ses commandes, ses extractions de marchandises et de denrées.

De ces deux points, elle fait passer ses remises en Allemagne, en Hollande, en Angleterre, en Italie. Ses émissaires vont et viennent sans cesse ; des dépôts sont établis près des frontières pour recevoir les achats ; elle fait fabriquer 60 mille paires de souliers dans le Canton de Berne, et deux cent mille dans l'étendue de la Suisse. Elle tire d'Allemagne des cuirs, des draps, des toiles, des chevaux, des armes, du fer, de la fonte, du cuivre, des bestiaux, du souffre dont elle était à la veille de manquer.

Ces articles, ainsi que les grains dont nous parlerons plus bas, sont soldés libéralement, de manière à exciter les vendeurs timides à la contrebande, qui se fait chaque jour par l'imbécille incurie ou la collusion des régences allemandes.

Vous pouvez conclure de cet aperçu des ressources financières de la convention, aperçu établi sur des informations certaines, que la république est plus riche, et met en dehors plus de ressources que tous les souverains de la coalition réunis ; car ici c'est la richesse nationale d'un empire, et l'accumulation des richesses depuis un siècle dans cet empire, qui se battent contre les faibles revenus de quelques princes ; si l'on laisse échapper cette vérité, il ne sera pas étonnant de voir perpétuer le misérable système d'économie étroite et routinière qui a ruiné les causes des puissances dans les deux dernières campagnes.

Armée. Maintenant je passe à l'armée, à son commandement, à son entretien, à son état moral, aux principes sur lesquels on la dirige, et à sa force numérique. L'armée a changé pour ainsi dire sa nature ;

autrefois elle était soumise au ministre de la guerre, et au comité militaire de l'assemblée nationale ; ministre et comité soumis eux-mêmes à cette assemblée : aujourd'hui elle dépend, dans sa composition, dans son régime, sa discipline, ses chefs, ses mouvemens, d'un conseil tout-puissant, de douze chefs de parti réunis par le même péril individuel, par les mêmes vues générales, par les mêmes passions et investis d'un pouvoir presque illimité. Le ministre ne peut donner ni retirer un emploi, créer ou destituer un général, secourir ou faire assiéger une place, disposer des fonds, statuer sur un point de discipline, ni gouverner dans tel ou tel sens les cœurs comme les bras du soldat, sans l'attache du comité du salut public. Quelquefois il est vrai, ce comité a montré de la condescendance pour certaines nominations des bureaux de la guerre, fermé les yeux sur les friponneries, les manœuvres, les horreurs de quelques-uns de leurs protégés et repoussé les dénonciations qu'on lui adresse pour solliciter contre ces misérables l'exercice de la responsabilité. Ce cas est arrivé pendant la guerre de la Vendée où 27 généraux ont successivement paru sur la scène, et où, à l'exception de quatre, tous eussent mérité la mort par leur ânerie, par leurs vols, par leurs débauches affreuses; mais le comité avait ses raisons pour tolérer des coquins qui le servaient sous d'autres rapports ; aussi dès qu'il a jugé le moment favorable, il a fait arrêter *Ronsin*, *Vincent* et *Maillard*, trois des scélérats qualifiés qui ont figuré dans les revers de l'été dernier à Saumur et sur la Loire Inférieure. Le comité ménagera de même toute cabale qu'il a dans sa main, quelle que soit sa conduite, jusqu'à l'instant où il pourra la réprimer sans perdre des créatures utiles.

Il n'existe plus d'autre titre d'avancement qu'un zèle féroce et un dévouement sans bornes à la convention.

Quant au commandement en chef, les promotions sont déterminées moins par la capacité que par la fidélité du sujet. Il ne reste aucun général des premiers temps de la révolution, ni des 18 premiers mois de la guerre. Des officiers de fortune, des bas-officiers, des aventuriers actifs et entreprenans les ont remplacés. Dugommier qui a emporté Toulon et qui est allé prendre le commandement des Pyrénées passe pour le plus éclairé et le plus capable ; c'est un ancien officier d'artillerie.

Il était difficile qu'à force de mutations il ne sortît de ce ressassement continuel de généraux des hommes propres à la guerre révolutionnaire dans laquelle ils ont été élevés et pour laquelle ils montrent des talens analogues aux circonstances, à l'espèce de troupes qu'ils commandent, et encore au génie des généraux qui leur sont opposés.

En se confiant à des généraux tirés de la fange, le comité a senti que leur abaissement passé et leur élévation présente lui servaient de caution de leur loyauté. Nonobstant cela, il les a entourés d'Argus et des Mentors. Les commissaires conventionnels qui siègent auprès des armées sont dans le fait des espèces de consuls investis de la double autorité civile et militaire, tandis que les généraux représentent les lieutenans-généraux de cavalerie chez les Romains. Ils président aux conseils de guerre, sanctionnent, ou changent les plans et donnent à l'armée une impulsion souveraine. A leurs ordres se trouvent une nuée d'espions et de délateurs, qui leur rendent compte de la conduite de chaque chef, de ses discours, de ses relations, de ses habitudes ; cette surveillance tient en bride les agitateurs incommodes, dont le comité s'est débarrassé au dedans en leur donnant de l'emploi à la frontière. Les états-majors, qui forment le conseil de guerre sont l'âme de l'armée ; ils rédigent et préparent les opérations. La plupart, officiers d'artillerie et du génie, ont été choisis avec discernement. Aidés de secours immenses en cartes, plans, reconnoissances, recueillis au dépôt de la guerre, ils opèrent réellement d'après l'expérience et les lumières des plus grands généraux de l'ancienne monarchie.

Le général exécute ce que ces états-majors et les commissaires ont décidé ; il n'a que sa voix dans la délibération : partout ailleurs il est l'instrument subordonné : l'armée n'est nullement dans la main de son chef : il ne disposerait pas d'un bataillon ; sa suprématie expire le lendemain d'un jour de bataille, et ce jour-là, on ne connaît que le général et les soldats. Les officiers sont absolument effacés. Que le général soit pendu ou déifié, cela ne change rien à l'esprit de l'armée qu'on a rendu indépendant de celui de son chef ; on a prévenu l'influence de l'amour ou la confiance qu'elle pourrait mettre en lui ; elle obéit à la chose, nullement à la personne. Ainsi isolés, et avertis par la rigueur comme par la fréquence des supplices, les généraux actuels sont contraints de faire leur devoir et de le faire sans négligence.

L'entretien et la subsistance des armées se sont fort améliorés ; le comité a porté une attention scrupuleuse à prévenir le dénuement qui amène la défection et la mortalité. Le soldat est généralement mieux vêtu et mieux équipé : l'administration des vivres s'est perfectionnée par des châtimens, par la nécessité, et remplit plus facilement ses approvisionnemens, depuis que toutes les denrées sont en réquisition, et à un prix fixe ; en conséquence les armées ne se ressentent point encore de la disette qui afflige plusieurs parties du royaume. Les mêmes moyens tyranniques secondent le transport des subsistances. Après la prise des lignes de Weissembourg, il n'existait que 900 sacs de farine à Strasbourg, la ville ne pouvait tenir six jours. Les commissaires, les jacobins, les chefs du département avaient déjà chargé leurs effets ; les chevaux étaient attelés, on se préparait à évacuer. M. de Wurmser perdit 5 jours avant d'approcher ; pas un détachement de cavalerie ne s'avança pour soutenir la terreur. Strasbourg respira ; des détachemens révolutionnaires furent expédiés dans la haute Alsace et la Franche-Comté : au bout de douze jours, on eut rassemblé dans la ville 30 mille sacs.

On se tromperait fort de présumer que l'administration civile de l'armée est exempte d'abus ; des dilapidations monstrueuses se renouvellent et se perpétuent dans toutes les branches ; mais nonobstant cet esprit de rapine général qui est porté à des excès fabuleux, le service ne manque point, et si le comité punit les gaspillages et les vols, c'est plutôt pour ravir la dépouille du voleur, que pour réprimer des prévarications qui ne s'étendent pas jusqu'à laisser souffrir l'armée. Les contributions universelles et excessives, imposées pour son entretien, la soutiendront encore 6 mois dans une espèce d'aisance ; et le comité laissera plutôt périr de faim et aller tous nus la moitié des habitans que de diminuer l'embonpoint de ses défenseurs.

On travaille maintenant à la grande mesure si longtemps retardée de l'incorporation des volontaires dans les troupes de ligne, et de remplir les cadres de celle-ci avec les gens de la première levée ; jusqu'ici on n'avait osé tenter cette opération : la toute-puissance du comité a surmonté les difficultés ; l'armée aura désormais plus d'unité et de consistance. Le régime de terreur a passé du royaume dans les camps.

Il y a brisé tout esprit commun, toute intimité, tous rapports sociaux entre les officiers et les soldats, et des soldats entre eux. Nul n'ose confier sa pensée à son camarade. Chacun craint de trouver un traître dans un confident : cette défiance tient lieu de discipline ; toujours effacée dans l'intérieur, dans les camps, dans les garnisons, parce que la convention veut perpétuer le défaut de considération où est tombé l'officier, elle renaît au jour d'action : dans aucun temps, le général n'obtint de sa troupe plus d'obéissance en présence de l'ennemi.

Cet effet résulte de l'état moral de l'armée en général. Elle n'est plus, comme ci-devant, raisonneuse, politiquante, stimulée au désordre dans des clubs, ni excitée contre ses chefs et ses officiers. Les révolutions de l'intérieur, la discorde des parties, les constitutions faites et à faire, tout cela lui est devenu étranger et indifférent. On n'y souffre plus que des harangueurs soldés par les commissaires; on ne permet qu'avec mesure et choix l'usage des papiers publics, même aux officiers; autant qu'on le peut, on les entretient dans une ignorance profonde des désavantages qu'essuie la république, des pertes qu'elle éprouve, des disputes qui s'élèvent à Paris. Devenue étrangère à ces vicissitudes, l'armée a changé d'enthousiasme : ses passions sont concentrées dans une exaltation de haine fanatique contre les ennemis de la république, de désir ardent de les battre et de certitude enthousiaste d'y réussir.

Tel est aujourd'hui son esprit universel : mélange d'orgueil et de rage; de patriotisme furieux et d'amour de la gloire; il soutient la bravoure, le mépris de la mort, l'obéissance, la patience à supporter les privations, les travaux et le froid : l'armée est en quelque sorte ni royaliste ni républicaine; c'est une nation sauvage qui abhorre et qui poursuit les armes à main d'autres nations.

Les étrangers et les cabinets se nourrissent des idées les plus fausses à cet égard. Les flatteurs, les étourdis, les ignorans ne cessent de leur dire que l'armée est pleine de mécontens, et qu'on aura bon marché de rassemblemens forcés, agités par les dissensions. Oui, sans doute, le nombre des soldats et officiers mécontens égale peut-être celui des zélateurs de la convention. C'est un fait certain, que si les uns sont réunis sous le drapeau par le fanatisme de l'égalité, et de la licence, les autres le sont par violence et par terreur; beaucoup d'entre eux ne sont dans les camps que pour y chercher leur sûreté, et celle de leurs familles; réduits à opter entre le tranchant de la guillotine ou le fer de l'ennemi, ils ne balancent pas : mais l'erreur consiste à penser, qu'il résulte de cette différence d'opinions et de motifs une différence dans la manière de combattre.— Non; un esprit, un sentiment commun anime tous les soldats; nul ne veut avoir l'air d'être vaincu par des étrangers; les mécontens sont d'abord français et ensuite royalistes. La présence des armées ennemies affaiblit chez eux l'intérêt, qu'ils prennent au rétablissement de la monarchie; car le militaire, sans raisonner, ne veut ni penser ni surtout agir conformément à la pensée de celui avec qui il va se battre pour opinion. Cette observation est particulièrement vraie du soldat français dont la vanité forme l'instinct. Combinée avec l'enthousiasme du temps, cette passion entreprend tout et brave tout. Voilà le vrai caractère des armées françaises en ce moment.

Plusieurs causes, qui ne remontent pas au delà de la dernière campagne, l'ont produit, fortifié, et peuvent le perpétuer. La plus puissante est cet art d'électriser les têtes et les cœurs dont la convention fait un usage prodigieux, et habituel : pour cela elle met à profit tous les évènemens ; le mépris est versé à pleines mains sur les ennemis ; elle les peint à ses troupes, tantôt comme des anthropophages, tantôt comme des lâches imbéciles. Ces instructions se répètent non pas deux jours, mais tous les jours, et par mille voies.

Le délire du patriotisme s'augmente par l'opinion universelle dans l'armée et commune à tous les partis que les puissances n'ont d'autre but que de ruiner la France, de la démembrer, d'en saccager les villes et les campagnes ; que leur intérêt pour les malheurs de la famille royale n'est qu'hypocrisie, et que sans distinction de monarchie ou de république, c'est à la France même, non à la France anarchique qu'elles font la guerre.

Enfin la mollesse de leurs opérations, le décousu de leur ligue, leur éternelle défensive, l'étude particulière qu'ont faite leurs généraux de laisser toujours évanouir les fruits de la victoire, et de ne poursuivre aucun avantage, leurs armées toutes successivement battues, deux campagnes perdues, ont porté l'ivresse des Français au dernier point. La nouvelle de la prise de Toulon a excité des transports de folie dans les armées ; on y a joint des fêtes, des hymnes, des orgies ; l'exaltation actuelle passe toute croyance.

Vous pénétrerez facilement encore combien ce fanatisme belliqueux reçoit d'énergie par le genre de guerre auquel on l'emploie. La tactique du comité n'est pas compliquée ; attaquer toujours en grandes masses ; voilà son thème et nous venons de voir si c'est le bon. Or des soldats toujours agissans, toujours ébranlés par l'espérance d'enfoncer un ennemi plus circonspect, et auxquels cet élan ne permet ni de voir ni de calculer le danger, contractent une habitude de témérité et une ardeur impétueuse à marcher au combat. Célérité et impétuosité sont pour eux les deux élémens de la guerre, élémens parfaitement conformes à leur caractère et à une guerre révolutionnaire. Comment voudrait-on qu'ils redoutassent des ennemis sans cesse inférieurs, sans cesse culbutés par le nombre, sans cesse enfermés dans un cercle d'opérations défensives, et qui n'ont jamais voulu prendre la peine de leur montrer qu'ils étaient redoutables. Lorsqu'on voit un général autrichien retranché derrière quelques redoutes, se laisser attaquer trente et une fois en cinq semaines sans aller lui-même une seule fois à l'ennemi, se laisser écraser en détail, forcé ensuite à une déroute qu'on compare à celle de Rosbach et perdre en cinq jours le prix du sang de la plus belle armée; lorsque d'une autre part, on voit un sergent d'artillerie (Pichegru) devenu général en chef, ramener chaque jour pendant un mois ses soldats sur les Autrichiens et finir par un triomphe éclatant, on peut s'attendre à un excès d'enthousiasme dans ses troupes et à l'opinion la plus exagérée de leur irrésistible intrépidité.

Ainsi vous avez maintenant à combattre ce qu'il n'a tenu qu'aux généraux et aux cabinets de la coalition d'éviter: vous avez à combattre ce qui n'existait pas dans la première campagne et à un faible degré dans le début de la seconde, *des armées passionnées aux prises avec les passions des souverains, un peuple soldat, fanatisé, auquel on oppose des soldats matériels, indifférens à l'objet de la querelle et dont la discipline n'a pas prévenu les défaites.*

Cet immense désavantage est parfaitement connu du comité, des généraux, de chaque bataillon: ce ne sera pas le seul qu'on aura gagné en s'amusant à faire traîner la guerre jusqu'à une quatrième campagne et à spéculer tranquillement sur la révolution.

Vous ne trouverez plus des ennemis désorganisés, des constitutionels et des fédéralistes au commandement des troupes et des places, ni des armées en haillons et dissoutes comme l'était celle de Dumouriez.

Le comité élève ses sacrifices à la hauteur de ses dangers, de ses espérances, de ses plans. Non seulement il entretient dans l'armée la soumission, non seulement il redouble de moyens pour l'exalter, il a travaillé de plus à lui procurer les secours dont elle manquait. On a formé un corps innombrable de tirailleurs qui, à l'aide des positions que les états-majors choisissent toujours avec art, incommodera les armées alliées autant qu'il a incommodé celle de M. Wurmser en la forçant d'être toujours sur ses gardes. Ces troupes légères sont maintenant plus que doublées.

On a multiplié l'artillerie à cheval surtout dans les armées d'Alsace et du nord; on l'augmenterait encore ainsi que la grosse artillerie employée en campagne sans le manque de chevaux dont la perte a été incalculable. Au mois de novembre on avait pris de force en Alsace une partie des attelages de l'entreprise des charrois pour le service de l'artillerie à cheval; d'après les renseignemens que m'a fournis un des chefs de cette entreprise, échappé de Strasbourg au commencement de l'année, il me paraît impossible que ce déficit de chevaux de trait ne mette pas hors de combat une partie de l'artillerie si la campagne s'ouvre avec vivacité.

Quant au service du canon, tous les témoignages que j'ai consultés me confirment qu'il est aujourd'hui très inférieur à ce qu'il était au commencement de la guerre. En officiers et en artilleurs on a fait des pertes qui ne se remplacent pas comme celle d'un simple fantassin, mais l'exercice continuel et la quantité de gens des professions mécaniques qui ont repeuplé les anciens régimens de canonniers diminuent chaque jour l'imperfection du service.

La cavalerie s'est trouvée presque anéantie au milieu de l'été dernier; elle n'était encore un peu considérable que dans l'armée d'Alsace où les régimens de chasseurs à cheval ont fait leur devoir avec distinction, et ont soutenu le choc de la cavalerie autrichienne.

La convention se flatte et le comité de salut public annonce que l'armée aura 60 *mille cavaliers* et *dragons*, et 40 *mille* hommes de cavalerie légère, pour la prochaine campagne. Cette promesse est-elle une gasconnade? Je ne puis le décider; mais des rapports auxquels j'ai confiance m'attestent unanimement qu'on fait des efforts prodigieux pour en remonter. Le comité achète des chevaux à tout prix; depuis trois mois la Suisse lui vend les siens, il en est sorti 3 à 400 chaque semaine par le compte de Neuchâtel, autant chaque semaine par Bâle, d'autres convois ont traversé Genève. Cette exportation que les cantons ont défendue et dont les ministres étrangers n'ont daigné se plaindre que lorsqu'elle a été achevée, a tellement épuisé le pays que s'il avait besoin de six cents cavaliers il ne trouverait pas aujourd'hui à les monter. Je parle d'après les connaissances positives parvenues aux chefs du gouvernement.

Ce n'est pas tout; 8,000 chevaux ont été achetés dans le Wirtembourg: on en fait sortir chaque jour d'Allemagne par la Suisse. J'en ai rencontré avant-hier un convoi de 180 qui se rendait en Savoie. Un de mes amis en a vu passer un près de Soleure de 270, venant de la Souabe et allant dans le *Sundgau*. Cette foire ne discontinue pas: l'appât d'un gain exorbitant l'emporte sur les risques de la contrebande; paysans, marchands, entremetteurs, chacun la favorise. A ma connaissance un seul paysan du voisinage de Berne avait il y a 15 jours 20 quintaux d'écus en dépôt pour achat de chevaux. Ce canal de la Suisse que les puissances ont laissé ouvert avec tant d'imprudence sert au comité à l'acquisition des fournitures quelconques qui lui sont nécessaires, et de plus à transmettre ses manœuvres et ses corruptions au dehors.

Pratiques au dehors. Trop préoccupée l'année dernière de ses divisions intestines et ne vivant que d'assignats, la convention avait ralenti le cours de ses pratiques extérieures. Elle a repris, étendu, alimenté ce genre d'hostilités par des sacrifices pécuniaires. Dans les villes qui avoisinent ses armées, dans les capitales où siègent les gouvernemens, dans les camps même, elle paye des espions, des traîtres, des révélateurs. Voici des faits constans. Les commissaires savaient à Strasbourg jusqu'aux moindres détails de l'armée de Wurmser et de ses projets. Quoique Landau fût bloqué, tous les deux jours les commissaires en recevaient le bulletin. Les membres du comité de salut public et leurs affidés annoncèrent la prise certaine de Toulon près de 20 jours avant l'attaque : ce fut par suite de la connaissance exacte qu'ils avoient de la faiblesse de la garnison, des divisions existant entre les Espagnols et les Anglais et des détachemens chargés de la défense de chacun des forts, que le comité ordonna à l'armée assiégeante d'attaquer d'assaut. La flotte anglaise n'a pas fait un mouvement ni préparé une sortie que les Jacobins n'en aient été instruits d'avance.

Ils se vantent assez publiquement, et le comité avec plus de discrétion, des intelligences qu'ils ont au dehors : ils prodiguent trop d'argent pour le prodiguer en vain : ce que je sais de certain c'est que par l'entremise de Genève, Bâle, Zurich, Hambourg et Gênes ils font passer, ainsi que je l'ai rapporté plus haut, des remises considérables, en Italie, en Allemagne, en Angleterre.

Ils ont des émissaires et des correspondans nationaux en Saxe, en Bavière, à Berlin, à Turin, à Milan, à Londres.

N'espérant rien obtenir en Autriche, ni y faire réussir des intrigues trop directes, ils se contentent d'y semer des bruits alarmans et d'y provoquer le désir de la paix. Leur politique à l'égard de cette puissance se réduit à travailler à la priver de ses alliés.

Ils se reposent sur l'ancienne rivalité des deux couronnes, sur la durée de la guerre, et sur le parti qui est mécontent à Berlin, pour dissoudre l'alliance des deux chefs de la coalition en Allemagne ; ils entretiennent des amis secrets chargés de fomenter des divisions de déclarer contre la guerre et de leur faire des pensionnaires dans les états-majors et dans les bureaux.

Ils destinent Gênes à être le brûlot de l'Italie ; de là leurs émissaires très nombreux et très actifs dans cette ville empoisonnent le Piémont et la Lombardie ; divers commis et même des chefs sont soupçonnés dans plus d'une cour d'Italie d'être à leur solde. Et ce soupçon n'est peut-être pas calomnieux.

Mais leurs efforts en ce genre se dirigent principalement sur l'Angleterre. J'ai appris par plusieurs canaux différens, mais tous venant de Paris et aboutissant au comité, qu'il se vante d'avoir des gens à lui dans les bureaux de l'amirauté, de la guerre et des affaires étrangères. Certainement quelques-uns des chefs de la convention d'Ecosse étaient gagés par lui. Il entretient des messagers *anglais* qui vont et viennent pour son compte tantôt par Ostende, tantôt par Helvoet, qui se rendent en France et qui en ressortent.

Ce commerce se fait à l'aide de faux passeports, ou avec des passeports surpris aux ambassadeurs, à leurs secrétaires, aux régences des états neutres. Très récemment un agent du comité de salut public nommé Mazelière est arrivé à Bâle ; là il a mis un bras en écharpe, a coupé ses moustaches et s'est dit venant de l'armée du Prince de Condé. Son dessein était d'obtenir un passeport de Lord Fitzgerald ou du ministre impérial pour se rendre en Angleterre : il avait apporté une somme forte en or, outre un portefeuille d'assignats qu'il a échangés à Bâle contre des traites sur Londres et Amsterdam. Instruit du projet de ce coquin par une personne qui avait acheté sa protection pour sortir de Paris, j'en ai prévenu Lord Fitzgerald.

Mais le plan favori du comité consiste à renverser le ministère actuel, à former en Angleterre un foyer révolutionnaire, ainsi que le rapporte l'écrivain d'une des lettres annexées à ce *résumé*, à faire baisser les fonds publics et prévaloir des propositions de paix ou de guerre défensive.

On poursuit ce projet par toutes les voies imaginables ; il fait oublier au comité toutes ses entreprises étrangères. Ce conseil s'efforce d'attaquer le gouvernement anglais par les revers, par l'opinion, par l'argent, par la corruption des subalternes, dont la vénalité n'est malheureusement que trop constatée ; et dès qu'il sera parvenu à susciter quelque secousse intérieure il tentera une descente dont on prépare les élémens.

La semaine dernière, il est échappé à Barthélemi, ministre de France auprès du corps helvétique, de dire à un magistrat suisse de qui je tiens ce discours : *Nous travaillons dans ce moment et avec activité à renverser le ministre anglais et à faire demander la paix au Parlement. Si cela réussit nous sommes sauvés, si cela manque, la révolution est perdue, nous n'irons pas à la fin de la campagne.*

Subsistances. Dans le nombre infini des prophéties, des illusions, des notions fausses qui ont exalté les têtes au dehors et produit tant d'absurdes combinaisons, la prétendue famine de la France a joué et joue encore un grand rôle. On trouve commode de reposer son incurie sur des fléaux extraordinaires qui tueront la révolution sans qu'on ait besoin d'inquiétudes et d'efforts pour s'en délivrer.

Cette histoire de la famine doit être reléguée parmi les fables, ainsi que l'espoir fondé sur l'anarchie, sur la lassitude, sur l'excès de la tyrannie, et autres billevesées de cette espèce.

Si l'on entend par la famine une rareté locale de grains, une diminution dans la consommation du pain, une altération de sa qualité, un défaut d'abondance porté jusqu'à ne laisser dans le royaume que le nécessaire, on a raison : mais toute idée au delà est exagération.

La récolte dernière a été généralement bonne en France et excellente dans quelques provinces. Après avoir mis tous les grains anciens ou nouveaux en réquisition, le Comité a ordonné un premier recensement dans chaque département : les administrations qui l'ont exécuté ont trouvé dans la pluralité un déficit sur la quantité nécessaire à la consommation annuelle.

Instruit que ce déficit résultait des fraudes et des réticences et qu'il existait des grains cachés, le Comité a fait faire un second recensement par les agens révolutionnaires : alors le déficit a disparu, et il s'est trouvé partout un excédant plus ou moins considérable, excepté dans le petit nombre de provinces qui ne recueillent jamais assez de grains pour leur consommation : j'ai vu les relevés des deux recensemens faits sur 27 départemens, ils emportent un excédant de 15, 20, 30, 35 mille setiers de grains.

Il n'y a donc pas disette effective, mais les besoins énormes des armées et l'approvisionnement des places entraînent une accumulation de subsistances dans les magasins publics, les gaspillages inévitables dans la formation et la distribution de ces magasins occasionnent des non-valeurs. Ainsi on peut présumer que le superflu existe aujourd'hui dans peu de départemens, et qu'en temps ordinaire on aurait peine à atteindre le niveau jusqu'à la récolte prochaine.

Cependant plusieurs circonstances modifient l'effet de cette rareté. 1°. Dans tout le royaume excepté à Paris on ne mange que d'un seul pain, nommé pain de l'Egalité. Il est mêlé de seigle ou d'orge et de son, il ne vaut pas le bon pain de munition ; mais le citadin et le villageois sont trop heureux d'en avoir de cette espèce et si un fermier ou un bourgeois s'avisait d'en fabriquer de meilleur pour son usage, en réservant le pain d'Egalité pour ses valets, il serait dénoncé, pillé, incarcéré et probablement égorgé. 2°. La quantité de grains nécessaire pour sa consommation étant fixée, personne ne s'avise de l'excéder par la crainte d'en manquer. 3°. Les administrations sont seules autorisées à faire vendre des grains dans les marchés ; et elles n'en délivrent en chacun qu'à raison du besoin de l'instant, et avec une extrême parcimonie. Dans les villes, la consommation de chaque famille est rigoureusement fixée ; nul boulanger n'oserait délivrer plus de pain que les arrêts municipaux n'en allouent à chaque individu. 4°. On a mis en réquisition les châtaignes, les pommes de terre, les navets, les maïs, le millet, tout ce qui peut suppléer au blé. On fait consommer ces derniers aux habitans des campagnes pour économiser les grains et augmenter d'autant la quantité disponible de ceux-ci. 5°. Enfin, malgré les précautions, (il est vrai, aussi faibles qu'imparfaites des puissances belligérantes) le Comité se procure des grains de l'extérieur par le concours des puissances neutres, et par celui du commerce de tous les pays qu'on attire à force d'or. Deux négocians du Havre m'ont affirmé que pendant le seul cours du mois de novembre, il était entré dans ce port 18 navires chargés de grain ; c'étaient des bâtimens *danois* et *hollandais* ; les derniers ne se font aucun scrupule de ce trafic ; ils prennent de faux connaissemens pour le Portugal et l'Espagne et vont décharger dans les ports de France. Leurs cargaisons sont payées en espèces sonnantes à très bon prix et avec toutes sortes d'encouragemens. Plusieurs ont déjà fait deux voyages.

Il échappe encore nombre de navires des Etats-Unis, et de toutes les parties du nord. A la fin de décembre un navire danois chargé de trente mille fusils entra au Havre après avoir été visité par une frégate anglaise, qui le laissa passer sur un faux connaissement pour la Corogne.

Gênes a approvisionné l'année dernière l'armée de Nice, celle de Marseille et la Provence. Lorsque Toulon fut pris par les alliés, ce trafic continua avec plus de difficultés et moins d'étendue, par la route de terre ou par le cabotage clandestin à Nice et à Antibes.

Il vient de reprendre sa funeste activité ; le blocus tardif du port de Gênes, et des croisières que la saison rend insuffisantes, le gênent, il est vrai, depuis quelques semaines ; mais le mal est fait, les magasins de Provence sont alimentés pour quelque temps : l'inconstance des mesures employées envers Gênes par les alliés, ces demandes hautaines, hasardées et retirées ; ces déclarations qui ont irrité les esprits ; ces menaces non exécutées et devenues un sujet de dérision ; la perte de Toulon ; la fermentation et la prépondérance du parti français ; enfin l'inconcevable indolence des alliés à l'égard de cette ville, qui devient le brûlot de l'Italie et qui bientôt, si on ne prend un parti décisif, en ouvrira les portes aux Français ; tout cela a fortifié la hardiesse, la cupidité et l'émulation des interlopes.

Depuis que le comité de salut public a fixé les rênes dans ses mains, l'administration des subsistances s'est améliorée : Paris s'est principalement ressenti de ce changement ; il est plus facilement, plus abondamment approvisionné qu'il ne l'était il y a trois mois : le pain est meilleur et en plus grande quantité : les inquiétudes sont ajournées.

Si vous faites attention, que les grands consommateurs, les riches propriétaires sont ou retranchés de la population, ou réduits au moindre taux de subsistance ; que plus de 200 mille d'entre eux, détenus dans les différentes villes du royaume, ne vivent, dans leurs prisons, ou maisons d'arrêts, que d'une faible ration de pain ; si vous observez que chaque jour la population diminue par les supplices, par les pertes de la guerre, par l'émigration, vous serez convaincu que la France ne se trouve encore qu'à un degré de disette relative, qui anciennement eût amené la famine et que le régime du jour peut soutenir.

D'ailleurs tenez pour certain que le principe fondamental du comité est de nourrir la capitale et les armées : les besoins du reste de la république ne lui donnent pas une heure de soucis ; au contraire il spécule sur ses souffrances, il sait qu'elles tendent à transformer en soldats ceux qui ne peuvent plus vivre en citoyens. La disette grossit les levées par réquisitions ; la disette excite les affamés à chercher leur subsistance dans les camps et aux invasions qui promettent le pillage des contrées et des magasins ennemis ; c'est tête levée, sans pudeur, avec l'affiche, que le comité, les Jacobins, les agens révolutionnaires proposent et projettent des massacres ; pour diminuer la consommation des vivres, si besoin est, ils viendront à égorger leurs prisonniers, les femmes, les vieillards, comme autant de bouches inutiles.

Quel sera l'effet de cet étrange état de choses ? Nous le dirons dans la seconde partie de ce *résumé* où je vous développerai le caractère et la classification des sentimens du peuple ; ce qu'il faut penser des divisions actuelles entre les Jacobins, de la durée, de la politique, du but général du comité de salut public ; et enfin des bases de conduite que cette masse de notions indique aux puissances.

Je commencerai cette seconde partie par un aperçu exact de la force des armées ; du nombre auquel elles seront portées ; des limites peu connues où cette masse militaire doit nécessairement rester ; et de l'emploi actuel des levées de première réquisition.

Finis.

Endorsed
In Lord Elgin's, *Feb. 14th.*

Extrait d'une lettre adressée à Milord Elgin.

16 fév., 1794.

Voici, My Lord, la suite du premier dépouillement, dont vous recevrez la dernière partie par l'un des courriers de la semaine. Je voudrais pouvoir rendre ces bases historiques très complètes, pour fixer votre jugement, et prévenir les erreurs de fait sur lesquelles je persiste à craindre qu'on n'édifie les plans de conduite pour cette année. Ne perdez point de vue que vous avez affaire à gens qui ont *organisé la désorganisation* et que vous finirez mal une guerre malheureuse qu'il faudra recommencer bientôt, si elle n'entr'ouvre pas avant six mois le cœur même de la révolution.

J'ai reçu un billet timide et couvert de mon voyageur à Paris. Il me demandait des explications ; aussitôt qu'il les aura reçues il doit se remettre en route. Il *renvoie* à ce moment de me rendre compte, n'osant pas, avec raison, se confier à la poste. Il a eu beaucoup de peine à s'accréditer auprès des personnes que je lui ai désignées; on n'ose se fier à son meilleur ami, à plus forte raison à un visage étranger, avant d'avoir bien authentiqué son caractère et sa mission.

Par les derniers avis que j'ai reçus en date du 2 et du 6 j'apprends que le comité va lever la seconde réquisition de 25 à 45 ans ; preuve de plus que la première n'a servi qu'au complément des cadres de l'armée : la seconde donnera plus de sujets, ainsi que vous le verrez dans le travail inclus.

Par un nouvel état plus correct, qui m'a été fourni, je crois qu'à la date du 24 janvier, le comité avait 75 millions monnayés au trésor public, et pour au delà de 330 millions de matières d'or et d'argent. Cette somme est un peu plus forte que celle que je vous avais indiquée. On en verrait bientôt la fin, si de nouvelles rapines ne remplaçaient les vides. Les assignats sont retombés au dehors à 56 p. 100 de perte : dans l'intérieur, point de prix fixe : il varie depuis *le pair* jusqu'à 33 : le papier étant devenu rare surtout dans les campagnes, et personne n'osant payer en espèces, pour vivre les particuliers sont obligés de sortir leur or et leurs écus, et d'aller les échanger au pair au bureau de leur district ou de leur municipalité.

Le comité va faire fondre des espèces qu'on réduira en lingots, pour s'en servir au dehors et masquer la source. Cette manœuvre n'a point suspendu les remises et les opérations, que l'on fait aux trois chefs-lieux, Gênes, Bâle et Genève. Là entr'autres, il rachète les assignats à 55 ou 56 de perte, pour les replacer dans l'intérieur au pair à 10, 20, 30, suivant les lieux et les circonstances.

Ses plans de corruption extérieure continuent à regarder essentiellement l'Angleterre et l'Italie. Voilà les deux points fortement travaillés. Le Piémont l'est à outrance ; l'esprit du peuple s'y gâte visiblement, et à la manière dont les choses y sont dirigées, on peut croire que l'argent de Paris n'y a pas été semé en vain.

Quant à l'Angleterre ils espèrent toujours y exciter quelque *ébranlement* et y former un embryon révolutionnaire que l'on soutiendrait ensuite à *main armée*. Les troupes ci-dev[t] employées contre la Vendée doivent renforcer celles des côtes de la Manche. Mais pour l'instant le grand effort va se porter sur la Flandre ; l'attaque de Valenciennes et une irruption dans les Pays-Bas sont à l'ordre du jour : si l'on pénètre dans la Belgique, le projet est de la châtier en la mettant à feu et à sang. On compte employer 100 mille h. et les garnisons à cette entreprise : vous ne tarderez pas à être vigoureusement attaqués, et l'on ne vous laissera sûrement pas le temps de finir vos longs préparatifs, ni terminer vos quartiers d'hiver. La seconde réquisition sera encore plusieurs mois hors de service, car on est hors d'état de l'équiper, de l'armer et de la nourrir ; mais si l'on fait la même faute que l'année dernière, si l'on se moque de cette levée et qu'on lui laisse le temps de s'organiser, cette nouvelle pépinière vous tombera sur les bras au milieu de l'été.

Le nombre de malades dans l'armée est prodigieux ; la mortalité y est terrible : il en est mort 6000 dans les seuls hôpitaux de Besançon : une fièvre épidémique les moissonne et est même passée aux habitans. Elle vient aussi de se déclarer à Lyon, où elle peut devenir pestilentielle par l'infection des cadavres qu'on laisse presque sans sépulture, ou qu'on jette dans le Rhône, d'où ils sont portés sur la côte, où ils pourrissent. Toutes les campagnes des environs de Lyon sont infectées de cette puanteur.

Le système pillard des massacres ne discontinue point à Paris. Tous les banquiers, négocians et marchands y passeront. On a formellement exclu de l'admission aux Jacobins tous les individus de ces classes : c'est assez vous dire qu'elles sont destinées à la boucherie. Il y a des départemens où les $\frac{7}{8}$ des propriétés sont aux mains de la Convention.

Robespierre, toujours meneur en chef, commence à sentir le poids de sa dignité, le danger de son élévation, et des embarras de toute espèce. Il voudrait arrêter l'action du gouvernement révolutionnaire, et ne sait comment s'y prendre. Il emploie Camille Desmoulins à lui ramener l'opinion populaire, qu'on lui enlève, jour par jour : il est observé par ses coadjuteurs, qui épient le moment de le culbuter et qui font son tourment. Quoique son crédit actuel soit encore très supérieur au leur, il n'ose les attaquer de front. Il a perdu sa cause dans l'affaire de Ronsin, Vincent, et Maillard, qui sont élargis, et qui vont travailler avec ses ennemis à lui débaucher l'armée révolutionnaire qui formait son corps de Janissaires. Si les alliés faisaient autrement la guerre, et qu'ils poussassent de grands et rapides succès en débutant, le comité de salut public volerait en pièces : Robespierre et Danton seraient égorgés.

Il a péri 350 mille âmes dans la guerre de la Vendée, y compris les vieillards, femmes et enfans. Les cinq départemens qui en ont été le théâtre sont en cendres.

Par les derniers renseignemens que j'ai eus, je vois que la disette de plusieurs articles essentiels est au plus haut degré. Les bestiaux manquent généralement, il est défendu au peuple de manger du bœuf et de la vache ; cette viande étant réservée aux troupes. Dans beaucoup de départemens il ne reste pas un mouton. Cela est vrai, même du Dauphiné et de la Provence, qui en abondaient : la loi du *maximum* a achevé cette dépopulation, en mettant la viande à la portée de toutes les classes du peuple. La disette des bestiaux a entraîné celle des cuirs, celle des moutons, la rareté des laines. On ne trouve presque plus de marchandises dans les villes, bourgs, et villages de la province. Au pied de la lettre, il est impossible en Franche-Comté et en Bourgogne, par exemple, d'acheter une culotte.

La conversion des rentes viagères en annuités à un prix très onéreux pour les rentiers est arrêtée et passera au premier jour à la Convention.

Le blocus du port de Gênes continue toujours à ne rien bloquer ; tout passe à Nice, grains, vivres, marchandises, poudres &c. Les grains de la Lombardie par l'impardonnable négligence du Ministre de l'Empereur Cte de Wilseek ont été exportés par les Génois : ils ont enlevé aussi une bonne partie de ceux de la Toscane, et des états du Pape ; en sorte que les grains ont renchéri partout, et surtout en Piémont, et en Lombardie.

Les troupes qui étaient survenues en Savoie sont reparties pour les Pyrénées.

On poursuit les exécutions à Lyon, 40, 50, 80 par semaine : 140 maisons à démolir par mois. Mêmes scènes à Marseille et à Bordeaux.

In Ld Elgin's N° 24.

Première suite du résumé.

15 *fév.*, 1794.

Force des armées. Les militaires et les ministres se sont obstinés jusqu'à ce jour de rire du nombre dénué d'exercice et de discipline ; mais l'expérience, plus savante que l'art, vient de nous apprendre à ne plus mépriser le nombre, quand il est animé par les passions et quand il est dirigé par des hommes à qui leur péril personnel a fait un besoin de tout prévoir comme une loi de tout oser.

Je ne puis fournir aucun état rigoureusement exact des différentes armées de la Convention, ni de la distribution arithmétique des forces qui sont en ce moment sous les drapeaux. Quant au nombre total d'hommes disponibles pour le service militaire déjà employés ou à employer en vertu des deux dernières réquisitions générales qui embrassent tous les individus de 18 à 45 ans, je me suis procuré des relevés, dont l'exactitude approximative me parait démontrée par le calcul de vérification, que je joins à cet envoi : cet accord des notions positives, et des évaluations résultant de la table de la vie humaine, est un puissant indice de vérité.

On peut regarder sans crainte de commettre une erreur importante, le *maximum* des forces actuelles en exercice comme étant d'environ 400 à 450 mille hommes, et l'excédant que fourniront au printemps les levées d'individus de 18 à 45 ans, comme borné au plus haut à 250,000 h. Voilà à quoi se réduisent le gigantesque appareil de cette nation de soldats et ces fameuses masses dont l'imagination grossit le nombre indéfiniment.

Ce total de 6 à 700 mille hommes sera diminué avant l'ouverture de la campagne de toutes les pertes que les blessures et les maladies ont préparées à la fin de l'automne. Cette mortalité est prodigieuse depuis un mois dans les hôpitaux, où il s'est manifesté, entr'autres à Strasbourg et à Besançon, une épidémie d'un caractère pestilentiel ; la rareté des drogues médicinales dont la France commence à manquer, fait empirer journellement le service.

Mais d'autre part, il faut observer que les provinces frontières où séjournent les armées sont obligées, au besoin, de leur fournir subsidiairement toute la population mâle, capable de porter les armes et de seconder ces irruptions impétueuses, en grandes masses, dans lesquelles le comité a placé une confiance justifiée par le succès.

Il est d'ailleurs indubitable que si les circonstances l'exigent, un décret et la guillotine feront marcher les habitans mariés, comme les célibataires et les adolescens de 15 à 18 ans, ainsi que les personnes de 45 à 60. Et qu'on ne s'y trompe pas ; le père partira de même qu'il a laissé partir son fils, et l'épouse n'osera pas plus retenir son mari qu'elle n'a osé retenir ses enfans.

Malgré la férocité de la tyrannie, cette mesure cependant échouera en grande partie, dans les provinces éloignées du théâtre de la guerre ; l'on ne trouvera dans ce ramassis, ni le désir, ni l'aptitude à sucer le fanatisme militaire, l'on manquera de temps et de facilités pour l'exercer aux armes; et, inutile pour la défensive, impossible à maintenir en permanence dans les camps, on ne s'en servira qu'à l'un de ces efforts du nombre qui va continuer à faire la tactique du comité.

La répartition des armées à la fin de l'automne, soit des 400,000 h., que je considère comme leur dernier nombre effectif, était à peu près conforme aux aperçus suivans :

Armée d'Alsace	45,000
Armée de la Moselle	25,000
Corps de la Haute Alsace	10,000
Armée des Alpes, et de Lyon	12,000
Armée assiégante de Toulon	40,000
Armée de Nice	18,000
Armée de la Vendée, du Poitou aux côtes de Bretagne et de Normandie	70,000
Armée du Rousillon et de Bayonne	45,000
Armée des Ardennes et du Nord	55,000
Garnisons	80,000
Total	400,000

Ce dénombrement correspond très également à ceux qu'ont représentés souvent les relations des alliés. On les a entendus dire par exemple qu'en Alsace, ils avaient à se défendre contre *cent mille hommes*. Il n'en est pas moins certain, que l'armée française du Rhin, n'atteignait pas à la moitié de cette force. Celle-ci, il est vrai, n'était que trop suffisante contre 18 à 20 mille Autrichiens ruinés de fatigues, d'épuisement, manquant de tout, et réduits par leur général au rôle de Stoïciens, qui 40 jours de suite, ont dû attendre et recevoir la mort en détail sans se permettre une seule attaque contre l'ennemi.

La même remarque s'applique à Toulon; eussent-ils été d'accord, et aussi intrépides que la moitié d'entr'eux ont été lâches, les 11,000 hommes qui défendaient la place ne pouvaient la conserver, contre 40,000 assaillans, se précipitant à la fois sur les ouvrages.

Ainsi l'extrême infériorité relative des armées alliées a causé leurs revers, beaucoup plus que les énumérations fabuleuses des forces de leurs ennemis: l'orgueil fait exagérer ces dénombremens après les défaites comme la présomption les affaiblit, lorsqu'il faudrait se mettre en mesure de leur résister.

C'est encore un désavantage essentiel que la distance où les armées alliées se trouvent les unes des autres; l'isolation de leurs parties, le peu de concert qui a régné dans les opérations, tandis qu'au premier geste du comité de salut public, les divisions plus contiguës de ses forces militaires se soutiennent, se réunissent, se fortifient avec une rapidité que leurs ennemis n'ont su dans aucune occasion, ni prévoir, ni prévenir, ni imiter.—

Les gens de la première réquisition de 18 à 25 ans sont tous rendus aujourd'hui à leur destination *provisoire*; généralement on les a laissés sur les derrières des armées, dans les chefs-lieux de districts, où on les arme, où on les exerce, où l'on enivre leur esprit, en ayant soin de leur corps—dans les différens lieux de leurs cantonnemens, il est défendu aux habitans de consommer du bœuf et de la vache : on réserve cette nourriture aux bataillons en noviciat. Vers la fin du mois dernier [janvier] en Alsace, Lorraine, Franche-Comté telle était la proportion existante dans ces miliciens de nouvelle levée, que 10 hommes étaient armés de fusils et 10 de piques par compagnie : plus de la moitié manquait encore d'uniformes : cette proportion à peu près générale dans les provinces voisines des frontières est plus faible en individus armés dans celles de l'intérieur.

Le plus grand nombre a marché par contrainte, beaucoup ont déserté, soit à l'étranger, soit pour revenir chez eux : le chagrin et la fatigue ont occasionné des maladies, et c'est grossir la vérité, loin de la réduire, que de porter à 100,000 h. *l'ultimatum effectif* de cette première levée.

La seconde de 18 à 45 fournira plus de sujets. Des fermiers riches m'ont informé que sur dix valets ou journaliers à leur gages, la première réquisition de 18 à 25 ne leur en avait enlevé que deux ; que la seconde leur en enlèverait trois de plus, et que le reste se composait de gens mariés ou au-dessus de 45 ans.

L'éducation militaire de ces malheureux avait été jusqu'au mois de janvier aussi nulle que grotesque ; ils s'exerçaient avec des bâtons ; ayant le droit de choisir, et ayant choisi dans leur sein des officiers aussi ignorans qu'eux ; à peine savaient-ils le pas de marche, mais depuis cette époque, des bas officiers tirés des armées sont chargés de dresser celles des milices qu'on n'a pas encore incorporées dans les cadres des anciens régimens. Quant à leur éducation morale, elle est confiée à des clubistes d'élite, qui les catéchisent, et qui leur inspirent l'exaltation commune aujourd'hui à une grande partie des soldats.

Afin de briser l'esprit de fraternité, prévenir l'effet des mécontentemens, et détruire les inclinations locales, on a divisé chaque bataillon en deux moitiés, pour les mêler à d'autres demi-bataillons qui leur fussent étrangers : par cet arrangement, et en exportant ces corps hors du territoire de leurs foyers, on les a entièrement dépaysés.

Après vous avoir développé la généralité des faits, dont j'ai pu me procurer une connaissance exacte, et qui peuvent fonder votre jugement touchant l'état politique de la France, celui de ses ressources, de ses finances, de son armée, de ses forces disponibles, de ses subsistances, de ses manœuvres au dehors, il me reste à vous présenter le caractère des dispositions publiques de la nation, et de la conduite, comme des desseins généraux du comité du salut public. Cet exposé complétera la carte morale du royaume.

Quand l'esprit français serait aussi susceptible qu'il l'est peu de persévérer longtemps dans les mêmes sentimens, la violence des vicissitudes de la révolution l'eût forcément modifié. Aucun objet d'observation n'est cependant plus difficile à constater que ce changement d'opinion; rien ne mérite autant de défiance que les rapports journaliers que l'on entend chaque jour à cet égard; rien de si dangereux que les hypothèses tranchantes et les plans de conduite construits sur la fausse base de ces rapports.

Au mois de novembre dernier l'esprit public en France différait déjà de celui qui existait durant l'été, et aujourd'hui les sentimens ne sont plus les mêmes qu'ils étaient au mois de novembre : les événemens ultérieurs développeront sans doute de nouvelles variations : ainsi les faiseurs de tableaux et de descriptions devraient soigneusement ajouter la date à leurs peintures, et surtout se garder de prendre des nuances pour un caractère général et des localités passagères pour une situation universelle et permanente.

On se trompe d'ailleurs journellement sur les causes qui produisent telle ou telle disposition publique; on en tire des inductions erronées pour les futurs contingens; on édifie sur des êtres de raison la probabilité de tels ou tels événemens prochains.

Cette réflexion m'est dictée par plusieurs passages des discours que viennent de prononcer dans les deux chambres du Parlement, les principaux membres ministériels, qui ont voté l'adresse à S. M. Ils se sont tous accordés à conclure du régime effréné de la Convention qu'il généralisait le mécontentement, et que le mécontentement amènerait la fin de la tyrannie. Cette manière de voir annonce une counaissance superficielle de la nature et des motifs du mécontentement, ainsi que des conséquences qui pourraient en résulter.

Chaque jour on répète que la grande majorité des habitans de la France est asservie par la minorité; en cela on répète une vérité incontestable, dont néanmoins on méconnaît les limites, et dont on discerne mal les conséquences. La très petite minorité gouverne en effet avec un sceptre d'acier tranchant; une autre minorité marche volontairement à la suite de la première, dont elle partage les passions, et exécute les desseins : l'autorité, l'attachement à la révolution toute entière, un vœu commun de la conserver, de la défendre, d'en jouir par toute espèce de crimes, sont l'apanage de ces deux classes dominantes : réunies par des intérêts, et par des périls communs, elles tendent au même but avec une égale énergie, quoiqu'il existe quelquefois entr'elles des dissidences sur la distribution des rôles et des profits.

La majorité, au contraire, est un faisceau épars, subdivisé en plusieurs branches sans analogie.

Une portion de cette majorité improuve l'usage que l'on fait maintenant du régime anarchique et révolutionnaire sans improuver le régime même. Adoucissez la tétricité des mesures ; resserrez le cercle des délations, des supplices, des confiscations, des recrues forcées ; diminuez la rareté des comestibles et la perte des assignats, cette classe nombreuse redeviendra presque aussi ardente que les deux premières pour le service de la révolution et pour les succès de la guerre. Son improbation actuelle, fruit de la crainte et du malaise, ne lui inspire ni ne lui inspirera jamais une pensée de révolte : elle obéit sans murmure et se console des souffrances qu'elle ressent par l'espoir plus ou moins stupide d'un avenir prospère, aussitôt que la guerre sera finie et la révolution consolidée.

Dans la majorité se trouvent encore tous ceux qui ont différé, ou qui diffèrent encore d'opinion avec la minorité régnante, soit dans la formation de la république, soit dans la proscription de la royauté. Les Monarchistes, les Feuillans, les Fédéralistes, et beaucoup de républicains chancelans, que le malheur a corrigés, forment cette classe sous le couteau, généralement frappée d'anathème, et qui sent que la soumission la plus humble ne suffit plus aujourd'hui à garantir sa vie et sa propriété.

Ajoutez à ce dénombrement, les hommes étrangers aux systèmes politiques, qui s'accommoderaient de la république, du gouvernement révolutionnaire comme de la monarchie, pourvu qu'on les laissât paisibles, et qui dans leur égoïsme recevraient Robespierre pour roi, aussi bien que Louis XVII, s'ils pouvaient boire, manger, dormir, spéculer, et se divertir sans inquiétudes. Désigner cette classe, c'est indiquer suffisamment, qu'elle n'est pas la moins nombreuse de la majorité mécontente.

Il faut encore placer en ligne de compte la section intermédiaire des indifférens, qui n'ayant ni une idée, ni une volonté, traînent une vie animale entre les assassins et les voleurs, et sont prêts constamment à penser, et à faire tout ce que le plus fort exige d'eux. Considérant, maintenant, la population politique sous d'autres rapports nous en trouvons un quart de chefs, de satellites, ou de fauteurs prononcés de la tyrannie actuelle. Environ un autre quart mécontent dans un sens relatif, mais disposé à se joindre aux premiers dès qu'il y verrait un avantage, ou qu'on lui montrerait plus de ménagement. Un quart de la seconde moitié, suit le torrent de la nécessité, sans regarder au passé ni à l'avenir, et borne l'expression de son mécontentement à quelques gémissemens tacites. Tout le reste, c'est à dire plus des deux cinquièmes des habitans, abhorre la Convention et les Jacobins, le régime et les régisseurs : pour cette classe la France est un vaste cachot, où chacun au moindre bruit croit voir arriver son bourreau, où nul ne s'endort sans la crainte de se réveiller chargé de fers, où le soupçon de la richesse est un délit irrémissible, où l'on se regarde sans oser se parler, où l'on se parle sans se confier, où le vœu général et continuel est de s'enfuir, et où l'on ne prolonge son affreuse existence que par des démonstrations hypocrites et inefficaces du civisme le plus emporté.

Ces deux cinquièmes que l'on peut même sans hyperbole pousser à la grande moitié des habitans, ne connaissent que deux sentimens : celui de l'effroi et le vœu le plus ardent pour être délivrés de leurs oppresseurs.

Ce nombre, ou la majorité en général comprend les six huitièmes des grands, des médiocres, et des petits propriétaires. Parmi ces derniers il en est encore beaucoup qui tiennent à la révolution actuelle par les envahissemens qu'on leur permet à très bas prix sur les domaines du clergé et des émigrés. Cette majorité renferme encore la grande pluralité des marchands, des fabricans, des chefs d'établissemens d'industrie, des négocians, des gens d'affaires, des gens de robe, des artisans jadis aisés, des fermiers, et des gens vivant de leur travail, qui ont conservé quelque principe de religion, et de probité, ou qui sont dépourvus de l'activité et de l'effervescence nécessaires pour sortir du néant, et sentir les avantages de la condition de *sans-culottes*.

En répartissant cette majorité tacitement rebelle sur les villes, et sur les campagnes, on trouvera trois bourgeois contre un dans les villes, et un habitant contre deux dans les campagnes. On ne fait pas compte ici des différences locales ; cette proportion varie suivant les départemens, mais elle est exacte en résultat total.

Sous un autre point de vue, et en généralisant encore davantage, il est de fait que l'attachement à la révolution pris dans le sens absolu, et à la république même n'existe plus que chez cette population vague, bâtarde et scélérate de misérables qui n'avaient, il y a quatre ans, ni état, ni existence; dont l'oisiveté, la licence, et l'impunité ont grossi le nombre, qui promènent leurs affreux talens sur les divers théâtres de l'anarchie, la servent à prix d'argent, ou aspirent à être délivrés de la nécessité du travail en participant aux fruits des brigandages publics.

Cette foule toujours croissante d'opprimés et de mécontens est beaucoup moins divisée dans ses sentimens politiques qu'elle ne l'était il y a six mois; les opinions, plus ou moins révolutionnaires se sont successivement atténuées; en sorte que les constitutionnels ont généralement abandonné la constitution de 1791; les fédéralistes et les Brissotins, la république; et beaucoup de républicains, le Jacobinisme et le régime du jour. Il serait donc infiniment plus aisé de trouver aujourd'hui un point de contact entre les anciens partis et de rallier unanimement à des principes communs, ou du moins de prévenir toute résistance de la part de quelqu'un d'entr'eux.

Les royalistes restés dans l'intérieur sont beaucoup plus raisonnables que les émigrés: la persécution et l'infortune dont ils supportent tout le poids, les ont rendus accessibles aux idées de conciliation avec leurs anciens ennemis, qu'ils voient maintenant punis et en partie corrigés.

On peut définir la progression des idées et le vœu de la majorité en disant qu'avant tout et par dessus tout elle désire voir renverser la domination actuelle, qu'elle demande ensuite la monarchie, qu'enfin elle voudrait en dernière analyse la monarchie plus ou moins limitée.

Mais l'on s'abuserait de supposer à ces dispositions assez d'énergie pour faire entreprendre aucune démarche de salut. Non: cette masse si nombreuse est abattue par l'effroi, par ses défaites, par le plus profond découragement: loin d'être en état de rien oser, elle n'a pas même la pensée d'une résistance possible; sa douleur est inerte et passive; elle appréhende de montrer ses souffrances; elle ressemble aux nègres qui s'étranglent avec leurs langues plutôt que de se plaindre; et la plupart cherchent leur sûreté dans la dissimulation, ou affectent le civisme le plus outré.

Il ne faut donc attendre aucun mouvement spontané de la majorité tyrannisée. Je vais plus loin en vous certifiant que tout ardent et universel qu'est parmi ses membres le vœu d'un changement, la moindre partie d'entr'eux ne s'arrête pas là et porte des vues moins étroites sur l'établissement de la monarchie, et sur la manière de la composer. Je m'explique. Cette pluralité n'est pas contraire à ces deux fins, elle les désire, mais vaguement comme l'on désire une chose dont on désespère, et dont la possession trop difficile ne vaut ni un effort ni un sacrifice.

Tel est le thermomètre d'un grand nombre d'esprits. L'idée et l'image, l'habitude de la royauté s'effacent en raison de l'intervalle qui s'écoule depuis la destruction du trône et en raison de la consistance que prend la république. On s'accoutume à regarder le retour du roi comme un château en Espagne, et de ce sentiment à une tendance naturelle vers le premier ordre de choses qui promettra paix, et sûreté, ou seulement trêve, la distance n'est rien. Aussi le vœu non moins général de cette classe considérable de mécontens, se trouve-t-il vers la fin de la guerre, en laquelle l'été dernier ils plaçaient toutes leurs espérances, parce qu'ils considèrent la guerre comme la cause efficiente de la puissance de leurs tyrans, des persécutions, des pillages, des proscriptions dans l'intérieur.

Si la lassitude et les énormités de la révolution ont détaché une masse très nombreuse d'adhérens, beaucoup s'unissent à leurs ennemis dans la crainte de retomber sans conditions sous le joug des émigrés et tous, dans la défiance et l'aversion pour la force étrangère. Les Jacobins abhorrent celle-ci comme dangereuse à leur sûreté; les mécontens la haïssent comme dangereuse à la monarchie et comme impuissante ou mal disposée à les secourir.

L'éloignement pour les émigrés diminue chaque jour, il s'éteindrait tout à fait, il ferait place aux sentimens opposés, si les princes paraissaient armés de quelques moyens secourables et si leur étendard cessait une fois de conserver la couleur chevaleresque, exclusive et tyrannique qu'on a l'aveuglement de ne pas abandonner.

Mais la prévention contre les étrangers a des racines profondes et nationales. Non seulement la guerre extérieure sert de point de ralliement aux diverses factions jacobines, qui s'entredéchireraient; elle alimente de plus l'inertie des mécontens, elle les livre pieds et poings liés à la Convention. Elle les force à se battre pour leurs bourreaux, parce qu'elle n'a offert jusqu'ici aucune perspective de consolation ou de succès et qu'elle s'est toujours présentée sous l'image d'une guerre faite à la France même, par des rivaux, par des ennemis de la France, d'une guerre où on ne veut rien obtenir que par la force armée, dont le véritable but est un mystère qui écrase la monarchie sans offrir aucun secours à la majorité souffrante et dont les revers perpétuels ont généralisé l'opinion, que le pire danger pour les mécontens était de compter sur elle.

Voilà l'exacte vérité; quiconque, my Lord, vous tiendra un autre langage cherche à vous tromper. Vous ne terminerez pas heureusement la guerre sans contre-révolution ; si vous ne changez le caractère, les moyens, et le but de la guerre. Voulez-vous réunir toute la France contre vous sans distinction de parti ? il suffira de poursuivre le plan de conduite observé jusqu'à présent. Voulez-vous rendre absolument inutile le concours de cette immensité de mécontens, perdu dans une océan de conjectures sinistres sur vos desseins et étouffer le principe de réaction qui menacerait les Jacobins ? continuez à laisser croire que peu vous importe le salut de la France et que vous êtes là pour l'asservir et non pour la sauver.

Persuadez-vous que cette défiance très augmentée des projets des alliés contrebalance l'effet et le nombre des haines intérieures conjurées pour l'anéantissement de la révolution, persuadez-vous que, soldat de gré ou de force, chaque Français vous combattra opiniâtrement, et qu'en vous bornant à essayer sur les frontières une contre-révolution indécise, des tâtonnements militaires, vous succomberez en 1794 comme en 1793.

On vous a crus longtemps très redoutables et vous l'étiez ; mais les alliés n'ayant su ni profiter des circonstances, ni poursuivre un seul avantage, à l'opinion de votre infériorité s'est unie en France celle de votre inhabileté. Depuis que les Jacobins n'ont plus craint de se mesurer avec vous et à outrance, les mécontens ont perdu tout espoir, toute confiance dans vos armes. Ils savent, ils disent, ils répètent partout que les Piémontais et la prise de Toulon ont fait sacrifier Lyon, que la discorde des alliés, la faiblesse de leurs moyens et le désir d'anéantir la marine française ont fait sacrifier Toulon; qu'on a préparé quelques démonstrations de secours pour la Vendée au moment où elle était exterminée, et qu'en un mot, les puissances seraient bien fâchées qu'il s'élevât dans l'intérieur une réunion capable de sauver la France qu'elles n'aspirent qu'à envahir.

Voilà l'opinion populaire, générale : or, tout opprimé qui en est imbu préférera jouer le Jacobinisme et aller se battre aux frontières pour sa sûreté plutôt que de courir le risque de former un vœu dangereux pour vos succès qui lui serait inutile ou de passer les frontières pour être chassé de lieu en lieu comme un pestiféré et mourir de faim au coin d'une route.

Dans la prochaine suite de ce travail, je vous exposerai, my Lord, les moyens qui me paraissent seuls capables de détruire ces dispositions et de les faire servir au but commun.

Endorsed
In Lord ELGIN's No. 24.

A MILORD ELGIN,
    Bruxelles.

Informations additionnelles.

Le 15 mars, 1794.

La mobilité des variations qu'éprouvent les différentes parties du tableau de la France, nécessite de six semaines en six semaines des correctifs ou des additions. Vous ne devez pas donc trouver contradictoires des rapports faits à divers intervalles : c'est la scène qui change, et non la tête de l'observateur. D'ailleurs, l'instruction se rectifie, s'étend, se fixe, avec plus de précision, à mesure que les informations s'augmentent et se perfectionnent.

Complément du comité de salut public. Les bases générales que je vous ai développées sont immuables, mais plusieurs détails ont varié, ou me sont mieux connus. Je vais les réunir dans un bref supplément.

Le douzième membre du comité de salut public dont j'avais laissé le nom en blanc est *St Just*. Relégué longtemps dans une espèce d'obscurité, il en est sorti par des déclamations furieuses, où l'on découvre de l'esprit, de la facilité, un emploi quelquefois heureux du néologisme du jour. Ses principes paraissent aussi emportés que ses discours. Quant à ses mœurs, il en a fait l'essai au mois de 9re à Strasbourg, où le comité l'envoya exercer en son nom le proconsulat. Les prisons et les échafauds ne suffisaient pas à ses poursuites : il accabla de taxes exorbitantes ceux qu'il ne fit pas égorger, et couvrit cette ville de sang et de deuil. Les Jacobins y avaient perdu leur prédominance ; un parti puissant appelait hautement les Autrichiens. La grande majorité des habitans, de l'état-major, de la municipalité et du district, s'étaient prononcés contre les Maratistes. St Just remit les choses en ordre et sortit triomphant de Strasbourg, sur les cadavres de plus de 2000 guillotinés. Fut-on affecté de son éloquence? On le supposerait plutôt bel esprit révolutionnaire que factieux ardent: on pourrait douter de la sincérité de son zèle, et en trouver la cause, en dernière analyse, dans la nécessité d'échapper au supplice. Ce soupçon est fortifié par l'inclination que montre St Just à embrasser la cause la plus effrénée, si celle de Roberspierre vient à décliner.

Religion. Il est surprenant qu'on a mis en doute dans la chambre haute de votre parlement l'adoption publique et légale de l'athéisme, comme seule religion de la France. L'hypocrisie de quelques entortillages de Robespierre, au moment où l'on décréta *le culte de la raison*, n'a pas empêché que ce culte ne soit devenu exclusif et national. Aucune église n'est ouverte à la religion chrétienne; tous les clochers sont abattus; tous les ustensiles du service divin, volés; les autels, démolis, et les prêtres qui refusent de rendre leurs lettres de prêtrise et d'abjurer le sacerdoce, incarcérés. Voilà la règle générale; la célébration plus ou moins secrète du culte religieux dans quelques villages en fait l'exception.

La Convention et la municipalité de Paris ont remplacé la religion par les spectacles: 40 théâtres sont ouverts dans la capitale et journellement peuplés d'ouvriers et de canaille des deux sexes. On y joue des pièces civiques et historiques sur les évènemens de la guerre, ou de la révolution; la population s'y infecte d'un fanatisme atroce; l'autorité en a fait un de ses ressorts, et a positivement transformé l'art dramatique, ramené à son enfance, en sacerdoce public.

Force des armées. Depuis les premiers résultats que je vous ai présentés, on m'a communiqué l'état des bataillons de la première levée, dans chacun des 549 districts. Ce relevé, dont je n'ai pu obtenir copie, offre une différence considérable avec le dénombrement approximatif, annexé à la *première suite du résumé*. Lorsque les districts ont fourni trois bataillons de 800 à 1100 hommes, plusieurs en ont donné deux; la pluralité, un, complet ou incomplet. 64 districts restent *pour mémoire* et n'ont pu lever une compagnie, (ceux de la Vendée, des Deux-Sèvres, de la Mayenne, de Maine et Loire, du Morbihan, quelques-uns du Var, des Pyrénées orientales, du Nord et du Bas-Rhin forment ce nombre négatif).

Des 485 restans, 166 n'avaient encore fourni que des compagnies, et non un bataillon à la date du 15 février.

319 ont levé, et fait partir, au delà de 286,000 hommes, qui joints aux troupes de ligne et aux anciens volontaires formeront une armée totale pour 1794 de près 700,000 hommes.

Les désertions, qui ont été très nombreuses dans la première levée, compensent à peu près la force additionnelle des compagnies auxquelles se réduit le contingent de 166 districts. Ainsi la somme de 700,000 soldats de toute classe constitue l'état très probable de l'armée nationale aujourd'hui en exercice.

Dans mon premier dénombrement elle était réduite à 650 mille en y comprenant les deux réquisitions. Voici la source de cette différence.

La famine, qui en 1707 procura 150 mille hommes à Louis quatorze, et la terreur, non moins énergique que la famine, ont précipité dans *la première levée de* 18 *à* 25 *ans*, une foule de sujets au-dessous de 18 ans et au-dessus de 25.

Elle n'embrassait que les célibataires : beaucoup de gens mariés, ont marché par le même motif, *pour subsister.*

La seconde réquisition de 25 à 45 ans ne tardera pas d'être exigée, le comité s'en occupe depuis quelques semaines. Outre les célibataires, le décret qui l'ordonnera, doit embrasser *les gens mariés sans enfans*, et les gens mariés sans enfans, dont néanmoins les femmes sont enceintes. Cette disposition tend à obvier à l'abus d'une quantité de mariages qui ont eu lieu, et surtout à Paris, pour échapper au devoir de marcher.

On remarqua que les premiers volontaires nationaux de 1792 contractèrent de jour en jour un esprit analogue à celui des troupes de ligne. Quelques revers un peu décisifs amortiraient leur exaltation de gloire, et feraient éclater la lassitude, le dégoût, le mécontentement, le désir d'un changement. Mais les derniers venus aux armées sont en général exécrables, comme moins rassasiés de la vie licencieuse et pillarde, et comme faisant journellement la comparaison de l'abondance où ils se trouvent, avec la misère de leurs habitations domestiques, où ils crevaient de faim sous des haillons.

La fabrication des armes a pris une grande activité : outre les anciennes manufactures on en a monté plusieurs nouvelles. Paris est un vaste atelier. Au commencement de février on y fabriquait 700 fusils par jour, 100 sautent ou se détériorent à l'épreuve. On espère pousser la fabrication journalière à mille fusils parce que les ouvriers se perfectionnent.

La fonte des canons va également grand train ; environ 100 sortent des fourneaux de la capitale tous les douze jours ; il y en avait 3,000 à l'arsenal le 16 février.

L'extraction du salpêtre a occupé à Paris un monde infini. On ne voyait que chaudières et lessives de terre dans les sections, mais ce grand travail a été très stérile, et ne peut se soutenir, car le comité ne paye que 24 sols la livre d'un salpêtre qui revient à 12 francs de fabrication, et qu'il faut ensuite raffiner.

Subsistances. Leur disette se manifeste journellement ; diverses consommations, jadis de première nécessité, sont épuisées ; d'autres deviennent rares de plus en plus, la source de la reproduction est tarie dans plusieurs provinces. Quant au pain, toujours suffisant aux besoins de la capitale, on ne s'en procure pas, sans peine, dans la grande pluralité des départemens. Les habitans ont été mis à la *ration* journalière, c'est à dire à demi-livre, ou trois quarts de livre de pain par individu.

À Lyon, dans les provinces environnantes, dans la plupart des villes du second ou du troisième ordre, on manque même souvent de pain, des semaines entières. Une infinité de familles ne s'en procurent qu'en l'achetant des soldats de l'armée révolutionnaire, auxquels on en donne deux livres par jour, et qui en revendent la moitié.

Le peuple dans les villes et les campagnes vit de choux, de fèves, de pommes de terre, de racines ; mais ces denrées diminuent rapidement. Peu d'auberges sur les routes où l'on ne trouve d'autre nourriture qu'un pain noir et desséché (de véritable biscuit) et que des légumes en petite quantité.

La viande a presque généralement disparu : on ne voit plus que quelques moutons épars dans les provinces méridionales, ci-devant couvertes d'innombrables troupeaux.

La loi du maximum a dévoré ce que les armées n'avaient pas encore englouti, parce que, dans les premiers temps de son émanation, le paysan, le journalier, tous ceux qui ne mangeaient de la viande qu'une fois par semaine, excités par le bas prix, ont augmenté la consommation.

On a tué les vaches faute de fourrage, ou l'administration des subsistances militaires et l'armée révolutionnaire les ont enlevées; les veaux sont encore plus rares que les moutons. Quant au bœuf, son usage, ainsi que celui de la vache, est généralement interdit excepté à Paris et dans les armées. Vous voyez que depuis plusieurs semaines la disette de viande a gagné même la capitale. Elle est privée de savon, d'huile, de café, de sucre que les apothicaires ont remplacé par un sirop de mélasse : le peu de cassonade qu'on se procure est noire comme la suie. Plus de gibier ni de volailles : un chapon s'est payé 47 francs, le 20 février ; les gens de la campagne ayant mangé leurs poules faute de grains pour les nourrir, et fait de leurs vaches des salaisons, les œufs, le lait, le beurre sont devenus denrées de luxe : la rareté de la morue et des légumes ne permet qu'à un très petit nombre d'individus d'en faire usage. Aussi quand Barrère, effrayé de la disette de viande, a proposé un *carême civique*, il proposait un ordre aux dix-huit vingtièmes des Parisiens de se nourrir de pain. Le vin consommé dans la capitale n'est pas altéré, car les marchands le fabriquent, et vendent cette boisson qu'on dit détestable, par l'impossibilité d'acheter, de transporter et de revendre de véritables vins, au prix du *maximum*.

Cette calamité vient d'exciter à Paris des murmures, des clameurs à la halle, quelques placards menaçans; mais dans le reste du royaume, tels sont l'inconcevable effroi et la soumission du peuple, qu'un village sans pain voit passer chaque jour des convois de vivres pour l'armée sans oser y porter la main.

La disette de bestiaux a amené celle des cuirs: la disette des moutons paralyse les fabriques, qui n'ont plus de laines. Afin de suppléer au cuir, il a été défendu à tout cordonnier de faire une paire de souliers pour aucun particulier, sous peine de 4 ans de fers. Leur travail et la matière sont en réquisition forcée; aussi à Paris, ainsi que dans le royaume, les deux sexes sont en sabots: on devient suspect en portant des bottes ou des souliers. Quant aux étoffes de tout genre, on ne trouve à acheter que le rebut des magasins, que des hardes de friperie, ou clandestinement, à des prix excessifs, quelques étoffes moins mauvaises et cachées par les marchands et qu'ils vendent en secret au risque de passer pour des *accapareurs*.

Je vous ai déjà annoncé les efforts et les sacrifices par lesquels le comité de salut public cherche à soutenir les choses dans cet équilibre entre les privations et la famine rigoureuse. Je vous ai indiqué les théâtres de ses achats, ses courtiers à l'étranger et le succès de ses profusions en ce genre. Nous venons de voir un nouvel exemple de celles-ci dans une foire de bestiaux tenue à Berne il y a quinze jours, et où en 6 heures les agens de la Convention ont acheté pour *huit cent mille livres* de bestiaux; huit paires de bœufs ont été vendues douze mille livres. Tous les achats payés en espèces, et au comptant, l'avidité d'un gain exorbitant a fait passer les vendeurs sur toute espèce de prudence: tel fermier a vendu ses attelages sans se douter qu'il ne trouverait plus à les racheter, ou qu'il les rachèterait à l'usure. Enfin lorsqu'une immense quantité de bestiaux a été enlevée et la viande renchérie, lorsque les boucheries ont été en souffrance, ainsi que les consommateurs, le gouvernement a rendu une prohibition générale et sévère d'exporter; mais le mal était fait en très grande partie.

Cette défense embrasse aussi les chevaux, dont le seul canton de Berne avait vendu au 1er mars 4,800, passés en France.

Les autres cantons ont imité cette mesure tardive ; ceux de Fribourg et de Soleure les avaient devancés.

Il serait superflu de vous redire, ce dont plusieurs de mes lettres vous ont instruit, que les fournitures de la Suisse même en bestiaux, chevaux, cuirs, toiles, fromages, bornées par la nature du pays, et par les défenses des gouvernemens, ne pourraient soulager six semaines les détresses de la France. Mais les exportations d'Italie, d'Allemagne, du nord &c. pour le compte des marchands de Bâle, Neuchatel, Genève, Gênes, et transmises aux Français par les commissionnaires, procurent des ressources plus étendues, et en procureraient d'intarissables. Il est sorti de la Lombardie, et de la Souabe 60 mille bêtes à cornes et chevaux, qui par l'intermédiaire de la Suisse, ont passé en Alsace. Les draps, les cuirs, nombre d'articles et même des grains ont pris la même route. D'après la multiplicité et l'accord des rapports qui me sont parvenus, je ne puis douter que des régences allemandes entraînées par l'amour du gain, ou séduites par les corruptions françaises, n'aient secondé de leurs invigilance cette contrebande ; les grands propriétaires, soit en Lombardie, soit en Souabe, s'empressent aussi à la favoriser pour vendre leurs blés à haut prix aux ennemis de toute propriété.

L'association de banquiers formée à Paris dans le dessein de provoquer et de solder ces versemens étrangers de marchandise et de denrées est une conspiration sur laquelle les puissances doivent porter une prompte et sévère attention : le fond de cette entreprise est de 60 millions fournis par 40 maisons de banque. Le comité de salut public les a obligées à cette réunion et a taxé chacune d'elles à sa quote part.

Celle de Mallet, père et fils, est rançonnée de 1200 mille livres : les autres à proportion : le comité appelle cette contribution une *avance* à rembourser après les fournitures faites. La crainte de la mort et de la confiscation ont concouru avec l'infernal esprit de commerce à la condescendance de ces banquiers. Je vous ai instruit que trois d'entr'eux s'étaient rendus à leur destination, savoir, Grivel associé de Fulchiron à Gênes, Perrigaux, à Neuchatel, et un *anonyme* à Hambourg. Ils ont ordre d'acheter à tout prix, grains, draps, cuirs, bestiaux, salpêtre &c. &c.

Finances. Malgré les dépenses énormes en espèces, la Convention soutient son trésor, entre quatre à cinq cent millions, par l'accaparement journalier de numéraire et des matières d'or et d'argent ; la terreur et l'armée révolutionnaire les font sortir avec une abondance proportionnée au danger. On court en foule aux hôtels des monnaies où l'on échange ses espèces et sa vaisselle contre des assignats *au pair*. Une personne qui, le 26 du mois dernier, avait accompagné une dame à la monnaie, où elle allait porter sa vaisselle, m'a assuré qu'elles attendirent 3 heures et demie sans pouvoir entrer à cause de la foule. À cette date l'or se vendait clandestinement à 40, à 100 de bénéfice sur l'assignat.

Par les informations que j'ai recueillies touchant le pillage de Lyon, il paraît qu'au milieu de février les commissaires avaient recueilli 20 millions espèces ou assignats, qu'une somme aussi forte était enfouie, et que 30 millions ont été exportés par les propriétaires.

Quant à la valeur des marchandises saisies, elle est inappréciable.

J'ai reçu avant-hier par deux témoins dignes de créance des informations sur l'état de la campagne, et de l'armée aux frontières d'Espagne vers le milieu du mois dernier.

Il en résulte que l'armée de Rousillon a été renouvelée deux fois, et qu'elle a perdu l'année dernière 40,000 hommes par les combats, la disette, le climat, les épidémies. Avec plus de célérité les Espagnols se fussent emparés de Perpignan, où un parti nombreux se disposait à les recevoir ; le moment ayant été manqué, ce parti a succombé et expié dans les supplices sa connivence avec l'ennemi.

L'armée de M. *De Ricardos* avait perdu environ 12,000 hommes pendant la campagne. Depuis la prise de Collioure, Bellegarde, Fort St Elme et Port-Vendres, elle a pris une position retranchée qu'on regarde comme inexpugnable. Sa cavalerie fait de fréquentes excursions et extermine tous les détachemens qui s'écartent de l'armée française.

Celle-ci à laquelle on a envoyé partie de l'armée de Toulon, de celle de Lyon et tout ce qu'on a pu tirer de bataillons de volontaires dans le midi est aujourd'hui de *cent mille hommes*, en deux divisions inégales : l'une sur Bayonne, l'autre sur Perpignan.

    Endorsed
    Intelligence
    R. 7th April.
      (1.)

A Milord Elgin,
  Bruxelles.

> 20 *mars*, 1794.

Un retour d'indisposition, qui ne m'a permis de reprendre le travail qu'avant-hier, retarde encore d'un courrier la conclusion que vous attendez : voici celle des informations.

Vous aurez vu, Milord, dans les papiers de France, l'appel du club des Cordeliers à l'insurrection, la députation fraternelle des Jacobins à ce club, le pas rétrograde de celui-ci, et leur réunion par le ministère de Collot d'Herbois. Je vous dois la clef de cette comédie. Elle ne signifie autre chose que les deux partis, jugeant leurs forces respectives balancées, veulent se donner le temps de recruter chacun de leur côté, et d'assurer leurs moyens de guerre. Collot d'Herbois, en feignant d'improuver les Cordeliers, n'a dans le fait improuvé que leur précipitation : il a soufflé à Roberspierre toujours malade, le rôle de médiateur, et saura profiter, en temps et lieu, du crédit que vient de lui donner cette démarche. Cette trêve entre les deux factions va être scellée par le massacre des 61 députés détenus, par celui de 99 membres de la Convention, et probablement par celui d'une partie des détenus particuliers. Roberspierre et Couthon gardent toujours leur maison. Le choc ne sera pas aussi prompt qu'on pouvait le croire et son issue dépendra absolument des premiers événemens de la campagne. Si vous la brusquez, si vous obtenez de grands succès, le comité est perdu, et vu la détresse de Paris pour les subsistances, la commotion pourra s'étendre jusqu'à la Convention elle-même.

Vous aurez lu aussi un décret rendu sur un rapport de Barrère et qui permet l'exportation aux neutres des *marchandises surabondantes.* J'ai appris d'une manière sûre le but d'un décret en apparence contradictoire avec tous ceux qui l'ont précédé : c'est une parade : il ne s'agit uniquement que de faciliter la vente à l'étranger des diamans de la couronne, des soieries prises à Lyon et autres effets précieux invendables dans l'intérieur. Les 42 banquiers qui ont fourni 60 millions pour achats au dehors, l'ont fait, non en espèces, ni assignats, mais par leurs billets solidaires, délivrés au comité. Celui-ci, pour faciliter le crédit et le placement de ces billets, leur a donné, pour hypothèque, les diamans et autres effets désignés plus haut ; les vendeurs étrangers pourront se payer avec ces valeurs ou bien elles leur serviront de nantissement pour la sûreté des billets.

La nouvelle de la prise de Bastia était prématurée. Rien d'Italie depuis huit jours.

L'armée du Rhin est à cinq livres de fourrage par jour pour chaque cheval.

Plus d'avoine; les magasins pris sur l'ennemi ayant été pillés en détail par les escortes, les conducteurs, les paysans, ils n'ont été d'aucun secours.

Endorsed
Intelligence
R. 7th April.
(2.)

Extrait d'une lettre de la frontière en date du 22 mai 1794.

S'il pouvait en exister un plus terrible que celui sous lequel nous sommes, je vous dirais, que nous allons au galop vers le despotisme. À force de faire jouer la hache, le comité de salut public s'en tirera à honneur. Vous devez remarquer qu'elle tranche de toutes parts; aristocrates, démocrates, patriotes, peu importe. Tout ce qui a un nom, de la fortune, du génie y passera. Le dernier rapport de Roberspierre a laissé tout le monde stupéfait; parce qu'on ne voulait pas lui accorder du talent. Pour cette fois il n'y a plus moyen de nier; ce n'est plus la plume virile de Siéyès son ancien faiseur : c'est trop doux, trop redondant. Si ce rapport est de Roberspierre, vous n'avez plus qu'à lire l'histoire d'Auguste. Avec la guillotine et du talent nous arriverons au même point. Les membres de la Commune sont arrêtés depuis deux jours : on n'ose en souffler mot.

Je doute qu'en aucun temps il ait existé un peuple plus discret que les Français d'aujourd'hui. On a affiché une récompense, pour qui pourrait donner des nouvelles de l'armée du nord, elle n'a tenté personne. Ne croyez nullement aux grands progrès ultérieurs de Cobourg: il tâtera le manche de la guillotine et voilà tout: il affermira le gouvernement, qui voudra ensuite se mettre en posture de faire la paix.

Deux personnes différentes échappées de Paris et arrivées, il y a peu de jours, m'ont tenu à peu près le même langage. Il résulte de leurs informations et de celles que j'ai recueillies récemment, qu'il n'y a rien, absolument rien, à attendre de l'intérieur ni de Paris. Les provinces abattues tremblent au seul nom de cette capitale, et marcheront éternellement sur ses traces, à moins qu'une force très supérieure ne vienne les ressusciter. On s'est habitué à la misère et à toutes les calamités ; personne n'ose ni ne songe à en murmurer.

Quant à Paris, ses habitans n'appartiennent plus à l'espèce humaine. Les uns plus féroces et plus redoutables à chaque nouveau crime sont liés irrémissiblement et chaque jour de plus en plus à la cause de Roberspierre. Le reste des habitans ne vaut guère mieux. Hébétés par les événemens journaliers, ils n'y sont plus même sensibles, chacun s'attend à finir par le dernier supplice et cherche à reculer ce dernier moment à force de précautions et de bassesses. Cette multitude animalisée n'a plus même l'instinct de sa propre défense, résignée à tout elle se verrait mourir de faim sans oser proférer un murmure. Soit par complicité, soit par égarement stupide, soit par lâcheté, Paris entier est une argile dans les mains du comité. Plus une étincelle d'espérance dans le cœur de qui que ce soit. Je vous avais annoncé, My Lord, ces dispositions depuis longtemps et combien il était absurde de compter sur le désespoir, sur la tyrannie, sur la famine, sur quelques succès des frontières.

Le crédit de Roberspierre s'affermit et s'augmente à vue d'œil : il est plus puissant, que ne fut jamais Louis XIV. Je vous certifie que personne n'a la hardiesse de penser à lui disputer son autorité. St Just, pour avoir manifesté quelques opinions différentes de celles du chef dans le comité, s'est mis au pied de l'échelle ; il cherche à s'en tirer par des bassesses, et par un dévouement plus servile ; mais il n'échappera pas à sa destinée.

La terreur a tué le germe des factions, et l'anéantissement du pouvoir populaire en a éteint l'aliment. Les Commissaires auprès des armées, les bureaux du gouvernement, les administrateurs, les accusateurs publics sont autant de créatures de Roberspierre. Sa cruauté ne fait point baisser sa popularité ; d'abord parce que le peuple de Paris n'est plus touché de la cruauté, ensuite parce que Roberspierre agit comme il parle, a des mœurs conformes à son rôle, n'aspire ni à la fortune, ni aux dignités, et a persuadé le vulgaire de la sincérité de son républicanisme.

Fouquier Tinville accusateur public au Trib. Révol. de Paris était ami de Danton, qui l'avait placé ; au premier mot de Roberspierre il n'hésita pas à faire périr son bienfaiteur.

Ces exemples sont innombrables. Le tribunal ne se donne plus la peine d'interroger les accusés. Le comité paye 1500 francs par jour à la galerie qui va applaudir aux sentences et courir aux exécutions. Celles-ci tiennent lieu de spectacles : c'est une erreur de penser que le peuple en est rassasié ; au contraire il murmure lorsque les charrettes qui traînent les condamnés au supplice se réduisent à une ou deux.

Il n'est pas plus question, à Paris, de la Vendée, de ses exploits, de ce prétendu siège de Nantes annoncé dans vos gazettes, que si elle n'existait pas. Le comité n'a pour le moment aucune inquiétude de ce côté-là ; du moins il ne la montre par aucune disposition.

Toujours du pain assez abondant, et rareté extrême d'autres comestibles, surtout de viande ; tel est l'état actuel des subsistances à Paris. Dans les provinces on se nourrit de légumes de printemps : la récolte est généralement belle et très avancée : on moissonne les orges en Provence, en Languedoc, dans le Bas-Dauphiné : tous les grains seront recueillis à l'est et au midi avant la fin de juin. Quant à l'extérieur, le plan du comité est seulement de vous résister en Flandre, de prévenir vos progrès en Picardie, de vous harasser par des combats journaliers et des diversions, et de vous laisser consumer en sièges la campagne. Pour la guerre offensive je vous répète qu'ils la destinent et qu'ils la portent impétueusement avec de grandes forces à l'Italie et à l'Espagne.

Extrait d'une lettre de la frontière, en date du 29 mai 1794.

La fabrique des fusils, et des canons augmente tous les jours d'activité : on a du salpêtre ; quoique les anciens canonniers soient presque tous tués, les élèves faits cet hiver commencent à les remplacer avantageusement. Il reste encore deux cent mille hommes de la première réquisition non employés, et disponibles. On ne procédera à la 2ᵉ levée que sur la fin de la campagne pour opposer des troupes fraîches à des troupes harassées : ces réquisitions, n'en doutez pas, marcheront sans la moindre résistance au premier ordre du comité.

Paris est approvisionné en blé pour six semaines ; il n'y a pas de viande, on ne tue que 32 moutons par jour, chaque individu ne peut avoir qu'une livre de viande par décade ; les œufs et le beurre sont rares, le jardinage, très abondant.

On s'est fait à cette vie, on la supporte sans murmurer : d'ailleurs on a levé des animaux, l'enlèvement de 30 à 40 mille chevaux de luxe, rend les fourrages abondans et les a fait refluer aux armées.

Plus de factions proprement dites, plus de partis prononcés, le comité plane sur tout. Les factions ne naissent et ne se soutiennent que par l'espoir, et il n'y a plus d'espoir quelconque dans le cœur de personne, pas plus du dehors que de l'intérieur.

Les excès moins cruels peut-être mais plus grossièrement nécessaires d'Hébert, de Ronsin et autres sans-culottes à moustaches et à sabres roulans font trouver l'état actuel de Paris plus supportable. L'exercice fréquent de la guillotine n'empêche pas le grand nombre de s'en croire encore éloigné, tant qu'on reste dans la soumission, le silence, et le dévouement au comité. D'ailleurs on peut aujourd'hui s'habiller décemment même avec goût : plus de bonnets rouges, plus de tutoiement affecté : on peut aller aux spectacles, et chez les filles, sans y être insulté par les sans-culottes ou par les satellites de l'armée révolutionnaire. Ainsi, à tout prendre, notre situation est un peu moins mauvaise.

Ce n'est pas en outre sur le comité de salut public que retombe la haine qu'inspire la fréquence des supplices, c'est sur celui de sûreté générale, son agent, et qui sera bientôt sa victime. On parle de la clémence de Roberspierre avec la même bonne foi, qu'on parlait à Rome de celle d'Auguste.

C'est à force d'adresse et d'habileté que le chef a su éviter les bénédictions, qu'on voulait lui prodiguer aux spectacles et aux Jacobins. Ce n'est pas que des succès éclatans et rapides des Autrichiens, que l'occupation de la Picardie, et une marche accélérée ne changeassent bien vite ces dispositions ; mais ces victoires, cette marche, on les a tant de fois attendues, et toujours si vainement que l'on n'ose plus même y penser.

On attend un immense convoi de l'Amérique : c'est pour le protéger que notre flotte est sortie de Brest ; la dernière division vient de mettre à la voile. Si nous pouvions attendre la récolte, nous sommes approvisionnés pour deux ans. Jamais autant de semence ne fut jetée en terre : jamais elle ne promit une si abondante restitution. Tout a été mis en culture ; jachères, bruyères, allées, avenues, promenades, biens royaux, jardins nationaux. On a soin de dire aux paysans que depuis qu'ils ne prient plus le bon Dieu, la nature leur donne toutes ses richesses.

Quoiqu'il n'y ait plus de factions, Roberspierre a du moins des jaloux dans le comité ; mais ces rivalités sourdes n'ont ni effet, ni influence. Par le moyen des Jacobins on vient de détruire les sociétés sectionnaires, ou populaires : plus de rassemblemens excepté aux Jacobins, qu'on conserve pendant la guerre pour exciter l'enthousiasme ; mais qu'on fera casser par la convention, lorsqu'il en sera temps. Collot et Couthon sont chargés du gouvernement de cette société. Roberspierre ne veut d'autre titre que celui de membre du comité de S.P. Il se contente de gouverner sous son nom.

Ses collègues ont une assez belle part pour en être contens. Ils disposent de la fortune, des places, des revenus pour leurs amis et leurs cliens.

   Endorsed
 In Lord ELGIN's, *June* 10*th*.

De la frontière. 30 *mai* 1794.

Il n'est pas douteux que mes correspondans de Paris sont moins exacts, l'un tient de si près aux guillotineurs, qu'il appréhende toujours d'être guillotiné, l'autre sans le mériter autant, a la même crainte ; ils me l'ont fait savoir tous deux par écrit, et de vive voix par des émigrés : ce que je vous écrivis le 27 de ce mois était le résultat d'une lettre du premier, et d'une longue conversation avec un de ses intimes, ci-devant lié avec les faiseurs. Il m'apprenait en outre, dans sa lettre, que la crainte et la terreur étaient encore plus à l'ordre du jour dans l'âme des membres du comité de S. P. que dans celle des autres Français, il entrait même à cet égard dans quelques détails sur les précautions que prend Roberspierre pour échapper aux coups que sa conscience sans doute lui fait appréhender dès lors ; dans une lettre reçue avant-hier, il me mande l'assassinat manqué de Collot, m'ajoutant que cette entreprise ne servira pas peu les projets des chefs, et qu'ils songent à en tirer parti pour leur autorité : l'exemple de Pisistrate est déjà dans l'esprit de tout le monde ; qu'au reste ce coup va servir de prétexte à de nouvelles cruautés, qu'on les fera porter sur plusieurs membres de la Convention dont on voulait encore se défaire. Les papiers ne nous disent pas que Collot était avec un de ses amis qui a reçu un coup de couteau à la gorge: Robespierre n'a pas osé sortir le lendemain, mais sa peur fera verser bien du sang. Les commissions populaires sont composées uniquement de gens sous sa main, aussi s'attend on qu'elles feront beaucoup de mal et peu de bien ; tout ce qui est riche sera guillotiné ; soyez-en sûr ; nous avons de mauvaises nouvelles de Flandre, nous les tenons secrètes, pour ne parler que de quelques avantages du côté de Thuin, et sur les

bords de la Sambre. Voilà monsieur l'extrait de ma lettre de mercredi, et mon correspondant m'ajoute : "Je comprends vos plain-
"tes sur mon silence, mais vous ne jugez plus Paris ce qu'il est ;
"l'égoïsme est dans tous les cœurs ; l'apathie est dans tous les esprits ;
"ne vous figurez plus qu'on s'intéresse au sort de tel ou tel membre
"du Comité de S. P. ou de ses adversaires, ce qu'on désire uniquement
"et ardemment, c'est qu'il domine en paix ; les partis qui se sont
"élevés ont tous entraîné, dans leur chute, la ruine et la mort d'une
"infinité d'honnêtes gens, et les factions de Brissot, Dumourier, Hébert,
"Danton ont toutes prouvé que même parmi les scélérats : Quidquid
"delirant Reges, plectuntur Achivi : Il est vrai qu'ici les Grecs sont
"bien les plus lâches des hommes : Que m'importe, pourvu que je ne
"porte pas les coups : voilà la pensée de tous ces fiers républicains
"de Paris. Je ne saurais trop vous le répéter : Il y a des jaloux
"secrets, mais point de factieux hardis, point de parti prononcé :
"obtenez quelque succès sur les frontières et vous les verrez renaître
"avec l'espoir de réussir : vous verrez le comité de S. P. harcelé, et
"environné de contradicteurs, mais il faut des revers, sans quoi le
"mot de faction n'existera pas même. Il y a plus : nous en sommes au
"point que l'on est plus prêt à donner à Robespierre des bénédictions,
"qu'à le charger de reproches, et pour peu qu'il paraisse s'adoucir, il
"sera bientôt traité comme un Dieu ! Je vous écrirais tous les jours
"que je ne vous en dirais pas davantage. Si d'ailleurs il y avait
"quelque chose d'important soit pour l'intérieur, soit pour des projets
"sur l'étranger, ou de descente en Angleterre à laquelle personne ne
"pense plus, je vous en ferais part. Quand je ne vous écris rien, c'est
"qu'il n'y a rien, du moins à ma connaissance ; soyez sûr d'ailleurs que
"nous vivons beaucoup au jour le jour."

Voilà, monsieur, tout ce que j'ai à vous mander aujourd'hui ; j'ai été si occupé ce matin par le retour des Bernois pour la transaction des solidaires que je n'ai pu encore vous envoyer prendre mes lettres d'Italie : veuillez faire dire à notre ami que j'ai reçu sa lettre, et que je lui écrirai demain.

  Endorsed
In Lord ELGIN's *June* 17th.

               Mercredi matin, 4 *juin*.

Je viens de recevoir votre lettre ; vous paraissez ajouter foi à l'affaire du 22 ; c'est un motif de plus pour moi d'y croire ; nous languissons comme vous d'en apprendre les résultats.

On me confirme de Gênes la prise de Bastia, qui s'est rendu le 19 faute de vivres ; de Turin, rien de plus sûr que l'arrivée de bon nombre d'Autrichiens ; la cour a pris enfin l'allure ferme ; si elle va bien, les peuples iront de même : il y a plusieurs personnes arrêtées ; on parle d'une conspiration assez grave, on dit qu'un million avait été offert au commandant d'Exilles, et que ce brave homme a repoussé l'offre et les offrans ; je n'ai pas sur ces objets de détails officiels, la lettre qui les contiendra, si le fait est vrai, ne me sera donnée que dans une heure, je vous les transmettrai vendredi. Une indiscrétion française m'a fait connaître une lettre récente d'un membre du comité de sal. pub. ; elle exprime les plus vives inquiétudes ; il parle de chercher un lieu de retraite, il dit que la pluralité du comité voit les choses comme lui ; c'est-à-dire appréhende l'extérieur et l'intérieur ; mais s'ils doivent périr, ce sera dans les flots de sang qu'ils auront fait verser dans l'intérieur, et sur les cadavres des victimes qu'ils se seront immolées : mon correspondant m'écrit aussi dix lignes, pour me parler des assassinats à peu près comme vrais ; il m'assure qu'ils seront le prétexte d'une effroyable tragédie, qu'elle portera en grande partie sur la Convention, et sur les détenus actuels : la terreur règne chez tous les Conventionnels, ils redoutent à chaque instant l'œil et le geste de Robespierre et de Barrère qui doit les désigner au supplice : il m'assure qu'il ne font aucun fond sur les succès de Pichegru, et qu'ils s'attendent à le voir battu ; il croit même que dans la nuit du jour qu'il m'écrit, le 28, ils ont reçu de mauvaises nouvelles ; il me confirme que la Vendée, quoique faible, existe et a des succès. Malgré tout cela, il ne peut croire aux résultats décidément contre-révolutionnaires et aux succès décisifs des alliés ; il croit que Robers-pierre trouvera, dans sa cruauté et le génie de Siéyès, des ressources si effroyables, que la terreur renforcée de tous leurs autres moyens exagérés, leur procurera des armées sans cesse renaissantes ; à moins, termine-t-il toujours, que des coups rapides et considérables, ne jettent une alarme salutaire, jusqu'au cœur de la capitale.

Je n'écris pas à notre ami ; ce sera vendredi ; il y a six jours que je n'ai rien de lui. Je l'embrasse ainsi que vous, excellent et vertueux homme. J'espère que notre ami n'a pas été fâché de la lettre que je lui écrivis samedi sur la reconnaissance.

Berne, le 8 *juin* 1794.

Ce que vous lirez de Paris, My Lord, dans *la lettre ci-incluse* m'a été confirmé hier par le même correspondant par une lettre que j'ai reçue moi-même de la capitale en date du 30 et que je n'ai pas encore eu le temps de déchiffrer en entier ; enfin par le témoignage d'une de mes connaissances, homme d'un esprit supérieur et d'une rare énergie, sorti de Paris il y a 12 jours. À son départ, ainsi qu'à celui des lettres, on avait la plus sinistre opinion de l'armée du nord, et l'on parlait du rappel de Pichegru, auquel on nommait pour successeur Scherer, Alsacien, qui commandait l'hiver dernier à Huningue.

Le comité a de vives craintes ; c'est un fait avéré : sa confiance existe principalement dans les moyens multipliés de corruption et d'intelligence par lesquels il travaille à opérer des soulèvemens et des troubles chez ses ennemis. Regardez ces efforts comme le fond de sa politique extérieure. Quant à l'intérieur, il prépare de nouveaux massacres. Il va continuer à supposer des complots dans les prisons, des projets d'assassinats, des préparatifs de révolte, et il égorgera. La terreur a encore augmenté à Paris parce qu'on y pressent cet orage, comme les animaux par leurs mugissemens annoncent ceux de l'atmosphère. Tout projet de descente en Angleterre est absolument abandonné.

J'ai dans mes mains les matériaux d'un quatrième mémoire historique sur l'intérieur actuel de la France. J'ai remis cette rédaction à un autre temps, je me borne à vous en indiquer les résultats que voici :

1°. Aucun espoir de soulèvement intérieur ni à Paris ni dans les départemens. Les hommes ne sont plus que des cadavres marchant dans les rues, et plus vils que des vermisseaux, il n'existe encore quelque reste de courage que chez les femmes.

2°. Cet état moral ne changera qu'après des succès éclatans et successifs de la part des alliés, et au moment où leurs armes inspireront plus de terreur que le comité.

3°. La Vendée sur laquelle on débite toutes sortes de fables à Londres et à Bruxelles, est réduite à 18 mille hommes cernés par 50 mille : elle a repoussé plusieurs attaques sur son terrain, où elle se défendra sans faire de progrès : elle a perdu tout ce qu'elle avait de troupes régulières, et le plus marquant, le plus utile de ses chefs, Mr de Lescure. Il était animé d'un fanatisme communicatif qui magnétisait tous ces paysans : nul ne le remplace dans cet ascendant. Le Pr. Talmont a certainement été pris, jugé, décapité à Laval, où sa tête est encore plantée devant la porte de sa maison. Les seules provinces desquelles on pourrait attendre quelque chose, après un changement de circonstances, sont la Normandie, la Franche-Comté et une partie de la Bretagne.

4°. Le projet du comité est de renverser la Convention. Brissot, Hébert, Danton eurent le même dessein : le comité l'a fort avancé ; les représentans tremblent devant lui ; il prépare le massacre de la moitié de ceux qui restent et des 42 détenus.

5°. Robespierre domine ; mais a besoin des bras du comité : il n'est pas encore assez fort pour se défaire de ses coopérateurs, il est douteux qu'il le soit jamais. Voici la distribution des rôles. Robespierre fait les plans, tient la tribune, prépare les décisions : on lui donne l'abbé Siéyès pour souffleur.

Couthon très influent antérieurement, s'est fait le valet et l'écho de Robespierre. Collot d'Herbois est chargé de la partie des crimes, des massacres, des fourberies. Barrère conserve les rapports et la manœuvre de l'enthousiasme. St Just administre : ses collègues n'y entendant rien, sa capacité lui a donné cette branche presque exclusivement ; elle le mènera loin ; Robespierre le ménage ; Carnot tient toujours la guerre ; les autres membres ne sont que des commis.

6°. On poursuit le plan de faire périr successivement les propriétaires, pour faire vivre la république de confiscations.

7°. Il ne faut absolument compter ni sur la famine, ni même sur la disette. Chacun s'est habitué à la pénurie actuelle qui va diminuer par l'abondance des récoltes. Jamais la France ne fut cultivée comme elle l'est ; il n'y a pas un arpent qui ne soit ensemencé, sauf dans les lieux où opèrent les armées belligérantes. Cette culture universelle a été forcée par les Directrices, là où on ne la faisait pas volontairement.

8°. On manque entièrement d'articles essentiels qui ne sont pas des subsistances ; par exemple de savon : aux armées on ne fait que laver le linge ; les miasmes infects y restent imprégnés ; il en est résulté une gale lépreuse du caractère le plus virulent : les soldats l'ont communiquée aux bourgeois : elle fait des ravages immenses partout où les troupes séjournent ou ont séjourné ; on est obligé de la traiter comme la vérole, par 24 frictions mercurielles.

9°. La 2e réquisition de 25 à 45 ans sera levée généralement après les récoltes, ainsi que je vous l'ai mandé, ce qui n'empêche pas qu'on ne l'ait déjà exécutée dans beaucoup de districts. Elle s'opérera sans murmure. Tout ce qui restait de disponible dans les provinces orientales vient de partir pour l'Alsace presque sans défense. Si l'armée autrichienne du Rhin valait celle de Prusse, il ne fût pas échappé un bataillon de tout ce que les Français avaient du Rhin au Vosges, et de Spire à Bitche.

10°. Le but du décret qui défend de faire prisonniers les Anglais et les Hanovriens, du rapport de Barrère et de l'adresse de la Convention à ce sujet, est de provoquer la désertion dans vos troupes, d'arrêter les levées, de fournir un texte à l'opposition, d'exalter la haine nationale contre vous, et de forcer les patriotes à se battre en désespérés. Vous verrez se multiplier les mesures de ce genre et le comité ordonner ensuite des forfaits, devant lesquels tout ce qu'il s'est permis sera des actes de vertu.

Ainsi, My Lord, je vous répète ce que je vous disais dans mon dernier mémoire, tant que l'on aura la simplicité de se conduire avec douceur, de respecter le droit des gens, et celui de la guerre, de croire éviter les représailles, de traiter les Français d'aujourd'hui comme on les traitait en 1756, en un mot, de rester sur un système militaire incompatible avec la révolution, les circonstances, et la nature de vos ennemis, vous n'en viendrez jamais à bout.

Le courrier d'Italie arrivé hier nous confirme la prise de Bastia ; la garnison reste prisonnière de guerre. Le bruit courait que Paoli venait de déclarer la guerre aux Génois : une escadre espagnole considérable arrivait dans la Méditerranée. Les neiges nouvelles ont fait partout rétrograder les Français en Piémont, où l'on a repris courage ; les arrestations ont continué à Turin : deux officiers d'artillerie sont détenus, outre les personnes que je vous désignais dans ma dernière lettre. Il n'y avait pas de véritable conspiration, mais les préliminaires ; intelligences, correspondances, corruptions ; tout cela avait des ramifications étendues, même jusqu'en Suisse.

Endorsed
In Mr Bruce's *June* 1794.

Extraits.

Les frontières le 19 *juin* 1794.

J'ai reçu hier une lettre de la capitale en date du 13, on me mande que le rapport, et le décret sur le tribunal révolutionnaire ont pétrifié de stupeur cet amas de bêtes brutes qu'on appelle les Parisiens. Chacun se prépare à recevoir la mort ; nul n'ose avoir la pensée de la donner. Plusieurs membres de la Convention, Collot-d'Herbois, Bourdon de L'Oise, Tallien, Ruamps, Bernard de Saintes, et d'autres vont être immolés : puis 80 à 100 meurtres par jour. Je vous avais déjà mandé le présage de ce redoublement de fureur. Le comité n'est jamais satisfait de la terreur qu'il inspire ; plus il frappe, plus il sent le besoin de frapper; il a autant de craintes que les victimes. Au surplus, il n'existe qu'un sentiment, *la peur*; qu'une opinion, *la peur*; qu'un parti, celui de la *peur*. Jacobins, patriotes, aristocrates, tous se regardent comme destinés à être atteints tôt ou tard.

Depuis 15 jours, la moitié de Paris, ne vivait que de pain, et d'herbes bouillies, mais pas une plainte. On finit par me répéter, ce qui est maintenant bien inutile à dire, et que j'eus l'honneur de vous exprimer dès le mois de mars, c'est que l'effet d'une défaite, et d'une marche rapide des alliés eût été et serait encore incalculable; mais le comité ne l'appréhende guère, et connaît parfaitement la situation où les alliés se sont réduits par leur opiniâtreté à persister dans les mesures médiocres et décousues, qui leur ont déjà coûté deux campagnes.

Depuis que les Suisses ont fermé leurs frontières à l'exportation des objets nécessaires au comité, celui-ci diminue chaque jour de tendresse à leur égard, et s'il continue à être victorieux, il ne tardera pas à leur montrer que la reconnaissance n'est pas une vertu républicaine. Il ne leur déclarera pas la guerre, mais il attaquera de front leur tranquillité; il les inondera d'incendiaires et soutiendra les premiers perturbateurs qui se déploieront. La contrebande de l'Allemagne continue avec d'immenses accroissemens. 20,000 bœufs ont été achetés par les Français en Souabe: il en est déjà sorti 3,000 qui traversent la Suisse: même trafic pour les blés. La friponnerie des préposés et l'avidité des propriétaires allemands soutiennent ce commerce en dépit des ordonnances du cercle.

Milord ELGIN.

II.

À Monsieur D. S. Curtis à Paris.

Monsieur,

Vous avez sans doute lu quelques ouvrages sur la révolution française dans lesquels se trouve rapportée l'arrestation de la famille royale à Varennes; les différentes versions diffèrent plus ou moins entre elles. Je pense que vous lirez avec plaisir la seule vraie qui a été écrite par l'aîné des six enfants de mon grand-père; mon oncle Simon Fouché, né à Metz le 3 janvier 1772, était le 20 juin 1791, âgé d'un peu plus de 19 ans et se trouvait en état de rendre un compte exact de ce qu'il a vu et entendu ce jour-là et les suivants.

Ses deux sœurs aînées, mes tantes, m'ont raconté plusieurs fois ce qui s'était passé et différaient du récit de mon oncle en un seul point; suivant elles, mon grand-père ignorait, quand il s'est adressé à la reine, à qui il parlait, mais Drouet et son ami Guillaume, seuls, le savaient. J'avais lu cette relation en 1852, lors d'un voyage que je fis à Epinal (Vosges), ville dans laquelle mon grand-père et les deux aînés de la famille ont terminé leurs jours : ce n'est qu'après le décès de ma tante Catherine, arrivé en 7bre 1860, que l'idée m'est venue de chercher dans ses papiers cette relation qui ne s'y trouvait plus, parce que son auteur en avait fait don au commissaire de police d'Epinal, lequel a bien voulu permettre au plus jeune de mes oncles et à moi d'en prendre copie.

Agréez en même temps l'assurance
de ma considération distinguée,

S. FOUCHÉ.

Paris, rue Neuve des Petits Champs, 6.

Relation du voyage de la famille royale à Varennes.

Le 20 juin 1791, à onze heures du soir, ma sœur entendant du bruit dans la rue, en avertit mon père, qui, à demi habillé, sort de la maison, et se trouve vis-à-vis de Mr Drouet maître de poste de Ste Menehould accompagné de Mr Guillaume.—" Vous êtes le commandant de la garde nationale?—Oui.—Eh bien! Deux voitures qui se trouvent à l'entrée de la ville vont arriver ; c'est la famille royale qui fuit, il faut l'arrêter ; faites battre la générale, et assemblez la garde nationale, pendant que j'irai chez le procureur de la commune et que je barricaderai le pont."

Mon père rentre chez lui, passe son uniforme, m'avertit d'en faire autant, et nous nous rendons à l'auberge du bras d'or, où Leblanc et son frère Poulot déjà avertis se trouvaient sur la porte ; le tambour qui demeure vis-à-vis reçoit l'ordre de battre la générale et le bruit des deux voitures se fait entendre.

Drouet, les deux Leblanc, mon père, moi, et deux autres personnes avec le procureur de la commune, Sausse, à l'arrivée des voitures, se trouvaient comme un poste, et mettant la main sur la bride des chevaux, l'un de nous cria: " Halte là! vos passeports."

Une voix de femme avait crié, de la voiture, de passer outre ; mais il fallut montrer le passeport au nom de Mme la Bne de Korff signé Montmorin.

Après la lecture qui en fut faite, Drouet dit ; que quoique le passeport fût bon, cependant il y manquait la signature du président de l'assemblée nationale pour passer à l'étranger ; qu'ainsi il fallait de toute nécessité s'arrêter puisque l'on n'avait point de chevaux de rechange, Varennes n'étant point un lieu de poste et que d'ici à demain on chercherait à se procurer des chevaux. On descendit donc de la voiture; l'auberge ne convenant pas pour s'y arrêter, Mr Sausse offrit son logement.

On accepta, on descendit la rue, on entra d'abord au rez de chaussée qui servait à la fabrique de chandelles ; il y sentait le suif, les femmes se plaignirent qu'il était impossible de supporter cette odeur ; on leur dit qu'on préparait la chambre qui leur était destinée, et un moment après on y monta par un escalier tournant et étroit. Mon père me dit alors : "Tu resteras dans la chambre ; tu m'avertiras si tu vois des dispositions de fuite, je serai à la porte de la maison." Je suivis donc la famille royale dans cette chambre assez grande qui donnait sur un jardin ou une cour, il s'y trouvait des bancs et des chaises, deux fauteuils, une table, un lit à colonnes, une cheminée, un portrait du roi en plâtre colorié ; le roi prit place dans un fauteuil qui se trouvait au milieu de la chambre, les dames sur les bancs et les chaises adossées aux croisées, les 3 gardes du corps au coin. Quand toute la famille fut placée, le procureur de la commune vint avec sa femme demander quels ordres on avait à lui donner ; et regardant le roi, le comparant au portrait, il dit : "Sire, je vois que j'ai le bonheur de posséder la famille royale, et je viens vous offrir mon respect et mes services.— Oui, je suis votre roi, voilà mon épouse, mes enfants et ma sœur, nous vous conjurons de nous traiter avec les égards qui nous sont dus et nous nous reposons sur votre loyauté." Cette espèce d'effusion passée, la reine demanda de l'eau chaude, des œufs, du vin, des draps de lit, que l'on plaça pendant que l'on mangeait et après ce repas improvisé les 2 enfants furent couchés et presque aussitôt ils s'endormirent.

La générale battue, la garde nationale fut bientôt sur pied ; les messagers envoyés dans les villages avec ordre de communiquer partout la nouvelle de l'arrivée du roi à Varennes en amenèrent de toutes parts.

Les postes placés aux entrées de la ville n'avaient pu refuser aux 40 hussards de Lauzun de passer pour retourner à leur quartier. Mon père, les voyant arriver et s'arrêter dans la rue qu'il occupait, les fit mettre en bataille au lieu de rester en colonne, aborda l'officier qui les commandait et lui ordonna de conduire sa troupe au quartier ; l'officier, au lieu d'exécuter cet ordre, remit son commandement à un maréchal des logis et partit.

Cette troupe après être restée 16 heures à cheval ne demandait que du repos et les hussards se trouvèrent heureux de recevoir l'ordre de retourner aux Cordeliers (leur caserne).

Ils y allèrent donc en criant vive la nation, et mon père fit adosser sa garde aux maisons pour les laisser passer. En se débarrassant de ces hommes suspects, il faisait place aux détachements qui arrivaient, renforçait les postes à mesure et fermait les issues de la ville. J'étais donc de planton dans la chambre. J'y vis arriver successivement des officiers qui venaient très humblement se justifier auprès de la reine ; elle paraissait très irritée ; le roi restait sur son fauteuil, regardait ses trois gardes du corps couchés l'un sur l'autre et ronflant; ce qui excitait son sourire.

Messieurs de Goguelat, Charles de Damas et de Choiseul se trouvant réunis, le roi se leva, prit place près de la reine, et, pendant que ce conseil délibérait, madame Elisabeth vint à moi, me prit par les revers de mon uniforme, m'attira près du lit où les enfants dormaient, et me dit: "Ne serait-ce pas dommage qu'il arrivât malheur à ces innocentes créatures?—Il faut espérer, madame, qu'il n'en arrivera pas.—Vous le croyez?—J'en suis persuadé.—Vous pensez donc que nous pourrons continuer notre voyage?—Je le présume." Elle me retint assez longtemps en me faisant diverses autres questions. Mais je n'étais pas dupe du motif qui m'éloignait du conseil; elle voulait m'empêcher d'entendre ce que l'on y disait et je ne pus entendre que le nom de Bouillé souvent répété.

Après que les officiers furent sortis, vers cinq heures du matin, Mr de Romeuf et son compagnon, en assez mauvais équipage, arrivèrent en se disant envoyés par l'assemblée nationale et portant l'ordre d'arrêter le roi et sa famille et de les ramener à Paris. Cette déclaration fut comme un coup de foudre; la reine surtout en paraissait indignée; le roi dit alors: "Il n'y a plus de roi en France."

La chambre donnant sur la rue était pleine de monde; on la fit évacuer. On demandait à voir le roi, et le procureur de la commune vint prier le roi de vouloir bien se montrer à la croisée de cette chambre. Il y alla, non pour entendre l'acclamation qu'il attendait sans doute, mais le cri de vive la nation, que toute la garde nationale jeta à sa vue. Il prononça quelques paroles et retourna à la chambre de derrière, d'où bientôt après il descendit pour monter dans sa berline et partir pour son retour à Paris.

Lorsque l'heure du départ, vers 7 heures, fut arrivée, Messrs de Choiseul et de Damas rentrèrent et redescendirent avec la famille royale; les voitures étaient devant la porte; la rue était encombrée de gardes nationales, enfin le roi et sa famille y reprirent leur place et elles partirent fort lentement.

Peu de gardes nationales de Varennes suivirent les voitures, bien assez d'autres le firent. Mais le fils de Mr Georges, le commandant d'honneur, Poulot Leblanc et d'autres les accompagnèrent jusqu'à Paris. Lorsque ces deux jeunes gens furent présentés par la commune de Paris à l'assemblée Nat^{le} et accueillis par elle, on admira leur courage et on leur en fit compliment. Mais Mr Georges fils ne pouvait se parer des plumes qui ne lui appartenaient pas;

mon père homme prudent et expérimenté fut prié par le procureur de la commune, son ami, de ne pas abandonner Varennes, au moment où la vengeance de Mr de Bouillé pouvait leur faire payer cher l'audace d'avoir déjoué tous ses plans. En effet le fils cadet de Mr de Bouillé, qui était parti de Varennes pour Stenay à l'instant où le roi avait été arrêté, reparut sur les hauteurs de la ville du côté de Chipy avec des compagnies du Régt de Royal-Allemand. Ils purent voir le convoi de la place qu'ils occupaient, mais ils ne furent pas assez hardis pour entrer dans Varennes ni forcer les gardes nationales qui en défendaient l'entrée.

Ce fut un bonheur sans doute que 10 mille hommes au moins se trouvassent dans la ville; un plus grand nombre y arriva dans la journée de sorte que la municipalité et mon père n'eurent rien autre chose à faire qu'à loger les arrivants et à leur fournir des vivres. Si les principaux acteurs eurent une faible indemnité en assignats, la répartition n'en fut pas très équitable, car mon père n'eut que trois mille francs sur la somme décrétée le 11 juillet suivant.

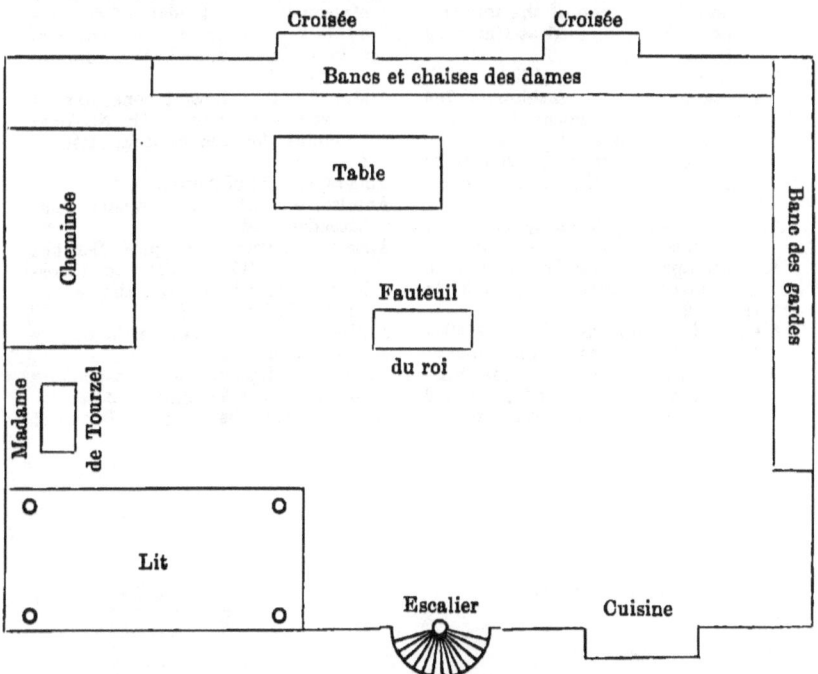

Mon oncle s'est borné à écrire ce qu'il a vu, et pour le détail du retour à Paris, il renvoie aux journaux du temps.

INDEX.

Abancourt, M. d' (Charles-Xavier-Joseph Franqueville d') (1758—1792), nephew of Calonne; minister of war after June 20, 1792; accused after August 10; imprisoned at Orleans and assassinated with other prisoners at Versailles. 202, 209

Abbadie, Mr d', an Englishman; settled at Rochefort as broker and interpreter. 172

Abbema, Balthazar, M., a Dutch patriot; took part in the insurrection against the Stadtholder in 1784; fled to France in 1787, and established a bank; returned to Holland and was minister at Hamburg. 190, 197

Aelders, Baronne d'; see Palm, Etta

Affry (Louis Augustin Philippe, Comte d'), 1743—1810. Lieutenant general in the French service; commander of the Swiss Guards; retired to Switzerland after August 10, 1792. 212, 228, 249

Aguylar, Marquis d', mayor of Perpignan, 1790. 8

Aiguillon, Duc d', son of the minister of Louis XV.; he died at Hamburg in 1800. 21, 240

Ainslie, Sir Robert, Bart. (1730—1812), ambassador at Constantinople 1776-1794; M.P. and numismatist. 42

Aire, at the junction of the Lys and the Laquette, a town in the county of Artois about 10 miles from St Omer. 284

Aix (Aquæ Sextiæ), formerly the capital of the county of Provence. 205

Aix-la-Chapelle, an old Imperial town, it belonged to France from 1794 to 1814. 262

Albert, M., Comte de Rioms (1740—1806), a distinguished sailor; fought under d'Estaing and de Grasse; commanded at Toulon in 1789; received the command of the fleet intended to support Spain against England in 1790; emigrated. 11, 34, 37

Algiers was from the beginning of the 16th century a nest of pirates. The Dey made himself independent of the Porte from the beginning of the 18th century. It was first conquered by the French in 1830. 11, 133, 139

Alkirch (Altkirch) in the Sundgau, the southern part of Alsace, a district which was long possessed by Austria. 66

Alsace formed at this time a military government with Strasburg as the capital. As a *pays d'étranger effectif* it had a line of customs on the side of France. The *three bishoprics* were Metz, Toul and Verdun in Lorraine, conquered by Henri II. in 1552, and definitely ceded to France in 1648. 19, 20, 41, 52, 59, 61, 65, 70

Alvarez, a Spanish general. 248

Amelot, M., son of a ministre de la Maison du roi; intendant of Burgundy 1786; commissaire au département de la caisse de l'extraordinaire in 1790. 243

André, M. d', ci-devant conseiller au parlement; member of the National Assembly for the Sénéchaussée of Aix. 78

Angers, capital of Anjou. 33

Anselm, servant to the Swedish ambassador. 147

Anselme, General (Jacques Bernard Modeste d') (1740—1812), conquered Nice 1792; retired from the service 1793. 258, 264, 275

Antibes, a fortified town in the county of Provence. 338

Ardèche, a department corresponding to the ancient Vivarais. 32 n.

Ardres, a town between Calais and St

378 INDEX.

Omer in the *pays reconquis*. Near Ardres the interview of the field of the Cloth of Gold took place in 1520. 284

Arnay-le-duc, in Burgundy near Beaune. 64, 68

Arras, the capital of Artois. 284

Artois, Comte d', born at Versailles October 9, 1757; died at Göritz Nov. 6, 1836; married Marie-Thérèse of Savoy 1773; emigrated 1789; lived in England after 1795; succeeded to the throne of France as Charles X. 1824; abdicated August 2, 1830. 5, 8, 48, 49, 59, 65, 87, 92, 94, 102, 115, 118

Artois, Comtesse d', Marie Thérèse, daughter of King Victor Amadeus III. of Sardinia; born Jan. 31, 1756; died June 2, 1805; married the Comte d'Artois Nov. 16, 1773. 8

Aubert du Bayet, M. (1759—1797), fought in America under La Fayette; député to the Legislative from the Isère and to the Convention; minister of war under the Directory. 169, 170, 171, 230

Aurillac, the chief town of Haute Auvergne. 18

Autun, Bishop of (Charles Maurice de Talleyrand-Périgord), Prince of Benevento (1754—1838), agent-general of the French clergy in 1780; bishop of Autun in 1788; member of the States General; celebrated mass at the Fête of the federation, July 14, 1790; asserted the civil constitution of the clergy; executor of Mirabeau; sent as envoy to London; minister of foreign affairs 1797, 1799, 1825; ambassador to London 1830. 47, 48, 51, 60, 73, 75, 82, 83, 95, 98, 140, 147, 148, 149, 158, 162, 167, 168, 176, 191

Auxerre in the N. W. corner of Burgundy, formerly capital of the county of Auxerre; bought by Charles V. in 1370; given by the Treaty of Arras 1435 to the Duke of Burgundy; and finally joined to France in 1477. 63

Avesnes, a frontier fortress in Hainault, taken by the Russians in 1814, and by the Prussians in 1815. 19

Avignon, Avenio, capital of the Cavari, on the Rhone. It was part of the kingdom of Arles, and afterwards became an imperial town governed by consuls but did homage to the Marquises of Provence, Counts of Toulouse. The Pope settled there in 1309 and Clement VI. bought it from Joanna of Naples in 1348; when the Pope returned to Rome in 1376 Avignon and the Venaissin were governed by papal legates down to 1791. 7, 50, 76, 83, 84, 89, 90, 123, 126, 183

Bailly, M. (Jean Sylvain), 1736—1793, a man of great literary and scientific distinction, member of the Académie des sciences 1763; of the French Academy 1784; member of the States General for Paris; President of the Constituent Assembly 1789; mayor of Paris July 16, 1789—Nov. 18, 1791. Guillotined Nov. 10, 1793. His chief work is the history of Astronomy. 7, 8, 9, 15, 17, 22, 37, 64, 80, 125, 173

Bâle, the ancient seat of a Prince Bishop; it became a free town in 1527; and was joined to France in May, 1793. 334, 335, 341, 358

Balfour, M. 93

Bannes, a castle in the Ardèche. 200

Bapaume, a town on the frontier of Artois, ceded to France by Spain at the Treaty of the Pyrenees. 284

Bar-le-duc, in Lorraine on the river Ornain. 24, 235, 247

Barmond, Abbé, deputy of the clergy to the States General; opposed the union of the Three Orders; emigrated; was taken with Bonne-Savardin at Châlons sur Marne; was tried at the Châtelet but acquitted. 21

Barnave, M. (Antoine Pierre Joseph-Marie), 1761—1793, deputy from Dauphiné to the States General. The best orator after Mirabeau; tried to reconcile the court with the constitutional party; guillotined Nov. 28, 1793. 25, 46, 55, 56, 68, 78, 79, 83, 87, 98, 101, 106, 114, 122

Barrère (Bertrand Barère de Vieuzac), 1755—1841, deputy to the States General; presided over the assembly Dec. 1, 1792 when the execution of the king was decreed; member of the comité de salut public; supported the Terror; was member of the conseil général des Hautes Pyrénées till 1840. 360, 367, 370

Barthélemy, François Marquis de, 1747—1830, a distinguished diplomatist; negotiated the peace of Bâle in 1795. 146, 158, 160, 177, 215, 236, 336

Bastia, on the east coast of Corsica, capital of Corsica under the Genoese. 100, 367, 370

Bastille, The; the fortress standing at the end of the Rue St Antoine in 1789. Begun 1369; finished 1382; captured July 14, 1789; and entirely destroyed. 6, 7

Bauchman, Major of the Swiss Guards. 228

Bavay in Hainault became French in 1678. 204, 206

Bayonne, a sea-port of Guienne on the Adour in the South of France. 256, 359

Beaulieu, General, John Peter Baron de, 1725—1819, born in Brabant; fought in the seven years war, in the revolutionary war, and against Napoleon who beat him at Mintenotte and Lodi. 180, 193

Béfort or Belfort, part of the Sundgau belonging to Austria, became French in 1636. 41, 186

Bellegarde, a fortress in the Pyrenees near the Col des Pertûs, between Perpignan and Figueras; taken by the Spaniards in 1793; retaken by Dugommier in 1794. 359

Bellevue, a village between Sèvres and Meudon, with a country house built by Madame de Pompadour in 1748, and destroyed in the Revolution. 63, 304

Belport, M., a spy. 156

Berenger, M., French minister at the diet of Ratisbon. 144

Bergen (Bergheim), a town on the road from Erkelens to Cologne. 262

Berkenrod, M. de, Dutch ambassador. 218

Bernard de Saintes (Adrien Antoine), so called because he was president of the tribunal of Saintes in 1791; member of the legislature, and the Convention; he was imprisoned in 1793 but was amnestied; he went to America in 1816, and died there. 370

Berne, capital of Switzerland. 357

Bernis, Cardinal de (François Joachim de Pierres de), 1715—1794; favoured by Madame de Pompadour; academician 1744; ambassador at Venice and Rome; lost everything by refusing to take the oath in 1791; lived upon a pension of the Spanish government. 56

Bertrand de Molleville (Antoine François Marquis de), 1744—1818;

intendant of Brittany; minister of Marine 1791; after August 10 took refuge in England; wrote a history of the Revolution and memoirs. 10, 127, 128, 161, 184, 186, 289

Besançon, a town on the Doubs, capital of Franche Comté; became French in 1679. 344

Béthune, a town of Artois ceded to France in 1659. 284

Béthune-Charost, M. de (Armand Joseph de Béthune, duc de Charost), 1738—1800; a distinguished soldier and philanthropist; imprisoned under the Terror, but escaped. 171, 175

Beureyer, M., is probably a mistake for Beauharnais (Alexandre Vicomte de), 1760—1794; born at Martinico; married Joséphine Tascher de la Pagerie who afterwards became Empress; deputy of the nobility to the States General; supported the Revolution; served under Custine; was guillotined. 234

Beurnonville (Pierre de Ruel Marquis de), 1752—1821; minister of war; sent to arrest Dumouriez; taken prisoner and remained so till 1795; joined the Bourbons; Marshal of France in 1816. 263

Bicêtre, a castle outside Paris built in the thirteenth century by John Bishop of Winchester; at first a hospital for invalid soldiers, then half a hospital and half a prison. Bicêtre is said to be a corruption of Winchester. 309

Bidermann, M., banker. 192

Bigot de Sainte-Croix, M. de, minister to the Elector of Trêves. 144, 206

Billaud-Varennes (Jacques Nicolas), 1756—1819; a member of the Jacobin Club, and of the Convention; one of the leaders of the Terror; exiled to Cayenne in 1795. 320

Biron (Armand Louis de Gontaut), (1747—1793), first Duc de Lauzun, then Duc de Gontaut-Biron; deputy of the nobility of Quercy to the States General; partisan of the Duke of Orleans; employed against Mons and in La Vendée; guillotined December 31, 1793. 44, 149, 150, 177, 178, 180, 194, 202, 221

Bitche, a small fortress in Lorraine attacked without success by the Prussians in 1793. 369

Blancheland, M. (Philibert François Rouxel de), 1735—1793; governor of San Domingo; brought to France and imprisoned after August 10. 90, 160

Blumendorf, chargé d'affaires of the Court of Vienna. 176, 179, 184

Bombelles (Marc Marie Marquis de), born 1744; ambassador at Lisbon and at Venice; emigrated; became a priest in 1792, and in 1819 bishop of Amiens. Before the Revolution he married two wives, one by the protestant, the other by the catholic ritual. 76

Bonchage, M. de, Le Vicomte Dubouchage, born 1750; minister of Marine and Foreign Affairs in 1792; emigrated; minister of Marine under Louis XVIII. 202

Bonne-Carrère (Guillaume), born 1754; president of the Société des Amis de la Constitution; expelled from the Jacobin Club in 1791; director general of foreign affairs in 1792. 75, 76, 147

Bonne-Savardin, Le Chevalier de, a Sardinian officer who opposed the Revolution. In 1790 he became intermediary of a correspondence between the Comte de Maillebois and the Count of Turin; he was imprisoned and escaped, but was taken at Châlons sur Marne, July 29, 1790; was tried at Orleans in 1791 and acquitted. 17, 21

Borde, M. la, F. L. J. de Laborde Méréville, son of the court banker; deputy of Étampes to the States General; retired to England and died in London 1801. 150

Bordeaux, capital of Guyenne; became French in 1453. 26, 198, 237, 318, 319, 324, 343

Bouchotte (Jean Baptiste Noel), 1754—1840; captain of cavalry in 1789; Minister of War after Beurnonville until April 1, 1794; a man of high character, lived in retirement at Metz. 320

Bougainville (Louis Antoine de), 1729—1814; the celebrated navigator, travelled in the South Seas 1766—1768; created Senator and Count by Napoleon. 40, 60, 125

Bouillé, M. de (François Claude Amour Marquis de), 1739—1800; fought in the seven years war, governor of Alsace, Lorraine and the three Bishoprics till 1791; after the failure of the flight to Varennes he retired to England and wrote memoirs. 19, 24, 29, 30, 31, 41, 97, 98, 100, 101, 110, 115, 376

Boulay, a town in Lorraine near Metz. 240, 245

Bourbon, Fort, the capital of Martinico, now called Fort de France, or Fort Royal. 86.

Bourdon de l'Oise (François Louis), a member of the Convention, attacked the Girondists; defended the Terror; aided in the fall of Robespierre; exiled after 18 Fructidor and died in 1797.

Bourget, Le, a port between Senlis and Paris. 285

Bourgoing, Jean François Baron de, 1748—1811; a distinguished diplomatist. 147, 154, 172

Bouvignes, a town close to Dinan on the left bank of the Meuse. 182

Brailow, a fortress in Roumania on the left bank of the Danube; also called Braila and Thaila; declared a free port in 1836. 86

Brasseur, M. le (J. A.), 1745—1794; intendant of San Domingo; chosen as minister of Marine in 1792, but La Coste was appointed instead; condemned to death June 15, 1794. 125

Brest, in Basse Bretagne, the chief war port of France; erected by Colbert. 12, 32, 33, 34, 35, 36, 37, 40, 42, 44, 53, 60, 72, 79, 198, 203, 262, 267, 364

Breteuil, Louis Auguste le Tonnelier Baron de, 1733—1807; ambassador at various courts; minister of state 1783; opposed the States General; succeeded Necker; emigrated; treated on behalf of the king with foreign powers; returned to France in 1802. 115

Briche, M., arrested with Prince Victor Broglie. 240

Brienne, Cardinal de (Étienne Charles de Loménie de Brienne) (1727—1794), archbishop of Toulouse 1763; academician 1770; friend of Turgot; succeeded Calonne as finance minister 1787; chief minister the same year; Bishop of Sens 1788—1794; summoned the States General 1789; resigned August 25; made cardinal December 15; took the civic oath; arrested at Sens November 9, 1793 and died soon afterwards. 56, 63, 70, 73, 75, 121, 125

Brissac, de (M. Louis Hercule Timoleon de Cossé, duc de Brissac), 1734—1792; captain-colonel of the Swiss Guard, and governor of Paris; refused to emigrate; imprisoned at Orléans

INDEX. 381

and massacred at Versailles. 130, 187, 239
Brissot (Jean Pierre), 1754—1793, born at Warville near Chartres; of humble origin; member of the legislature and of the Convention; was proscribed with the Girondists, and was guillotined with them October 31, 1793. 124, 141, 149, 203, 278, 287, 366, 369
Brittany became French in 1532. 57, 59, 61, 65
Broglie, Maréchal de (Victor Francis, duc de Broglie), 1718—1804; was made Marshal of France in the seven years war; minister of war in 1789 and commanded the émigrés in 1792. 73
Broglie, Prince de (Claude Victor), 1757—1794; fought in America; deputy to the States General and president of the Constituent Assembly; condemned to death by the revolutionary tribunal June 27, 1794. 73, 195, 240
Brune, General (Guillaume Marie Anne), 1763—1815; founder of the Cordeliers Club; entered the army 1792; served under Napoleon and became Marshal of France; murdered by the populace at Avignon. 275
Brunswick-Lüneburg (Charles William Ferdinand, Duke of) 1735—1806; generalissimo of the Austrian and Prussian troops invading France in 1792; resigned in 1794; mortally wounded in the campaign of Jena 1806. 206, 214, 217, 233, 235, 238, 243, 246, 254
Brunswick, the capital of the Duchy of the same name. 60, 265
Bruxelles, capital of the Duchy of Brabant on the Senne, taken by the French in 1746 and 1792. 265
Buzot, M. (François Nicolas Léonard), 1760—1793; member of the States General; one of the heads of the Girondist party; poisoned himself with Pétion; was found half eaten by wolves. 90, 108

Cahier de Gerville, a lawyer; sent to Nancy in 1790; minister of the interior from Nov. 27, 1791, to Feb. 18, 1792. 139, 155, 161
Cailhaisson, M., financier. 169
Calonne (Charles Alexander de), 1734—1802; controller general of finances 1783; convoked the Notables in 1787; exiled by the King to Lorraine; withdrew to England; assisted the émigrés at Coblentz; returned to France a month before his death. 43, 52, 62, 145
Cambon (Joseph), 1754—1820; member of the legislature, and of the Convention; erected the *grand livre* of the public debt. 169
Camus (Armand Gaston), 1740—1804, deputy from Paris to the States General; strict Jansenist; one of those sent to arrest Dumouriez and imprisoned by the Austrians. 6, 252
Capes, M., commissary of arms and ammunition. 234
Carnot (Lazare Nicolas Marguerite, comte), 1753—1823; a brilliant officer of engineers; deputy to the legislature, and the Convention; voted the death of Louis XVI.; member of the Comité de Salut Public; took no part in the Terror; was the chief author of the new military tactics and organization which caused the triumph of the revolutionary armies; died in exile. 369
Carpentras, capital of the Comtat Venaissin which belonged to the Popes from 1274 to 1791. Carpentras remained faithful to the Pope. 50, 53, 54, 85, 86, 89, 92
Carra (Jean Louis), 1743—1793; published with Mercier the Annales Patriotiques, and the Journal de l' Empire et de Citoyen; a leader of the Jacobins; member of the Convention; fell with the Girondins; executed Nov. 1, 1793. 184
Carthagena, a seaport town on the coast of Murcia in Spain. 41
Castelnaudary, Castellum Novum Arianorum, a town in Languedoc. 8
Castries (Armand Charles Augustin, duc de), 1756—1842; member of the States General; fought a duel with Charles de Lameth; son of the Marquis de Castries, maréchal de France. 43
Cavaillon, a town of the Venaissin, once a bishopric. 50
Cayenne, an island in French Guyana. 57, 247
Cazalès, M. (Jacques Antoine Marie de), 1758—1806; deputy of the nobility to the States General; opposed the union of the Three Orders; defended the royal authority in the Constituante; left Paris after August 10, and assisted the émigrés; refused to serve under Napoleon. 25, 79, 101

Cernon, M., Baron de Cernon-Pinteville; deputy of Châlons sur Marne to the Constituante; spoke against the division of France into departments. 74

Cette, a town in Languedoc founded by Louis XIV. 1666—1678. 21

Cevennes, a chain of mountains in the S.E. of France. 65

Chabot (François), 1759—1794, son of a cook; a Capuchin; member of the legislature and the Convention; belonged to the extreme left; guillotined April 5, 1794. 237, 243

Chaillot, a village on the right bank of the Seine, joined to Paris in 1659. 99

Châlons sur Marne, a town in Champagne. 21, 216, 233, 235, 236, 241, 242, 248, 250, 254

Chambéry, the capital of Savoy. 20, 262—273

Chambonas (Marquis de); minister of foreign affairs June, 1792; went to England after August 10, where he gained his living as jeweller and watchmaker. He died in London very poor 1807. 193

Champion, M. (de Villeneuve), son of a royal valet; minister of the Interior July, 1792. 202

Chandernagor, a town in Bengal not far from Calcutta; belonged to France from 1676—1688; taken by the English in 1757; restored in 1763; since that time alternately taken and restored. 52

Chantilly, a property belonging first to the Montmorency family, then 1632 to the house of Condé, since 1830 to the Duc d'Aumale. 59

Chapariellan, a place in Savoy or Piedmont not identified. 243

Chapelier (Jean René Gui le), 1754—1792; deputy of the Tiers État; a distinguished member of the Girondist party; guillotined. 102

Chapelle en Serval, a post between Senlis and Paris. 285

Charles II., King of England, 1660—1685. 2

Charleville, a town in Champagne; founded by Charles of Gonzaga duc de Nevers in 1606. 19, 236

Charton, M., French general; commanded at Aix; named maréchal du camp at Soissons; was killed in the battle of Castellaro Sept. 1796. 234

Châtelet, M. de, Colonel of the Régiment du Roy. 30

Châtelet, the Grand Châtelet, a fortress on the right bank of the Seine; was destroyed in 1802; it was the seat of the ordinary royal justice, and was also a prison. 24, 34, 45

Chaton, M., commanded the National Guard Oct. 1791. 129

Chauvelin (François Bernard, Marquis de), 1766—1832. When the Revolution broke out was master of the King's wardrobe; ambassador in London 1790—1793; on his return to France imprisoned for eleven months; held many public appointments. 167, 168, 176

Chazot, General, commanded a division under Dumouriez in 1792. 247, 249

Cherbourg, a town of the Côtentin in Basse Normandie. A great war port opposite Portsmouth; the sea wall, begun in 1783 under Louis XVI., was finished in 1853 under Napoleon III. 48, 205

Chipy (Cheppy), a village close to Varennes. 376

Choiseul (Claude Antoine Gabriel, duc de), 1760—1838, made duc et pair 1787; helped to prepare the flight of the Royal family to Varennes in 1791; was imprisoned at Verdun and at Orleans; emigrated after September 1792; was made peer of France at the restoration; was aide-de-camp to Louis Philippe. 100

Choiseul-Gouffier (Marie Gabriel Florent Auguste, comte de), 1752—1817; travelled in Greece; ambassador to Constantinople in 1784; refused the embassy to England 1791; retired to Russia in 1792; returned to France in 1802; left his antiquities to the Louvre. 86, 144

Clairfait, General (Francis Sebastian Charles Joseph de Croix, comte de Clerfayt), 1733—1798; a Belgian; general in the Austrian Service; fought in the seven years war, against the Turks, and in the invasion of France; was superseded by Archduke Charles in 1796. 245

Clavière (Etienne), 1735—1793; born at Geneva; made a fortune at Paris as a financier; a friend of Mirabeau; joined the Girondins; killed himself in prison December 8, 1793. 162, 163, 167, 190, 191, 208

Clermont en Argonne, capital of a country ceded to France at the Treaty of the Pyrenees 1609, and given at a later date to the House of Condé. 233

Clermont-Tonnerre (Stanislas, comte de), 1747—1792; grandson of the marshal; deputy of the nobility to the States General; president of the Constituante; founded the Société des Amis de la Monarchie; massacred by the mob after August 10. 53, 208

Clermontois, a county adjacent to the Bishopric of Beauvais N.E. of Paris; had counts since the tenth century; was given in 1250 by Louis IX. to his sixth son Robert. 71

Clichy la Garenne, a village on the right bank of the Seine close to St Denis. 234

Clootz (Jean Baptiste, Baron de), called Anacharsis; 1755—1794; very rich; posed as the apostle of universal philanthropy; proclaimed himself in 1790 the *orator of the human race*, and in 1792 the *personal enemy* of God; was made a French citizen; guillotined March 23, 1794. 142

Clostercamp, a town in Rhenish Prussia not far from Düsseldorf. 274

Coblence, a town formerly belonging to the elector of Trêves; at the junction of the Moselle and the Rhine; a favourite seat of the emigrés. 206

Coignie, Chevalier de (Duc de Coigny), died 1821; deputy of the nobility to the States General; emigrated in 1792; returned to France in 1814; made marshal of France. 111, 113, 115

Collioure, a fortified town in the Eastern Pyrenees; taken by the Spanish in 1793, and retaken by Dugommier in 1794. 359

Collot d'Herbois (Jean Marie), comedian, 1750—1796; member of the Convention; attacked the Girondists; member of the Committee of Public Safety; president of the Convention on Thermidor 9; transported to Guyana April 1795, where he died of yellow fever. 253, 360, 365, 369, 370

Colmar, a town in Haute Alsace; taken by Louis XIV. in 1673. 59, 65

Colmin, Captain, commanding the ship Emmanuel. 168, 189

Compiègne, a town in the Ile de France celebrated for its royal château. 96

Comtat, le, Comtat Venaissin, sometimes erroneously called the Comtat d'Avignon, called after Vénasque which was the capital before Carpentras. It belonged to the popes from 1274 to 1791. See Carpentras. 83, 84, 90, 93, 123, 126

Conchy (Chouchy les Pots), a post between Roye and Pont St Maxence. 285

Condé (Louis Joseph de Bourbon, Prince de), 1736—1818; was the first to emigrate after the capture of the Bastille; founded an army of emigrés; took refuge in England in 1801 and returned to France with Louis XVIII. 21, 24, 43, 48, 49, 51, 52, 59, 60, 62, 65, 70, 71, 79, 85, 92, 94, 95, 114, 145, 336

Consaarbruck, a village on the Sarre, a short distance from Trêves. 263, 264

Conway, Mr, returns from the Ile de France. 46

Cordeliers (Club des), a political club founded in 1790; its chiefs were Danton, Camille Desmoulins, Marat, Hébert and Chaumette. It was the first to demand the overthrow of the King, to establish the power of the commune, and to attack the Girondists. After the destruction of the Hébertists and the Dantonists it coalesced with the Jacobins. 360

Cordon, Abbé, Comte de, a relation of the Sardinian minister. 10

Corff, Baronne de, the Russian lady in whose name the passport was made out under which the Royal family escaped to Varennes. 100

Corsica, an island in the Mediterranean, finally joined to France 15 May—15 August, 1768; it tried to place itself under England, 1794—1796. 102

Court, M. de, a gentleman from the West Indies who dropped a dagger in the Queen's apartment on the Journée des Poignards, Feb. 28, 1791. In the Tableaux Historiques de la Révolution he is called apparently the Marquis de Curl. 66

Courtray, a town on the Lys taken by the French in 1643, 1646, 1679, 1683, 1744, 1792 and 1794. 194

Couthon (Georges), 1756—1794; member of the legislature and of the Convention; a close follower of Robespierre; guillotined with him 13 Thermidor, an II. (July 28, 1794). 320, 360, 365

Crevelt, a town near Düsseldorf; founded by the Protestant refugees in the 17th century. 274

Croix-aux-Bois, La, a defile of the Ardennes; a short distance from Vouziers. 247

Curt, M., deputy of Guadeloupe to the Constituent Assembly. 21

INDEX.

Custine (Adam Philippe, comte de), 1740—1793; served under Rochambeau in the American war; commanded the army of the Rhine after Luckner; took Mayence; guillotined. 181, 189, 194, 205, 258, 262, 264, 266, 274, 279

Cuvilly, a post between Roye and Pont St Maxence. 285

Damas, M. de, governor of Martinico. 42, 53

Damas (Joseph François Louis Charles, comte de), fought in the American war; was arrested at Varennes; emigrated; became duke in 1825, and died in 1829. 100

Dampier (Dampierre), a village near Ste Menehould. 254

Danton (Georges Jacques), 1759—1794; founded the Club of the Cordeliers; as minister of justice organized or permitted the massacres of Sept. 1793; lost his credit after the fall of the Girondists and was guillotined April 5, 1794. 109, 208, 216, 252, 320, 362, 366, 369

Darfort, M. de (Durfort), minister at Florence and Venice. 76

Dauphin, The (Louis Charles de France), born March 27, 1785, died June 8, 1795; became dauphin after the death of his brother Louis Joseph in 1789. 101, 102

Dawson, Mr, an English subject who complained to Lord Gower. 49

Defresney, M. (Dufresney), secretary of the Cardinal de Rohan. 68, 75

Delasny, General, a Spanish general. 248

Delessart, M. (Antoine de Valdec de Lessart), 1742—1792; a friend of Necker; controller general in 1790; minister of the interior and afterwards of foreign affairs; one of the Orleans prisoners murdered at Versailles Sept. 9, 1792. 45, 54, 66, 68, 239

Denoue, M., commander of the Regiment du Roy at Nancy. 30

Desilles, M., born 1767; on August 31, 1790, during the insurrection at Nancy, he threw himself in front of the cannon of the insurgents pointed against his fellow-citizens, but was killed in the attempt to prevent bloodshed. 57

D'Esterno, 1739—1790, minister of France at Madrid. 36

Deuxponts, Duke of (Karl August Christian), 1746—1795; his brother was Maximilian Joseph 1756—1825, succeeded on his death; he became elector of Bavaria Feb. 16, 1799, and King of Bavaria Dec. 26, 1805. 72

de Witt, M., a Dutch patriot. 190

Dietrich (Philippe Frédéric, Baron de) 1748—1793; first constitutional mayor of Strasbourg; a learned mineralogist; perished on the scaffold. 162

Dillon (Théobald, comte de), 1745—1792, born at Dublin; commander of Lille; murdered by his troops April 29, 1792. 180, 245

Dorset (John Frederick Sackville, Duke of), 1744—1799, succeeded 1769; ambassador in France 1784—1790. 5

Douai, a town of French Flanders, finally joined to France in 1668; before the Revolution the seat of a famous university. 74, 112

Drôme, la, a department in the S.E. of France formed partly from Dauphiné and partly from Provence. 54

Drouet (Jean Baptiste), 1763—1824; was post-master of Sainte Menehould in 1791; arrested the king at Varennes; deputy to the Convention; was favoured under the Empire, but proscribed after 1815; died at Macon under the name of Merger. 372, 373

Du Barry (Marie Jeanne Gomard de Vaubernier, comtesse de), 1746—1793; mistress of Louis XV.; of humble birth; presented at court April 22, 1769; went to England July 1792, but returned; guillotined Dec. 8, 1793. 62

Dubazet, M., see Aubert du Bayet

Dubois de Crancé (Edmond Louis Alexis), 1747—1814; lieutenant of the marshals in 1789; deputy to the States General; voted the death of Louis XVI., and the destruction of the Girondists; supported the Directory who made him minister of war in 1799; opposed the coup d'état of Brumaire 18. 168

Duchâtelet, Achille, one of the officers in command of the camp at Paris. 234

Dugommier (Jean François Coquille), 1736—1794; born at Guadeloupe; represented Martinico in the Convention; took Toulon Dec. 1793; died in the Catalonian war 1794. 328

Dumas (Mathieu Comte), 1755—1837; served under Rochambeau in America;

member of the legislature; exiled by the Convention; served under Napoleon I., Joseph King of Naples, the restoration, and the government of July. His memoirs are published. 125

Dumouriez (Charles Francis Dupérier), 1739—1823; fought in the seven years war; minister of foreign affairs March 15—June 1792; won the battle of Jemappes Nov. 6; beaten at Neeuwinden March 18, 1793; deserted to Austria; died in England. 162, 163, 164, 167, 171, 172, 178, 188, 189, 190, 191, 192, 195, 216, 224, 234, 236, 240, 244, 245, 247, 249, 254, 262, 264, 266, 275, 276, 366

Duport (Adrien), 1759—1798, deputy of the nobility to the States General; joined the Tiers État; formed a triumvirate with Barnave and Alexandre Lameth; paid special attention to judicial legislation; escaped after August 10, 1792; died at Appenzell in Switzerland. 101, 168

Duport-Dutertre (Marguerite Louis François), 1754—1793; minister of war 1790; guillotined with Barnave Nov. 28, 1793. 45, 49, 90, 91

Duportail, M. (N), an officer of engineers; fought in America; minister of war in 1790; concealed himself during the Terror, and escaped, but died on the passage from America 1802. 43, 50, 65, 73, 91, 105, 109, 118, 120, 125, 129, 133, 140

Duranteau (Duranton), 1736—1793; minister of justice in March 1792; guillotined Dec. 20, 1793. 166, 173, 193, 199

Duveyrier (Honoré Nicolas Marie), born 1753; a distinguished advocate; sent in 1796 to appease the troubles at Nancy; imprisoned in 1792, and just escaped being massacred; held various appointments under the consulate and the empire. 106, 110, 111

Écluse, L', a fortress on the Rhone not far from Bellegarde on the frontier of France and Switzerland. 185

Ecouen, the château was built by the constable Montmorency. 285

Elizabeth (Philippine Marie Helene de France, madame), 1764—1794; sister of Louis XVI.; a pure, brave and excellent character; guillotined May 9, 1794. 197

Elliot, Hugh, The Honble., brother of the first Lord Minto; 1752—1830; a distinguished diplomatist; sent by Pitt on a secret mission to Mirabeau. 38, 40

Emmery, M. (Jean Louis Claude, comte de Grozyeulx), born 1752; deputy from Metz to the States General; retired into private life after August 10, 1792, but was employed under the consulate. 109

Ephraim, a Jew employed by the King of Prussia; a Jew of that name was employed by Frederick the Great to coin false money in 1759. 107, 109, 110

Épinal, a town in Lorraine in the Vosges district. 372

Epresménil (Jean Jacques Duval d'), 1746—1794; opposed the king in parliament; as deputy of the noblesse to the States General defended the ancien régime; after August 10, returned to Havre; condemned to death April 21, 1794, and guillotined. 204

Estaing (Charles Henri, comte d'), 1729—1794; served in India and America; member of the assembly of notables in 1787; admiral 1792; guillotined 1794. 37

Estampes, a town in the Bearne; part of the domain of the House of Capet. 159

Exilles, a fortress in Piedmont, not far from Susa. 367

Expilly (Jean Joseph, abbé d'), 1719—1793; a great traveller and geographer. 48

Ezmar (Abbé d'Eymard), deputy from Alsace to the Constituante. 68

Fabre d'Eglantine (Philippe François Noyaire), 1755—1794; poet and writer of comedies; called after the flower with which he was crowned at the floral games; Danton's secretary; member for Paris to the Convention; proposed the maximum, and the republican calendar; guillotined April 5, 1794. 325

Fauchet (Claude), 1744—1793; priest, led the people to the attack of the Bastille; made constitutional bishop of Calvados in 1791; member of the legislative and the Convention; perished on the scaffold with the Girondists October 31, 1793. 124, 168, 255

Fénétrange, Fenestrange, or Finstringen, a town in Lorraine. 62

Fernan-Nunez, M. de, ambassador of Spain at Paris. 9, 16, 22

Ferrières, M., commanded some troops at Avignon at the time of the massacres. 131

Fersen (Axel, Count of), 1750—1810; colonel of the regiment *Royal Suédois* in France; prepared and assisted the flight of the king to Varennes in 1791; murdered by the populace at Stockholm in 1810. 100

Feuillans (Club des); when the Club Breton became the Club des Jacobins, the Club des Feuillans was established for those who wished to maintain the constitution. La Fayette and Bailly were at its head. It disappeared after August 10, 1792. It derived its name from the convent in which the sittings were held. 145

Fini, Claude, alias Chameron. 50, 60

Fitzherbert, Mr Alleyne, afterwards Lord St Helens; English ambassador to the Court of Spain. 9, 24

Fleurien (Charles Pierre Claret, comte de Fleurieu), 1738—1810; took part as sailor in the seven years war; director of ports and arsenals in 1776; directed the naval war in America 1778—1783; made minister of marine 1790; governor of the dauphin 1792; imprisoned after the king's death; senator under the Empire. 40, 77, 78, 85

Florian (Jean Pierre Claris de), 1755—1794; became academician in 1788; published *Fables* in 1792. 308

Florida Blanca (Don José Monina, Count of), 1728—1808; ambassador of Spain to Pope Clement XIV.; minister of foreign affairs; imprisoned and exiled by Godoy in 1792. 9, 24

Fonches, a post between Péronne and Roye. 285

Fontainebleau, a town in the pays de Gat; seat of a royal palace built by Francis I., Henri II. and Henri IV. 63, 65

Fontenay aux Roses, a village close to Sceaux and not far from Paris. 301

Fouché, Simon, born 1772; a resident at Varennes where he witnessed the arrest of the king. 372

Fouquier-Tinville (Antoine Quentin), 1747—1795; public prosecutor at the revolutionary tribunal of 1793; he was condemned to death and executed May 8, 1795. 362

Fraser, Mr, under secretary in the Foreign office. 46

Fredenburg (Freudenburg), a town near the Sarre between Saarburg and Mentzig. 261

Friteau, M. (Emmanuel Marie Freteau de St Just), 1745—1794; member of the parliament of Paris and afterwards of the Constituante; guillotined June 14, 1794. 22, 113, 114

Fulchiron, a banker at Genoa. 358

Garat l'aîné (Dominique), 1735—1799; deputy to the States General; of moderate opinions. The story of him in the text is told differently: "Un jour l'abbé Grégorie descendait de chez M. Talleyrand. Garat montait: Adieu aristocrate! dit l'évêque de Blois; Adieu, beau masque! repliqua l'avocat; et les rieurs furent de son côté." *Biographie Universelle*, 65, 103. 301

Garat le jeune (Dominique Joseph), 1749—1833; avocat to the parlement of Bordeaux; deputy to the States General; a strong liberal; succeeded Danton as minister of justice October 12, 1792; and Roland as minister of the Interior March 14, 1793; professor at the École Normale; served under Napoleon in 1814; voted the déchéance of Napoleon; disgraced after 1815. 301

Garnier (le comte Germain), 1754—1821; member of the States General; refused the ministry of justice in 1792; retired to Switzerland; afterwards joined the consular government; translated Adam Smith. 164

Garran de Coulon (Jean Philippe), 1748—1816; lawyer in 1789; member of the legislative in 1791; member of the Institute. 121

Gônes (Genoa), a republic and free port on the Mediterranean between Nice and Pisa. 188, 335, 341, 343, 358, 367

Geneva in Switzerland was a republic from 1535 to 1798. 57, 63, 65, 179, 188, 334, 335, 341, 358

Gex, Pays de, between the Jura and Geneva, was taken from the Duke of Savoy in 1601, and joined to France by Henry IV. 71

Ghent, capital of Flemish Flanders, at the junction of the Scheldt and the Lys; capital of the county of Flanders in 1180; revolted against Charles V. in 1538; taken by the French in 1678, 1708, 1745, 1792, 1794. 194

Gisors, capital of the Vexin Normand. 236

Givet, a frontier town of France on the Meuse; belonged originally to

Luxemburg; ceded to France in 1678. 182

Gobel (Jean Baptiste Joseph), 1727—1794; bishop of Lydda in partibus in 1772; bishop suffragan of Bâle in 1789; member of the States General; took the civil oath Jan. 3, 1791; guillotined with the Hébertistes 24 Germinal, an II. (April 13, 1794). 48, 71

Goltz (Bernhard von der), 1730—1795; ambassador of Prussia to Paris 1772; made count 1786; returned to Prussia in May 1792; went to Bâle to conduct the negociation of peace with Barthélémy but died there. 153, 184

Goguelat (Francis Baron Goguelas), aide de camp of Bouillé in 1791; sent by him with a detachment of hussars in 1791 to help the escape of Louis XVI.; was wounded in the shoulder; entered the service of Austria, but returned at the restoration. 375

Gonpillian (Jean François Goupilleau) of Fontenay; deputy to the legislative and the Convention. 253

Goupel (Goupil-Préfeln), deputy from Alençon to the Constituante; died Feb. 18, 1801. 287

Gournay (sur Aronde), a port between Roye and Pont S. Maxence. 285

Gouvernet, M. de, son of M. Tour du Pin; minister of France to the Hague. 75, 171

Gouvion, M. (Jean Baptiste), served under La Fayette in America, and in France; killed in action June 11, 1792. 29, 182, 189, 192

Gouy d'Arcy (Louis Henri, marquis de), 1753—1794; deputy of S. Domingo to the National Assembly; sent to Najac as Maréchal-de-camp; accused of cowardice and guillotined. 156

Gower (George Granville, Earl), 1758—1833; ambassador to France 1790—1792; became Marquis of Stafford and was created Duke of Sutherland, having married Elizabeth Countess of Sutherland in her own right. 1, 5

Grand Pré, a town in the Réthelois near a defile of the Argonne. 245

Grave, M. de (Le Chevalier de Grave); minister of war in 1792; fled from France to England; returned in 1800. 162, 181, 182

Grégoire (Henri), 1750—1831; sent to the States General by the clergy of Lorraine; took an active part; constitutional bishop of Blois; elected to the Convention 1792; wished to Christianize the Revolution; senator in 1801; count of the Empire; ended his life in study. 237

Grenoble, the capital of Dauphiné; became French in 1349. 13

Grevenmaker (Grevenmachem), a town near Luxemburg. 261

Grivel, a banker at Genoa. 358

Groschlag, Baron de; minister plenipotentiary from the King of France to the circle of the Upper Rhine. 52, 70

Groves, Mr, King's messenger. 50

Guadeloupe, a West Indian island; one of the Lesser Antilles; discovered by Columbus 1493; occupied by the French in 1635. 21, 95

Guibert, M., representative of the Island of Guadeloupe. 21

Guignard (François Emmanuel, comte de S. Priest), 1735—1831; a diplomatist; minister of the Interior in 1789; emigrated in December 1790, and returned in 1814. 17

Guillaume, M., a clerk at Ste Menehould, accompanied Drouet to Varennes. 372, 373

Guy, M. (Pierre Augustin Guys), 1724—1801; a distinguished and erudite navigator in the Mediterranean. 24

Guyanne (French Guyana) lies between Dutch Guyana and Brazil on the N. E. coast of S. America. 57

Hamburg, a free town of Germany at the mouth of the Elbe; a great seat of commerce. 335, 358

Havre, Le, a port on the Channel founded by Francis I. in 1557, and first called Ville Françoise, then Havre de Grâce. 338

Hébert (Jacques René), 1755—1794; published a disgraceful journal; called the *Père Duchêne;* organized the worship of the goddess Reason; executed with the leaders of his party March 24, 1794. 364, 366, 369

Hector (Le comte d'), intendant of marine in the port of Brest. 36

Helvoetsluis, the part of Rotterdam taken by the French in 1795. 336

Henilly (Louis Charles, comte d'), 1755—1795; fought in America; commanded the infantry (other accounts say the cavalry) in the constitutional guard 1791; emigrated to England and was mortally wounded in the expedition to Quiberon. 130

Hérault, L', the department of France of which Montpellier is the capital;

25—2

it was formerly part of Bas-Languedoc. 32 n.
Herkelens (Erkelens), a town in the province of Jülich. 262
Hervillers (Ervillers), a post between Arras and Bapaume. 284
Hesse, Prince Charles, Landgrave of Hesse Cassel, 1744—1831; stadtholder of the Schleswig and Holstein Duchies. 17, 79, 168
Hoc, M. le, talked of as minister of Marine after the resignation of Fleurieu May 1791; afterwards minister at Hamburg. 86, 171
Huber, M., a friend and correspondent of Lord Auckland; one of the Commissaires de la Trésorerie. 78, 86
Huningue, a town on the left bank of the Rhine in Haute Alsace. 66, 240, 368

Ile de France, an island in the Indian Ocean. It was discovered by the Portuguese in 1505, who called it Cerno; occupied by the Dutch from 1598 to 1712, who called it Mauritius; became French in 1721; it was taken by the English in 1810. 45, 46, 76, 133
Isnard (Maximin), 1751—1830; born at Grasse; member of the legislative and the Convention; joined the Jacobins; left public life on the advent of Napoleon to power, and died in his native town. 139, 146

Jacobins, Club des, founded a few days after the meeting of the States General under the name of Club Breton; after the removal of the king to Paris, the club established itself in the convent of the Jacobin or Dominican friars in the Rue St Honoré; became very important and corresponded with 1200 clubs; it became all powerful after August 10. The club was closed after the fall of Robespierre Nov. 11, 1794. 9, 38, 53, 55, 56, 66, 99, 106, 108, 145, 154, 287
Jalès, Château de, in the Ardèche. Some nobles met here under the name of the Camp of Jalès to correct a rising against the Constituante. The castle was burnt in 1792. 32, 65, 68, 70, 200
Jarjaye, M. de, Maréchal du Camp at Soissons. 234
Jarre, M. de la (Pierre Auguste de Lajard), 1757-1837; aide de camp to La Fayette; minister of war in 1792; fled to England and returned to France after Brumaire 18; was member of the Corps Législatif from 1808 to 1815. 193, 197
Jarry, M. de, sent on a mission to Berlin; perhaps Baron Etienne Anastase Gedean, born 1764. 147
Joly, M. de (Dejoly), minister of justice June 29, 1792, between Duranton and Danton; served under Napoleon till the Restoration. 199
Jones (John Paul), 1747—1792; born in Scotland; took service in America 1775; received at Versailles; served in Russia; died at Paris. 202
Jourdan (Mathieu Jouve-), called Coupe-Tête 1749—1794; organized the massacre of the *glacière* at Avignon in 1791; was guillotined May 27, 1793. 173

Kaunitz (Wenceslas Antony, count of Rietberg, prince of Kaunitz), 1711—1794; diplomat; signed the treaty of Aix-la-Chapelle in 1748 and the alliance between Austria and France in 1756. 165
Kavel cannot be identified; perhaps a mistake for Doeil = Dyle. 261
Kellermann (François Christophe, duc de Valmy), 1735—1820; won the battle of Valmy Sept. 20, 1792; made Duke by Napoleon I. 216, 235, 236, 240, 243, 245, 247, 254, 258, 262
Kerkalin, M. (Kerguelen), either the famous navigator Yves Joseph de Kerguelen-Tremarec (1745—1797) or one of his sons. 179
Koch, Christian Guillaume de, 1737—1813; professor of public law at Strasburg, 1780; elected to the legislative in 1791; imprisoned after August 10; member of the Tribunal 1802—1807; author of *Abrégé des Traités de Paix*. 199

La Bourdonnaie (Anne François Auguste, comte de), 1747—1793; served in the seven years war; general of division in 1792; died at Dax in Feb. 1793. 240, 245
La Corogne (La Coruña), a harbour of Galicia in Spain, called in old English books The Groyne. 338
La Coste (N), minister of marine from March to July 10, 1792; ambassador in Tuscany. 162, 170, 193
Lacroix (J. F. de), 1754—1794; member of the legislative and the Convention; friend of Danton; opposed the Girondists; perished in the ruin of Danton and the Mountain. 203

INDEX. 389

La Fayette (Marie Jean Paul Roch Yves Gilbert Mottier, marquis de), 1757—1834; married 1774; went to America 1777; deputy from the noblesse of Auvergne 1789; took an active part in the Revolution; emigrated after August 10, and was imprisoned by the Austrians; was set free by the Treaty of Campo Formio; took part in the Revolution of 1830. 7, 9, 17, 21, 22, 29, 31, 33, 37, 38, 42, 44, 45, 54, 63, 64, 67, 80, 81, 82, 98, 99, 102, 107, 121, 124, 129, 136, 138, 143, 158, 163, 172, 173, 178, 189, 195, 196, 198

La Harpe (Jean François de), 1739—1803; critic and man of letters; admitted to the Academy 1776; most successful as a lecturer on literature; his lectures began 1786, were interrupted during the Revolution and continued in 1794; he must not be confounded with the Swiss tutor of the Emperor Alexander. 208

Lajaille, M. de, commander of one of the vessels destined for Domingo. 139

La Lande, M. de (M. Delalande), chargé d'affaires in Savoy in 1792. 176

La Marck (Auguste Marie Raymond d'Aremberg), 1755—1833; grandson of Leopold Philip de Ligne prince of Aremberg; deputy to the States General; friend of Mirabeau who died in his arms; died in the Dutch service. 80, 83

Lamballe (Marie Thérèse Louise de Savoie-Carignan, princesse de), 1748—1792; daughter of Louis Victor de Savoie-Carignan; married in 1767 the duc de Lamballe son of the duc de Penthièvre; left a widow in 1768; a great friend of Marie Antoinette; accompanied her to the Temple; perished in the massacres of September 3, 1792. 187, 228, 232, 235

Lambert, M. (C. G.), 1726—1793; controller general for a short time; guillotined. 35, 45

Lamel, M. Du (M. Duhamel), a young broker; killed by the Fédérés of Marseilles in the Champs Elysées August 1792. 205

Lameth (Alexandre Victor Théodore, comte de), 1760—1829; deputy of the nobility to the States General; imprisoned with La Fayette in Austria; fled to London; employed by Louis XVIII.; wrote several books. 55, 68, 110

Lameth (Charles Malo François, comte de), 1757—1832; fought with his brothers Theodore and Alexandre in America; deputy of the nobility to the States General; fought a duel with the duc de Castries 1790. After August 10 fled to Hamburg; employed by Napoleon and Louis XVIII.; took part in the Revolution of 1830. He formed with his brother Alexandre (1760—1829) and Barnave a kind of triumvirate who put themselves into opposition against Mirabeau. 12, 18, 44, 68, 78, 87

Lamorlière, General (Alexandre), 1707—1793; commanded Alsace in 1792. 195, 274

Landau, a town in the Bavarian Palatinate; belonged to France from 1697 to 1815. 111, 239, 240

Landolphe (Antoine), a French officer; director of a philanthropic establishment on the coast of Africa; attacked treacherously in 1792 by two vessels belonging to Messrs Dobson and Co. of Liverpool. 49, 111, 112

Languedoc, a French province of which Toulouse was the capital. In old days the Loire divided the Langue d'oc from the Langue d'oil; it did not become entirely French till 1589. 21, 26, 36

Lanvres (Louvres), a post between Senlis and Paris. 285

La Porte (Arnauld de), 1724—1792; intendant of the Civil List; guillotined. 96

Laqueuille, marquis de; deputy of the nobility to the States General; one of the earliest emigrés; died abroad. 145

La Recourse, a post-station between Ardres and St Omer. 284

La Réole, a town on the Garonne; capital of the Gironde; it contains an old castle of the Visigoths. 318

La Rochefoucauld d'Enville (Louis Alexandre, duc de la Roche Guyon et de), 1743—1792; deputy of Paris to the States General; was one of the first to join the *Tiers état*; was president de l'administration du département de Paris; massacred at Gisors Sept. 14, 1792. 83, 101, 102, 236

Lasource (Marie David Albin), 1762—1793; born at Anglès near Montpellier; was a member of the legislative assembly and the Convention; joined the Girondins and perished with them. 252

Latouche-Levassor, chancellor of the

Duke of Orleans; deputy from Montargis to the Constituante. 13

La Tour-Maubourg (Marie de Victor de Fay, marquis de), 1766—1850; lieutenant of the gardes du corps who defended Marie Antoinette on Oct. 6; taken prisoner by the Austrians with La Fayette; fought under Napoleon; ambassador to London under Louis XVIII. 98

La Tour du Pin Gouvernet (Jean Frederic de), 1727—1794; fought in the war of the Austrian succession, and the seven years war; deputy to the States General; minister of war 1789; was imprisoned August 1792; guillotined. 24, 29, 30, 75

Laval, a town in Maine, formerly capital of the duchy of Laval; the Vendeans gained a victory here in 1793. 368

Lavivière (Pierre François Joachim Henri de Larivière), 1761—1838; deputy to the legislative; joined with the Girondists; member of the Convention; fled to London and returned at the Restoration. 230

Lavoisier, M. (Antoine Laurent), 1743—1794; became member of the Academy in 1768; deputy to the National Assembly; guillotined. He was a great chemist and the discoverer of oxygen. 78

Lebrun, Charles François, duc de Plaisance, 1739—1824; a friend of Maupeou; member of the Constituante; third consul with Napoleon, under whom he afterwards held important offices. 208, 211

Le Cointre (Laurent), 1750—1805; cloth-merchant when the Revolution broke out; member of the Legislative and the Convention; member of the Comité de Surveillance. 186

Leeward Islands, part of the Antilles, comprising Antigua, Montserrat, S. Kitts, Nevis, Dominica and the Virgin Islands. They possessed a common legislature as far back as William and Mary. 24

Lémontey (Pierre Edouard), 1762—1826; lawyer; deputy to the Legislative; fled to Switzerland after August 10; returned to Paris in 1797; academician in 1819. 142

Lescure (Louis Marie, marquis de), 1766—1793; a leader of the Vendean insurrection; was mortally wounded at La Tremblaye Oct. 15, 1793, and died Nov. 3. 368

L'Escuyer or Lescuyer, one of those who took part in the murders of the *glacière* at Avignon 1791. 130

Lessart (Antoine de Valdée de), 1742—1792; maître des requêtes in 1768; controller general in 1790; accused by Brisson in March 1792; sent as prisoner to Orleans and massacred at Versailles Sept. 9. 136, 137, 144, 145, 147, 150, 156, 161, 162, 168

Liège in Belgium, became a bishopric in 708; was conquered by the French in 1801; passed to Holland in 1814, and to Belgium in 1830. 76

Ligne (Charles, prince de), the eldest son of the famous Prince de Ligne (1735—1814); was killed in the campaign of 1792. 250

Ligny, on the Ornain; the chief town of a county which belonged successively to Bar, Luxemburg and Lorraine. 243, 245

Lille, the capital of French Flanders; conquered by Louis XIV. in 1667. 69, 182, 318

Lillers, in Artois, ten miles from Béthune. The first Artesian well was made here. 284

Linange, Prince of (Charles Frederick, prince of Leiningen), 1779—1807. 72

Lisle (Lille), a fortress on the north frontier of France. It was taken by France in 1667; the Duke of Saxe-Teschen bombarded it for eight days in 1792. 240

Longwy, a fortress near the Belgian frontier belonging to the Duchy of Bar. 215, 221, 241

L'Orient, in Brittany; one of the five great war ports of France; founded by the East India Company of Louis XIV.; it was bought for the government by Louis XV. 18, 51, 57, 65

Louis, abbé, ambassador of France to Denmark; took the civil oath. 115

Louis XVI. (Louis Auguste) (August 23, 1754—Jan. 21, 1793), King of France; son of the dauphin Louis and of Maria Josepha of Saxony; called first the Duc de Berry; lost his father in 1765; his mother in 1767; succeeded his grandfather Louis XV. 1774; married May 16, 1770, Marie-Antoinette daughter of Maria Theresa. 5, 6, 12, 14, 16, 22, 96

Lozère, a department of France, formerly part of Languedoc. 32 n.

Luckner (Nicolas, baron de), 1722—1794; a Bavarian by birth; served under Frederick the Great; joined the French service in 1763; commanded the army of the Rhine, and then that of the North; was repulsed by Kellermann after the battle of Longwy in 1792; was condemned to death as a conspirator at the end of 1793. 113, 158, 163, 171, 176, 177, 181, 182, 184, 185, 188, 189, 194, 197, 202, 216, 224, 233, 234, 240, 241, 243, 245, 254

Lunéville, a town in Lorraine. 30

Luxembourg, Palais de, on the left bank of the Seine at Paris; built by Marie de Medicis 1615—1620; bought by Louis XV. from the Orleans family and given by Louis XVI. to his brother the Comte de Provence. 63

Luzerne (Charles Henri, comte de la), 1737—1799; minister of Marine 1787; died in Austria 1799. 18, 21, 30, 31, 34, 41, 42, 44

Luzerne (M. Anne César, Chevalier de la), 1741—1791; ambassador in Bavaria 1776, America 1778, England 1788. 124

Lydda, Bishop of; see Gobel

Lyons (Lyon), once capital of the Kingdom of Provence; annexed to France by Philippe le Bel. 10, 19, 34, 49, 185, 241, 247, 255, 256, 319, 324, 343, 356, 359, 360

Macnamara, Mr, killed in the Mauritius. 76

Maillard (Stanislas), 1745—1805; arrested de Launay, governor of the Bastille; directed the march to Versailles Oct. 5, 1789; presided over the massacres of September; changed his name during the Empire, and died in misery. 328

Maillé, M. de, governor of S. Domingo. 160

Maillebois (Yves Marie Desmarets, comte de), 1715—1791; accused of a conspiracy in 1790; he took refuge in Liège where he died. 17

Mallet du Pan (Jacques), 1749—1800; a publicist; obtained reputation as a writer before the Revolution; wandered in Switzerland and Belgium from 1792 to 1798 when he went to England; died there in 1800. 358

Malouet (Pierre Victor, baron), 1740—1814; deputy of the commons to the States General; in favour of a constitutional monarchy; fled to London in September 1792; returned in 1801; died as minister of Marine. 56

Malseigne (Le Chevalier Guyot de); sent to Nancy 1790; emigrated and fought against France; died 1800 at Anspach. 25, 29, 30

Mandat (Jean Antoine Galyot de), 1731—1792; commanded the National Guard on August 10, and was shot at the Hotel de Ville. 208

Mangin, M., a surgeon at Varennes sent to announce the capture of the King to the Assembly. 97

Manuel, M. (Pierre Louis), 1751—1793; member of the Convention; guillotined November 14, 1793. (Misspelt Manuda in 200.) 208, 270, 281

Marat (Jean Paul), 1744—1793; a doctor; published the *Ami du Peuple* (1789—1793); implicated in the massacres of Sept. 1792; murdered by Charlotte Corday July 13, 1793. 244, 251, 256, 258, 271

Marboeuf (Yves-Alexandre, M.), 1734—1791; bishop of Autun; archbishop of Lyons; his younger brother, the Marquis de Marboeuf, was governor of Corsica and arrested the Napoleon family. 243

Marbois, M. de, ambassador of France at the diet of Ratisbon and at Vienna. 144, 152

Marche-le-Pot, a post between Péronne and Roye. 285

Marel, a place near La Croix aux Bois not mentioned in the despatch of the *Moniteur* and not to be identified. 247

Marmontel (Jean François), 1723—1799; a versatile man of letters; became permanent secretary of the French Academy in 1783. 307

Mars, Champ de, a large plain to the S.W. of Paris between the Seine and the École Militaire; made about 1770 as a field of exercise for the pupils. The name is obviously an imitation of Campus Martius. 6, 9, 11, 13, 51, 58, 68, 72, 75, 76, 78, 79, 80

Marseilles on the Mediterranean; the first harbour of France; it suffered deeply in the Revolution. 49, 198, 203, 205, 319, 324, 343

Martigues, Les, a decayed port in the South of France, W. of Marseilles. 11

Martineau, M. (N.) lawyer; deputy from Paris to the Constituante; escaped the Terror and died 1800. 19, 20

Martinique, an island in the Smaller Antilles; discovered by Columbus on Saint Martin's day 1493; colonized by the French in 1635; taken by the English in 1794 and 1802; restored to France in 1815. 10, 42, 45, 53, 57, 74, 80, 95, 112

Maubeuge, a town on the Sambre; acquired by France through the treaty of Nimeguen; besieged by the Austrians in 1793, and saved by the victory of Wattignies. 182, 204

Mauduit, M., colonel of a regiment at Port-au-Prince in the Island of Hayti; assassinated there in 1791. 83

Maulde, M. de (Étienne); ambassador of France at the Hague; arrested during the Terror but escaped. 171

Maulde, a village in Belgian Hainault near Tournay; a camp was formed here by the French which was abandoned at the approach of the Austrians Sept. 1792. 245

Maureau, M., judge of the Admiralty. 172

Maury (Jean Siffrein), 1746—1817; son of a shoemaker; deputy of the clergy to the States General; emigrated; made Cardinal in 1794; took office under Napoleon I.; was disgraced at his fall. 57, 75, 79

Mayence, Elector of, Friedrich Karl Joseph von Erthal, from 1774 to 1802. 65

Mayence, a fortified town on the Rhine; formerly the seat of a prime archbishop; it was taken by the French in 1644, 1688 and 1792, but recovered by the Germans in 1793; was ceded to France in 1797. 266, 274

Mazelière, agent of the Comité de Salut Public. 336

Meaux, capital of the Brie on the Marne. 216, 242, 275

Mercy-Argenteau (Florimand Claude, comte de), 1722—1794; Austrian ambassador to France from 1766 to 1790; afterwards governor of the Low Countries; died in England. 19, 116

Mertzieg, a town on the Sarre, between Sarre Louis and Saarburg. 261

Metz, a fortress of Lorraine; one of the three bishoprics acquired for France by Henri II. in 1553; ceded definitely in 1648; ceded to Germany in 1870. 18, 24, 31, 44, 105, 216, 235, 238, 372

Meurthe, department de la; forms part of Lorraine, and contains the towns of Nancy, Lunéville and Toul. 25

Meuse, a river flowing through France, Belgium where it is called Maes, and Holland where it is called Maas. 19, 20

Mézières, a town in the Ardennes, separated by the Meuse from Charleville. 18, 19

Mirabeau (André Boniface Louis Riquetti, vicomte de), 1754—1792; representative of the nobility in the States General; an aristocrat; emigrated; called Mirabeau-Tonneau from his fatness. 8, 145

Mirabeau (Honoré Gabriel Riquetti, comte de), 1749—1791. Treated harshly by his father during his youth, and often imprisoned; deputy of the *Tiers état* to the States General; tried to reconcile the Revolution and the monarchy. 21, 24, 26, 31, 34, 51, 55, 58, 68, 73, 74, 76, 77, 78, 80

Miranda, Francis, 1750—1816; a Spaniard by birth; served under Dumouriez; fled to England in 1793, to America in 1806. 259, 261

Mollegaert, Capt., complained of ill-treatment by the Captain of the Nemesis. 170

Monaco, Prince of (Honoré III. Camillus Leonor Grimaldi), 1720—1795; resigned Monaco to France Feb. 14, 1793. 15

Monge (Gaspard), 1746—1818; geometrician; minister of Marine August 1792—April 1793; went to Egypt with Napoleon; was greatly honoured by him; but was disgraced under the restoration. 208

Mons, the capital of Belgian Hainault called Bergen in Flemish. It was taken by the French in 1691 and 1746. It is the key of Belgium on the side of France. 180, 182, 184, 185

Montmédi, a fortress; formerly part of the Duchy of Luxemburg; joined to France in 1659. 105

Montmorin, M. de, a relation of the foreign minister who commanded at Fontainebleau in Feb. 1791. 65, 373

Montmorin - Saint - Hérem (Armand Marc, comte de), 1745—1792; succeeded Vergennes as minister of foreign affairs; perished in the September massacres. 7, 9, 15, 16, 19, 21, 22, 24, 28, 31, 32, 35, 36, 38, 40, 41, 44, 46, 47, 49, 50, 82, 83, 86, 87, 91, 93, 97, 100, 102, 105, 111, 115, 132, 172, 186, 187, 211, 221, 223

Moras, M., member of the Jacobin Club. 230

Moret, a small town a short distance S. E. of Fontainebleau. 65

Moreton-Chabillart, Gen., 1750—1793; served in the American war; ardent revolutionist; served under Dumouriez; died at Douai. 240

Morris (Gouverneur), 1752—1816; American member of the Convention 1787; ambassador in France 1792—1794; member of the American Senate 1799—1803. 192, 218

Mortand, a place near St Dizier; not mentioned in the despatch of the *Moniteur* and which cannot be identified. 247

Mossy, M., member of the Jacobin Club. 230

Mourgues (Jacques Augustin), born 1734; Minister of the Interior June 1792, between Roland and Terrier de Monciel; escaped the Terror; and lived in retirement. 190

Moustier (Eléonora François Elie, comte, and afterwards marquis de), 1752—1817; served as diplomate at Lisbon, Naples, Trèves, London, Washington, Berlin, Constantinople; helped the *émigrés*. 36, 86, 87, 127, 128, 129, 130, 144, 153

Moysset, M. de (Guillaume Monysset); judge; member of the legislative; served under the consulate and empire. 157

Mulot, abbé (François Valentin), 1749—1804; mixed up in the affair of the diamond necklace; member of the legislative; imprisoned during the Terror but escaped; wrote numerous works. 131

Muy (Jean Baptiste Louis Philippe de Felix, comte de), 1751—1820; served in America; at Avignon, in the army of the South; went to Egypt with Napoleon; served in the campaign of Jena; became Peer of France after the Restoration. 171

Naillac, M. de, minister of France to the Duke of Deux Ponts in 1792; minister of war the same year for a short time; minister at Genoa till 1794. 190

Namur, a town of Belgium at the confluence of the Meuse and the Sambre; taken by Louis XIV. in 1692; recovered in 1695, by William of Orange; retaken by the French in 1746, 1792 and 1794, after which it remained French till 1814. 181

Nancy, capital of Lorraine, taken by Louis XIII. in 1633, and by Louis XIV. in 1660. 25, 29, 31, 46, 258

Nantes, a town on the Lower Loire; it suffered greatly in the Revolution; repulsed the army of the Vendeans under Cathelineau in 1793. 363

Nantucket, an island belonging to the State of Massachusetts in America. 186

Naples, king and queen of, Ferdinand IV., Anton Pascal John Nepomuk; Seraphin Januarius Benedict de Bourbon (1751—1825); regent of Naples and Sicily, 1759; king, 1767; married Mary Caroline Louisa Johanna Josepha Antonia (1752—1814), daughter of the Emperor Francis I.; they had 16 children, 7 sons and 9 daughters. 62

Narbonne-Lara (Le Comte Louis de), 1755—1814; made minister of war Dec. 1791; disgraced March 10, 1792; emigrated after August 10; returned 1800. 133, 141, 142, 144, 149, 161, 163, 167, 171, 172, 176, 200

Necker, M. (Jacques), 1732—1804; a banker; born at Geneva; controller general in 1777; retired in 1781; recalled in 1788; dismissed July 1789; recalled immediately afterwards; retired definitely in Sept. 1790. 12, 28, 31, 33, 78, 125, 162

Neuchâtel, a town and canton in the west of Switzerland. The county of Neuchâtel belonged to Burgundy in the 12th century and then to the Empire; it came to Prussia in 1707 and remained under Prussian suzerainty till 1856; it became a canton in 1814. 334, 358

Neuilly, a village on the Seine below St Cloud; the bridge was built by Peronnet. 302

Nevers, capital of the Nivernais on the right bank of the Loire. 241

Nice, on the Mediterranean; capital of a county of that name; dependent upon Savoy after 1388; taken by the French in 1792 and remained French till 1814; ceded again to France in 1860. 20, 49, 348

Nîmes, a town in Languedoc; became French in 1259; a sect of Calvinistic Protestants. 5, 6

Noailles (Louis Marie, vicomte de), 1756—1804; second son of the Maréchal de Mouchy; fought in America under La Fayette; deputy to the States General; proposed the abolition of orders on August 4; emigrated to England and America but returned mortally wounded in a naval action 1804. 174, 188, 285, 288

Noel (François Joseph Michel), 1755—1841; at school with Robespierre; employed in many diplomatic missions under the Revolution; the author of a number of school-books, including a French grammar. 218

Nootka Sound, a bay on the W. coast of Vancouver's Island, the subject of a dispute between England and Spain in 1790. 9 n., 23 n., 39 n.

Noyon, a town in France, N.E. of Paris. 158, 159

Nyon, a town on the Lake of Geneva, not far from Lausanne. 48

O'Dunn, French ambassador at the court of Lisbon. 135

Oraczewski, court minister from Poland to the court of France in 1791. 76

Oran, a town in Algeria; founded by the Moors driven out of Spain; belonged to the Spanish from 1509 to 1708; taken by the French in 1831. 41

Orléans, a town of France, S. of Paris, on the Loire. 69, 70, 74, 78, 186, 187

Orléans, bishop of, Louis François Jarente Senac d'Orgeval; appointed 1788; took the civil oath in 1791; died 1810. 56, 73

Orléans, Duchess of (Maria Louisa Adelaide), 1755—1821; married 1769, divorced 1792; imprisoned and exiled to Spain; returned to France in 1814. 79

Orléans (Louis Philippe Joseph, duc d'), 1747—1793; surnamed Égalité, became very rich by marrying the daughter of the duc de Bourbon-Penthièvre; deputy of the nobility to the States General; belonged to the Jacobin Club; elected to the Convention under the name of Philippe-Égalité; joined the Mountain; guillotined November 6, 1793. 9, 13, 14, 24, 26, 31, 35, 37, 79, 103, 104, 118, 188, 192, 249, 259, 281, 290

Osmond (René Eustache, marquis d'), minister of France to the Hague in 1789 and to St Petersburg in 1791; remained abroad till the Restoration; minister in London 1815. 75

Ostend, a seaport town in West Flanders. 282

Oxon, an English malefactor whom they requested the French to deliver up. 146

Pache (Jean Nicolas), 1746—1825; minister of war October 1792—Feb. 1793; mayor of Paris; joined the Hébertists; died in obscurity. 320

Paine (Thomas), 1737—1809; born at Thetford in Norfolk; wrote the Rights of Man; chosen a member of the Convention; pleaded there the cause of Louis XVI., and was imprisoned; died in America. 237, 250, 253, 260, 268, 272

Palm, Etta, née Baronne d'Aelders, wrote Appel aux Françaises sur la régénération des mœurs et la nécessité de l'influence des femmes dans un gouvernement libre, 1791. 109, 110

Paoli (Pascal), 1726—1807; defended the independence of Corsica against the Genoese, and at a later period against the French; gave the island to the English; went to England in 1796 and died there in 1807. 100, 370

Paris, bishop of, Antoine Leonore Leo Leclerc de Juigne; bishop 1781—1801; died in Paris, March 19, 1811. 73

Péronne, a fortress in Picardie. 284

Perpignan, bishop of, Antoine Felix de Legris Desponchez 1788—1801; died at Maline. 239

Perpignan, the ancient capital of Rousillon in the Pyrenees; taken by the French from the Spanish in 1475 and 1642; left to the French by the treaty of the Pyrenees in 1659. 8, 256, 318, 359

Perrigaux, a banker at Neuchâtel. 358

Perry, Captain, an English supporter of the Revolution. 277

Pétion de Villeneuve (Jérôme), 1753—1794; deputy to the States General; sent to Varennes to bring back the royal family; mayor of Paris; first president of the Convention; joined the party of the Gironde; arrested June 1793 and fled; was found with Buzot June 1794, their bodies half eaten by wolves. 79, 98, 108, 136, 188, 194, 200, 203, 208, 220, 225, 229, 232, 237, 239, 252, 270

Peynier, M., governor of St Domingo, 45

Peyroux, M. la, misspelling for Jean François Galaup de La Pérouse; born 1741; a celebrated navigator; started in 1781 on a long voyage of discovery from which he never returned; the remains of his ships were found in 1826. 246

Pichegru (Charles), 1761—1804; general of the army of the Rhine 1793; commanded the army of the North 1794; arrested and transported after 18 Fructidor (Sept. 1797); went to London and Germany; joined the conspiracy of Georges Cadoudal and died in prison at Paris. 333, 367, 368

Pierre Encise, a prison near Lyons. 47

Pisani, Le Chevalier de; ambassador from Venice to Paris. 211

INDEX. 395

Polignac (Gabrielle de Polastron, comtesse and duchesse de), 1749—1793; married 1767; governor of the infants of France 1782; emigrated July 1789 and died at Vienna. 62

Polignac (Jules, comte and duc de), the husband of the favourite friend of Marie Antoinette; he emigrated and died in Russia 1817. 62

Poncharra, a place in Savoy or Piedmont not to be identified. 243

Pondèves, M. de, navigator. 24

Pondicherry, a French settlement in India, founded in 1675; taken by the English in 1761 and restored at the peace of 1763. 46, 51

Pons, marquis de, French ambassador, first to Sweden and then to Spain. 11

Pont à Mousson, a town on the Moselle in Lorraine, at the foot of the mountain of Mousson. 236

Pont de Beauvoisin, a village on the frontier between France and Savoy, between Lyons and Chambéry. 10

Ponthieu, duc de, a mistake for Louis Jean Marie de Bourbon, duc de Penthièvre (1725—1793), son of the Comte de Toulouse and father of the Duchess of Orleans, step-father of the Princesse de Lamballe. 79

Pont-l'abbé, M., commander of the cavalry October, 1791. 130

Pont St Maxence, a town of the duchy of Valois on the Oise; the bridge across the Oise was built by Peronnet. 285

Porentruy was, before the Revolution, the seat of the sovereign bishop of Bâle, and might in case of war be garrisoned by the French; joined to France in 1793. 76, 84

Port au Prince, formerly the capital of St Domingo; now of the republic of Hayti; founded in 1745. 10, 148

Port-Vendres (Portus Veneris), a fortress and harbour of France in the Eastern Pyrenees. 359

Priestley, Dr (Joseph), 1733—1804; dissenting minister; librarian to Lord Shelburne, 1773—1780; wrote on electricity; discovered oxygen, 1774; replied to Burke on the Revolution; went to America in 1794. 238, 250

Queille, de la, see Laqueuille, Marquis de.

Quercy, part of Aquitaine; divided into Haut-Quercy, capital Cahors; and Bas-Quercy, capital Montauban; it belonged for some time to the English and became definitely French in 1472. 59

Quievrain, a town of Belgian Hainault not far from Mons on the frontier of France; taken by the French, April 29, 1792. 180, 181, 182

Rabaut-Saint-Etienne (Jean Paul), 1743—1793; a protestant minister; deputy to the Constituante; member of the Convention; joined the Girondists; executed Dec. 5, 1793. 252, 317

Rabi, a general in the Spanish service. 248

Ratisbonne (Regensburg in German), a town on the Danube; the diet of the Empire was held here from 1663 to 1803. 20, 72

Raynal (Guillaume Thomas François, called l'abbé), 1713—1796; pupil of the Jesuits; exiled from France, 1781—1788; deputy from Marseilles to the States General; died at Chaillot. 91

Réthel, formerly capital of the Réthelois, on the Aisne. 245

Rheims, on the Vesle; capital of the Remois in Champagne; famous for the cathedral in which the French kings were crowned. 233, 250, 254

Ricardos (Antonio, comte de), 1727—1794; a Spanish general; governor of Catalonia in 1793; he was made Captain General in 1794, and died perhaps by poison in the same year. 359

Riccé, M. de, member of the Society of Friends of the Constitution; appointed ambassador of France to Berlin. 184

Richebourg, M. de, postmaster-general at Paris. 150

Rivière, M. de, captain of the ship La Forme. 36

Robespierre (François Joseph Maximilien Isidore de), 1759—1794; born at Arras; deputy to the States General; member of the Convention; attacked Louis XVI.; established the revolutionary tribunal; during the Terror was dictator of France; guillotined July 28, 1794. 11, 79, 108, 109, 149, 163, 237, 256, 258, 271, 273, 278, 281, 320, 353, 360, 361, 362, 364, 365, 366, 367, 369

Rochambeau (Donatien Marie Joseph de Vimeur, vicomte de), 1750—1813; son of the Marshal; served in America; reduced Saint Domingo to obedience; sent to Martinico in 1793; in Italy in 1802; for some time prisoner in England; killed at the battle of Leipsig. 135, 140, 143, 185

Rochambeau (Jean Baptiste Donatien de Vimeur, comte de), 1725—1807; marshal of France; served in the war of the Austrian succession; in America; commander of the army of the North, 1791; retired in 1792; nearly executed in the Terror. 112, 151, 158, 163, 178, 181, 182, 184, 185

Rochefort-sur-Mer, a port of war in Aunis; established by Colbert in 1666. 31, 234

Rocroy, a town in the Ardennes, on the Meuse. It was fortified by Francis I., Henry II., and Louis XIII. 19

Rohan (Louis René Edouard, cardinal de), 1734—1803; made coadjutor of the bishop of Strasburg in 1760; ambassador to Vienna 1772—1774; grand almoner of France 1777; cardinal 1778; bishop of Strasburg 1779; involved in the affair of the diamond necklace; was arrested and sent to the Bastille; deputy to the States General 1789; emigrated 1791. 20, 21, 68, 78, 92, 246

Roland de La Platière (Jean Marie), 1734—1793; deputy from Lyons to the Constituante; joined the Girondist party; minister of the interior for three months from March 1792; returned to the ministry after August 10, until Jan. 23, 1793; killed himself on hearing of his wife's execution. 164, 190, 208, 234, 244, 258

Romeuf, M. de, aide de camp of La Fayette; sent to arrest the Royal Family. 375

Ronsin (Charles-Philippe), 1752—1794; began life as a man of letters; then general in the army; joined the Hébertistes and was executed with them. 328, 364

Rosbach, a village in Saxony between Merseburg and Naumburg; the French were defeated here by Frederic the Great, Nov. 5, 1787. 333

Rouen, the capital of the province of Normandy. 234, 255

Rouen, bishop of, Cardinal Dominique de la Rochefoucauld de Saint Elpis; bishop 1759—1800; died at Münster. 135

Rouger, M. (Jean Pascal Rouger), deputy from the Hérault to the legislative. 204

Rouillé de l'Étang, M., Commissioner of the Treasury. 78

Roume-St Laurent, M., sent as Royal commissary to St Domingo; made a commercial treaty with the United States. 105, 115

Rousillon, a county in the South of France; joined to France by the Treaty of the Pyrenees 1659. 359

Roveray, M. du, a Genoese sent with Talleyrand and Chauvelin as an embassy to England. 66, 169

Roye, a town in Picardie on the Arre. 285

Ruamps (Pierre Charles), deputy to the legislative and the Convention; member of the Comité de sûreté générale; a member of the Mountain; remained neutral during the events of Thermidor; was condemned for complicity in the rising of 1 Germinal; but was amnestied and died in obscurity. 370

Ruremonde, a town at the junction of the Meuse and the Roer; from 1702 to 1793 capital of Austrian Guelders. 258, 274

Russia, Empress of, Catherine II.; born May 2, 1729—died Nov. 17, 1796; daughter of the Prince of Anhalt-Zerbst; married 1745, Charles Peter Ulric, duke of Holstein Gottorp, who succeeded his aunt Elizabeth, Empress of Russia. 105

Saarbruck, a town on the Sarre near the French frontier; formerly the residence of the Princes of Nassau-Saarbrück. 261

Saarlouis, a town on the Sarre; built by Louis XIV. in 1680; given to Prussia in 1815. 264

Saillant (comte Dusaillant), M. de, counter-revolutionist; accused of exciting conspiracy at Perpignan; procures the surrender of the castle of Bannes; killed July 1792. 200, 202

Sailly, a post between Bapaume and Péronne. 284

Saint Domingo, an island at the entrance of the Gulf of Mexico; discovered by Columbus in 1492 and called by him Hispaniola; the western portion was seized by France in 1664, and called Haiti; the other half remained Spanish till 1795, when it was surrendered to France by the peace of Bâle; an insurrection broke out in 1791. 21, 33, 34, 45, 83, 88, 90, 102, 106, 108, 131, 134, 139, 146, 148, 179

Sainte Ménéhould, a town of the Perthois; formerly capital of the Argonne. 97, 216, 245, 373

Saint Just (Louis Antoine de), 1767—1794; deputy to the Convention; closely allied with Robespierre; one of the principal authors of the Terror;

INDEX.   397

guillotined with Robespierre. 269, 353, 362
Salm-Kyrbourg (Frederick, Prince of), 1746—1794; he built a large hôtel at Paris; which afterwards became the palace of the legion of honour; he was guillotined during the Terror as an aristocrat. 305
Santerre (Antoine Joseph), 1752—1809; a brewer; commander of a section of the national guard; took part in the émeute of the Champ de Mars 1791; commander general of the national guard; died in retirement. 203, 208, 278
Sardinia, King of, Victor Amadeus III., born June 26, 1726; King of Sardinia March 20, 1773; died October 16, 1796. 17, 20, 48, 49
Sausse, M. (Sauce), procureur of the commune of Varennes in 1791. 373
Schérer (Barthélemi Louis Joseph), 1747—1804; made general in 1794; served in the army of Italy; minister of war in 1797; lost the battle of Magnano in 1799. 368
Ségneville, M. de, Sécrétaire à la Conduite des Ambassadeurs. 15
Ségur (Louis Philippe, comte de), 1753—1830; took part in the American war; ambassador to Russia in 1784; sent ambassador to Rome 1791, but was dismissed; failed in his embassy to Prussia 1792; held high office under Napoleon; supported the Revolution of July. 75, 76, 124, 130, 132, 133, 144, 147, 152, 153
Sémonville (Charles Louis Huguet, marquis de), 1759—1839; a diplomat; sent to Belgium 1790, Genoa 1791, Turin, where he was not received, 1792; imprisoned by the Austrians 1792—1795; senator 1805; took office under the Restoration. 176, 201
Senlis, a town in the Ile de France. 285
Servan de Gerbey (Joseph), 1741—1808; wrote in the Encyclopédie; joined the Girondins; minister of war under Roland; imprisoned in the Abbaye 1793. 182, 190, 193, 205, 208
Sèvres (Sève), a town on the left bank of the Seine; famous for the manufacture of porcelain, established there in 1750. 56, 187
Siéyès, abbé (Emmanuel Joseph, afterwards comte), 1748—1836; author of Qu'est-ce que le tiers état? 1789; a prominent member of the States General, and of the Convention; invented the consular constitution;

served under Napoleon. 71, 81, 82, 83, 361, 367
Simolin, M., Russian ambassador at Paris. 49, 100, 105, 147, 154
Soissons, capital of the Soissonnais, one of the ten *pays* of the Ile de France. 196, 233, 245
Soleure, on the Aar; capital of a canton of Switzerland. 334
Sombreuil (Charles François Vérot, marquis de), 1727—1794; governor of the Invalides; imprisoned at the Abbaye, and saved during the massacres of September by the devotion of his daughter (Marie-Mantille), 1774—1823. 228
Sospello, a town in the Maritime Alps on the Bevena; the French beat the Piedmontese here in 1793. 258
Spire, bishop of, Damianus Augustus Philip Charles of Limburg-Styrum; bishop 1770—1797. 52, 70
Spires, a town in Rhenish Bavaria; formerly an important imperial city. 369
Staël-Holstein (Anne Louise Germaine Necker, baronne de), 1766—1817; daughter of the banker Necker; married the Swedish ambassador; retired to Switzerland after the massacres of September; was exiled by Napoleon, and went to Germany; resided at Coppet on the lake of Geneva; returned to Paris at the Restoration. 255
Staël-Holstein (Gui Marquis, Baron of), 1749—1802; Swedish Ambassador in France 1783; married Mlle Necker 1786; welcomed the Revolution; was recalled 1792; returned in 1795 and was again recalled in 1799. 9 n., 15, 150
Stanhope, Lord, president of the Society of Friends of the Revolution; Charles Earl Stanhope 1753—1816; educated at Geneva; married Pitt's sister; a man of deep and various attainments; a strong Liberal. 18
St Arold (St Avold), a town in Lorraine. 240, 245
St Cloud, a village on the Seine; about five miles N. E. of Versailles. The domain was given by Louis XIV. to his brother the Duke of Orleans who built the palace about 1658; it was bought by Marie Antoinette in 1789, and was restored by Napoleon; it was burnt by the Germans in 1871. 26, 80, 81
Ste Brice, Madame de, saved by Tallien in the massacres of September. 228, 232

Ste Croix, M. de, a French diplomat. 69, 149, 160

St Denys, the Abbey church was built between 1130 and 1285. 285

St Dizier, a town in Champagne on the Marne. 245, 248

Ste Foy, M. de, destined to accompany the embassy to England, Jan. 1792. 150

St Elme, a frontier fortress of France in the Eastern Pyrenees. 359

Stenay, a town belonging to the house of Condé near Montmédy on the Meuse. 236, 376

St Germain-en-Laye, a town not far from Versailles on a height above the Seine; the palace was built by Charles V. in 1370. 302

Stockholm, capital of Sweden. 22, 206

St Omer, on the Aa; a town in Artois, famous for its Jesuit College. 284

St Pol, Bishop of, Jean François de la Marche; bishop 1772—1802; died in London Nov. 25, 1806. 61

Strasburg, on the Rhine; during the middle ages a free town of the Empire governed by its bishop; it embraced Protestantism at the Reformation; Louis XIV. annexed it in 1681; it was the capital of Alsace till 1790. 21, 44, 59, 68, 76, 78, 221, 264, 324, 326, 330, 344

Sturt, Miss, married M. Huber. 78

Stuttgard, the capital of Würtemberg. 51, 60, 62

Sundgau, the southern part of Alsace containing Béfort and Huningue. It belonged for some time to Austria, after the rest of Alsace was French. 334

Talleyrand, M. de; see Autun, Bishop of.

Tallien (Jean Lambert), 1769—1820; member of the Jacobin Club; took part in the massacres of September, and directed those of Bordeaux; attacked Robespierre; member of the Comité du Salut Public; afterwards became more moderate; followed Bonaparte to Egypt; after 1802 lived in obscurity. 319, 370

Talmont, Prince de (Antoine Philippe de la Trémouille), aide de camp of the comte d'Artois in 1792; joined the Vendean insurrection in 1793; he fled after the defeat of Mans, but was arrested and executed at Laval in 1794. 368

Tangiers, a port on the Atlantic belonging to the Empire of Morocco; belonged to the Portuguese from 1472 to 1662; it came into English hands as part of the dowry of Catherine of Braganza 1662, and remained till 1684. 34

Tarascon, a town on the Rhone; not far from Arles. 85

Tarbé, M. (Louis Hardouin), ministre des contributions publics 1791; afterwards minister of finance; escaped with difficulty after August 10, 1792; died 1806. 92

Tarente, Madame de, dame d'honneur to Marie Antoinette; massacred in September 1792. 221, 224

Ternant, chevalier de, ambassador from France to the United States. 69, 93

Terrier de Monciel (Antoine Marie René), 1757—1831; minister of the interior June 18, 1792; emigrated; returned to France in 1806. 192, 201

Thévenard (Antoine Jean Marie, comte), 1733—1815; naval officer; minister of the marine, May 16—September 17, 1791; took office under the Empire. 87, 102, 111

Thionville (Diedenhoven), a fortress on the Moselle; belonged successively to Luxemburg, Burgundy, Austria and Spain; taken by Condé in 1643; and remained French; besieged by the Prussians in 1792. 216, 235, 238, 247

Thuin, a town of Hainault on the Sambre not far from Charleroi. 365

Thuriot-Larosière (Jacques Alexis), deputy to the legislative and the Convention; member of the Comité du Salut Public; presided at the famous sitting of 9 Thermidor; served under Napoleon; after the Revolution settled down as a lawyer at Liège. 164

Tippoo Saib, 1749—1799; Rajah of Mysore; fought against the Mahrattas 1775—1779, and against the English 1780—1782; succeeded 1783; fell at the siege of Seringapatam 1799. 51, 52

Tobago, discovered by Columbus in 1498; claimed by the English in 1580, and 1608; given by Charles I. in 1645 to James Duke of Courland; Dutch settled in the island also; in 1662 the island was claimed by the French; in 1748 the island was declared neutral, but in 1763 was ceded to the English; in 1781 it was captured by the French and secured to them in 1783; in 1793 it

INDEX. 399

was taken by the English and secured to them in 1814. 9, 10, 31, 60, 77, 78, 145, 154, 188, 199
Touchet (Souchez), a post between Béthune and Arras. 284
Toul, an imperial town governed by sovereign bishops; one of the *three bishoprics* seized by Henri II. in 1552; secured to France by the Treaty of Westphalia 1648. 30
Toulon, the principal arsenal of France in the Mediterranean; it owes its magnificence to Louis XIV.; it was delivered up to the English for a short time in 1793. 18, 32, 34, 36, 37, 262, 319, 328, 332, 345, 352, 359
Toulouse has been the capital of the kingdom of the Visigoths; of the duchy of Aquitaine, and of the county of Toulouse. 37, 65, 76
Tournay, a town of Belgian Hainault on the Scheldt; it was lost by France in 1709; retaken in 1745; given up in 1748; taken again in 1792; restored to the Low Countries in 1814. 182, 185
Tour-Taxis, Prince de; the family is of Italian origin; united the titles of Torre, and Tasso near Bergamo. They were post-masters of the empire from an early period. 72
Tourzelle (Louise Elisabeth Félicité Françoise de Croy d'Havré, marquise and afterwards duchesse de), 1748—1832; in 1789 succeeded Madame de Polignac as gouvernante des enfants de France; accompanied the Queen in the flight to Varennes and to the Temple; arrested in 1793, 1794, 1795; exiled during the Empire; made duchess by Louis XVI. 224, 228, 232
Treguier, Bishop of, Augustin Louis René le Mointier, 1780—1801; died at London. 61
Treilhard (Jean Baptiste, comte), 1742—1810; deputy to the States General 1789; presided over the trial of Louis XVI.; refused the ministry of justice 1796; member of the Directory May 15, 1798; minister of State and comte in 1808; took a large share in preparing the Code Civil. 270
Tremblay, M., commissioner of the treasury. 78
Trèves, a town on the Moselle; capital of a spiritual electorate from 1356 to 1794. 73, 264
Trist, Mr, an Englishman. 161
Trompette, Château; a castle at Bordeaux built by Charles VII. and destroyed in 1817. 319
Tronchin, M., minister from Geneva to the court of Versailles. 179
Troyes, formerly capital of the county of Champagne. 255
Truguet (Laurent Jean François, comte), 1752—1839; a distinguished sailor; fought in America under D'Estaing and de Grasse; commanded a squadron in 1792; minister of marine under the Directory in 1795. 179
Turin, the capital of Piedmont; a favourite residence of the emigrés. 10, 48, 65, 367

Ukraine, an expression meaning frontier in Polish; the Russian Ukraine was conquered from Poland in 1667 and 1686; the Polish Ukraine in 1793. 68
Ulm, formerly a fortress of the German confederation, now belonging to Würtemberg. 94
Uzès, a town in Bas-Languedoc, not far from Nîmes. 65

Val-de-Grace, a Benedictine convent founded by Anne of Austria as a thanksgiving for the birth of Louis XIV. under the name of Val-de-Grace de Notre-Dâme de la Crêche; built between 1645 and 1665; it became a military hospital under the Empire. 99
Valence (Cyrus Marie Alexandre de Timbrune, comte de), 1757—1822; married daughter of Madame de Genlis; deputy to the States General; served under Luckner and Dumouriez; commanded the reserve at Valmy; deserted with Dumouriez; returned to France in 1799; served under Napoleon and Louis XVIII. 197
Valenciennes, capital of French Hainault; became French in 1677. 68, 181, 182, 184, 188, 204
Valmy, a village of the Perthois near Ste Ménéhould where the duke of Brunswick was defeated by Kellermann Sept. 20, 1792. 254
Vandémont, Princesse de. 187
Van-der-Noot (Henry Charles Nicolas), 1735—1827; raised the insurrection of the Belgian patriots against the Austrian government in 1789; he was defeated; returned to Belgium in 1797 and died in obscurity. 29
Vannes, a small sea-port town in Brittany. 61
Var, a river in the south of France which formerly divided Provence from Nice. 185, 266

Varennes en Argonne, the town where Louis XVI. was arrested June 22, 1791. 373, 374, 376
Vaucluse, the French department which contains Avignon. 84
Vayne, M. de, commissioner of the public treasury. 78
Venaissin, le Comtat. See Comtat.
Venice, an Italian republic on the Adriatic. 49, 62
Verdun, formerly capital of the bishopric and county of Verdun; one of the *three bishoprics* conquered by Henry II. in 1552. 30, 216, 221, 225, 232, 235, 241, 242
Vergniaud, M. (Pierre Victurnien), 1753—1793; administrator of the department of the Gironde 1790; elected to the legislative 1791; became a distinguished member of the Girondist party; executed October 31, 1793. 149
Versailles, the favourite seat of the French court; Louis XIV. dwelt in the Château from 1672, and the court was established there in 1682. 41, 56, 69, 84
Vibraye, M. de, diplomat; minister of France to Sweden and Denmark; remained faithful to the king. 75, 135, 172
Vienna (Wien), capital of Austria. 24, 62
Villages, M. de, *commandant de la station* at St Domingo. 87
Villars, M., diplomatist; minister at Mayence and Genoa. 172
Villette (Charles, marquis de), 1756—1793; served in the seven years war; a friend of Voltaire, who died in his house; was deputy to the Convention. 280
Villette, La, a suburb of Paris to the North. 54
Vincennes, a short distance from Paris; the Château was built by Philip Augustus, and was a royal residence till Louis XIII. 67, 68, 70
Vincent (François Nicolas), 1767—1794; revolutionary agent; member of the club of Cordeliers; took part in August 10; perished with the Hébertists. 328
Vitry le François, a town of the Perthois in Champagne; founded by Francis I. in 1545 to receive the inhabitants of Vitry le Brûlé, burnt by Louis VII. and Charles V. 240, 245

Vivarois, a district of France with capital Viviers; became part of the royal domain in 1229. 32
Voltaire (François Marie Arouet de), born 1694; died May 30, 1778. 105

Waldeck, Prince of, a general in the Austrian service; killed September 1792. 247
Walkiers, Edouard de; Belgian officer who took part in the Belgian revolution. 177, 182
Weissemburg; the lines of Weissemburg extended in front of the river Lauter from Weissemburg to Lauterburg. They were erected by the Austrians and occupied by the French, who were driven from them by Würmser in 1793; they soon recovered them under Hoche and Pichegru. 330
Wilseek, Cte de, minister of the Emperor in Lombardy. 343
Wimpfen (Félix de), 1745—1814; served in America; deputy of the nobility to the States General; defended Thionville against the Prussians; commanded the coast of Cherbourg; general of the army of Calvados in favour of the Girondins, but had little success; served under the Empire. 318
Wittenkopf, General, commanding the troops of Nagor. 158
Wittgenstein, M. de, lieutenant general commanding the second military division in April 1792; superseded by General Montesquiou. 171
Worms, an imperial town from the 11th century; now belonging to Hesse Darmstadt; it became part of the French Empire in 1802. 94
Würmser (Dagobert Sigismund, comte de), 1724—1797; an Austrian general of Alsacian origin; he fought in the seven years war, and died soon after his ineffectual defence of Mantua against Napoleon in 1797. 330, 333
Würtemberg, Duke of (Charles Eugene), from 1737 to 1793. 70, 72

Yriarté, M., Spanish Minister in Paris, 190

Zurich, a town in Switzerland, capital of a Canton; situated on the lake of Zurich, and on the Limmat; it joined the Swiss confederation in 1351. 335

CAMBRIDGE: PRINTED BY C. J. CLAY, M.A. AND SON, AT THE UNIVERSITY PRESS

UNIVERSITY PRESS, CAMBRIDGE
January, 1890

CATALOGUE OF

WORKS

PUBLISHED FOR THE SYNDICS

OF THE

Cambridge University Press.

London: C. J. CLAY AND SONS,
CAMBRIDGE UNIVERSITY PRESS WAREHOUSE,
AVE MARIA LANE.

GLASGOW: 263, ARGYLE STREET.

Cambridge: DEIGHTON, BELL AND CO.
Leipzig: F. A. BROCKHAUS.

500
8/1/90

PUBLICATIONS OF

The Cambridge University Press.

THE REVISED VERSION

OF THE

OLD AND NEW TESTAMENTS.

The Revised Version is the Joint Property of the Universities of Oxford and Cambridge.

(The Cambridge & Oxford Editions are uniform in Type, Size, & Price.)

The following Editions of the Revised Version of the Holy Bible and New Testament have been already published and may be had in a great variety of cloth and leather bindings of all booksellers.

THE HOLY BIBLE.

N.B. *The Pearl* 16mo., *the Ruby* 16mo., *and the Minion* 8vo., *are* **facsimile** *editions and correspond page for page with each other.*

Cheap edition for use in Schools.

1. Pearl type, 16mo.   prices from   1/6
2. Ruby type, 16mo.   do.   4/6
3. Minion type, 8vo.   do.   7/6

A large type edition in one volume.

4. Small Pica type, Imperial 8vo. prices from   18/-

LIBRARY EDITIONS.

In five vols., or the Old Testament only, in four volumes.

5. Pica type, Demy 8vo.   5 vols., prices from £2
6. Pica type, Demy 8vo. Old Testament only, 4 vols.,   do.   £1. 12s.
7. Pica type, Royal 8vo.   5 vols., do. £3. 2s. 6d.
8. Pica type, Royal 8vo. Old Testament only, 4 vols.,   do.   £2. 10s.

THE PARALLEL BIBLE.

Being the AUTHORISED VERSION arranged in Parallel columns with the REVISED VERSION.

9. Minion type, Crown 4to. prices from   £1. 6s.

London: C. J. CLAY & SONS, Cambridge University Press Warehouse, Ave Maria Lane.

THE REVISED VERSION OF
THE NEW TESTAMENT.

Cheap editions for use in Schools.

1. Nonpareil type, 32mo.   prices from   -/6
2. Brevier type, 16mo.   do.   1/-
3. Long Primer type, 8vo.   do.   1/6

LIBRARY EDITIONS.

4. Pica type, Demy 8vo. prices from   8/-
5. Pica type, Royal 8vo.   do.   12/6

THE PARALLEL NEW TESTAMENT.

Giving the Authorised and Revised Versions side by side.

6. Pearl type, 16mo. (Pocket Edition) prices from   1/6
7. Minion type, 8vo.   do.   4/6
8. Long Primer type, 4to.   do.   7/6

STUDENT'S LARGE PAPER EDITION.

9. Minion type, Crown 4to. prices from   10/6

All Editions of the Parallel New Testament correspond page for page with each other.

THE PARALLEL NEW TESTAMENT, Greek and English. The Greek Text edited by the Rev. F. H. A. SCRIVENER, M.A., LL.D., and printed on alternate pages with the English Parallel Minion Edition of the Revised Version.

Minion type, Crown 8vo. prices from   12/6

THE NEW TESTAMENT IN GREEK, according to the Text followed in the Authorised Version with the variations adopted in the Revised Version. Edited by the Rev. F. H. A. SCRIVENER, M.A., LL.D.

Crown 8vo. prices from   6/-

Specimens of type and size of pages with prices sent on application.

London: C. J. CLAY & SONS, Cambridge University Press Warehouse,
Ave Maria Lane.

THE HOLY SCRIPTURES, &c.

THE CAMBRIDGE PARAGRAPH BIBLE of the Authorized English Version, with the Text Revised by a Collation of its Early and other Principal Editions, the Use of the Italic Type made uniform, the Marginal References remodelled, and a Critical Introduction prefixed, by F. H. A. SCRIVENER, M.A., LL.D., Editor of the Greek Testament, Codex Augiensis, &c., and one of the Revisers of the Authorized Version. Crown 4to. gilt. 21s.

From the *Times*.
"Students of the Bible should be particularly grateful (to the Cambridge University Press) for having produced, with the able assistance of Dr Scrivener, a complete critical edition of the Authorized Version of the English Bible, an edition such as, to use the words of the Editor, 'would have been executed long ago had this version been nothing more than the greatest and best known of English classics.' Falling at a time when the formal revision of this version has been undertaken by a distinguished company of scholars and divines, the publication of this edition must be considered most opportune."

From the *Athenæum*.
"Apart from its religious importance, the English Bible has the glory, which but few sister versions indeed can claim, of being the chief classic of the language, of having, in conjunction with Shakspeare, and in an immeasurable degree more than he, fixed the language beyond any possibility of important change. Thus the recent contributions to the literature of the subject, by such workers as Mr Francis Fry and Canon Westcott, appeal to a wide range of sympathies; and to these may now be added Dr Scrivener, well known for his labours in the cause of the Greek Testament criticism, who has brought out, for the Syndics of the Cambridge University Press, an edition of the English Bible, according to the text of 1611, revised by a comparison with later issues on principles stated by him in his Introduction. Here he enters at length into the history of the chief editions of the version, and of such features as the marginal notes, the use of italic type, and the changes of orthography, as well as into the most interesting question as to the original texts from which our translation is produced."

From the *London Quarterly Review*.
"The work is worthy in every respect of the editor's fame, and of the Cambridge University Press. The noble English Version, to which our country and religion owe so much, was probably never presented before in so perfect a form."

THE CAMBRIDGE PARAGRAPH BIBLE. STUDENT'S EDITION, on *good writing paper*, with one column of print and wide margin to each page for MS. notes. This edition will be found of great use to those who are engaged in the task of Biblical criticism. Two Vols. Crown 4to. gilt. 31s. 6d.

THE AUTHORIZED EDITION OF THE ENGLISH BIBLE (1611), ITS SUBSEQUENT REPRINTS AND MODERN REPRESENTATIVES. Being the Introduction to the Cambridge Paragraph Bible (1873), re-edited with corrections and additions. By F. H. A. SCRIVENER, M.A., D.C.L., LL.D., Prebendary of Exeter and Vicar of Hendon. Crown 8vo. 7s. 6d.

THE LECTIONARY BIBLE, WITH APOCRYPHA, divided into Sections adapted to the Calendar and Tables of Lessons of 1871. Crown 8vo. 3s. 6d.

THE NEW TESTAMENT IN GREEK according to the text followed in the **Authorised Version**, with the Variations adopted in the **Revised Version**. Edited by F. H. A. SCRIVENER, M.A., D.C.L., LL.D. Crown 8vo. 6s. Morocco boards or limp. 12s.
The Revised Version is the Joint Property of the Universities of Cambridge and Oxford.

BREVIARIUM ROMANUM a FRANCISCO CARDINALI QUIGNONIO editum et recognitum iuxta editionem Venetiis A.D. 1535 impressam curante JOHANNE WICKHAM LEGG Societatis Antiquariorum atque Coll. Reg. Medicorum Londin. Socio. Demy 8vo. 12s.

London: C. J. CLAY & SONS, Cambridge University Press Warehouse, Ave Maria Lane.

BREVIARIUM AD USUM INSIGNIS ECCLESIAE SARUM. Juxta Editionem maximam pro CLAUDIO CHEVALLON ET FRANCISCO REGNAULT A.D. MDXXXI. in Alma Parisiorum Academia impressam: labore ac studio FRANCISCI PROCTER, A.M., ET CHRISTOPHORI WORDSWORTH, A.M.

FASCICULUS I. In quo continentur KALENDARIUM, et ORDO TEMPORALIS sive PROPRIUM DE TEMPORE TOTIUS ANNI, una cum ordinali suo quod usitato vocabulo dicitur PICA SIVE DIRECTORIUM SACERDOTUM. Demy 8vo. 18s.

"The value of this reprint is considerable to liturgical students, who will now be able to consult in their own libraries a work absolutely indispensable to a right understanding of the history of the Prayer-Book, but which till now usually necessitated a visit to some public library, since the rarity of the volume made its cost prohibitory to all but a few."—*Literary Churchman.*

FASCICULUS II. In quo continentur PSALTERIUM, cum ordinario Officii totius hebdomadae juxta Horas Canonicas, et proprio Completorii, LITANIA, COMMUNE SANCTORUM, ORDINARIUM MISSAE CUM CANONE ET XIII MISSIS, &c. &c. Demy 8vo. 12s.

"Not only experts in liturgiology, but all persons interested in the history of the Anglican Book of Common Prayer, will be grateful to the Syndicate of the Cambridge University Press for forwarding the publication of the volume which bears the above title."—*Notes and Queries.*

"Cambridge has worthily taken the lead with the Breviary, which is of especial value for that part of the reform of the Prayer-Book which will fit it for the wants of our time."—*Church Quarterly Review.*

FASCICULUS III. In quo continetur PROPRIUM SANCTORUM quod et sanctorale dicitur, una cum accentuario. Demy 8vo. 15s.

*** An Introduction of 130 pages, prefixed to this volume, contains (besides other interesting information as to the Breviary and its contents) Mr BRADSHAW'S exhaustive lists of editions and copies of the Breviary and allied liturgical books.

FASCICULI I. II. III. complete, £2. 2s.

GREEK AND ENGLISH TESTAMENT, in parallel Columns on the same page. Edited by J. SCHOLEFIELD, M.A. Small Octavo. New Edition, with the Marginal References as arranged and revised by Dr SCRIVENER. Cloth, red edges. 7s. 6d.

GREEK AND ENGLISH TESTAMENT. THE STUDENT'S EDITION of the above, on *large writing paper.* 4to. 12s.

GREEK TESTAMENT, ex editione Stephani tertia, 1550. Small 8vo. 3s. 6d.

THE PARALLEL NEW TESTAMENT, GREEK AND ENGLISH, being the **Authorised Version** set forth in 1611 arranged in Parallel Columns with the **Revised Version** of 1881, and with the original Greek, as edited by F. H. A. SCRIVENER, M.A., D.C.L., LL.D. Crown 8vo. 12s. 6d. *The Revised Version is the Joint Property of the Universities of Cambridge and Oxford.*

THE BOOK OF ECCLESIASTES, with Notes and Introduction. By the Very Rev. E. H. PLUMPTRE, D.D., Dean of Wells. Large Paper Edition. Demy 8vo. 7s. 6d.

London: C. J. CLAY & SONS, Cambridge University Press Warehouse, Ave Maria Lane.

THE OLD TESTAMENT IN GREEK ACCORDING TO THE SEPTUAGINT. Edited by H. B. SWETE, D.D., Honorary Fellow of Gonville and Caius College. Vol. I. Genesis—IV Kings. Crown 8vo. 7s. 6d.

Volume II. By the same Editor. [*In the Press.*

"Der Zweck dieser Ausgabe, den ganzen in den erwähnten Hss. vorliegenden kritischen Stoff übersichtlich zusammenzustellen und dem Benützer das Nachschlagen in den Separatausgaben jener Codices zu ersparen, ist hier in compendiösester Weise vortrefflich erreicht. Bezüglich der Klarheit, Schönheit und Correctheit des Drucks gebürt der Ausgabe das höchste Lob. Da zugleich der Preis sehr niedrig gestellt ist, so ist zu hoffen und zu wünschen, dass sie auch ausserhalb des englischen Sprachkreises ihre Verbreitung finden werde. Bezüglich der Accente und Spiritus der Eigennamen sind die Herausg. ihre eigenen Wege gegangen."—*Deutsche Litteraturzeitung.*

"The Edition has been executed in the very best style of Cambridge accuracy, which has no superior anywhere, and this is enough to put it at the head of the list of editions for manual use."—*Academy.*

"An edition, which for ordinary purposes will probably henceforth be that in use by readers of the Septuagint."—*Guardian.*

THE BOOK OF PSALMS IN GREEK ACCORDING TO THE SEPTUAGINT, being a portion of Vol. II. of the above. Crown 8vo. 2s. 6d.

THE GOSPEL ACCORDING TO ST MATTHEW in Anglo-Saxon and Northumbrian Versions, synoptically arranged: with Collations exhibiting all the Readings of all the MSS. Edited by the Rev. W. W. SKEAT, Litt.D., Elrington and Bosworth Professor of Anglo-Saxon. **New Edition.** Demy 4to. 10s.

"By the publication of the present volume Prof. Skeat has brought to its conclusion a work planned more than a half century ago by the late J. M. Kemble... Students of English have every reason to be grateful to Prof. Skeat for the scholarly and accurate way in which he has performed his laborious task. Thanks to him we now possess a reliable edition of all the existing MSS. of the old English Gospels."—*Academy.*

THE GOSPEL ACCORDING TO ST MARK, uniform with the preceding, by the same Editor. Demy 4to. 10s.

THE GOSPEL ACCORDING TO ST LUKE, uniform with the preceding, by the same Editor. Demy 4to. 10s.

THE GOSPEL ACCORDING TO ST JOHN, uniform with the preceding, by the same Editor. Demy 4to. 10s.

"*The Gospel according to St John, in Anglo-Saxon and Northumbrian Versions:* completes an undertaking designed and commenced by that distinguished scholar, J. M. Kemble, some forty years ago. Of the particular volume now before us, we can only say it is worthy of its two predecessors. We repeat that the service rendered to the study of Anglo-Saxon by this Synoptic collection cannot easily be overstated."—*Contemporary Review.*

THE FOUR GOSPELS (as above) bound in one volume, price 30s.

THE POINTED PRAYER BOOK, being the Book of Common Prayer with the Psalter or Psalms of David, pointed as they are to be sung or said in Churches. Royal 24mo. 1s. 6d.

The same in square 32mo. cloth. 6d.

THE CAMBRIDGE PSALTER, for the use of Choirs and Organists. Specially adapted for Congregations in which the "Cambridge Pointed Prayer Book" is used. Demy 8vo. cloth extra, 3s. 6d. cloth limp, cut flush. 2s. 6d.

London: C. J. CLAY & SONS, Cambridge University Press Warehouse, Ave Maria Lane.

THE PARAGRAPH PSALTER, arranged for the use of Choirs by BROOKE FOSS WESTCOTT, D.D., Regius Professor of Divinity in the University of Cambridge. Fcap. 4to. 5s.

The same in royal 32mo. Cloth 1s. Leather 1s. 6d.

THE MISSING FRAGMENT OF THE LATIN TRANSLATION OF THE FOURTH BOOK OF EZRA, discovered, and edited with an Introduction and Notes, and a facsimile of the MS., by ROBERT L. BENSLY, M.A., Lord Almoner's Professor of Arabic. Demy 4to. 10s.

"It has been said of this book that it has added a new chapter to the Bible, and, startling as the statement may at first sight appear, it is no exaggeration of the actual fact, if by the Bible we understand that of the larger size which contains the Apocrypha, and if the Second Book of Esdras can be fairly called a part of the Apocrypha."—*Saturday Review.*

THE HARKLEAN VERSION OF THE EPISTLE TO THE HEBREWS, Chap. xi. 28—xiii. 25. Now edited for the first time with Introduction and Notes on this Version of the Epistle. By ROBERT L. BENSLY, M.A. Demy 8vo. 5s.

NOTITIA CODICIS QUATTUOR EVANGELIORUM Græci Membranacei viris doctis hucusque incogniti quem in museo suo asservat EDUARDUS REUSS Argentoratensis. 2s.

THE ORIGIN OF THE LEICESTER CODEX OF THE NEW TESTAMENT. By J. RENDEL HARRIS, M.A. With 3 plates. Demy 4to. 10s. 6d.

THE REST OF THE WORDS OF BARUCH: A Christian Apocalypse of the Year 136 A.D. The Text revised with an Introduction. By J. RENDEL HARRIS, M.A. Royal 8vo. 5s.

CODEX S. CEADDAE LATINUS. Evangelia SSS, Matthaei, Marci, Lucae ad cap. III. 9 complectens, circa septimum vel octavum saeculum scriptvs, in Ecclesia Cathedrali Lichfieldiensi servatus. Cum codice versionis Vulgatae Amiatino contulit, prolegomena conscripsit, F. H. A. SCRIVENER, A.M., D.C.L., LL.D., With 3 plates. £1. 1s.

THEOLOGY—(ANCIENT).

THE GREEK LITURGIES. Chiefly from original Authorities. By C. A. SWAINSON, D.D., late Master of Christ's College, Cambridge. Crown 4to. Paper covers. 15s.

"Jeder folgende Forscher wird dankbar anerkennen, dass Swainson das Fundament zu einer historisch-kritischen Geschichte der Griechischen Liturgien sicher gelegt hat."— ADOLPH HARNACK, *Theologische Literatur-Zeitung.*

London: C. J. CLAY & SONS, Cambridge University Press Warehouse, Ave Maria Lane.

THEODORE OF MOPSUESTIA'S COMMENTARY
ON THE MINOR EPISTLES OF S. PAUL. The Latin Version with the Greek Fragments, edited from the MSS. with Notes and an Introduction, by H. B. SWETE, D.D. In Two Volumes. Volume I., containing the Introduction, with Facsimiles of the MSS., and the Commentary upon Galatians—Colossians. Demy 8vo. 12s.

"It is the result of thorough, careful, and patient investigation of all the points bearing on the subject, and the results are presented with admirable good sense and modesty."—*Guardian.*

"In dem oben verzeichneten Buche liegt uns die erste Hälfte einer vollständigen, ebenso sorgfältig gearbeiteten wie schön ausgestatteten Ausgabe des Commentars mit ausführlichen Prolegomena und reichhaltigen kritischen und erläuternden Anmerkungen vor."—*Literarisches Centralblatt.*

"Auf Grund dieser Quellen ist der Text bei Swete mit musterhafter Akribie hergestellt. Aber auch sonst hat der Herausgeber mit unermüdlichem Fleisse und eingehender Sachkenntniss sein Werk mit allen denjenigen Zugaben ausgerüstet, welche bei einer solchen Text-Ausgabe nur irgend erwartet werden können.... Von den drei Haupthandschriften ... sind vortreffliche photographische Facsimile's beigegeben, wie überhaupt das ganze Werk von der *University Press* zu Cambridge mit bekannter Eleganz ausgestattet ist."—*Theologische Literaturzeitung.*

"Hernn Swete's Leistung ist eine so tüchtige dass wir das Werk in keinen besseren Händen wissen möchten, und mit den sichersten Erwartungen auf das Gelingen der Fortsetzung entgegen sehen."—*Göttingische gelehrte Anzeigen* (Sept. 1881).

VOLUME II., containing the Commentary on 1 Thessalonians—Philemon, Appendices and Indices. 12s.

"Eine Ausgabe ... für welche alle zugänglichen Hülfsmittel in musterhafter Weise benützt wurden ... eine reife Frucht siebenjährigen Fleisses."—*Theologische Literaturzeitung.*

(Sept. 23, 1882).
"Mit derselben Sorgfalt bearbeitet die wir bei dem ersten Theile gerühmt haben."—*Literarisches Centralblatt* (July 29, 1882).

SAYINGS OF THE JEWISH FATHERS, comprising
Pirqe Aboth and Pereq R. Meir in Hebrew and English, with Critical and Illustrative Notes. By CHARLES TAYLOR, D.D., Master of St John's College, Cambridge. Demy 8vo. 10s.

"The 'Masseketh Aboth' stands at the head of Hebrew non-canonical writings. It is of ancient date, claiming to contain the dicta of teachers who flourished from B.C. 200 to the same year of our era. Mr Taylor's explanatory and illustrative commentary is very full and satisfactory."—*Spectator.*

"A careful and thorough edition which does credit to English scholarship, of a short treatise from the Mishna, containing a series of sentences or maxims ascribed mostly to Jewish teachers immediately preceding, or immediately following the Christian era..."—*Contemporary Review.*

A COLLATION OF THE ATHOS CODEX OF THE
SHEPHERD OF HERMAS. Together with an Introduction by SPYR. P. LAMBROS, PH. D., translated and edited with a Preface and Appendices by J. ARMITAGE ROBINSON, M.A., Fellow and Dean of Christ's College, Cambridge. Demy 8vo. 3s. 6d.

THE PALESTINIAN MISHNA. By W. H. LOWE, M.A.,
Lecturer in Hebrew at Christ's College, Cambridge. Royal 8vo. 21s.

SANCTI IRENÆI EPISCOPI LUGDUNENSIS libros
quinque adversus Hæreses, versione Latina cum Codicibus Claromontano ac Arundeliano denuo collata, præmissa de placitis Gnosticorum prolusione, fragmenta necnon Græce, Syriace, Armeniace, commentatione perpetua et indicibus variis edidit W. WIGAN HARVEY, S.T.B. Collegii Regalis olim Socius. 2 Vols. 8vo. 18s.

M. MINUCII FELICIS OCTAVIUS. The text revised
from the original MS., with an English Commentary, Analysis, Introduction, and Copious Indices. Edited by H. A. HOLDEN, LL.D. Examiner in Greek to the University of London. Crown 8vo. 7s. 6d.

London: C. J. CLAY & SONS, Cambridge University Press Warehouse,
Ave Maria Lane.

THEOPHILI EPISCOPI ANTIOCHENSIS LIBRI TRES AD AUTOLYCUM edidit, Prolegomenis Versione Notulis Indicibus instruxit G. G. HUMPHRY, S.T.B. Post 8vo. 5s.

THEOPHYLACTI IN EVANGELIUM S. MATTHÆI COMMENTARIUS, edited by W. G. HUMPHRY, B.D. Prebendary of St Paul's, late Fellow of Trinity College. Demy 8vo. 7s. 6d.

TERTULLIANUS DE CORONA MILITIS, DE SPECTACULIS, DE IDOLOLATRIA, with Analysis and English Notes, by GEORGE CURREY, D.D. Preacher at the Charter House, late Fellow and Tutor of St John's College. Crown 8vo. 5s.

FRAGMENTS OF PHILO AND JOSEPHUS. Newly edited by J. RENDEL HARRIS, M.A., Fellow of Clare College, Cambridge. With two Facsimiles. Demy 4to. 12s. 6d.

THE TEACHING OF THE APOSTLES. Newly edited, with Facsimile Text and Commentary, by J. RENDEL HARRIS, M.A. Demy 4to. £1. 1s.

THEOLOGY—(ENGLISH).

WORKS OF ISAAC BARROW, compared with the Original MSS., enlarged with Materials hitherto unpublished. A new Edition, by A. NAPIER, M.A. 9 Vols. Demy 8vo. £3. 3s.

TREATISE OF THE POPE'S SUPREMACY, and a Discourse concerning the Unity of the Church, by ISAAC BARROW. Demy 8vo. 7s. 6d.

PEARSON'S EXPOSITION OF THE CREED, edited by TEMPLE CHEVALLIER, B.D. New Edition. Revised by R. SINKER, B.D., Librarian of Trinity College. Demy 8vo. 12s.

"A new edition of Bishop Pearson's famous work *On the Creed* has just been issued by the Cambridge University Press. It is the well-known edition of Temple Chevallier, thoroughly overhauled by the Rev. R. Sinker, of Trinity College......Altogether this appears to be the most complete and convenient edition as yet published of a work which has long been recognised in all quarters as a standard one."—*Guardian*.

AN ANALYSIS OF THE EXPOSITION OF THE CREED written by the Right Rev. JOHN PEARSON, D.D. late Lord Bishop of Chester, by W. H. MILL, D.D. Demy 8vo. 5s.

WHEATLY ON THE COMMON PRAYER, edited by G. E. CORRIE, D.D. late Master of Jesus College. Demy 8vo. 7s. 6d.

TWO FORMS OF PRAYER OF THE TIME OF QUEEN ELIZABETH. Now First Reprinted. Demy 8vo. 6d.

CÆSAR MORGAN'S INVESTIGATION OF THE TRINITY OF PLATO, and of Philo Judæus, and of the effects which an attachment to their writings had upon the principles and reasonings of the Fathers of the Christian Church. Revised by H. A. HOLDEN, LL.D. Crown 8vo. 4s.

London: C. J. CLAY & SONS, Cambridge University Press Warehouse, Ave Maria Lane.

SELECT DISCOURSES, by JOHN SMITH, late Fellow of Queens' College, Cambridge. Edited by H. G. WILLIAMS, B.D. late Professor of Arabic. Royal 8vo. 7s. 6d.

"The 'Select Discourses' of John Smith, collected and published from his papers after his death, are, in my opinion, much the most considerable work left to us by this Cambridge School [the Cambridge Platonists]. They have a right to a place in English literary history."—Mr MATTHEW ARNOLD, in the *Contemporary Review*.

"Of all the products of the Cambridge School, the 'Select Discourses' are perhaps the highest, as they are the most accessible and the most widely appreciated...and indeed no spiritually thoughtful mind can read them unmoved. They carry us so directly into an atmosphere of divine philosophy, luminous with the richest lights of meditative genius... He was one of those rare thinkers in whom largeness of view, and depth, and wealth of poetic and speculative insight, only served to evoke more fully the religious spirit, and while he drew the mould of his thought from Plotinus, he vivified the substance of it from St Paul."—Principal TULLOCH, *Rational Theology in England in the 17th Century*.

THE HOMILIES, with Various Readings, and the Quotations from the Fathers given at length in the Original Languages. Edited by the late G. E. CORRIE, D.D. Demy 8vo. 7s. 6d.

DE OBLIGATIONE CONSCIENTIÆ PRÆLECTIONES decem Oxonii in Schola Theologica habitæ a ROBERTO SANDERSON, SS. Theologiæ ibidem Professore Regio. With English Notes, including an abridged Translation, by W. WHEWELL, D.D. late Master of Trinity College. Demy 8vo. 7s. 6d.

ARCHBISHOP USHER'S ANSWER TO A JESUIT, with other Tracts on Popery. Edited by J. SCHOLEFIELD, M.A. late Regius Professor of Greek in the University. Demy 8vo. 7s. 6d.

WILSON'S ILLUSTRATION OF THE METHOD OF explaining the New Testament, by the early opinions of Jews and Christians concerning Christ. Edited by T. TURTON, D.D. 8vo. 5s.

LECTURES ON DIVINITY delivered in the University of Cambridge, by JOHN HEY, D.D. Third Edition, revised by T. TURTON, D.D. late Lord Bishop of Ely. 2 vols. Demy 8vo. 15s.

S. AUSTIN AND HIS PLACE IN THE HISTORY OF CHRISTIAN THOUGHT. Being the Hulsean Lectures for 1885. By W. CUNNINGHAM, D.D. Demy 8vo. Buckram, 12s. 6d.

THE GOSPEL HISTORY OF OUR LORD JESUS CHRIST IN THE LANGUAGE OF THE REVISED VERSION, arranged in a Connected Narrative, especially for the use of Teachers and Preachers. By Rev. C. C. JAMES, M.A., Rector of Wortham, Suffolk, and late Fellow of King's College. Crown 8vo. [*Nearly ready.*

ARABIC, SANSKRIT, SYRIAC, &c.

THE DIVYÂVADÂNA, a Collection of Early Buddhist Legends, now first edited from the Nepalese Sanskrit MSS. in Cambridge and Paris. By E. B. COWELL, M.A., Professor of Sanskrit in the University of Cambridge, and R. A. NEIL, M.A., Fellow and Lecturer of Pembroke College. Demy 8vo. 18s.

London: C. J. CLAY & SONS, Cambridge University Press Warehouse, Ave Maria Lane.

POEMS OF BEHA ED DIN ZOHEIR OF EGYPT.
With a Metrical Translation, Notes and Introduction, by E. H. PALMER, M.A., Barrister-at-Law of the Middle Temple, late Lord Almoner's Professor of Arabic, formerly Fellow of St John's College, Cambridge. 2 vols. Crown 4to.
> Vol. I. The ARABIC TEXT. 10s. 6d.
> Vol. II. ENGLISH TRANSLATION. 10s. 6d.

"We have no hesitation in saying that in both Prof. Palmer has made an addition to Oriental literature for which scholars should be grateful; and that, while his knowledge of Arabic is a sufficient guarantee for his mastery of the original, his English compositions are distinguished by versatility, command of language, rhythmical cadence, and, as we have remarked, by not unskilful imitations of the styles of several of our own favourite poets, living and dead."—*Saturday Review.*

"This sumptuous edition of the poems of Behá-ed-dín Zoheir is a very welcome addition to the small series of Eastern poets accessible to readers who are not Orientalists."—*Academy.*

THE CHRONICLE OF JOSHUA THE STYLITE, composed in Syriac A.D. 507, with an English translation and notes, by the late W. WRIGHT, LL.D., Professor of Arabic. Demy 8vo. 10s. 6d.

"Die lehrreiche kleine Chronik Josuas hat nach Assemani und Martin in Wright einen dritten Bearbeiter gefunden, der sich um die Emendation des Textes wie um die Erklärung der Realien wesentlich verdient gemacht hat ... Ws. Josua-Ausgabe ist eine sehr dankenswerte Gabe und besonders empfehlenswert als ein Lehrmittel für den syrischen Unterricht; es erscheint auch gerade zur rechten Zeit, da die zweite Ausgabe von Roedigers syrischer Chrestomathie im Buchhandel vollständig vergriffen und diejenige von Kirsch-Bernstein nur noch in wenigen Exemplaren vorhanden ist."— *Deutsche Litteraturzeitung.*

KALĪLAH AND DIMNAH, OR, THE FABLES OF BIDPAI; being an account of their literary history, together with an English Translation of the same, with Notes, by I. G. N. KEITH-FALCONER, M.A., late Lord Almoner's Professor of Arabic in the University of Cambridge. Demy 8vo. 7s. 6d.

NALOPÁKHYÁNAM, OR, THE TALE OF NALA;
containing the Sanskrit Text in Roman Characters, followed by a Vocabulary and a sketch of Sanskrit Grammar. By the late Rev. THOMAS JARRETT, M.A. Trinity College, Regius Professor of Hebrew. Demy 8vo. 10s.

NOTES ON THE TALE OF NALA, for the use of Classical Students, by J. PEILE, Litt. D., Master of Christ's College. Demy 8vo. 12s.

CATALOGUE OF THE BUDDHIST SANSKRIT MANUSCRIPTS in the University Library, Cambridge. Edited by C. BENDALL, M.A., Fellow of Gonville and Caius College. Demy 8vo. 12s.

"It is unnecessary to state how the compilation of the present catalogue came to be placed in Mr Bendall's hands; from the character of his work it is evident the selection was judicious, and we may fairly congratulate those concerned in it on the result... Mr Bendall has entitled himself to the thanks of all Oriental scholars, and we hope he may have before him a long course of successful labour in the field he has chosen."—*Athenæum.*

THE HISTORY OF ALEXANDER THE GREAT,
being the Syriac version of the Pseudo-Callisthenes. Edited from Five Manuscripts, with an English Translation and Notes, by E. A. W. BUDGE, M.A., Assistant in the Department of Egyptian Antiquities, British Museum. Demy 8vo. 25s. (*The Edition is limited to* 250 *copies.*)

London: C. J. CLAY & SONS, Cambridge University Press Warehouse,
Ave Maria Lane.

GREEK AND LATIN CLASSICS, &c.

SOPHOCLES: The Plays and Fragments, with Critical Notes, Commentary, and Translation in English Prose, by R. C. JEBB, Litt.D., LL.D., Regius Professor of Greek in the University of Cambridge.

Part I. Oedipus Tyrannus. Demy 8vo. *New Edition.* 12s. 6d.
Part II. Oedipus Coloneus. Demy 8vo. *New Edition.* 12s. 6d.
Part III. Antigone. Demy 8vo. 12s. 6d.
Part IV. Philoctetes. [*In the Press.*

"Of his explanatory and critical notes we can only speak with admiration. Thorough scholarship combines with taste, erudition, and boundless industry to make this first volume a pattern of editing. The work is made complete by a prose translation, upon pages alternating with the text, of which we may say shortly that it displays sound judgment and taste, without sacrificing precision to poetry of expression."—*The Times.*

"Professor Jebb's edition of Sophocles is already so fully established, and has received such appreciation in these columns and elsewhere, that we have judged this third volume when we have said that it is of a piece with the others. The whole edition so far exhibits perhaps the most complete and elaborate editorial work which has ever appeared."—*Saturday Review.*

"Prof. Jebb's keen and profound sympathy, not only with Sophocles and all the best of ancient Hellenic life and thought, but also with modern European culture, constitutes him an ideal interpreter between the ancient writer and the modern reader."—*Athenæum.*

"It would be difficult to praise this third instalment of Professor Jebb's unequalled edition of Sophocles too warmly, and it is almost a work of supererogation to praise it at all. It is equal, at least, and perhaps superior, in merit, to either of his previous instalments; and when this is said, all is said. Yet we cannot refrain from formally recognising once more the consummate Greek scholarship of the editor, and from once more doing grateful homage to his masterly tact and literary skill, and to his unwearied and marvellous industry."—*Spectator.*

AESCHYLI FABULAE.—IKETIΔEΣ XOHΦOPOI IN LIBRO MEDICEO MENDOSE SCRIPTAE EX VV. DD. CONIECTURIS EMENDATIUS EDITAE cum Scholiis Graecis et brevi adnotatione critica, curante F. A. PALEY, M.A., LL.D. Demy 8vo. 7s. 6d.

THE AGAMEMNON OF AESCHYLUS. With a Translation in English Rhythm, and Notes Critical and Explanatory. **New Edition Revised.** By the late BENJAMIN HALL KENNEDY, D.D., Regius Professor of Greek. Crown 8vo. 6s.

"One of the best editions of the masterpiece of Greek tragedy."—*Athenæum.*

THE THEÆTETUS OF PLATO with a Translation and Notes by the same Editor. Crown 8vo. 7s. 6d.

ARISTOTLE.—ΠΕΡΙ ΨΥΧΗΣ. ARISTOTLE'S PSYCHOLOGY, in Greek and English, with Introduction and Notes, by EDWIN WALLACE, M.A., late Fellow and Tutor of Worcester College, Oxford. Demy 8vo. 18s.

"The notes are exactly what such notes ought to be,—helps to the student, not mere displays of learning. By far the more valuable parts of the notes are neither critical nor literary, but philosophical and expository of the thought, and of the connection of thought, in the treatise itself. In this relation the notes are invaluable. Of the translation, it may be said that an English reader may fairly master by means of it this great treatise of Aristotle."—*Spectator.*

"Wallace's Bearbeitung der Aristotelischen Psychologie ist das Werk eines denkenden und in allen Schriften des Aristoteles und grösstenteils auch in der neueren Litteratur zu denselben belesenen Mannes... Der schwächste Teil der Arbeit ist der kritische... Aber in allen diesen Dingen liegt auch nach der Absicht des Verfassers nicht der Schwerpunkt seiner Arbeit, sondern."—Prof. Susemihl in *Philologische Wochenschrift.*

---

*London: C. J. CLAY & SONS, Cambridge University Press Warehouse
Ave Maria Lane.*

ARISTOTLE.—ΠΕΡΙ ΔΙΚΑΙΟΣΤΝΗΣ. THE FIFTH BOOK OF THE NICOMACHEAN ETHICS OF ARISTOTLE. Edited by HENRY JACKSON, Litt.D., Fellow of Trinity College, Cambridge. Demy 8vo. 6s.

"It is not too much to say that some of the points he discusses have never had so much light thrown upon them before.... Scholars will hope that this is not the only portion of the Aristotelian writings which he is likely to edit."—*Athenæum*.

ARISTOTLE. THE RHETORIC. With a Commentary by the late E. M. COPE, Fellow of Trinity College, Cambridge, revised and edited by J. E. SANDYS, Litt.D. With a biographical Memoir by the late H. A. J. MUNRO, Litt.D. 3 Vols., Demy 8vo. **Now reduced to 21s.** (*originally published at* 31s. 6d.)

"This work is in many ways creditable to the University of Cambridge. If an English student wishes to have a full conception of what is contained in the *Rhetoric* of Aristotle, to Mr Cope's edition he must go."—*Academy*.

"Mr Sandys has performed his arduous duties with marked ability and admirable tact. ...... In every part of his work—revising, supplementing, and completing—he has done exceedingly well."—*Examiner*.

PINDAR. OLYMPIAN AND PYTHIAN ODES. With Notes Explanatory and Critical, Introductions and Introductory Essays. Edited by C. A. M. FENNELL, Litt. D., late Fellow of Jesus College. Crown 8vo. 9s.

"Mr Fennell deserves the thanks of all classical students for his careful and scholarly edition of the Olympian and Pythian odes. He brings to his task the necessary enthusiasm for his author, great industry, a sound judgment, and, in particular, copious and minute learning in comparative philology."—*Athenæum*.

—— **THE ISTHMIAN AND NEMEAN ODES.** By the same Editor. Crown 8vo. 9s.

"... As a handy and instructive edition of a difficult classic no work of recent years surpasses Mr Fennell's 'Pindar.'"—*Athenæum*.
"This work is in no way inferior to the previous volume. The commentary affords valuable help to the study of the most difficult of Greek authors, and is enriched with notes on points of scholarship and etymology which could only have been written by a scholar of very high attainments."—*Saturday Review*.

DEMOSTHENES. PRIVATE ORATIONS OF, with Introductions and English Notes, by the late F. A. PALEY, M.A. and J. E. SANDYS, Litt.D. Fellow and Tutor of St John's College, and Public Orator in the University of Cambridge.

PART I. Contra Phormionem, Lacritum, Pantaenetum, Boeotum de Nomine, Boeotum de Dote, Dionysodorum. **New Edition.** Crown 8vo. 6s.

"Mr Paley's scholarship is sound and accurate, his experience of editing wide, and if he is content to devote his learning and abilities to the production of such manuals as these, they will be received with gratitude throughout the higher schools of the country. Mr Sandys is deeply read in the German literature which bears upon his author, and the elucidation of matters of daily life, in the delineation of which Demosthenes is so rich, obtains full justice at his hands. ... We hope this edition may lead the way to a more general study of these speeches in schools than has hitherto been possible."—*Academy*.

PART II. Pro Phormione, Contra Stephanum I. II.; Nicostratum, Cononem, Calliclem. **New Edition.** Crown 8vo. 7s. 6d.

"It is long since we have come upon a work evincing more pains, scholarship, and varied research and illustration than Mr Sandys's contribution to the 'Private Orations of Demosthenes'."—*Saturday Review*.
" ...... the edition reflects credit on Cambridge scholarship, and ought to be extensively used."—*Athenæum*.

DEMOSTHENES. LEPTINES. With Introductory Essay and Critical and Explanatory Notes. Edited by J. E. SANDYS, Litt.D. Demy 8vo. [*Nearly ready*.

London: C. J. CLAY & SONS, Cambridge University Press Warehouse, Ave Maria Lane.

DEMOSTHENES AGAINST ANDROTION AND AGAINST TIMOCRATES, with Introductions and English Commentary, by WILLIAM WAYTE, M.A., late Professor of Greek, University College, London. Crown 8vo. 7s. 6d.

"These speeches are highly interesting, as illustrating Attic Law, as that law was influenced by the exigencies of politics... As vigorous examples of the great orator's style, they are worthy of all admiration... Besides a most lucid and interesting introduction, Mr Wayte has given the student effective help in his running commentary."—*Spectator.*

PLATO'S PHÆDO, literally translated, by the late E. M. COPE, Fellow of Trinity College, Cambridge, revised by HENRY JACKSON, Litt.D., Fellow of Trinity College. Demy 8vo. 5s.

P. VERGILI MARONIS OPERA, cum Prolegomenis et Commentario Critico edidit B. H. KENNEDY, S.T.P., Extra Fcap. 8vo. 3s. 6d.

THE BACCHAE OF EURIPIDES. With Introduction, Critical Notes, and Archæological Illustrations, by J. E. SANDYS, Litt.D. New and Enlarged Edition. Crown 8vo. 12s. 6d.

"Of the present edition of the *Bacchae* by Mr Sandys we may safely say that never before has a Greek play, in England at least, had fuller justice done to its criticism, interpretation, and archæological illustration, whether for the young student or the more advanced scholar. The Cambridge Public Orator may be said to have taken the lead in issuing a complete edition of a Greek play, which is destined perhaps to gain redoubled favour now that the study of ancient monuments has been applied to its illustration."—*Saturday Review.*

"The volume is interspersed with well-executed woodcuts, and its general attractiveness of form reflects great credit on the University Press. In the notes Mr Sandys has more than sustained his well-earned reputation as a careful and learned editor, and shows considerable advance in freedom and lightness of style.... Under such circumstances it is superfluous to say that for the purposes of teachers and advanced students this handsome edition far surpasses all its predecessors."—*Athenæum.*

THE TYPES OF GREEK COINS. By PERCY GARDNER, Litt. D., F.S.A. With 16 Autotype plates, containing photographs of Coins of all parts of the Greek World. Impl. 4to. Cloth extra, £1. 11s. 6d.; Roxburgh (Morocco back), £2. 2s.

"Professor Gardner's book is written with such lucidity and in a manner so straightforward that it may well win converts, and it may be distinctly recommended to that omnivorous class of readers—'men in the schools'."—*Saturday Review.*

ESSAYS ON THE ART OF PHEIDIAS. By C. WALDSTEIN, Litt. D., Phil. D., Reader in Classical Archæology in the University of Cambridge. Royal 8vo. With numerous Illustrations. 16 Plates. Buckram, 30s.

"His book will be universally welcomed as a very valuable contribution towards a more thorough knowledge of the style of Pheidias."—*The Academy.*

"'Essays on the Art of Pheidias' form an extremely valuable and important piece of work.... Taking it for the illustrations alone, it is an exceedingly fascinating book."—*Times.*

AN INTRODUCTION TO GREEK EPIGRAPHY. Part I. The Archaic Inscriptions and the Greek Alphabet by E. S. ROBERTS, M.A., Fellow and Tutor of Gonville and Caius College. Demy 8vo. With illustrations. 18s.

"We will say at once that Mr Roberts appears to have done his work very well. The book is clearly and conveniently arranged. The inscriptions are naturally divided according to the places to which they belong. Under each head are given illustrations sufficient to show the characteristics of the writing, one copy in letters of the original form (sometimes a facsimile) being followed by another in the usual cursive. References, which must have cost great labour, are given to the scattered notices bearing on each document. Explanatory remarks either accompany the text or are added in an appendix. To the whole is prefixed a sketch of the history of the alphabet up to the terminal date. At the end the result is resumed in general tables of all the alphabets, classified according to their connexions; and a separate table illustrates the alphabet of Athens. The volume contains about five hundred inscriptions, and forms a moderate octavo of about four hundred pages."—*Saturday Review.*

London: C. J. CLAY & SONS, Cambridge University Press Warehouse,
Ave Maria Lane.

M. TULLI CICERONIS AD M. BRUTUM ORATOR.
A revised text edited with Introductory Essays and with critical and explanatory notes, by J. E. SANDYS, Litt.D. Demy 8vo. 16s.

"This volume, which is adorned with several good woodcuts, forms a handsome and welcome addition to the Cambridge editions of Cicero's works."—*Athenæum.*

"A model edition."—*Spectator.*
"The commentary is in every way worthy of the editor's high reputation."—*Academy.*

M. TULLI CICERONIS DE FINIBUS BONORUM ET MALORUM LIBRI QUINQUE. The text revised and explained; with a Translation by JAMES S. REID, Litt. D., Fellow and Tutor of Gonville and Caius College. 3 Vols. [*In the Press.*
VOL. III. Containing the Translation. Demy 8vo. 8s.

M. T. CICERONIS DE OFFICIIS LIBRI TRES, with Marginal Analysis, English Commentary, and copious Indices, by H. A. HOLDEN, LL.D. **Sixth Edition**, Revised and Enlarged. Cr. 8vo. 9s.

"Few editions of a classic have found so much favour as Dr Holden's *De Officiis*, and the present revision (sixth edition) makes the position of the work secure."—*American Journal of Philology.*

M. T. CICERONIS DE OFFICIIS LIBER TERTIUS, with Introduction, Analysis and Commentary, by H. A. HOLDEN, LL.D. Crown 8vo. 2s.

M. TVLLI CICERONIS PRO C RABIRIO [PERDVELLIONIS REO] ORATIO AD QVIRITES, with Notes, Introduction and Appendices by W. E. HEITLAND, M.A., Fellow and Tutor of St John's College, Cambridge. Demy 8vo. 7s. 6d.

M. TULLII CICERONIS DE NATURA DEORUM Libri Tres, with Introduction and Commentary by JOSEPH B. MAYOR, M.A., together with a new collation of several of the English MSS. by J. H. SWAINSON, M.A.
Vol. I. Demy 8vo. 10s. 6d. Vol. II. 12s. 6d. Vol. III. 10s.

"Such editions as that of which Prof. Mayor has given us the first instalment will doubtless do much to remedy this undeserved neglect. It is one on which great pains and much learning have evidently been expended, and is in every way admirably suited to meet the needs of the student... The notes of the editor are all that could be expected from his well-known learning and scholarship."—*Academy.*

See also Pitt Press Series, pp. 30—34.

MATHEMATICS, PHYSICAL SCIENCE, &c.

MATHEMATICAL AND PHYSICAL PAPERS. By Sir W. THOMSON, LL.D., D.C.L., F.R.S., Professor of Natural Philosophy in the University of Glasgow. Collected from different Scientific Periodicals from May 1841, to the present time. Vol. I. Demy 8vo. 18s. Vol. II. 15s. [Volume III. *In the Press.*

MATHEMATICAL AND PHYSICAL PAPERS, by Sir G. G. STOKES, Sc.D., LL.D., F.R.S., Lucasian Professor of Mathematics in the University of Cambridge. Reprinted from the Original Journals and Transactions, with Additional Notes by the Author. Vol. I. Demy 8vo. 15s. Vol. II. 15s. [Vol. III. *In the Press.*

London: C. J. CLAY & SONS, *Cambridge University Press Warehouse, Ave Maria Lane.*

A HISTORY OF THE THEORY OF ELASTICITY AND OF THE STRENGTH OF MATERIALS, from Galilei to the present time. Vol. I. Galilei to Saint-Venant, 1639–1850. By the late I. TODHUNTER, Sc.D., F.R.S., edited and completed by Professor KARL PEARSON, M.A. Demy 8vo. 25s.
Vol. II. By the same Editor. *[In the Press.*

THE ELASTICAL RESEARCHES OF BARRÉ DE SAINT-VENANT (Extract from Vol. II. of TODHUNTER'S History of the Theory of Elasticity), edited by Professor KARL PEARSON, M.A. Demy 8vo. 9s.

A TREATISE ON GEOMETRICAL OPTICS. By R. S. HEATH, M.A., Professor of Mathematics in Mason Science College, Birmingham. Demy 8vo. 12s. 6d.

AN ELEMENTARY TREATISE ON GEOMETRICAL OPTICS. By R. S. HEATH, M.A. Crown 8vo. 5s.

A TREATISE ON ELEMENTARY DYNAMICS. By S. L. LONEY, M.A., Fellow of Sidney Sussex College. Crown 8vo. 7s. 6d.

A TREATISE ON PLANE TRIGONOMETRY. By E. W. HOBSON, M.A., Fellow and Lecturer of Christ's College, Cambridge. Demy 8vo. *[In the Press.*

CATALOGUE OF SCIENTIFIC PAPERS COMPILED BY THE ROYAL SOCIETY OF LONDON: Vols. 1—6 for the years 1800—1863, Royal 4to. cloth (vol. 1 in half morocco) £4 (**net**); half morocco £5. 5s. (**net**). Vols. 7—8 for the years 1864—1873, cloth £1. 11s. 6d. (**net**); half morocco £2. 5s. (**net**). Single volumes cloth 20s. or half-morocco 28s. (**net**). New Series for the years 1874—1883. *[In the Press.*

THE COLLECTED MATHEMATICAL PAPERS OF ARTHUR CAYLEY, Sc.D., F.R.S., Sadlerian Professor of Pure Mathematics in the University of Cambridge. Demy 4to. 10 vols. Vols. I. and II. 25s. each. [Vol. III. *In the Press.*

THE SCIENTIFIC PAPERS OF THE LATE PROF. J. CLERK MAXWELL. Edited by W. D. NIVEN, M.A. In 2 vols. Royal 4to. *[Nearly ready.*

A HISTORY OF THE STUDY OF MATHEMATICS AT CAMBRIDGE. By W. W. ROUSE BALL, M.A., Fellow and Lecturer on Mathematics of Trinity College, Cambridge. Crown 8vo. 6s.

A TREATISE ON ANALYTICAL STATICS, by E. J. ROUTH, Sc.D., F.R.S., Fellow of the University of London, Honorary Fellow of St Peter's College, Cambridge. *[In the Press.*

A CATALOGUE OF THE PORTSMOUTH COLLECTION OF BOOKS AND PAPERS written by or belonging to SIR ISAAC NEWTON. Demy 8vo. 5s.

London: C. J. CLAY & SONS, Cambridge University Press Warehouse,
Ave Maria Lane.

A TREATISE ON NATURAL PHILOSOPHY. By Sir W. Thomson, LL.D., D.C.L., F.R.S., and P. G. Tait, M.A. **Part I.** Demy 8vo. 16s. **Part II.** Demy 8vo. 18s.

ELEMENTS OF NATURAL PHILOSOPHY. By Professors Sir W. Thomson and P. G. Tait. Demy 8vo. 9s.

AN ATTEMPT TO TEST THE THEORIES OF CAPILLARY ACTION, by Francis Bashforth, B.D., and J. C. Adams, M.A., F.R.S. Demy 4to. £1. 1s.

A TREATISE ON THE THEORY OF DETERMINANTS and their applications in Analysis and Geometry, by R. F. Scott, M.A., Fellow of St John's College. Demy 8vo. 12s.

HYDRODYNAMICS, a Treatise on the Mathematical Theory of the Motion of Fluids, by H. Lamb, M.A. Demy 8vo. 12s.

THE ANALYTICAL THEORY OF HEAT, by Joseph Fourier. Translated, with Notes, by A. Freeman, M.A., formerly Fellow of St John's College, Cambridge. Demy 8vo. 12s.

PRACTICAL WORK AT THE CAVENDISH LABORATORY. HEAT. Edited by W. N. Shaw, M.A. Demy 8vo. 3s.

THE ELECTRICAL RESEARCHES OF THE Hon. H. Cavendish, F.R.S. Written between 1771 and 1781. Edited from the original MSS. in the possession of the Duke of Devonshire, K. G., by the late J. Clerk Maxwell, F.R.S. Demy 8vo. 18s.

An ELEMENTARY TREATISE on QUATERNIONS. By P. G. Tait, M.A. *3rd Edition. Enlarged.* Demy 8vo. 18s.

COUNTERPOINT. A Practical Course of Study, by the late Professor Sir G. A. Macfarren, M.A., Mus. Doc. New Edition, revised. Crown 4to. 7s. 6d.

A TREATISE ON THE GENERAL PRINCIPLES OF CHEMISTRY, by M. M. Pattison Muir, M.A. **Second Edition.** Demy 8vo. 15s.

"The value of the book as a digest of the historical developments of chemical thought is immense."—*Academy.*

"Theoretical Chemistry has moved so rapidly of late years that most of our ordinary text books have been left far behind. German students, to be sure, possess an excellent guide to the present state of the science in 'Die Modernen Theorien der Chemie' of Prof. Lothar Meyer; but in this country the student has had to content himself with such works as Dr Tilden's 'Introduction to Chemical Philosophy', an admirable book in its way, but rather slender. Mr Pattison Muir having aimed at a more comprehensive scheme, has produced a systematic treatise on the principles of chemical philosophy which stands far in advance of any kindred work in our language."—*Athenæum.*

ELEMENTARY CHEMISTRY. By M. M. Pattison Muir, M.A., and Charles Slater, M.A., M.B. Crown 8vo. 4s. 6d.

PRACTICAL CHEMISTRY. A Course of Laboratory Work. By M. M. Pattison Muir, M.A., and D. J. Carnegie, B.A. Crown 8vo. 3s.

NOTES ON QUALITATIVE ANALYSIS. Concise and Explanatory. By H. J. H. Fenton, M.A., F.I.C., Demonstrator of Chemistry in the University of Cambridge. Cr. 4to. *New Edition.* 6s.

London: C. J. Clay & Sons, Cambridge University Press Warehouse, Ave Maria Lane.

LECTURES ON THE PHYSIOLOGY OF PLANTS,
by S. H. VINES, Sc.D., Professor of Botany in the University of Oxford. Demy 8vo. With Illustrations. 21s.

"To say that Dr Vines' book is a most valuable addition to our own botanical literature is but a narrow meed of praise: it is a work which will take its place as cosmopolitan: no more clear or concise discussion of the difficult chemistry of metabolism has appeared.... In erudition it stands alone among English books, and will compare favourably with any foreign competitors."—*Nature*.
"The work forms an important contribution to the literature of the subject....It will be eagerly welcomed by all students."—*Academy*.

A SHORT HISTORY OF GREEK MATHEMATICS.
By J. GOW, Litt.D., Fellow of Trinity College. Demy 8vo. 10s. 6d.

DIOPHANTOS OF ALEXANDRIA; a Study in the
History of Greek Algebra. By T. L. HEATH, M.A., Fellow of Trinity College, Cambridge. Demy 8vo. 7s. 6d.

"This study in the history of Greek Algebra is an exceedingly valuable contribution to the history of mathematics."—*Academy*.
"The most thorough account extant of Diophantus's place, work, and critics."—*Athenæum*.

THE MATHEMATICAL WORKS OF ISAAC BARROW, D.D.
Edited by W. WHEWELL, D.D. Demy 8vo. 7s. 6d.

THE FOSSILS AND PALÆONTOLOGICAL AFFINITIES OF THE NEOCOMIAN DEPOSITS OF UPWARE AND BRICKHILL
with Plates, being the Sedgwick Prize Essay for 1879. By the late W. KEEPING, M.A. Demy 8vo. 10s. 6d.

THE BALA VOLCANIC SERIES OF CAERNARVONSHIRE AND ASSOCIATED ROCKS,
being the Sedgwick Prize Essay for 1888 by A. HARKER, M.A., F.R.S., Fellow of St John's College. Demy 8vo. 7s. 6d.

A CATALOGUE OF BOOKS AND PAPERS ON PROTOZOA, CŒLENTERATES, WORMS,
and certain smaller groups of animals, published during the years 1861—1883, by D'ARCY W. THOMPSON, M.A. Demy 8vo. 12s. 6d.

ASTRONOMICAL OBSERVATIONS
made at the Observatory of Cambridge by the late Rev. J. CHALLIS, M.A. from 1846 to 1860.

ASTRONOMICAL OBSERVATIONS from 1861 to 1865.
Vol. XXI. Royal 4to. 15s. From 1866 to 1869. Vol. XXII. Royal 4to. 15s.

A CATALOGUE OF THE COLLECTION OF BIRDS
formed by the late H. E. STRICKLAND, now in the possession of the University of Cambridge. By O. SALVIN, M.A. Demy 8vo. £1. 1s.

A CATALOGUE OF AUSTRALIAN FOSSILS,
Stratigraphically and Zoologically arranged, by R. ETHERIDGE, Jun., F.G.S. Demy 8vo. 10s. 6d.

ILLUSTRATIONS OF COMPARATIVE ANATOMY,
VERTEBRATE AND INVERTEBRATE, for the Use of Students in the Museum of Zoology and Comparative Anatomy. Second Edition. Demy 8vo. 2s. 6d.

London: C. J. CLAY & SONS, Cambridge University Press Warehouse,
Ave Maria Lane.

A CATALOGUE OF THE COLLECTION OF CAMBRIAN AND SILURIAN FOSSILS contained in the Geological Museum of the University of Cambridge, by J. W. SALTER, F.G.S. With a Portrait of PROFESSOR SEDGWICK. Royal 4to. 7s. 6d.

CATALOGUE OF OSTEOLOGICAL SPECIMENS contained in the Anatomical Museum of the University of Cambridge. Demy 8vo. 2s. 6d.

LAW.

ELEMENTS OF THE LAW OF TORTS. A Text-book for Students. By MELVILLE M. BIGELOW, Ph.D., Lecturer in the Law School of the University of Boston, U.S.A. Crown 8vo. 10s. 6d.

"It is based on the original American edition, but it is an English Text-book with English authorities and statutes and illustrations substituted very generally for the American... The style is easy and lucid, though condensed, showing great grasp of subject... A very full index enhances the value of this book, which should take a prominent place among the really trustworthy text-books for the use of students."—*Law Times.*

A SELECTION OF CASES ON THE ENGLISH LAW OF CONTRACT. By GERARD BROWN FINCH, M.A., of Lincoln's Inn, Barrister at Law. Royal 8vo. 28s.

"An invaluable guide towards the best method of legal study."—*Law Quarterly Review.*

THE INFLUENCE OF THE ROMAN LAW ON THE LAW OF ENGLAND. Being the Yorke Prize Essay for 1884. By T. E. SCRUTTON, M.A. Demy 8vo. 10s. 6d.

"Legal work of just the kind that a learned University should promote by its prizes."—*Law Quarterly Review.*

LAND IN FETTERS. Being the Yorke Prize Essay for 1885. By T. E. SCRUTTON, M.A. Demy 8vo. 7s. 6d.

COMMONS AND COMMON FIELDS, OR THE HISTORY AND POLICY OF THE LAWS RELATING TO COMMONS AND ENCLOSURES IN ENGLAND. Being the Yorke Prize Essay for 1886. By T. E. SCRUTTON, M.A. 10s. 6d.

HISTORY OF THE LAW OF TITHES IN ENGLAND. Being the Yorke Prize Essay for 1887. By W. EASTERBY, B.A., LL.B., St John's College and the Middle Temple. Demy 8vo. 7s. 6d.

HISTORY OF LAND TENURE IN IRELAND. Being the Yorke Prize Essay for 1888. By W. E. MONTGOMERY, M.A., LL.M. Demy 8vo. 10s. 6d.

AN ANALYSIS OF CRIMINAL LIABILITY. By E. C. CLARK, LL.D., Regius Professor of Civil Law in the University of Cambridge, also of Lincoln's Inn, Barrister-at-Law. Crown 8vo. 7s. 6d.

PRACTICAL JURISPRUDENCE, a Comment on AUSTIN. By E. C. CLARK, LL.D. Crown 8vo. 9s.

"Damit schliesst dieses inhaltreiche und nach allen Seiten anregende Buch über Practical Jurisprudence."—König. *Centralblatt für Rechtswissenschaft.*

London: C. J. CLAY & SONS, Cambridge University Press Warehouse, Ave Maria Lane.

PUBLICATIONS OF

A SELECTION OF THE STATE TRIALS. By J. W. WILLIS-BUND, M.A., LL.B., Professor of Constitutional Law and History, University College, London. Crown 8vo. Vols. I. and II. In 3 parts. **Now reduced to 30s.** (*originally published at 46s.*)

"This work is a very useful contribution to that important branch of the constitutional history of England which is concerned with the growth and development of the law of treason, as it may be gathered from trials before the ordinary courts."—*The Academy.*

THE FRAGMENTS OF THE PERPETUAL EDICT OF SALVIUS JULIANUS, collected, arranged, and annotated by BRYAN WALKER, M.A., LL.D., late Law Lecturer of St John's College, and Fellow of Corpus Christi College, Cambridge. Crown 8vo. 6s.

"In the present book we have the fruits of the same kind of thorough and well-ordered study which was brought to bear upon the notes to the Commentaries and the Institutes... Hitherto the Edict has been almost inaccessible to the ordinary English student, and such a student will be interested as well as perhaps surprised to find how abundantly the extant fragments illustrate and clear up points which have attracted his attention in the Commentaries, or the Institutes, or the Digest."—*Law Times.*

BRACTON'S NOTE BOOK. A Collection of Cases decided in the King's Courts during the reign of Henry the Third, annotated by a Lawyer of that time, seemingly by Henry of Bratton. Edited by F. W. MAITLAND of Lincoln's Inn, Barrister at Law, Downing Professor of the Laws of England. 3 vols. Demy 8vo. Buckram, £3. 3s. Net.

AN INTRODUCTION TO THE STUDY OF JUSTINIAN'S DIGEST. Containing an account of its composition and of the Jurists used or referred to therein. By HENRY JOHN ROBY, M.A., formerly Prof. of Jurisprudence, University College, London. Demy 8vo. 9s.

JUSTINIAN'S DIGEST. Lib. VII., Tit. I. De Usufructu, with a Legal and Philological Commentary. By H. J. ROBY, M.A. Demy 8vo. 9s.

Or the Two Parts complete in One Volume. Demy 8vo. 18s.

"Not an obscurity, philological, historical, or legal, has been left unsifted. More informing aid still has been supplied to the student of the Digest at large by a preliminary account, covering nearly 300 pages, of the mode of composition of the Digest, and of the jurists whose decisions and arguments constitute its substance. Nowhere else can a clearer view be obtained of the personal succession by which the tradition of Roman legal science was sustained and developed."—*The Times.*

THE COMMENTARIES OF GAIUS AND RULES OF ULPIAN. With a Translation and Notes, by J. T. ABDY, LL.D., Judge of County Courts, late Regius Professor of Laws in the University of Cambridge, and the late BRYAN WALKER, M.A., LL.D., New Edition by BRYAN WALKER. Crown 8vo. 16s.

"As scholars and as editors Messrs Abdy and Walker have done their work well... For one thing the editors deserve special commendation. They have presented Gaius to the reader with few notes and those merely by way of reference or necessary explanation. Thus the Roman jurist is allowed to speak for himself, and the reader feels that he is really studying Roman law in the original, and not a fanciful representation of it."—*Athenæum.*

THE INSTITUTES OF JUSTINIAN, translated with Notes by J. T. ABDY, LL.D., and the late BRYAN WALKER, M.A., LL.D. Crown 8vo. 16s.

"We welcome here a valuable contribution to the study of jurisprudence. The text of the *Institutes* is occasionally perplexing, even to practised scholars, whose knowledge of classical models does not always avail them in dealing with the technicalities of legal phraseology. Nor can the ordinary dictionaries be expected to furnish all the help that is wanted. This translation will then be of great use. To the ordinary student, whose attention is distracted from the subject-matter by the difficulty of struggling through the language in which it is contained, it will be almost indispensable."—*Spectator.*

"The notes are learned and carefully compiled, and this edition will be found useful to students."—*Law Times.*

London: C. J. CLAY & SONS, Cambridge University Press Warehouse, Ave Maria Lane.

SELECTED TITLES FROM THE DIGEST, annotated by the late B. WALKER, M.A., LL.D. Part I. Mandati vel Contra. Digest XVII. 1. Crown 8vo. 5s.

—— Part II. De Adquirendo rerum dominio and De Adquirenda vel amittenda possessione. Digest XLI. 1 and 11. Crown 8vo. 6s.

—— Part III. De Condictionibus. Digest XII. 1 and 4—7 and Digest XIII. 1—3. Crown 8vo. 6s.

GROTIUS DE JURE BELLI ET PACIS, with the Notes of Barbeyrac and others; accompanied by an abridged Translation of the Text, by W. WHEWELL, D.D. late Master of Trinity College. 3 Vols. Demy 8vo. 12s. The translation separate, 6s.

HISTORICAL WORKS, &c.

THE LIFE AND LETTERS OF THE REVEREND ADAM SEDGWICK, LL.D., F.R.S., Fellow of Trinity College, Cambridge, and Woodwardian Professor of Geology from 1818 to 1873. (Dedicated, by special permission, to Her Majesty the Queen.) By JOHN WILLIS CLARK, M.A., F.S.A., formerly Fellow of Trinity College, and THOMAS McKENNY HUGHES, M.A., Woodwardian Professor of Geology. 2 vols. Demy 8vo.   [*Nearly ready.*

THE DESPATCHES OF EARL GOWER, English Ambassador at the court of Versailles from June 1790 to August 1792, to which are added the Despatches of Mr Lindsay and Mr Munro, and the Diary of Lord Palmerston in France during July and August 1791. Edited by OSCAR BROWNING, M.A. Demy 8vo. 15s.

LIFE AND TIMES OF STEIN, OR GERMANY AND PRUSSIA IN THE NAPOLEONIC AGE, by J. R. SEELEY, M.A., Regius Professor of Modern History in the University of Cambridge, with Portraits and Maps. 3 Vols. Demy 8vo. 30s.

"DR BUSCH's volume has made people think and talk even more than usual of Prince Bismarck, and Professor Seeley's very learned work on Stein will turn attention to an earlier and an almost equally eminent German statesman.... He was one, perhaps the chief, of the illustrious group of strangers who came to the rescue of Prussia in her darkest hour, about the time of the inglorious Peace of Tilsit, and who laboured to put life and order into her dispirited army, her impoverished finances, and her inefficient Civil Service. Englishmen will feel very pardonable pride at seeing one of their countrymen undertake to write the history of a period from the investigation of which even laborious Germans are apt to shrink."—*Times.*

"In a notice of this kind scant justice can be done to a work like the one before us; no short *résumé* can give even the most meagre notion of the contents of these volumes, which contain no page that is superfluous, and none that is uninteresting.... To understand the Germany of to-day one must study the Germany of many yesterdays, and now that study has been made easy by this work, to which no one can hesitate to assign a very high place among those recent histories which have aimed at original research."—*Athenæum.*

THE GROWTH OF ENGLISH INDUSTRY AND COMMERCE DURING THE EARLY AND MIDDLE AGES. By W. CUNNINGHAM, D.D., University Lecturer. Demy 8vo. 16s.

CHRONOLOGICAL TABLES OF GREEK HISTORY. Accompanied by a short narrative of events, with references to the sources of information and extracts from the ancient authorities, by CARL PETER. Translated from the German by G. CHAWNER, M.A., Fellow of King's College, Cambridge. Demy 4to. 10s.

London: C. J. CLAY & SONS, Cambridge University Press Warehouse, Ave Maria Lane.

THE ARCHITECTURAL HISTORY OF THE UNI-
VERSITY OF CAMBRIDGE AND OF THE COLLEGES OF
CAMBRIDGE AND ETON, by the late ROBERT WILLIS, M.A.
F.R.S., Jacksonian Professor in the University of Cambridge. Edited
with large Additions and brought up to the present time by JOHN
WILLIS CLARK, M.A., formerly Fellow of Trinity College, Cambridge. Four Vols. Super Royal 8vo. £6. 6s.

Also a limited Edition of the same, consisting of 120 numbered
Copies only, large paper Quarto; the woodcuts and steel engravings
mounted on India paper; price Twenty-five Guineas net each set.

THE UNIVERSITY OF CAMBRIDGE FROM THE
EARLIEST TIMES TO THE ROYAL INJUNCTIONS OF
1535. by J. B. MULLINGER, M.A., Lecturer on History and Librarian
to St John's College. Part I. Demy 8vo. (734 pp.), 12s.

Part II. From the Royal Injunctions of 1535 to the Accession of
Charles the First. Demy 8vo. 18s.

"He shews in the statutes of the Colleges, the internal organization of the University, its connection with national problems. its studies, its social life. All this he combines in a form which is eminently readable."—PROF. CREIGHTON in *Cont. Review.*

"Mr Mullinger displays an admirable thoroughness in his work. Nothing could be more exhaustive and conscientious than his method: and his style...is picturesque and elevated."—*Times.*

SCHOLAE ACADEMICAE: some Account of the Studies
at the English Universities in the Eighteenth Century. By C.
WORDSWORTH, M.A., Fellow of Peterhouse. Demy 8vo. 10s. 6d.

"Mr Wordsworth has collected a great quantity of minute and curious information about the working of Cambridge institutions in the last century, with an occasional comparison of the corresponding state of things at Oxford.

... To a great extent it is purely a book of reference. and as such it will be of permanent value for the historical knowledge of English education and learning."—*Saturday Review.*

HISTORY OF THE COLLEGE OF ST JOHN THE
EVANGELIST, by THOMAS BAKER, B.D., Ejected Fellow. Edited
by JOHN E. B. MAYOR, M.A. Two Vols. Demy 8vo. 24s.

HISTORY OF NEPĀL, translated by MUNSHĪ SHEW
SHUNKER SINGH and PANDIT SHRĪ GUNĀNAND; edited with an
Introductory Sketch of the Country and People by Dr D. WRIGHT,
late Residency Surgeon at Kāthmāndū, and with facsimiles of native
drawings, and portraits of Sir JUNG BAHĀDUR, the KING OF NEPĀL,
&c. Super-royal 8vo. 10s. 6d.

KINSHIP AND MARRIAGE IN EARLY ARABIA,
by W. ROBERTSON SMITH, M.A., LL.D., Professor of Arabic and
Fellow of Christ's College. Crown 8vo. 7s. 6d.

"It would be superfluous to praise a book so learned and masterly as Professor Robertson Smith's; it is enough to say that no student of

early history can afford to be without *Kinship in Early Arabia.*"—*Nature.*

TRAVELS IN ARABIA DESERTA IN 1876 AND
1877. BY CHARLES M. DOUGHTY, of Gonville and Caius College.
With Illustrations and a Map. 2 vols. Demy 8vo. £3. 3s.

"This is in several respects a remarkable book. It records the ten years' travels of the author throughout Northern Arabia, in the Hejas and Nejd, from Syria to Mecca. No doubt this region has been visited by previous travellers, but none, we venture to think, have done their work with so much thoroughness and with more enthusiasm and love."—*Times.*

"We judge this book to be the most remarkable record of adventure and research which has been published to this generation."—*Spectator.*

"Its value as a storehouse of knowledge simply cannot be exaggerated."—*Saturday Review.*

London: C. J. CLAY & SONS, Cambridge University Press Warehouse,
Ave Maria Lane.

A JOURNEY OF LITERARY AND ARCHÆOLOGICAL RESEARCH IN NEPAL AND NORTHERN INDIA, during the Winter of 1884-5. By CECIL BENDALL, M.A., Professor of Sanskrit in University College, London. Demy 8vo. 10s.

THE CONSTITUTION OF CANADA. By J. E. C. MUNRO, LL.M., Professor of Law and Political Economy at Victoria University, Manchester. Demy 8vo. 10s.

CAMBRIDGE HISTORICAL ESSAYS.

POLITICAL PARTIES IN ATHENS DURING THE PELOPONNESIAN WAR, by L. WHIBLEY, M.A., Fellow of Pembroke College, Cambridge. (Prince Consort Dissertation, 1888.) *Second Edition.* Crown 8vo. 2s. 6d.

POPE GREGORY THE GREAT AND HIS RELATIONS WITH GAUL, by F. W. KELLETT, M.A., Sidney Sussex College. (Prince Consort Dissertation, 1888.) Crown 8vo. 2s. 6d.

THE CONSTITUTIONAL EXPERIMENTS OF THE COMMONWEALTH, being the Thirlwall Prize Essay for 1889, by E. JENKS, B.A., LL.B. Crown 8vo. [*In the Press.*

MISCELLANEOUS.

THE LITERARY REMAINS OF ALBRECHT DÜRER, by W. M. CONWAY. With Transcripts from the British Museum MSS., and Notes by LINA ECKENSTEIN. Royal 8vo. 21s. (*The Edition is limited to 500 copies.*)

A LATIN-ENGLISH DICTIONARY. Printed from the (Incomplete) MS. of the late T. H. KEY, M.A., F.R.S. Cr. 4to. 31s. 6d.

THE COLLECTED PAPERS OF HENRY BRADSHAW, including his Memoranda and Communications read before the Cambridge Antiquarian Society. *With 13 fac-similes.* Edited by F. J. H. JENKINSON, M.A., Fellow of Trinity College. Demy 8vo. 16s.

THE LATIN HEPTATEUCH. Published piecemeal by the French printer WILLIAM MOREL (1560) and the French Benedictines E. MARTÈNE (1733) and J. B. PITRA (1852—88). Critically reviewed by JOHN E. B. MAYOR, M.A., Professor of Latin in the University of Cambridge. Demy 8vo. 10s. 6d.

A CATALOGUE OF ANCIENT MARBLES IN GREAT BRITAIN, by Prof. ADOLF MICHAELIS. Translated by C. A. M. FENNELL, Litt. D. Royal 8vo. Roxburgh (Morocco back), £2. 2s.

"The book is beautifully executed, and with its few handsome plates, and excellent indexes, does much credit to the Cambridge Press. All lovers of true art and of good work should be grateful to the Syndics of the University Press for the liberal facilities afforded by them towards the production of this important volume by Professor Michaelis."—*Saturday Review.*

London: C. J. CLAY & SONS, Cambridge University Press Warehouse, Ave Maria Lane.

CONTRIBUTIONS TO THE TEXTUAL CRITICISM OF THE DIVINA COMMEDIA. Including the complete collation throughout the *Inferno* of all the MSS. at Oxford and Cambridge. By the Rev. EDWARD MOORE, D.D. Demy 8vo. 21*s.*

RHODES IN ANCIENT TIMES. By CECIL TORR, M.A. With six plates. Demy 8vo. 10*s.* 6*d.*

RHODES IN MODERN TIMES. By the same Author. With three plates. Demy 8vo. 8*s.*

THE WOODCUTTERS OF THE NETHERLANDS during the last quarter of the Fifteenth Century. In 3 parts. I. History of the Woodcutters. II. Catalogue of their Woodcuts. III. List of Books containing Woodcuts. By W. M. CONWAY. Demy 8vo. 10*s.* 6*d.*

THE LITERATURE OF THE FRENCH RENAISSANCE. An Introductory Essay. By A. A. TILLEY, M.A. Cr. 8vo. 6*s.*

FROM SHAKESPEARE TO POPE: an Inquiry into the causes and phenomena of the rise of Classical Poetry in England. By EDMUND GOSSE, M.A. Crown 8vo. 6*s.*

CHAPTERS ON ENGLISH METRE. By Rev. JOSEPH B. MAYOR, M.A. Demy 8vo. 7*s.* 6*d.*

A GRAMMAR OF THE IRISH LANGUAGE. By Prof. WINDISCH. Translated by Dr NORMAN MOORE. Crown 8vo. 7*s.* 6*d*

LECTURES ON TEACHING, delivered in the University of Cambridge in the Lent Term, 1880. By J. G. FITCH, M.A., LL.D. Her Majesty's Inspector of Training Colleges. Cr. 8vo. New Edit. 5*s.*

"Mr Fitch's book covers so wide a field and touches on so many burning questions that we must be content to recommend it as the best existing *vade mecum* for the teacher."—*Pall Mall Gazette.*

LECTURES ON THE SCIENCE OF EDUCATION. By FRANCIS WARNER, M.D., F.R.C.P. [*In the Press.*

OCCASIONAL ADDRESSES ON EDUCATIONAL SUBJECTS. By S. S. LAURIE, M.A., LL.D. Crown 8vo. 5*s.*

A MANUAL OF CURSIVE SHORTHAND. By H. L. CALLENDAR, M.A., Fellow of Trinity College. Ex. Fcap. 8vo. 2*s.*

A SYSTEM OF PHONETIC SPELLING ADAPTED TO ENGLISH. By H. L. CALLENDAR, M.A. Ex. Fcap. 8vo. 6*d.*

A PRIMER OF CURSIVE SHORTHAND. By H. L. CALLENDAR, M.A. Ex. Fcap. 8vo. 6*d.*

READING PRACTICE IN CURSIVE SHORTHAND. Easy Extracts for Beginners. The Gospel according to St Mark, (First half). The Vicar of Wakefield. Chaps. I.—V. Alice in Wonderland. Chap. VII. 3*d.* each.

For other books on Education, see Pitt Press Series, p. 39.

London: C. J. CLAY & SONS, Cambridge University Press Warehouse, Ave Maria Lane.

STUDIES IN THE LITERARY RELATIONS OF ENGLAND WITH GERMANY IN THE SIXTEENTH CENTURY. By C. H. HERFORD, M.A. Crown 8vo. 9s.

ADMISSIONS TO GONVILLE AND CAIUS COLLEGE in the University of Cambridge March 1558—9 to Jan. 1678—9 Edited by J. VENN, Sc.D., and S. C. VENN. Demy 8vo. 10s.

ECCLESIAE LONDINO—BATAVAE ARCHIVVM. TOMVS PRIMVS. ABRAHAMI ORTELII et virorum eruditorum ad eundem et ad JACOBVM COLIVM ORTELIANVM Epistulae, 1524—1628. TOMVS SECVNDVS. EPISTVLAE ET TRACTATVS cum Reformationis tum Ecclesiae Londino-Batavae Historiam Illustrantes 1544—1622. Ex autographis mandante Ecclesia Londino-Batava edidit JOANNES HENRICVS HESSELS. Demy 4to. Each volume, separately, £3. 10s. Taken together £5. 5s. *Net.*

CATALOGUE OF THE HEBREW MANUSCRIPTS preserved in the University Library, Cambridge. By Dr S. M. SCHILLER-SZINESSY. Volume I. containing Section I. *The Holy Scriptures;* Section II. *Commentaries on the Bible.* Demy 8vo. 9s.

A CATALOGUE OF THE MANUSCRIPTS preserved in the Library of the University of Cambridge. Demy 8vo. 5 Vols. 10s. each. INDEX TO THE CATALOGUE. Demy 8vo. 10s.

A CATALOGUE OF ADVERSARIA and printed books preserved in the Library of the University of Cambridge. 3s. 6d.

THE ILLUMINATED MANUSCRIPTS IN THE LIbrary of the Fitzwilliam Museum, Catalogued with Descriptions, and an Introduction, by W. G. SEARLE, M.A. Demy 8vo. 7s. 6d.

A CHRONOLOGICAL LIST OF THE GRACES, Documents, and other Papers in the University Registry which concern the University Library. Demy 8vo. 2s. 6d.

CATALOGUS BIBLIOTHECÆ BURCKHARDTIANÆ. Demy 4to. 5s.

GRADUATI CANTABRIGIENSES: SIVE CATALOGUS exhibens nomina eorum quos gradu quocunque ornavit Academia Cantabrigiensis (1800—1884). Cura H. R. LUARD S. T. P. Demy 8vo. 12s. 6d.

STATUTES OF THE UNIVERSITY OF CAMBRIDGE and for the Colleges therein, made, published and approved (1878—1882) under the Universities of Oxford and Cambridge Act, 1877. With an Appendix. Demy 8vo. 16s.

STATUTES OF THE UNIVERSITY OF CAMBRIDGE. With Acts of Parliament relating to the University. 8vo. 3s. 6d.

ORDINANCES OF THE UNIVERSITY OF CAMBRIDGE. Demy 8vo., cloth. 7s. 6d.

TRUSTS, STATUTES AND DIRECTIONS affecting (1) The Professorships of the University. (2) The Scholarships and Prizes. (3) Other Gifts and Endowments. Demy 8vo. 5s.

COMPENDIUM of UNIVERSITY REGULATIONS. 6d.

London: C. J. CLAY & SONS, Cambridge University Press Warehouse, Ave Maria Lane.

The Cambridge Bible for Schools and Colleges.

GENERAL EDITOR: THE VERY REVEREND J. J. S. PEROWNE, D.D., DEAN OF PETERBOROUGH.

"It is difficult to commend too highly this excellent series."—*Guardian.*

"The modesty of the general title of this series has, we believe, led many to misunderstand its character and underrate its value. The books are well suited for study in the upper forms of our best schools, but not the less are they adapted to the wants of all Bible students who are not specialists. We doubt, indeed, whether any of the numerous popular commentaries recently issued in this country will be found more serviceable for general use."—*Academy.*

"One of the most popular and useful literary enterprises of the nineteenth century."—*Baptist Magazine.*

"Of great value. The whole series of comments for schools is highly esteemed by students capable of forming a judgment. The books are scholarly without being pretentious: information is so given as to be easily understood."—*Sword and Trowel.*

The Very Reverend J. J. S. PEROWNE, D.D., Dean of Peterborough, has undertaken the general editorial supervision of the work, assisted by a staff of eminent coadjutors. Some of the books have been already edited or undertaken by the following gentlemen:

Rev. A. CARR, M.A., *late Assistant Master at Wellington College.*
Rev. T. K. CHEYNE, M.A., D.D., *Canon of Rochester.*
Rev. S. COX, *Nottingham.*
Rev. A. B. DAVIDSON, D.D., *Professor of Hebrew, Edinburgh.*
The Ven. F. W. FARRAR, D.D., *Archdeacon of Westminster.*
Rev. C. D. GINSBURG, LL.D.
Rev. A. E. HUMPHREYS, M.A., *late Fellow of Trinity College, Cambridge.*
Rev. A. F. KIRKPATRICK, B.D., *Fellow of Trinity College, Regius Professor of Hebrew.*
Rev. J. J. LIAS, M.A., *late Professor at St David's College, Lampeter.*
Rev. J. R. LUMBY, D.D., *Norrisian Professor of Divinity.*
Rev. G. F. MACLEAR, D.D., *Warden of St Augustine's College, Canterbury.*
Rev. H. C. G. MOULE, M.A., *late Fellow of Trinity College, Principal of Ridley Hall, Cambridge.*
Rev. E. H. PEROWNE, D.D., *Master of Corpus Christi College, Cambridge.*
The Ven. T. T. PEROWNE, B.D., *Archdeacon of Norwich.*
Rev. A. PLUMMER, M.A., D.D., *Master of University College, Durham.*
The Very Rev. E. H. PLUMPTRE, D.D., *Dean of Wells.*
Rev. H. E. RYLE, M.A., *Hulsean Professor of Divinity.*
Rev. W. SIMCOX, M.A., *late Rector of Weyhill, Hants.*
W. ROBERTSON SMITH, M.A., *Professor of Arabic and Fellow of Christ's College.*
The Very Rev. H. D. M. SPENCE, M.A., *Dean of Gloucester.*
Rev. A. W. STREANE, M.A., *Fellow of Corpus Christi College, Cambridge.*

London: C. J. CLAY & SONS, Cambridge University Press Warehouse, Ave Maria Lane.

THE CAMBRIDGE BIBLE FOR SCHOOLS & COLLEGES. *Cont.*

Now Ready. Cloth, Extra Fcap. 8vo.

THE BOOK OF JOSHUA. By the Rev. G. F. MACLEAR, D.D. With 2 Maps. 2s. 6d.

THE BOOK OF JUDGES. By the Rev. J. J. LIAS, M.A. With Map. 3s. 6d.

THE FIRST BOOK OF SAMUEL. By the Rev. Professor KIRKPATRICK, B.D. With Map. 3s. 6d.

THE SECOND BOOK OF SAMUEL. By the Rev. Professor KIRKPATRICK, B.D. With 2 Maps. 3s. 6d.

THE FIRST BOOK OF KINGS. By Rev. Prof. LUMBY, D.D. 3s. 6d.

THE SECOND BOOK OF KINGS. By the same Editor. 3s. 6d.

THE BOOK OF JOB. By the Rev. A. B. DAVIDSON, D.D. 5s.

THE BOOK OF ECCLESIASTES. By the Very Rev. E. H. PLUMPTRE, D.D. 5s.

THE BOOK OF JEREMIAH. By the Rev. A. W. STREANE, M.A. With Map. 4s. 6d.

THE BOOK OF HOSEA. By Rev. T. K. CHEYNE, M.A., D.D. 3s.

THE BOOKS OF OBADIAH AND JONAH. By Archdeacon PEROWNE. 2s. 6d.

THE BOOK OF MICAH. By Rev. T. K. CHEYNE, D.D. 1s. 6d.

THE BOOKS OF HAGGAI AND ZECHARIAH. By Archdeacon PEROWNE. 3s.

THE GOSPEL ACCORDING TO ST MATTHEW. By the Rev. A. CARR, M.A. With 2 Maps. 2s. 6d.

THE GOSPEL ACCORDING TO ST MARK. By the Rev. G. F. MACLEAR, D.D. With 4 Maps. 2s. 6d.

THE GOSPEL ACCORDING TO ST LUKE. By Archdeacon F. W. FARRAR. With 4 Maps. 4s. 6d.

THE GOSPEL ACCORDING TO ST JOHN. By the Rev. A. PLUMMER, M.A., D.D. With 4 Maps. 4s. 6d.

THE ACTS OF THE APOSTLES. By the Rev. Professor LUMBY, D.D. With 4 Maps. 4s. 6d.

THE EPISTLE TO THE ROMANS. By the Rev. H. C. G. MOULE, M.A. 3s. 6d.

THE FIRST EPISTLE TO THE CORINTHIANS. By the Rev. J. J. LIAS, M.A. With a Map and Plan. 2s.

THE SECOND EPISTLE TO THE CORINTHIANS. By the Rev. J. J. LIAS, M.A. 2s.

THE EPISTLE TO THE EPHESIANS. By the Rev. H. C. G. MOULE, M.A. 2s. 6d.

THE EPISTLE TO THE PHILIPPIANS. By the Rev. H. C. G. MOULE, M.A. 2s. 6d.

London: C. J. CLAY & SONS, Cambridge University Press Warehouse, Ave Maria Lane.

THE CAMBRIDGE BIBLE FOR SCHOOLS & COLLEGES. *Cont.*

THE EPISTLE TO THE HEBREWS. By Arch. FARRAR. 3s. 6d.

THE GENERAL EPISTLE OF ST JAMES. By the Very Rev. E. H. PLUMPTRE, D.D. 1s. 6d.

THE EPISTLES OF ST PETER AND ST JUDE. By the same Editor. 2s. 6d.

THE EPISTLES OF ST JOHN. By the Rev. A. PLUMMER, M.A., D.D. 3s. 6d.

Preparing.

THE BOOK OF GENESIS. By the Very Rev. the DEAN OF PETERBOROUGH.

THE BOOKS OF EXODUS, NUMBERS AND DEUTERONOMY. By the Rev. C. D. GINSBURG, LL.D.

THE BOOKS OF EZRA AND NEHEMIAH. By the Rev. Prof. RYLE, M.A.

THE BOOK OF PSALMS. By the Rev. Prof. KIRKPATRICK, B.D.

THE BOOK OF ISAIAH. By Prof. W. ROBERTSON SMITH, M.A.

THE BOOK OF EZEKIEL. By the Rev. A. B. DAVIDSON, D.D.

THE BOOK OF MALACHI. By Archdeacon PEROWNE.

THE EPISTLE TO THE GALATIANS. By the Rev. E. H. PEROWNE, D.D.

THE EPISTLES TO THE COLOSSIANS AND PHILEMON. By the Rev. H. C. G. MOULE, M.A.

THE EPISTLES TO TIMOTHY AND TITUS. By the Rev. A. E. HUMPHREYS, M.A.

THE BOOK OF REVELATION. By the Rev. W. SIMCOX, M.A.

The Smaller Cambridge Bible for Schools.

The Smaller Cambridge Bible for Schools *will form an entirely new series of commentaries on some selected books of the Bible. It is expected that they will be prepared for the most part by the Editors of the larger series (The Cambridge Bible for Schools and Colleges). The volumes will be issued at a low price, and will be suitable to the requirements of preparatory and elementary schools.*

Now ready. Price 1s. each.

THE FIRST AND SECOND BOOKS OF SAMUEL. By Rev. Prof. KIRKPATRICK, B.D.

THE GOSPEL ACCORDING TO ST MATTHEW. By Rev. A. CARR, M.A.

THE GOSPEL ACCORDING TO ST MARK. By Rev. G. F. MACLEAR, D.D.

Nearly ready.

THE GOSPEL ACCORDING TO ST LUKE. By ARCHDEACON FARRAR, D.D.

London: C. J. CLAY & SONS, Cambridge University Press Warehouse Ave Maria Lane.

The Cambridge Greek Testament for Schools and Colleges,

with a Revised Text, based on the most recent critical authorities, and English Notes, prepared under the direction of the General Editor, THE VERY REVEREND J. J. S. PEROWNE, D.D.

Now Ready.

THE GOSPEL ACCORDING TO ST MATTHEW. By the Rev. A. CARR, M.A. With 4 Maps. 4s. 6d.

"Copious illustrations, gathered from a great variety of sources, make his notes a very valuable aid to the student. They are indeed remarkably interesting, while all explanations on meanings, applications, and the like are distinguished by their lucidity and good sense."—*Pall Mall Gazette.*

THE GOSPEL ACCORDING TO ST MARK. By the Rev. G. F. MACLEAR, D.D. With 3 Maps. 4s. 6d.

"The Cambridge Greek Testament, of which Dr Maclear's edition of the Gospel according to St Mark is a volume, certainly supplies a want. Without pretending to compete with the leading commentaries, or to embody very much original research, it forms a most satisfactory introduction to the study of the New Testament in the original... Dr Maclear's introduction contains all that is known of St Mark's life, an account of the circumstances in which the Gospel was composed, an excellent sketch of the special characteristics of this Gospel; an analysis, and a chapter on the text of the New Testament generally... The work is completed by three good maps."—*Saturday Review.*

THE GOSPEL ACCORDING TO ST LUKE. By Archdeacon FARRAR. With 4 Maps. 6s.

THE GOSPEL ACCORDING TO ST JOHN. By the Rev. A. PLUMMER, M.A., D.D. With 4 Maps. 6s.

"A valuable addition has also been made to 'The Cambridge Greek Testament for Schools,' Dr Plummer's notes on 'the Gospel according to St John' are scholarly, concise, and instructive, and embody the results of much thought and wide reading."—*Expositor.*

THE ACTS OF THE APOSTLES. By the Rev. Prof. LUMBY, D.D., with 4 Maps. 6s.

THE FIRST EPISTLE TO THE CORINTHIANS. By the Rev. J. J. LIAS, M.A. 3s.

THE SECOND EPISTLE TO THE CORINTHIANS. By the Rev. J. J. LIAS, M.A. [*Preparing.*

THE EPISTLE TO THE HEBREWS. By Arch. FARRAR, D.D. 3s. 6d.

THE EPISTLES OF ST JOHN. By the Rev. A. PLUMMER, M.A., D.D. 4s.

London: C. J. CLAY & SONS, Cambridge University Press Warehouse, Ave Maria Lane.

THE PITT PRESS SERIES.

[*Copies of the Pitt Press Series may generally be obtained bound in two parts for Class use, the text and notes in separate volumes.*]

I. GREEK.

ARISTOPHANES—AVES—PLUTUS—RANAE. With English Notes and Introduction by W. C. GREEN, M.A., late Assistant Master at Rugby School. 3s. 6d. each.

EURIPIDES. HERACLEIDÆ. With Introduction and Explanatory Notes by E. A. BECK, M.A., Fellow of Trinity Hall. 3s. 6d.

EURIPIDES. HERCULES FURENS. With Introductions, Notes and Analysis. By A. GRAY, M.A., Fellow of Jesus College, and J. T. HUTCHINSON, M.A., Christ's College. New Edition. 2s.

EURIPIDES. HIPPOLYTUS. By W. S. HADLEY, M.A. Fellow of Pembroke College. 2s.

EURIPIDES. IPHIGENEIA IN AULIS. By C. E. S. HEADLAM, B.A., Fellow of Trinity Hall. 2s. 6d.

HERODOTUS, BOOK V. Edited with Notes, Introduction and Maps by E. S. SHUCKBURGH, M.A., late Fellow of Emmanuel College. 3s.

HERODOTUS, BOOK VI. By the same Editor. 4s.

HERODOTUS, BOOK VIII., CHAPS. 1—90. By the same Editor. 3s. 6d.
"We could not wish for a better introduction to Herodotus."—*Journal of Education.*

HERODOTUS, BOOK IX., CHAPS. 1—89. By the same Editor. 3s. 6d.

HOMER—ODYSSEY, BOOKS IX. X. With Introduction, Notes and Appendices. By G. M. EDWARDS, M.A., Fellow and Classical Lecturer of Sidney Sussex College. 2s. 6d. each.

HOMER—ODYSSEY, BOOK XXI. By the same Editor. 2s.

LUCIANI SOMNIUM CHARON PISCATOR ET DE LUCTU, with English Notes by W. E. HEITLAND, M.A., Fellow of St John's College, Cambridge. New Edition, with Appendix. 3s. 6d.

PLATONIS APOLOGIA SOCRATIS. With Introduction, Notes and Appendices by J. ADAM, M.A., Fellow and Classical Lecturer of Emmanuel College. 3s. 6d.
"A worthy representative of English Scholarship."—*Classical Review.*

—— CRITO. With Introduction, Notes and Appendix. By the same Editor. 2s. 6d.
"Mr Adam, already known as the author of a careful and scholarly edition of the Apology of Plato, will, we think, add to his reputation by his work upon the Crito."—*Academy.*
"A scholarly edition of a dialogue which has never been really well edited in English."—*Guardian.*

—— EUTHYPHRO. By the same Editor. [*In the Press.*

London: C. J. CLAY & SONS, Cambridge University Press Warehouse, Ave Maria Lane.

PLUTARCH. LIVES OF THE GRACCHI. With Introduction, Notes and Lexicon by Rev. HUBERT A. HOLDEN, M.A., LL.D. 6*s*.

PLUTARCH. LIFE OF NICIAS. With Introduction and Notes. By Rev. HUBERT A. HOLDEN, M.A., LL.D. 5*s*.
"This edition is as careful and thorough as Dr Holden's work always is."—*Spectator.*

PLUTARCH. LIFE OF SULLA. With Introduction, Notes, and Lexicon. By the Rev. HUBERT A. HOLDEN, M.A., LL.D. 6*s*.

PLUTARCH. LIFE OF TIMOLEON. With Introduction, Notes and Lexicon. By Rev. HUBERT A. HOLDEN, M.A., LL.D. 6*s*.

SOPHOCLES.—OEDIPUS TYRANNUS. School Edition, with Introduction and Commentary, by R. C. JEBB, Litt. D., LL.D., Regius Professor of Greek in the University of Cambridge. 4*s*. 6*d*.

THUCYDIDES. BOOK VII. With Notes and Introduction By H. R. TOTTENHAM, M.A., Fellow of St John's College. [*In the Press.*

XENOPHON.—AGESILAUS. The Text revised with Critical and Explanatory Notes, Introduction, Analysis, and Indices. By H. HAILSTONE, M.A., late Scholar of Peterhouse. 2*s*. 6*d*.

XENOPHON.—ANABASIS, BOOKS I. III. IV. and V. With a Map and English Notes by ALFRED PRETOR, M.A., Fellow of St Catharine's College, Cambridge. 2*s*. each.
"Mr Pretor's 'Anabasis of Xenophon, Book IV.' displays a union of accurate Cambridge scholarship, with experience of what is required by learners gained in examining middle-class schools. The text is large and clearly printed, and the notes explain all difficulties. . . . Mr Pretor's notes seem to be all that could be wished as regards grammar, geography, and other matters."—*The Academy.*

— — **BOOKS II. VI. and VII.** By the same. 2*s*. 6*d*. each.
"Had we to introduce a young Greek scholar to Xenophon, we should esteem ourselves fortunate in having Pretor's text-book as our chart and guide."—*Contemporary Review.*

XENOPHON.—ANABASIS. By A. PRETOR, M.A., Text and Notes, complete in two Volumes. 7*s*. 6*d*.

XENOPHON.—CYROPAEDEIA. BOOKS I. II. With Introduction, Notes and Map. By Rev. H. A. HOLDEN, M.A., LL.D. 2 vols. Vol. I. Text. Vol. II. Notes. 6*s*.
"The work is worthy of the editor's well-earned reputation for scholarship and industry."—*Athenæum.*

— — **BOOKS III., IV., V.** By the same Editor. 5*s*.
"Dr Holden's Commentary is equally good in history and in scholarship."—*Saturday Review.*

II. LATIN.

BEDA'S ECCLESIASTICAL HISTORY, BOOKS III., IV., the Text from the very ancient MS. in the Cambridge University Library, collated with six other MSS. Edited, with a life from the German of EBERT, and with Notes, &c. by J. E. B. MAYOR, M.A., Professor of Latin, and J. R. LUMBY, D.D., Norrisian Professor of Divinity. Revised edition. 7*s*. 6*d*. BOOKS I. and II. *In the Press.*
"In Bede's works Englishmen can go back to *origines* of their history, unequalled for form and matter by any modern European nation. Prof. Mayor has done good service in rendering a part of Bede's greatest work accessible to those who can read Latin with ease. He has adorned this edition of the third and fourth books of the 'Ecclesiastical History' with that amazing erudition for which he is unrivalled among Englishmen and rarely equalled by Germans. And however interesting and valuable the text may be, we can certainly apply to his notes the expression, *La sauce vaut mieux que le poisson*. They are literally crammed with interesting information about early English life. For though ecclesiastical in name, Bede's history treats of all parts of the national life, since the Church had points of contact with all."—*Examiner.*

London: C. J. CLAY & SONS, Cambridge University Press Warehouse, Ave Maria Lane.

CAESAR. DE BELLO GALLICO COMMENT. I. With Maps and English Notes by A. G. PESKETT, M.A., Fellow of Magdalene College, Cambridge. 1s. 6d.

CAESAR. DE BELLO GALLICO COMMENT. II. III. By the same Editor. 2s.

CAESAR. DE BELLO GALLICO COMMENT. I. II. III. by the same Editor. 3s.

CAESAR. DE BELLO GALLICO COMMENT. IV. AND V. and COMMENT. VII. by the same Editor. 2s. each.

CAESAR. DE BELLO GALLICO COMMENT. VI. AND COMMENT. VIII. by the same Editor. 1s. 6d. each.

CICERO. ACTIO PRIMA IN C. VERREM. With Introduction and Notes. By H. COWIE, M.A., Fellow of St John's College, Cambridge. 1s. 6d.

CICERO. DE AMICITIA. Edited by J. S. REID, Litt.D., Fellow and Tutor of Gonville and Caius College. New Edition. 3s. 6d.

"Mr Reid has decidedly attained his aim, namely, 'a thorough examination of the Latinity of the dialogue.'..... The revision of the text is most valuable, and comprehends sundry acute corrections. ... This volume, like Mr Reid's other editions, is a solid gain to the scholarship of the country."—*Athenæum*.

"A more distinct gain to scholarship is Mr Reid's able and thorough edition of the *De Amicitiâ* of Cicero, a work of which, whether we regard the exhaustive introduction or the instructive and most suggestive commentary, it would be difficult to speak too highly. . . . When we come to the commentary, we are only amazed by its fulness in proportion to its bulk. Nothing is overlooked which can tend to enlarge the learner's general knowledge of Ciceronian Latin or to elucidate the text."—*Saturday Review*.

CICERO. DE SENECTUTE. Edited by J. S. REID, Litt.D. Revised Edition. 3s. 6d.

"The notes are excellent and scholarlike, adapted for the upper forms of public schools, and likely to be useful even to more advanced students."—*Guardian*.

CICERO. DIVINATIO IN Q. CAECILIUM ET ACTIO PRIMA IN C. VERREM. With Introduction and Notes by W. E. HEITLAND, M.A., and HERBERT COWIE, M.A., Fellows of St John's College, Cambridge. 3s.

CICERO. PHILIPPICA SECUNDA. With Introduction and Notes by A. G. PESKETT, M.A., Fellow of Magdalene College. 3s. 6d.

CICERO. PRO ARCHIA POETA. Edited by J. S. REID, Litt.D. Revised Edition. 2s.

"It is an admirable specimen of careful editing. An Introduction tells us everything we could wish to know about Archias, about Cicero's connexion with him, about the merits of the trial, and the genuineness of the speech. The text is well and carefully printed. The notes are clear and scholar-like. . . . No boy can master this little volume without feeling that he has advanced a long step in scholarship."—*The Academy*.

CICERO. PRO BALBO. Edited by J. S. REID, Litt.D. 1s. 6d.

"We are bound to recognize the pains devoted in the annotation of these two orations to the minute and thorough study of their Latinity, both in the ordinary notes and in the textual appendices."—*Saturday Review*.

London: C. J. CLAY & SONS, Cambridge University Press Warehouse,
Ave Maria Lane.

CICERO. PRO MILONE, with a Translation of Asconius' Introduction, Marginal Analysis and English Notes. Edited by the Rev. JOHN SMYTH PURTON, B.D., late President and Tutor of St Catharine's College. 2s. 6d.
"The editorial work is excellently done."—*The Academy.*

CICERO. PRO MURENA. With English Introduction and Notes. By W. E. HEITLAND, M.A., Fellow and Classical Lecturer of St John's College, Cambridge. **Second Edition, carefully revised.** 3s.
"Those students are to be deemed fortunate who have to read Cicero's lively and brilliant oration for L. Murena with Mr Heitland's handy edition, which may be pronounced 'four-square' in point of equipment, and which has, not without good reason, attained the honours of a second edition."—*Saturday Review.*

CICERO. PRO PLANCIO. Edited by H. A. HOLDEN, LL.D., Examiner in Greek to the University of London. Second Edition. 4s. 6d.

CICERO. PRO SULLA. Edited by J. S. REID, Litt.D. 3s. 6d.
"Mr Reid is so well known to scholars as a commentator on Cicero that a new work from him scarcely needs any commendation of ours. His edition of the speech *Pro Sulla* is fully equal in merit to the volumes which he has already published... It would be difficult to speak too highly of the notes. There could be no better way of gaining an insight into the characteristics of Cicero's style and the Latinity of his period than by making a careful study of this speech with the aid of Mr Reid's commentary... Mr Reid's intimate knowledge of the minutest details of scholarship enables him to detect and explain the slightest points of distinction between the usages of different authors and different periods... The notes are followed by a valuable appendix on the text, and another on points of orthography; an excellent index brings the work to a close."—*Saturday Review.*

CICERO. SOMNIUM SCIPIONIS. With Introduction and Notes. By W. D. PEARMAN, M.A., Head Master of Potsdam School, Jamaica. 2s.

HORACE. EPISTLES, BOOK I. With Notes and Introduction by E. S. SHUCKBURGH, M.A. 2s. 6d.

LIVY. BOOK IV. With Notes and Introduction, by Rev. H. M. STEPHENSON, M.A. 2s. 6d.

LIVY. BOOK V. With Notes and Introduction by L. WHIBLEY, M.A., Fellow of Pembroke College. 2s. 6d., [*Shortly.*

LIVY. BOOKS XXI., XXII. With Notes, Introduction and Maps. By M. S. DIMSDALE, M.A., Fellow of King's College. 2s. 6d. each.

LUCAN. PHARSALIA LIBER PRIMUS. Edited with English Introduction and Notes by W. E. HEITLAND, M.A. and C. E. HASKINS, M.A., Fellows and Lecturers of St John's College, Cambridge. 1s. 6d.
"A careful and scholarlike production."—*Times.*
"In nice parallels of Lucan from Latin poets and from Shakspeare, Mr Haskins and Mr Heitland deserve praise."—*Saturday Review.*

LUCRETIUS. BOOK V. With Notes and Introduction by J. D. DUFF, M.A., Fellow of Trinity College. 2s.

OVID. FASTI. LIBER VI. With a Plan of Rome and Notes by A. SIDGWICK, M.A., Tutor of Corpus Christi College, Oxford. 1s. 6d.
"Mr Sidgwick's editing of the Sixth Book of Ovid's *Fasti* furnishes a careful and serviceable volume for average students. It eschews 'construes' which supersede the use of the dictionary, but gives full explanation of grammatical usages and historical and mythical allusions, besides illustrating peculiarities of style, true and false derivations, and the more remarkable variations of the text."—*Saturday Review.*

London: C. J. CLAY & SONS, *Cambridge University Press Warehouse,*
Ave Maria Lane.

QUINTUS CURTIUS. A Portion of the History.
(ALEXANDER IN INDIA.) By W. E. HEITLAND, M.A., Fellow and Lecturer of St John's College, Cambridge, and T. E. RAVEN, B.A., Assistant Master in Sherborne School. 3s. 6d.

"Equally commendable as a genuine addition to the existing stock of school-books is *Alexander in India*, a compilation from the eighth and ninth books of Q. Curtius, edited for the Pitt Press by Messrs Heitland and Raven.... The work of Curtius has merits of its own, which, in former generations, made it a favourite with English scholars, and which still make it a popular text-book in Continental schools...... The reputation of Mr Heitland is a sufficient guarantee for the scholarship of the notes, which are ample without being excessive, and the book is well furnished with all that is needful in the nature of maps, indices, and appendices." —*Academy*.

VERGIL. AENEID. LIBRI I., II., III., IV., V., VI., VII. VIII., IX., X., XI., XII. Edited with Notes by A. SIDGWICK, M.A., Tutor of Corpus Christi College, Oxford. 1s. 6d. each.

"Mr Sidgwick's Vergil is......we believe, the best school edition of the poet."—*Guardian*.
"Mr Arthur Sidgwick's 'Vergil, Aeneid, Book XII.' is worthy of his reputation, and is distinguished by the same acuteness and accuracy of knowledge, appreciation of a boy's difficulties and ingenuity and resource in meeting them, which we have on other occasions had reason to praise in these pages."—*The Academy*.
"As masterly in its clearly divided preface and appendices as in the sound and independent character of its annotations.... There is a great deal more in the notes than mere compilation and suggestion.... No difficulty is left unnoticed or unhandled."—*Saturday Review*.

VERGIL. AENEID. LIBRI IX. X. in one volume. 3s.

VERGIL. AENEID. LIBRI X., XI., XII. in one volume. 3s. 6d.

VERGIL. BUCOLICS. With Introduction and Notes, by the same Editor. 1s. 6d.

VERGIL. GEORGICS. LIBRI I. II. By the same Editor. 2s. LIBRI III. IV. 2s.

"This volume, which completes the Pitt Press edition of Virgil's Georgics, is distinguished by the same admirable judgment and first-rate scholarship as are conspicuous in the former volume and in the "Aeneid" by the same talented editor."—*Athenæum*.

VERGIL. The Complete Works, edited with Notes, by A. SIDGWICK, M.A., Two vols. Vol. I. containing the Text. Vol. II. The Notes.   [*Nearly ready*.

III. FRENCH.

CORNEILLE. LA SUITE DU MENTEUR. A Comedy in Five Acts. Edited with Fontenelle's Memoir of the Author, Voltaire's Critical Remarks, and Notes Philological and Historical. By the late GUSTAVE MASSON. 2s.

DE BONNECHOSE. LAZARE HOCHE. With Four Maps, Introduction and Commentary, by C. COLBECK, M.A., late Fellow of Trinity College, Cambridge. Revised Edition. 2s.

D'HARLEVILLE. LE VIEUX CÉLIBATAIRE. A Comedy. With a Biographical Memoir, and Grammatical, Literary and Historical Notes. By GUSTAVE MASSON. 2s.

London: C. J. CLAY & SONS, Cambridge University Press Warehouse, Ave Maria Lane.

DE LAMARTINE. JEANNE D'ARC. With a Map
and Notes Historical and Philological and a Vocabulary by Rev. A. C.
CLAPIN, M.A., St John's College, Cambridge, and Bachelier-ès-Lettres of
the University of France. Enlarged Edition. 2*s*.

DE VIGNY. LA CANNE DE JONC. Edited with Notes
by Rev. H. A. BULL, M.A. 2*s*.

ERCKMANN-CHATRIAN. LA GUERRE. With Map,
Introduction and Commentary by the Rev. A. C. CLAPIN, M.A. 3*s*.

LA BARONNE DE STAËL-HOLSTEIN. LE DIRECTOIRE. (Considérations sur la Révolution Française. Troisième et quatrième parties.) With a Critical Notice of the Author, a Chronological Table, and Notes Historical and Philological, by G. MASSON, B.A., and G. W. PROTHERO, M.A. Revised and enlarged Edition. 2*s*.

"Prussia under Frederick the Great, and France under the Directory, bring us face to face respectively with periods of history which it is right should be known thoroughly, and which are well treated in the Pitt Press volumes. The latter in particular, an extract from the world-known work of Madame de Staël on the French Revolution, is beyond all praise for the excellence both of its style and of its matter."—*Times*.

LA BARONNE DE STAËL-HOLSTEIN. DIX ANNÉES D'EXIL. LIVRE II. CHAPITRES 1—8. With a Biographical Sketch of the Author, a Selection of Poetical Fragments by Madame de Staël's Contemporaries, and Notes Historical and Philological. By GUSTAVE MASSON and G. W. PROTHERO, M.A. Revised and enlarged edition. 2*s*.

LEMERCIER. FRÉDÉGONDE ET BRUNEHAUT. A
Tragedy in Five Acts. Edited with Notes, Genealogical and Chronological Tables, a Critical Introduction and a Biographical Notice. By GUSTAVE MASSON. 2*s*.

MOLIÈRE. LE BOURGEOIS GENTILHOMME, Comédie-Ballet en Cinq Actes. (1670.) With a life of Molière and Grammatical and Philological Notes. By Rev. A. C. CLAPIN. Revised Edition. 1*s*. 6*d*.

MOLIÈRE. L'ÉCOLE DES FEMMES. Edited with Introduction and Notes by GEORGE SAINTSBURY, M.A. 2*s*. 6*d*.

"Mr Saintsbury's clear and scholarly notes are rich in illustration of the valuable kind that vivifies textual comment and criticism."—*Saturday Review*.

MOLIÈRE. LES PRÉCIEUSES RIDICULES. With
Introduction and Notes by E. G. W. BRAUNHOLTZ, M.A., Ph.D. University Lecturer in French. 2*s*.

PIRON. LA METROMANIE, A Comedy, with a Biographical Memoir, and Grammatical, Literary and Historical Notes. By G. MASSON. 2*s*.

RACINE. LES PLAIDEURS. With Introduction and
Notes by E. G. W. BRAUNHOLTZ, M.A., Ph.D. 2*s*.

SAINTE-BEUVE. M. DARU (Causeries du Lundi, Vol. IX.).
With Biographical Sketch of the Author, and Notes Philological and Historical. By GUSTAVE MASSON. 2*s*.

SAINTINE. LA PICCIOLA. The Text, with Introduction, Notes and Map, by Rev. A. C. CLAPIN. 2*s*.

---

*London: C. J. CLAY & SONS, Cambridge University Press Warehouse,
Ave Maria Lane.*

SCRIBE AND LEGOUVÉ. BATAILLE DE DAMES.
Edited by Rev. H. A. BULL, M.A. 2s.

SCRIBE. LE VERRE D'EAU. With a Biographical Memoir, and Grammatical, Literary and Historical Notes. By C. COLBECK, M.A. 2s.

"It may be national prejudice, but we consider this edition far superior to any of the series which hitherto have been edited exclusively by foreigners. Mr Colbeck seems better to understand the wants and difficulties of an English boy. The etymological notes especially are admirable. ... The historical notes and introduction are a piece of thorough honest work."—*Journal of Education.*

SÉDAINE. LE PHILOSOPHE SANS LE SAVOIR.
Edited with Notes by Rev. H. A. BULL, M.A., late Master at Wellington College. 2s.

THIERRY. LETTRES SUR L'HISTOIRE DE FRANCE (XIII.—XXIV.). By GUSTAVE MASSON, B.A. and G. W. PROTHERO, M.A. With Map. 2s. 6d.

THIERRY. RÉCITS DES TEMPS MÉROVINGIENS I—III. Edited by GUSTAVE MASSON, B.A. Univ. Gallic., and A. R. ROPES, M.A. With Map. 3s.

VILLEMAIN. LASCARIS, OU LES GRECS DU XVE. SIÈCLE, Nouvelle Historique, with a Biographical Sketch of the Author, a Selection of Poems on Greece, and Notes Historical and Philological. By GUSTAVE MASSON, B.A. 2s.

VOLTAIRE. HISTOIRE DU SIÈCLE DE LOUIS XIV.
Part I. Chaps. I.—XIII. Edited with Notes Philological and Historical, Biographical and Geographical Indices, etc. by G. MASSON, B.A. Univ. Gallic., and G. W. PROTHERO, M.A., Fellow of King's College, Cambridge. 2s. 6d.

—— Part II. Chaps. XIV.—XXIV. With Three Maps of the Period. By the same Editors. 2s. 6d.

—— Part III. Chap. XXV. to the end. By the same Editors. 2s. 6d.

XAVIER DE MAISTRE. LA JEUNE SIBÉRIENNE.
LE LÉPREUX DE LA CITÉ D'AOSTE. With Biographical Notice, Critical Appreciations, and Notes. By G. MASSON, B.A. 1s. 6d.

IV. GERMAN.

BALLADS ON GERMAN HISTORY. Arranged and Annotated by W. WAGNER, Ph. D., late Professor at the Johanneum, Hamburg. 2s.

"It carries the reader rapidly through some of the most important incidents connected with the German race and name, from the invasion of Italy by the Visigoths under their King Alaric, down to the Franco-German War and the installation of the present Emperor. The notes supply very well the connecting links between the successive periods, and exhibit in its various phases of growth and progress, or the reverse, the vast unwieldy mass which constitutes modern Germany."—*Times.*

London: C. J. CLAY & SONS, Cambridge University Press Warehouse,
Ave Maria Lane.

BENEDIX. DOCTOR WESPE. Lustspiel in fünf Aufzügen. Edited with Notes by KARL HERMANN BREUL, M.A. 3s.

FREYTAG. DER STAAT FRIEDRICHS DES GROSSEN. With Notes. By WILHELM WAGNER, Ph.D. 2s.

GERMAN DACTYLIC POETRY. Arranged and Annotated by the same Editor. 3s.

Goethe's Knabenjahre. (1749—1759.) GOETHE'S BOYHOOD: being the First Three Books of his Autobiography. Arranged and Annotated by the same Editor. 2s.

GOETHE'S HERMANN AND DOROTHEA. With an Introduction and Notes. By the same Editor. Revised edition by J. W. CARTMELL, M.A. 3s. 6d.

"The notes are among the best that we know, with the reservation that they are often too abundant."—*Academy*.

GUTZKOW. ZOPF UND SCHWERT. Lustspiel in fünf Aufzügen von. With a Biographical and Historical Introduction, English Notes, and an Index. By H. J. WOLSTENHOLME, B.A. (Lond.). 3s. 6d.

"We are glad to be able to notice a careful edition of K. Gutzkow's amusing comedy 'Zopf and Schwert' by Mr H. J. Wolstenholme.... These notes are abundant and contain references to standard grammatical works."—*Academy*.

HAUFF. DAS BILD DES KAISERS. Edited by KARL HERMANN BREUL, M.A., Ph.D. 3s.

HAUFF. DAS WIRTHSHAUS IM SPESSART. Edited by A. SCHLOTTMANN, Ph.D., late Assistant Master at Uppingham School. 3s. 6d.

HAUFF. DIE KARAVANE. Edited with Notes by A. SCHLOTTMANN, Ph.D. 3s. 6d.

IMMERMANN. DER OBERHOF. A Tale of Westphalian Life. With a Life of Immermann and English Notes, by WILHELM WAGNER, Ph.D., late Professor at the Johanneum, Hamburg. 3s.

KOHLRAUSCH. Das Jahr 1813 (THE YEAR 1813). With English Notes. By W. WAGNER. 2s.

LESSING AND GELLERT. SELECTED FABLES. Edited with Notes by KARL HERMANN BREUL, M.A., Lecturer in German at the University of Cambridge. 3s.

MENDELSSOHN'S LETTERS. Selections from. Edited by JAMES SIME, M.A. 3s.

RAUMER. Der erste Kreuzzug (THE FIRST CRUSADE). Condensed from the Author's 'History of the Hohenstaufen', with a life of RAUMER, two Plans and English Notes. By W. WAGNER. 2s.

"Certainly no more interesting book could be made the subject of examinations. The story of the First Crusade has an undying interest. The notes are, on the whole, good."—*Educational Times*.

RIEHL. CULTURGESCHICHTLICHE NOVELLEN. With Grammatical, Philological, and Historical Notes, and a Complete Index, by H. J. WOLSTENHOLME, B.A. (Lond.). 3s. 6d.

London: C. J. CLAY & SONS, Cambridge University Press Warehouse, Ave Maria Lane.

SCHILLER. WILHELM TELL. Edited with Introduction and Notes by KARL HERMANN BREUL, M.A., University Lecturer in German. 2s. 6d.

UHLAND. ERNST, HERZOG VON SCHWABEN. With Introduction and Notes. By H. J. WOLSTENHOLME, B.A. (Lond.), Lecturer in German at Newnham College, Cambridge. 3s. 6d.

V. ENGLISH.

ANCIENT PHILOSOPHY. A SKETCH OF, FROM THALES TO CICERO, by JOSEPH B. MAYOR, M.A. 3s. 6d.
"Professor Mayor contributes to the Pitt Press Series *A Sketch of Ancient Philosophy* in which he has endeavoured to give a general view of the philosophical systems illustrated by the genius of the masters of metaphysical and ethical science from Thales to Cicero. In the course of his sketch he takes occasion to give concise analyses of Plato's Republic, and of the Ethics and Politics of Aristotle; and these abstracts will be to some readers not the least useful portions of the book."—*The Guardian.*

ARISTOTLE. OUTLINES OF THE PHILOSOPHY OF. Compiled by EDWIN WALLACE, M.A., LL.D. (St Andrews), late Fellow of Worcester College, Oxford. Third Edition Enlarged. 4s. 6d.
"A judicious selection of characteristic passages, arranged in paragraphs, each of which is preceded by a masterly and perspicuous English analysis."—*Scotsman.*
"Gives in a comparatively small compass a very good sketch of Aristotle's teaching."—*Sat. Review.*

BACON'S HISTORY OF THE REIGN OF KING HENRY VII. With Notes by the Rev. J. RAWSON LUMBY, D.D. 3s.

COWLEY'S ESSAYS. With Introduction and Notes. By the Rev. J. RAWSON LUMBY, D.D., Norrisian Professor of Divinity; Fellow of St Catharine's College. 4s.

MORE'S HISTORY OF KING RICHARD III. Edited with Notes, Glossary and Index of Names. By J. RAWSON LUMBY, D.D. to which is added the conclusion of the History of King Richard III. as given in the continuation of Hardyng's Chronicle, London, 1543. 3s. 6d.

MORE'S UTOPIA. With Notes by the Rev. J. RAWSON LUMBY, D.D. 3s. 6d.
"It was originally written in Latin and does not find a place on ordinary bookshelves. A very great boon has therefore been conferred on the general English reader by the managers of the *Pitt Press Series*, in the issue of a convenient little volume of *More's Utopia* not in the original Latin, but in the quaint *English Translation thereof made by Raphe Robynson*, which adds a linguistic interest to the intrinsic merit of the work. . . . All this has been edited in a most complete and scholarly fashion by Dr J. R. Lumby, the Norrisian Professor of Divinity, whose name alone is a sufficient warrant for its accuracy. It is a real addition to the modern stock of classical English literature."—*Guardian.*

THE TWO NOBLE KINSMEN, edited with Introduction and Notes by the Rev. Professor SKEAT, Litt.D., formerly Fellow of Christ's College, Cambridge. 3s. 6d.
"This edition of a play that is well worth study, for more reasons than one, by so careful a scholar as Mr Skeat, deserves a hearty welcome."—*Athenæum.*
"Mr Skeat is a conscientious editor, and has left no difficulty unexplained."—*Times.*

VI. EDUCATIONAL SCIENCE.

COMENIUS. JOHN AMOS, Bishop of the Moravians. His Life and Educational Works, by S. S. LAURIE, M.A., F.R.S.E., Professor of the Institutes and History of Education in the University of Edinburgh. New Edition, revised. 3s. 6d.

London: C. J. CLAY & SONS, Cambridge University Press Warehouse, Ave Maria Lane.

EDUCATION. THREE LECTURES ON THE PRAC-
TICE OF. I. On Marking, by H. W. Eve, M.A. II. On Stimulus, by
A. Sidgwick, M.A. III. On the Teaching of Latin Verse Composition, by
E. A. Abbott, D.D. 2s.

LOCKE ON EDUCATION. With Introduction and Notes
by the Rev. R. H. Quick, M.A. 3s. 6d.
"The work before us leaves nothing to be desired. It is of convenient form and reasonable price, accurately printed, and accompanied by notes which are admirable. There is no teacher too young to find this book interesting; there is no teacher too old to find it profitable."—*The School Bulletin, New York.*

MILTON'S TRACTATE ON EDUCATION. A facsimile reprint from the Edition of 1673. Edited, with Introduction and Notes, by Oscar Browning, M.A. 2s.
"A separate reprint of Milton's famous letter to Master Samuel Hartlib was a desideratum, and we are grateful to Mr Browning for his elegant and scholarly edition, to which is prefixed the careful *résumé* of the work given in his 'History of Educational Theories.'"—*Journal of Education.*

MODERN LANGUAGES. LECTURES ON THE
TEACHING OF, delivered in the University of Cambridge in the Lent
Term, 1887. By C. Colbeck, M.A., Assistant Master of Harrow School. 2s.

ON STIMULUS. A Lecture delivered for the Teachers'
Training Syndicate at Cambridge, May 1882, by A. Sidgwick, M.A. 1s.

TEACHER. GENERAL AIMS OF THE, AND FORM
MANAGEMENT. Two Lectures delivered in the University of Cambridge
in the Lent Term, 1883, by Archdeacon Farrar, D.D., and R. B. Poole,
B.D. Head Master of Bedford Modern School. 1s. 6d.

TEACHING. THEORY AND PRACTICE OF. By the
Rev. Edward Thring, M.A., late Head Master of Uppingham School
and Fellow of King's College, Cambridge. New Edition. 4s. 6d.
"Any attempt to summarize the contents of the volume would fail to give our readers a taste of the pleasure that its perusal has given us."—*Journal of Education.*

BRITISH INDIA, A SHORT HISTORY OF. By
Rev. E. S. Carlos, M.A., late Head Master of Exeter Grammar School. 1s.

GEOGRAPHY, ELEMENTARY COMMERCIAL. A
Sketch of the Commodities and the Countries of the World. By H. R.
Mill, Sc.D., F.R.S.E., Lecturer on Commercial Geography in the Heriot-
Watt College, Edinburgh. 1s.

AN ATLAS OF COMMERCIAL GEOGRAPHY. In-
tended as a Companion to the above. By J. G. Bartholomew,
F.R.G.S. With an Introduction by Dr H. R. Mill. 3s.

VII. MATHEMATICS.

EUCLID'S ELEMENTS OF GEOMETRY. Books I.
& II. Edited by H. M. Taylor, M.A., Fellow and formerly Tutor of
Trinity College, Cambridge. 1s. 6d.

[*Other Volumes are in preparation.*]

---

*London: C. J. Clay & Sons, Cambridge University Press Warehouse,
Ave Maria Lane.*

University of Cambridge.

LOCAL EXAMINATIONS.

Examination Papers, for various years, with the *Regulations for the Examination.* Demy 8vo. 2s. each, or by Post 2s. 2d.

Class Lists, for various years, Boys 1s., Girls 6d.

Annual Reports of the Syndicate, with Supplementary Tables showing the success and failure of the Candidates. 2s. each, by Post 2s. 3d.

HIGHER LOCAL EXAMINATIONS.

Examination Papers for various years, *to which are added the Regulations for the Examination.* Demy 8vo. 2s. each, by Post 2s. 2d.

Class Lists, for various years. 1s. each. By Post 1s. 2d.

Reports of the Syndicate. Demy 8vo. 1s., by Post 1s. 2d.

LOCAL LECTURES SYNDICATE.

Calendar for the years 1875—80. Fcap. 8vo. *cloth*. 2s.; for 1880—81. 1s.

TEACHERS' TRAINING SYNDICATE.

Examination Papers for various years, *to which are added the Regulations for the Examination.* Demy 8vo. 6d., by Post 7d.

CAMBRIDGE UNIVERSITY REPORTER.

Published by Authority.

Containing all the Official Notices of the University, Reports of Discussions in the Schools, and Proceedings of the Cambridge Philosophical, Antiquarian and Philological Societies. 3d. weekly.

CAMBRIDGE UNIVERSITY EXAMINATION PAPERS.

These Papers are published in occasional numbers every Term, and in volumes for the Academical year.

VOL. XVI. Parts 44 to 65. PAPERS for the Year 1886—87, 15s. *cloth.*
VOL. XVII. ,, 65 to 86. ,, ,, 1887—88, 15s. *cloth.*
VOL. XVIII. ,, 87 to 107. ,, ,, 1888—89, 15s. *cloth.*

Oxford and Cambridge Schools Examinations.

Papers set in the Examination for Certificates, July, 1888. 2s. 6d.

List of Candidates who obtained Certificates at the Examination held in 1889; and Supplementary Tables. 6d.

Regulations of the Board for 1890. 9d.

Regulations for the Commercial Certificate, 1890. 3d.

Report of the Board for the year ending Oct. 31, 1889. 1s.

Studies from the Morphological Laboratory in the University of Cambridge. Edited by ADAM SEDGWICK, M.A., Fellow and Lecturer of Trinity College, Cambridge. Vol. II. Part I. Royal 8vo. 10s. Vol. II. Part II. 7s. 6d. Vol. III. Part I. 7s. 6d. Vol. III. Part II. 7s. 6d. Vol. IV. Part I. 12s. 6d. Vol. IV. Part II. 10s. Vol. IV. Part III. 5s.

London: C. J. CLAY AND SONS,
CAMBRIDGE UNIVERSITY PRESS WAREHOUSE,
AVE MARIA LANE.

GLASGOW: 263, ARGYLE STREET.

www.ingramcontent.com/pod-product-compliance
Lightning Source LLC
Chambersburg PA
CBHW022057300426
44117CB00007B/490